American Map® Corporation

S0-CEY-458

Road Atlas

United States • Canada • Mexico

Contents

Time Zone and Area Code Map
. . . . Facing Page
Mileage Chart 2-3
U.S. Interstate Highway Map 4-5
National Parks and Landmarks Map 6-7

Canada 8-9
Mexico 10-11
State Maps 12-89
City Maps 90-150
Index to Cities and Towns 151-176

State Maps

Alabama   13
Alaska   14
Arizona   16-17
Arkansas   15
California   18-21
Colorado   22-23
Connecticut   24-25
Delaware   43
Florida   26-27
Georgia   28-29
Hawaii   30
Idaho   31
Illinois   32-33
Indiana   34-35
Iowa   36
Kansas   37
Kentucky   38-39
Louisiana   40
Maine   41
Maryland   42-43
Massachusetts   24-25
Michigan   44-45
Minnesota   46-47
Mississippi   50
Missouri   48-49
Montana   51

Nebraska   52-53
Nevada   54
New Hampshire   55
New Jersey   56-57
New Mexico   62
New York   58-61
North Carolina   64-65
North Dakota   63
Ohio   66-67
Oklahoma   68-69
Oregon   70-71
Pennsylvania   72-73
Rhode Island   24-25
South Carolina   64-65
South Dakota   74
Tennessee   38-39
Texas   75-79
Utah   80-81
Vermont   55
Virginia   82-83
Washington   84-85
West Virginia   82-83
Wisconsin   86-87
Wyoming   88-89

City Maps

Atlanta, GA   90
Baltimore, MD   91
Birmingham, AL   92
Boston, MA   93
Buffalo, NY   94
Charlotte, NC   95
Chicago, IL   96-99
Cincinnati, OH   100
Cleveland, OH   101
Columbus, OH   102
Denver, CO   103
Dallas, TX   104-105
Detroit, MI   106-107
Fort Lauderdale, FL   120
Fort Myers, FL   108
Fort Worth, TX   104-105
Houston, TX   109
Indianapolis, IN   110
Jacksonville, FL   111
Kansas City, MO   112
Las Vegas, NV   113
Los Angeles, CA   114-117
Louisville, KY   118
Memphis, TN   119
Miami, FL   120
Milwaukee, WI   121
Minneapolis, MN   122-123
Nashville, TN   124

New Orleans, LA   125
New York, NY   126-129
Norfolk, VA   130
Oakland, CA   144-145
Oklahoma City, OK   131
Omaha, NE   132
Orlando, FL   133
Philadelphia, PA   134
Phoenix, AZ   135
Pittsburgh, PA   136
Portland, OR   137
Raleigh, NC   138
Richmond, VA   139
Rochester, NY   138
Sacramento, CA   141
Saint Louis, MO   140
Saint Paul, MN   122-123
Saint Petersburg, FL   148
Salt Lake City, UT   141
San Antonio, TX   142
San Diego, CA   143
San Francisco, CA   144-145
San Jose, CA   146
Seattle, WA   147
Tampa, FL   148
Tucson, AZ   149
Washington, DC   150
West Palm Beach, FL   120

Mileage Chart

	Albany, NY	Albuquerque, NM	Amarillo, TX	Atlanta, GA	Austin, TX	Baltimore, MD	Billings, MT	Birmingham, AL	Boise, ID	Boston, MA	Brownsville, TX	Buffalo, NY	Charleston, SC	Charleston, WV	Charlotte, NC	Chicago, IL	Cincinnati, OH	Cleveland, OH	Columbia, SC	Columbus, OH	Dallas, TX	Daytona Beach, FL	Denver, CO	Des Moines, IA	Detroit, MI	El Paso, TX	Fargo, ND	Fort Lauderdale, FL	Fort Wayne, IN	Fort Worth, TX	Grand Rapids, MI	Greensboro, NC	Hartford, CT	Houston, TX	Indianapolis, IN	Jackson, MS	Jacksonville, FL	Kansas City, MO	Knoxville, TN	Las Vegas, NV	Lincoln, NE	Little Rock, AK
Albany, NY	0	2125	1825	1007	1882	332	2073	1112	2601	170	2007	292	932	639	795	795	729	496	823	657	1679	1209	1853	1193	690	2327	1463	1403	705	1682	710	661	106	1825	836	1320	1111	1279	836	2609	1336	1370
Albuquerque, NM	2125	0	300	1387	716	1881	1022	1260	970	2214	988	1801	1695	1583	1628	1346	1394	1606	1598	1468	673	1716	446	1013	1537	267	1314	1953	1410	632	1491	1677	2084	870	1289	1087	1678	811	1407	576	837	883
Amarillo, TX	1825	300	0	1087	485	1581	1037	965	1235	1914	784	1501	1517	1304	1338	1046	1094	1306	1298	1168	363	1467	454	806	1289	508	999	1670	1109	344	1191	1377	1822	608	989	787	1378	552	1107	876	596	607
Atlanta, GA	1007	1387	1087	0	884	669	1804	160	2252	1068	1175	912	300	495	251	695	438	692	211	543	805	446	1401	924	726	1453	1364	681	612	837	749	348	969	816	543	397	329	810	204	1947	1013	540
Austin, TX	1882	716	485	884	0	1550	1449	793	1716	1930	331	1566	1247	1251	1237	1100	1127	1371	1095	1233	203	1158	1009	897	1330	583	1333	1326	1200	192	1288	1281	1867	162	1111	519	1057	680	1051	1297	851	520
Baltimore, MD	332	1881	1581	669	1550	0	1875	804	2416	409	1825	352	567	339	430	697	510	355	513	405	1347	876	1692	997	511	1997	1339	1036	550	1379	624	346	308	1409	584	1006	770	1078	503	2408	1192	1037
Billings, MT	2073	1022	1037	1804	1449	1875	0	1759	586	2232	1771	1857	2222	1762	2027	1214	1479	1662	2075	1654	1395	2173	579	959	1579	1284	625	2466	1405	1406	1396	1958	2169	1739	1400	1743	2227	1078	1723	1060	836	1439
Birmingham, AL	1112	1260	965	160	793	804	1759	0	2101	1267	1065	941	460	539	411	669	468	722	359	584	637	505	1370	838	721	1304	1311	764	610	702	739	493	1058	676	497	251	472	724	255	1822	953	394
Boise, ID	2601	970	1235	2252	1716	2416	586	2101	0	2794	1921	2271	2503	2246	2408	1777	1983	2058	2289	2069	1610	2576	870	1402	2020	1241	1245	2820	1871	1598	1917	2408	2652	1854	1890	2091	2579	1476	2022	662	1205	1781
Boston, MA	170	2214	1914	1068	1930	409	2232	1267	2794	0	2255	454	989	728	828	965	875	632	928	738	1727	1257	1953	1305	795	2376	1623	1492	847	1761	908	739	105	1878	933	1395	1167	1435	871	2765	1500	1472
Brownsville, TX	2007	988	784	1175	331	1825	1909	1065	1921	2255	0	1865	1500	1479	1426	1430	1426	1670	1360	1533	526	1353	1251	1184	1694	806	1601	1542	1455	518	1585	1480	2094	357	1427	791	1264	1008	1320	1573	1216	819
Buffalo, NY	292	1801	1501	912	1566	352	1857	941	2271	454	1865	0	947	430	666	543	438	195	822	333	1363	1069	1602	867	366	2011	1185	1400	381	1395	419	641	397	1492	512	1119	1068	1007	671	2254	1057	1046
Charleston, SC	932	1695	1517	300	1247	567	2222	460	2503	989	1500	947	0	479	203	912	628	750	113	670	1164	351	1743	1185	874	1729	1557	586	740	1116	959	271	867	1027	743	702	248	1135	368	2247	1287	814
Charleston, WV	639	1583	1304	495	1251	339	1762	539	2246	728	1479	430	479	0	276	469	178	284	376	156	1134	726	1377	761	371	1672	1126	1004	284	1056	457	227	662	1246	328	790	676	777	284	2119	960	707
Charlotte, NC	795	1628	1338	251	1237	430	2027	411	2408	828	1426	666	203	276	0	738	446	543	100	453	1054	469	1548	1029	607	1710	1414	721	602	1061	791	89	763	1053	551	640	413	940	219	2173	1151	743
Chicago, IL	795	1346	1046	695	1100	697	1214	669	1777	965	1430	543	912	469	738	0	291	348	794	340	932	1096	1037	357	284	1435	649	1348	159	945	178	729	875	1160	186	762	999	543	537	1749	527	675
Cincinnati, OH	729	1394	1094	438	1127	510	1479	468	1983	875	1426	438	628	178	446	291	0	249	502	105	924	861	1199	583	260	1472	940	1086	184	956	357	458	746	1053	105	680	786	591	246	1921	715	608
Cleveland, OH	496	1606	1306	692	1371	355	1662	722	2058	632	1670	195	750	284	543	348	249	0	627	138	1168	952	1407	672	171	1716	997	1232	211	1200	284	486	539	1297	317	924	908	803	489	2059	867	851
Columbia, SC	823	1598	1298	211	1095	513	2075	359	2289	928	1360	822	113	376	100	794	502	627	0	513	1032	381	1616	1126	745	1668	1446	622	671	1057	858	188	836	1066	625	610	290	1025	267	2162	1199	759
Columbus, OH	657	1469	1168	543	1233	405	1654	584	2069	738	1533	333	670	156	453	340	105	138	513	0	1030	901	1270	657	195	1540	989	1126	150	1062	311	381	641	1159	179	786	850	665	351	1995	776	713
Dallas, TX	1679	673	363	805	203	1347	1395	637	1610	1727	526	1363	1164	1134	1054	932	924	1168	1032	1030	0	1123	806	714	1203	648	1131	1097	1030	33	1110	1122	1664	243	908	422	1005	511	820	1249	648	317
Daytona Beach, FL	1209	1716	1467	446	1158	876	2173	505	2576	1257	1353	1069	351	726	469	1096	883	952	381	901	1123	0	1823	1329	1103	1728	1714	227	1006	1126	1143	551	1138	952	880	688	97	1209	603	2316	1401	904
Denver, CO	1853	446	454	1401	1009	1692	579	1370	870	1953	1251	1602	1743	1377	1548	1037	1199	1407	1616	1270	806	1823	0	695	1321	705	915	2067	1186	773	1201	1621	1988	1060	1091	1246	1779	608	1341	743	507	992
Des Moines, IA	1193	1013	806	924	897	997	959	838	1402	1305	1184	867	1185	761	1029	357	583	672	1126	657	714	1329	695	0	600	1114	475	1581	516	747	502	1028	1283	930	478	846	1270	203	821	1399	203	562
Detroit, MI	690	1537	1289	726	1330	511	1579	721	2020	795	1694	366	874	371	607	284	260	171	745	195	1203	1103	1321	600	0	1701	922	1346	170	1240	162	567	701	1304	293	923	1046	791	506	2011	819	850
El Paso, TX	2327	267	508	1453	583	1997	1274	1304	1241	2376	806	2011	1729	1672	1710	1435	1372	1716	1668	1540	648	1728	705	1114	1701	0	1460	1869	1573	609	1554	1783	2263	743	1460	1070	1626	915	1488	722	946	960
Fargo, ND	1463	1314	999	1364	1333	1339	625	1311	1245	1625	1601	1185	1557	1126	1414	649	940	997	1446	989	1131	1714	915	475	922	1460	0	2007	808	1072	827	1412	1531	1334	835	1335	1704	609	1195	1535	451	1091
Fort Lauderdale, FL	1435	1953	1670	681	1326	1036	2466	764	2820	1492	1542	1400	586	1004	721	1348	1086	1232	622	1126	1097	227	2067	1581	1346	1869	2007	0	1271	1129	1342	786	1403	1191	1232	883	332	1459	860	2530	1670	1184
Fort Wayne, IN	705	1410	1109	612	1200	550	1405	610	1871	847	1455	381	740	284	602	159	184	219	671	150	1030	1006	1186	516	170	1573	808	1271	0	1053	172	551	768	1176	122	784	929	648	430	1878	686	711
Fort Worth, TX	1682	632	344	837	192	1379	1406	702	1598	1761	518	1395	1116	1056	1061	945	956	1200	1057	1062	33	1126	773	747	1236	609	1072	1129	1053	0	1121	1154	1696	264	912	446	1037	513	853	1203	648	349
Grand Rapids, MI	710	1491	1191	749	1288	624	1396	739	1917	908	1585	419	959	457	791	178	357	284	858	311	1110	1143	1201	502	162	1554	827	1342	172	1121	0	707	794	1196	263	957	1071	638	573	1889	699	799
Greensboro, NC	661	1677	1377	348	1281	346	1958	493	2408	739	1480	641	271	227	89	729	458	486	188	381	1122	551	1621	1028	567	1783	1412	786	551	1154	707	0	650	1167	563	770	483	1013	283	2237	1202	778
Hartford	106	2084	1822	969	1867	308	2169	1058	2652	105	2044	397	867	662	763	875	746	539	836	641	1664	1138	1988	1283	701	2263	1531	1403	768	1696	794	650	0	1773	805	1306	1071	1297	841	2675	1378	1344
Houston, TX	1825	870	608	816	162	1409	1639	676	1854	1878	357	1492	1027	1246	1053	1160	1053	1297	1066	1159	243	952	1060	930	1304	743	1334	1191	1176	264	1196	1167	1773	0	1041	406	891	754	922	1468	892	446
Indianapolis, IN	836	1289	989	543	1111	584	1400	497	1890	933	1427	512	743	328	551	186	105	317	625	179	908	980	1091	478	293	1460	835	1232	122	912	263	563	805	1041	0	681	867	486	351	1816	673	608
Jackson, MS	1320	1087	787	397	519	1006	1743	251	2091	1395	991	1119	702	790	640	762	680	924	610	786	422	688	1246	846	923	1070	1335	883	784	446	957	770	1306	406	681	0	591	716	506	1650	874	251
Jacksonville, FL	1111	1678	1378	329	1057	770	2227	472	2579	1167	1264	1068	248	676	413	999	786	908	290	850	1005	97	1779	1270	1046	1626	1704	332	929	1037	1071	483	1071	891	867	591	0	1110	555	2238	1321	843
Kansas City, MO	1279	811	552	810	680	1078	1078	724	1476	1435	1008	1007	1135	777	940	543	591	803	1025	665	511	1209	608	203	791	916	609	1459	648	513	638	1013	1297	754	486	716	1110	0	752	1345	211	409
Knoxville, TN	836	1407	1107	204	1051	503	1723	255	2022	871	1320	671	368	284	219	537	246	489	267	351	820	603	1341	821	506	1488	1195	860	430	872	573	283	841	922	351	506	555	752	0	1983	944	523
Las Vegas, NV	2609	576	876	1947	1297	2408	1060	1822	662	2765	1573	2254	2247	2119	2173	1749	1921	2059	2162	1995	1249	2316	743	1399	2011	722	1535	2530	1878	1203	1889	2237	2675	1468	1816	1650	2238	1345	1983	0	1224	1483
Lincoln, NE	1386	837	596	1013	851	1192	836	953	1205	1500	1216	1057	1287	960	1151	527	802	867	1199	776	648	1401	507	203	819	946	451	1670	686	648	699	1202	1378	892	673	874	1321	211	944	1224	0	616
Little Rock, AK	1370	883	607	540	520	1037	1439	394	1781	1472	819	1046	814	707	743	675	608	851	759	713	317	904	992	562	850	960	1091	1184	711	349	799	778	1344	446	608	251	843	409	523	1483	616	0
Los Angeles, CA	2911	823	1095	2197	1410	2676	1254	2067	837	2993	1678	2587	2521	2394	2617	1989	2164	2392	2426	2254	1401	2407	1009	1654	2270	818	1844	2704	2137	1361	2148	2478	2829	1581	2075	1880	2402	1589	2201	275	1476	1678
Louisville, KY	868	1332	1041	421	1022	608	1550	373	1908	976	1321	543	608	258	438	300	105	349	494	211	819	801	1127	591	365	1467	949	1078	222	851	373	462	867	948	129	575	729	519	246	1861	730	502
Memphis, TN	1232	1021	721	397	658	900	1557	239	1833	1379	957	908	689	653	604	551	469	713	612	575	455	749	1151	599	712	1103	1224	989	592	487	690	640	1209	584	470	211	697	470	385	1581	647	138
Miami, FL	1439	1994	1694	665	1338	1095	2580	788	2860	1516	1580	1524	630	1046	745	1338	1086	1264	658	1210	1321	259	2131	1582	1386	1958	1986	24	1326	1353	1356	810	1427	1207	1208	907	356	1475	859	2570	1673	1208
Milwaukee, WI	933	1443	1143	784	1203	794	1143	766	1777	1078	1530	640	1032	566	835	92	388	445	891	448	1013	1180	1070	365	389	1528	576	1443	256	1059	275	826	948	1155	283	884	1067	568	643	1752	560	772
Minneapolis, MN	1215	1256	1062	1105	1120	1105	812	1088	1488	1362	1456	948	1316	874	1143	405	696	753	1276	753	1013	1458	956	251	698	1520	244	1723	564	1001	583	1135	1257	1266	591	1123	1376	459	932	1630	409	881
Mobile, AL	1322	1265	965	340	656	990	1854	269	2343	1379	851	1184	607	825	575	908	745	989	555	834	592	502	1372	954	988	1236	1413	705	839	624	1006	681	1290	478	749	178	413	819	449	1841	1039	430
Montgomery, AL	1178	1345	1042	164	804	833	1836	93	2346	1232	1041	1076	464	632	405	762	561	815	379	707	677	458	1412	1311	814	1325	1521	671	686	701	819	512	1133	709	590	255	379	867	348	2015	975	470
Nashville, TN	993	1232	932	243	869	688	1640	195	2059	1062	1168	722	576	458	399	474	283	527	458	389	666	639	1167	712	536	1314	1136	900	385	698	534	429	973	795	302	422	592	590	174	1792	770	349
New Orleans, LA	1453	1187	875	493	535	1136	1820	352	2191	1526	730	1273	727	891	721	925	820	1078	701	940	530	632	1323	978	1077	1127	1494	843	916	519	1071	810	1436	367	857	193	551	857	607	1800	1114	430
New York City, NY	146	1995	1695	855	1728	201	1926	1019	2571	203	2002	390	786	524	625	794	628	446	715	551	1525	1054	1775	1070	620	2173	1450	1289	691	1557	706	561	101	1679	730	1192	957	1192	771	2520	1274	1235
Norfolk, VA	505	1905	1632	551	1403	237	2098	711	2551	660	1735	569	454	369	341	851	681	493	412	559	1359	702	1800	1202	711	1998	1581	964	709	1382	802	227	471	1362	669	948	632	1179	412	2534	1354	1025
Oakland, CA	2982	1134	1430	2488	1786	2864	1218	2321	671	3124	2034	2745	2788	2600	2755	2098	2317	2498	2703	2391	1803	2831	1223	1742	2350	1194	1870	3041	2257	1723	2308	2809	2909	1957	2212	2270	2771	1799	2509	582	1604	1984
Oklahoma City, OK	1523	559	267	863	414	1322	1168	701	1451	1659	680	1242	1176	1031	1069	804	835	1047	1091	909	211	1257	660	576	1030	708	989	1481	852	210	932	1118	1546	454	730	575	1181	373	847	1119	433	324
Omaha, NE	1308	905	754	989	847	1143	904	904	1274	1443	1249	1005	1303	899	1135	464	721	824	1283	795	693	1402	559	146	726	1256	464	1604	634	634	640	1208	1321	949	616	914	1305	195	930	1249	57	690
Orlando, FL	1249	1751	1451	446	1142	917	2277	545	2695	1297	2034	1306	401	814	559	1127	892	1046	440	997	1078	81	1896	1363	1143	1735	1826	208	1059	1110	1188	648	1208	964	989	697	138	1266	665	2311	1452	965
Philadelphia, PA	251	1922	1622	766	1630	97	2051	880	2488	327	1954	397	688	517	522	757	559	430	627	460	1427	914	1762	998	585	2075	1370	1127	604	1459	672	438	220	1581	624	1094	859	1134	646	2449	1260	1110
Phoenix, AZ	2512	446	746	1810	1030	2311	1220	1700	1022	2644	1289	2269	2222	2045	2061	1776	1808	2045	2025	1907	1013	2101	802	1497	2019	438	1791	2244	1831	983	1906	2099	2523	1110	1719	1500	2100	1277	1845	284	1236	1379
Pittsburgh, PA	471	1654	1354	712	1412	245	1681	778	2203	584	1713	219	778	211	504	470	291	128	572	186	1209	859	1475	770	304	1833	1112	1216	336	1241	397	438	486	1345	349	965	882	851	515	2181	965	899
Portland, Or	2869	1378	1636	2763	2059	2765	867	2571	439	3149	2468	2677	2952	2615	2757	2140	2474	2416	2972	2478	2051	3018	1283	1816	2368	1661	1484	3204	2299	2003	2251	2823	2877	2369	2335	2518	3042	1809	2550	991	1641	2270
Providence, RI	178	2156	1856	1027	1898	356	2238	1189	2701	41	2222	454	956	699	785	924	790	600	888	713	1695	1201	1961	1256	746	2335	1566	1459	799	1727	859	706	73	1849	892	1362	1127	1378	935	2683	1451	1395
Raleigh, NC	656	1759	1459	397	1355	324	2273	557	2560	713	1506	721	300	297	162	802	540	559	215	453	1152	559	1694	1123	643	1800	1485	794	603	1184	754	73	624	1233	635	815	486	1086	356	2319	1263	851
Reno, NV	2763	1056	1345	2411	1775	2562	1021	2363	404	2871	2068	2433	2765	2407	2570	1897	2221	2238	2626	2295	1731	2758	1030	1606	2190	1183	1660	3008	2056	1608	2067	2591	2749	1932	2116	2143	2716	1606	2363	478	1411	1986
Richmond, VA	482	1833	1533	527	1463	155	1655	699	2594	544	1646	552	462	251	280	788	356	583	390	498	1313	713	1904	1293	609	2023	1481	946	635	1333	722	191	455	2291	907	946	693	1205	440	2406	1249	963
Rochester,NY	219	1857	1557	1015	1623	300	1922	965	2352	381	1891	81	871	495	689	608	502	268	789	397	1420	1176	1637	932	424	2036	1249	1410	464	1452	499	600	324	1555	551	1183	1102	1062	710	2371	1135	1111
Saint Louis, MO	1028	1054	754	588	806	827	1381	539	1727	1184	1216	747	884	544	689	292	340	552	737	414	641	956	859	377	585	1238	872	1208	369	698	437	762	1030	835	251	495	859	251	497	1581	462	422
Saint Paul, MN	1215	1362	1062	1105	1120	1095	812	1118	1398	892	1565	948	1316	870	1143	405	696	753	1320	745	1013	1458	956	251	698	1541	244	1753	564	987	583	1138	1257	1266	591	1160	1376	459	951	1630	408	881
Salt Lake City, UT	2290	621	1324	1900	1341	2051	579	1825	349	2417	1775	1922	2254	1896	2059	1386	1710	1727	2115	1711	1287	2283	519	1085	1679	892	1172	2578	1527	1184	1556	2059	2238	1460	1605	1742	2286	1095	1766	413	900	1462
San Antonio, TX	1986	684	530	965	81	1646	1600	895	1709	2052	300	1638	1371	1419	1272	1208	1208	1443	1180	1305	284	1175	975	1022	1500	576	1402	1378	1269	283	1353	1321	1965	203	1200	649	1086	795	1150	1273	916	592
San Diego, CA	2855	787	1078	2174	1313	2714	1309	2034	1010	2992	1574	2613	2505	2402	2423	2335	2193	2334	2389	2277	1369	2418	1054	1760	2419	721	1934	2621	2189	1332	2269	2457	2944	1484	2067	1783	2329	1627	2269	349	1573	1743
San Francisco, CA	2966	1135	1396	2511	1776	2765	1239	2371	595	3133	2044	2403	2923	2616	2756	2108	2329	2408	2738	2461	1865	2827	1233	1832	2360	1184	1886	3073	2304	1735	2318	2740	3019	1947	2224	2183	2781	1869	2549	592	1614	1994
Seattle, WA	2855	1500	1805	2656	2157	2685	815	2475	524	2961	2521	2531	2960	2748	2765	2043	2334	2336	2971	2408	2203	3070	1371	1889	2299	1775	1440	3882	2202	2071	2221	2773	2918	2498	2229	2585	3090	1884	2553	1209	1636	2320
Shreveport, LA	1599	868	568	624	340	1229	1691	474	1912	1618	644	1265	945	899	885	916	826	1070	833	592	196	903	1112	827	1069	844	1229	1144	909	228	1018	937	1519	271	827	223	814	624	729	1468	727	219
Spokane, WA	2652	1346	1563	2367	1981	2417	541	2469	369	2693	2359	2263	2700	2503	2505	1775	2066	2068	2572	2115	1978	2811	1095	1556	2020	1686	1166	3014	1921	1978	1941	2503	2650	2222	1961	2205	2822	1727	2298	1119	1460	2092
Tallahassee, FL	1249	1508	1208	268	899	932	2306	302	2512	1312	1094	1155	364	868	559	957	706	949	408	828	835	259	1727	1216	957	1492	1598	462	871	867	1022	608	1223	721	818	421	170	1045	584	2068	1227	679
Tampa, FL	1281	1759	1459	476	1150	949	2143	553	2763	1329	1345	1346	479	903	584	1143	908	1091	497	1013	1086	141	1858	1460	1200	1743	1849	268	1092	1118	1219	673	1240	972	1069	672	195	1296	730	2319	1477	958
Toledo, OH	633	1526	1220	641	1315	454	1557	673	2020	742	1622	309	973	284	533	243	203	114	683	138	1112	1063	1272	567	65	1699	885	1289	105	1144	170	516	624	1249	243	876	989	717	449	1954	762	803
Tuscon, AZ	2442	486	656	1785	908	2246	1342	1621	1144	2571	1176	2166	2100	2039	1913	1711	1750	1971	2080	1833	964	1999	835	1484	1938	316	1897	2271	1783	932	1856	2059	2433	1079	1668	1378	2010	1281	1755	389	1246	1257
Tulsa, OK	1409	674	336	803	462	1208	1293	636	2020	1532	835	1128	1103	941	989	673	721	933	1018	795	259	1156	714	471	916	788	972	1409	738	305	818	1037	1411	504	616	510	1167	283	782	1224	416	259
Washington, DC	378	1864	1564	630	1509	41	2006	781	2441	430	1787	429	559	299	334	697	478	341	498	418	1306	802	1654	1054	506	1954	1322	1062	531	1338	608	309	341	1220	551	965	730	1046	554	2376	1184	832
West Palm Beach, FL	1396	1938	1638	632	1329	1046	2736	702	2942	1426	1524	1443	568	982	673	1289	1063	1192	586	1146	1265	195	2157	1646	1305	1922	2028	41	1157	1297	1476	737	1339	1151	1176	851	284	1052	806	2498	1598	1101
Youngstown, OH	462	1632	1346	719	1368	298	1632	738	2090	568	1695	190	709	251	502	413	275	74	561	170	1193	986	1421	737	239	1804	1038	1219	275	1225	340	482	470	1322	341	949	958	843	521	2124	923	876

Mileage Chart

	Los Angeles, CA	Louisville, KY	Memphis, TN	Miami, FL	Milwaukee, WI	Minneapolis, MN	Mobile, AL	Montgomery, AL	Nashville, TN	New Orleans, LA	New York City NY	Norfolk, VA	Oakland,CA	Oklahoma City, OK	Omaha, NE	Orlando, FL	Philadelphia, PA	Phoenix, AZ	Pittsburgh, PA	Portland, OR	Providence, RI	Raleigh, NC	Reno, NV	Richmond, VA	Rochester, NY	Saint Louis, MO	Saint Paul, MN	Salt Lake City, UT	San Antonio, TX	San Diego, CA	San Francisco, CA	Seattle, WA	Shreveport, LA	Spokane, WA	Tallahassee, FL	Tampa, FL	Toledo, OH	Tucson, AZ	Tulsa, OK	Washington, DC	West Palm Beach, FL	Youngstown, OH
Albany, NY	2911	868	1232	1439	933	1215	1322	1178	993	1453	146	505	2982	1523	1308	1249	251	2512	471	2869	178	656	2763	482	219	1028	1215	2290	1986	2855	2966	2855	1599	2652	1249	1281	633	2442	1409	378	1396	462
Albuquerque, NM	823	1332	1021	1994	1443	1256	1265	1345	1232	1187	1995	1905	1134	559	905	1751	1922	446	1654	1378	2156	1759	1056	1833	1857	1054	1362	621	684	787	1135	1500	868	1346	1508	1759	1526	486	674	1864	1938	1646
Amarillo, TX	1095	1041	721	1694	1143	1062	965	1045	932	875	1695	1632	1430	267	754	1451	1622	746	1354	1636	1856	1458	1345	1533	1557	754	1062	917	530	1078	1396	1805	568	1563	1208	1459	1220	656	336	1564	1638	1346
Atlanta, GA	2197	421	397	665	784	1105	340	164	243	493	855	551	2488	863	989	446	766	1810	712	2763	1027	397	2411	527	1015	588	1105	1900	965	2174	2511	2656	624	2367	268	476	641	1785	803	630	632	719
Austin, TX	1410	1022	658	1338	1203	1120	656	804	869	535	1728	1403	1786	414	847	1142	1630	1030	1412	2059	1898	1355	1775	1463	1623	806	1120	1341	81	1313	1776	2157	340	1981	899	1150	1315	908	462	1509	1329	1368
Baltimore, MD	2676	608	900	1095	794	1105	990	833	688	1136	201	237	2864	1322	1143	917	97	2311	245	2765	356	324	2562	155	300	827	1095	2051	1646	2714	2765	2686	1229	2417	932	949	454	2246	1208	41	1046	298
Billings, MT	1254	1550	1557	2580	1143	812	1854	1836	1640	1820	1926	2098	1218	1168	904	2277	2051	1220	1681	867	2238	2273	1021	1655	1922	1381	812	579	1600	1309	1239	815	1691	541	2306	2143	1557	1342	1293	2006	2736	1632
Birmingham, AL	2067	373	239	788	766	1088	269	93	195	352	1019	711	2321	701	904	545	880	1700	778	2571	1189	557	2363	699	965	539	1118	1825	895	2034	2371	2475	474	2469	302	553	673	1621	636	781	702	738
Boise, ID	837	1908	1833	2860	1777	1488	2143	2346	2059	2191	2571	2551	671	1451	1274	2695	2498	1022	2203	439	2701	2560	404	2594	2352	1727	1398	349	1709	1010	595	524	1912	369	2512	2763	2020	1144	1582	2441	2492	2090
Boston, MA	2993	976	1379	1516	1078	1362	1379	1232	1062	1525	203	560	3124	1659	1443	1297	327	2644	584	3149	41	713	2871	544	381	1184	892	2417	2052	2992	3133	2961	1618	2693	1312	1329	742	2571	1532	430	1426	568
Brownsville, TX	1678	1321	957	1580	1530	1456	851	1041	1168	730	2002	1735	2034	680	1249	2034	1954	1289	1713	2468	2222	1506	2068	1646	1891	1216	1565	1609	300	1574	2044	2521	644	2359	1094	1345	1622	1176	835	1787	1524	1695
Buffalo, NY	2587	543	908	1424	640	948	1184	1076	722	1273	390	569	2745	1242	1005	1306	397	2269	219	2677	454	721	2433	552	81	747	948	1922	1638	2613	2667	2531	1265	2263	1155	1346	309	2166	1128	429	1443	190
Charleston, SC	2521	608	689	630	1032	1316	607	464	576	727	787	454	2788	1176	1303	401	688	2222	778	2952	956	300	2765	462	871	884	1316	2254	1371	2505	2923	2960	945	2700	364	479	973	2100	1103	559	568	709
Charleston, WV	2394	258	653	1046	566	874	825	632	458	891	524	369	2600	1031	899	814	517	2045	211	2615	699	297	2407	251	495	544	870	1896	1419	2402	2616	2748	899	2503	868	903	284	2039	941	299	982	251
Charlotte, NC	2417	438	592	604	835	1143	575	415	399	721	625	341	2755	1069	1135	559	522	2061	504	2757	785	162	2570	280	689	689	1143	2059	1272	2423	2756	2765	885	2505	559	584	583	1913	989	334	673	502
Chicago, IL	1989	300	551	1338	92	405	908	762	474	925	794	851	2098	804	454	1127	757	1776	470	2140	924	802	1897	788	608	292	405	1386	1208	2306	2108	2043	916	1775	957	1143	243	1711	673	697	1289	413
Cincinnati, OH	2164	105	469	1086	388	696	712	561	283	810	628	601	2317	835	721	892	559	1808	291	2369	790	540	2201	503	502	340	696	1671	1208	2193	2329	2334	813	2066	706	908	203	1756	721	478	1051	275
Cleveland, OH	2392	349	713	1264	445	753	989	815	527	1078	446	493	2498	1047	824	1046	430	2045	128	2416	600	559	2238	583	268	552	753	1727	1443	2384	2408	2336	1070	2068	949	1091	114	1971	933	341	1192	74
Columbia, SC	2426	494	612	658	891	1276	555	379	458	701	715	412	2703	1091	1283	440	627	2025	572	2972	888	215	2626	390	789	737	1320	2115	1180	2389	2738	2971	833	2572	408	497	683	2080	1018	498	586	561
Columbus, OH	2254	211	575	1210	448	753	834	707	389	940	551	559	2391	909	795	997	460	1907	186	2478	713	453	2295	498	397	414	745	1711	1305	2277	2461	2408	592	2115	828	1513	138	1833	795	418	1146	170
Dallas, TX	1401	819	455	1321	1013	1013	592	677	666	530	1525	1359	1803	211	693	1078	1427	1013	1209	2059	1695	1152	1731	1313	1420	641	1013	1287	284	1369	1865	2203	196	1978	835	1086	1112	964	259	1306	1265	1193
Daytona Beach, FL	2407	801	749	259	1180	1458	502	458	639	632	1054	702	2831	1257	1402	81	914	2102	859	3018	1201	559	2758	713	1176	956	1458	2283	1175	2418	2827	3070	903	2811	259	141	1063	1999	1156	802	195	986
Denver, CO	1009	1127	1151	2131	1070	956	1372	1412	1167	1323	1775	1800	1223	660	559	1896	1762	802	1475	1283	1961	1694	1030	1904	1637	859	956	519	975	1054	1233	1371	1112	1095	1727	1858	1272	835	714	1654	2157	1421
Des Moines, IA	1654	591	599	1582	365	251	954	1131	712	978	1070	1202	1742	576	146	1363	1037	1479	770	1816	1256	1123	1606	1293	932	377	251	1085	1022	1760	1832	1889	827	1556	1216	1460	567	1484	471	1054	1646	737
Detroit, MI	2270	365	712	1386	389	698	988	814	536	1077	620	711	2350	1030	726	1143	585	2019	304	2368	746	643	2190	609	424	535	698	1679	1500	2419	2360	2299	1069	2020	957	1200	65	1938	916	506	1305	239
El Paso, TX	818	1467	1103	1958	1528	1520	1236	1325	1314	1127	2173	1998	1194	708	1256	1735	2073	438	1833	1661	2335	1800	1185	2023	2036	1238	1541	894	576	721	1184	1775	844	1686	1492	1743	1699	316	788	1954	1922	1804
Fargo, ND	1844	949	1224	1987	576	244	1413	1525	1138	1521	1450	1581	1870	989	464	1826	1370	1791	1112	1484	1566	1485	1660	1481	1249	872	244	1172	1402	1934	1886	1440	1229	1166	1598	1849	885	1897	972	1322	2028	1038
Fort Lauderdale, FL	2704	1078	989	24	1443	1723	705	671	900	843	1289	964	3041	1481	1604	208	1127	2244	1216	3204	1459	794	3008	946	1410	1208	1753	2578	1378	2621	3073	3382	1144	3014	462	268	1289	2271	1409	1062	41	1219
Fort Wayne, IN	2137	222	592	1326	256	564	839	686	385	916	691	709	2257	852	634	1059	604	1831	336	2299	799	603	2056	635	464	369	564	1527	1269	2189	2304	2202	909	1921	871	1092	105	1783	738	531	1157	275
Fort Worth, TX	1361	851	487	1353	1059	1001	624	701	698	519	1557	1382	1723	210	634	1110	1459	983	1241	2003	1727	1184	1608	1333	1452	698	987	1184	283	1332	1735	2071	228	1978	867	1118	1144	932	305	1338	1297	1225
Grand Rapids, MI	2148	373	690	1356	275	583	1006	819	534	1071	706	802	2308	932	640	1188	672	1906	397	2251	859	754	2067	722	499	437	583	1556	1353	2269	2318	2221	1018	1941	1022	1219	170	1856	818	608	1476	340
Greensboro, NC	2478	462	640	810	826	1135	681	512	429	810	561	227	2809	1118	1208	648	438	2099	438	2823	706	73	2591	191	600	762	1138	2059	1321	2457	2740	2773	937	2503	608	673	516	2059	1037	309	737	482
Hartford, CT	2829	867	1209	1427	948	1257	1290	1133	973	1436	101	471	2909	1546	1321	1208	220	2523	486	2877	73	624	2749	455	324	1030	1257	2238	1965	2944	3019	2918	1529	2656	1223	1240	624	2433	1411	341	1339	470
Houston, TX	1581	948	584	1207	1155	1266	478	709	795	367	1679	1362	1957	454	949	964	1581	1110	1345	2369	1849	1233	1932	2291	1555	835	1266	1460	203	1484	1947	2498	271	2222	721	972	1249	1079	504	1420	1151	1322
Indianapolis, IN	2075	129	470	1208	283	591	749	590	302	857	730	669	2212	730	616	989	624	1719	349	2335	892	635	2116	907	551	251	591	1605	1200	2067	2224	2229	827	1961	818	1069	243	668	616	551	1176	341
Jackson, MS	1880	575	211	907	884	1123	178	255	422	193	1192	948	2270	575	914	697	1094	1500	965	2518	1362	815	2143	946	1183	495	1160	1742	649	1783	2183	2585	223	2205	421	672	876	1378	510	965	851	949
Jacksonville, FL	2402	729	697	356	1067	1374	413	379	592	551	957	632	2771	1181	1305	138	859	2100	882	3030	1127	584	2716	693	1102	867	1374	2286	1086	2329	2781	3042	814	2822	170	195	989	2010	1167	730	284	958
Kansas City, MO	1589	519	470	1475	568	459	819	867	590	857	1192	1179	1799	373	195	1266	1134	1277	851	1809	1378	1086	1606	1205	1062	251	459	1095	795	1627	1869	1834	624	1727	1045	1296	717	1281	283	1052	144	843
Knoxville, TN	2201	246	385	859	643	932	449	348	174	607	753	412	2509	847	930	665	646	1845	515	2550	951	356	2363	440	710	497	935	1766	1150	2269	2549	2553	729	2298	584	730	449	1755	782	554	806	521
Las Vegas, NV	275	1861	1581	2570	1752	1630	1841	2015	1792	1800	2520	2534	582	1119	1249	2311	2449	284	2181	991	2683	2319	478	2406	2371	1581	1630	413	1273	349	592	1209	1468	1119	2068	2319	1954	389	1224	2376	2498	2124
Lincoln, NE	1476	730	647	1673	560	409	1039	975	770	1014	1274	1354	1604	433	57	1452	1260	1236	965	1641	1451	1263	1411	1249	1135	462	408	900	916	1573	1614	1636	727	1460	1227	1477	762	1246	416	1184	1598	923
Little Rock	1678	502	138	1208	772	881	430	470	349	430	1235	1025	1984	324	690	965	1110	1379	899	2270	1395	851	1986	963	1111	422	881	1462	592	1743	1994	2368	219	2092	679	958	803	1257	259	832	1101	876
Los Angeles, CA	0	2136	1816	2828	2238	1905	2013	2035	2027	1883	2790	2809	372	1354	1508	2585	2717	389	2449	989	2902	2554	511	2641	2400	1849	1905	672	1378	121	382	1159	1687	1406	2342	2578	2213	502	1459	2659	2772	2424
Louisville, KY	2136	0	364	1102	397	705	626	466	178	729	707	607	2333	738	671	907	664	1782	381	2298	421	525	2132	686	608	290	705	1638	1103	2119	2388	2320	721	2075	664	915	300	1697	633	533	1094	373
Memphis, TN	1816	364	0	1013	673	949	389	332	211	397	1095	876	2122	462	705	770	989	1444	795	2408	1257	712	2124	825	973	300	949	1613	730	1881	2132	2506	357	2230	527	778	665	1370	397	875	957	738
Miami, FL	2828	1102	1013	0	1435	1743	729	695	908	867	1313	988	3087	1524	1670	227	1215	2448	1248	3366	1483	818	3032	988	1435	1231	1743	2602	1402	2645	3097	3406	1130	3138	486	292	1293	2326	1483	1086	65	1264
Milwaukee, WI	2238	397	673	1435	0	332	981	859	571	1045	851	948	2171	884	503	1224	834	1873	567	2002	1021	899	1930	832	697	389	332	1419	1305	2109	2175	1970	1013	1702	1053	1240	332	1808	770	770	1386	510
Minneapolis, MN	1905	705	949	1743	332	0	1227	1281	892	1346	1160	1337	2065	803	381	1673	1126	1679	868	1670	1322	1241	1776	1237	1005	628	1	1475	1265	1975	2075	1638	985	1370	1354	1589	641	1702	705	1078	1737	794
Mobile, AL	2013	626	389	729	981	1227	0	176	462	146	1176	884	2351	786	1011	486	1078	1593	1050	2611	1346	738	2278	867	1273	673	1158	1903	697	1971	2361	2710	401	2342	243	494	940	1542	713	949	673	1005
Montgomery, AL	2035	466	332	695	859	1281	176	0	288	322	1010	715	2295	794	1037	452	930	1655	843	2632	1191	561	2456	792	1179	632	1281	1918	904	2127	2464	2838	478	2562	209	460	766	1633	765	794	639	831
Nashville, TN	2027	178	211	908	571	892	462	288	0	551	859	665	2374	673	735	689	761	1671	575	2376	1029	502	2189	614	770	323	892	1678	941	2092	2375	2384	669	2124	486	737	478	1581	608	632	875	543
New Orleans, LA	1883	729	397	867	1045	1346	146	322	551	0	1322	1054	2317	681	1021	624	1224	1540	1078	2505	1492	876	2278	1114	1362	681	1346	1842	551	1824	2327	2574	309	2409	381	632	1005	1419	657	1095	811	1095
New York, NY	2790	707	1095	1313	851	1160	1176	1010	859	1322	0	389	2876	1436	1208	1094	101	2425	381	2880	162	510	2635	366	320	941	1160	2124	1832	2773	2886	2837	1415	2569	1109	1126	556	2360	1331	252	1223	403
Norfolk, VA	2809	607	876	988	948	1337	884	715	665	1054	389	0	2957	1349	1362	770	268	2393	365	2968	527	197	2789	98	535	927	1337	2262	1606	2669	2967	2975	1203	2700	802	827	592	2271	1234	190	916	438
Oakland, CA	372	2333	2122	3087	2171	2065	2351	2295	2374	2317	2876	2957	0	1660	1596	2844	2913	744	2528	614	2974	2865	201	2988	2681	2003	2065	545	1734	493	9	777	2052	979	2601	2836	2233	878	1766	2772	3055	2463
Oklahoma City, OK	1354	738	462	1524	884	803	786	794	673	681	1436	1349	1660	0	495	1281	1363	998	1095	1946	1597	1200	1662	1287	1298	495	803	1151	478	1345	1670	2044	389	1768	1038	1289	961	908	105	1305	1468	1087
Omaha, NE	1508	671	705	1670	503	381	1110	1037	735	1021	1208	1362	1596	495	0	1421	1200	1427	908	1605	1394	1281	1395	1400	1078	446	381	947	949	1641	1606	1679	729	1403	1241	1492	705	1400	401	1151	1671	875
Orlando, FL	2585	907	770	227	1224	1673	486	452	689	624	1094	770	2844	1281	1421	0	1005	2205	1025	3123	1273	608	2789	776	1200	1030	1551	2359	1159	2402	2854	3163	920	2895	243	89	1086	2083	1240	876	194	1052
Philadelphia, PA	2717	664	989	1215	834	1126	1078	930	761	1224	101	268	2913	1363	1200	1005	0	2374	292	2830	259	412	2627	252	324	868	1126	2209	1734	2911	2923	2780	1270	2512	1020	1037	502	2287	1249	133	1134	357
Phoenix, AZ	389	1782	1444	2448	1873	1679	1593	1655	1671	1540	2425	2393	744	998	1427	2205	2374	0	2084	1322	2586	2172	754	2285	2281	1484	1808	673	989	357	754	1492	1282	1386	1962	2213	1950	122	1103	2367	2392	2061
Pittsburgh, PA	2449	381	795	1248	567	868	1050	843	575	1078	381	365	2528	1095	908	1025	292	2084	0	2538	559	519	2335	333	284	600	868	1824	1468	2441	2538	2513	1087	2190	932	998	227	2021	981	219	1111	65
Portland, OR	985	2298	2408	3366	2002	1670	2611	2632	2376	2505	2880	2968	614	1946	1605	3123	2830	1322	2538	0	3000	2903	616	3012	2676	2068	1670	764	2168	1078	624	170	2255	365	2880	3131	2311	1483	1987	2846	3310	2481
Providence, RI	2902	421	1257	1483	1021	1322	1346	1191	1029	1492	162	527	2974	1597	1394	1273	259	2586	559	3000	0	673	2814	511	381	1102	1322	2303	2002	2978	2984	2967	1585	2644	1288	1322	689	252	1483	397	1402	538
Raleigh, NC	2554	525	713	818	899	1241	738	561	502	876	510	197	2865	1200	1281	608	412	2172	519	2903	673	0	2716	175	600	835	1241	2205	1427	2529	2797	2911	538	2651	624	657	584	2124	1103	283	754	535
Reno, NV	511	2132	2124	3032	1930	1776	2278	2456	2189	2278	2635	2789	201	1662	1395	2789	2627	754	2335	616	2814	2716	0	2803	2489	1881	1776	511	1768	535	211	810	1927	770	2546	2797	2133	867	1702	2579	2976	2303
Richmond, VA	2641	686	825	988	832	1237	867	792	614	1114	366	98	2988	1287	1400	776	252	2285	333	3012	511	175	2803	0	455	976	1237	2324	1555	2643	2989	3029	1173	2761	794	827	630	2425	1222	114	924	662
Rochester, NY	2400	608	973	1435	697	1005	1273	1179	770	1362	320	535	2681	1298	1078	1200	324	2281	284	2676	381	600	2489	455	0	803	1005	1978	1686	2674	2691	2660	1361	2384	1208	1257	381	2222	1398	341	1346	265
Saint Louis, MO	1849	290	300	1231	389	628	673	632	323	681	941	927	2003	495	446	1030	868	1484	600	2068	1102	835	1881	976	803	0	628	1370	916	1840	2075	2076	624	1881	795	1030	466	1419	381	795	1241	592
Saint Paul, MN	1905	705	949	1743	332	1	1158	1281	892	1346	1160	1337	2065	803	381	1551	1126	1808	868	1670	1322	1241	1776	1237	1005	628	0	1475	1265	1975	2075	1638	985	1370	1354	1589	641	1702	705	1078	1737	794
Salt Lake City, UT	672	1638	1613	2602	1419	1475	1903	1918	1678	1842	2124	2262	545	1151	947	2359	2209	673	1824	764	2303	2205	511	2324	1978	1370	1475	0	1447	762	714	851	1563	706	2116	2318	1715	795	1223	2141	2490	1805
San Antonio, TX	1378	1103	730	1402	1305	1265	697	904	941	551	1832	1606	1734	478	949	1159	1734	989	1468	2168	2002	1427	1768	1555	1686	916	1265	1447	0	1274	1774	2255	474	2110	916	1151	1387	876	535	1605	1370	1477
San Diego, CA	121	2119	1881	2645	2109	1975	1971	2127	2092	1824	2773	2669	493	1345	1641	2402	2911	357	2441	1078	2978	2529	535	2643	2674	1840	1975	762	1274	0	527	1276	1565	1403	2213	2464	2604	405	1403	2733	2072	2456
San Francisco, CA	382	2388	2132	3097	2175	2075	2361	2464	2375	2327	2886	2967	9	1670	1606	2854	2923	754	2538	624	2984	2797	211	2989	2691	2075	2075	714	1774	527	0	787	2061	852	2611	2846	2415	868	1776	2949	3065	2569
Seattle, WA	1159	2343	2506	3406	1970	1638	2710	2838	2384	2574	2837	2975	777	2044	1679	3163	2780	1492	2513	170	2967	2911	810	3029	2660	2076	1638	851	2255	1276	787	0	2335	274	2920	3155	2231	1573	2034	2684	3388	2456
Shreveport, LA	1687	721	357	1130	1013	985	401	478	669	309	1415	1203	2052	389	729	920	1270	1282	1087	2255	1585	538	1927	1173	1361	624	985	1563	474	1565	2061	2335	0	2038	644	895	1099	1160	356	953	507	1081
Spokane, WA	1406	2075	2230	3138	1702	1370	2342	2562	2124	2409	2569	2700	979	1768	1403	2895	2512	1386	2190	365	2644	2651	770	2761	2384	1816	1370	706	2110	1403	852	274	2038	0	2652	2887	2100	1496	1727	2417	3196	2125
Tallahassee, FL	2342	664	527	486	1053	1354	243	209	486	381	1109	802	2601	1038	1241	243	1020	1962	932	2880	1288	624	2546	794	1208	795	1354	2116	916	2213	2611	2920	644	2652	0	251	900	1840	955	891	430	1005
Tampa, FL	2578	915	778	292	1240	1589	494	460	737	632	1126	827	2836	1289	1492	89	1037	2213	998	3131	1322	657	2797	827	1251	1030	1589	2318	1151	2464	2846	3155	895	2887	251	0	1143	2076	1182	908	219	1088
Toledo, OH	2213	300	665	1293	332	641	940	766	478	1005	556	592	2293	961	705	1086	502	1950	227	2311	689	584	2133	630	381	466	641	1715	1387	2604	2415	2231	1099	2100	900	1143	0	2051	867	438	1248	170
Tuscon, AZ	502	1697	1370	2326	1808	1702	1542	1633	1581	1419	2360	2271	878	908	1400	2083	2287	122	2021	1483	252	2124	867	2425	2222	1419	1702	795	876	405	868	1573	1160	1496	1840	2076	2051	0	1038	2254	2270	2003
Tulsa, OK	1459	633	397	1483	770	705	713	765	608	657	1331	1234	1766	105	401	1240	1249	1103	981	1987	1483	1103	1702	1222	1398	381	705	1223	535	1403	1776	2034	356	1727	955	1182	867	1038	0	1284	1167	964
Washington, DC	2659	533	875	1086	770	1078	949	796	632	1095	252	190	2772	1305	1151	876	133	2367	219	2846	397	283	2579	114	341	795	1078	2141	1605	2733	2949	2684	953	2417	891	908	438	2254	1284	0	1005	283
West Palm Beach, FL	2772	1094	957	65	1386	1737	673	639	875	811	1223	916	3055	1468	1671	194	1134	2392	1111	3310	1402	754	2976	924	1346	1241	1737	2490	1370	2072	3065	3388	507	3196	430	219	1248	2270	1167	1005	0	1167
Youngstown, OH	2424	373	738	1238	510	794	1005	831	543	1095	403	438	2463	1087	875	1052	357	2076	65	2481	527	535	2303	662	265	592	794	1877	1477	2432	2569	2456	1181	2125	1005	1088	170	2003	964	283	1167	0

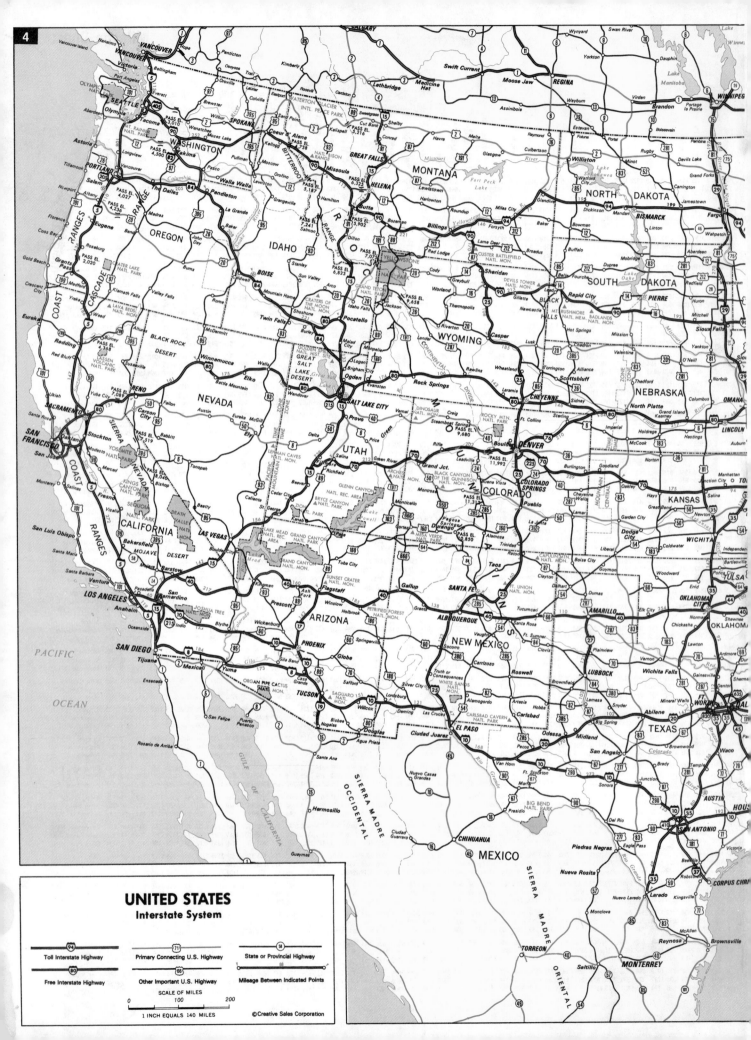

UNITED STATES
Interstate System

| Toll Interstate Highway | Primary Connecting U.S. Highway | State or Provincial Highway |
| Free Interstate Highway | Other Important U.S. Highway | Mileage Between Indicated Points |

SCALE OF MILES

0   100   200

1 INCH EQUALS 140 MILES

©Creative Sales Corporation

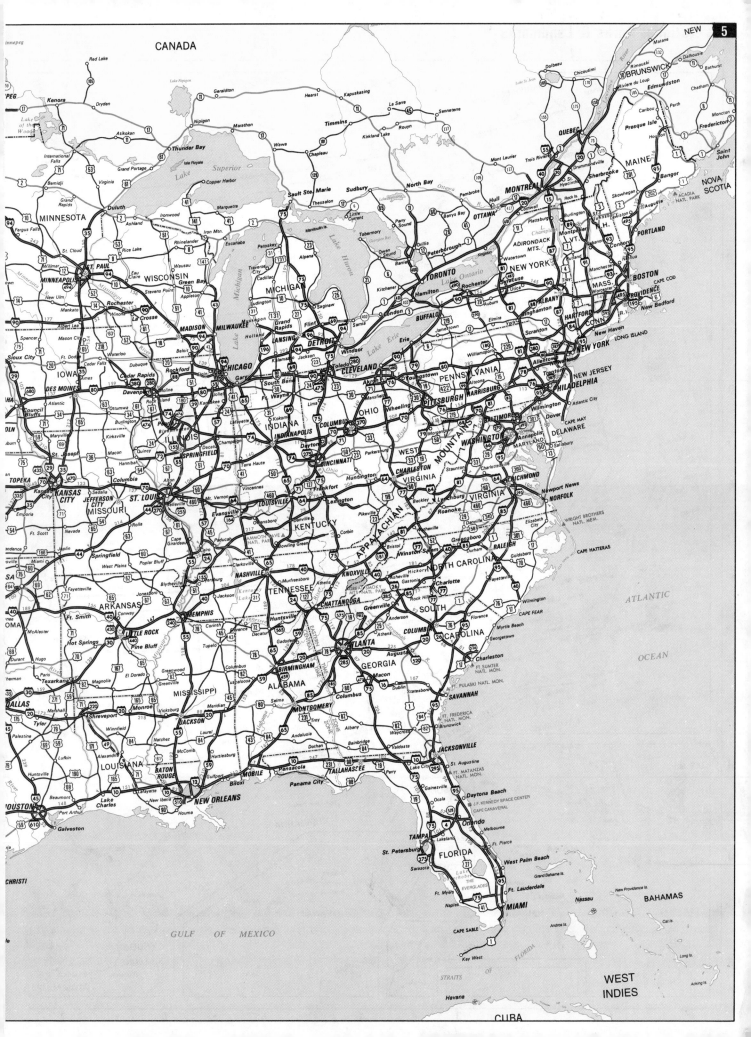

Grid columns: 1 2 3 4 5 6 7

Grid rows: A B C D E F G H J K

BRITISH COLUMBIA
ALBERTA
Calgary
Saskatoon
SASKATCHEWAN
Regina
Moose Jaw
MANITOBA
Winnipeg
Riding Mountain Nat'l Park
CANADA
UNITED STATES

Vancouver
Pacific Rim Nat'l Park
San Juan Island Nat'l Hist. Park
Olympic Nat'l Park
Olympic Nat'l Forest
Seattle
Tacoma
Mt. Rainier Nat'l Park
WASHINGTON
Spokane
Coeur d'Alene
MONTANA
Great Falls
Helena
Butte
Billings
Yellowstone Nat'l Park

Ft. Vancouver Nat'l Hist. Site and Museum
Astoria
Portland
Salem
Mt. Hood Nat'l Forest
Eugene
OREGON
John Day Fossil Beds Nat'l Mon.
Pendleton
Walla Walla
Umatilla Nat'l Forest
Wallowa Whitman Nat'l Forest
Malheur Nat'l Forest
IDAHO
Clearwater Nat'l Forest
Nezperce Nat'l Forest
Salmon Nat'l Forest
Payette Nat'l Forest
Boise
Sawtooth Nat'l Forest
Craters of the Moon Nat'l Mon.
Twin Falls
Pocatello
Jackson
Grand Teton Nat'l Park

Ft. Union Nat'l Hist. Site
Williston
Theodore Roosevelt Nat'l Park North
Theodore Roosevelt Nat'l Park South
Knife River Indian Village Nat'l Hist. Site
NORTH DAKOTA
Bismarck
Fargo
Ft. Peck Lake
Lake Sakakawea

Crater Lake Nat'l Park
Oregon Caves Nat'l Mon.
Redwood Nat'l Park
Grants Pass
Klamath Nat'l Forest
Lava Beds Nat'l Mon.
Modoc Nat'l Forest
Eureka
Six Rivers Nat'l Forest
Trinity Nat'l Forest
Shasta Nat'l Forest
Redding
Lassen Volcanic Nat'l Park
Mendocino Nat'l Forest
Plumas Nat'l Forest
Tahoe Nat'l Forest
Reno
Carson City
NEVADA
BLACK ROCK DESERT
Winnemucca
Humboldt Nat'l Forest
GREAT SALT LAKE DESERT
GREAT SALT LAKE
Golden Spike Nat'l Hist. Site
Wasatch Nat'l Forest
Ogden
Salt Lake City
Provo
UTAH
Dinosaur Nat'l Mon.
WYOMING
Casper
Cheyenne
Medicine Bow Nat'l Forest
Laramie
Rock Springs
Fossil Butte Nat'l Mon.
Shoshone Nat'l Forest
Bighorn Nat'l Forest
Custer Nat'l Forest
Custer Battlefield Nat'l Mon.
Devil's Tower Nat'l Mon.
BLACK HILLS
Rapid City
Mt. Rushmore Nat'l Mem.
Wind Cave Nat'l Park
Hot Springs
Badlands Nat'l Park
Pierre
SOUTH DAKOTA
Sioux Falls
Lake Oahe

Sacramento
Oakland
San Francisco
San Jose
Pt. Reyes Nat'l Seashore
John Muir Nat'l Hist. Site
Monterrey
Pinnacles Nat'l Mon.
Los Padres Nat'l Forest
Fresno
Yosemite Nat'l Park
Kings Canyon Nat'l Park
Sequoia Nat'l Forest
Sequoia Nat'l Park
Death Valley Nat'l Mon.
San Luis Obispo
Bakersfield
Los Angeles
Anaheim
Channel Islands Nat'l Park
Ventura
Santa Barbara
Cabrillo Nat'l Mon.
San Diego
Tijuana
Mexicali
BAJA CALIFORNIA
SIERRA NEVADA
COASTAL RANGES
MOJAVE DESERT
Barstow
CALIFORNIA
San Bernardino Nat'l Forest
Angeles Nat'l Forest
Cleveland Nat'l Forest
Joshua Tree Nat'l Mon.
Las Vegas
Lake Mead
ARIZONA
Ely
Lehman Caves Nat'l Mon.
Toiyabe Nat'l Forest
Manti-La Sal Nat'l Forest
Cedar Breaks Nat'l Mon.
Capitol Reef Nat'l Park
Arches Nat'l Park
Canyonlands Nat'l Park
Dixie Nat'l Forest
Zion Nat'l Park
Bryce Canyon Nat'l Park
Natural Bridges Nat'l Mon.
Lake Powell
Hovenweep Nat'l Mon.
Rainbow Bridge Nat'l Mon.
Kaibab Nat'l Forest
Grand Canyon Nat'l Park
Canyon De Chelly Nat'l Mon.
Wupatki Nat'l Mon.
Sunset Crater Nat'l Mon.
Flagstaff
Prescott
Walnut Canyon Nat'l Mon.
Coconino Nat'l Forest
Petrified Forest Nat'l Park
Tonto Nat'l Forest
Phoenix
Globe
Tonto Nat'l Mon.
Apache Nat'l Forest
Casa Grande Ruins Nat'l Mon.
Saguaro Nat'l Mon.
Organ Pipe Cactus Nat'l Mon.
Tucson
Coronado Nat'l Forest
Coronado Nat'l Mem.
Chiricahua Nat'l Mon.
Nogales
Douglas
COLORADO
Grand Mesa Nat'l Forest
White River Nat'l Forest
Routt Nat'l Forest
Roosevelt Nat'l Forest
Arapaho Nat'l Forest
Boulder
Denver
Colorado Springs
Pueblo
Gunnison Nat'l Forest
Black Canyon of the Gunnison Nat'l Mon.
Colorado Nat'l Mon.
Pike Nat'l Forest
Durango
Mesa Verde Nat'l Park
San Juan Nat'l Forest
Rio Grande Nat'l Forest
Comanche Nat'l Grassland
Pawnee Nat'l Grassland
NEBRASKA
Nebraska Nat'l Forest
Samuel R. McKelvie Nat'l Forest
Scottsbluff
North Platte
Lincoln
KANSAS
Dodge City
Wichita
NEW MEXICO
Albuquerque
Santa Fe
Bandelier Nat'l Mon.
Aztec Ruins Nat'l Mon.
Chaco Canyon Nat'l Mon.
El Morro Nat'l Mon.
Cibola Nat'l Forest
Santa Fe Nat'l Forest
Carson Nat'l Forest
Gran Quivira Nat'l Mon.
Gila Nat'l Forest
Gila Cliff Dwellings Nat'l Mon.
Pecos Nat'l Mon.
Kiowa Nat'l Grasslands
Capulin Mtn. Nat'l Mon.
Lincoln Nat'l Forest
White Sands Nat'l Mon.
Carlsbad
Carlsbad Caverns Nat'l Park
Guadalupe Mtns. Nat'l Park
El Paso
Ciudad Juarez
OKLAHOMA
Oklahoma City
Amarillo
Lubbock
Wichita Falls
Platt Nat'l Park
TEXAS
Ft. Worth
Dallas
Abilene
San Angelo
Midland
Odessa
Old Ft. Davis Nat'l Hist. Site
Big Bend Nat'l Park
Austin
Waco
San Antonio
Corpus Christi
Padre Island Nat'l Seashore
Brownsville
COAHUILA
NUEVO LEON
Monterrey
TAMAULIPAS
Piedras Negras
Nueva Rosita
Laredo
CHIHUAHUA
SONORA
SIERRA MADRE OCCIDENTAL
Nuevo Casas Grandes
Santa Ana
CONTINENTAL DIVIDE
MEXICO
UNITED STATES
Nogales
Yuma
Ensenada
PACIFIC OCEAN

U.S.S.R.
Arctic Ocean
Point Hope
Wainwright
Barrow
Prudhoe Bay
Noatak
Noatak Nat'l Preserve
Gates of the Arctic Nat'l Park & Preserve
Kobuk Valley Nat'l Park
Bering Land Bridge Nat'l Preserve
Noorvik
Nome
Kotzebue
CONTINENTAL DIVIDE
Fort Yukon
Fairbanks
College
Bering Sea
Hooper Bay
Norton Sound
Unalakleet
ALASKA
Denali Nat'l Park and Preserve
Yukon-Charley Nat'l Preserve
Delta Junction
Tok
U.S.
CANADA
YUKON
Togiak
Bristol Bay
Lake Clark Nat'l Park & Preserve
Anchorage
Palmer
Glennallen
Wrangell-St. Elias Nat'l Park
Chugach Nat'l Forest
Valdez
Cordova
Kluane Nat'l Park
Katmai Nat'l Park & Preserve
Kenai Fjords Nat'l Park
Seward
Kodiak
Kodiak Island
Aniakchak Nat'l Park & Preserve
Chugach Nat'l Forest
Gulf of Alaska
Tongass Nat'l Forest
Glacier Bay Nat'l Park
Juneau
Sitka
Ketchikan
B.C.
Pacific Ocean
Aleutian Islands

HAWAII
Wahiawa
Pearl City
Kaneohe
Honolulu
Lihue
Lahaina
Wailuku
Haleakala Nat'l Park
City of Refuge Nat'l Hist. Park
Hilo
Hawaii Volcanoes Nat'l Park
Pacific Ocean

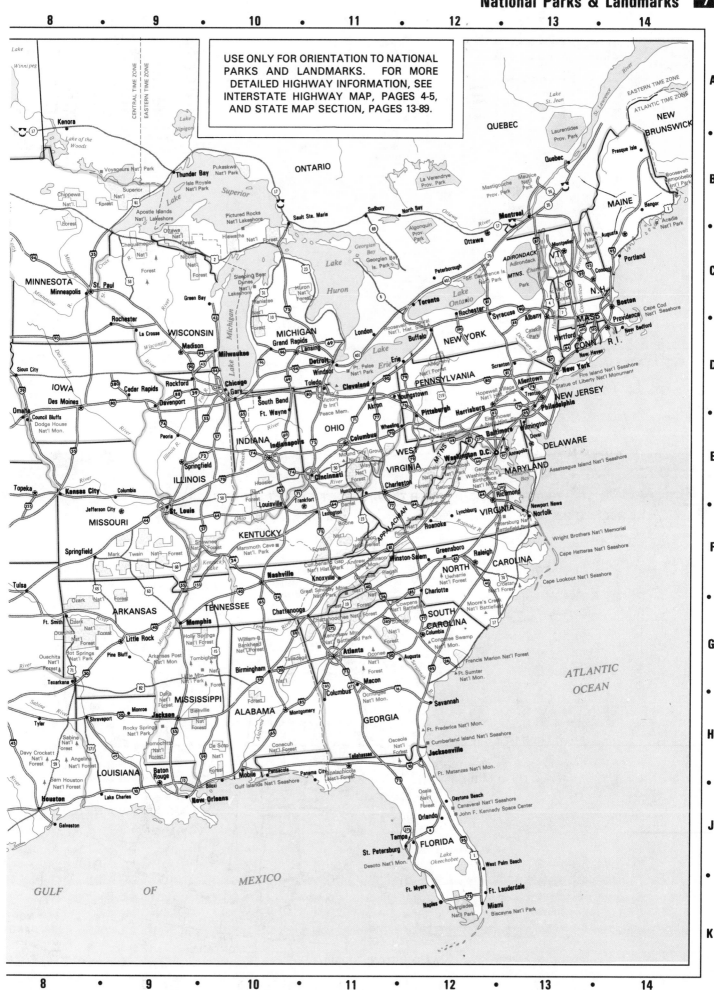

USE ONLY FOR ORIENTATION TO NATIONAL PARKS AND LANDMARKS. FOR MORE DETAILED HIGHWAY INFORMATION, SEE INTERSTATE HIGHWAY MAP, PAGES 4-5, AND STATE MAP SECTION, PAGES 13-89.

ALBERTA

Banff J-4
Calgary J-4
Camrose H-5
Cardston J-5
Drumheller . . . H-5
Edmonton H-5
Edson H-4
Fitzgerald F-5
Fort Chipewyn . F-4
Ft. McMurray . . G-5
Ft. Vermillion . . F-4

Grande Centre . . G-5
Grande Prairie . . G-4
Habay F-4
High Level F-4
High River J-4
Hinton H-4
Jasper H-4
Lethbridge J-5
Medicine Hat . . J-5
Peace River . . . G-4
Rainbow Lake . . F-4

Red Deer H-5
Rocky Mtn. House . H-4
Waterways G-5
Wetaskiwin . . . H-4
Whitecourt H-4

BRITISH COLUMBIA

Alert Bay J-2
Atlin F-2
Bella Coola . . . H-2
Campbell River . J-2

Cassiar F-2
Courtnay J-2
Cranbrook J-4
Dawson Creek . G-3
Ft. Nelson F-3
Ft. St. John . . . G-3
Hazelton G-2
Kamloops J-3
Kelowna J-3
Kimberley J-4
Kitimat H-2
Masset G-1
Nanaimo J-2

Nelson J-4
New Westminster J-3
Ocean Falls . . . H-2
Penticton J-4
Port Alberni . . . J-2
Port Alice J-2
Powell River . . . J-3
Prince George . . H-3
Prince Rupert . . G-2
Quesnel H-3
Revelstoke H-3
Sandpit H-1

Smithers G-2
Stewart G-2
Telegraph Creek . F-2
Trail J-4
Ucluelet J-2
Vancouver J-3
Vernon J-4
Victoria J-4
Ware G-3
Williams Lake . . H-3

MANITOBA

Berens River . . . G-7
Brandon H-7
Brochet F-6
Churchill F-7
Dauphin H-7
Flin Flon G-6
Gillam F-7
Gods Lake G-7
Grand Rapids . . G-7
Island Lake . . . G-7

Lynn Lake F-6
Norway House . . G-7
Portage la Prairie . H-7
Selkirk H-8
Snow Lake G-7
S. Indian Lake . . F-7
Swan River H-7
The Pas G-6
Thompson F-7
Virden J-7
Winnipeg H-8

NEW BRUNSWICK

Bathurst E-13
Campbellton . . . E-12
Chatam E-13
Edmundston . . . F-12
Fredricton F-13
Moncton E-13
Newcastle E-13
St. John F-13
St. Stephen . . . F-13
Tracadie E-13

Woodstock F-13

NEWFOUNDLAND

Battle Harbour . . C-13
Bonavista C-14
Cartwright C-12
Channel-Port aux
Basques D-14
Churchill Falls . . D-12
Corner Brook . . D-13
Gander C-14

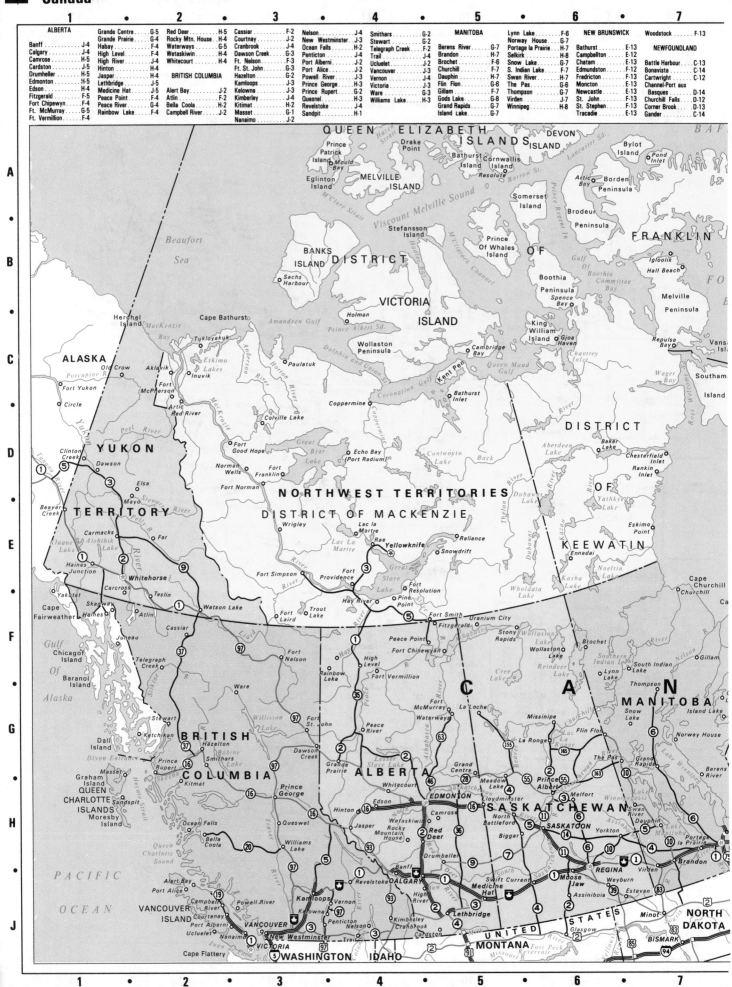

8	9	10	11	12	13	14

Goose Bay.....C-12
Grand Falls.....C-11
Hebron.....C-11
Hopedale.....C-11
Labrador City.....D-11
Makkovic.....C-12
Marystown.....D-14
Northwest River.....C-12
Nutak.....C-14
Placentia.....C-14
St. John's.....C-14

St. Pierre (France).....D-14
Stephenville.....D-13
Wabana.....C-14

N.W. TERRITORY
Aklavik.....C-2
Artic Bay.....A-6
Artic Red River.....D-2
Baker Lake.....D-6
Bathurst Inlet.....C-5
Cambridge Bay.....C-5
Cape Dorset.....C-8
Cape Dyer.....A-9
Chesterfield Inlet.....D-7
Clyde.....A-8
Colville Lake.....D-3
Coppermine.....D-4
Echo Bay (Port Radium).....D-4
Ennadai.....E-6
Eskimo Point.....E-7
Ft. Franklin.....D-3
Ft. Good Hope.....D-3
Ft. Laird.....F-3
Ft. McPherson.....D-2
Ft. Norman.....D-3
Ft. Providence.....E-4
Ft. Resolution.....F-4
Ft. Simpson.....E-3
Ft. Smith.....F-4
Frobisher Bay.....B-9
Gjoa Haven.....B-7
Hall Beach.....B-7
Hay River.....E-4
Igloolik.....B-7
Inuvik.....C-2
Lac la Martre.....E-4
Lake Harbour.....B-9
Mould Bay.....A-4
Norman Wells.....D-3
Panguirtung.....A-9
Paulatuk.....C-3
Pine Point.....E-4
Pond Inlet.....A-7
Rae.....E-4
Rankin Inlet.....D-7
Reliance.....E-5
Repulse Bay.....B-7
Resolute.....A-5
Resolution Island.....B-10
Sachs Harbour.....B-3
Snowdrift.....E-5
Spence Bay.....B-6
Trout Lake.....F-3
Tukloy,ckuk.....C-2
Wrigley.....E-3
Yellowknife.....E-4

NOVA SCOTIA
Amherst.....E-13
Bridgewater.....F-14
Canso.....E-14
Glace Bay.....E-14
Halifax.....F-14
Kentville.....F-13
New Glasgow.....E-14
Shelburne.....F-14
Sydney.....E-14
Truro.....E-13
Yarmouth.....F-13

ONTARIO
Armstrong.....G-9
Atikokan.....H-8
Barrie.....H-11
Belleville.....H-12
Blind River.....H-10
Brantford.....J-11
Brockville.....G-12
Chatham.....J-11
Cochrane.....G-10
Cornwall.....G-12
Deep River.....G-11
Favourable Lake.....G-8
Ft. Albany.....F-9
Ft. Frances.....H-8
Ft. Severn.....F-8
Geraldton.....H-9
Goderich.....J-11
Guelph.....H-11
Hamilton.....H-12
Hearst.....G-10
Kapuskasing.....G-10
Kenora.....H-8
Kingston.....H-12
Kirkland Lake.....G-10
Kitchener.....H-11
Lec Seul.....H-8
London.....J-11
Marathon.....H-9
Moosonee.....F-10
Nakina.....G-9
Niagra Falls.....H-12
Nipigon.....H-9
North Bay.....H-11
Oshawa.....H-11
Ottawa.....G-12
Owen Sound.....H-11
Parry Sound.....H-11
Pembroke.....G-11
Peterborough.....H-12
Pickle Lake.....G-9
Red Lake.....H-8
Renfrew.....G-11
St. Catharines.....H-12
St. Thomas.....J-11
Sault Ste. Marie.....H-10
Sioux Lookout.....H-8
Smith's Falls.....G-12
Sudbury.....H-10
Thunder Bay.....H-9
Timmins.....G-10
Toronto.....H-11
Trenton.....H-12
Wawa.....H-10
Windsor.....J-11
Winisk.....F-9

PRINCE EDWARD ISLAND
Charlottetown.....E-13
Summerside.....E-13

QUEBEC
Alma.....F-12
Amos.....G-11
Arvida.....F-12
Baie Comeau.....E-12
Belin (Payne).....C-10
Cape Smith.....D-9
Chandler.....E-12
Chicoutimi.....F-12
Deception.....C-9
Desmaraisville.....F-11
Drummondville.....G-12
Eastmain.....F-10
Ft. Chimo.....C-10
Ft. George.....F-10
Ft. Rupert.....F-10
Gagnon.....E-11
Gaspe.....E-12
Granby.....G-12
Harve St. Pierre.....D-12
Hull.....G-12
Inoucdjouac (Port Harrison).....D-9
Ivujivik.....C-9
Koartac.....C-9
La Tugue.....F-12
Lac-Allard.....D-12
Levis.....F-12
Manicourgan.....E-12
Maniwaki.....G-11
Maricourt (Wakeham).....C-9
Matagami.....F-10
Matane.....E-12
Mont-Laurier.....G-12
Montreal.....G-12
Nitchequon.....E-11
Noranda.....G-11
Nouveau-Quebec (George River).....C-10
Port Alfred.....F-12
Port Cartier.....E-12
Poste-de-la-Baleine.....E-10
Povungnitak.....D-9
Quebec.....F-12
Rimouski.....E-12
Riviere-du-Loup.....F-12
Rouyn.....G-11
St. Hyacinthe.....G-12
St. Jean.....G-12
St. Jerome.....G-12
Ste. Anne-des-Monts.....E-12
Schefferville.....D-11
Senneterre.....G-11
Sept. Iles.....E-12
Shawinigan.....G-12
Sherbrooke.....G-12
Shibougamau.....F-11
Sorel.....G-12
Thetford Mines.....F-12
Trois-Rivieres.....G-12
Val-d'Or.....G-11

SASKATCHEWAN
Assiniboia.....J-6
Biggar.....H-5
Estevan.....J-7
La Loche.....G-5
La Rouge.....G-5
Lloydminster.....H-5
Meadow lake.....H-5
Melfort.....H-5
Missinipe.....G-6
Moose Jaw.....J-6
North Battleford.....H-5
Prince Albert.....H-6
Regina.....J-6
Saskatoon.....H-6
Stoney Rapids.....F-5
Swift Current.....J-5
Uranium City.....F-5
Weyburn.....J-6
Wollaston Lake.....F-5
Yorkton.....H-6

YUKON
Beaver Creek.....E-1
Carcross.....E-1
Carmacks.....D-1
Clinton Creek.....D-1
Dawson.....D-1
Elsa.....D-2
Faro.....E-2
Haines Jct.....E-2
Mayo.....E-2
Old Crow.....C-1
Teslin.....F-2
Watson Lake.....F-2
Whitehorse.....E-2

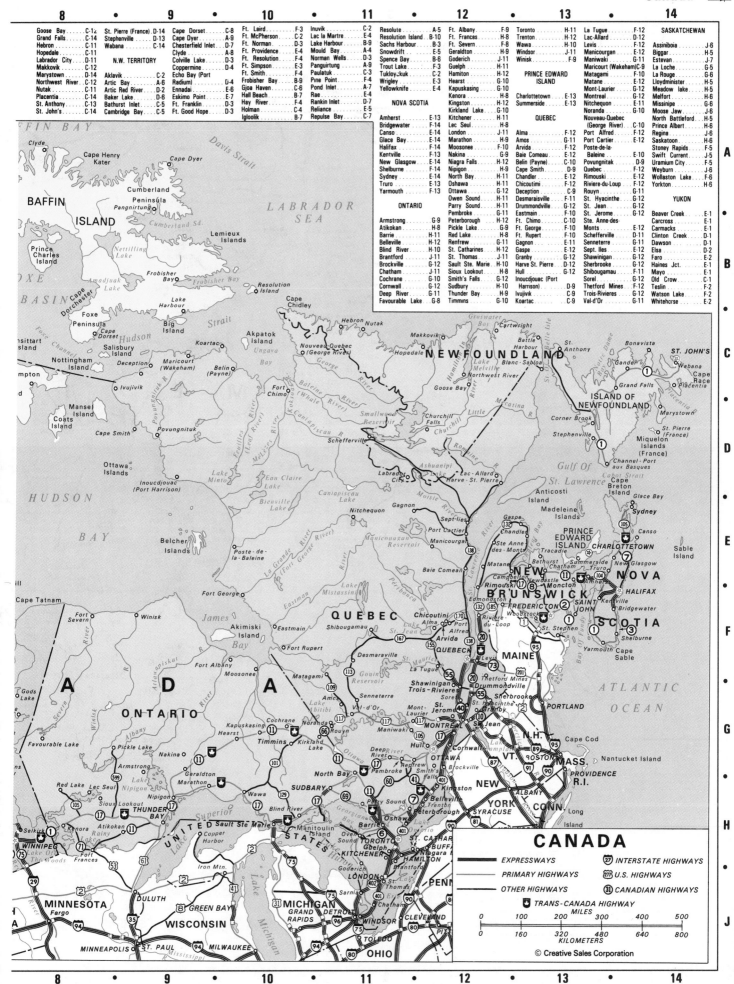

CANADA

▬▬ EXPRESSWAYS	(27) INTERSTATE HIGHWAYS
── PRIMARY HIGHWAYS	(27) U.S. HIGHWAYS
── OTHER HIGHWAYS	(31) CANADIAN HIGHWAYS
🛡 TRANS-CANADA HIGHWAY	

MILES
0   100   200   300   400   500

KILOMETERS
0   160   320   480   640   800

© Creative Sales Corporation

United States / Mexico Map

ARIZONA
NEW MEXICO
UNITED STATES
SONORA
BAJA CALIFORNIA
BAJA CALIFORNIA SUR
COAHUILA
CHIHUAHUA
DURANGO
SINALOA
ZACATECAS
NAYARIT
JALISCO
AGUASCALIENTES
COLIMA

M E X I C O

Gulf of California
Pacific Ocean
Rio Grande

Cities and places:

Tijuana, Tecate, Mexicali, San Luis, Yuma, Ensenada, San Felipe, El Rosario, Puerto Penasco, Ajo, Sonorita, Caborca, Altar, Santa Ana, Magdalena, Nogales, Agua Prieta, Cananea, Bavispe, Douglas, Safford, Silver City, Tucson, Las Cruces, Alamogordo, Artesia, Hobbs, Carlsbad, Midland, Odessa, Pecos, Rankin, Alpine, Sanderson, El Paso, Ciudad Juárez, Janos, Villa Ahumada, Moctezuma, Nueva Casas Grandes, Buenaventura, Gallego, Madera, El Sauz, Ciudad Guerrero, Chihuahua, Cuauhtémoc, La Perla, Ojinaga, Presidio, Boquillas del Carmen, La Cuesta, Nacimiento, Sabinas, Ocampo, Delicias, Ciudad Camargo, Jiménez, Escalón, Santa Barbara, Hidalgo del Parral, San Pedro de las Colonias, La Cadena, Gómez Palacio, TORREÓN, Parras, Concepción del Oro, Camacho, Puerto de la Libertad, Punta Prieta, Rasarito, Hermosillo, Bahia Kino, Sahuaripa, Tonichi, Yecora, Guaymas, Empalme, Rosario, San Ignacio, Santa Rosalia, Ciudad Obregón, Navojoa, El Fuerte, Sinaloa, Rosarito, Ejido Insurgentes, Los Mochis, Topolobampo, Guasave, Tameapa, Cosalá, Abasolo, Cuencamé, Canatlán, El Medano, Altata, Culiacán, Eldorado, Durango, Tepehuanes, La Paz, Todos Santos, San Jose del Cabo, La Cruz, El Salto, Sombrerete, Rio Grande, Mazatlán, Villa Union, Rosario, Fresnillo, Zacatecas, Monte Escobedo, Tuxpan, Los Corchos, Tepic, Jalpa, Lagos de Moreno, Moyahua, Aguascalientes, Las Varas, Puerto Vallarta, El Tuito, GUADALAJARA, Tlaquepaque, Ocotlán, Salamanca, Irapuato, Tepatitlan, Sahuayu, Uruapan, Autlán, Sayula, Ciudad Guzmán, Tomatlán, Melaque, Manzanillo, Colima, Apatzingán, Arteaga, Playa Azul, Ixtapa

Legend

MEXICO

EXPRESSWAYS	38 MEXICAN HIGHWAYS
PRIMARY THROUGH ROUTES	31 INTERSTATE HIGHWAYS
OTHER THROUGH ROADS	83 U.S. HIGHWAYS
OTHER ROADS	31 STATE HIGHWAYS

Approximate distances are shown between red markers on map.
Red numbers are kilometers, black numbers are miles.

MILES 0 — 100 — 200 — 300
KILOMETERS 0 — 160 — 320 — 480

© Creative Sales Corporation

MEXICO
Cities and Towns

Abasolo D-5	Ciudad del Maiz E-7	La Pesca D-7	Paraiso F-9	Sonorita A-2
Acambaro F-6	Coatzacoalcos F-9	La Piedad E-6	Parras C-6	Soto La Marina D-7
Acapulco G-6	Colima F-5	Las Varas E-5	Peto E-10	Tameapa C-4
Acatlan F-7	Comitan G-9	Leon E-6	Piedras Negras B-6	Tampico E-7
Acayucan F-8	Conception de Oro D-6	Linares D-7	Pijijiapan G-9	Tapachula G-9
Agua Prieta A-3	Cordoba F-8	Los Corchos E-5	Pinotepa Nacional G-7	Tapanatepec G-9
Aguascalientes E-6	Cosala D-4	Los Mochis C-3	Piste E-11	Taxco F-7
Altar A-3	Cuauhtemoc B-4	Madera B-4	Playa Azul F-6	Teapa F-9
Altata D-4	Cuencame D-5	Magdalena A-3	Pochutla G-8	Tecate A-1
Alvarado F-8	Cuernavaca F-7	Malpaso G-9	Poza Pica E-7	Tehuacan F-7
Apatzingan F-6	Culiacan D-4	Manuel E-7	Progreso E-10	Tehuantepec G-8
Arcelia F-6	Delicias B-5	Manzanillo F-5	Puebla F-7	Temporal E-7
Arriga G-9	Durango D-5	Matamoros C-7	Puerto de la	Tepatitlan E-6
Arteaga F-6	Dzilam de Bravo E-10	Matehuala D-6	Libertad B-2	Tepehuanes D-5
Arlixco F-7	Ejido Insurgentes C-3	Matias Romero G-8	Puerto Escondido G-8	Tepic E-5
Autlan F-5	Eldorado D-4	Mazatlan D-4	Puerto Juarez E-11	Ticul E-10
Bahia Kino B-2	El Fuerte C-4	Melaque F-5	Puerto Madero G-9	Tijuana A-1
Bavispe B-4	El Medana D-3	Merida E-10	Puerto Penasco A-2	Tiquicheo F-6
Becal E-10	El Rosario A-1	Mexicali A-1	Punta Prieta B-2	Tlaciaco G-7
Boquillas de	El Sauz B-4	Mexico City F-7	Queretaro E-6	Tlaxcala F-7
Carmen B-6	El Tuito E-5	Miahuatlan G-8	Rasarito B-2	Tlaxiaco G-7
Buenaventura B-4	Empalme B-3	Mier C-7	Reynosa C-7	Todos Santos D-3
Caborca A-2	Ensanada A-1	Minatitlan F-8	Rio Grande D-6	Toluca F-5
Camacho D-6	Escalon C-5	Moctezuma B-4	Rio Lagartos E-11	Tomatian B-3
Campeche E-10	Escarcega F-10	Molango E-7	Rosario C-3	Tonichi C-3
Cananea A-3	Fresnillo D-5	Moncloya C-6	Rosario D-4	Topolobampo C-3
Canatlan D-5	Gallego B-4	Monte Escobedo E-5	Sabinas C-6	Torreon C-5
Cardenas F-9	Gomez Palacio C-5	Montemorelos D-7	Sabinas Hidagalo C-6	Totolapan G-8
Celaya E-6	Guadalajara E-5	Monterrey C-6	Sahuaripa B-3	Tulancingo F-7
Celestun E-10	Guasave C-4	Morelia F-6	Salamanca E-6	Tulum E-11
Champoton F-10	Guaymas B-3	Morelos B-6	Salinas C-6	Tuxpan E-5
Chetumal F-11	Hermosillo B-3	Moyahua E-5	Salina Cruz G-8	Tuxpan E-7
Chihuahua B-5	Hidalgo del Parral C-5	Nacimiento C-6	Saltillo C-6	Tuxtepec F-8
Chilpancingo F-7	Hopelchen E-10	Nautla E-7	San Andres Tuxtla F-8	Tuxtla Gutierrez G-9
China C-7	Huajuapan de Leon F-7	Navojoa C-3	San Cristobal G-9	Uruapan F-6
Ciudad Acuna B-6	Iguala F-7	Nogales A-3	San Felipe A-2	Valladolid E-11
Ciudad Camargo C-5	Irapuato E-6	Nueva Casas	San Fernando D-7	Veracruz F-8
Ciudad Guerrero B-4	Iturbide F-10	Grandes B-4	San Ignacio C-2	Villa Ahumada A-4
Ciudad Guzman F-5	Jalapa F-8	Nueva Rosita C-6	San Jose del Cabo D-3	Villagran D-7
Ciudad Juarez A-4	Jalpa F-6	Nuevo Laredo C-7	San Luis A-2	Villahermosa F-9
Ciudad Madero E-7	Janos A-4	Oaxaca G-8	San Luis Potosi E-6	Villa Union D-4
Ciudad Mante E-7	Jimenez C-5	Ocampo C-6	San Pedro de las	Xcan E-11
Ciudad Victoria D-7	Juchitan G-8	Ocotlan E-6	Colonias C-6	Yecora B-4
Ciudad de Carmen F-9	La Cruz D-4	Ojinaga B-5	Santa Ana A-3	Zacatal F-9
Ciudad de Valles E-7	La Cadena B-6	Ometepec G-7	Santa Barbara C-5	Zacatecas E-6
	La Cuesta B-6	Orizaba F-8	Santa Rosalia C-2	Zamora F-6
	Lagos de Morena E-6	Pachuca E-7	Sayula F-5	Zihuatanejo F-6
	La Paz D-3	Palenque F-9	Sinaloa C-4	Zimapan E-7
	La Perla B-5	Papantla E-7	Sombrerete D-5	Zitacuaro F-6

STATE MAP LEGEND

ROAD CLASSIFICATIONS & RELATED SYMBOLS

Free Interstate Hwy.	90
Toll Interstate Hwy.	76
Divided Federal Hwy.	14
Federal Hwy.	20
Divided State Hwy.	31
State Hwy.	147
Other Connecting Road	258
Trans - Canada Hwy.	
Point to Point Milage	17
State Boundaries	

LAND MARKS & POINTS OF INTEREST

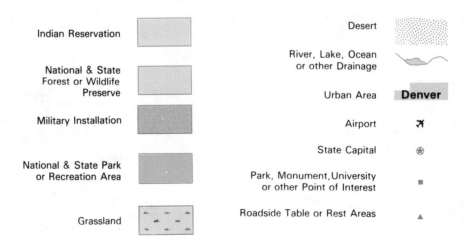

Indian Reservation		Desert	
National & State Forest or Wildlife Preserve		River, Lake, Ocean or other Drainage	
Military Installation		Urban Area	**Denver**
		Airport	✈
National & State Park or Recreation Area		State Capital	⊛
		Park, Monument, University or other Point of Interest	■
Grassland		Roadside Table or Rest Areas	▲

ABBREVIATIONS

A.F.B. - Air Force Base	Mgmt. - Management	Prov. - Province	S. F. - State Forest
Hist. - Historical	Mon. - Monument	Rec. - Recreation	St. Pk. - State Park
Mem. - Memorial	Nat. - Natural	Ref. - Refuge	W.M.A. - Wildlife Management Area

CITIES & TOWNS - Type size indicates the relative population of cities and towns

Mapleton	Kenhorst	Somerset	Butler	Auburn	Harrisburg	Madison	Chicago
under 1000	1000-5,000	5,000-10,000	10,000-25,000	25,000-50,000	50,000-100,000	100,000-500,000	500,000 and over

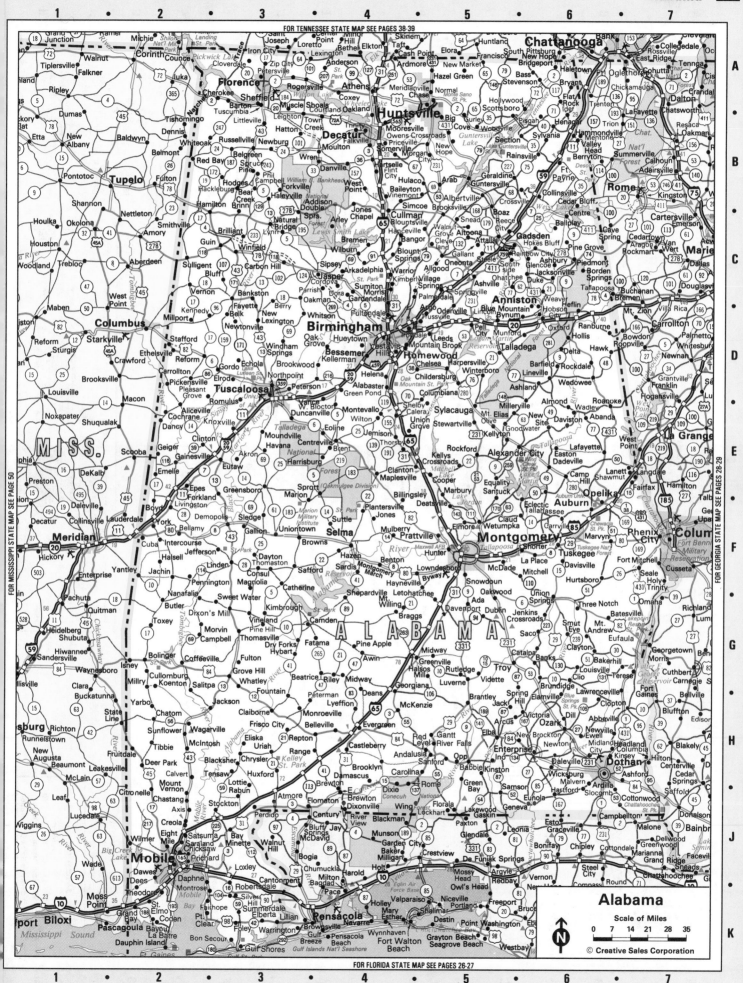

FOR TENNESSEE STATE MAP SEE PAGES 38-39

FOR FLORIDA STATE MAP SEE PAGES 26-27

FOR MISSISSIPPI STATE MAP SEE PAGE 50

FOR GEORGIA STATE MAP SEE PAGES 28-29

Alabama

Scale of Miles

0 7 14 21 28 35

N

© Creative Sales Corporation

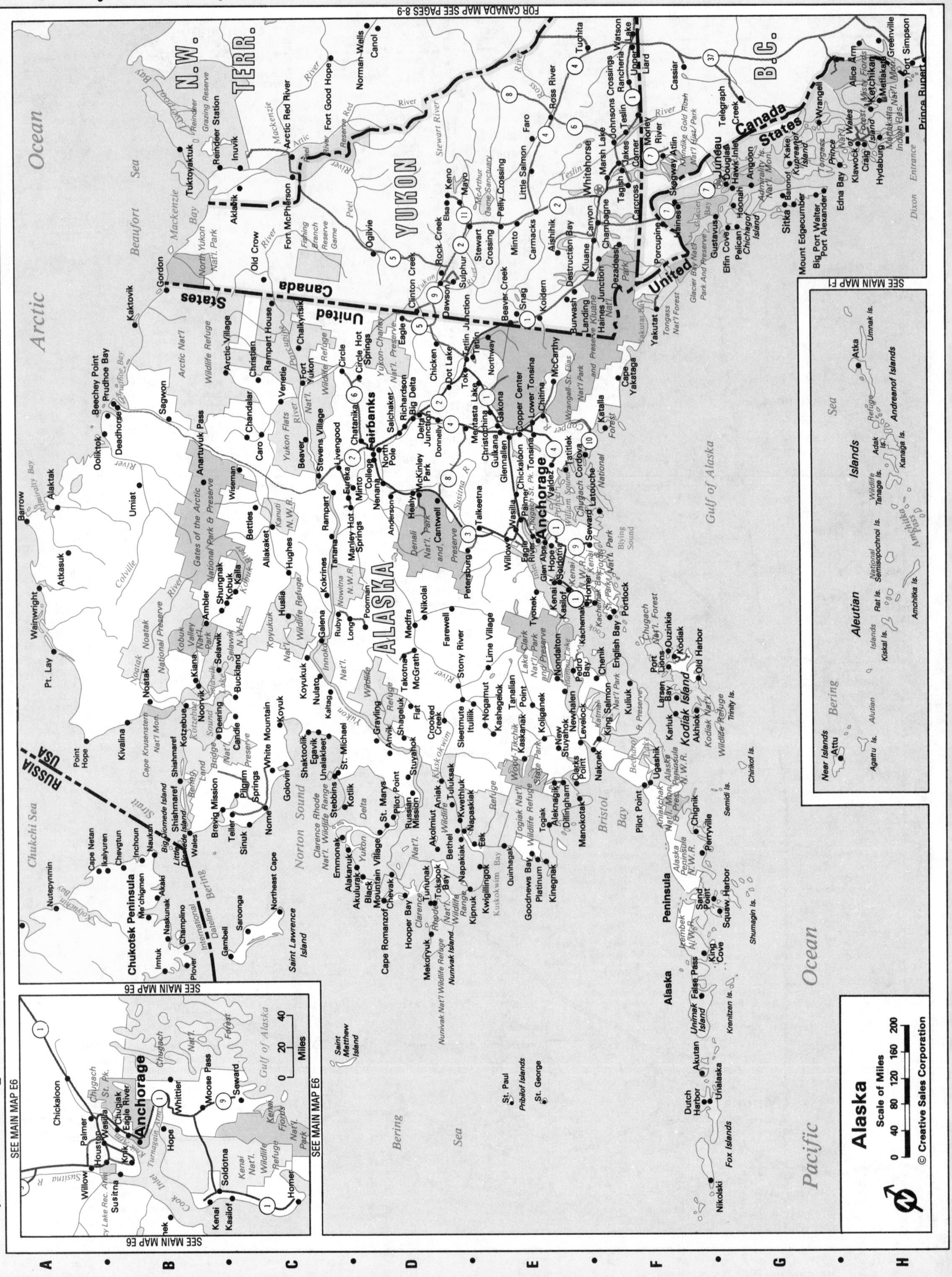

FOR CANADA SEE MAP PAGES 8-9

Alaska

Scale of Miles
0 40 80 120 160 200

© Creative Sales Corporation

SEE MAIN MAP F1

SEE MAIN MAP E6

RUSSIA
USA

United States
Canada

N.W. TERR.

YUKON

B.C.

ALASKA

Arctic Ocean

Beaufort Sea

Chukchi Sea

Bering Sea

Gulf of Alaska

Pacific Ocean

Norton Sound

Bristol Bay

Kotzebue Sound

Aleutian Islands

Andreanof Islands

Near Islands

Kodiak Island

Anchorage

Fairbanks

Juneau

Barrow

Nome

Miles
0 20 40

SEE MAIN MAP E6

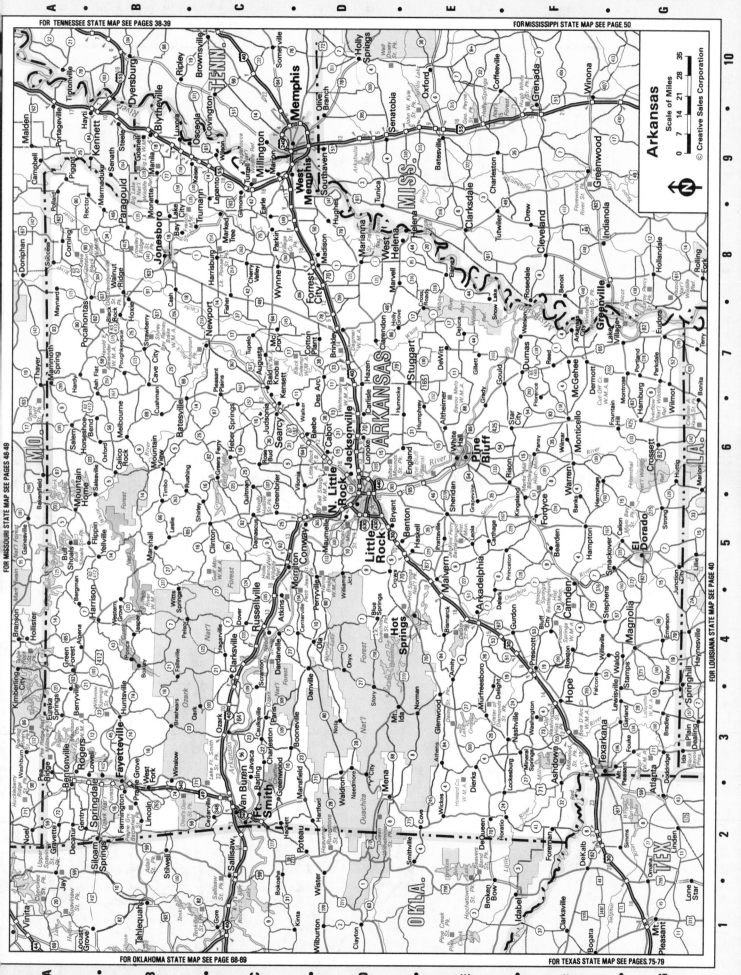

FOR TENNESSEE STATE MAP SEE PAGES 38-39

FOR MISSISSIPPI STATE MAP SEE PAGE 50

Arkansas

Scale of Miles

0 7 14 21 28 35

© Creative Sales Corporation

FOR MISSOURI STATE MAP SEE PAGES 48-49

FOR LOUISIANA STATE MAP SEE PAGE 40

FOR OKLAHOMA STATE MAP SEE PAGES 68-69

FOR TEXAS STATE MAP SEE PAGES 75-79

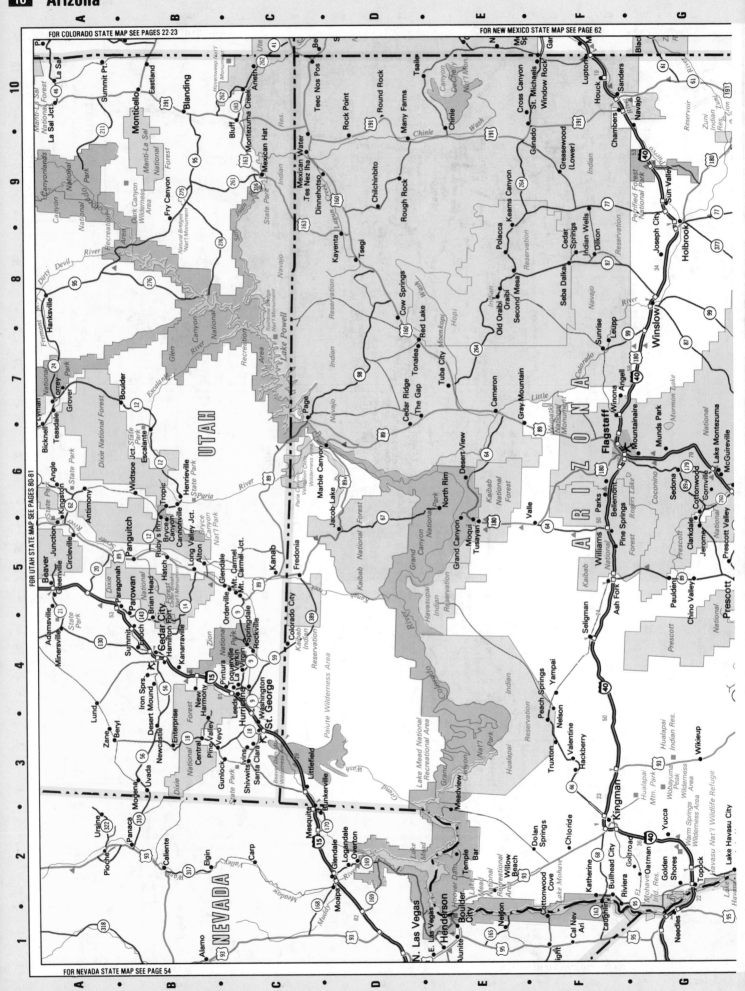

FOR COLORADO STATE MAP SEE PAGES 22-23

FOR NEW MEXICO STATE MAP SEE PAGE 62

FOR UTAH STATE MAP SEE PAGES 80-81

FOR NEVADA STATE MAP SEE PAGE 54

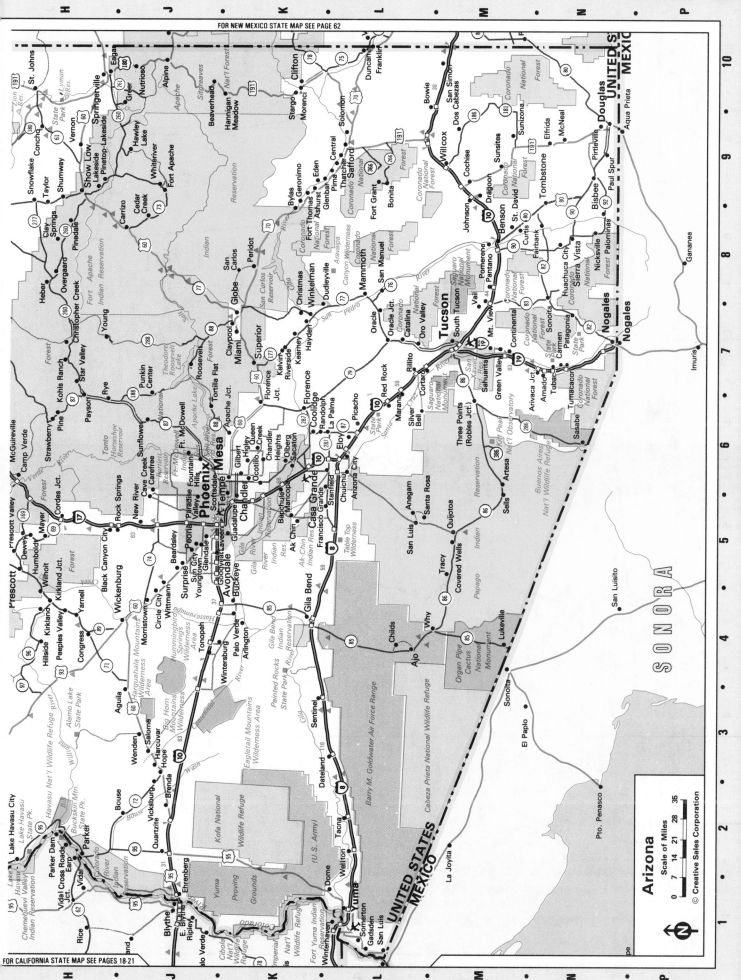

FOR NEW MEXICO STATE MAP SEE PAGE 62

FOR CALIFORNIA STATE MAP SEE PAGES 18-21

Arizona

Scale of Miles

0   7   14   21   28   35

© Creative Sales Corporation

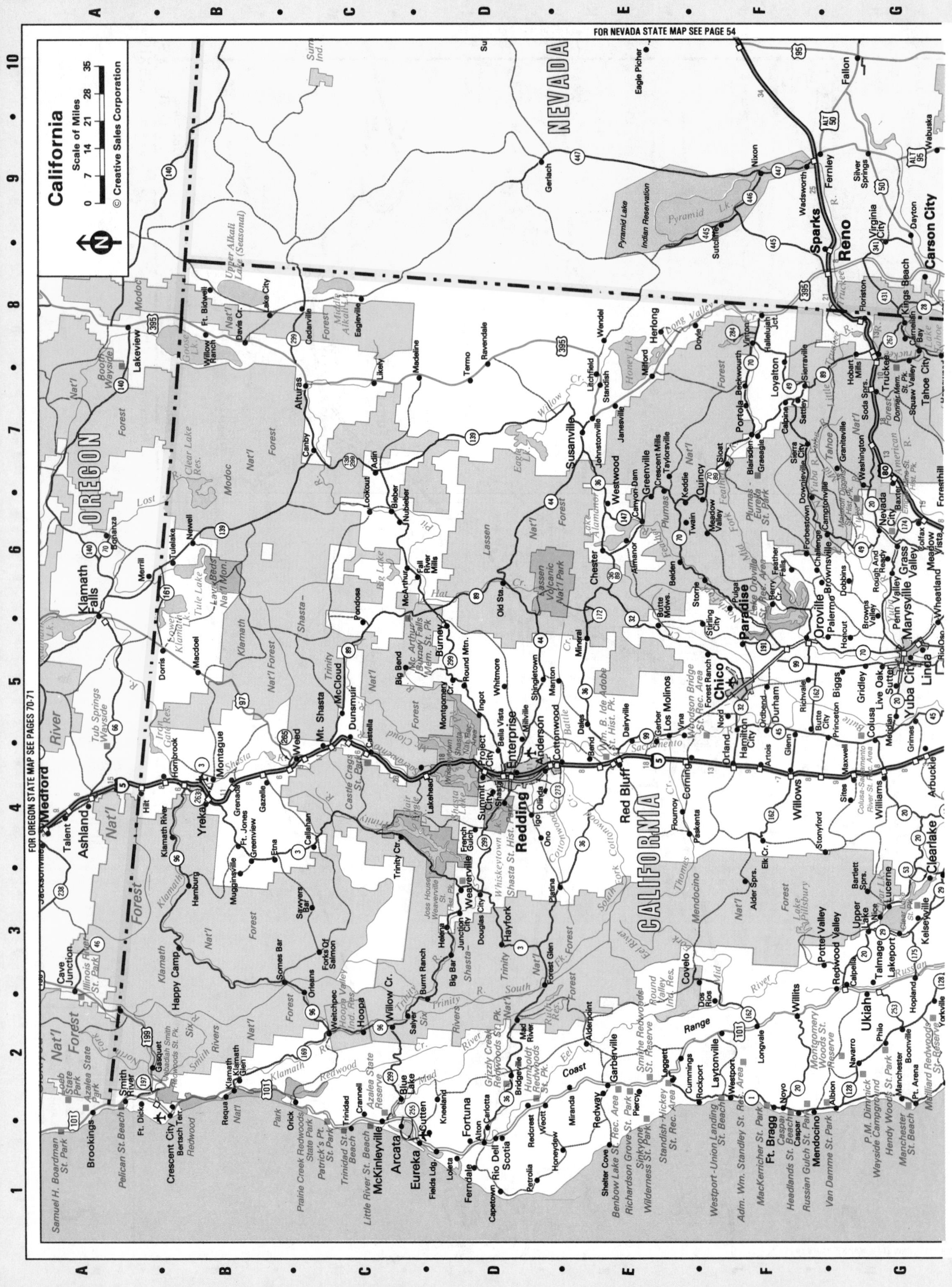

California

Scale of Miles

0 7 14 21 28 35

© Creative Sales Corporation

FOR NEVADA STATE MAP SEE PAGE 54

FOR OREGON STATE MAP SEE PAGES 70-71

NEVADA

OREGON

CALIFORNIA

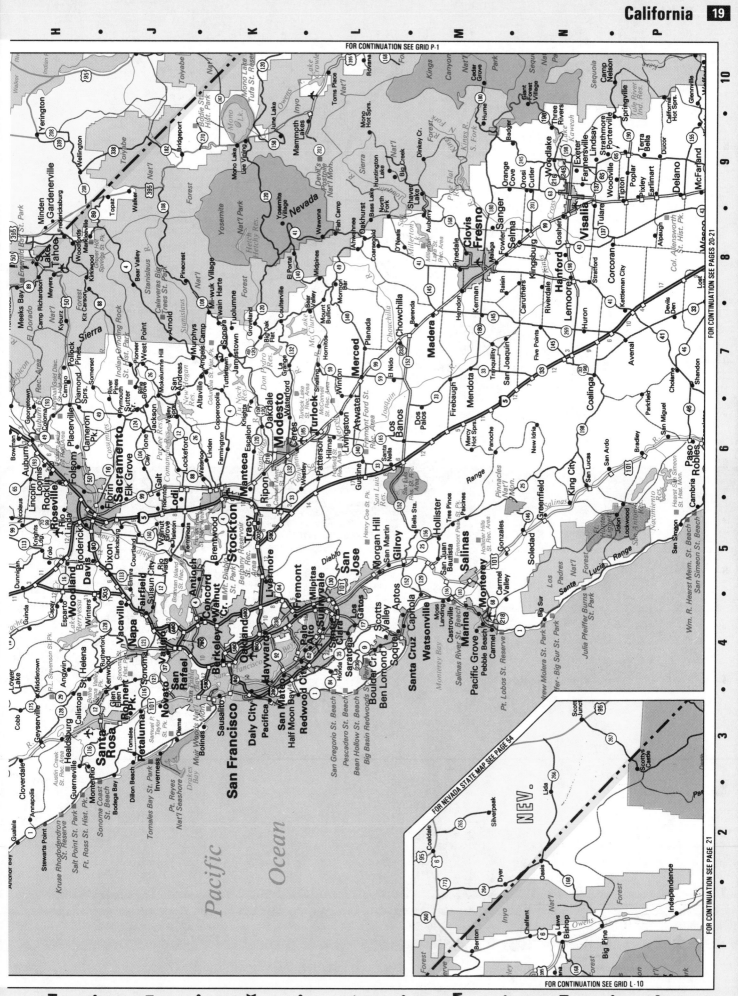

FOR CONTINUATION SEE GRID P-1

FOR CONTINUATION SEE PAGES 20-21

FOR CONTINUATION SEE PAGE 21

FOR NEVADA STATE MAP SEE PAGE 54

FOR CONTINUATION SEE GRID L-10

FOR CONTINUATION SEE PAGES 18-19

Carmel
Carmel Valley
Gonzales
Pinnacles Nat'l Mon.
Panoche
Tranquillity
Malaga
Fowler
Sanger
Orange Cove
Badger
Park
Pt. Lobos St. Reserve

Big Sur
Soledad
Greenfield
New Idria
San Joaquin
Raisin
Selma
Orosi
Cutler
Giant Forest Village
Sequoia Nat'l Park

Andrew Molera St. Park
Los Padres
Santa Nat'l Forest
King City
Caruthers
Kingsburg
201
Woodlake
Three Rivers
Lake Kaweah

Pfeiffer - Big Sur St. Park
San Lucas
Coalinga
Huron
Stratford
Visalia
Goshen
Exeter
Farmersville
Lindsay
Camp Nelson

Julia Pfeiffer Burns St. Park
Ft. Hunter Liggett
San Ardo
Corcoran
Tulare
Woodville
Strathmore
Porterville
Springville
Nat'l

Jolon
Lockwood
Bradley
Parkfield
Avenal
Kettleman City
Alpaugh
Tipton
Poplar
Earlimart
Terra Bella
Springville
Tule River Ind. Res.

San Antonio Res.
Nacimiento Res.
Cholame
Devils Den
Ducor
California Hot Sprs.
Forest

San Simeon
Hearst San Simeon St. Hist. Mon.
Paso Robles
Shandon
Lost Hills
Wasco
McFarland
Glennville
Kernville
Isabella Res.
Onyx

Wm. R. Hearst Mem. St. Beach
San Simeon St. Beach
Cambria
Templeton
Blackwells Corner
Woody
Wofford Heights

Cayucos St. Beach
Atascadero
Santa Margarita
Shafter
Green Acres
Bakersfield
Bodfish
Nat'l Forest

Morro Bay
Baywood Pk.
San Luis Obispo
Pozo
Simmler
Buttonwillow
McKittrick
Tule Elk St. Reserve
Edison
Caliente
Keene

Montana De Oro St. Park
Pismo Beach
Arroyo Grande
Fellows
Ford City
Pumpkin Center
Lamont
Arvin
Tehachapi

Grover City
Oceano
Nipomo
Taft
Maricopa
Cuyama
New Cuyama

Guadalupe
Orcutt
Santa Maria
Sisquoc
Madre
Los Padres Mtns.
Frazier Pk.
Ft. Tejon St. Hist. Pk.
Gorman
Willow Sprs.

Pt. Sal St. Beach
Casmalia
Los Alamos
Surf
Vandenberg Air Force Base
Lompoc
La Purisima Mission St. Hist. Park
Los Olivos
Buellton
Solvang
Lake Cachuma
Castaic Lake St. Rec. Area
Palmdale
Acton

Gaviota St. Pk.
Gaviota
El Capitan St. Beach
Montecito
Summerland
Carpinteria
Ojai
Castaic
Refugio St. Beach
Goleta
Santa Barbara
Carpinteria St. Beach
Emma Wood St. Beach
Santa Paula
Fillmore
Santa Clarita
San Fernando

Ventura
Oxnard
Port Hueneme
Saticoy
Moorpark
Simi Valley
Glendale
Pasadena

San Miguel Is.
Pt. Mugu St. Park
Leo Carrillo St. Beach
Thousand Oaks
Agoura Hills
Beverly Hills
Malibu

Santa Cruz Is.
Anacapa Is.
Channel Islands National Park
Santa Monica Mtns. Nat'l Rec. Area
Santa Monica
Los Angeles
Redondo Beach

Santa Rosa Is.
San Miguel Passage
Santa Cruz Channel
Santa Barbara Channel
Rancho Palos Verdes
Long Beach
Huntington Beach
Newport Beach
Laguna

Pacific

Ocean

Santa Barbara Is.
San Nicolas Is.
Santa Catalina Is.
Avalon
San Pedro Channel
Outer Santa Barbara Channel
San Clemente
Doheny

San Clemente Is.
Gulf
Santa Ca

California

Scale of Miles

0   7   14   21   28   35

N

© Creative Sales Corporation

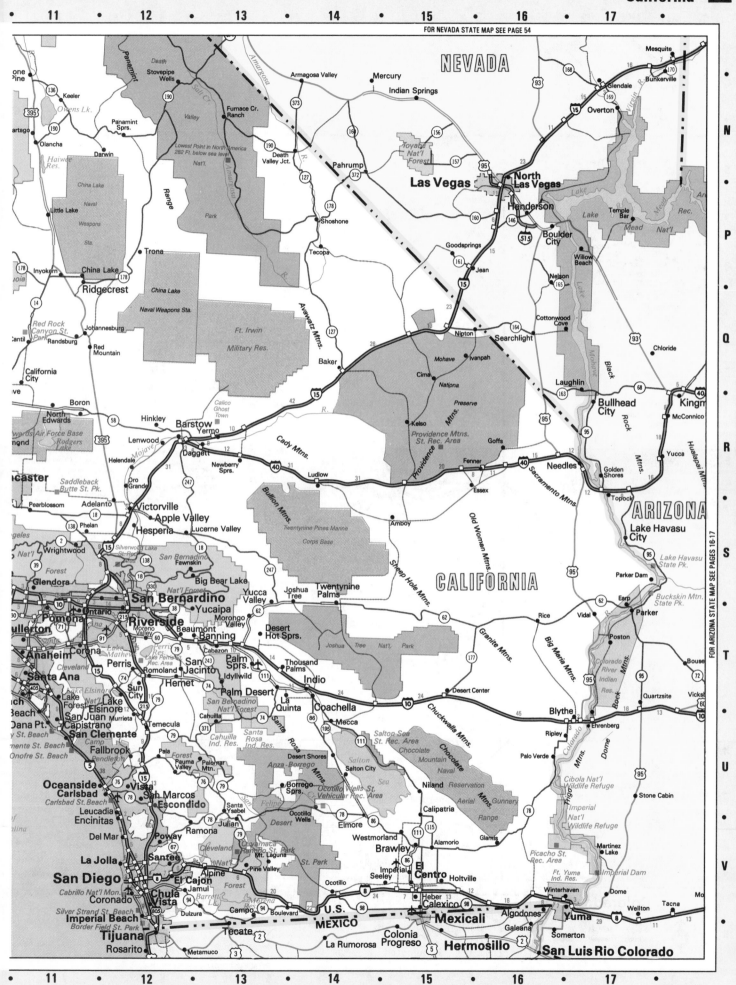

FOR NEVADA STATE MAP SEE PAGE 54

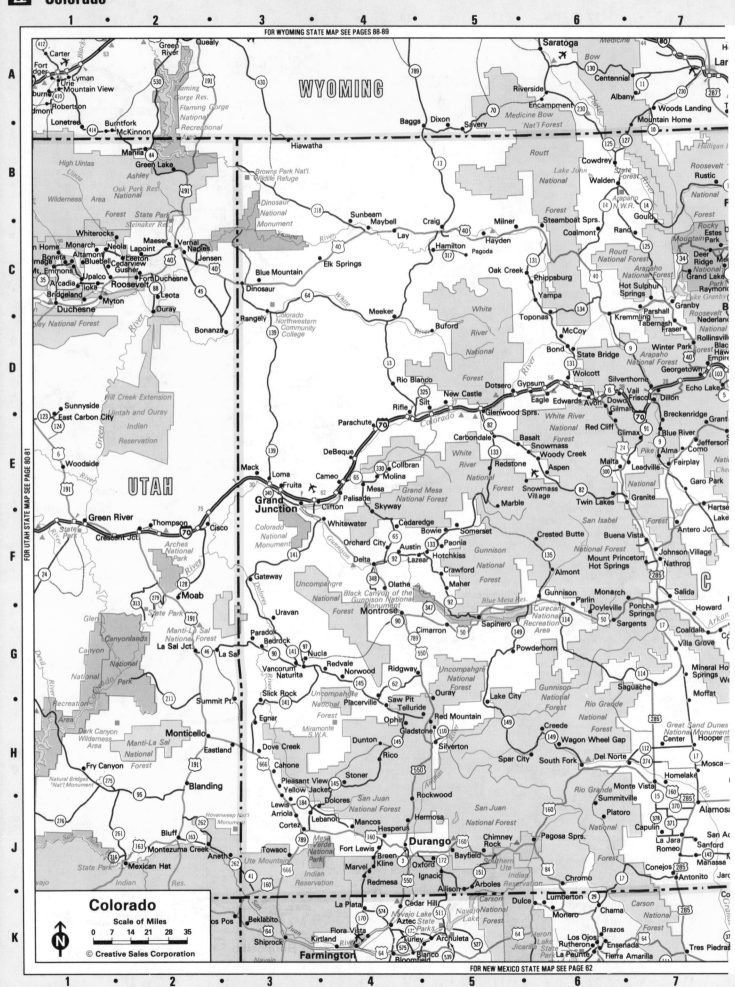

FOR WYOMING STATE MAP SEE PAGES 88-89

WYOMING

UTAH

FOR UTAH STATE MAP SEE PAGE 80-81

Colorado

Scale of Miles

0   7   14   21   28   35

N

© Creative Sales Corporation

FOR NEW MEXICO STATE MAP SEE PAGE 62

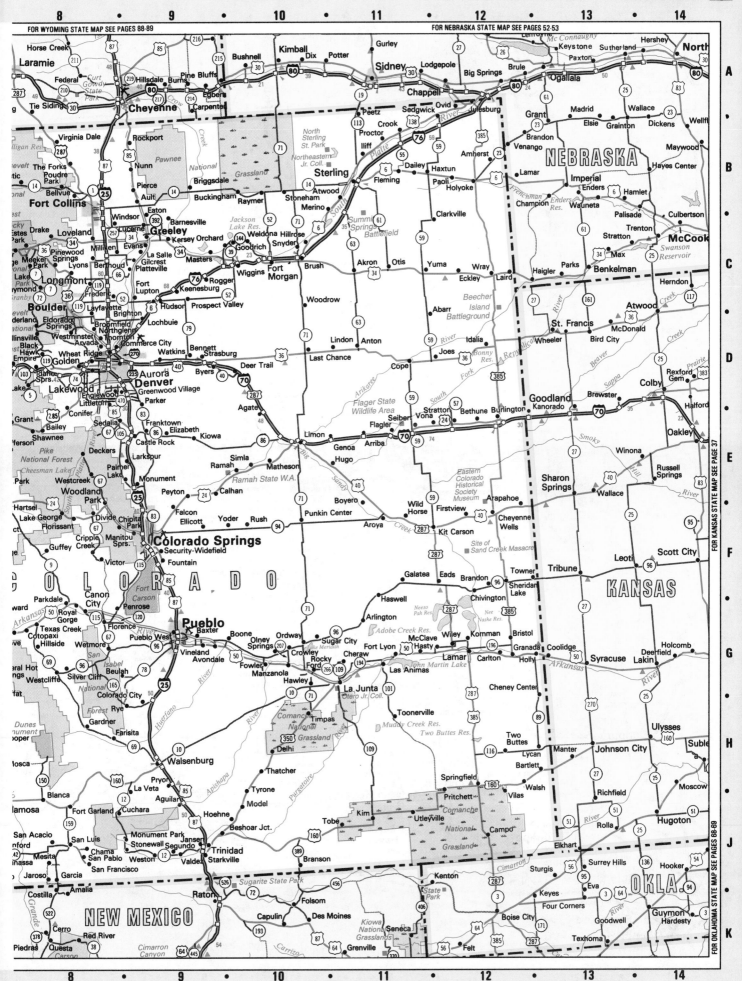

FOR VERMONT STATE MAP SEE PAGE 55

FOR NEW YORK STATE MAP SEE PAGES 58-61

N.H.

VT.

MASS.

CONN.

N.Y.

Long Island Sound

Albany Troy Rensselaer Pittsfield North Adams Adams Williamstown Greenfield Deerfield Northfield Winchendon Fitchburg Gardner Leominster Worcester Springfield Chicopee Holyoke West Springfield Agawam Northampton Easthampton Amherst Hartford West Hartford East Hartford Manchester New Britain Meriden Waterbury Middletown Bristol Torrington Danbury New Milford Bridgeport Stratford Milford New Haven West Haven East Haven Stamford Greenwich Norwalk Fairfield Westport Darien New London Groton Mystic Stonington Norwich Windsor Enfield Vernon Storrs Willimantic

FOR NEW HAMPSHIRE STATE MAP SEE PAGE 55

8 • 9 • 10 • 11 • 12 • 13 • 14 • 15

A B C D E F G H J K

Wilton Merrimack Derry Hampstead Amesbury Merrimac Salisbury
Milford Litchfield Londonderry Atkinson Newburyport Salisbury Beach St. Res.
Silver Lake St. Pk. Windham West Newbury Newbury Parker River Nat'l Wildlife Ref.
Nashua Hudson Salem Haverhill Newbury Plum Is.
Hollis Groveland Georgetown Rowley Plum Is. St. Pk.
Townsend Methuen Lawrence Ipswich Halibut Point State Park
Tyngsborough Boxford Topsfield Essex Rockport
Lowell Dracut Andover Wenham Hamilton Gloucester
Pepperell Tewksbury North Reading Danvers Manchester-by-the-Sea
Lunenburg Groton Westford Chelmsford Billerica Wilmington Lynnfield Reading Beverly Salem
Shirley Ayer Littleton Carlisle Wakefield Peabody Saugus Marblehead
Harvard Acton Bedford Concord Woburn Lexington Lynn Swampscott
Boxborough Lincoln Cambridge Revere Nahant
Sterling Clinton Stow Maynard Wayland Chelsea Winthrop
Boylston Hudson Marlborough Cochituate Newton Boston Massachusetts Bay
Northborough Shrewsbury Wellesley Milton Quincy Hull
Westborough Natick Framingham Dedham Hingham Scituate
Grafton Hopkinton Westwood Norwood Weymouth Norwell
Millbury Upton Medfield Canton Braintree Randolph Rockland Hanover
Northbridge Milford Millis Walpole Holbrook Avon Abington Hanson Marshfield
Hopedale Medway Sharon Stoughton Brockton Whitman Pembroke
Sutton Whitinsville Mendon Norfolk Wrentham Easton East Bridgewater Duxbury
Uxbridge Bellingham Foxborough Mansfield Bridgewater Halifax Kingston
Blackstone N. Attleborough Norton Plympton Plymouth
Slatersville Woonsocket Attleboro Raynham Carver
Harrisville Pascoag Ashton Berkley Taunton Middleborough Provincetown
Mapleville Chepachet Esmond Pawtucket Rehoboth Dighton Berkley Herring Cove Beach Truro
Glocester Harmony Providence Freetown Fall River Wellfleet
North Foster N. Scituate Cranston East Providence Seekonk Somerset Swansea Wareham Cape Cod Bay Eastham
Foster Center Clayville Auburn Warren Bristol Rochester Buzzards Bay Sagamore Orleans Brewster
Vernon Hope Lippitt Barrington Acushnet Sandwich Barnstable Dennis Yarmouth Chatham
West Greenwich Center Warwick Marion Mattapoisett Bourne Hyannis Harwich
Nooseneck East Greenwich Tiverton Westport Fairhaven New Bedford Otis A.F.B. Centerville West Yarmouth South Dennis Dennis Port
Exeter Homestead Dartmouth East Falmouth Osterville Monomoy Island
Millville Middletown West Is. Falmouth Buzzards Bay
Kingston Jamestown Newport Little Compton Naushon Is. Vineyard Haven Oak Bluffs Nantucket Sound
Hope Valley Wickford Saunderstown Tisbury Edgartown Chappaquiddick Island
Wood River Jct. Woodville Carolina Narragansett Pier Cuttyhunk Nashawena Is. Martha's Vineyard St. Forest Muskeget Is.
Charlestown Gay Head Chilmark West Tisbury Martha's Vineyard Island Nantucket
Westerly Trustom Pond Vineyard Sound Nantucket Island Nantucket State Forest
Block Island Sound Block Island Nat'l W.R. Nantucket Mem. Airport
Block Island
Block Island State Beach

Atlantic Ocean

Rhode Island Sound

Buzzards Bay

Connecticut
Massachusetts
Rhode Island

Scale of Miles
0 3 6 9 12 15

N

© Creative Sales Corporation

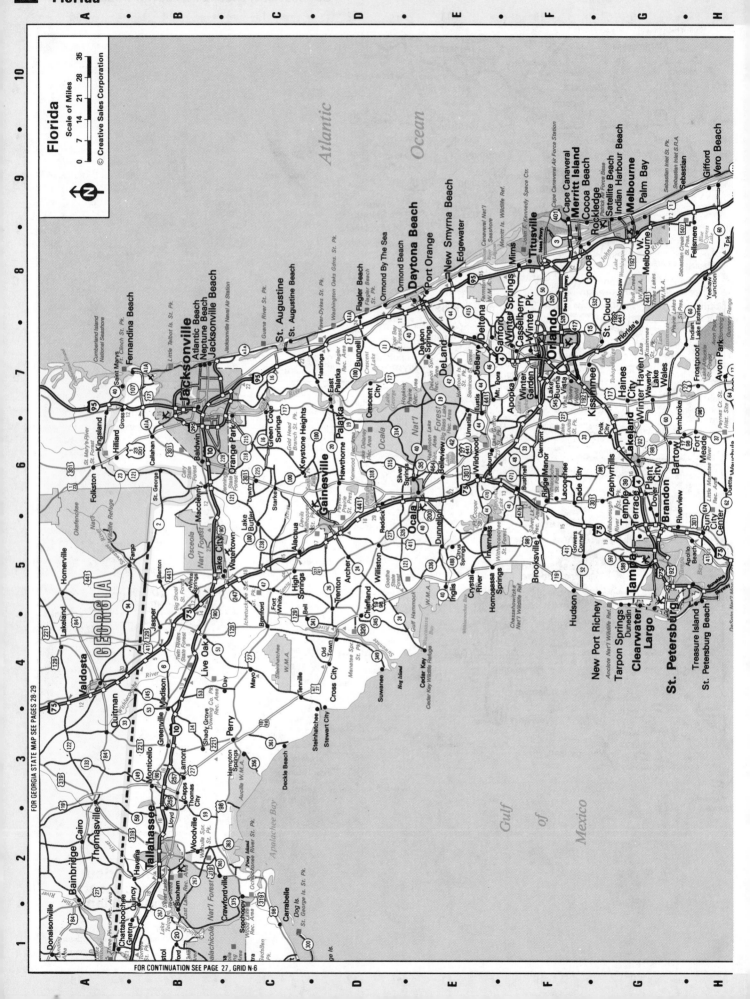

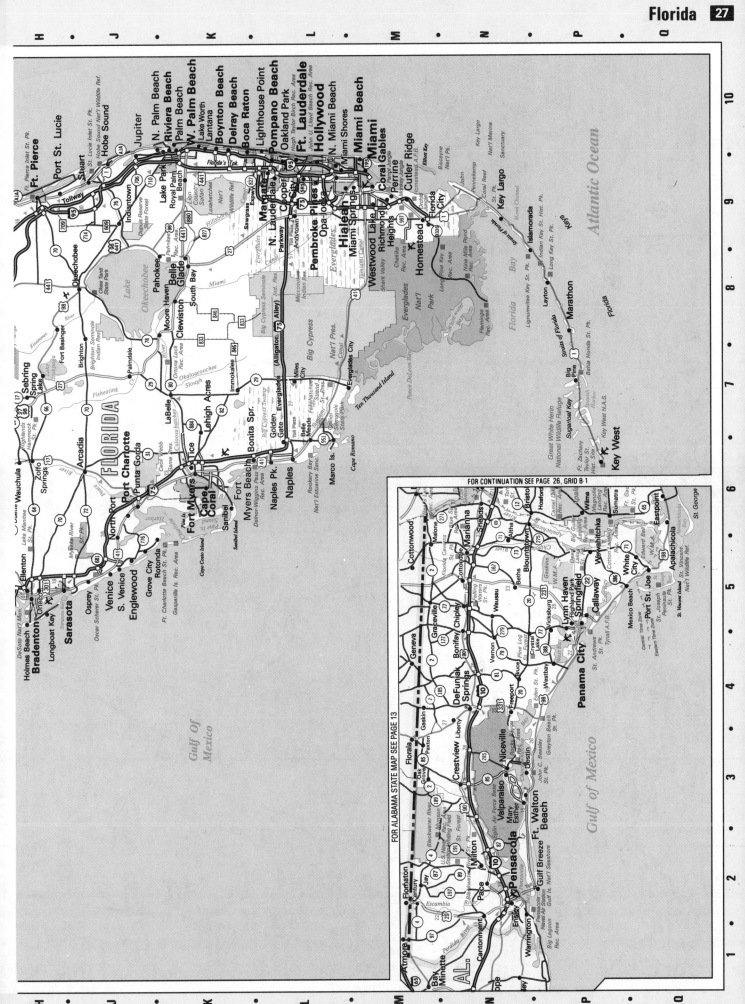

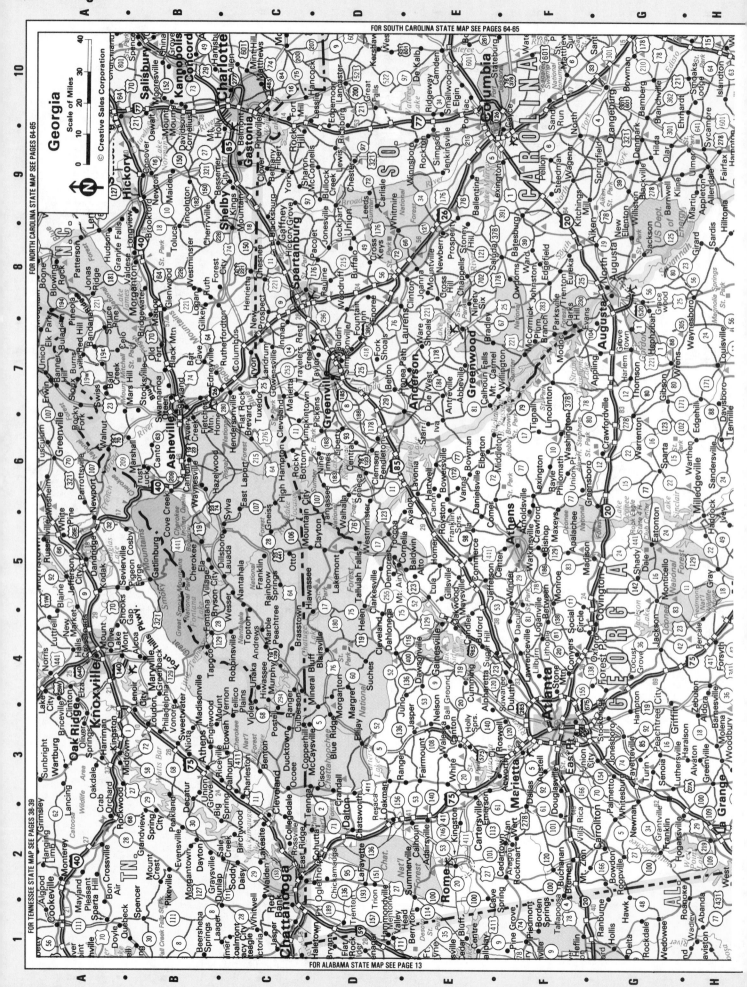

FOR SOUTH CAROLINA STATE MAP SEE PAGES 64-65

FOR NORTH CAROLINA STATE MAP SEE PAGES 64-65

FOR TENNESSEE STATE MAP SEE PAGES 38-39

FOR ALABAMA STATE MAP SEE PAGE 13

Georgia

Scale of Miles

© Creative Sales Corporation

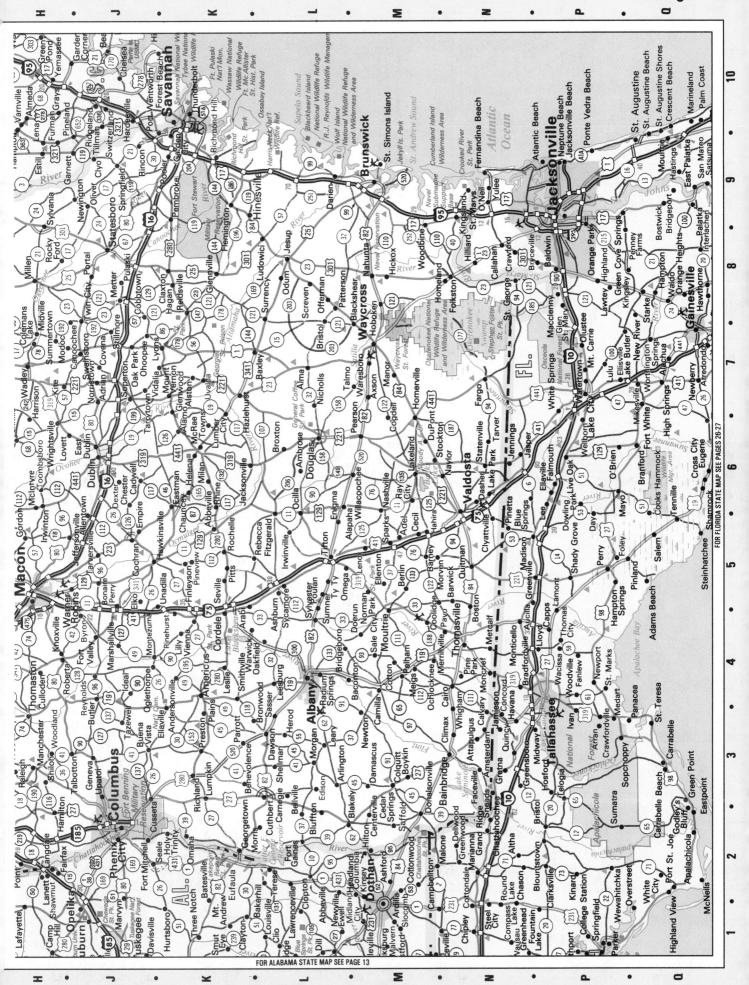

Hawaii

Scale of Miles

© Creative Sales Corporation

0 4 8 12 16 20

Maui

Nakalele Pt., Honokahua, Kahakuloa Pt., Wailee Pt., Pauwela Pt., Kahului Bay, Maalaea Bay, Kaanapali, Pauwela, Paia, Spreckelsville, Haiku, Makawao, Puunene, Puunene, Kahului, Wailuku, Waiehu, Iao Valley, Olowalu, Mopua, Maalaea, Lahaina, Honokahua, Hekili Pt., Kihei, Waiea, Makena, Keokea, Ulupalakua, Keoneoio, Nukuele Pt., Cape Hanamanioa, Kaupo, Apole Pt., Kipahulu, Mokulau, Hana, Kaupo, Kalahu Pt., Pukaulua Pt., Waianapanapa St. Pk., Haleakala Crater, Haleakala Nat'l Park, Alenuihaha Channel, Kamaole Beach Park, Pacific Ocean

360, 378, 377, 37, 31, 36, 311, 30, 340

Hawaii

Waikea, Pohoiki, Black Sands, Kapoho, Ophihikao, Kalapana, Apua Pt., Kaena Pt., Kaimu Black Beach, Pahoa, Keaau, Hilo, Honohina, Hakalau, Papaikou, Papaaloa, Paukaa, Rainbow Falls, Pepeekeo, Papaeeko Pt., Ookala, Honokaa, Kukuihaele, Kukaiau, Waimea, Kurtistown, Mountain View, Glenwood, Kalaoa, Kaloa, Puna, Hawi, Niulii, Mahukona, Kawaihae, Upolu Pt., Keahole Pt., Kailua, Keauhou, Napoopoo, Captain Cook, Kainaliu, Honaunau, Kealakekua, Keokea, Hookena, Hookena, Papa, Miloli, Hanamalo Pt., Kauna Pt., Honuapo, Naalehu, Waiohinu, Kaalualu, Waiahukini, Ka Lae, Pahala, Punaluu Black Sand Beach, Hawaii Volcanoes National Park, Mauna Kea 13,796 ft., Mauna Loa 13,680 ft.

130, 11, 19, 200, 190, 250, 270, 19

Molokai

Lamaloa Head, Halawa, Cape Halawa, Waialua, Pauwalu, Pukoo, Ualapue, Kahiipu Pt., Kaiwa Pt., Makanalua Pen., Kalaupapa, Kalae, Kualapuu, Kaunakakai, Kamiloloa, Kamalo, Mauna Loa, Kolo, Ilio Pt., Laau Pt., Pailolo Channel, Kalohi Channel, Pacific Ocean

450, 460

Kauai (small inset)
Anahola, Lihue, Lawaii, Waimea, Mana, Haena, Kauai, Pacific Ocean
56, 50

Niihau (Private), Puuwai, Kaulakahi Channel

Lanai
Halawa, Kualapuu, Mauna Loa, Koele, Lanai City, Kaumalapau, Kamalo, Maunalei, Kaohai Pt., Kaa Pt., Kahoolawe, Kealaikahiki Channel, Auau Channel, Kalohi Channel, Kaiwi Channel
450, 460

Maui (inset)
Hana, Haleakala Nat'l Park, Honokahua, Kahului, Lahaina, Ulupalakua
360, 36, 37, 31, 30

Oahu (inset)
Kahuku, Kahana, Kaneohe, Kailua, Waikiki, Haleiwa, Pearl City, Honolulu, Makaha, Nanakuli
83, H-2, H-1

HAWAII

Maui Co. — Hawaii Co.
Honolulu Co. — Maui Co.
Kauai Co. — Honolulu Co.

Pacific Ocean

Oahu
Mokapu Pt., Kaneohe Marine Air Station, Kailua, Waimanalo, Bellows Air Force Station, Makapuu, Sea Life Park, Koko Head, Koko Head Park, Diamond Head, Waikiki, Honolulu, Pearl Harbor, Aiea, Pearl City, Waipahu, Ewa, Waimanalo, Mililani Town, Schofield Barracks, Wahiawa, Waialua, Haleiwa, Waialee, Kahuku, Laie, Hauula, Sacred Falls, Kahana, Kahana Beach, Kaaawa, Kualoa Pt., Kaneohe Bay, Kahaluu, Polynesian Cultural Center, Koolau, Range, Waianae, Maili, Nanakuli, Makaha, Kapuhi Pt., Kaena Pt., Kahuku Pt., Barbers Pt., Dillingham Air Force Base, Barbers Pt. Air Sta., Honolulu Int'l Airport, Kaneohe, Kahana, Waimalu, Pali Lookout, Range, Waianae, Mokuleia, Maunalua Bay
H-3, 61, 63, 83, 72, H-1, 92, 78, 99, 93, 76, 750, 95, 99, 930, H-2

Pacific Ocean, Kaneohe Bay, Kaiwi Channel

Kauai
Moloaa, Anahola, Kealia, Kapaa, Wailua, Hanamaulu, Lihue, Nawiliwili, Ninini Pt., Kilauea, Hanalei, Haena, Haena Pt., Puhi, Koloa, Lawai, Kalaheo, Eleele, Port Allen, Hanapepe, Waimea, Kaumakani, Koheo Pt., Makahuena Pt., Kekaha, Mana, Makaha Pt., Kalalau, Kokee State Park, Mt. Waialeale 5,148 ft., Waimea Canyon, Lihue Airport
56, 580, 583, 50, 56, 550, 550

Pacific Ocean, Kauai Channel

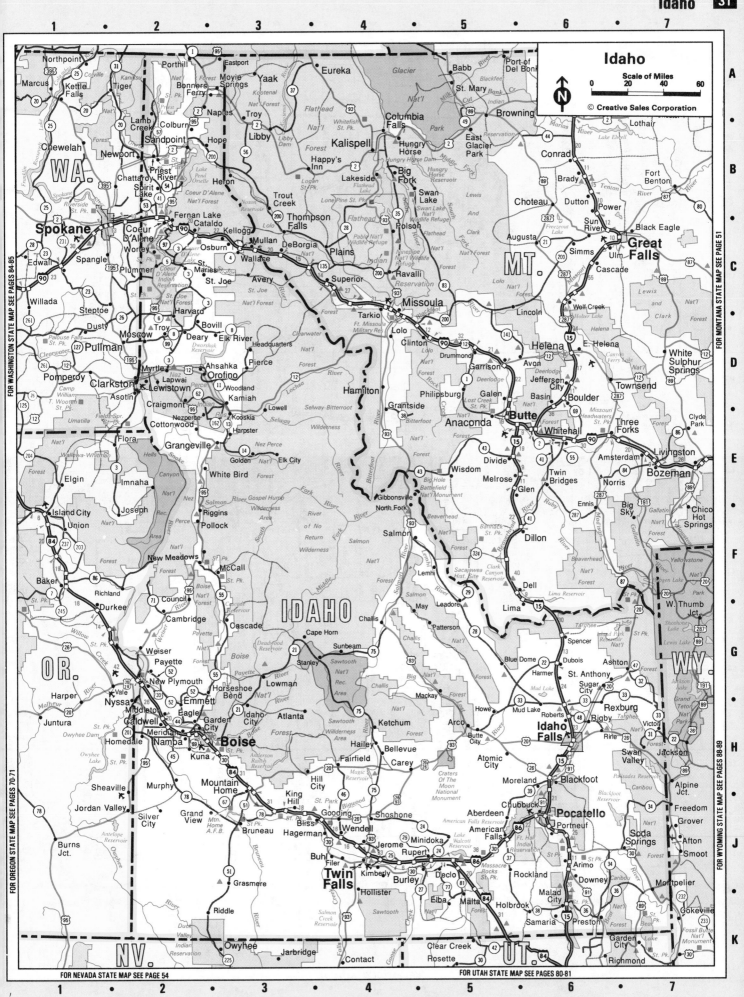

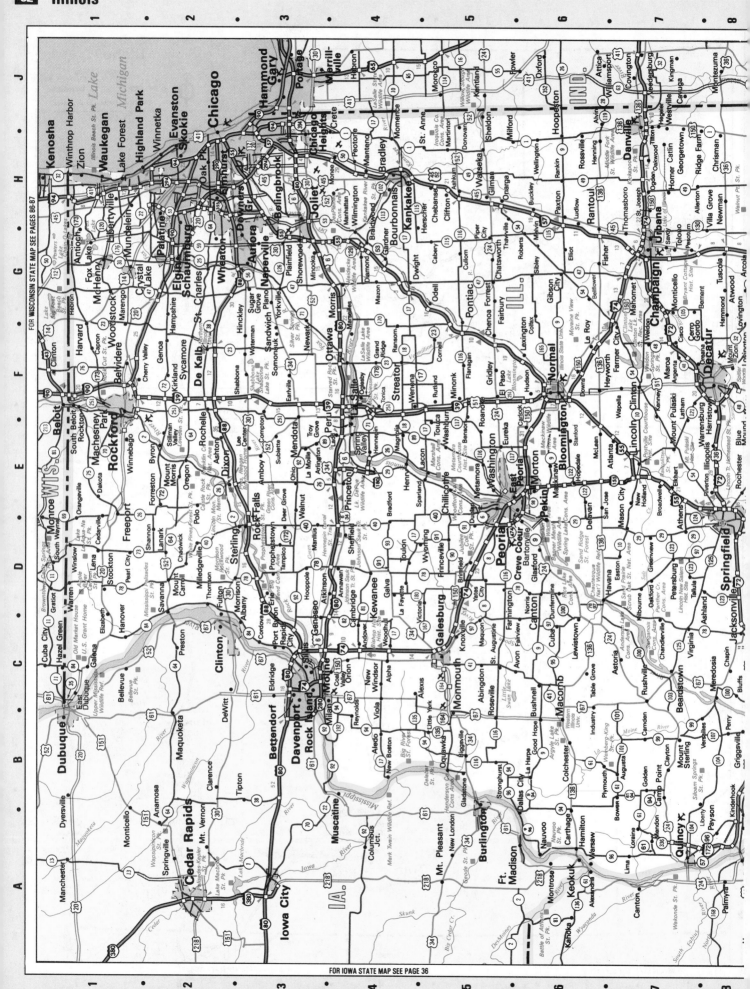

FOR WISCONSIN STATE MAP SEE PAGES 86-87

FOR IOWA STATE MAP SEE PAGE 36

FOR INDIANA STATE MAP SEE PAGES 34-35

FOR KENTUCKY STATE MAP SEE PAGES 38-39

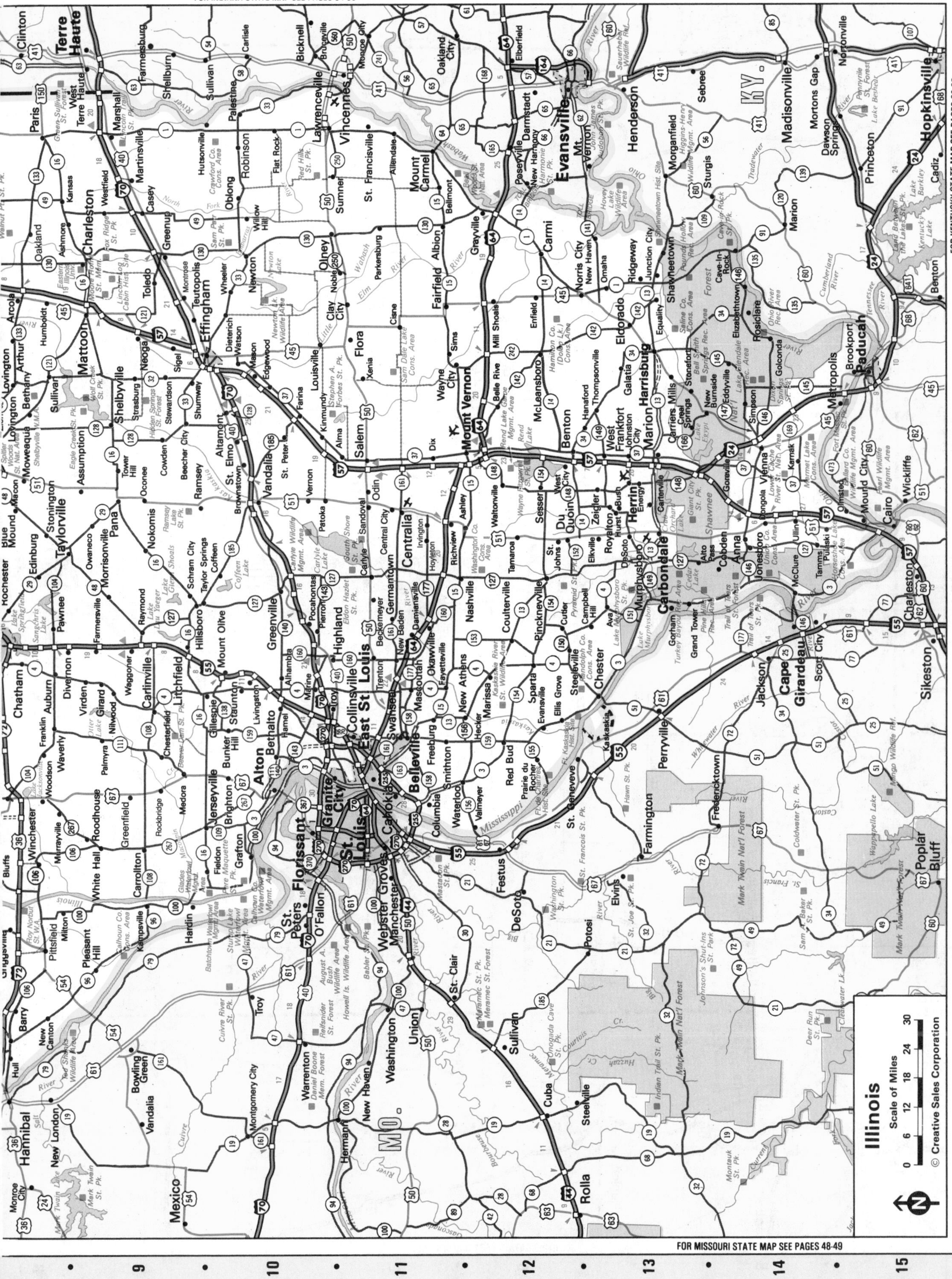

Illinois

Scale of Miles

0 6 12 18 24 30

© Creative Sales Corporation

N

FOR OHIO STATE MAP SEE PAGES 66-67

FOR MICHIGAN STATE MAP SEE PAGES 44-45

FOR ILLINOIS STATE MAP SEE PAGES 32-33

MI

IL

INDIANA

Major cities and places:

Chicago, Oak Lawn, Naperville, Aurora, Downers Grove, Joliet, Hammond, Whiting, East Chicago, Gary, Hobart, Portage, Valparaiso, Crown Point, Merrillville, Schererville, Lansing, Munster, Lake Station, Michigan City, Michiana Shores, New Buffalo, Grand Beach, Union Pier, Three Oaks, Niles, South Bend, Mishawaka, Elkhart, Goshen, Bristol, Middlebury, Lagrange, Angola, Fremont, Sturgis, White Pigeon, Howe, Shipshewana, Nappanee, Warsaw, Winona Lake, Syracuse, Ligonier, Albion, Kendallville, Auburn, Garrett, Waterloo, Butler, Edgerton, New Haven, Ft. Wayne, Huntertown, Columbia City, S. Whitley, N. Manchester, Wabash, Peru, Logansport, Rochester, Plymouth, Bremen, Bourbon, Argos, Knox, La Porte, Westville, Valparaiso

Huntington, Andrews, Marion, Gas City, Jonesboro, Fairmount, Elwood, Alexandria, Anderson, Muncie, New Castle, Cambridge City, Centerville, Richmond, Hagerstown, Economy, Winchester, Union City, Portland, Geneva, Berne, Bluffton, Decatur, Kokomo, Tipton, Noblesville, Carmel, Westfield, Sheridan, Lebanon, Zionsville, Indianapolis, Lawrence, Crawfordsville, Lafayette, W. Lafayette, Frankfort, Thorntown, Brownsburg, Danville

Delphi, Monticello, Brookston, Attica, Covington, Williamsport, Fowler, Rensselaer, Remington, Monon, Wolcott, Brook, Kentland, Morocco, Kankakee, Watseka, Hoopeston

Indianapolis

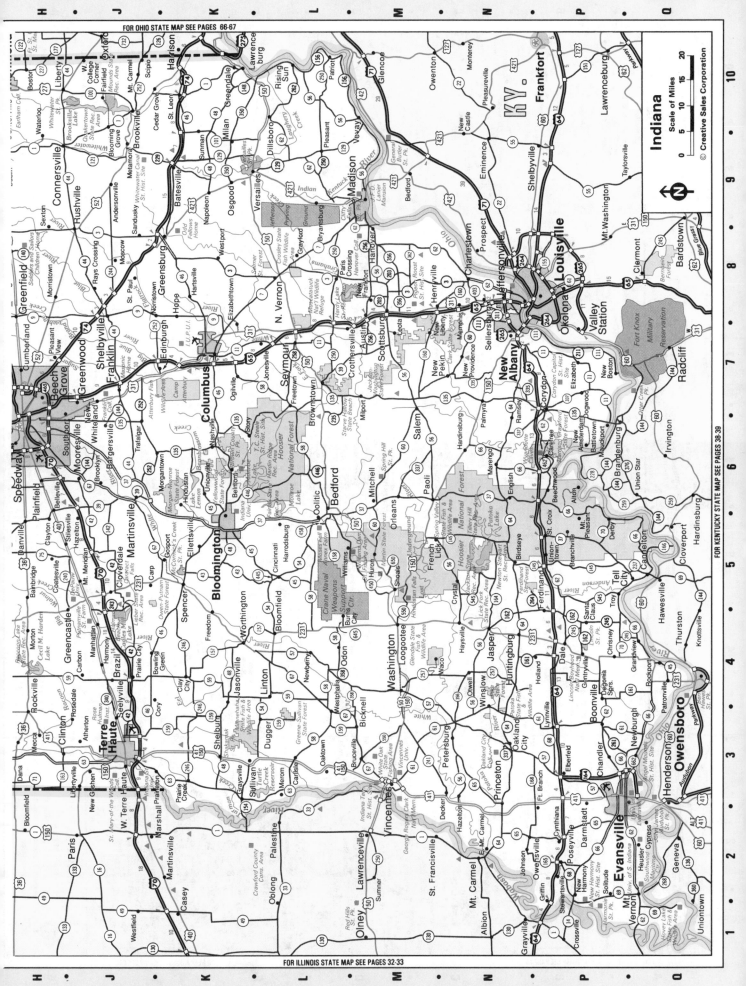

FOR OHIO STATE MAP SEE PAGES 66-67

FOR ILLINOIS STATE MAP SEE PAGES 32-33

FOR KENTUCKY STATE MAP SEE PAGES 38-39

Indiana

Scale of Miles

© Creative Sales Corporation

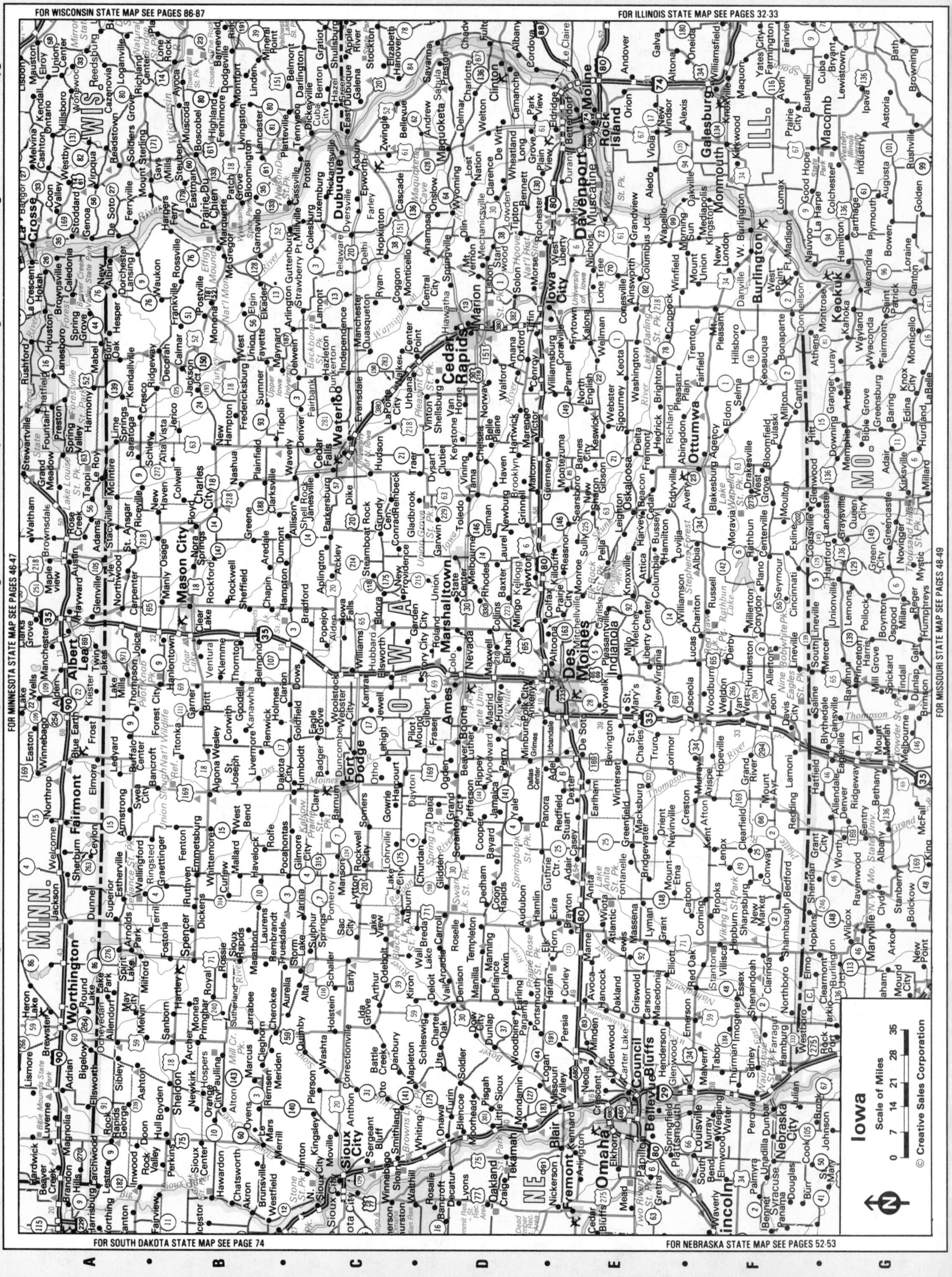
FOR WISCONSIN STATE MAP SEE PAGES 86-87
FOR ILLINOIS STATE MAP SEE PAGES 32-33
FOR MINNESOTA STATE MAP SEE PAGES 46-47
FOR MISSOURI STATE MAP SEE PAGES 48-49
FOR SOUTH DAKOTA STATE MAP SEE PAGE 74
FOR NEBRASKA STATE MAP SEE PAGES 52-53
Iowa
Scale of Miles
0 7 14 21 28 35
© Creative Sales Corporation
Des Moines
Cedar Rapids
Davenport
Sioux City
Council Bluffs
Waterloo
Dubuque
Iowa City
Ames
Mason City
Burlington
Ottumwa
Fort Dodge
Marshalltown
Keokuk
Omaha
Rock Island
Moline

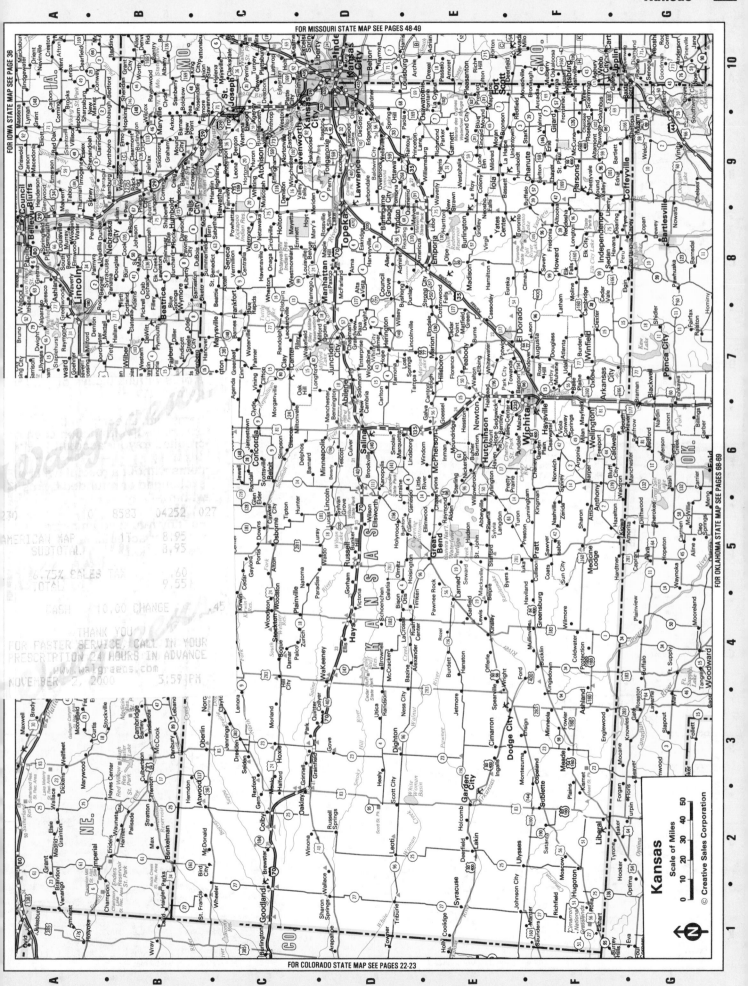

FOR MISSOURI STATE MAP SEE PAGES 48-49

FOR IOWA STATE MAP SEE PAGE 36

FOR OKLAHOMA STATE MAP SEE PAGES 88-89

FOR COLORADO STATE MAP SEE PAGES 22-23

Kansas

Scale of Miles

0 10 20 30 40 50

© Creative Sales Corporation

Kentucky/Tennessee

Scale of Miles
0 7 14 21 28 35

N

© Creative Sales Corporation

FOR ILLINOIS STATE MAP SEE PAGES 32-33
FOR INDIANA STATE MAP SEE PAGES 34-35
FOR MISSOURI STATE MAP SEE PAGES 48-49
FOR ARKANSAS STATE MAP SEE PAGE 15
FOR MISSISSIPPI STATE MAP SEE PAGE 50
FOR ALABAMA STATE MAP SEE PAGE 13

Terre Haute, Martinsville, Trafalgar, Charleston, Mattoon, Windsor, Shelbyville, Pana, Cowden, Toledo, Casey, Greenup, Marshall, Riley, Clay City, Spencer, Bloomington, Litchfield, Hillsboro, Staunton, St. Elmo, Effingham, Robinson, Sullivan, Linton, Worthington, Cincinnati, Oolitic, Alton, Greenville, Vandalia, Newton, Carlisle, Bloomfield, Bedford, Mitchell, St. Charles, O'Fallon, Edwardsville, Louisville, Olney, Lawrenceville, Vincennes, Washington, Shoals, Orleans, St. Louis, East St. Louis, Highland, Carlyle, Flora, Bicknell, Plainville, Loogootee, French Lick, Paoli, Ballwin, Belleville, Swansea, Mascoutah, Centralia, Salem, Mount Carmel, Albion, Patoka, Princeton, Jasper, Marengo, Arnold, Waterloo, Mount Vernon, Fairfield, Wayne City, New Harmony, Huntingburg, Birdseye, English, Corydon, Saint Clair, Hillsboro, Festus, Redbud, Coulterville, Ashley, Carmi, Boonville, Tennyson, Dale, Santa Claus, Oriole, Brandenburg, DeSoto, Sparta, Tamaroa, McLeansboro, Enfield, Norris City, Evansville, Mt. Vernon, Chrisney, Tell City, Webster, Irvington, Potosi, Pinckneyville, DuQuoin, Benton, Thompsonville, Henderson, Hawesville, Cloverport, Hardinsburg, Deslodge, Flat River, Chester, Zeigler, West Frankfort, Eldorado, Shawneetown, Uniontown, Corydon, Waverly, Audubon, Owensboro, Whitesville, Fordsville, Elizabeth, Harned, Elvins, Belleview, Murphysboro, Harrisburg, Morganfield, Sebree, Beech Grove, Leitchfield, Caneyville, Farmington, Carbondale, Marion, Carrier Mills, Sturgis, Dixon, Slaughters, Island, Hartford, Centertown, McHenry, Rockport, Ironton, Fredericktown, Creal Springs, Caseyville, Clay, Providence, Hanson, Nebo, Bremen, Central City, Drakesboro, Morgantown, Hogan, Jonesboro, Anna, Vienna, Elizabethtown, Marion, Madisonville, Earlington, Nortonville, Greenville, Brownsville, Glover, Jackson, Tamms, Dixon Springs, Carrsville, Fredonia, Dawson Sprgs., Princeton, Crofton, Dunmor, Oakland, Smiths Grove, Annapolis, Cape Girardeau, Marble Hill, Chaffee, Karnak, Metropolis, Smithland, Eddyville, Cerulean, Kirkmansville, Bowling Green, Piedmont, Grassy, Zalma, Scott City, Monkeys Eyebrow, Dycusburg, Calvert City, Kuttawa, Grand Rivers, Rockcastle, Cadiz, Hopkinsville, Fairview, Russellville, Lewisburg, Auburn, Greenville, Arab, Idlewild, Advance, Oran, Barlow, Cairo, Paducah, Reidland, Benton, Golden Pond, Pembroke, Elkton, Allensville, Franklin, Woodburn, Ellsinore, Bloomfield, Bell City, Sikeston, Wickliffe, Arlington, Hardin, Dexter, La Fayette, Trenton, Guthrie, Adairville, Poplar Bluff, Dexter, East Prairie, Columbus, Bardwell, Clinton, Wingo, Mayfield, Murray, Hazel, Saint Bethlehem, Adams, Cedar Hill, Portland, Grandin, Bernie, Columbus, New Madrid, Sedalia, Water Valley, Midway, Dover, Clarksville, Palmyra, Pleasant View, Cross Plains, White House, Greenbrier, Ridgetop, Gallatin, Doniphan, Qulin, Malden, Parma, Hickman, Fulton, South Fulton, Puryear, Bumpus Mills, Oakwood, Joelton, Goodlettsville, Corning, Clarkton, Portageville, Reelfoot Lake St. Pk., Woodland Mills, Union City, Latham, Paris, Erin, Cumberland City, Charlotte, Ashland City, Hendersonville, Inglewood, Lebanon, Piggott, Campbell, Tiptonville, Troy, Rives, Martin, Dresden, Gleason, Big Sandy, Tennessee Ridge, McEwen, Nashville, Donelson, Mt. Juliet, Beech Grove, Kennett, Senath, Steele, Caruthersville, Obion, Kenton, Sharon, Greenfield, McKenzie, Camden, Dickson, Burns, White Bluff, Pegram, Belle Meade, Brentwood, La Vergne, Smyrna, Paragould, Cardwell, Hayti, Miston, Bogota, Newbern, Rutherford, Bradford, Gibson, Medina, Clarksburg, New Johnsonville, Waverly, Lyles, Fairview, Franklin, Triune, Arrington, Kirkland, Murfreesboro, Blytheville, Monette, Manila, S. Dyersburg, Dyersburg, Central, Dyer, Trezevant, Atwood, Milan, Huntingdon, Leach, Bruceton, Camden, Nunnelly, Leipers Fork, Centerville, Pinewood, Columbia, Trumann, Caraway, Ashport, Halls, Trenton, Friendship, Humboldt, Alamo, Gadsden, Springcreek, Milan, Lexington, Parsons, Linden, Hohenwald, Mt. Pleasant, Hampshire, Aetna, Allisona, Lepanto, Ripley, Gates, Maury City, Bells, Fruitvale, Medina, Darden, Scotts Hill, Decaturville, Flat Woods, Summertown, Culleoka, Lewisburg, Belfast, Shelbyville, Manchester, Marked Tree, Burlison, Covington, Henning, Stanton, Jackson, Malesus, Mercer, Pinson, Henderson, Sardis, Clifton, Waynesboro, Webber, Waco, Lynnville, Cornersville, Tullahoma, Millington, Braden, Atoka, Munford, Brighton, Keeling, Mason, Dancyville, Toone, Medon, Milledgeville, Bethel Sprs., Morris Chapel, Olivehill, Lawrenceburg, Ethridge, Pulaski, Frankewing, Petersburg, Lynchburg, West Memphis, Raleigh, Bartlett, Oakland, Williston, Somerville, Whiteville, Bolivar, Hornsby, Adamsville, Savannah, Highland, Lutts, Collinwood, Goodspring, Minor Hill, Fayetteville, Winchester, Memphis, Arlington, Germantown, Collierville, Rossville, Grand Junction, Hickory Valley, Middleton, Selmer, Ramer, Nixon, Shiloh, Walkertown, Eastview, Michie, Saint Joseph, Loretto, Bethel, Elkton, Taft, Elora, Capleville, Byhalia, Michigan City, Moscow, Williston, Walnut, Corinth, Counce, Iron City, Lexington, Anderson, Cash Point, Ardmore, New Market, Hernando, Coldwater, Independence, Holly Springs, Ashland, Ripley, Tiptonville, Falkner, Iuka, Zip City, Petersburg, Athens, Meridianville, Chase, Florence, Rogersville, Sheffield, Muscle Shoals, Barton, Cherokee, Coxey, Wheeler Lake

Mississippi River, Ohio River, Wabash River, Tennessee River, Cumberland River, Kentucky Lake, Lake Barkley, Reelfoot Lake, Rend Lake, Carlyle Lake, Shawnee National Forest, Land Between the Lakes, Fort Campbell, Fort Donelson, Shiloh Nat'l Mil. Park, Pickwick Lake

MO. ILL. IND. KY. TENN. ARK. MS. ALA.

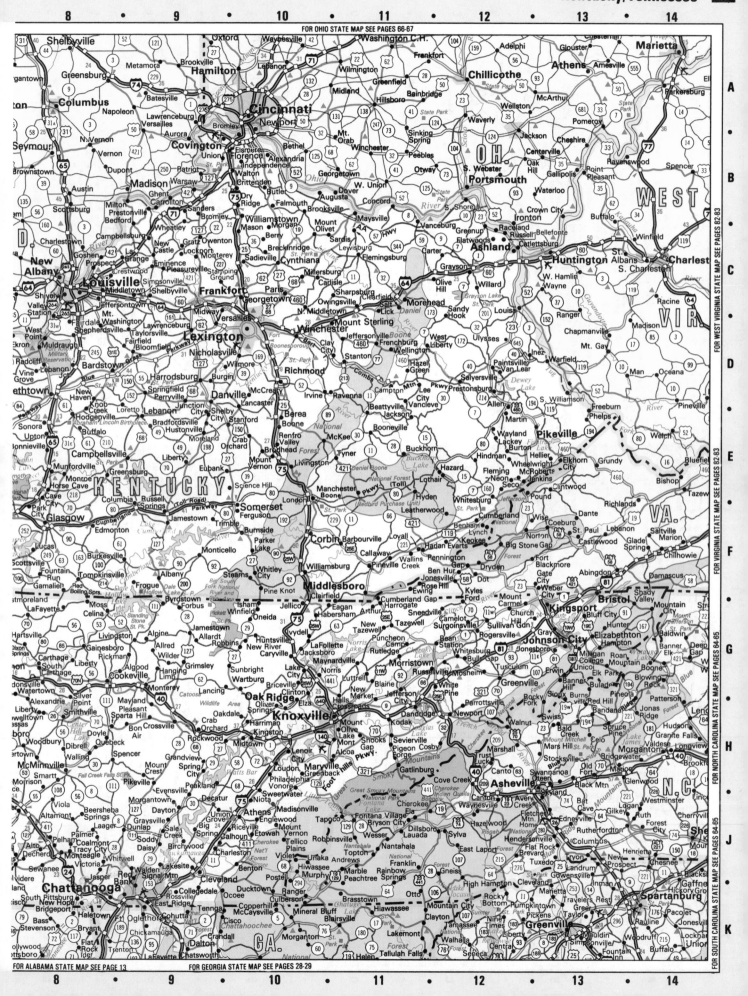

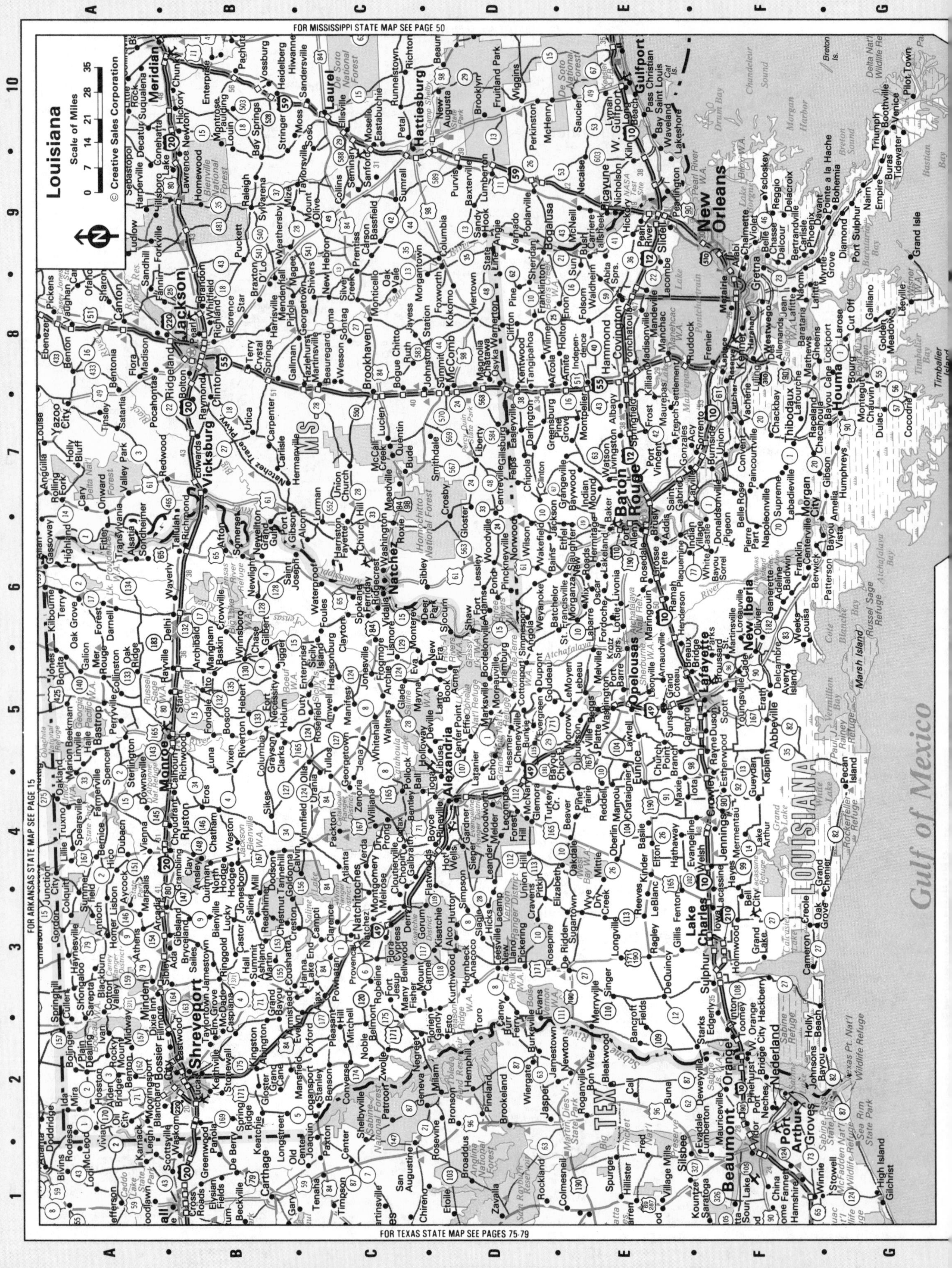

A B C D E F G

FOR MISSISSIPPI STATE MAP SEE PAGE 50

Louisiana

Scale of Miles

0 7 14 21 28 35

© Creative Sales Corporation

FOR ARKANSAS STATE MAP SEE PAGE 15

Gulf of Mexico

LOUISIANA

MS

TEX

New Orleans
Baton Rouge
Shreveport
Monroe
Alexandria
Lafayette
Lake Charles
Houma
New Iberia
Opelousas
Hammond
Slidel
Covington
Natchez
Vicksburg
Jackson
Meridian
Hattiesburg
Laurel
Gulfport
Beaumont
Port Arthur
Orange

FOR TEXAS STATE MAP SEE PAGES 75-79

A B C D E F G

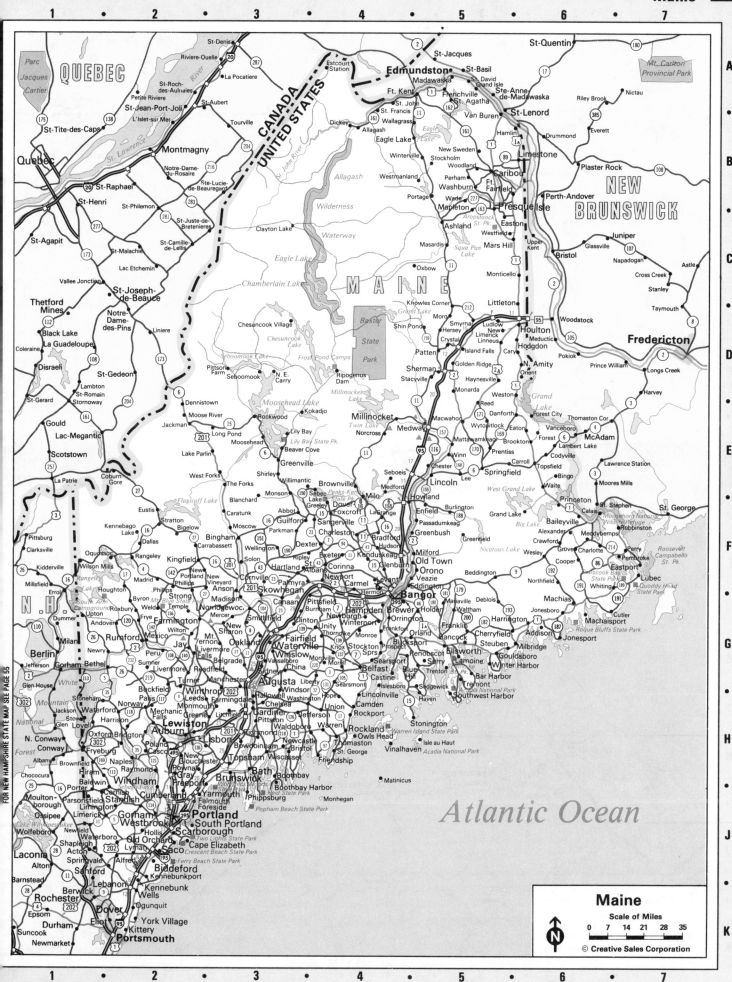

Atlantic Ocean

Maine
Scale of Miles
0   7   14   21   28   35
© Creative Sales Corporation

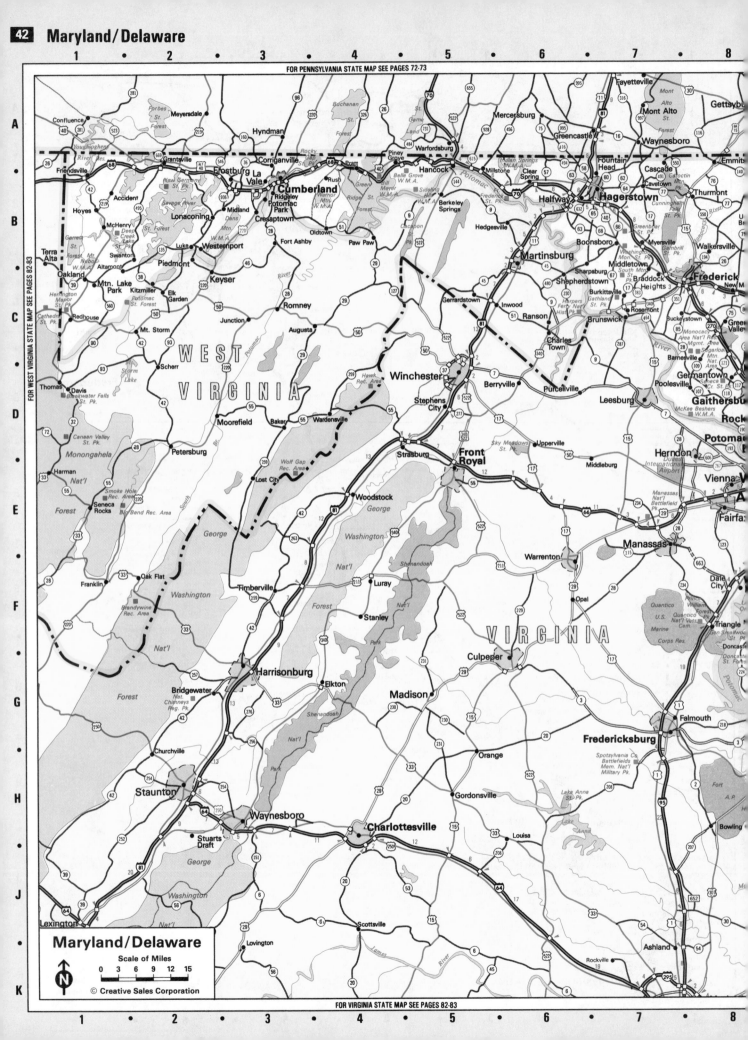

8 9 10 11 12 13 14 15

FOR PENNSYLVANIA STATE MAP SEE PAGE 72-73 FOR NEW JERSEY STATE MAP SEE PAGES 56-57

PENN

N. J.

DEL

MARYLAND

Chesapeake Bay

Atlantic Ocean

Delaware Bay

Quarryville, Red Lion, Spring Grove, Airville, Kennett Square, Paulsboro, Runnemede, Woodbury, Lindenwold, Pitman, Williamstown, Franklinville, Elmer, Vineland, Millville, Bridgeton, Shiloh, Centerton, Woodstown, Salem, Penns Grove, Swedesboro, Wilmington, Elsmere, Newark, New Castle, Delaware City, Porter, Middletown, Odessa, Townsend, Smyrna, Clayton, Leipsic, Dover, Camden, Wyoming, Cheswold, Hartly, Frederica, Bowers Beach, Milford, Slaughter Beach, Harrington, Houston, Felton, Greensboro, Greenwood, Ellendale, Milton, Lewes, Bridgeville, Harbeson, Georgetown, Angola, Dewey Beach, Millsboro, Seaford, Blades, Laurel, Delmar, Selbyville, Fenwick Is., Bethany Beach, Frankford, Millville, Gumboro, Willards, Pittsville, Salisbury, Fruitland, Powellville, Berlin, Ocean City, Longridge, Princess Anne, Snow Hill, Public Landing, Stockton, Pocomoke City, Crisfield, Chincoteague

McSherrystown, Hanover, Stewartstown, Shrewsbury, Manchester, Melrose, Harkins, Whiteford, Dublin, Rising Sun, Fair Hill, Newport, Elkton, North East, Charlestown, Cecilton, Galena, Kennedyville, Chestertown, Sudlersville, Barclay, Templeville, Ridgely, Denton, Harmony, Federalsburg, Hurlock, Preston, Easton, St. Michaels, Cambridge, Vienna, Hebron, Salisbury

Taneytown, Westminster, Reisterstown, Owings Mills, Pikesville, Towson, Baltimore, Dundalk, Columbia, Ellicott City, Catonsville, Glen Burnie, Severna Park, Annapolis, Bowie, Crofton, Laurel, Beltsville, Greenbelt, Washington, Bethesda, Silver Springs, Alexandria, Oxon Hill, Clinton, Waldorf, White Plains, La Plata, Leonardtown, Lexington Park, California

Chincoteague Nat'l Wildlife Refuge

FOR VIRGINIA STATE MAP SEE PAGES 82-83

8 9 10 11 12 13 14 15

A B C D E F G H J K

CANADA
UNITED STATES

Lake Huron

Lake Michigan

Lake Superior

CANADA
UNITED STATES

ONT.

MICH

FOR CONTINUATION SEE GRID B-1

FOR CONTINUATION SEE GRID A-10

FOR WISCONSIN STATE MAP SEE PAGES 86-87

When travelling in wilderness areas or on unfamiliar roads, it is always best to be cautious and particularly attentive to local driving conditions. Be alert at all times and use the designated rest areas as often as necessary.

Sault Ste. Marie

Marquette

Negaunee

Ishpeming

Escanaba

Gladstone

Houghton

Hancock

Alpena

Petoskey

Cheboygan

Gaylord

Grayling

Traverse City

Cadillac

Manistee

Ludington

Green Bay

Appleton

Oshkosh

Manitowoc

Two Rivers

Menominee

Marinette

Iron Mountain

Crystal Falls

L'Anse

Baraga

Calumet

Isle Royale Nat'l Park

Mackinac Bridge (TOLL)

St. Ignace

Mackinaw City

Pictured Rocks National Lakeshore

Sleeping Bear Dunes National Lakeshore

Hiawatha National Forest

Seney National Wildlife Refuge

Ottawa National Forest

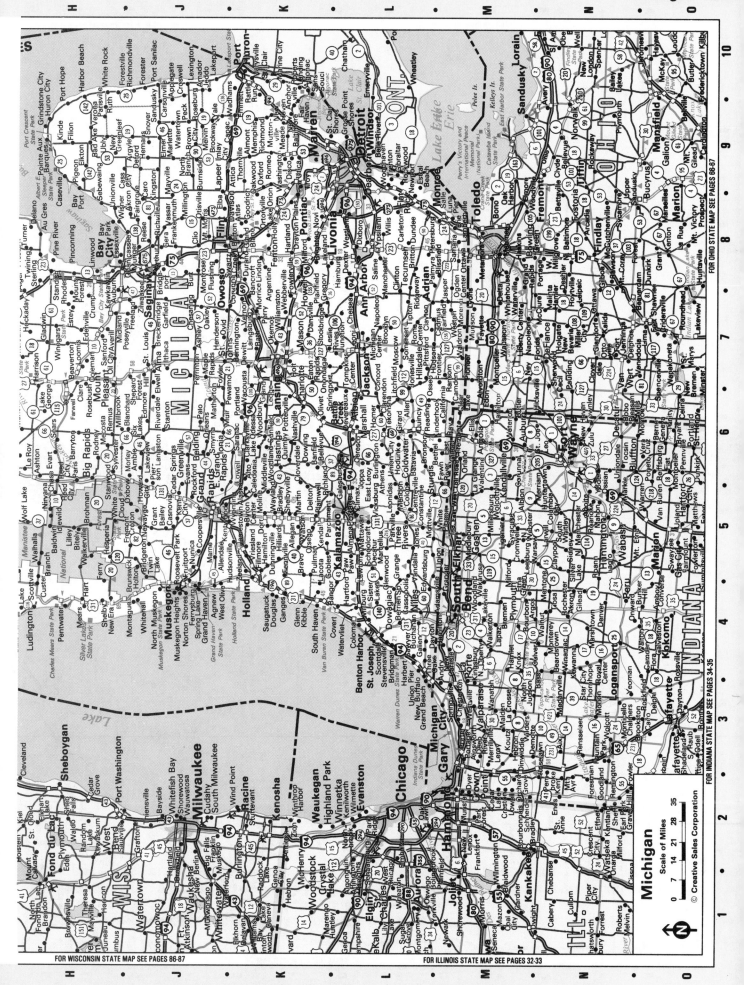

FOR INDIANA STATE MAP SEE PAGES 34-35

FOR OHIO STATE MAP SEE PAGES 66-67

Michigan

Scale of Miles

0   7   14   21   28   35

© Creative Sales Corporation

FOR CONTINUATION SEE GRID A-9
FOR WISCONSIN STATE MAP SEE PAGES 86-87
FOR CONTINUATION SEE GRID C-10
FOR NORTH DAKOTA STATE MAP SEE PAGE 74

Grid labels: A B C D E F G (top and bottom), 10 9 8 7 6 5 4 3 2 1 (sides)

Inset map: Isle Royale National Park, Grand Portage Indian Res., Hovland, Grand Portage, Grand Portage State Forest, Croftville, Grand Marais, Cascade River St. Park, Lutsen, Arrow Lake

ONTARIO, CANADA, UNITED STATES

Lake Superior, Lake of the Woods, Rainy Lake, Vermillion Lake, Leech Lake, Red Lake, Upper Red Lake, Lower Red Lake, Mille Lacs Lake

Duluth, Superior, Virginia, Hibbing, Bemidji, International Falls, Grand Rapids, Brainerd, Moorhead, Fargo, Fergus Falls, Wahpeton, Alexandria, Detroit Lakes, Thief River Falls, Crookston, East Grand Forks, Ashland, Washburn, Bayfield

Hallock, Warroad, Roseau, Badger, Greenbush, Baudette, Pitt, Williams, Warren, Stephen, Argyle, Alvarado, Oslo, Fisher, Climax, Shelly, Halstad, Ada, Borup, Felton, Hawley, Barnesville, Comstock, Wolverton, Breckenridge, Doran, Campbell, Tintah, Wheaton, Herman, Dumont, Norcross, Elbow Lake, Hoffman, Kensington, Barrett, Ashby, Dalton, Underwood, Battle Lake, Henning, Ottertail, Perham, Frazee, Audubon, Callaway, Ogema, Waubun, Mahnomen, Bagley, Clearbrook, Gonvick, Trail, Gully, McIntosh, Fosston, Erskine, Mentor, Brooks, Plummer, Red Lake Falls, St. Hilaire, Goodridge, Grygla, Gatzke, Strathcona, Middle River, Holt, Newfolden, Strandquist, Karlstad, Halma, Lancaster, Kennedy, Donaldson, Humboldt, St. Vincent, Lake Bronson, Tolstoi

Grand Marais, Lutsen, Tofte, Schroeder, Taconite Harbor, Little Marais, Silver Bay, Beaver Bay, Two Harbors, Knife River, Larsmont, Finland, Isabella, Ely, Winton, Tower, Babbitt, Aurora, Biwabik, Hoyt Lakes, Gilbert, Eveleth, Mountain Iron, Chisholm, Buhl, Kinney, Keewatin, Nashwauk, Calumet, Marble, Coleraine, Bovey, Taconite, Goodland, La Prairie, Cohasset, Deer River, Remer, Longville, Walker, Akeley, Nevis, Park Rapids, Menahga, Sebeka, Nimrod, Verndale, Wadena, Staples, Motley, Pillager, Baxter, Nisswa, Pequot Lakes, Crosslake, Pine River, Backus, Hackensack, Outing, Emily, Crosby, Ironton, Deerwood, Garrison, Isle, Wahkon, Onamia, Milaca, Princeton, Mora, Ogilvie, Hinckley, Sandstone, Askov, Moose Lake, Cromwell, Barnum, Carlton, Cloquet, Proctor, Hermantown, Scanlon, Floodwood, Meadowlands, Cotton, Canyon

Cass Lake, Bena, Boy River, Federal Dam, Remer, Longville

MINNESOTA

Roads/highways: US 2, US 10, US 53, US 59, US 71, US 75, US 169, US 210, US 12, US 61, I-29, I-35

Bad River Ind. Res., Apostle Islands Nat'l Lakeshore, Madeline Island State Park, Chequamegon National Forest, Brule River State Forest, St. Croix State Forest, Fond du Lac Ind. Res., Superior National Forest, Boundary Waters Canoe Area, Voyageurs National Park, Quetico Provincial Park, Chippewa National Forest, Red Lake Indian Reservation, Leech Lake Reservation, White Earth Indian Reservation, Itasca State Park, Tamarac Nat'l Wildlife Ref.

Iron River, Hurley, Montreal, Mellen, Cable, Hayward, Spooner, Siren, Webster, Grantsburg, Pine City, Rush City, North Branch, Cambridge, Braham, Mille Lacs, Foley, Gilman, Rice, Royalton, Little Falls, Sauk Centre, Melrose, Freeport, Albany, Avon, St. Cloud

Mellen, Mason, Gordon, Solon Springs, Minong, Trego, Radisson, Winter, Park Falls, Fifield, Phillips, Butternut

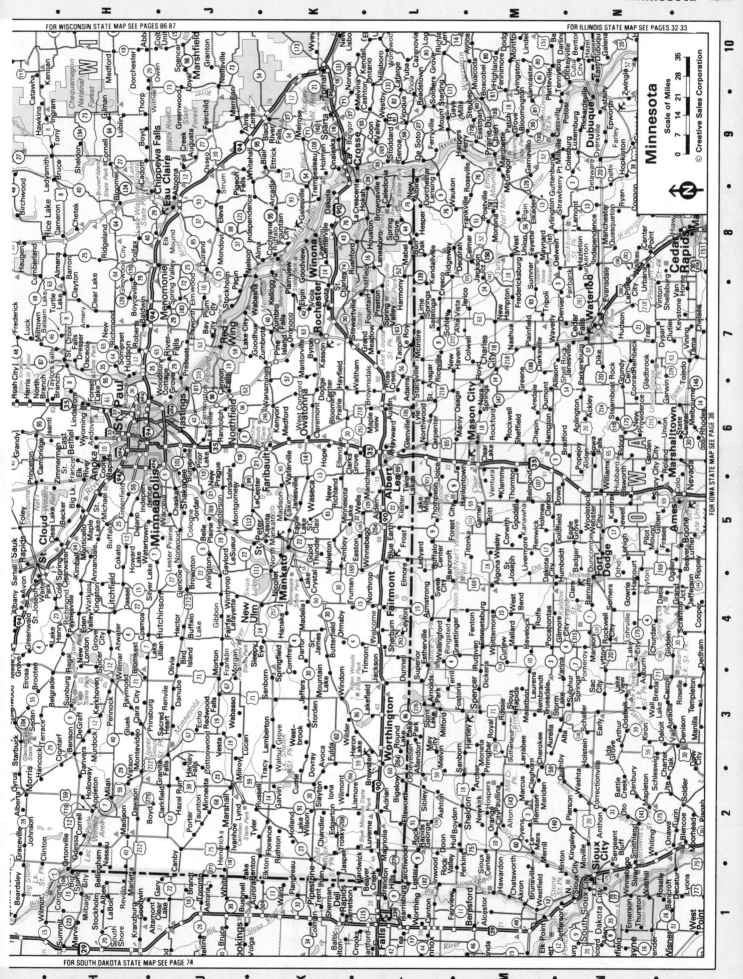

FOR WISCONSIN STATE MAP SEE PAGES 86-87

FOR ILLINOIS STATE MAP SEE PAGES 32-33

Minnesota

Scale of Miles

0   7   14   21   28   35

© Creative Sales Corporation

FOR IOWA STATE MAP SEE PAGE 36

FOR SOUTH DAKOTA STATE MAP SEE PAGE 74

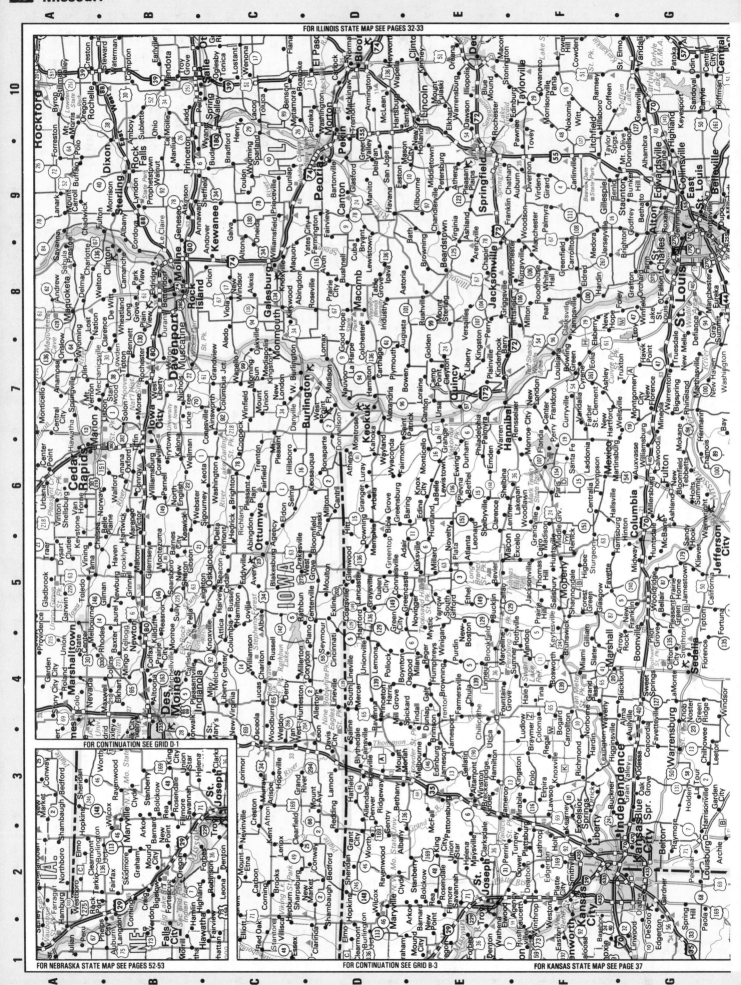

FOR ILLINOIS STATE MAP SEE PAGES 32-33

FOR CONTINUATION SEE GRID D-1

FOR NEBRASKA STATE MAP SEE PAGES 52-53

FOR CONTINUATION SEE GRID B-3

FOR KANSAS STATE MAP SEE PAGE 37

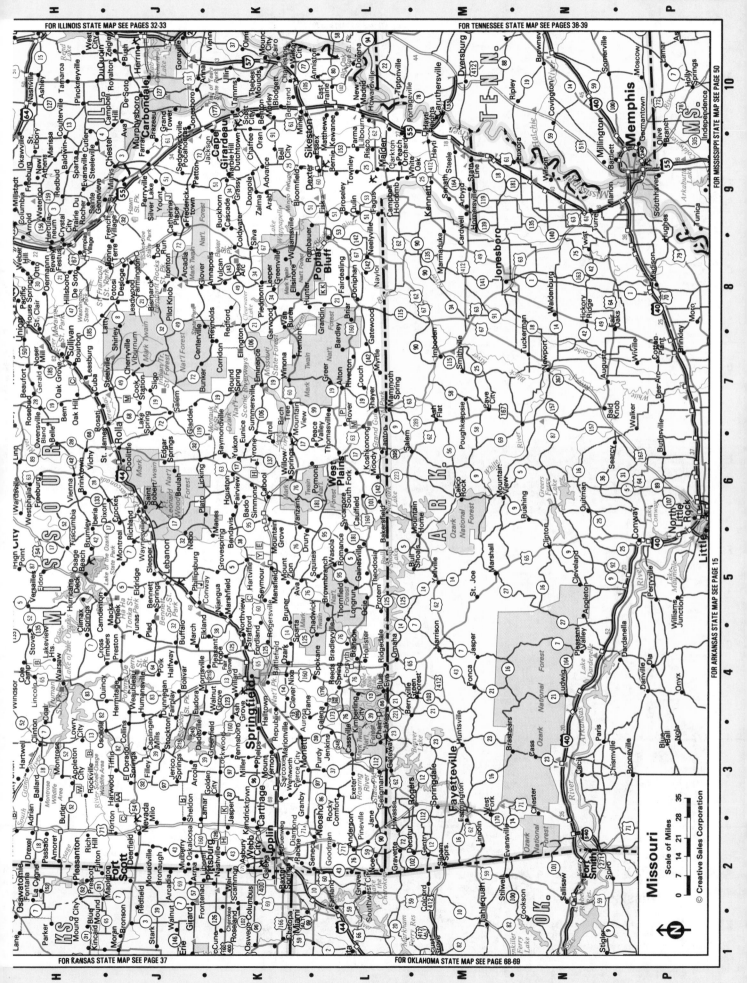

Missouri

Scale of Miles

0   7   14   21   28   35

© Creative Sales Corporation

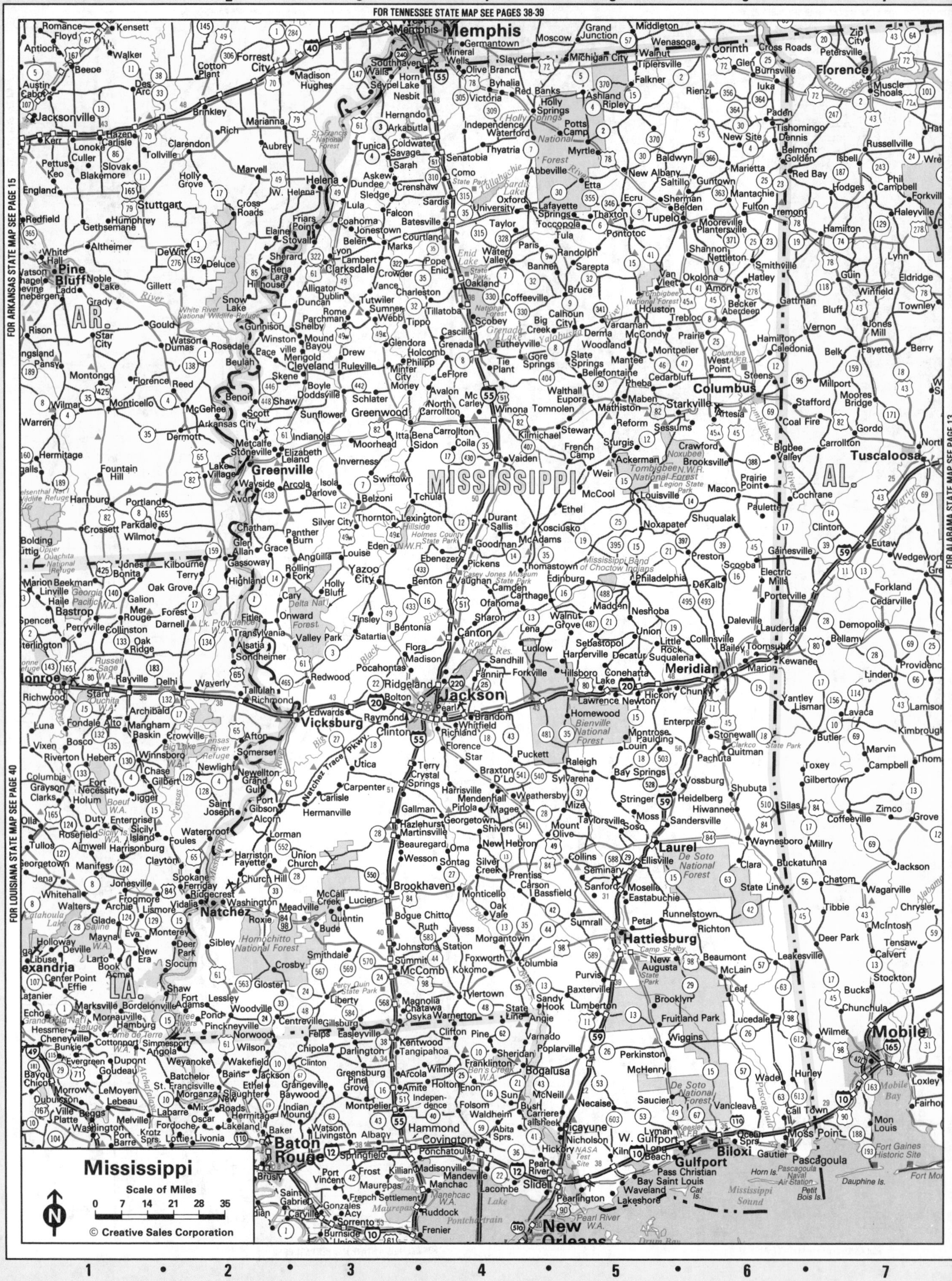

FOR TENNESSEE STATE MAP SEE PAGES 38-39

FOR ARKANSAS STATE MAP SEE PAGE 15

FOR LOUISIANA STATE MAP SEE PAGE 40

FOR ALABAMA STATE MAP SEE PAGE 13

MISSISSIPPI

AR.

LA.

AL.

Memphis

Jackson

Vicksburg

Natchez

Meridian

Hattiesburg

Laurel

Biloxi

Gulfport

Pascagoula

Mobile

Baton Rouge

New Orleans

Tuscaloosa

Florence

Columbus

Starkville

Tupelo

Corinth

Greenville

Greenwood

Yazoo City

Brookhaven

McComb

Mississippi

Scale of Miles

0 7 14 21 28 35

N

© Creative Sales Corporation

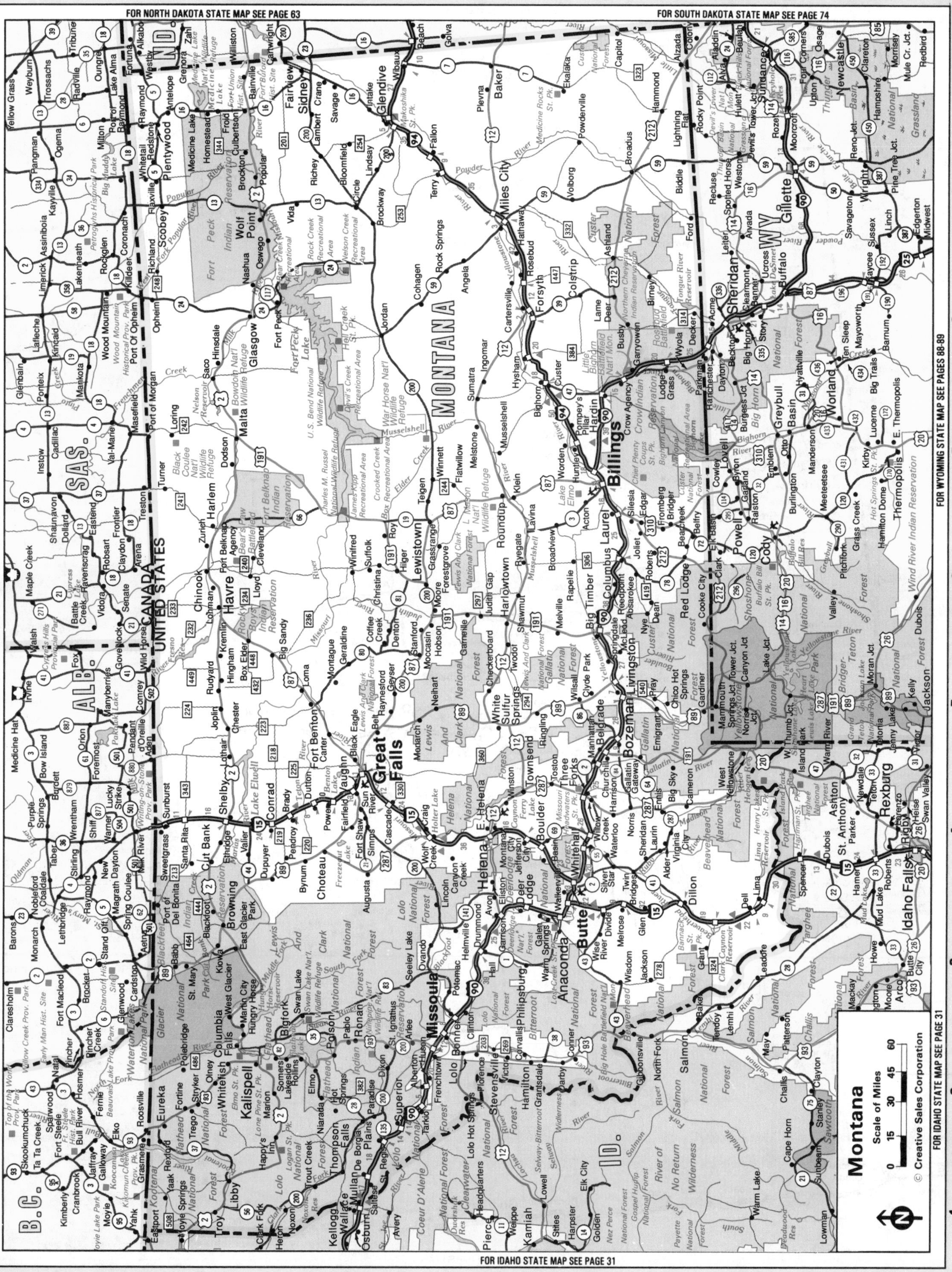

FOR NORTH DAKOTA STATE MAP SEE PAGE 63

FOR SOUTH DAKOTA STATE MAP SEE PAGE 74

FOR WYOMING STATE MAP SEE PAGES 88-89

FOR IDAHO STATE MAP SEE PAGE 31

Montana

Scale of Miles

0 15 30 45 60

© Creative Sales Corporation

CANADA
UNITED STATES

SASK.
ALBERTA

N.D.
S.D.
WY
ID.

MONTANA

Great Falls

Billings

Missoula

Butte

Helena

Bozeman

Kalispell

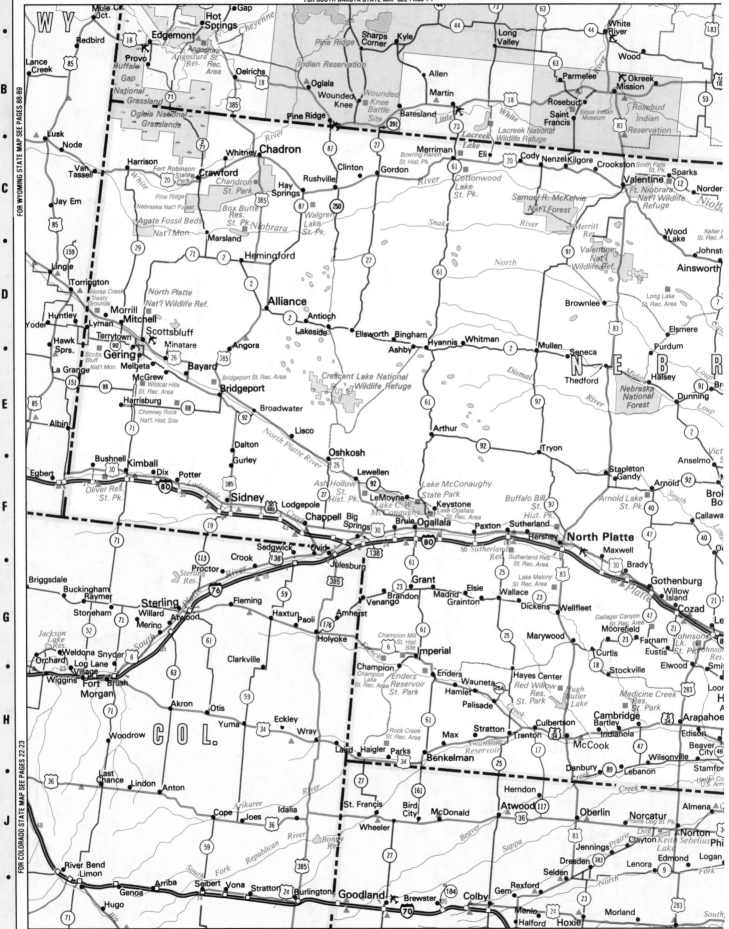

FOR SOUTH DAKOTA STATE MAP SEE PAGE 74

FOR WYOMING STATE MAP SEE PAGES 88-89

FOR COLORADO STATE MAP SEE PAGES 22-23

FOR KANSAS STATE MAP SEE PAGE 37

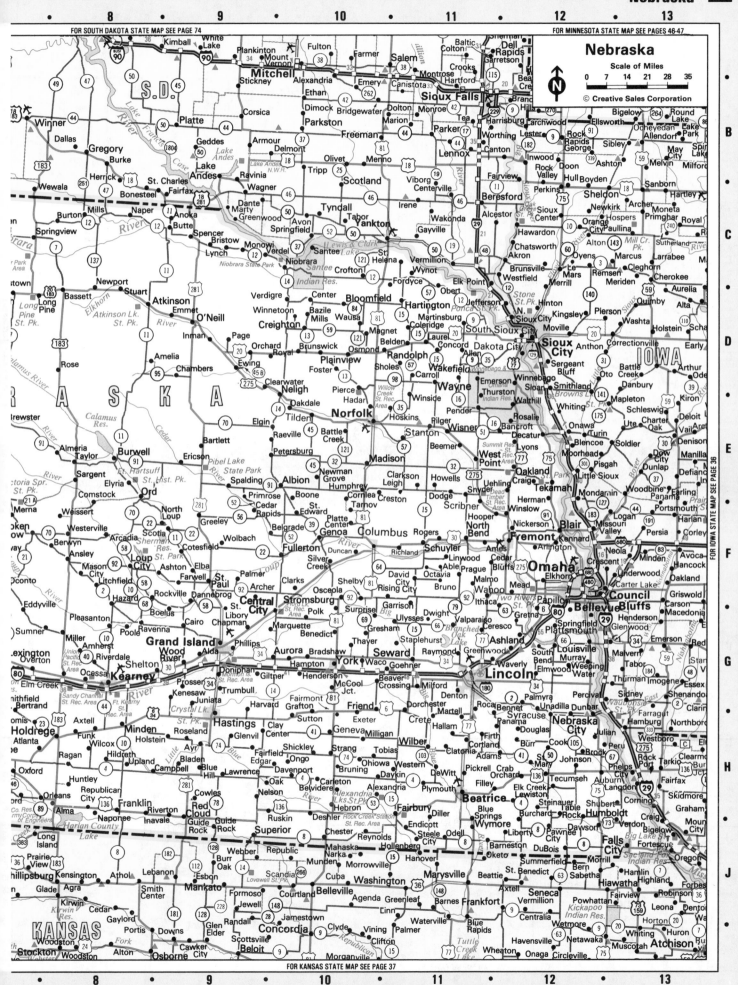

FOR OREGON STATE MAP SEE PAGES 70-71

FOR IDAHO STATE MAP SEE PAGE 31

OR.   ID.

CA.

NEVADA

UT.

AZ.

CA.

Riddle, Rogerson, Sawtooth National Forest, McDermitt, Three Creek, Jackpot, Owyhee, Duck Valley Indian Reservation, Mountain City, Jarbidge, Contact, Ft. McDermitt Indian Reservation, Humboldt National Forest, Thousand Springs, Montello, Orovada, Paradise Valley, Jack Creek, Tuscarora, Wells, Oasis, Midas, Halleck, Deeth, Winnemucca, Golconda, Valmy, Battle Mountain, Elko, Lamoille, Wendover, Sulphur, Carlin, Gerlach, Imlay, Mill City, Beowawe, Beowawe Geysers, Te-Moak Indian Res., Lee, South Fork Indian Res., Wendover Range, Empire, Unionville, Crescent Valley, Jiggs, Ruby Valley, Currie, Dugway Proving Grounds, Lovelock, Eagle Picher Mine, Oreana, Shantytown, Ruby Lake National Wildlife Refuge, Desert Test Center, Nixon, Lage's, Cherry Creek, Goshute Indian Reservation, Sutcliffe, Doyle, Herlong, Austin, Eureka, Pony Express Station Site, Trout Cr., Reno, Sparks, Wadsworth, Fallon, Fallon Naval Air Station, Fernley, Silver Springs, Cold Springs, Pony Express Station Site, McGill, Gandy, Virginia City, Silver City, Carson City, Frenchman, Middle Gate, Ruth, Ely, East Ely, Lehman Caves Nat'l Mon., Weed Heights, Schurz, Ione, Toiyabe National Forest, Kimberly, Copper Pit, Baker, Yerington, Gabbs, Carver's, Duckwater, Preston, Major's Place, Garrison, Great Basin National Park, Wellington, Babbitt, Round Mountain, Duckwater Indian Res., Lund, Wheeler Peak Scenic Area, Hawthorne, Luning, Currant, Mina, Pancake Range, Nyala, Adaven, Warm Springs, Railroad Valley W.M.A., Bridgeport, Coaldale, Tonopah, Pioche, Ursine, Lund, Beryl, Lee Vining, June Lake, Benton, Dyer, Silver Peak, Goldfield, Rachel, Hiko, Caselton, Panaca, Uvada, Mammoth Lakes, Toms Place, Lida, Nellis A.F. Bombing & Gunnery Range, Ash Springs, Alamo, Caliente, Round Valley, Bishop, Oasis, Laws, Gold Point, Scotty's Junction, Elgin, Carp, Shivwits, Independence, Beatty, Mercury, Indian Springs, Glendale, Mesquite, Lone Pine, Keeler, Death Valley, Cactus Springs, Moapa, Overton, Bunkerville, Hanford, Camp Nelson, Little Lake, Panamint Springs, Death Valley Jct., N. Las Vegas, Henderson, Las Vegas, Blue Diamond, Sloan, Boulder City, Shoshone, Tecopa, Goodsprings, Sandy, Nelson, Onyx, Weldon, China Lake, Westend, Argus, Jean, Searchlight, Nipton, Baker, Cima, Laughlin, Kingman, Barstow

Nevada

Scale of Miles
0   20   40   60

N

© Creative Sales Corporation

FOR CALIFORNIA STATE MAP SEE PAGES 18-21

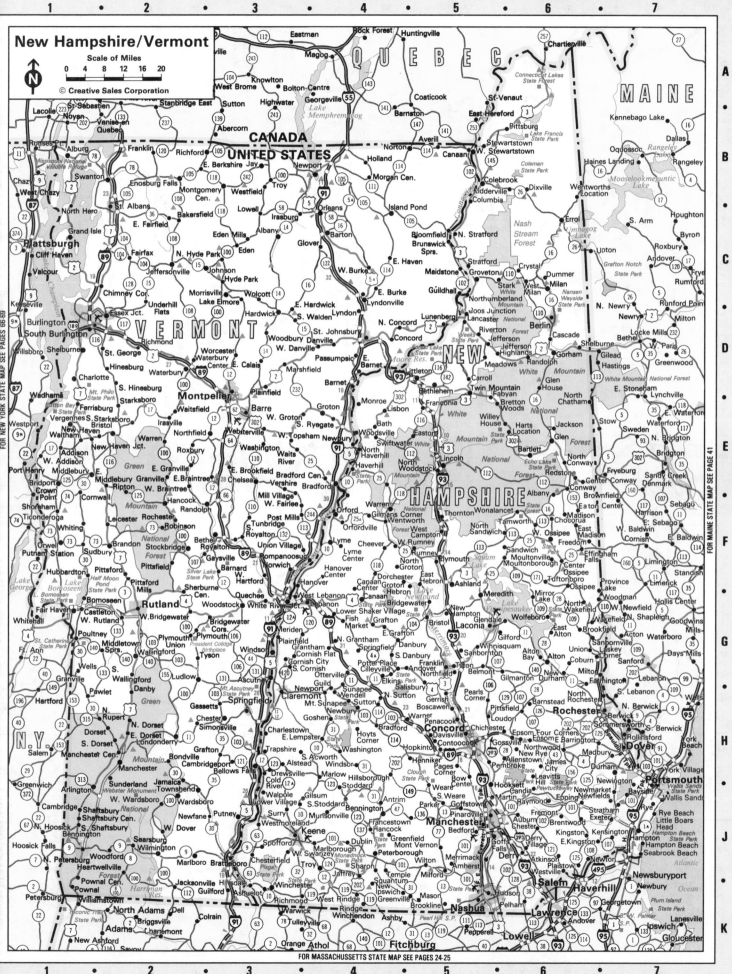

FOR NEW YORK STATE MAP SEE PAGES 58-61

FOR PENNSYLVANIA STATE MAP SEE PAGES 72-73

FOR PENNSYLVANIA STATE MAP SEE PAGES 72-73

NEW YORK

PENNSYLVANIA

Ocean

Atlantic Ocean

Long Island Sound

Hudson River

Delaware River

Raritan Bay

Staten Is.

White Plains · Yonkers · Mt. Vernon · New York · Jersey City · Newark · Elizabeth · Bayonne · Hoboken · Union City · West New York · Englewood · Tenafly · Bergenfield · Hackensack · Paramus · Passaic · Garfield · Clifton · Paterson · West Paterson · Hawthorne · Fair Lawn · Ridgewood · Waldwick · Nutley · Bloomfield · Belleville · Irvington · Orange · East Orange · West Orange · Summit · New Providence · Watchung · Plainfield · South Plainfield · Westfield · Roselle · Roselle Park · Kenilworth · Linden · Rahway · Metuchen · Carteret · Perth Amboy · South Amboy · Sayreville · South River · Highland Park · New Brunswick · Bound Brook · Somerville · Manville · Raritan · Millstone · Milltown · Spotswood · Old Bridge · South Brunswick · Cranbury · Princeton · Hightstown · Hopewell · Pennington · Lawrence · Trenton · Ewing · Morrisville · Levittown · Warminster · Lansdale · Doylestown · Quakertown · Allentown · Bethlehem · Easton · Phillipsburg · Alpha · Spring Mills · Milford · Frenchtown · Flemington · Lambertville · Stockton · Lebanon · Clinton · High Bridge · Califon · Long Valley · Chester · Peapack · Bedminster · Whitehouse · Readington · Oldwick · Washington · Broadway · Oxford · Belvidere · Hackettstown · Hope · Blairstown · Johnsonburg · Hainesburg · Delaware · Columbia · Knowlton · Newton · Fredon · Andover · Sparta · Stanhope · Netcong · Hopatcong · Budd Lakes · Allamuchy · Great Meadows · Stephens St. Pk. · Bernardsville · Liberty Corner · Warren · Dunellen · New Edison · Morristown · Madison · Chatham · Florham Park · Hanover · Morris Plains · Parsippany-Troy Hills · Mendham · Dover · Wharton · Rockaway · Denville · Boonton · Montville · Lincoln Park · Pompton Lakes · Butler · Bloomingdale · Kinnelon · Riverdale · Wanaque · Ringwood · West Milford · Stockholm · Franklin · Hamburg · Ogdensburg · Lafayette · Branchville · Ross Corner · Tuttles Corner · Montague · Colesville · Sussex · Vernon · McAfee · Glenwood · Warwick · Florida · Monroe · Central Valley · New City · Spring Valley · Nyack · Tappan · Tarrytown · Ossining · Peekskill · Pt. Jervis · Port Jervis · Scranton · Moscow · Sterling · Gouldsboro · Stroudsburg · Bangor · Nazareth · Northampton · Catasauqua · Macungie · Pottstown · Pennsburg · New Berlinsville · Newtown · Yardville · Hamilton Sq. · Robbinsville · Allentown · Roosevelt · Jamesburg · Englishtown · Freehold · Manalapan · Marlboro · Holmdel · Matawan · Keyport · Union Beach · Keansburg · Atlantic Highlands · Highlands · Rumson · Red Bank · Shrewsbury · Oceanport · Eatontown · Tinton Falls · Fair Haven · Long Branch · West Long Branch · Neptune · Farmingdale · Adelphia · Freewood Acres · Asbury Park · Bradley Beach · Belmar · Spring Lakes Heights · Long Beach · Atlantic Beach · Valley Stream · Great Neck

Sandy Hook Light · Sandy Hook Nat'l Hist. Landmark · Gateway Nat'l Rec. Area

Great Swamp Nat'l Wildlife Refuge · Delaware Water Gap Nat'l Rec. Area · High Point St. Pk. · Stokes St. Forest · Worthington St. Forest · Wawayanda St. Pk. · Norvin Green St. Forest · Ramapo Mtn. Co. Res. · Greenwood Lake · Wanaque Res. · Palisades · Black River Wildlife Mgmt. Area · Pequest Wildlife Mgmt. Area · Assunpink Wildlife Mgmt. Area · Amwell Lk. Wildlife Mgmt. Area · Delaware & Raritan Canal St. Pk. · Round Valley Res. · Spruce Run Res. · Merrill Creek Res. · Promised Land St. Pk. · Tobyhanna St. Pk. · Big Pocono St. Pk.

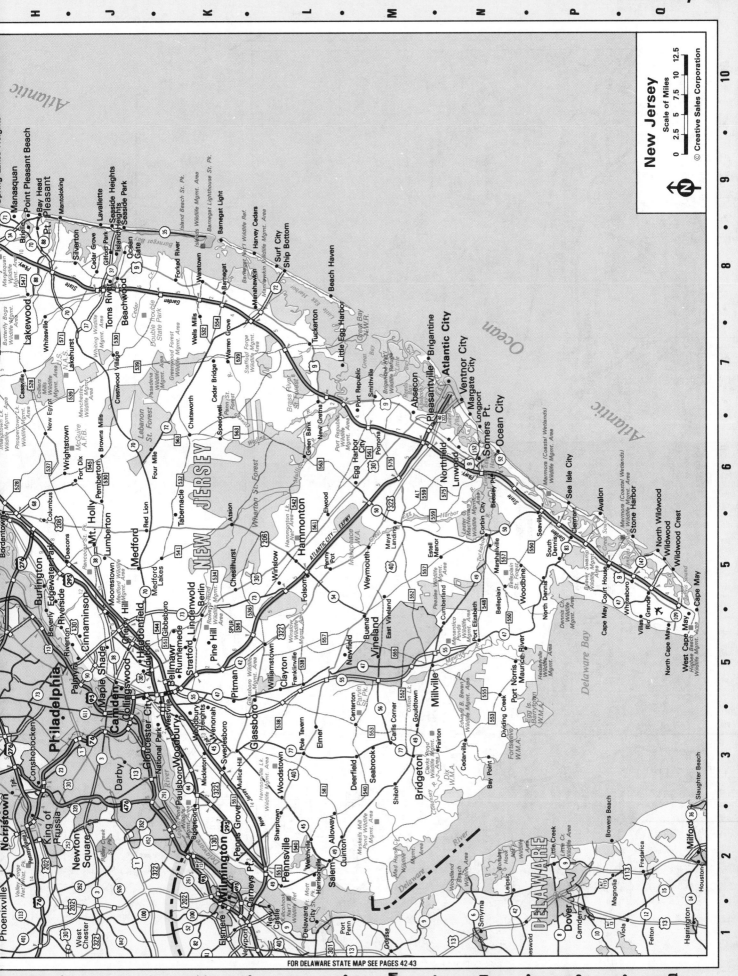

New Jersey

Scale of Miles

0 2.5 5 7.5 10 12.5

© Creative Sales Corporation

FOR DELAWARE STATE MAP SEE PAGES 42-43

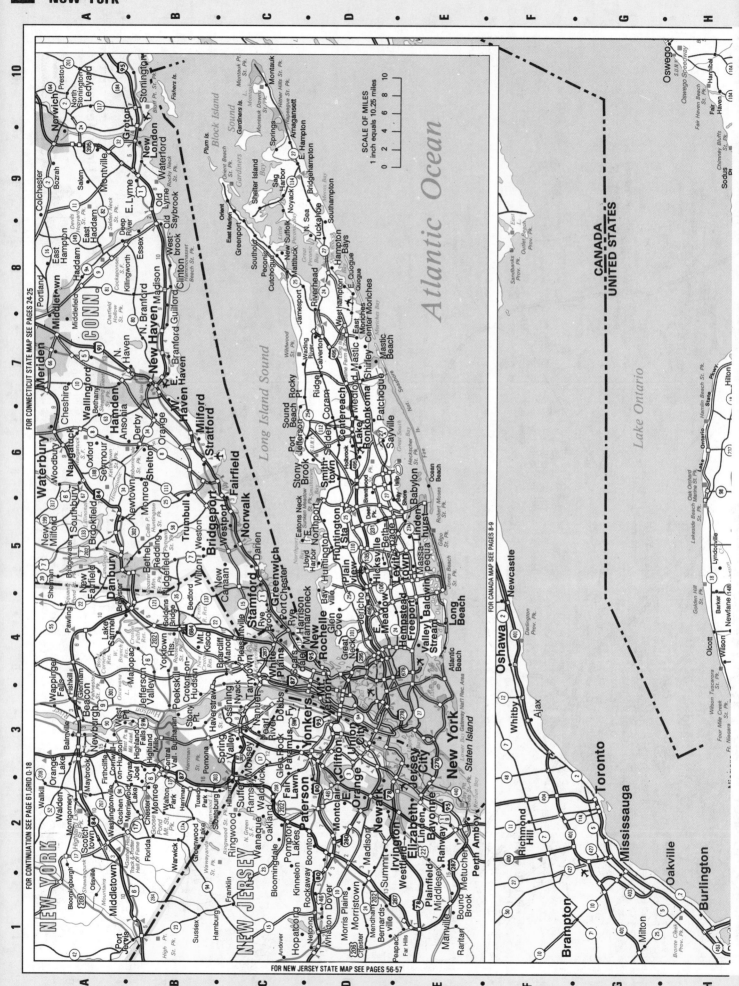

FOR CONTINUATION SEE PAGE 61, GRID Q-18

FOR CONNECTICUT STATE MAP SEE PAGES 24-25

FOR CANADA MAP SEE PAGES 8-9

SCALE OF MILES
1 inch equals 10.25 miles
0 2 4 6 8 10

Atlantic Ocean

Long Island Sound

Block Island
Sound

Lake Ontario

CANADA
UNITED STATES

NEW YORK

NEW JERSEY

CONN

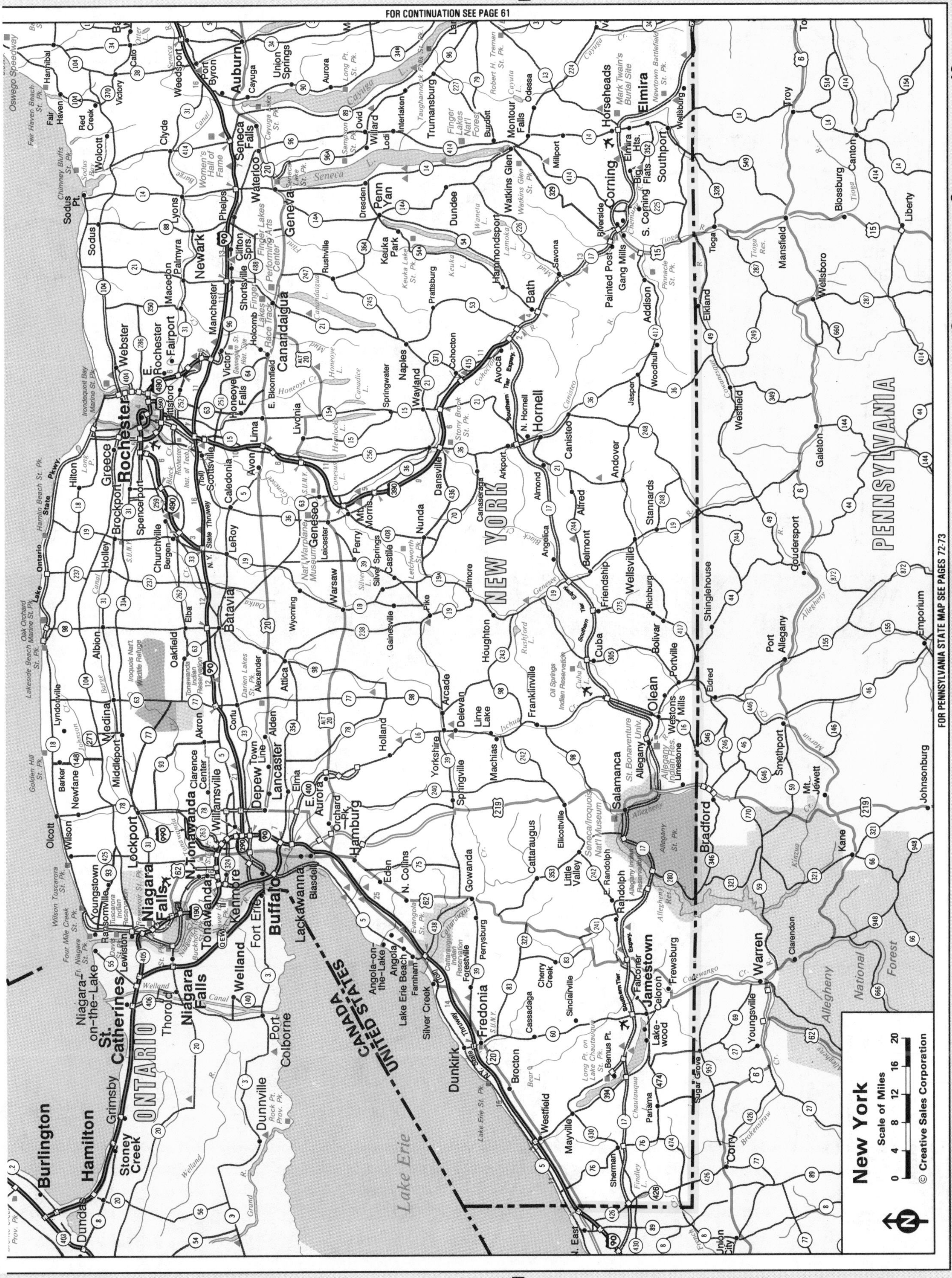

FOR CONTINUATION SEE PAGE 61

FOR PENNSYLVANIA STATE MAP SEE PAGES 72-73

New York

Scale of Miles

0 4 8 12 16 20

© Creative Sales Corporation

NEW YORK

PENNSYLVANIA

ONTARIO

CANADA
UNITED STATES

Lake Erie

Lake Ontario

Allegheny National Forest

Major cities and towns: Rochester, Buffalo, Niagara Falls, Elmira, Corning, Horseheads, Auburn, Seneca Falls, Geneva, Canandaigua, Batavia, Genesco, Hornell, Olean, Salamanca, Bradford, Warren, Jamestown, Dunkirk, Fredonia, Lackawanna, Tonawanda, Lockport, Welland, St. Catharines, Hamilton, Burlington

FOR VERMONT STATE MAP SEE PAGE 55

New York
Scale of Miles
0 4 8 12 16 20
© Creative Sales Corporation

N

QUEBEC
CANADA
UNITED STATES
ONTARIO
VERMONT
NEW YORK
Adirondack Park
Adirondack Mountains
Lake Champlain

St. Albans, Swanton, Alburg, Milton, Colchester, Essex Jct., Shelburne, Hinesburg, Ferrisburg, Bristol, New Haven, Middlebury, Vergennes, Addison, Orwell, Castleton, Fair Haven, Poultney, Pawlet, Whitehall, Granville, Hudson Falls, Ft. Edward, Argyle, Glens Falls, Corinth

Venise-en-Québec, Lacolle, Rouses Pt., Champlain, Moers, Plattsburgh, W. Plattsburgh, Morrisonville, Peru, Keeseville, Port Henry, Witherbee, Mineville, Westport, Ticonderoga, Lake George, Lake Luzerne, Hadley, Warrensburg

Ormstown, Barrington, Huntingdon, Port-Lewis, Dundee, Burke, Chateaugay, Malone, Brushton, Dannemora, Saranac Lake, Lake Placid, Olympic Site Tour, Bloomingdale, Tupper Lake, Blue Mountain, Speculator, Northville

Cornwall, Barnhart Is., Finch, Chesterville, Winchester, Kemptville, Smiths Falls, Morrisburg, Iroquois, Waddington, Massena, Norfolk, Norwood, Winthrop, Brasher Falls, Potsdam, Canton, Hermon, Edwards, Star Lake, Old Forge, Atwell, Remsen, Prospect, Barneveld, Boonville, Constableville

Prescott, Ogdensburg, Heuvelton, Rensselaer Falls, Richville, Gouverneur, Antwerp, Philadelphia, Ft. Drum Military Reserve, Deferiet, Herrings, Carthage, Croghan, Lowville, Turin, Port Leyden, Lyons Falls

Brockville, Athens, Morristown, Hammond, Theresa, Alexandria Bay, Evans Mills, Watertown, Black River, W. Carthage, Copenhagen, Castorland, Denmark

Gananoque, Kingston, Wolfe Is., Thousand Islands, Clayton, Cape Vincent, Chaumont, Brownville, Glen Park, Dexter, Sackets Harbor, Adams, Mannsville, Lacona, Pulaski, Altmar, Camden

Henderson, Ellisburg, Sandy Creek, Parish, Central Square, Mexico, Minetto, Fulton, Constantia, Mt. Marcy Highest Pt. in NY

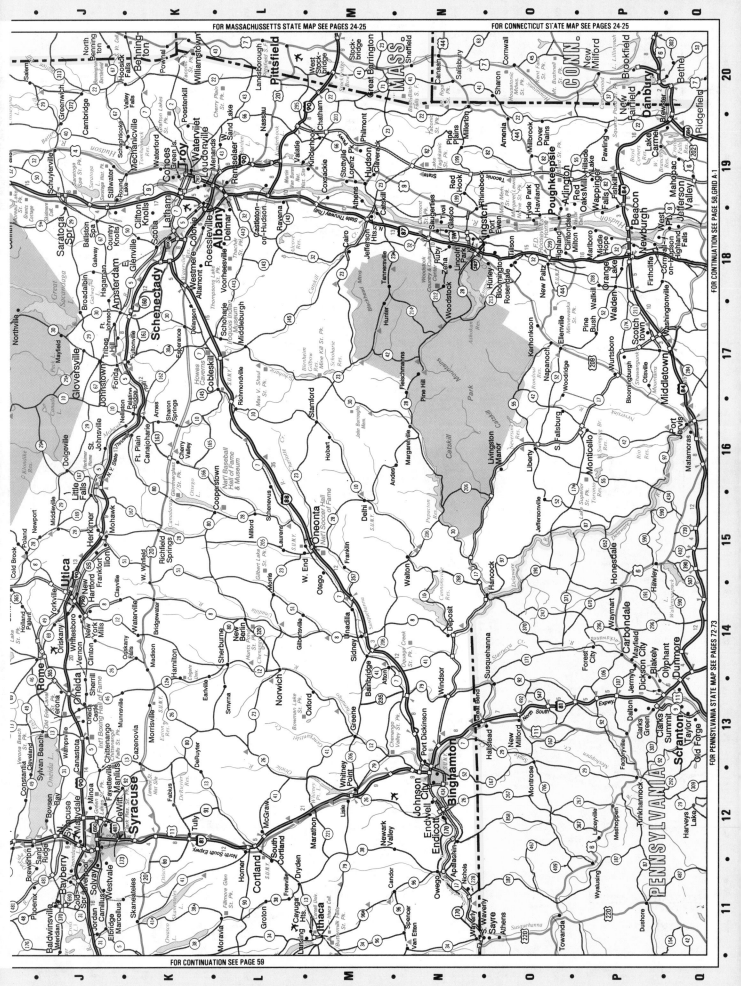

FOR MASSACHUSSETTS STATE MAP SEE PAGES 24-25

FOR CONNECTICUT STATE MAP SEE PAGES 24-25

FOR CONTINUATION SEE PAGE 58, GRID A-1

FOR PENNSYLVANIA STATE MAP SEE PAGES 72-73

FOR CONTINUATION SEE PAGE 59

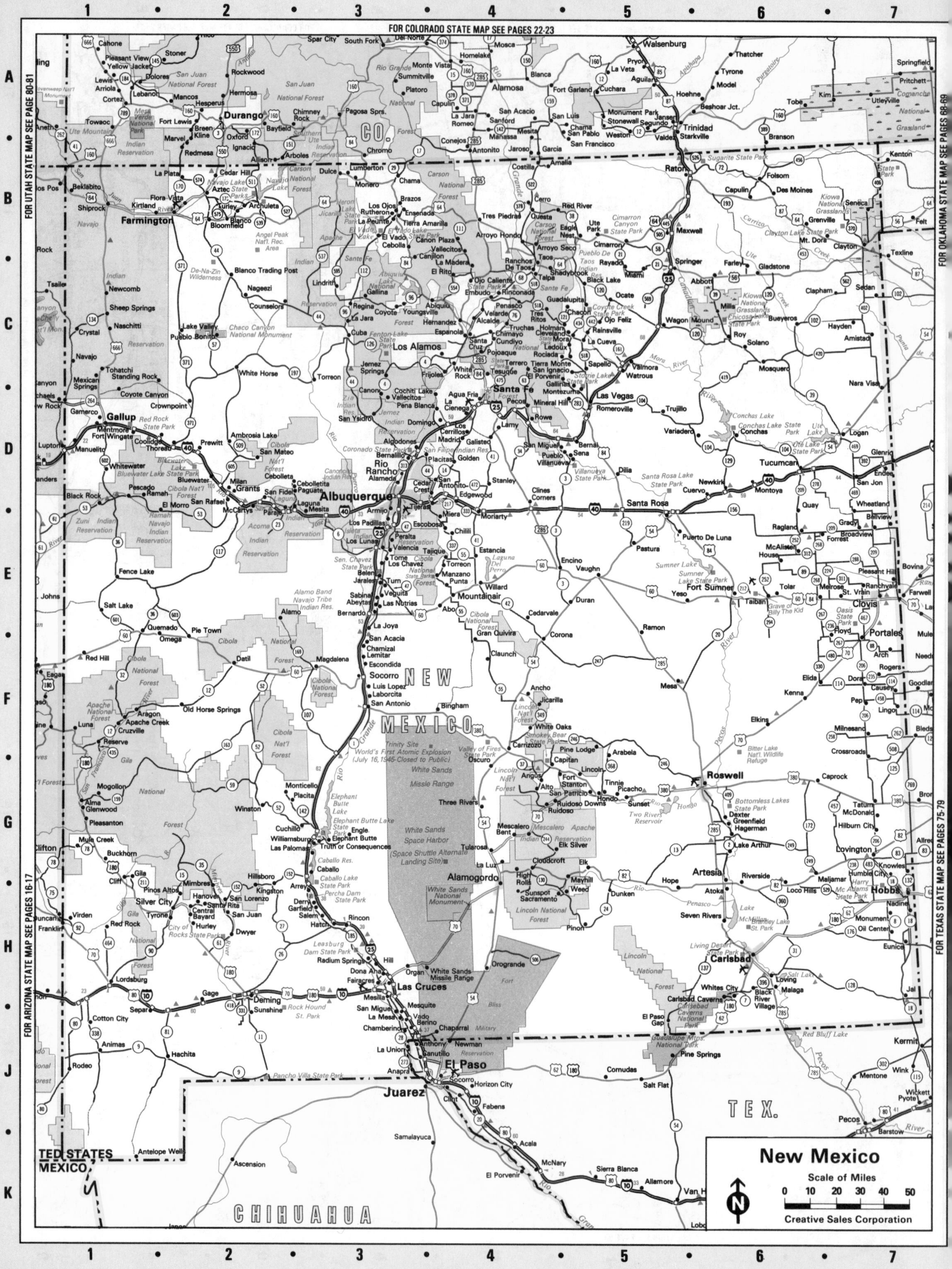

FOR COLORADO STATE MAP SEE PAGES 22-23

FOR UTAH STATE MAP SEE PAGE 80-81
FOR OKLAHOMA STATE MAP SEE PAGES 68-69
FOR ARIZONA STATE MAP SEE PAGES 16-17
FOR TEXAS STATE MAP SEE PAGES 75-79

New Mexico

Scale of Miles

0 10 20 30 40 50

N

Creative Sales Corporation

CO.

NEW MEXICO

TEX.

CHIHUAHUA

UNITED STATES
MEXICO

Durango, Farmington, Shiprock, Gallup, Santa Fe, Los Alamos, Albuquerque, Rio Rancho, Grants, Socorro, Truth or Consequences, Silver City, Deming, Las Cruces, El Paso, Juarez, Roswell, Artesia, Carlsbad, Hobbs, Portales, Clovis, Fort Sumner, Tucumcari, Santa Rosa, Raton, Las Vegas, Alamogordo, Ruidoso, Lordsburg

World's First Atomic Explosion (July 16, 1945-Closed to Public)
Trinity Site
White Sands Missile Range
White Sands National Monument
White Sands Space Harbor (Space Shuttle Alternate Landing Site)

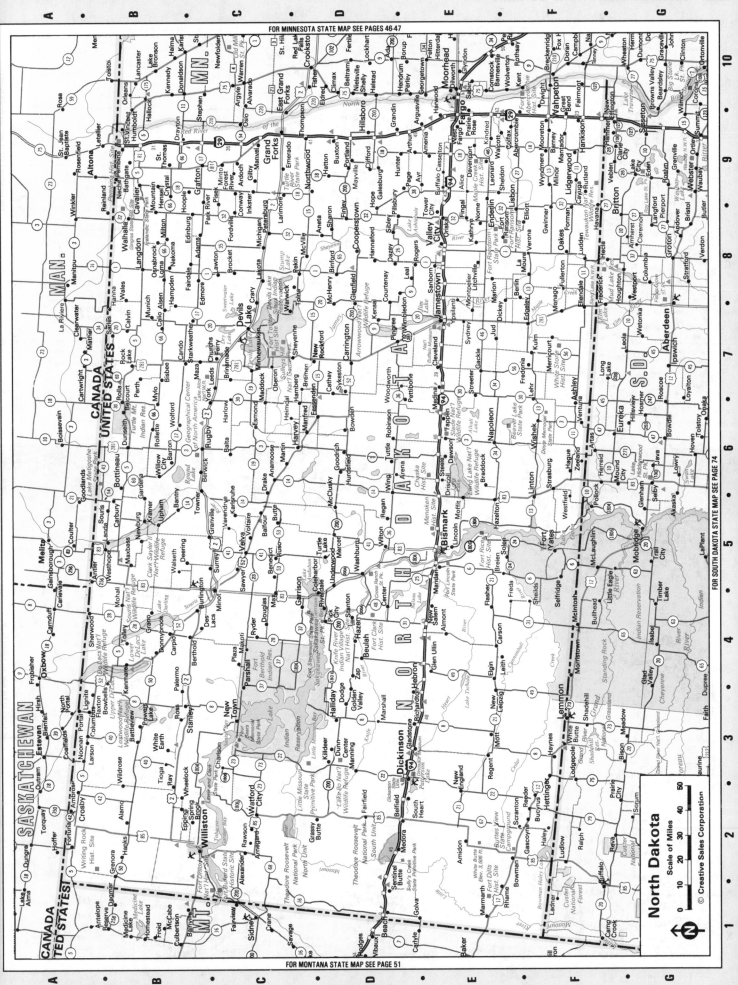

FOR SOUTH DAKOTA STATE MAP SEE PAGE 74

North Dakota

Scale of Miles

0   10   20   30   40   50

© Creative Sales Corporation

FOR KENTUCKY STATE MAP SEE PAGES 38-39

FOR VIRGINIA STATE MAP SEE PAGES 82-83

FOR TENNESSEE STATE MAP SEE PAGES 38-39

FOR GEORGIA STATE MAP SEE PAGES 28-29

KY. VIR. TENN NORTH SOUTH CAROLINA GEORGIA

Corbin Middlesboro Knoxville Bristol Kingsport Johnson City Winston-Salem High Point Statesville Hickory Salisbury Kannapolis Concord Charlotte Gastonia Asheville Shelby Spartanburg Greenville Anderson Greenwood Columbia Sumter Atlanta Athens Augusta Macon Warner Robins Savannah Hilton Head Island

FOR VIRGINIA STATE MAP SEE PAGES 82-83

Atlantic Ocean

North Carolina South Carolina

Scale of Miles

0 7 14 21 28 35

N

© Creative Sales Corporation

Martinsville, Danville, S. Boston, Chatham, Halifax, Clarksville, South Hill, Lawrenceville, Emporia, Franklin, Corapeake, Morgans Corner, Barco, Coinjock, Bertha, Grandy, Jarvisburg, Powells Point, Point Harbor, Harbinger

Yanceyville, Casville, Hightowers, Leasburg, Brooksdale, Picks, Roxboro, Oxford, Henderson, Middleburg, Liberia, Jackson, Woodland, Rich Square, Ahoskie, Colerain, Hertford, Edenton, Columbia, East Lake, Manns Harbor, Nags Head, Whalebone, Manteo, Wanchese

Burlington, Durham, Greensboro, Chapel Hill, Raleigh, Hillsborough, Carrboro, Cary, Wake Forest, Zebulon, Wendell, Wilson, Rocky Mount, Tarboro, Battleboro, Williamston, Plymouth, Creswell, Rodanthe, Waves, Salvo

Asheboro, Seagrove, Sanford, Goldston, Moncure, Fuquay-Varina, Smithfield, Selma, Kenly, Fremont, Goldsboro, Greenville, Washington, Belhaven, Bath, New Holland, Englehard, Lake Landing, Avon, Buxton, Frisco, Hatteras

Aberdeen, Southern Pines, Pinebluff, Fayetteville, Spring Lake, Lillington, Benson, Dunn, Mount Olive, Kinston, New Bern, Trenton, Pollocksville, Maysville, Ocracoke, Portsmouth

Rockingham, Hamlet, Raeford, Red Springs, Lumberton, Clinton, Warsaw, Kenansville, Beulaville, Jacksonville, Swansboro, Morehead City, Beaufort, Newport, Fort Macon St. Park

Laurinburg, Maxton, Pembroke, Bladenboro, Elizabethtown, White Oak, Wallace, Burgaw, Hampstead, Surf City, Topsail Beach, West Onslow Beach, Del Mar Beach

McColl, Clio, Rowland, Fairmont, Whiteville, Chadbourn, Wilmington, Wrightsville Beach, Seabreeze, Carolina Beach, Wilmington Beach, Kure Beach, Southport, Long Beach, Smith Island

Bennettsville, Society Hill, Blenheim, Dillon, Latta, Mullins, Nichols, Tabor City, Loris, Shallotte, Supply, Winnabow

Florence, Marion, Galivants Ferry, Green Sea, Aynor, Conway, Myrtle Beach, Surfside Beach, Garden City, Litchfield Beach, Pawleys Island, Little River, Cresent Beach

Lake City, Kingstree, Hemingway, Andrews, Georgetown, North Island, Debidue Beach

Moncks Corner, Goose Creek, Hanahan, Awendaw, Mt. Pleasant, Isle of Palms, Sullivans Island, Charleston, James Island, Folly Beach

Albemarle Sound, Pamlico Sound, Raleigh Bay, Onslow Bay, Long Bay, Bulls Bay, Atlantic Ocean

Roanoke Rapids, Roanoke Rapids Lake, John H. Kerr Reservoir, Lake Mattamuskeet, Dismal Swamp, Cape Hatteras, Cape Lookout, Cape Romain National Wildlife Refuge

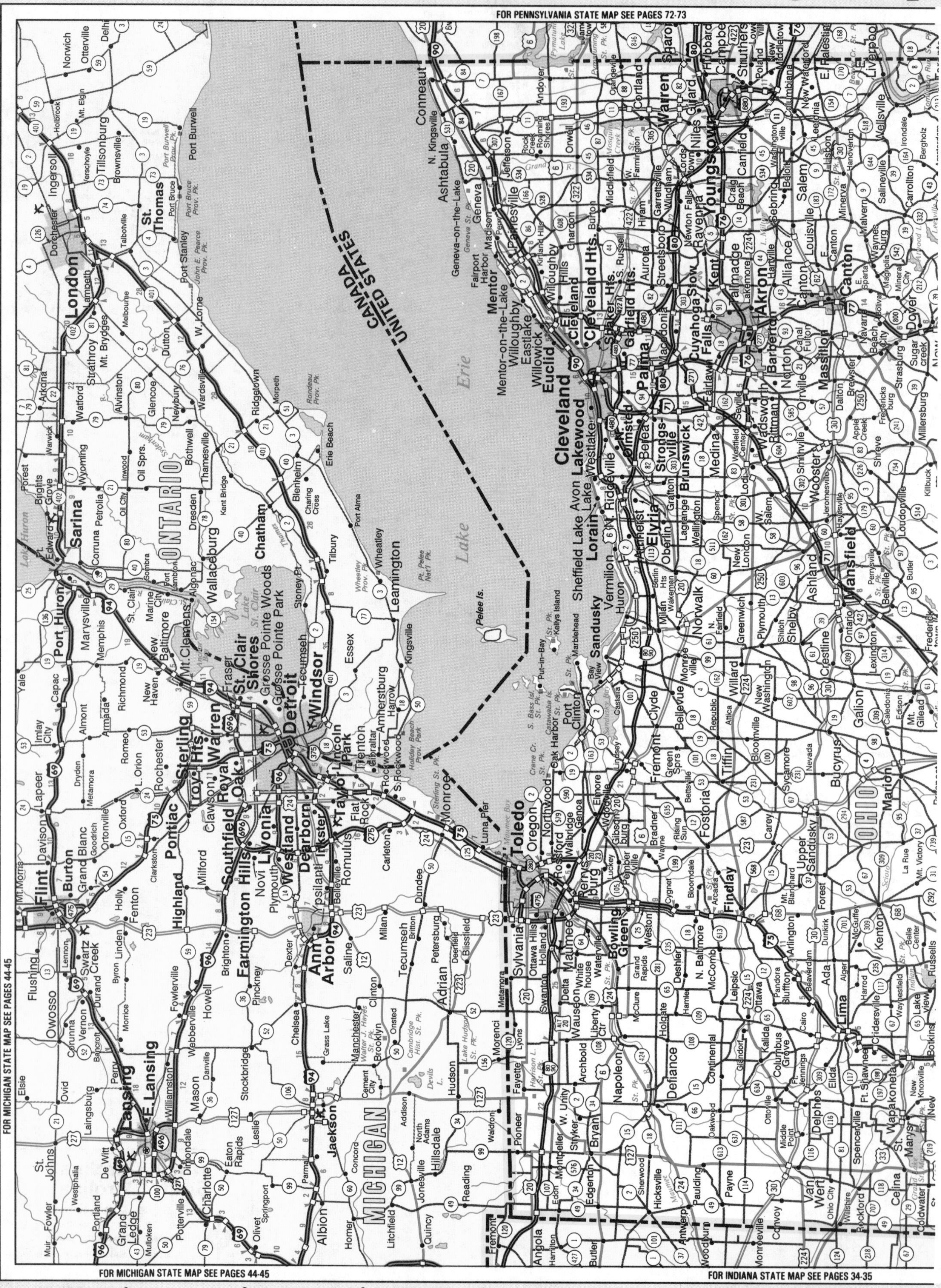

FOR PENNSYLVANIA STATE MAP SEE PAGES 72-73

FOR MICHIGAN STATE MAP SEE PAGES 44-45

FOR INDIANA STATE MAP SEE PAGES 34-35

CANADA
UNITED STATES

Lake Erie

Lake Huron
Lake St. Clair

MICHIGAN
ONTARIO
OHIO

Cleveland
Detroit
Windsor
Toledo
Akron
Canton
Youngstown
Warren
Mansfield
Marion
Findlay
Lima
Sandusky
Lorain
Elyria
Euclid
Lakewood
Parma
E. Lansing
Flint
Pontiac
Ann Arbor
Jackson
Sarnia
Port Huron
London
St. Thomas
Chatham
Leamington
Bowling Green
Sylvania
Maumee
Defiance
Van Wert
St. Marys
Wapakoneta
Wooster
Ashland
Wadsworth
Medina
Brunswick
Strongsville
Berea
North Olmsted
Westlake
Avon Lake
Vermilion
Huron
Norwalk
Tiffin
Fostoria
Fremont
Bucyrus
Galion
Crestline
Shelby
Willoughby
Mentor
Eastlake
Wickliffe
Ashtabula
Conneaut
Geneva
Painesville
Chardon
Ravenna
Kent
Cuyahoga Falls
Barberton
Alliance
Salem
Niles
Hubbard
Sharon
Struthers
Campbell
Dover
Massillon

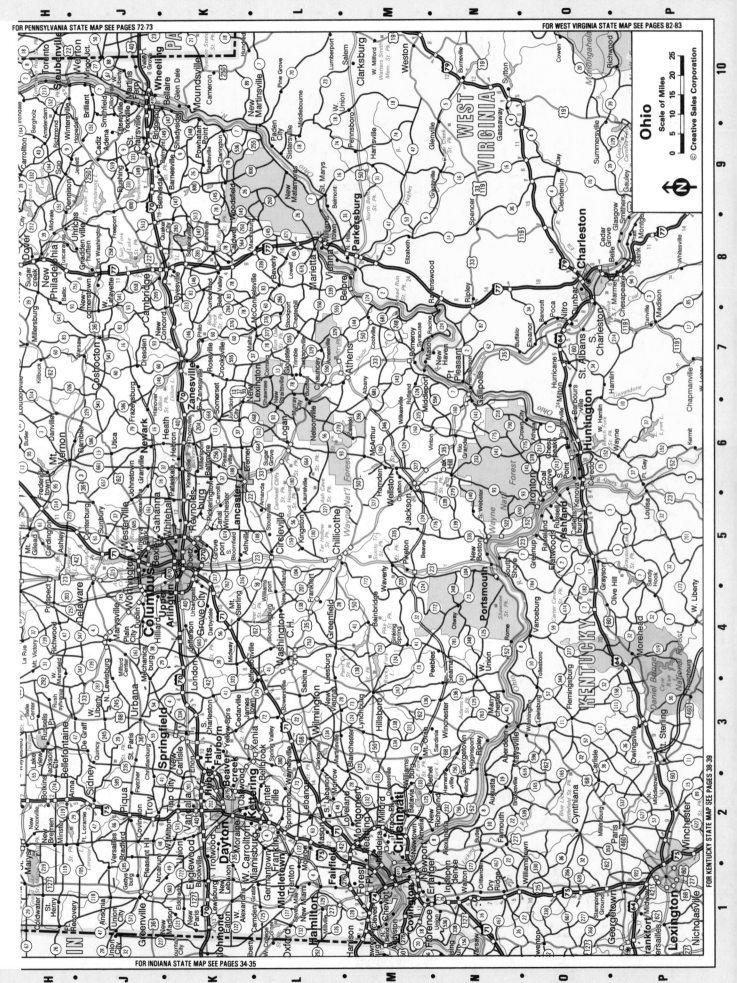

FOR PENNSYLVANIA STATE MAP SEE PAGES 72-73

FOR WEST VIRGINIA STATE MAP SEE PAGES 82-83

Ohio

Scale of Miles

© Creative Sales Corporation

FOR INDIANA STATE MAP SEE PAGES 34-35

FOR KENTUCKY STATE MAP SEE PAGES 38-39

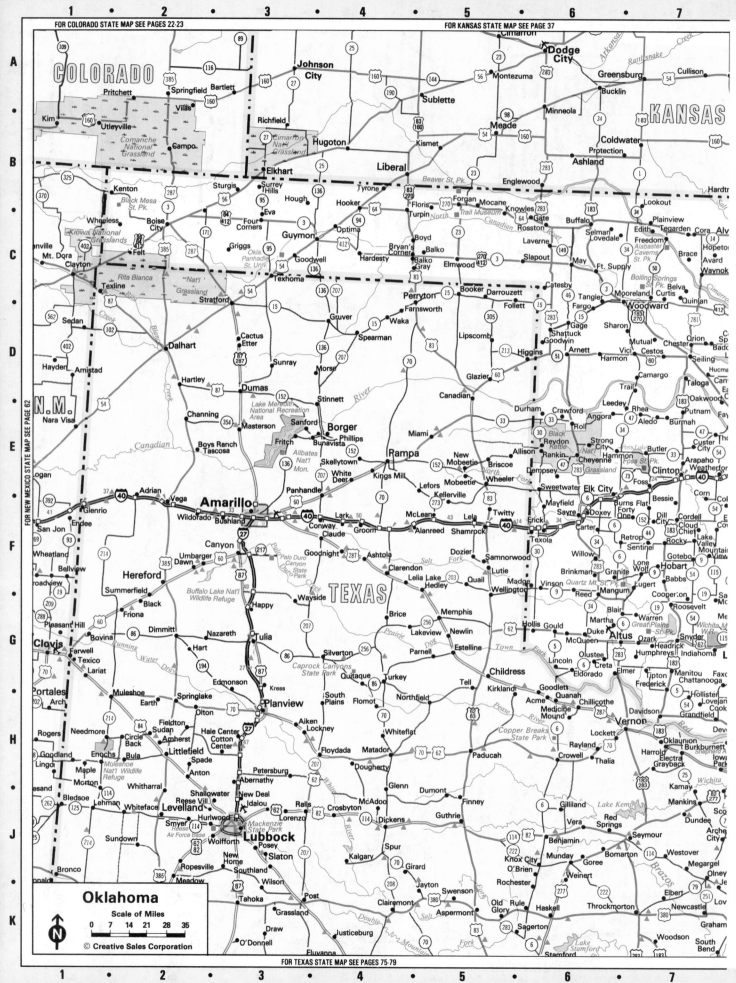

FOR NEW MEXICO STATE MAP SEE PAGE 62

Oklahoma

Scale of Miles

0 7 14 21 28 35

N

© Creative Sales Corporation

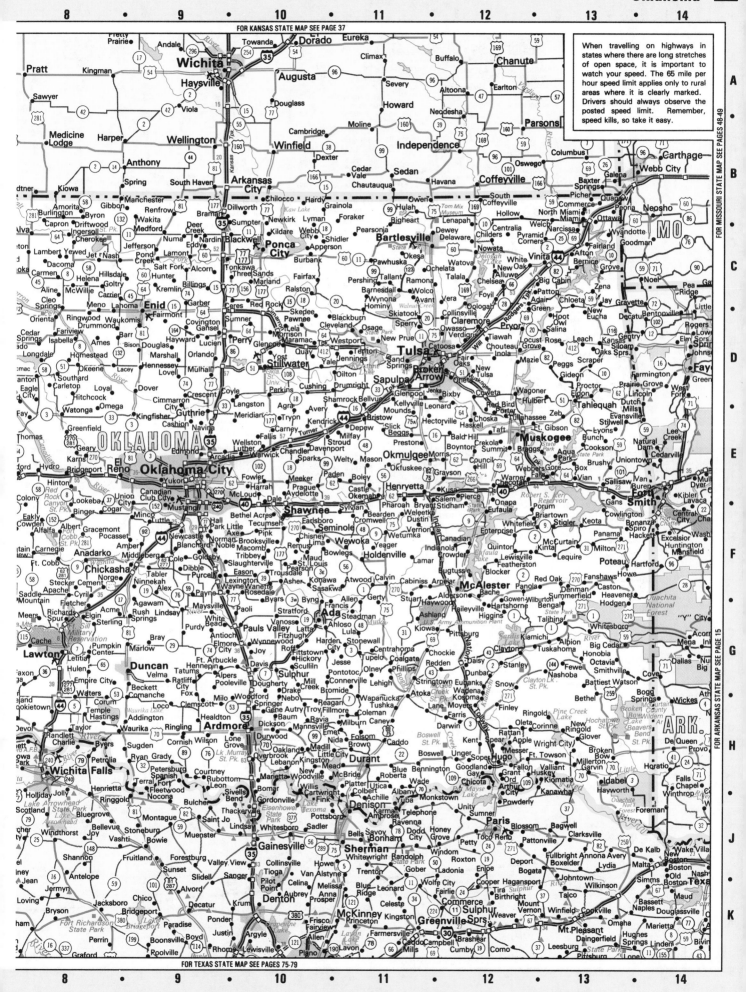

When travelling on highways in states where there are long stretches of open space, it is important to watch your speed. The 65 mile per hour speed limit applies only to rural areas where it is clearly marked. Drivers should always observe the posted speed limit. Remember, speed kills, so take it easy.

FOR MISSOURI STATE MAP SEE PAGES 48-49

FOR ARKANSAS STATE MAP SEE PAGE 15

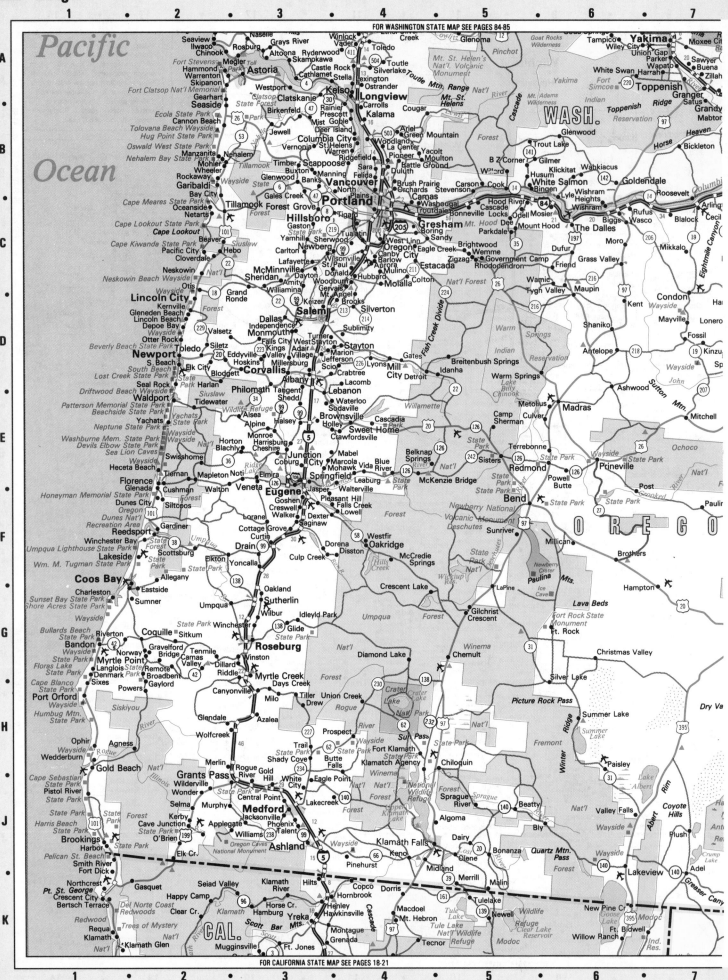

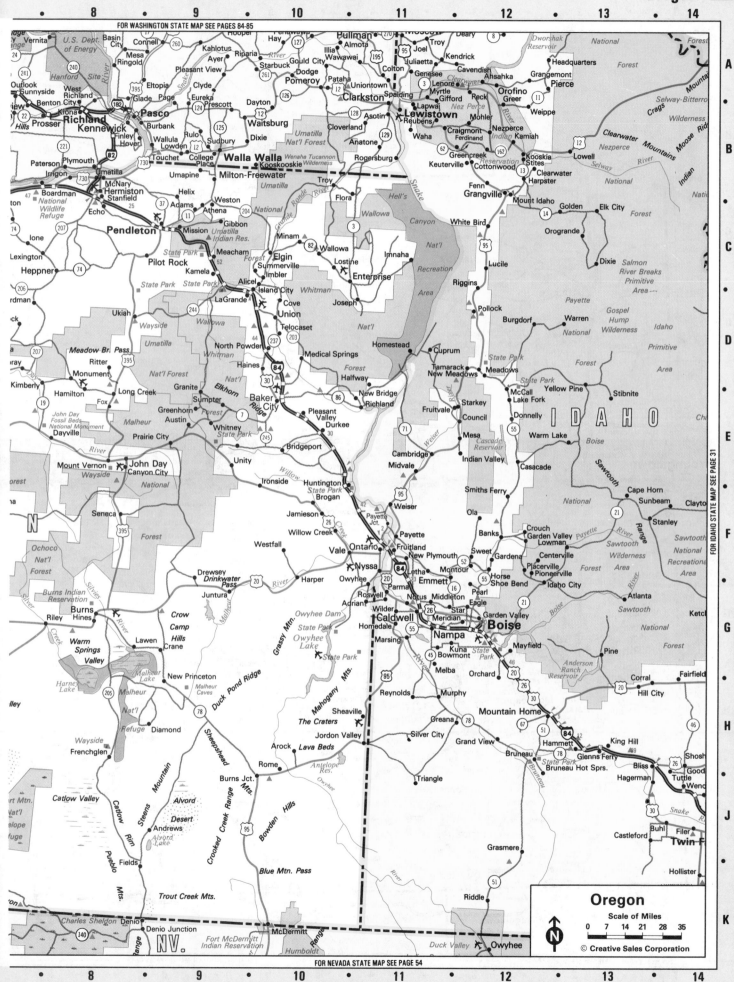

FOR IDAHO STATE MAP SEE PAGE 31

Oregon

Scale of Miles

0 7 14 21 28 35

N

© Creative Sales Corporation

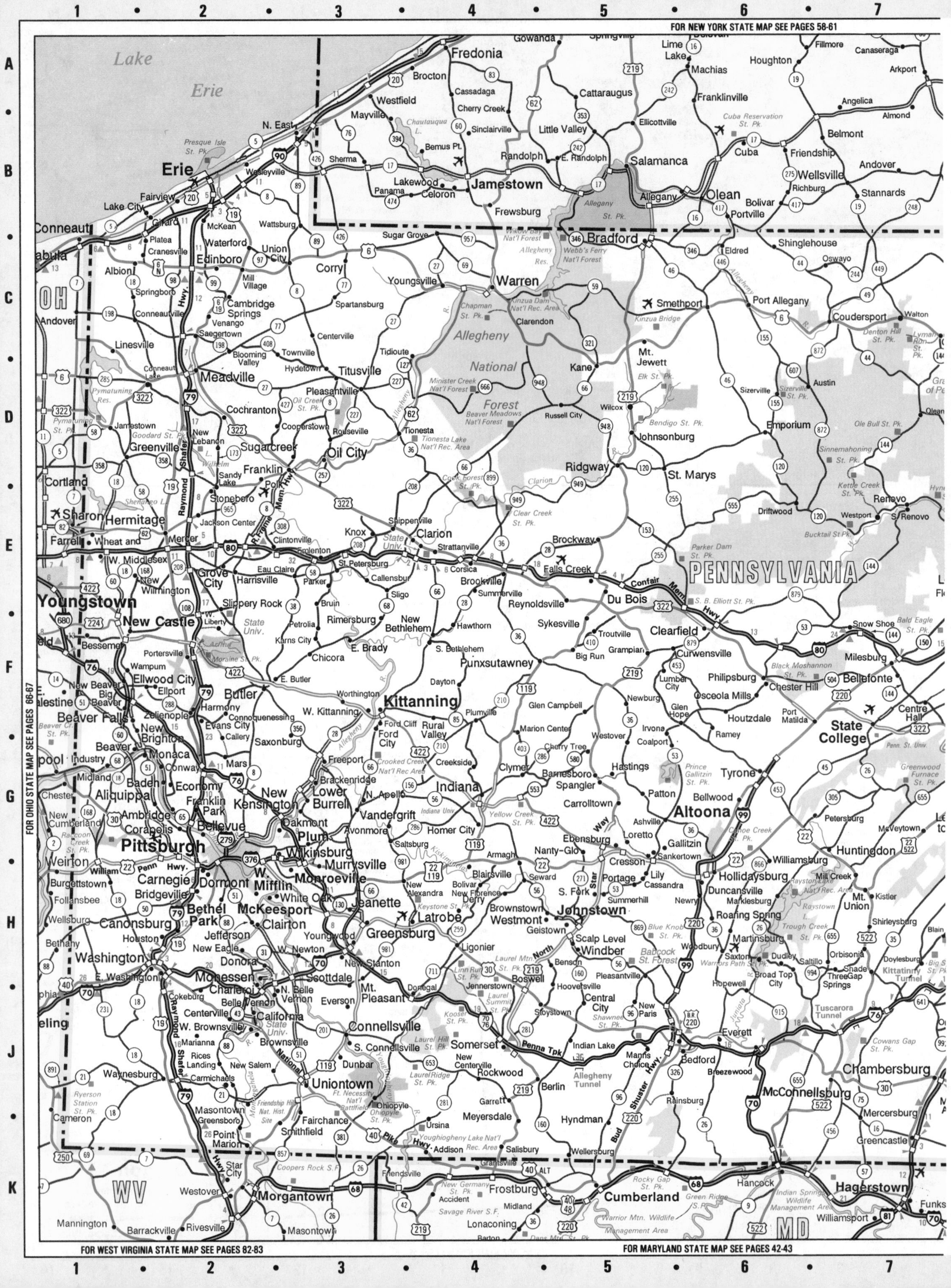

FOR NEW YORK STATE MAP SEE PAGES 58-61

Lake Erie

PENNSYLVANIA

OH

WV

MD

Allegheny National Forest

Major cities and towns: Erie, Fredonia, Jamestown, Warren, Bradford, Olean, Coudersport, Emporium, Renovo, Meadville, Oil City, Franklin, Clarion, Ridgway, St. Marys, Du Bois, Clearfield, Sharon, Hermitage, Greenville, Grove City, Butler, Kittanning, Indiana, Altoona, State College, Youngstown, New Castle, Beaver Falls, Pittsburgh, Monroeville, Greensburg, Johnstown, Hollidaysburg, Huntingdon, Bedford, Washington, Uniontown, Connellsville, Somerset, McConnellsburg, Chambersburg, Morgantown, Cumberland, Hagerstown

FOR OHIO STATE MAP SEE PAGES 66-67

FOR WEST VIRGINIA STATE MAP SEE PAGES 82-83

FOR MARYLAND STATE MAP SEE PAGES 42-43

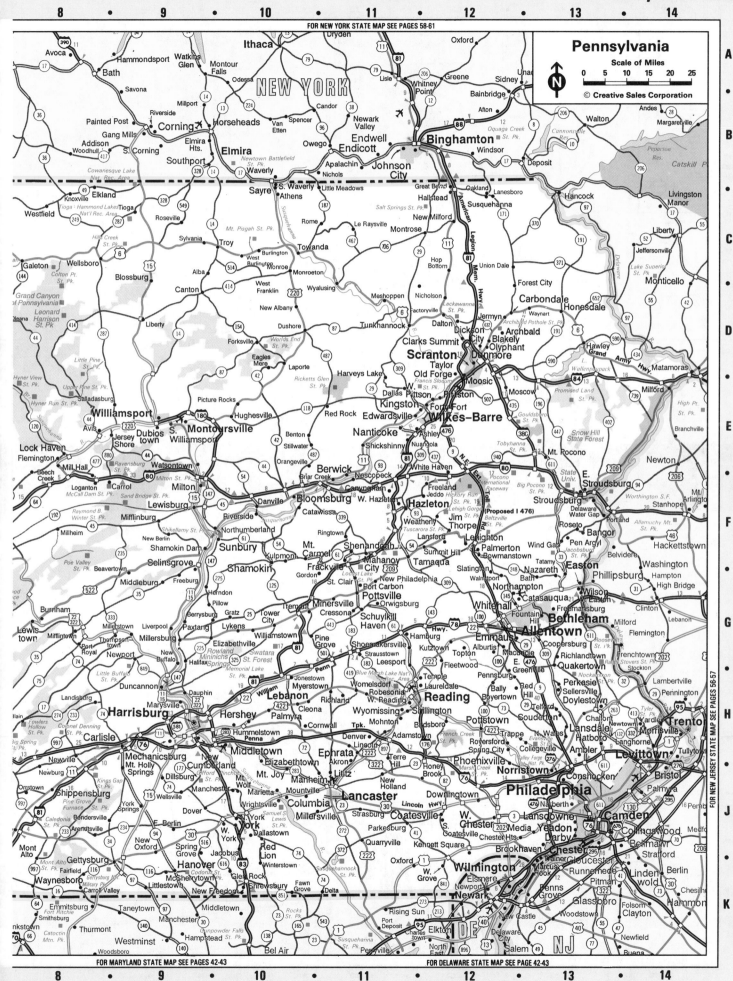

Pennsylvania
Scale of Miles
0 5 10 15 20 25
© Creative Sales Corporation

FOR NEW JERSEY STATE MAP SEE PAGES 56-57

South Dakota

Scale of Miles

0 10 20 30 40 50

© Creative Sales Corporation

N

FOR MINNESOTA STATE MAP SEE PAGES 46-47
FOR IOWA STATE MAP SEE PAGE 36
FOR NORTH DAKOTA STATE MAP SEE PAGE 63 
FOR NEBRASKA STATE MAP SEE PAGES 52-53
FOR MONTANA STATE MAP SEE PAGE 51
FOR WYOMING STATE MAP SEE PAGES 88-89

SOUTH DAKOTA

N.D.

MT.

WY.

NE.

IA

MN

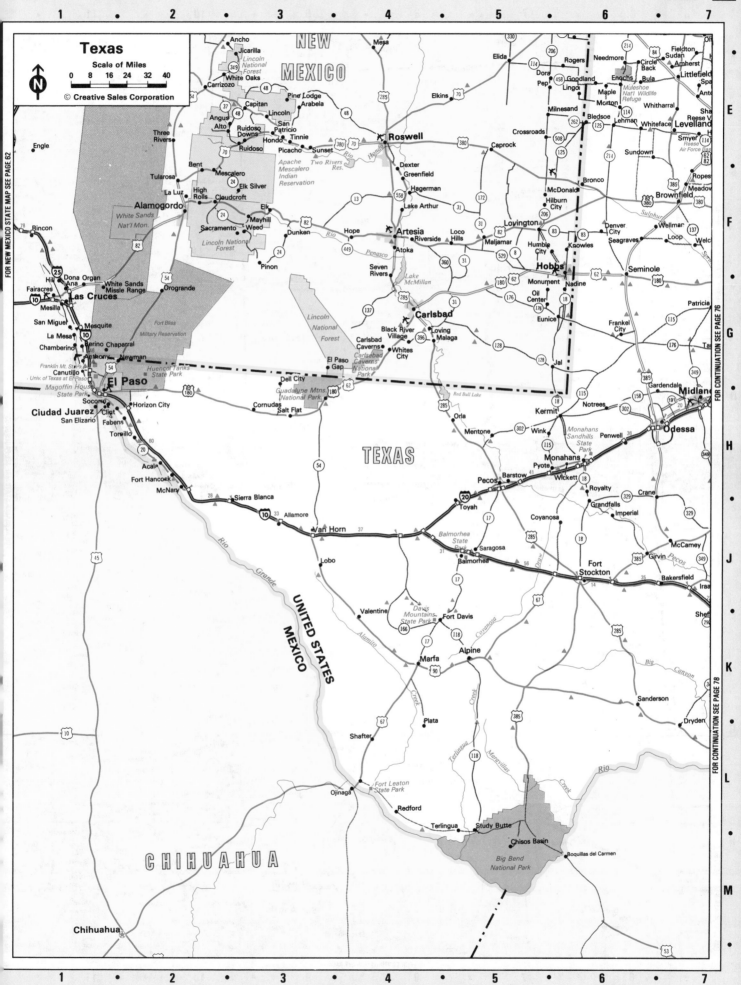

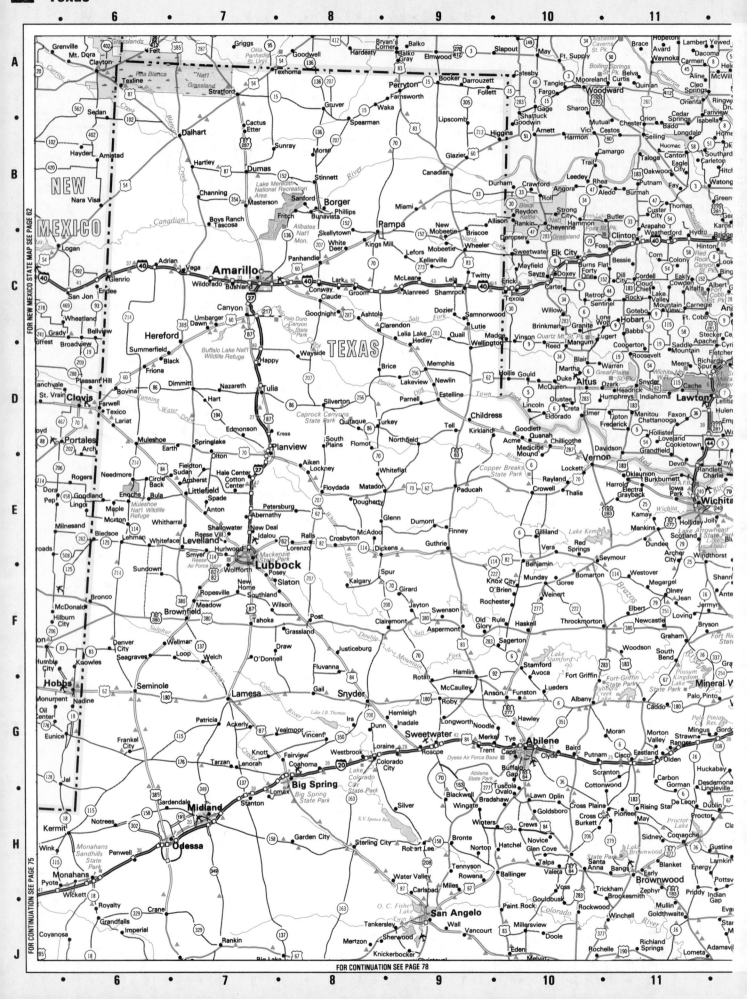

FOR NEW MEXICO STATE MAP SEE PAGE 62

FOR CONTINUATION SEE PAGE 75

FOR CONTINUATION SEE PAGE 78

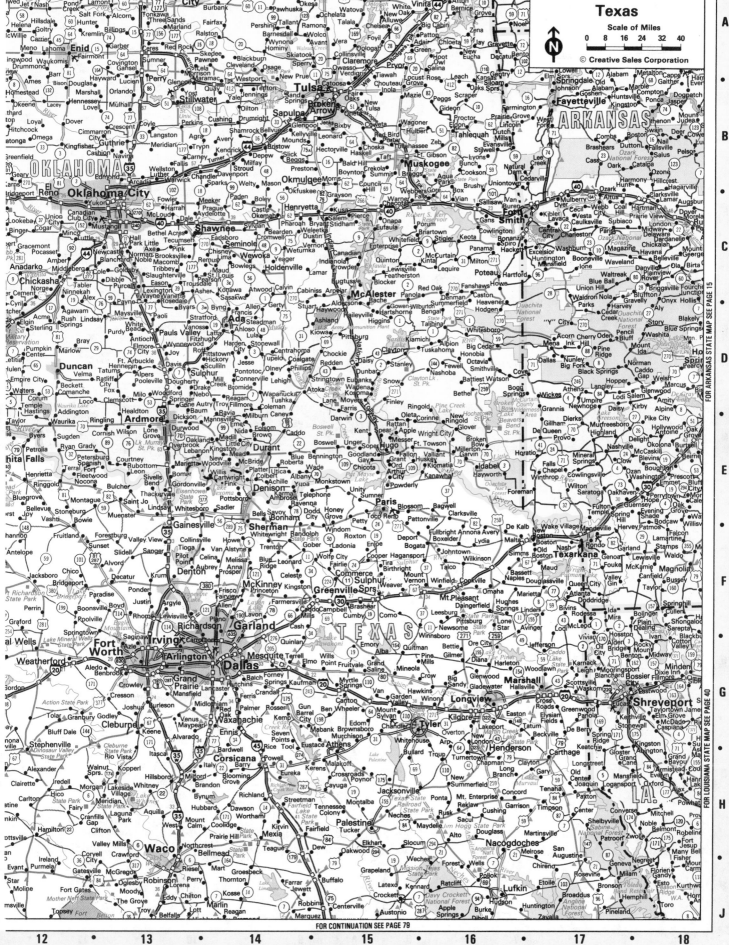

FOR CONTINUATION SEE PAGE 76

FOR CONTINUATION SEE PAGE 75

J K L M N P Q R S

6 7 8 9 10 11

Rankin
McCamey
Big Lake
Mertzon
Knickerbocker
Christoval
Eden
Melvin
Rochelle
Richland Springs
Lometa
Adamsvil
Copp
Lampasa
San Saba

Girvin
Barnhart
Brady
71
Voca
Cherokee
Tow
Bluffton
Buchanan
Lake

Fort Stockton
Bakersfield
Iraan
190
Calf Creek
Menard
Hext
Katemcy
Fredonia
Valley Spring
Pontotoc
Llano
Buchanan Dam
Lake

Sheffield
Ozona
Eldorado
Fort McKavett
Fort McKavett State Park
190
London
29
Grit
Mason
29
Kingsland
Lake LBJ
Marble Falls

Fort Lancaster State Park
290
10
137
Sonora
Roosevelt
Junction
377
Doss
Cherry Spring
Willow City
Round Mountain
Spicew

Sanderson
163
Segovia
Harper
Enchanted Rock State Park
Fredericksburg
Johnson City
Stonewall

Dryden
349
Juno
Telegraph
54
290
Hye
Luckenbach
Lyndon B. Johnson State Park

90
Langtry
Loma Alta
Rocksprings
41
Mountain Home
Hunt
Ingram
Kerrville
Center Pt.
Comfort
Sisterdale
Spring Branch
Blanco
Blanco State Park

Rio Grande
Seminole Canyon State Park
Comstock
Carta Valley
377
Barksdale
Camp Wood
Vanderpool
Kerrville State Park
Lost Maples State Park
Medina
Camp Verde
Pipecreek
10
Leon Springs
281
Bra

Amistad National Recreation Area
Devils Lake
Lake Walk
55
Garner State Park
Utopia
Tarpley
Bandera
Lake Hills
Mico
16
Riomedina
San
Leon Valley
Sa

Basin
Boquillas del Carmen
Del Rio
Ciudad Acuna
Fort Clark Springs
Brackettville
Concan
127
D'Hanis
Knippa
Sabinal
Hondo
Castroville
410
Martinez
Elm

Spofford
Dabney
Blewett
90
Uvalde
Frio River
Dunlay
Natalia
Somerset

131
Quemado
Normandy
La Pryor
Batesville
Frio Town
Moore
Devine
Lytle
Bigfoot
Leming
Pleasant

Eagle Pass
Piedras Negras
277
57
Crystal City
Divot
Derby
Hindes
Christine
Campbellton
Whitsett

53
Brundage
Big Wells
Woodward
Millett
Los Angeles
Cotulla
35
Dilley
85
97
Three Rivers
Tilden
72

Carrizo Springs
Asherton
Catarina
83
Artesia Wells
97
Fowlerton
16
Calliham
George We

TEXAS
Nueces

Nueva Rosita
UNITED STATES
MEXICO
Encinal
44
44
Freer
Ora

COAHUILA
Rio Grande
44
San Diego
Ben
339

Laredo St. Univ.
59
Benavides
Rio
Ora

Lake Casa Blanca State Park
16
Oilton
Realitos
359
Concepcion
Ramirez

Nuevo Laredo
Laredo
85
Mirando City
Bruni
Hebbronville
285

30
Monclova
San Ygnacio
Escobas
Randado
83
16
Bustamante

Falcon Res.
2
Lopeno
Falcon
La Gloria
Santa Elen
San Isidro

57
Sabinas Hidalgo
Nuevo Guerrero
Falcon State Park
El Sauz
La Reforma

53
Cd. Mier
Roma
Rio Grande City
Edinbur

30
NUEVO LEON
Cd. Camargo
83
La Grulla
La Joya
Mission
Sullivan City
107

Presa De El Azucar
Bentsen Rio Grande Valley State Park
Hidalgo

54
Reynosa

San Pedro de las Colonias
40
Monterrey

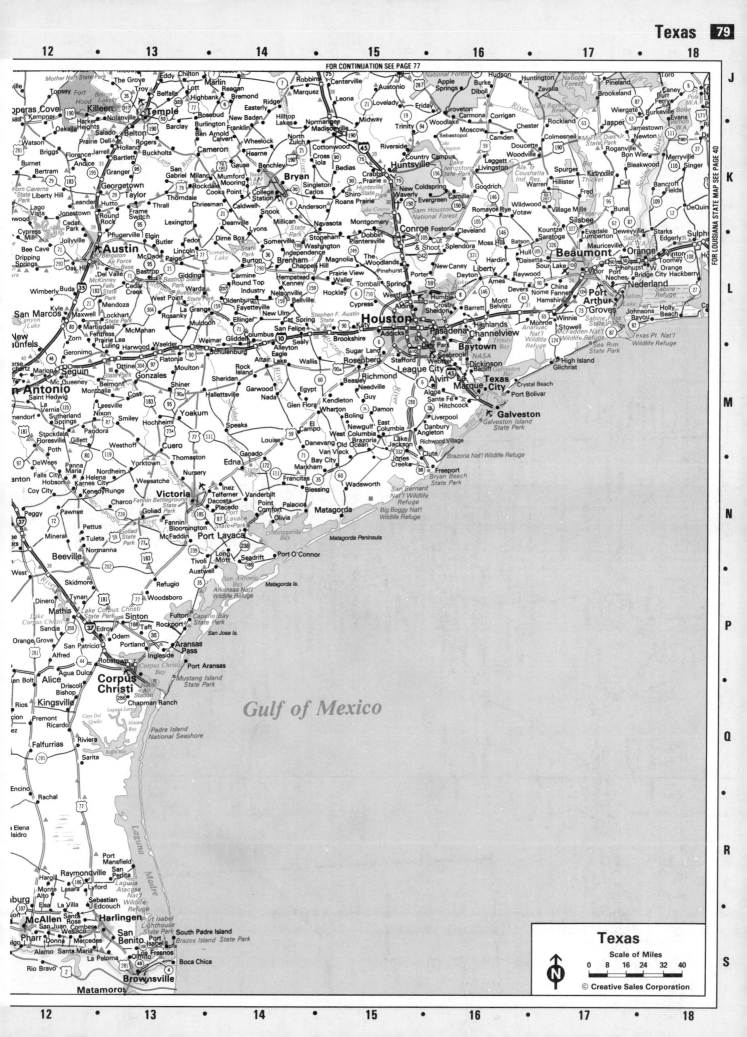

FOR CONTINUATION SEE PAGE 77

FOR LOUISIANA STATE MAP SEE PAGE 40

Gulf of Mexico

Texas

Scale of Miles

0 8 16 24 32 40

N

© Creative Sales Corporation

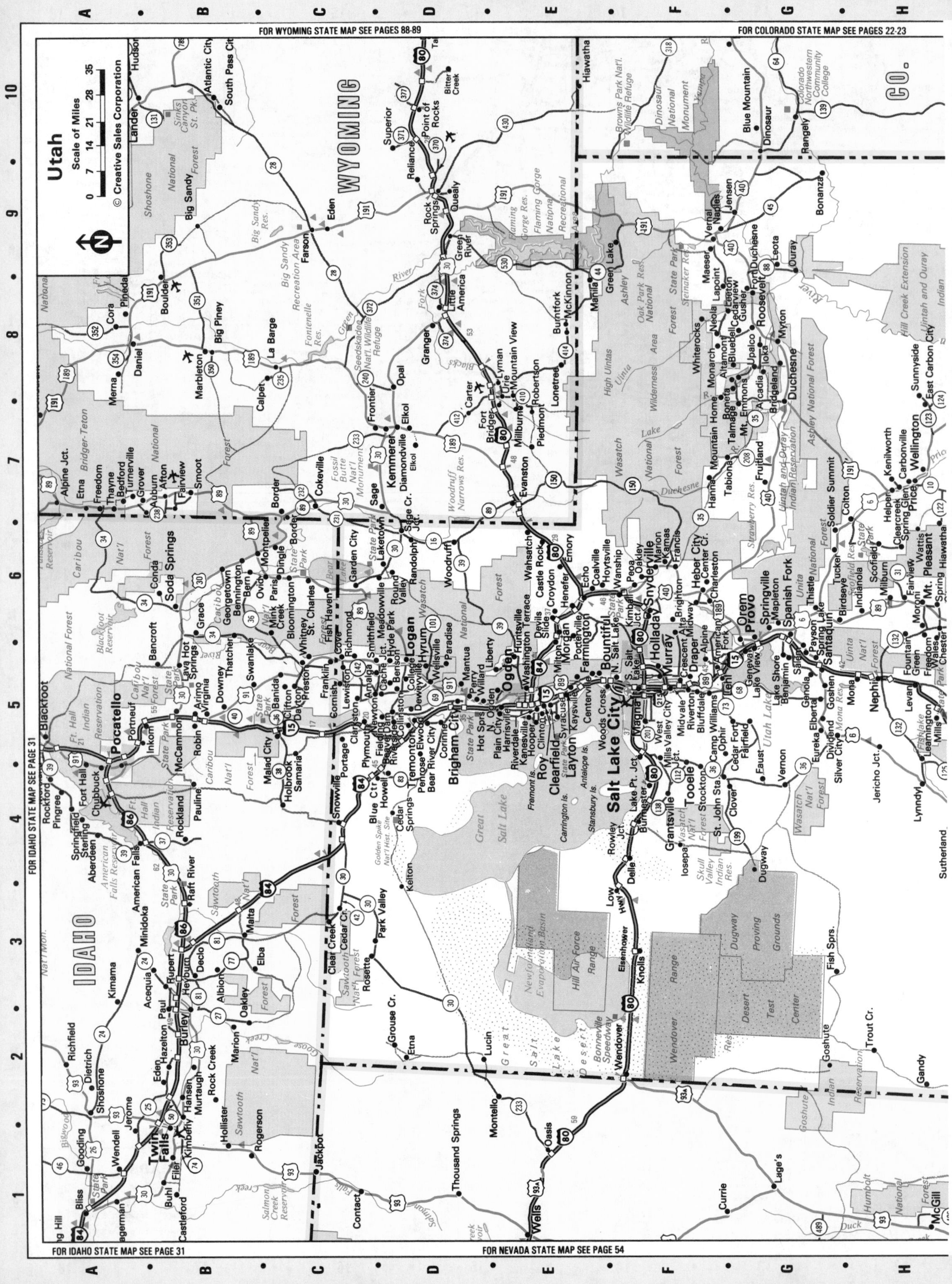

Utah

Scale of Miles

0   7   14   28   35

© Creative Sales Corporation

FOR WYOMING STATE MAP SEE PAGES 88-89

FOR COLORADO STATE MAP SEE PAGES 22-23

FOR IDAHO STATE MAP SEE PAGE 31

WYOMING

IDAHO

CO.

FOR IDAHO STATE MAP SEE PAGE 31

FOR NEVADA STATE MAP SEE PAGE 54

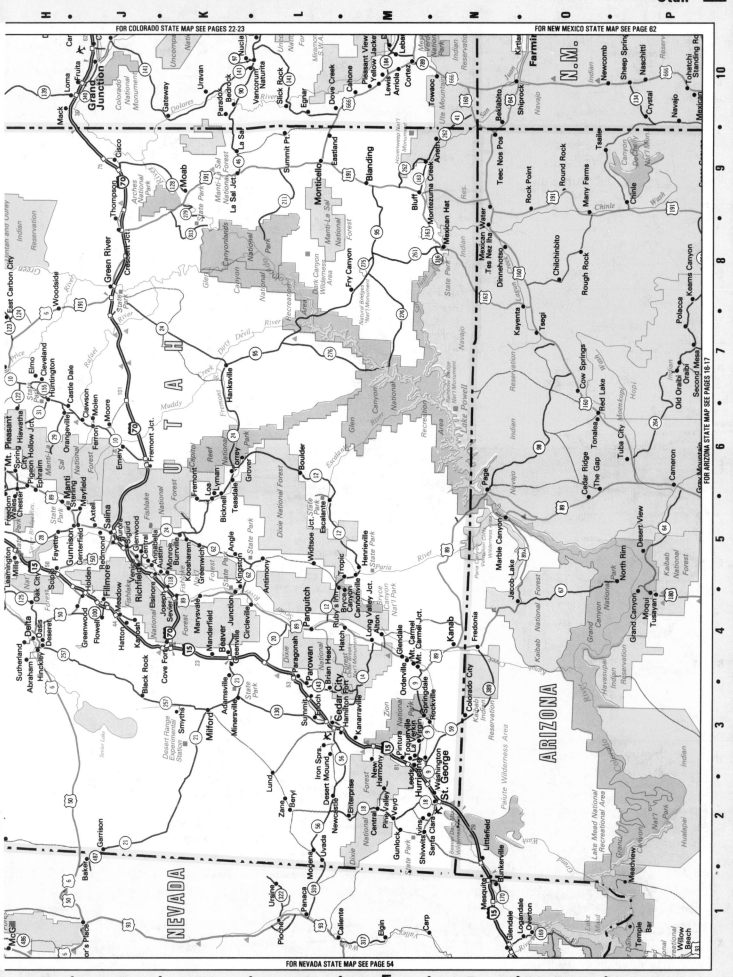

FOR COLORADO STATE MAP SEE PAGES 22-23

FOR NEW MEXICO STATE MAP SEE PAGE 62

FOR ARIZONA STATE MAP SEE PAGES 16-17

FOR NEVADA STATE MAP SEE PAGE 54

FOR OHIO STATE MAP SEE PAGES 66-67
FOR PENNSYLVANIA STATE MAP SEE PAGES 72-73
FOR OHIO STATE MAP SEE PAGES 66-67
FOR KENTUCKY STATE MAP SEE PAGES 38-39
FOR TENNESSEE STATE MAP SEE PAGES 38-39
FOR NORTH CAROLINA STATE MAP SEE PAGES 64-65

Grid columns: 1 2 3 4 5 6 7
Grid rows: A B C D E F G H J K

States: OHIO, WEST VIRGINIA, KENTUCKY, TENN

Selected cities and towns:

Kenton, Marion, Richwood, Cardington, Mt. Gilead, Bellville, Butler, Fredericktown, Killbuck, Strasburg, Millersburg, Salineville, Carrollton, E. Liverpool, Chester, Aliquippa, New Kensington, Lower Burrell, Natrona Hts.

Delaware, Mt. Vernon, Danville, Warsaw, Sugarcreek, New Philadelphia, Uhrichsville, Amsterdam, Richmond, Weirton, Follansbee, Pittsburgh, Murrysville, McKeesport, Jeannette, Greensburg

Columbus, Newark, Hebron, Zanesville, Cambridge, St. Clairsville, Wheeling, Triadelphia, Bethel Park, Cannonsburg, Washington, Monessen, Connellsville

London, Winchester, Lancaster, Somerset, Crooksville, Caldwell, Woodsfield, Barnesville, Powhatan Pt., Bellaire, Glen Dale, Moundsville, Cameron, Blacksville, Morristown, Uniontown, Farmington

Circleville, Logan, New Lexington, McConnelsville, Beverly, New Matamoras, Paden City, Pine Grove, New Martinsville, Hundred, Fairview, Westover, Morgantown, Masontown, Terra Alta

Chillicothe, Athens, McArthur, Chauncey, Glouster, Marietta, Williamstown, Vienna, St. Marys, Belmont, Friendly, Middlebourne, West Union, Smithfield, Center, Clarksburg, Salem, Bridgeport, Fairmont, Monongah, Shinnston, Kingwood, Oakland

Waverly, Jackson, Hamden, Pomeroy, Parkersburg, Harrisville, Pennsboro, Cairo, Ellenboro, Nutter Fort, Stonewood, Philippi, Parsons, Davis, Hambleton

Vinton, Mason, New Haven, Ravenswood, Reedy, Elizabeth, Cox Mills, Linn, Grantsville, Glenville, Weston, Belington, Buckhannon, Junior, Elkins, Beverly, Harman, Seneca Rocks

Oak Hill, Rio Grande, Gallipolis, Pt. Pleasant, Leon, Ripley, Spencer, Arnoldsburg, Gilmer, Burnsville, Rock Cave, Mill Creek, Huttonsville, Durbin, Thornwood, Franklin

West Union, Portsmouth, South Shore, Greenup, Ironton, Ashton, Buffalo, Eleanor, Gandeeville, Newton, Gassaway, Sutton, Webster Spr., Valley Head, Monterey, Vanderpool

Vanceburg, Ashland, Huntington, Kenova, Hurricane, Milton, Nitro, Dunbar, Poca, Pocatalico, Clendenin, Clay, Big Otter, Birch River, Monterey, Dunmore

Morehead, Olive Hill, Barboursville, S. Charleston, St. Albans, Charleston, East Bank, Cedar Grove, Big Chimney, Muddlety, Summersville, Camden-on-Gauley, Slatyfork, Richwood, Marlinton, Warm Springs

Sandy Hook, Webbville, Louisa, Ft. Gay, Hamlin, Yawkey, Racine, Marmet, Smithers, Gauley Bridge, Nettie, Hillsboro, Renick, Neola, Goshen

Wayne, Prichard, Midkiff, Danville, Chesapeake, Montgomery, Fayetteville, Mossy, Oak Hill, Rainelle, Rupert, White Sulphur Spr., Clifton Forge, Lexington

West Liberty, Kermit, Chapmanville, Madison, Whitesville, Sylvester, Mt. Hope, Meadow Bridge, Lewisburg, Covington, Iron Gate

Salyersville, Paintsville, Inez, West Logan, Van, Naoma, Bradley, Grandview St. Pk., Alderson, Ronceverte, Eagle Rock, Buchanan

Prestonsburg, Williamson, Logan, Omar, Man, Lester, Beckley, Mabscott, Hinton, Union, New Castle, Big Island

Lee City, Rosseau, Delbarton, Matewan, Gilbert, Oceana, Sophia, Rhodell, Mullens, Forest Hill, Gap Mills, Buchanan, Lynchburg

Jackson, Mayflower, Phelps, Iaeger, Pineville, Baileysville, Camp Cr. St. Forest, Pipestem, Peterstown, Pearisburg, Hollins, Roanoke, Bedford

Hazard, Pikeville, Garrett, Welch, Kimball, Matoaka, Athens, Ripplemead, Pembroke, Salem, Vinton

Isom, Dorton, Grundy, Jolo, War, Gary, Keystone, Bramwell, Princeton, Ingleside, Narrows, Blacksburg, Dublin, Christiansburg, Boones Mill

Whitesburg, Pound, Clinchco, Vansant, Red Ash, Raven, Richlands, Bluefield, Bastian, Radford, Floyd, Rocky Mount, Sydnorsville

Cutshin, Norton, Wise, Coeburn, Dante, Lebanon, Cedar Bluff, Tazewell, Pulaski, Wytheville, Dugspur

Harlan, Appalachia, Big Stone Gap, St. Paul, Castlewood, Saltville, Marion, Rural Retreat, Hillsville, Stanleytown, Martinsville, Fieldale

Pennington Gap, Jonesville, Gate City, Weber City, Abingdon, Chilhowie, Sugar Grove, Woodlawn, Fries, Galax, Stuart, Patrick Springs

Ewing, Kingsport, Bristol, Damascus, Independence, Claudville, Mt. Airy, Danville, Eden

Sparta, Lansing

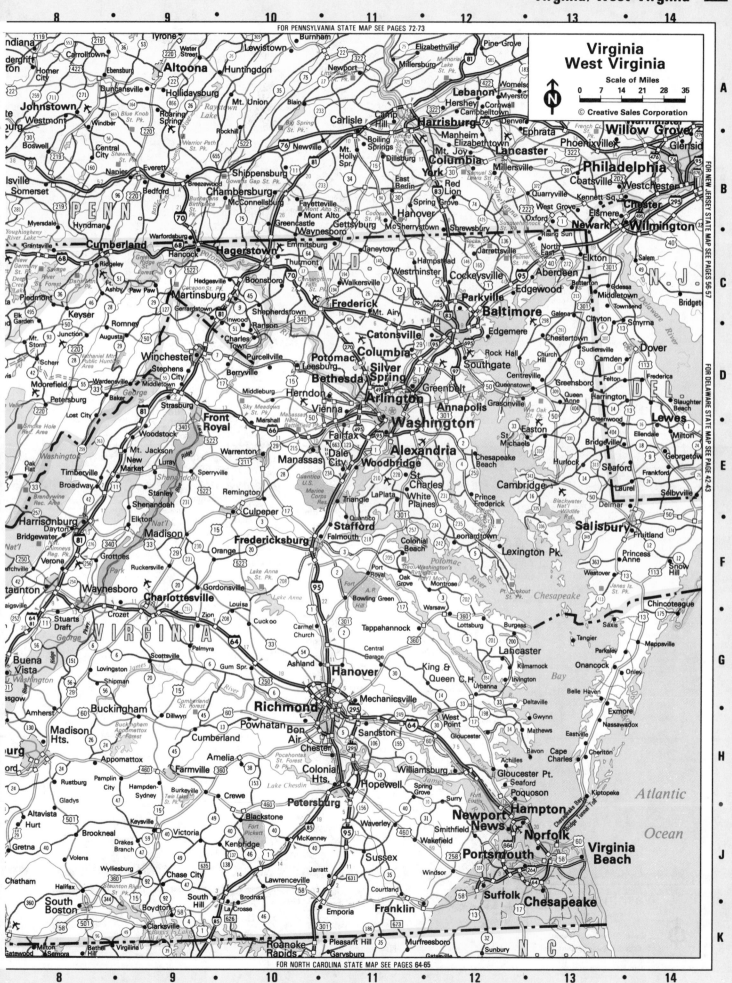

Virginia
West Virginia

Scale of Miles

0   7   14   21   28   35

© Creative Sales Corporation

1 • 2 • 3 • 4 • 5 • 6 • 7 • 8

A B C D E F G H J K

BRITISH COLUMBIA

Vancouver Island

CANADA
U.S.

Strait of Juan De Fuca

Strait of Georgia

Barkley Sound
Nitinat Lake
Cowichan Lake
Ladysmith
Duncan
Sidney
Sooke Lake
Port Renfrew
Sooke
Victoria
Neah Bay
Ozette
Lake Ozette
Sappho
Forks
La Push
Queets
Taholah
Pacific Beach
Ocean Shores
Copalis Beach
Ocean City St. Pk.
Westhaven St. Pk.
Westport
Twin Harbors St. Pk.
Grayland Beach St. Pk.
North Cove
Ocean Park
Long Beach
Ilwaco
Ft. Canby St. Pk.
Seaside
Cannon Beach
Manzanita
Garibaldi
Tillamook

Olympic National Park
Olympic Nat'l Forest

Joyce
Port Angeles
Sequim
Discovery Bay
Port Townsend
Coupeville
Oak Harbor
Stanwood
Marysville
Everett
Mukilteo
Lynnwood
Edmonds
Poulsbo
Seattle
Bremerton
Port Orchard
Mercer Island
Renton
Des Moines
Kent
Auburn
Tacoma
Fircrest
Steilacoom
Shelton
McCleary
Elma
Montesano
Aberdeen
Hoquiam
Cosmopolis
Raymond
South Bend
Menlo
Lebam
Pe Ell
Naselle
Rosburg
Altoona
Astoria
Warrenton
Cathlamet
Stella
Longview
Kelso
Kalama
Woodland
Ridgefield
La Center
Battle Ground
Vancouver
Camas
Washougal
Hillsboro
Gresham
Portland
Oregon City
Newberg
Forest Grove
Tillamook

Bellingham
Ferndale
Blaine
Lynden
Everson
Sumas
Deming
Acme
Wickersham
Mount Vernon
Sedro-Woolley
Burlington
Concrete
Rockport
Arlington
Darrington
Granite Falls
Lake Stevens
Snohomish
Sultan
Monroe
Gold Bar
Index
Duvall
Carnation
Redmond
Bellevue
Kirkland
Issaquah
North Bend
Snoqualmie
Black Diamond
Enumclaw
Buckley
Sumner
Puyallup
Bonney Lake
Orting
Carbonado
Eatonville
Yelm
Roy
Rainier
Tenino
Bucoda
Centralia
Chehalis
Napavine
Winlock
Toledo
Vader
Castle Rock
Morton
Randle
Packwood
Glenoma
Mossyrock
Trout Lake
Klickitat
White Salmon
Bingen
Stevenson
North Bonneville
Hood River
The Dalles
Wishram
Dufur

Mt. Rainier Nat'l Park
Gifford Pinchot Nat'l Forest
North Cascades Nat'l Park
Snoqualmie Nat'l Forest

Pacific Ocean

Columbia R.

Washington
Scale of Miles
0 6 12 18 24 30
N
© Creative Sales Corporation

FOR OREGON STATE MAP SEE PAGES 70-71

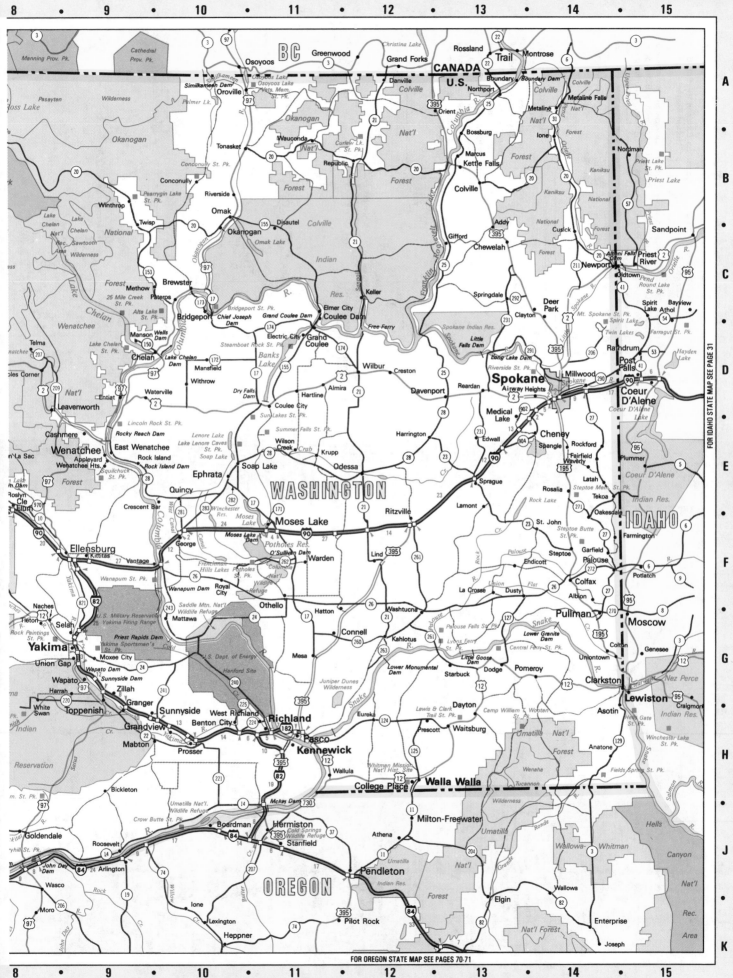

FOR IDAHO STATE MAP SEE PAGE 31

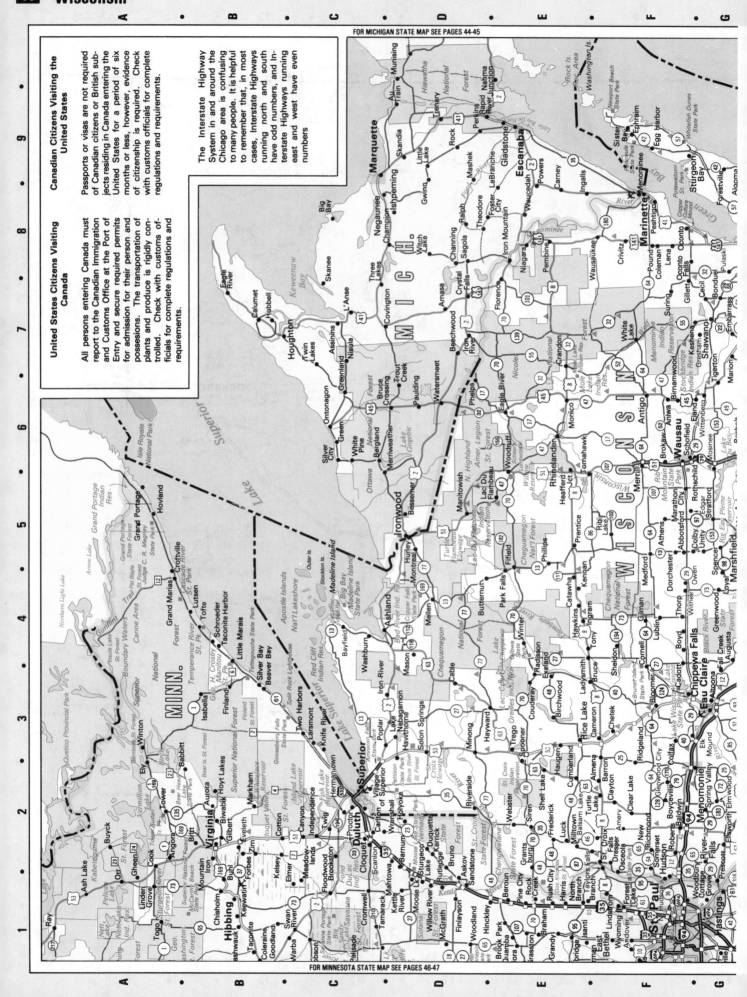

FOR MICHIGAN STATE MAP SEE PAGES 44-45

FOR MINNESOTA STATE MAP SEE PAGES 46-47

United States Citizens Visiting Canada

All persons entering Canada must report to the Canadian Immigration and Customs Office at the Port of Entry and secure required permits for admission for their person and possesions. The transportation of plants and produce is rigidly controlled. Check with customs officials for complete regulations and requirements.

Canadian Citizens Visiting the United States

Passports or visas are not required of Canadian citizens or British subjects residing in Canada entering the United States for a period of six months or less, however, evidence of citizenship is required. Check with customs officials for complete regulations and requirements.

The Interstate Highway System in and around the Chicago area is confusing to many people. It is helpful to remember that, in most cases, Interstate Highways running north and south have odd numbers, and Interstate Highways running east and west have even numbers

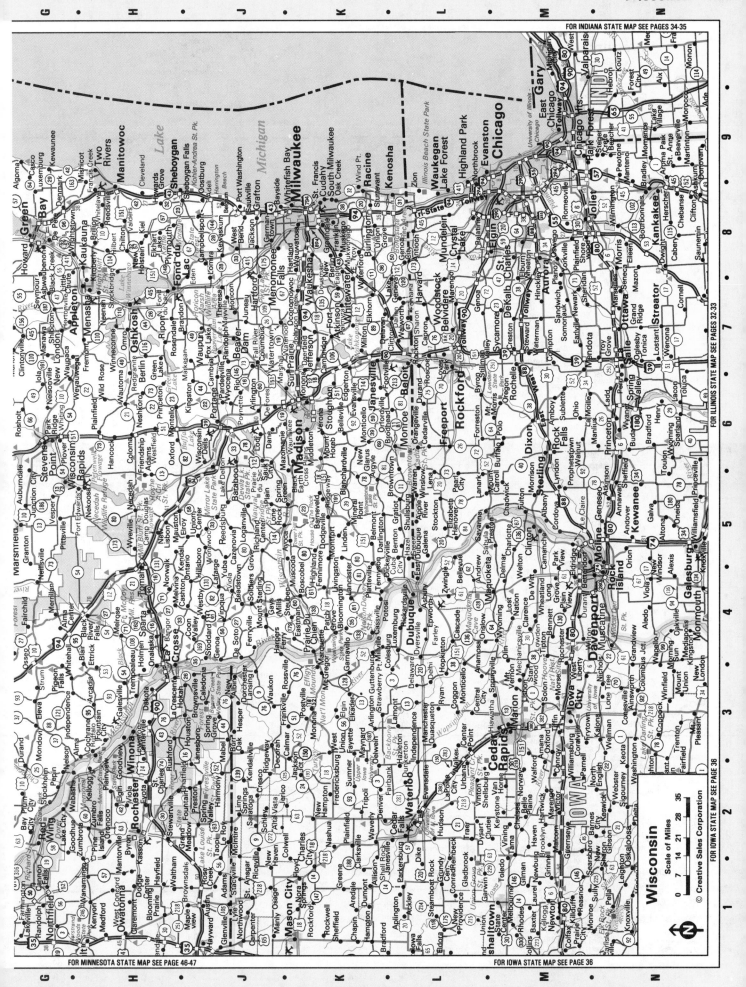

FOR INDIANA STATE MAP SEE PAGES 34-35

FOR ILLINOIS STATE MAP SEE PAGES 32-33

FOR IOWA STATE MAP SEE PAGE 36

Wisconsin

Scale of Miles

0 7 14 21 28 35

© Creative Sales Corporation

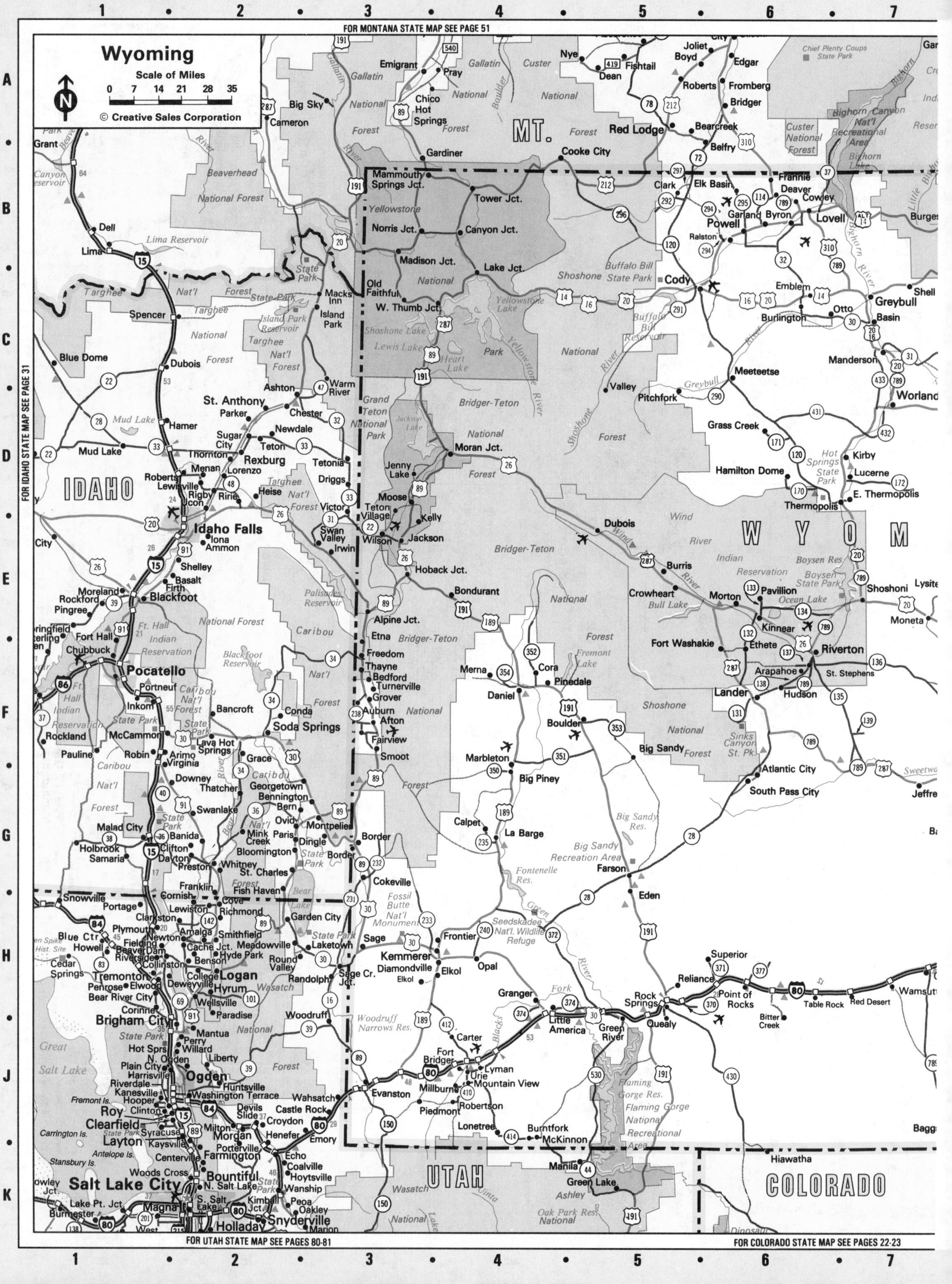

Wyoming

Scale of Miles
0 7 14 21 28 35

© Creative Sales Corporation

N

FOR MONTANA STATE MAP SEE PAGE 51

MT.

IDAHO

WYOM

UTAH

COLORADO

Salt Lake City

Idaho Falls

Pocatello

Logan

Ogden

Brigham City

Cody

Powell

Lovell

Greybull

Worland

Thermopolis

Riverton

Lander

Rock Springs

Green River

Evanston

Kemmerer

Jackson

Pinedale

Yellowstone
National
Park

Grand Teton
National Park

Old
Faithful

Mammouth
Springs Jct.

Norris Jct.

Madison Jct.

Canyon Jct.

Tower Jct.

Lake Jct.

W. Thumb Jct.

Red Lodge

Cooke City

Gardiner

Bridger-Teton
National
Forest

Shoshone
National
Forest

Targhee
National
Forest

Caribou
National
Forest

FOR MONTANA STATE MAP SEE PAGE 51

8 9 10 11 12 13

A B C D E F G H J K

FOR SOUTH DAKOTA STATE MAP SEE PAGE 74

FOR NEBRASKA STATE MAP SEE PAGES 52-53

MT.

SOUTH DAK.

NEBRASKA

CO.

WYOMING

Broadus, Birney, Hammond, Biddle, Ford, Lightning Flat, Rockypoint, Colony, Alzada, Zeona, Hoover, Mud Butte, Maurine, Castle Rock, Fairpoint, Stoneville, Red Owl

Lodge Grass, Wyola, Decker, Parkman, Ranchester, Dayton, Acme, Beckton, Big Horn, Sheridan, Leiter, Recluse, Spotted Horse, New Haven, Hulett, Alva, Aladdin, Belle Fourche, Newell, Nisland, Fruitdale, Beulah, Whitewood, Sturgis, Elm Springs, Union Center

Clearmont, Arvada, Weston, Oshoto, Devils Tower Nat'l Monument, Devil's Tower Jct., Spearfish, Central City, Deadwood, Lead, Pluma

Banner, Story, Ucross, Buffalo, Gillette, Rozet, Moorcroft, Sundance, Four Corners, Rochford, Silver City, Deerfield, Hisega, Rapid City, Box Elder, New Underwood

Hyattville, Ten Sleep, Mayoworth, Big Trails, Barnum, Kaycee, Sussex, Linch, Savageton, Wright, Reno Jct., Upton, Osage, Newcastle, Clareton, Rochelle, Hampshire, Morrisey, Mule Cr. Jct., Custer, Blue Bell, Pringle, Hill City, Keystone, Hermosa, Fairburn, Game Lodge, Caputa, Farmingdale, Buffalo Gap, Scenic

Lost Cabin, Arminto, Waltman, Hiland, Powder River, Natrona, Bar Nunn, Mills, Casper, Evansville, Glenrock, Orpha, Lost Springs, Manville, Lusk, Node, Van Tassell, Harrison, Chadron, Rushville, Edgemont, Redbird, Igloo, Provo, Ardmore, Oelrichs, Manderson, Oglala, Hot Springs, Oral, Smithwick, Buffalo Gap, Wind Cave National Park, Angostura Reservoir

Midwest, Edgerton, Pine Tree Jct., Bill, Lance Creek, Douglas, Shawnee, Keeline, Orin, Glendo, Guernsey, Sunrise, Hartville, Jay Em, Lingle, Torrington, Mitchell, Scottsbluff, Gering, Harrison, Crawford, Whitney, Hay Springs, Marsland, Hemingford, Alliance, Antioch, Angora

Boxelder, Glendo Res., Glendo St. Park, Guernsey St. Park, Fort Laramie, Veteran, Morrill, Lyman, Huntley, Yoder, Terrytown, Minatare, Melbeta, McGrew, Bayard, Bridgeport, Broadwater

Alcova, Shirley Basin, Wheatland, Slater, Chugwater, Hawk Sprs., La Grange, Albin, Bushnell, Kimball, Dix, Potter, Sidney, Dalton, Gurley

Bairoil, Lamont, Medicine Bow, Hanna, Elmo, Rock River, Iron Mountain, Horse Creek, Harrisburg, Gurley

Rawlins, Sinclair, Walcott, McFadden, Bosler, Laramie, Federal, Hillsdale, Burns, Egbert, Carpenter, Pine Bluffs

Creston Jct., Elk Mountain, Arlington, Saratoga, Medicine Bow Nat'l Forest, Centennial, Albany, Woods Landing, Mountain Home, Tie Siding, Cheyenne, Peetz, Crook, Proctor, Iliff

Riverside, Encampment, Dixon, Severy, Walden, Cowdrey, Rustic, The Forks, Roosevelt, Bellvue, Virginia Dale, Rockport, Nunn, Pierce, Ault, Briggsdale, Buckingham, Sterling, Atwood, Fleming, Stoneham

Fort Collins

FOR COLORADO STATE MAP SEE PAGES 22-23

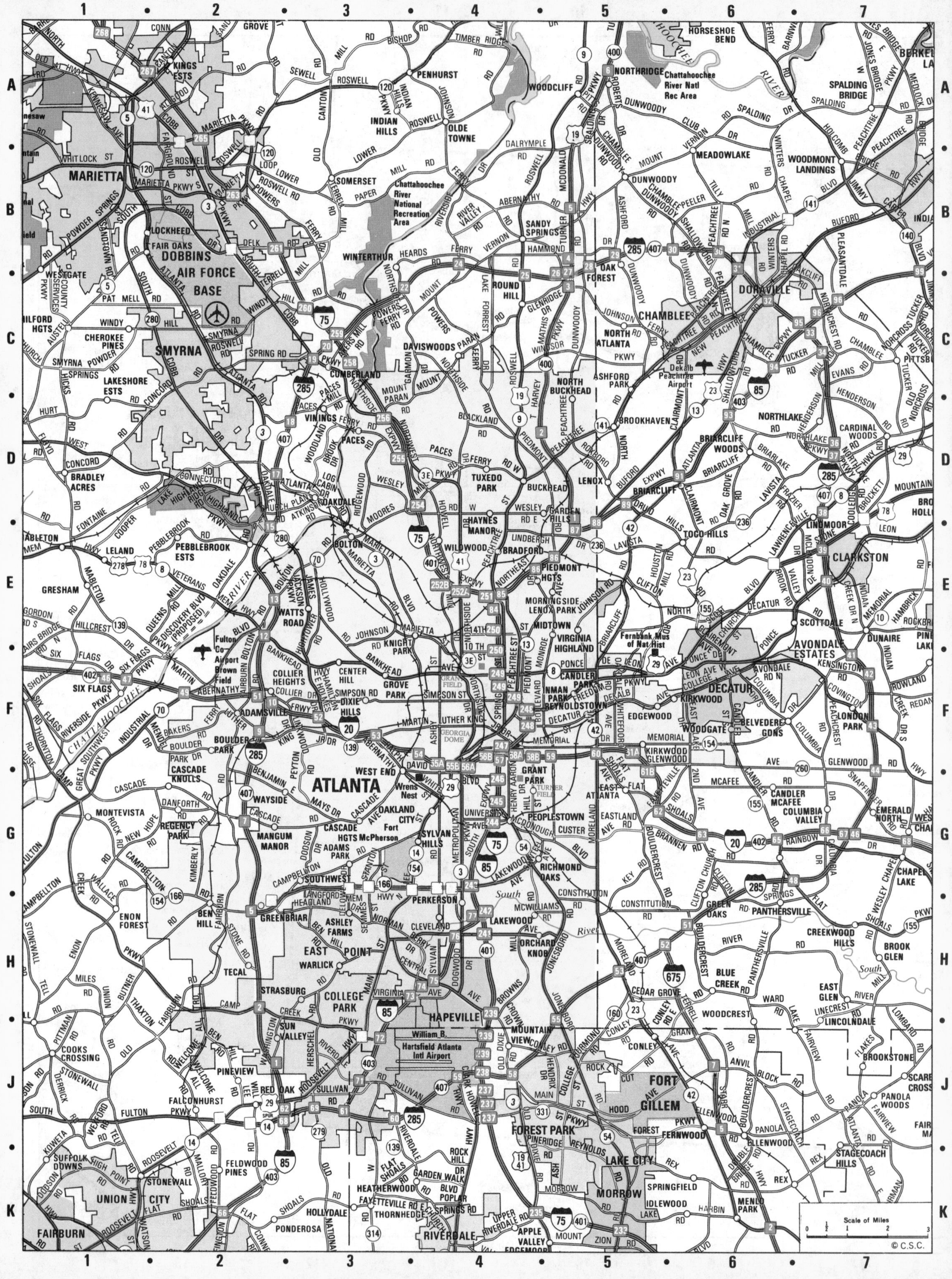
MARIETTA
KINGS ESTS
DOBBINS AIR FORCE BASE
SMYRNA
CHEROKEE PINES
LAKESHORE ESTS
BRADLEY ACRES
MILFORD HGTS
WESTGATE
LELAND
PEBBLEBROOK ESTS
GRESHAM
SIX FLAGS
Fulton Co. Airport Brown Field
ADAMSVILLE
BOULDER PARK
CASCADE KNOLLS
MONTEVISTA
REGENCY PARK
ENON FOREST
BEN HILL
TECAL
COOKS CROSSING
PINEVIEW
FALCONHURST
RED OAK
SUFFOLK DOWNS
UNION CITY
FAIRBURN
FELDWOOD PINES
PONDEROSA
HOLLYDALE
HEATHERWOOD
THORNHEDGE
RIVERDALE
PENHURST
INDIAN HILLS
OLDE TOWNE
SOMERSET
Chattahoochee River National Recreation Area
WINTERTHUR
VININGS
PACES
CUMBERLAND
DAVISWOODS
ROUND HILL
SANDY SPRINGS
WOODCLIFF
NORTHRIDGE
Chattahoochee River Natl Rec Area
HORSESHOE BEND
MEADOWLAKE
WOODMONT LANDINGS
SPALDING BRIDGE
OAK FOREST
CHAMBLEE
DORAVILLE
NORTH ATLANTA
Dekalb Peachtree Airport
ASHFORD PARK
NORTH BUCKHEAD
BROOKHAVEN
NORTHLAKE
BRIARCLIFF WOODS
CARDINAL WOODS
LENOX
BUCKHEAD
TUXEDO PARK
HAYNES MANOR
GARDEN HILLS
BRADFORD
WILDWOOD
TOCO HILLS
LINDMOOR
CLARKSTON
PIEDMONT HGTS
MORNINGSIDE LENOX PARK
MIDTOWN
VIRGINIA HIGHLAND
Fernbank Mus of Nat Hist
SCOTTDALE
DUNAIRE
AVONDALE ESTATES
WATTS ROAD
KNIGHT PARK
COLLIER HEIGHTS
CENTER HILL
GROVE PARK
DIXIE HILLS
GEORGIA DOME
CANDLER PARK
INMAN PARK
REYNOLDSTOWN
EDGEWOOD
KIRKWOOD
DECATUR
WOODGATE
BELVEDERE GDNS
LONDON PARK
WEST END
ATLANTA
Wrens Nest
GRANT PARK
TURNER FIELD
EAST ATLANTA
KIRKWOOD GLENWOOD
CANDLER MCAFEE
COLUMBIA VALLEY
EMERALD NORTH
WAYSIDE
MANGUM MANOR
CASCADE HGTS
Fort McPherson
OAKLAND CITY
SYLVAN HILLS
PEOPLESTOWN
RICHMOND OAKS
ADAMS PARK
SOUTHWEST
PERKERSON
LAKEWOOD
GREENBRIAR
ASHLEY FARMS
EAST POINT
WARLICK
STRASBURG
COLLEGE PARK
SUN VALLEY
HAPEVILLE
William B. Hartsfield Atlanta Intl Airport
MOUNTAIN VIEW
ORCHARD KNOB
GREEN OAKS
PANTHERSVILLE
CHAPEL LAKE
CREEKWOOD HILLS
BROOK GLEN
BLUE CREEK
EAST GLEN
LINCOLNDALE
BROOKSTONE
PANOLA WOODS
FORT GILLEM
FOREST PARK
LAKE CITY
MORROW
FERNWOOD
ELLENWOOD
STAGECOACH HILLS
MENLO PARK
SPRINGFIELD
IDLEWOOD
APPLE VALLEY
CHATTAHOOCHEE
Scale of Miles
0 1/2 1 2 3
© C.S.C.

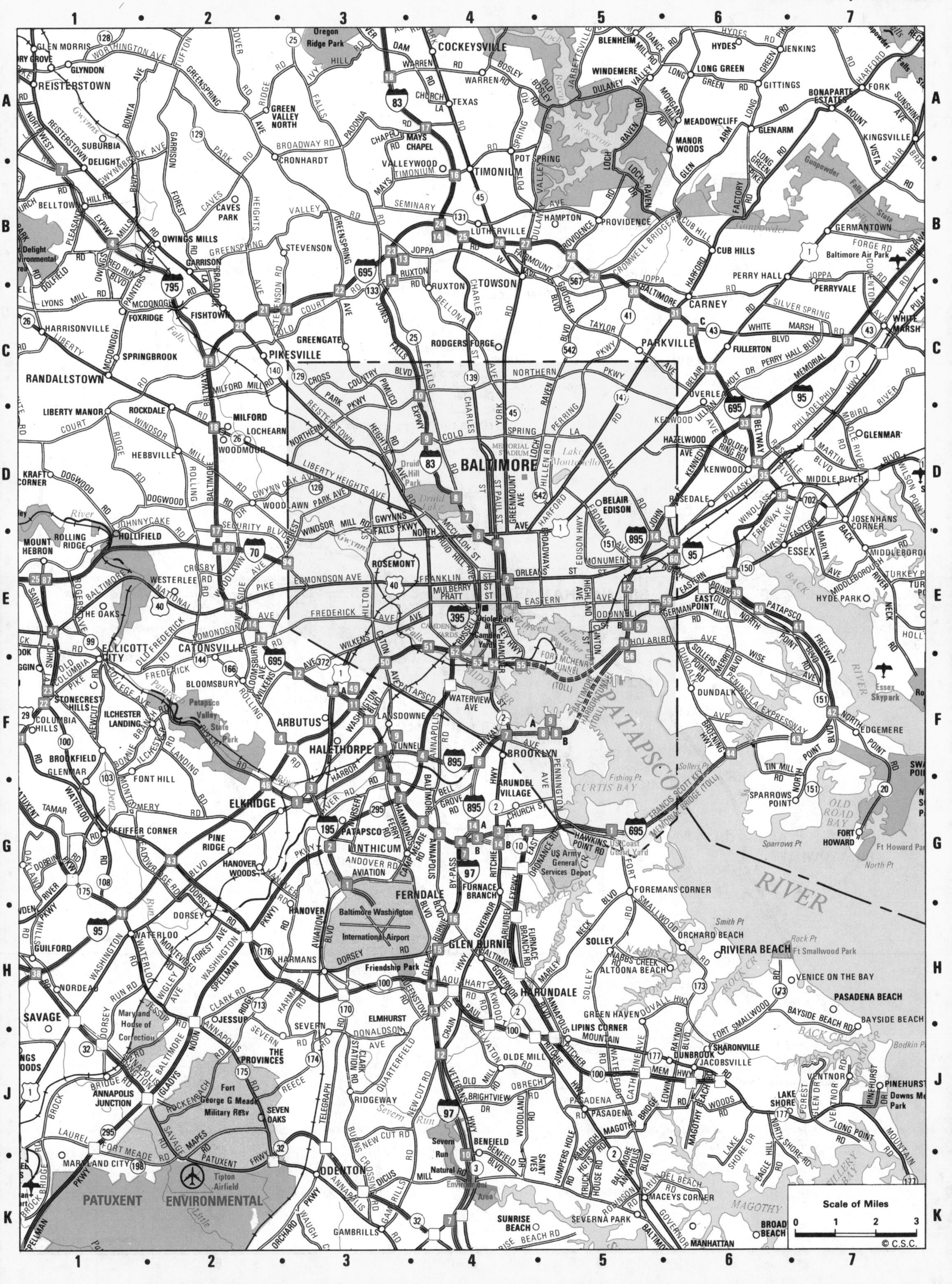

BALTIMORE

REISTERSTOWN
COCKEYSVILLE
TIMONIUM
TOWSON
PARKVILLE
CARNEY
PERRYVALE
WHITE MARSH
GLENMAR
ESSEX
DUNDALK
BROOKLYN
GLEN BURNIE
FERNDALE
ELKRIDGE
CATONSVILLE
ELLICOTT CITY
ARBUTUS
HALETHORPE
LINTHICUM
PIKESVILLE
RANDALLSTOWN
OWINGS MILLS
RIVIERA BEACH
PASADENA BEACH
BAYSIDE BEACH
SPARROWS POINT
FORT HOWARD
ODENTON
SAVAGE
ANNAPOLIS JUNCTION

PATAPSCO RIVER
BACK RIVER
MAGOTHY RIVER
CURTIS BAY
OLD ROAD BAY

Baltimore Washington International Airport

PATUXENT ENVIRONMENTAL
Tipton Airfield

Scale of Miles
0   1   2   3

© C.S.C.

A B C D E F G H J K

1 2 3 4 5 6 7

Forestdale
45 78 Blvd 4 5 SAYRE
KILGORE
71 109 DIVIDE STATION MT. OLIVE 77 3 Decatur
LINN CORSSING 12 Hwy
BESSIE 12 CARDIFF ALDEN BROOKSIDE FIELDSTOWN GARDENDALE NEW CASTLE
GRAYSVILLE 112 Cherry Brookside 18 Coalburg 238 112 31 Main GREENS STATION CHALKVILLE
LINDBERGH Ave. MINERAL SPRINGS 18 Walker Rd. St. Odom Rd. Tarrant Dr. Newcastle N. Carson Rd. Pinson CENTER POINT 128 157
ADAMSVILLE Forestdale Coalburg Chapel FULTONDALE 123 125 79 ROBINWOOD Carson Rd. Sun Valley Rd. Polly Reed Rd. Brewster
Village REPUBLIC 67 COALBURG WALKER CHAPEL 120 KETONA Black Creek Rd. 24 Springdale Rd. Huffman 75 11 7
UNION GROVE 78 105 LEWISBURG TARRANT CITY 31 Huntsville Rd. Tarrant Huffman Rd. West Blvd. 59 ROEBUCK PLAZA 94 ALTON Goat
BAY VIEW 4 5 Bankhead 3 35th Ave. 79 East Lake Blvd. Southern Museum of Flight Rufner Mtn. Nature Ctr. 147 Altona Billy
MULGA DOCENA 45 86 Finley Hwy. 27th St. Vanderbilt Birmingham Municipal Airport Airport Hwy. 20 Ruffner IRONDALE Karl Daly Rd. JEFFERSON PARK 143
MAYTOWN 57 Loop 65 Rd. BIRMINGHAM 65 Village Civic Center 13th St. Sloss Furnaces Georgia 11 64 Grants 78
SYLVAN SPRINGS 269 61 Birmingport EDGEWATER 80 Mulga Loop 20th St. 59 Museum of Art Civil Rights Inst. U.A.B. 28th St. Messer Crestwood BANKHEAD Bankhead 60 OVERTON GRANTS MILL
61 Pleasant Loop Lexington Rd. Ave. E. 20 3rd Cotton Ave. University of Alabama Medical Center Clairmont Montclair 62 Grants Mill
PLEASANT GROVE FAIRFIELD 76 59 Warrior Rd. 7 5 11 Birmingham Sou. College 6th Ave. King Jr. Vulcan Statue Green Montevallo 64 Old Leeds Rd.
Grove 56 Miles College Pearson Fayette Dennison Ave. 95 MOUNTAIN BROOK Brookwood
HUEYTOWN Forest 57 MIDFIELD Brighton Rd. ISHKOODA Wenonah Rd. Martin Luther Oxmoor HOMEWOOD Caraba 280 OVERTON Hollow
DOLOMITE 46 Warrior Fairfield-Dolomite 66 Spaulding 149 Samford University Cherokee Rd. 62 Lake Purdy
19th Ave. BROWNSVILLE Wenonah 31 Lake Shore Dr. 60 60
BRIGHTON Huntsville 3rd WENONAH OXMOOR 97 West Shades 65 149 99 Crest VESTAVIA HILLS CAHABA HEIGHTS Sicard 60
32 51 Jefferson Ave. LIPSCOMB 95 Tyler Rd. 3 Rocky Ridge Rd. Attalla 115 459
36 82 46 Bessemer SHANNON Chapel HOOVER Montgomery ROCKY RIDGE 17 119
36 Dartmouth BESSEMER 93 PATTON CHAPEL 459 JEFFERSON CO. 280 Route
59 20 MUSCODA SHELBY CO.
18 52 150 97 115
EASTERN VALLEY 52 ACTION 31 NEW HOPE 41
20 52 MORGAN Shades 17 Oak Mountain State Park 43
MC CALLA 53 GREENWOOD ELVIRA River 65 3 CHELSEA 280
18 Cahaba 111
53 GENERY

Scale of Miles
0 1 2 3

N

HELENA
PELHAM

© C.S.C.

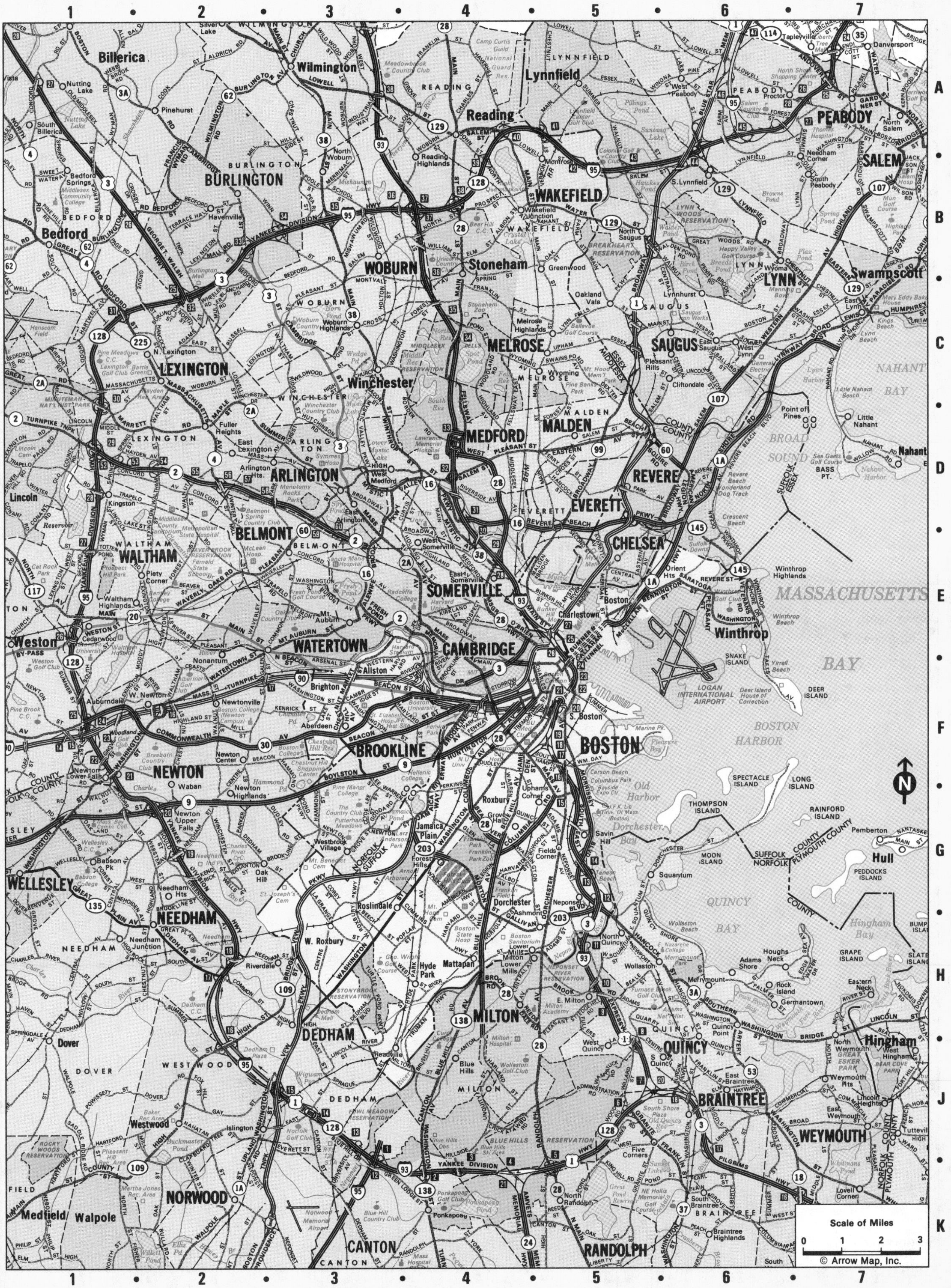

Billerica
Wilmington
Lynnfield
Reading
PEABODY
SALEM
BURLINGTON
WAKEFIELD
Swampscott
Bedford
WOBURN
Stoneham
SAUGUS
LYNN
N. Lexington
LEXINGTON
Winchester
MELROSE
MALDEN
REVERE
NAHANT BAY
ARLINGTON
MEDFORD
EVERETT
CHELSEA
Nahant
Lincoln
BELMONT
SOMERVILLE
MASSACHUSETTS
WALTHAM
Winthrop
Weston
WATERTOWN
CAMBRIDGE
Logan International Airport
DEER ISLAND
BAY
Newton
BROOKLINE
BOSTON
BOSTON HARBOR
WELLESLEY
Roxbury
SPECTACLE ISLAND
LONG ISLAND
NEEDHAM
Jamaica Plain
Roslindale
Dorchester
QUINCY BAY
Hull
Dover
Hyde Park
Mattapan
QUINCY
Hingham
Westwood
DEDHAM
MILTON
Weymouth
Medfield Walpole
NORWOOD
CANTON
RANDOLPH
BRAINTREE
WEYMOUTH

Scale of Miles
0 1 2 3

© Arrow Map, Inc.

NIAGARA FALLS · ECHOTA · BERKHOLTZ · BEACH RIDGE · PENDLETON · RAPIDS

NIAGARA FALLS · ST. JOHNSBURG · NASHVILLE · HOFFMAN · WENDELVILLE · MILLERSPORT · ELSERS CORNERS

LA SALLE · SAWYER · MARTINSVILLE · SWORMVILLE

CHIPPAWA · PEACH HAVEN · WURLITZER PARK · GETZVILLE · EAST AMHERST

SANDY BEACH · EDGEWATER · NORTH TONAWANDA · S.U.N.Y. Buffalo · CLARENCE CENTER

GRANDYLE VILLAGE · TONAWANDA · KENMORE · NORTH BAILEY AMHERST · EGGERTSVILLE · WILLIAMSVILLE · HARRIS HILL

SNYDER · FERRY VILLAGE · Beaver Island State Park · SNYDER · Buffalo International Airport · BOWMANSVILLE

STEVENSSVILLE · FORT ERIE NORTH · Fort Erie Airport · SUNY Golf Buffalo · Buffalo Zoo · DEPEW · LANCASTER

CRESCENT PARK · FORT ERIE · Fort Erie Race Track · SLOAN · CHEEKTOWAGA · BELLEVUE

POINT ABINO · RIDGEWAY · ERIE BEACH · Buffalo Museum of Science · War Mem. Stadium · BLOSSOM · ELMA

THUNDER BAY · CRYSTAL BEACH · GARDENVILLE · ELMA CENTER

BUFFALO · Buffalo Air Park · WEST SENECA · EAST SENECA

Buffalo Harbor · EBENEZER · SPRINGBROOK

LACKAWANNA · Botanical Gardens

BLASDELL · WOODLAWN · WINDOM · Orchard Park Airport · Proner Airport

Lake Erie · BAY VIEW · EAST HAMBURG · WEBSTER CORNERS

ATHOL SPRINGS · BIG TREE · ORCHARD PARK

LOCKSLEY PARK · MT. VERNON · WANAKAH · DUELLS CORNERS

CARNEGIE · ELLICOTT · ELLICOTT HEIGHTS

CLIFTON HEIGHTS · PINEHURST · SCRANTON · ARMOR · Erie Co. Fairgrounds · JEWETTVILLE · GRIFFINS MILLS

HIGHLAND-ON-THE-LAKE · LAKE VIEW · HAMBURG · WATER VALLEY · Chestnut Ridge Park · WEST FALLS

NORTH EVANS · Lakeview Airport · Eighteen Mile Creek

JERUSALEM CORNERS · DERBY · EDEN VALLEY · NORTH BOSTON

ANGOLA-ON-THE-LAKE · EVANS · EAST EDEN · PATCHIN

CANADA / UNITED STATES · ONTARIO / NEW YORK · WELLAND CO. / ERIE CO.

Scale of Miles: 0 1 2 3

©C.S.C.

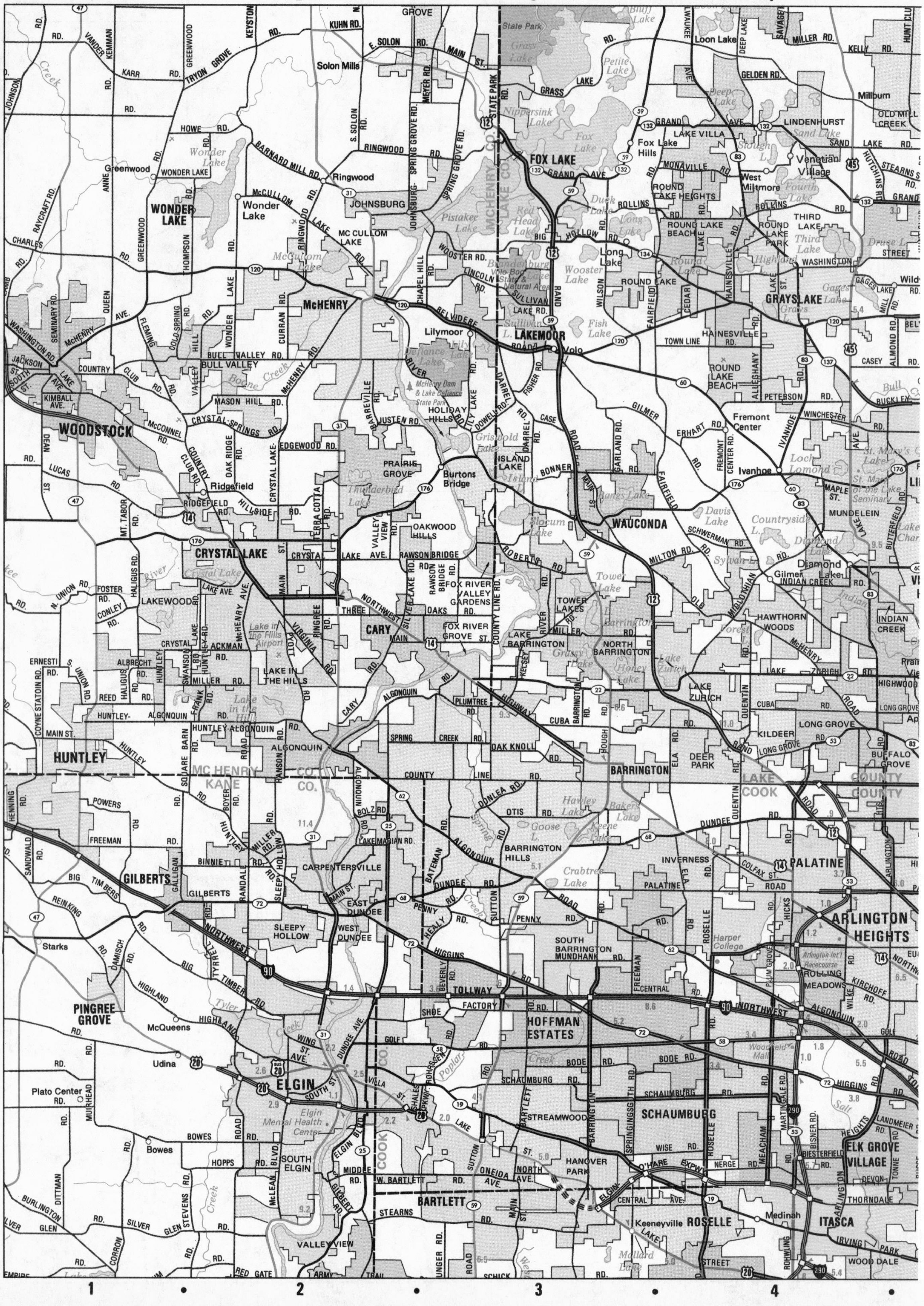

Map grid columns: 1, 2, 3, 4 (top and bottom); rows: B, C, D, E, F, G

Major place names:

WONDER LAKE, Wonder Lake, Greenwood, Solon Mills, Ringwood, Johnsburg, MC CULLOM LAKE, McHenry, Lilymoor, FOX LAKE, Fox Lake Hills, Lake Villa, LINDENHURST, Venetian Village, West Miltmore, Round Lake Heights, Round Lake Beach, Round Lake Park, Third Lake, Long Lake, Lakemoor, Volo, Round Lake, Hainesville, GRAYSLAKE, Round Lake Beach, Fremont Center, Ivanhoe, MUNDELEIN, WOODSTOCK, Ridgefield, CRYSTAL LAKE, Lakewood, Prairie Grove, Burtons Bridge, Oakwood Hills, Island Lake, WAUCONDA, Diamond Lake, Gilmer, Indian Creek, Hawthorn Woods, Cary, Fox River Grove, Fox River Valley Gardens, Tower Lakes, Lake Barrington, North Barrington, Lake Zurich, Kildeer, Long Grove, Buffalo Grove, HUNTLEY, Lake in the Hills, Algonquin, Spring Creek, BARRINGTON, Deer Park, PALATINE, GILBERTS, Carpentersville, East Dundee, West Dundee, Sleepy Hollow, Barrington Hills, Inverness, Palatine, ARLINGTON HEIGHTS, Rolling Meadows, PINGREE GROVE, McQueens, Udina, ELGIN, South Barrington, Mundhank, Harper College, HOFFMAN ESTATES, NORTHWEST, Plato Center, Bowes, South Elgin, Streamwood, Schaumburg, Hanover Park, Keeneyville, ROSELLE, Medinah, ELK GROVE VILLAGE, ITASCA, BARTLETT, Valley View, Wood Dale

Counties: McHENRY CO., LAKE CO., KANE CO., COOK CO., LAKE COOK COUNTY

Lakes and water features: Grass Lake, Fox Lake, Petite Lake, Nippersink Lake, Pistakee Lake, Wonder Lake, McCullom Lake, Griswold Lake, Thunderbird Lake, Slocum Lake, Davis Lake, Diamond Lake, Crystal Lake, Lake in the Hills, Honey Lake, Bangs Lake, Tower Lake, Crabtree Lake, Baker's Lake, Goose Lake, Woodfield Mall

LAKE MICHIGAN

ZION
WADSWORTH
BEACH PARK
WAUKEGAN
NORTH CHICAGO
GURNEE
Great Lakes Naval Training Station
Six Flags Great America
LIBERTYVILLE
LAKE FOREST
LAKE BLUFF
Lake Forest College
VERNON HILLS
METTAWA
DEERFIELD
HIGHLAND PARK
LINCOLNSHIRE
BANNOCKBURN
NORTHBROOK
GLENCOE
WINNETKA
KENILWORTH
WILMETTE
GLENVIEW
Glenview N.A.S. (Closed)
MORTON GROVE
NILES
SKOKIE
EVANSTON
Northwestern University
Kendall College
National College of Education
Loyola University
PARK RIDGE
DES PLAINES
MOUNT PROSPECT
PROSPECT HEIGHTS
BENSENVILLE
CHICAGO O'HARE INTERNATIONAL AIRPORT
ROSEMONT
HARWOOD HEIGHTS
NORRIDGE
LINCOLNWOOD

WHITING
EAST CHICAGO
HAMMOND
Gary Municipal Airport
GARY
MARQUETTE PARK
Grand Calumet River Lagoon
Purdue Univ. Regional Campus
MUNSTER
HIGHLAND
GRIFFITH
DYER
SCHERERVILLE
MERRILLVILLE
Indiana Univ. Regional Campus
NEW CHICAGO
LAKE STATION
Lake George
HOBART
Ainsworth
Deep River
ST. JOHN
CROWN POINT
Krietzburg
Wicker Memorial Park

INDIANA
ILLINOIS
LAKE CO.
COOK CO.
WILL CO.
LAKE COUNTY

CONTINUED ON PAGE 105, GRID L-8

LAKE MICHIGAN

Scale of Miles
0   1   2   3

© A.M.C.

Scale of Miles

0 1 2 3

© A.M.C.

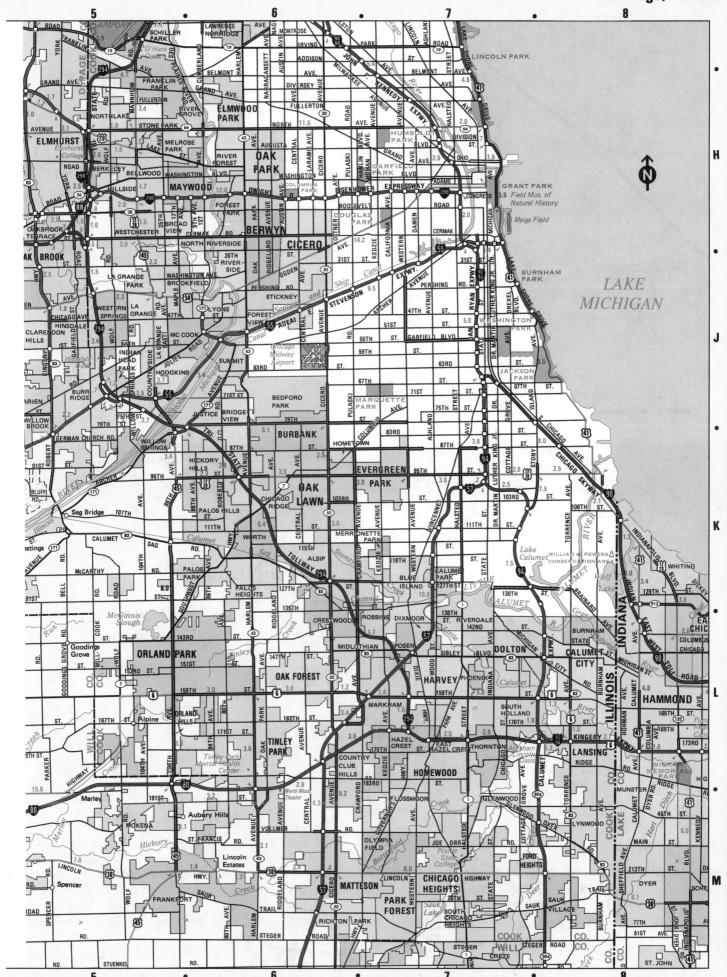

FOREST PARK

Greenhills

Dunlap

Springdale

Glendale

Woodlawn

EVENDALE

BLUE ASH

Sharonville

Sharon Woods

CINCINNATI BLUE ASH AIRPORT

Univ. of Cinci. Raymond Walters Campus

Mt. Healthy

WYOMING

Lincoln Hts.

Lockland

Reading

W. North College Hill

Arlington Hts.

Barnsburg

AMBERLEY

Deer Park

Silverton

Golf Manor

Madeira

Cheviot

Bridgetown

Mt. Airy Forest

Spring Grove Cemetery

St. Bernard

NORWOOD

Fairfax

Mariem

Westwood

Zoological Gardens

Xavier Univ.

Ault Park

University

Univ. of Cincinnati

CINCINNATI

Dayton

LUNKEN AIRPORT

City Hall

Sabin Convention Center

Bellevue

Art Museum

Eden Park

Ludlow

Bromley

COVINGTON

Newport

Ft. Thomas

Villa Hills

Fort Wright

Wilder

Southgate

Cresent Springs

Kenton Vale

Cresent Park

Fort Mitchell

Lakeview

Highland Hts.

Cold Spring

Erlanger

Crestview Hills

Lakeside Park

CINCINNATI & NORTHERN KENTUCKY INT'L AIRPORT

River Downs Race Track

OHIO

KENTUCKY

Ohio River

Scale of Miles
0   1   2   3

N

© C.S.C.

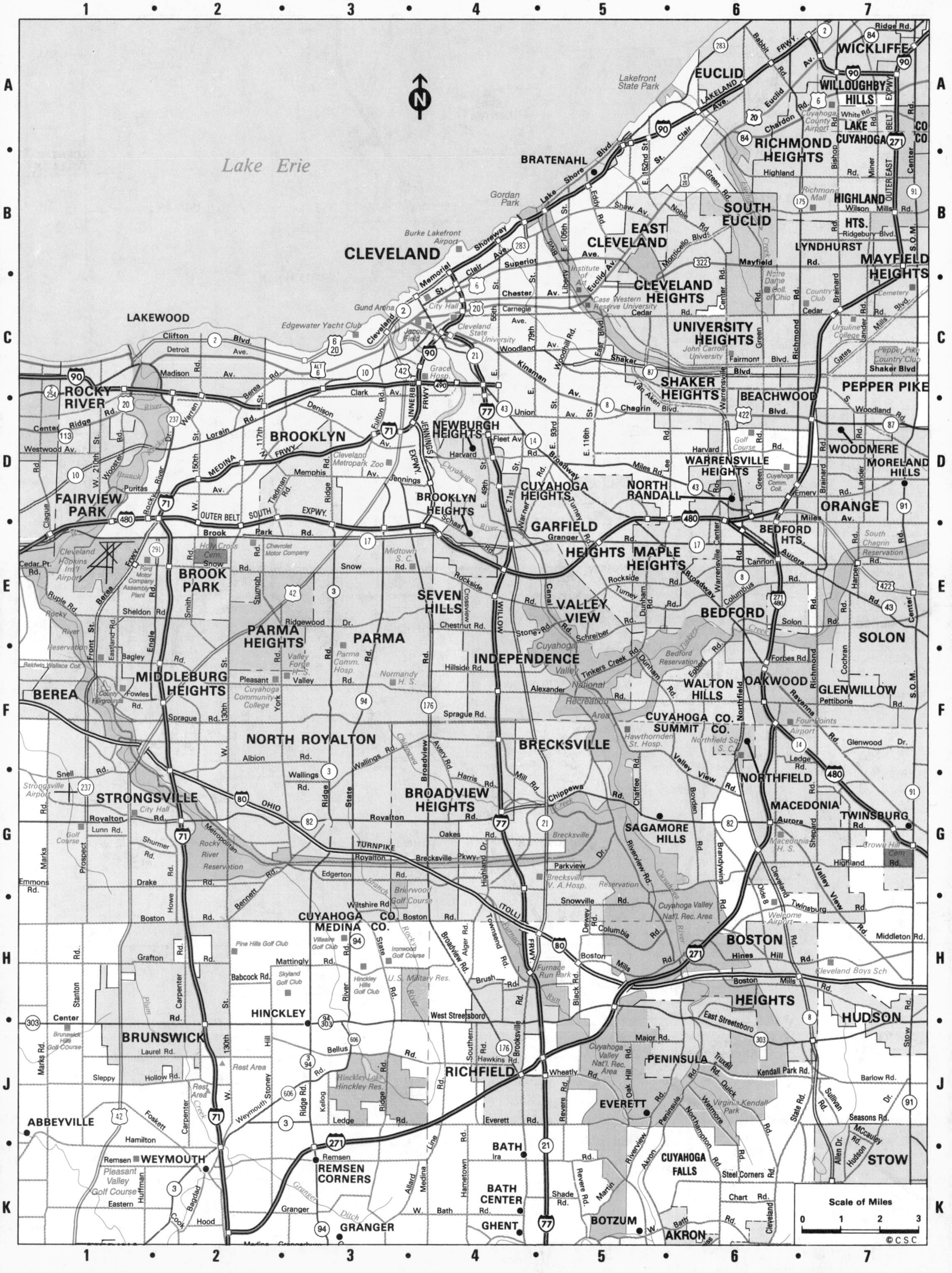

Lake Erie

N

LAKEWOOD
CLEVELAND
ROCKY RIVER
FAIRVIEW PARK
BEREA
BROOK PARK
MIDDLEBURG HEIGHTS
STRONGSVILLE
BRUNSWICK
ABBEYVILLE
WEYMOUTH
REMSEN CORNERS
GRANGER
HINCKLEY
RICHFIELD
NORTH ROYALTON
BROADVIEW HEIGHTS
PARMA
PARMA HEIGHTS
SEVEN HILLS
BROOKLYN
BROOKLYN HEIGHTS
NEWBURGH HEIGHTS
CUYAHOGA HEIGHTS
GARFIELD HEIGHTS
INDEPENDENCE
VALLEY VIEW
BRECKSVILLE
SAGAMORE HILLS
MACEDONIA
NORTHFIELD
WALTON HILLS
OAKWOOD
BEDFORD
BEDFORD HTS.
MAPLE HEIGHTS
NORTH RANDALL
WARRENSVILLE HEIGHTS
GLENWILLOW
SOLON
TWINSBURG
BOSTON HEIGHTS
HUDSON
PENINSULA
EVERETT
BATH
BATH CENTER
GHENT
BOTZUM
AKRON
CUYAHOGA FALLS
STOW
BRATENAHL
EAST CLEVELAND
CLEVELAND HEIGHTS
UNIVERSITY HEIGHTS
SHAKER HEIGHTS
BEACHWOOD
PEPPER PIKE
WOODMERE
MORELAND HILLS
ORANGE
EUCLID
SOUTH EUCLID
LYNDHURST
MAYFIELD HEIGHTS
HIGHLAND HTS.
RICHMOND HEIGHTS
WILLOUGHBY HILLS
WICKLIFFE
LAKE CO.
CUYAHOGA CO.
MEDINA CO.
SUMMIT CO.

Scale of Miles
0 1 2 3

© CSC

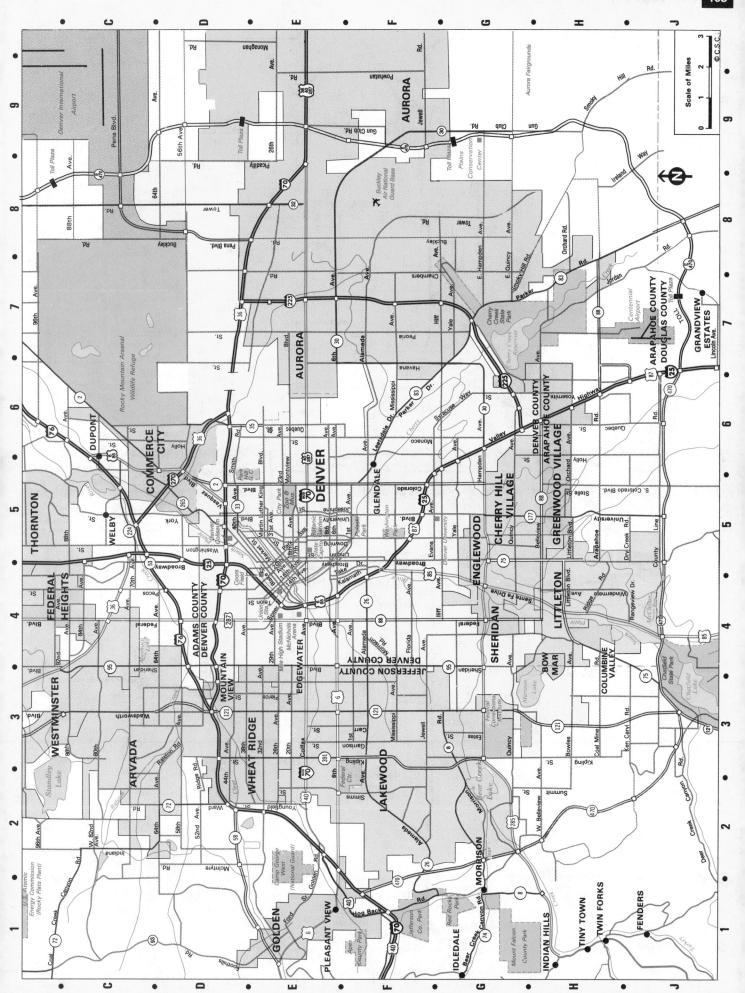

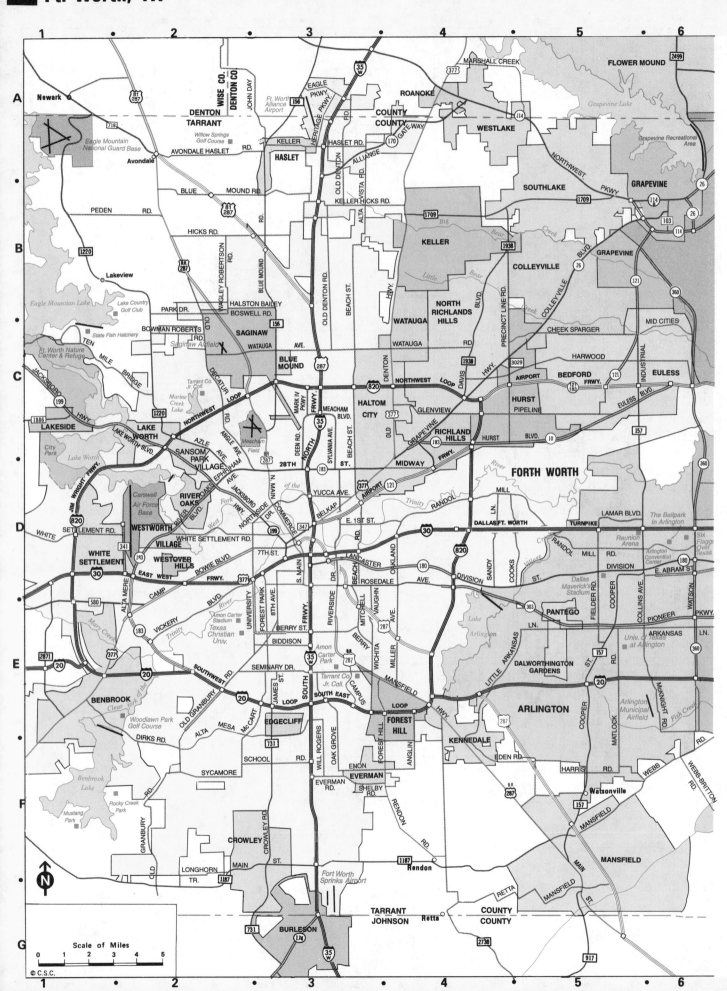

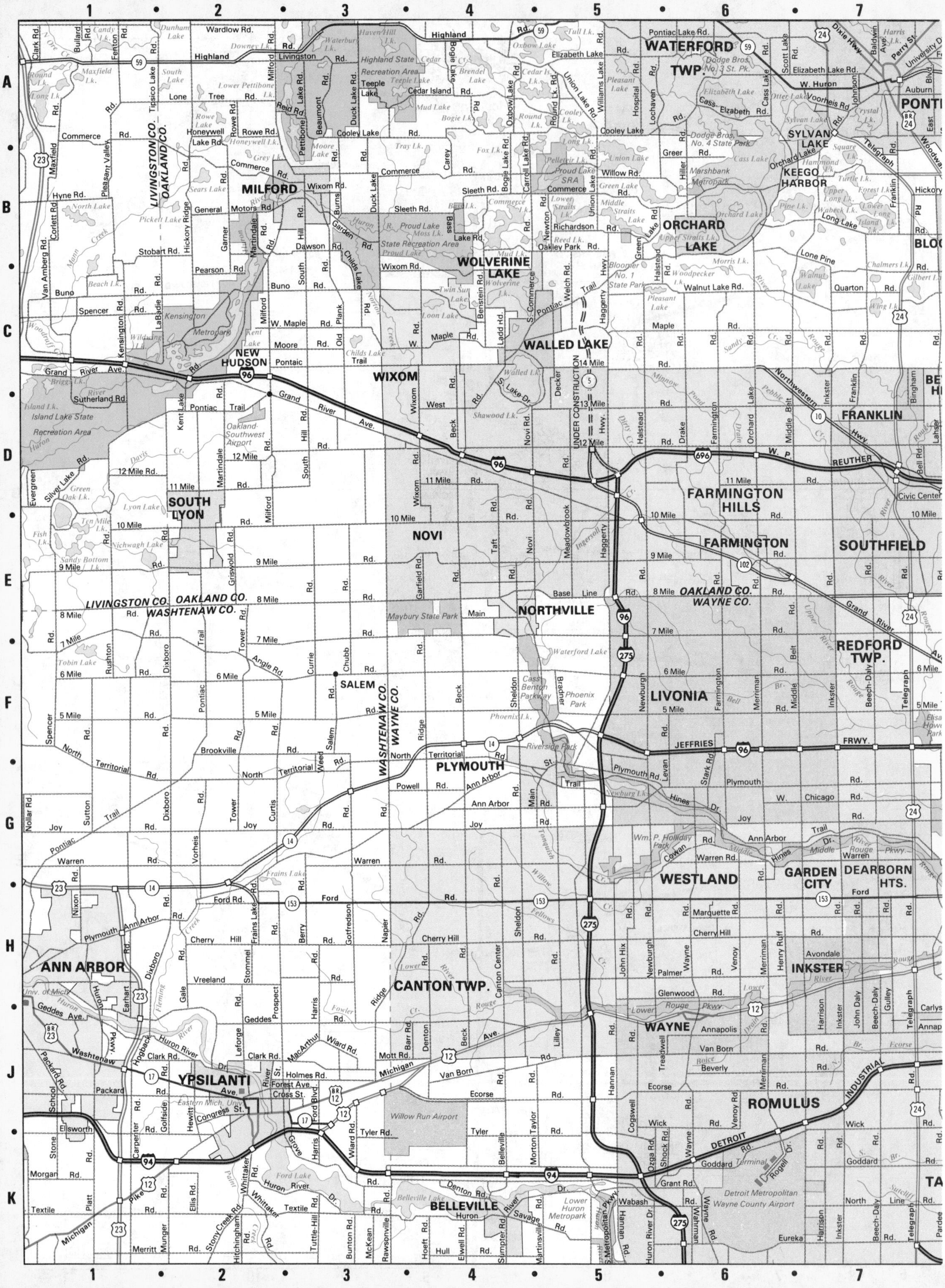

1 2 3 4 5 6 7

A

B

C

D

E

F

G

H

J

K

WATERFORD TWP.

PONTIAC

SYLVAN LAKE
KEEGO HARBOR

ORCHARD LAKE

BLOOMFIELD

MILFORD

WOLVERINE LAKE

WALLED LAKE

WIXOM

NEW HUDSON

FRANKLIN

FARMINGTON HILLS

FARMINGTON

SOUTHFIELD

NOVI

SOUTH LYON

NORTHVILLE

REDFORD TWP.

LIVONIA

PLYMOUTH

SALEM

WESTLAND

GARDEN CITY

DEARBORN HTS.

INKSTER

ANN ARBOR

CANTON TWP.

WAYNE

YPSILANTI

ROMULUS

BELLEVILLE

Willow Run Airport

Detroit Metropolitan Wayne County Airport

Livingston Co. / Oakland Co. / Washtenaw Co.

Oakland Co. / Wayne Co.

Washtenaw Co. / Wayne Co.

Kensington Metropark

Island Lake State Recreation Area

Proud Lake State Recreation Area

Highland State Recreation Area

Maybury State Park

Lower Huron Metropark

AnchorBay

AUBURN HILLS
Featherstone Ave.
PITIAC
ROCHESTER HILLS
WALDENBURG Rd.
Berz-Macomb Airport
22 Mile Rd.
21 Mile
UTICA
MOUNT CLEMENS
CLINTON TWP.
TROY
STERLING HEIGHTS
Oakland Troy Airport
BIRMINGHAM
CLAWSON
FRASER
BLOOMFIELD HILLS
BEVERLY HILLS
ROYAL OAK
MADISON HEIGHTS
WARREN
ST. CLAIR SHORES
LATHRUP VILLAGE
BERKLEY
HUNTINGTON WOODS
ROSEVILLE
HAZEL PARK
CENTER LINE
EAST DETROIT
OAK PARK
FERNDALE
State Fair Grounds
Derby Hill Park
Palmer Park
MACOMB CO. WAYNE CO.
HARPER WOODS
GROSSE POINTE SHORES
GROSSE POINTE WOODS
Univ. of Detroit
HIGHLAND PARK
Lake St. Claire
DETROIT
HAMTRAMCK
Detroit City Airport
GROSSE POINT FARMS
GROSSE POINTE
GROSSE POINTE PARK
Tiger Stadium
Wayne St. Univ.
Gabriel Richard Park
Memorial Park
Belle Isle Park
Windmill Point
U.S.A.
CANADA
Peche Is.
WAYNE CO. ESSEX CO.
DEARBORN
Ford Field
Greenfield Village
MELVINDALE
RIVER ROUGE
WINDSOR
Windsor Airport
MICH. ONT.
ALLEN PARK
ECORSE
LA SALLE
LINCOLN PARK
TECUMSAH
TAYLOR
SOUTH GATE
WYANDOTE
Grasse Is.
Fighting Is.

N

Scale of Miles
0 1 2 3

©C.S.C.

LEE COUNTY

CALOOSAHATCHEE NATIONAL WILDLIFE REFUGE

NORTH FORT MYERS

EAST FORT MYERS

Fort Myers

FORT MYERS PAGE FIELD

SOUTHWEST FLORIDA REGIONAL AIRPORT

LEMIGH ACRES

ESTERO

KORESHAN STATE PARK

KORESHAN STATE PARK

Cape Coral

ESTERO BAY AQUATIC PRESERVE

BONITA BEACH

FORT MYERS BEACH

ESTERO ISLAND

Estero Bay

San Carlos Bay

SANIBEL CAUSEWAY (TOLL)

J.N. "DING" DARLING NATIONAL WILDLIFE REFUGE

PERIWINKLE

SANIBEL-CAPTIVA RD

CAPTIVA

NORTH CAPTIVA ISLAND

CAPTIVA ISLAND

Pine Island Sound

PINE ISLAND

STRINGFELLOW RD

ST. JAMES CITY

FLAMINGO BAY

STRINGFELLOW BLVD

YORK ISLAND

MATLACHA PASS AQUATIC PRESERVE

WEST ISLAND

MATLACHA

Matlacha Pass

BOKEELIA

PINELAND

PINE ISLAND NATIONAL WILDLIFE REFUGE

MONEESHA ISLAND

EAST ISLAND

Cabbage Key

CHARLOTTE HARBOR

CAPE HAZE-GASPARILLA SOUND AQUATIC PRESERVE

BOCA GRANDE

Boca Grande

GULF OF MEXICO

GULF

Scale of Miles

0 1 2 3

© C.S.C.

N

FORT MYERS SHORES

BUCKINGHAM

IMMOKALEE

TAMIAMI TRAIL

CLEVELAND AV

COLONIAL

DANIELS PKWY

SIX MILE CYPRESS

METRO

SUMMERLIN

MCGREGOR BLVD

GLADIOLUS

SAN CARLOS BLVD

TRUCKLAND

DEL PRADO BLVD

PINE ISLAND RD

BURNT STORE RD

SALVISTA

BAYSHORE

N TAMIAMI TRAIL

PONDELLA

Caloosahatchee River

BASS RD

BULB RD

CYPRESS LAKE DR

COLLEGE

ANDERSON

ORTIZ

TICE

PALM BEACH

CREEK

DEAL RD

NALLE GRADE RD

NALLE RD

RICH RD

SLATER RD

LEE BLVD

GUNNERY

LEONARD

NEAL

ORANGE RIVER RD

BEAUTIFUL ISLAND

CORKSCREW

SPRING CREEK RD

COCONUT RD

ALICO

ESTERO

LAKE FRONT

ISLAND PARK

BIG HICKORY PASS

BIG HICKORY ISLAND

BLACK ISLAND

LOVERS KEY STATE PARK

ROUND KEY

FGCU

Hurricane Pass

Redfish Pass

Pine Island

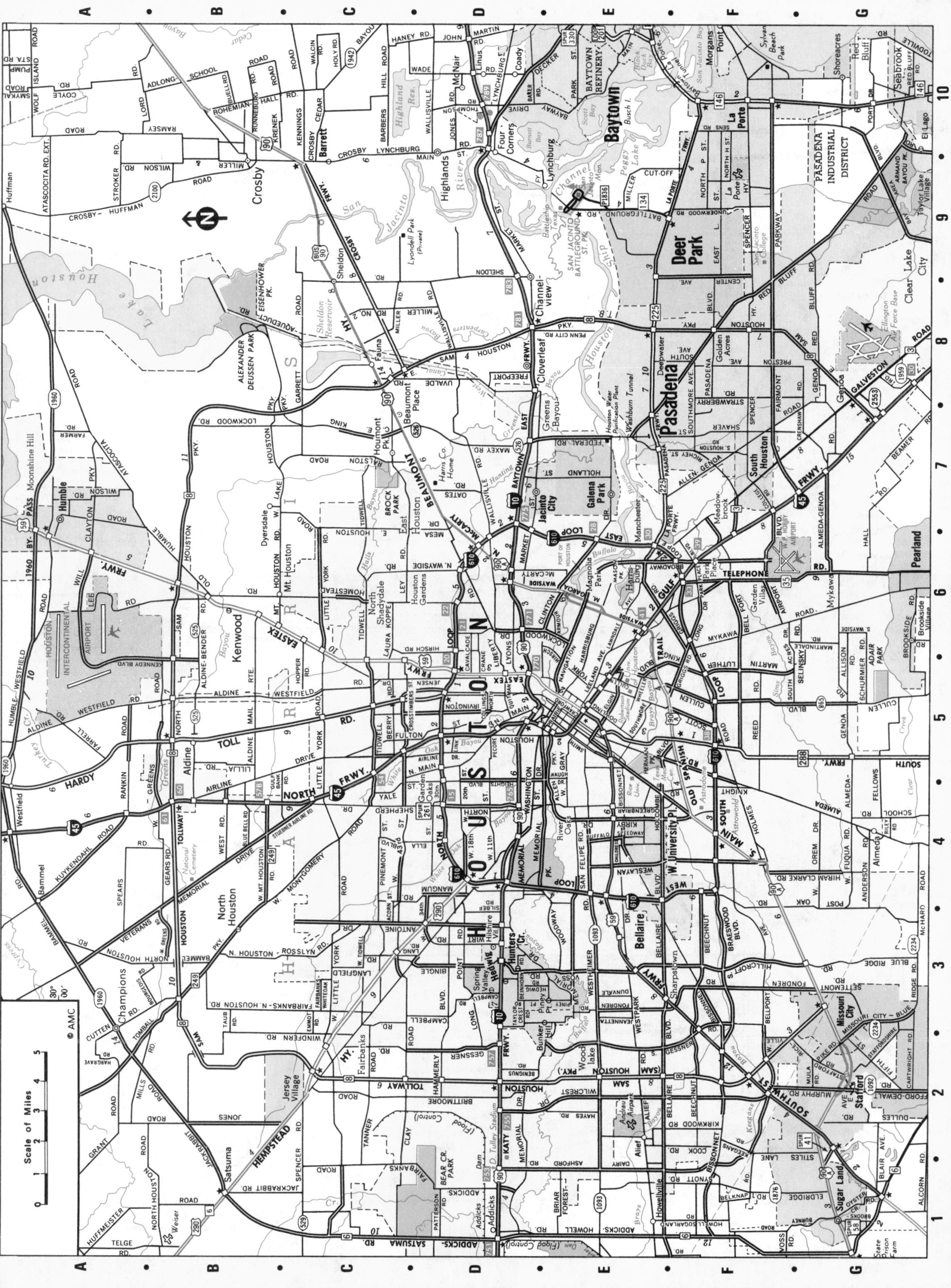

Houston
Baytown
Pasadena
Deer Park
La Porte
Galena Park
Jacinto City
South Houston
Bellaire
Humble
Crosby
Channelview
Highlands
Aldine
Kenwood
North Houston
Jersey Village
Katy
Addicks
Alief
Missouri City
Stafford
Sugar Land
Pearland
Seabrook
Shoreacres
Morgans Point
Clear Lake City
Pasadena Industrial District
Houston Intercontinental Airport
Lake Houston
Scale of Miles
© AMC

1 2 3 4 5 6

Eagle Village
116TH ST.
Carmel
Fishers
Zionville
Metropolitan Airport
Allisonville
Castleton
HAMILTON CO.
MARION CO.
96TH ST.
Sahm Park
82ND ST.
Fairbanks Hosp.
Castleton Square S.C.
86TH ST.
86TH ST.
Nora
Williams Creek
Traders Point
79TH ST.
79TH ST.
Augusta
Meridian Hills
Ravenswood
71ST ST.
71ST ST.
New Augusta
73RD ST.
Shore Acres
65TH ST.
Hillcrest C.C.
Fort Harrison State Park
Eagle Creek Pk.
62ND ST.
62ND ST.
Camp Belzer
North Westway Park
Fox Hill Dr.
North Crows Nest
Glendale S.C.
Washington Park North Cemetery
Highland Country Club
Crows Nest
Kessler Blvd.
56TH ST.
Lawrence Central H.S.
Fort Benjamin Harrison
Indianapolis Colts Training Facility
56TH
Broadmoor Country Club
Highwood
Rocky Ripple
State School For The Deaf
Cathedral H.S.
Eagle Creek Reservoir
Spring Hills
Butler University
State Fairgrounds
Arlington H.S.
Lawrence
Clermont
Eagle Creek Airport
Wynnedale
Woodstock
Crown Hill Cem.
46TH ST.
Pendleton Pike
Indianapolis Country Club
34TH ST.
Marian College
30TH ST.
38TH
34TH
Chrysler Corp.
Speedway H.S.
Coffin G.C.
South Grove Gr. Cr.
30TH
25TH
Indiana St. Police Hqts.
Camp Dellwood
21ST ST.
Indianapolis Motor Speedway
Speedway
16TH ST.
Benjamin Harrison Memorial
21ST
16TH
Warren Park
Tremont
10TH ST.
I.U.P.U.I.
War Memorial
Market Square Arena
10TH
Pleasant Run G.C.
INDIANAPOLIS
ROCKVILLE RD
Thatcher Golf Course
Indiana Univ. Medical Center
State Capitol
White River St. Pk.
New
Michigan
Ford Assembly Plant
Central State Hosp.
Indianapolis Zoo
RCA Dome
Washington
Willard Park
Six Points
Mickeyville
Morris
Nat'l Track & Field Hall Of Fame
Union Station Market Place
Prospect
Raymond Park
Ben Davis
Minnesota
Union Stock Yards
Bridgeport
Indiana Nat'l Guard
Raymond St.
Sarah Shank G.C.
Marion County Fair Grounds
Indianapolis International Airport
Mars Hill
Maywood
St. Francis Hospital
Troy
Five Points
Beech Grove
Hanna
Hanna Ave.
Univ. of Indianapolis
Wanamaker
Decatur Central H.S.
Thompson Rd.
Thompson Rd.
Franklin Central H.S.
Valley Mills
Epler Rd.
Edgewood
Camby
Antrim
Edgewood
Homecroft
West Newton
Southport Rd.
Southport
South Westway Park
STOP 11 RD.
Glenns Valley
Carl Smock Park
MARION COUNTY

Scale of Miles
0 5 1 2 3

© C.S.C.

SCALE IN MILES
1½
0   1.5   3
SCALE IN KILOMETERS
©1999 TRAKKER MAPS, INC.

Thomas Creek

To Waycross

JACKSONVILLE INTERNATIONAL AIRPORT

ARNOLD RD
YELLOW BLUFF RD
NASSAU CO.
DUVAL CO.
Nassau River
Amelia Island
Atlantic Ocean

NEW KINGS RD
LEM TURNER RD
TERRELL RD
PECAN PARK RD
AIRPORT RD
OWENS RD
DUVAL RD
STARRATT RD
DUVAL STATION RD
STARRATT RD
NEW BERLIN RD
CEDAR POINT RD

Broward River
EASTPORT RD
ANNHEUSER BUSCH BREWERY TOUR
JACKSONVILLE ZOO
HECKSCHER DR
Clapboard Cr
Fort George River
FORT GEORGE CULTURAL CENTER
Fort George Inlet

DUNN AV
TROUT RIVER BLVD
SOUTEL DR
MONCRIEF RD
EDGEWOOD AV
MAIN ST N
BROWARD RD
Trout River
St Johns River
Blount Island
Mill Cove
MAYPORT U.S. NAVAL AIR STATION
HANNA STATE PARK

PRITCHARD RD
OLD KINGS RD
CSX
NEW KINGS RD
COMMONWEALTH AV
BEAVER ST
NORMANDY BLVD
HERLONG RD
CASSAT AV
PARK ST
ORTEGA BLVD
ROOSEVELT BLVD
FT CAROLINE
JACKSONVILLE UNIVERSITY
MERRILL RD
ARLINGTON RD
GILMORE HTS RD
MONUMENT RD
MT PLEASANT RD
GRAIG MUNICIPAL AIRPORT
ATLANTIC BLVD
ATLANTIC BEACH
NEPTUNE BEACH

JACKSONVILLE
ALLTEL STADIUM
CONVENTION CENTER
CIVIC AUDITORIUM
MUSEUM OF SCIENCES
St Johns River
Ortega River
EMERSON ST
AUGUSTINE BLVD
UNIVERSITY BLVD
TIMUQUANA RD
WILSON BLVD
FOURAKER RD
RICKER RD
MORSE AV
TOWNSEND RD
JAMMES RD
BLANDING BLVD
PHILLIPS HWY
BAY MEADOWS RD
SUNBEAM RD
ST JOHNS BLUFF RD
BEACH BLVD
SAN PABLO RD
JACKSONVILLE BEACH
J. TURNER BUTLER BLVD
SOUTHSIDE BLVD

JACKSONVILLE NAVAL AIR STATION
BUCKMAN BRIDGE

DUVAL COUNTY / CLAY COUNTY
DUVAL COUNTY / ST JOHNS COUNTY

To Tallahassee
To Gainesville
OLD ST AUGUSTINE RD

Route numbers: 115, 95, 9, 17, 5, 104, 106, 1, 117, 23, 115A, 103, 111, 15, 21D, 21B, 129, 8, 10, 228, 211, 208, 21, 295, 9A, 13, 163, 105, 9A, 295, A1A, 109, 90, 212, 202, 152, 228

N

Mosby

Scale of Miles

© C.S.C.

James A. Reed

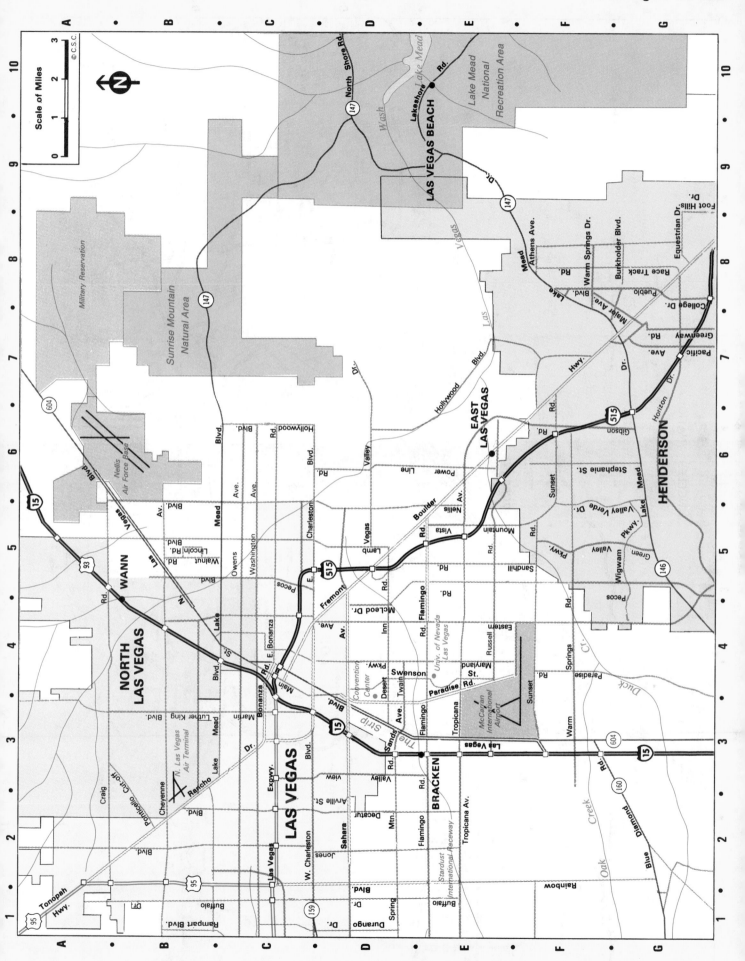

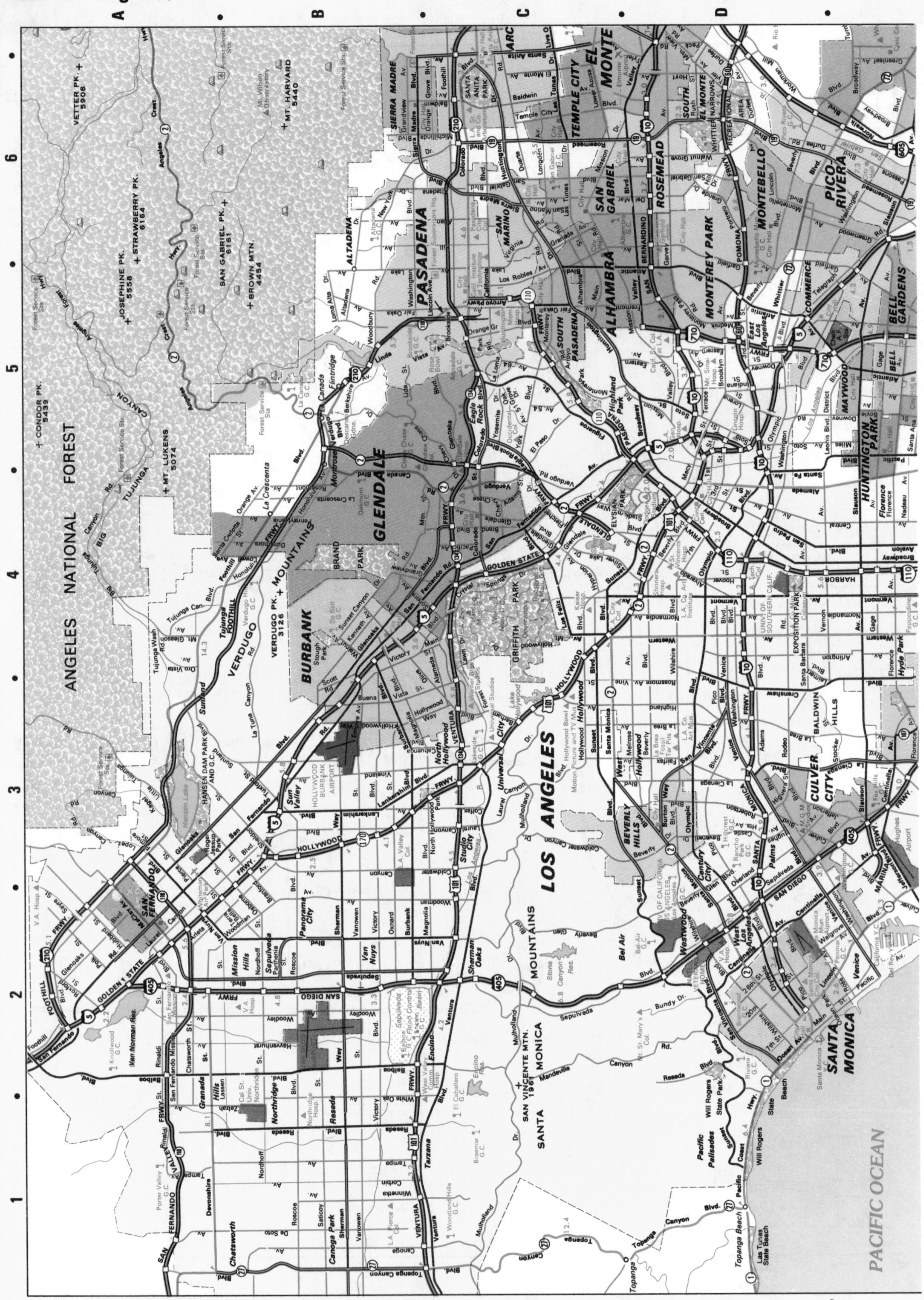
ANGELES NATIONAL FOREST
VERDUGO MOUNTAINS
SANTA MONICA MOUNTAINS
PACIFIC OCEAN
LOS ANGELES
PASADENA
GLENDALE
BURBANK
ALHAMBRA
SAN GABRIEL
ROSEMEAD
TEMPLE CITY
EL MONTE
SOUTH EL MONTE
MONTEREY PARK
MONTEBELLO
PICO RIVERA
COMMERCE
BELL GARDENS
BELL
MAYWOOD
HUNTINGTON PARK
EAST LOS ANGELES
SOUTH PASADENA
SAN MARINO
ALTADENA
SIERRA MADRE
ARCADIA
SAN FERNANDO
BEVERLY HILLS
WEST HOLLYWOOD
CULVER CITY
SANTA MONICA
Venice
Pacific Palisades
Topanga
La Crescenta
Canoga Park
Chatsworth
Northridge
Granada Hills
Mission Hills
Sepulveda
Panorama City
Van Nuys
Sherman Oaks
Studio City
North Hollywood
Sun Valley
Sunland
Tujunga
Tarzana
Encino
Reseda
Highland Park
Eagle Rock
Bel Air
Westwood
Century City
Hollywood
Baldwin Hills
GRIFFITH PARK
ELYSIAN PARK
BRAND PARK
HOLLYWOOD BURBANK AIRPORT
MT. LUKENS 5074
CONDOR PK. 5439
JOSEPHINE PK. 5558
STRAWBERRY PK. 6164
SAN GABRIEL PK. 6161
BROWN MTN. 4454
MT. HARVARD 5440
VETTER PK. 5906
VERDUGO PK. 3126
SAN VICENTE MTN. 1961
A
B
C
D
1
2
3
4
5
6

Scale of Miles
INGLEWOOD
HAWTHORNE
LAWNDALE
GARDENA
TORRANCE
COMPTON
CARSON
LYNWOOD
SOUTH GATE
HUNTINGTON PARK
MAYWOOD
BELL
BELL GARDENS
CUDAHY
DOWNEY
NORWALK
BELLFLOWER
PARAMOUNT
LAKEWOOD
LONG BEACH
SIGNAL HILL
ARTESIA
CYPRESS
SEAL BEACH
LOMITA
EL SEGUNDO
MANHATTAN BEACH
HERMOSA BEACH
REDONDO BEACH
PALOS VERDES ESTATES
ROLLING HILLS
MARINA DEL REY
Venice
San Pedro
TERMINAL ISLAND
U.S. NAVAL WEAPONS STATION
LOS ALAMITOS NAVAL AIR STATION
PT. FERMIN
PT. VINCENTE
PALOS VERDES PT.
FLATROCK PT.
LONG PT.

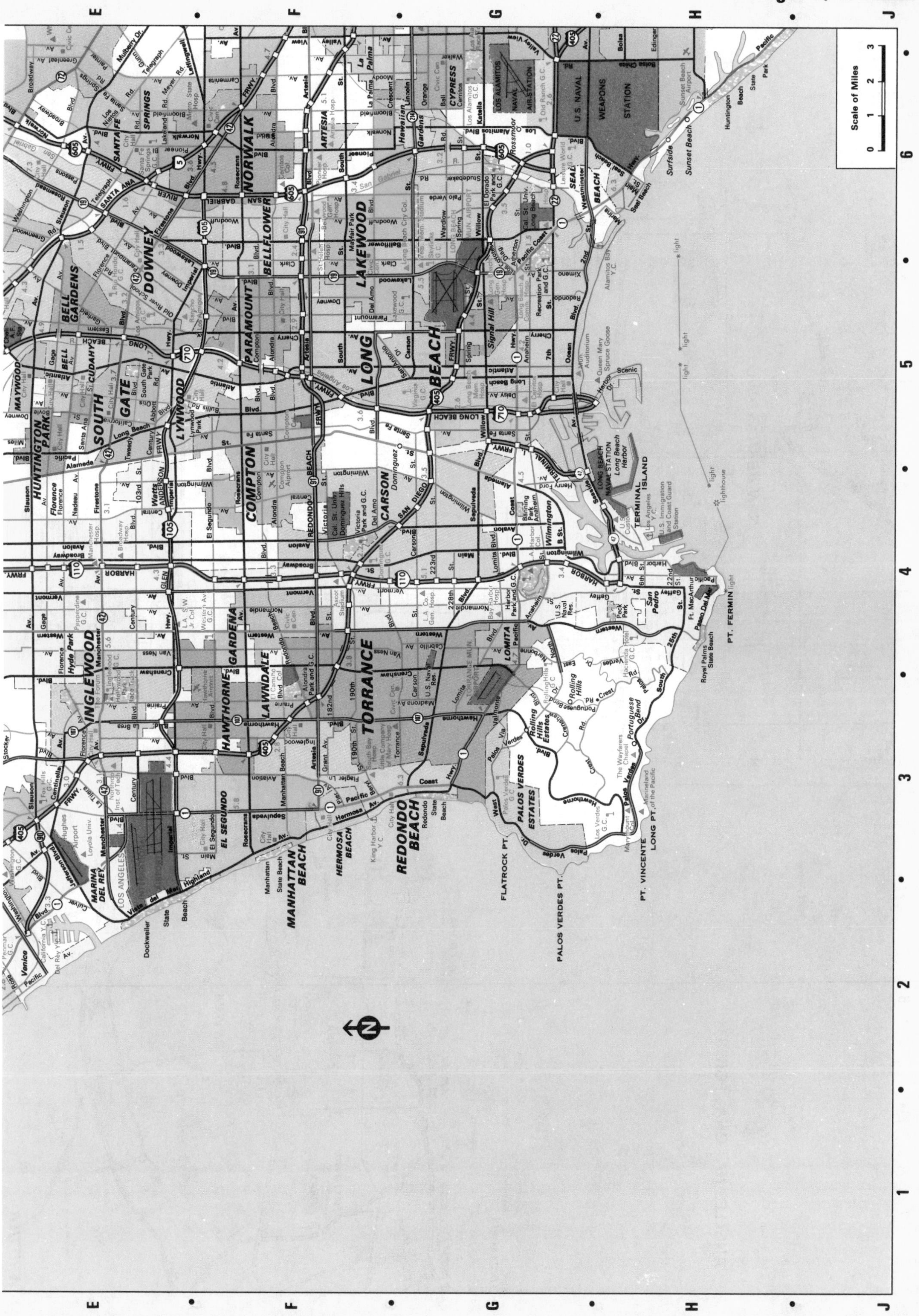

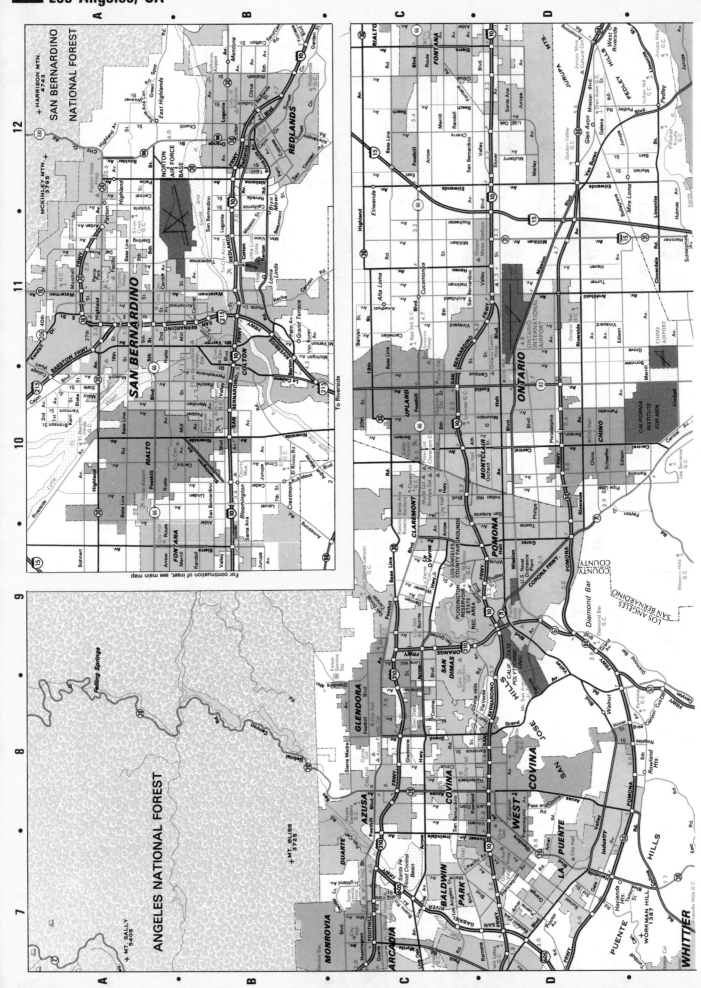

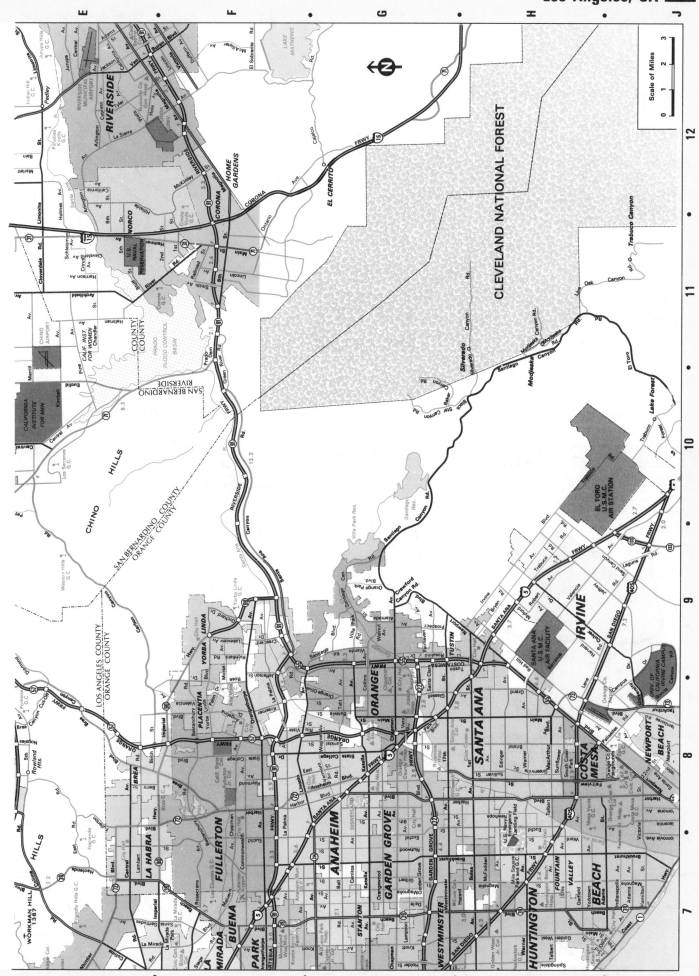

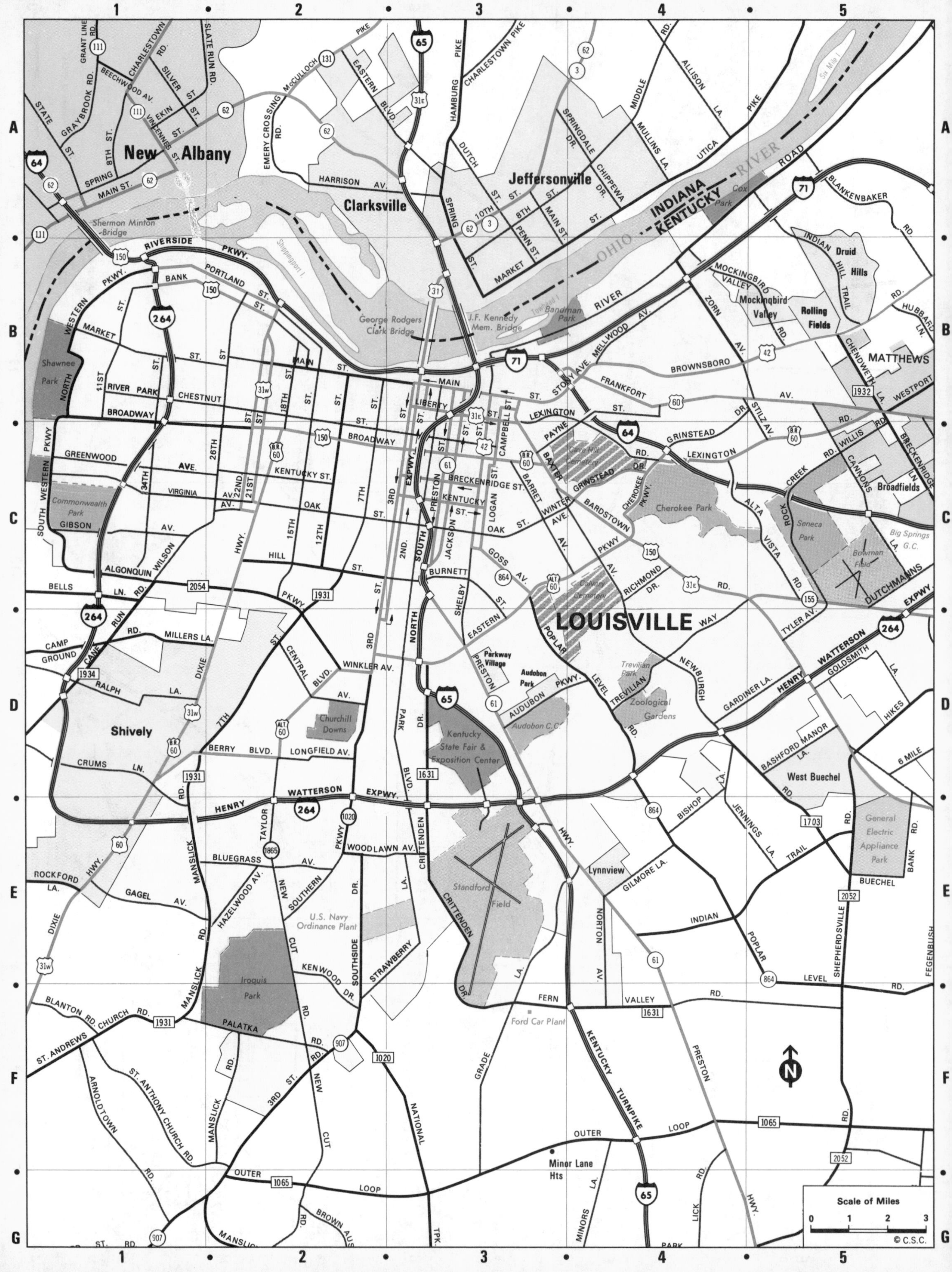

1
2
3
4
5
A
B
C
D
E
F
G
New Albany
Clarksville
Jeffersonville
LOUISVILLE
Shively
MATTHEWS
Lynnview
Minor Lane Hts
West Buechel
Broadfields
Druid Hills
Mockingbird Valley
Rolling Fields
INDIANA
KENTUCKY
OHIO
RIVER
Shermon Minton Bridge
George Rodgers Clark Bridge
J.F. Kennedy Mem. Bridge
Shippingport I.
Towhead I.
Six Mile I.
Shawnee Park
Commonwealth Park
Bandman Park
Cox Park
Cave Hill Cemetery
Cherokee Park
Seneca Park
Big Springs G.C.
Bowman Field
Calvary Cemetery
Trevilian Park
Zoological Gardens
Parkway Village
Audobon Park
Audobon C.C.
Churchill Downs
Kentucky State Fair & Exposition Center
Standford Field
U.S. Navy Ordinance Plant
Iroquis Park
Ford Car Plant
General Electric Appliance Park
RIVERSIDE PKWY.
WATTERSON EXPWY.
HENRY WATTERSON EXPWY.
KENTUCKY TURNPIKE
OUTER LOOP
PRESTON HWY.
DIXIE HWY.
NORTH SOUTH EXPWY.
BROADWAY
MAIN
MARKET
CHESTNUT
LEXINGTON
FRANKFORT AV.
BROWNSBORO
MELLWOOD AV.
BARDSTOWN
POPLAR LEVEL RD.
TAYLOR BLVD.
NEW CUT RD.
BERRY BLVD.
ALGONQUIN PKWY.
BELLS LN.
BLANKENBAKER
SHELBYVILLE
Scale of Miles
0
1
2
3
© C.S.C.

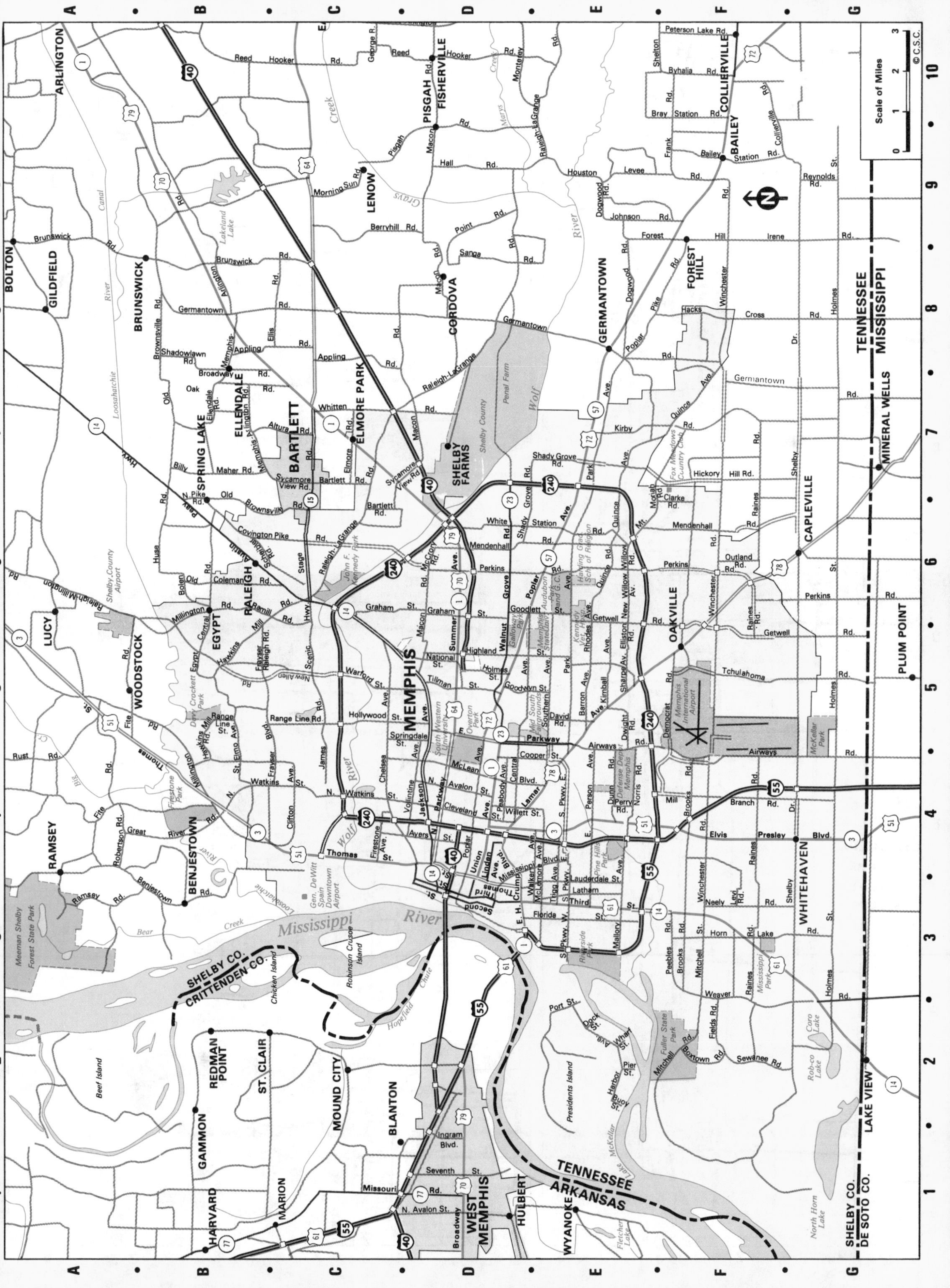

Scale of Miles
0 1 2 3
© C.S.C.

ARLINGTON
BOLTON
GILDFIELD
BRUNSWICK
PISGAH
FISHERVILLE
LENOW
COLLIERVILLE
BAILEY
TENNESSEE
MISSISSIPPI
MINERAL WELLS
CAPLEVILLE
CORDOVA
ELMORE PARK
GERMANTOWN
FOREST HILL
SHELBY FARMS
SPRING LAKE
BARTLETT
ELLENDALE
RALEIGH
EGYPT
WOODSTOCK
LUCY
RAMSEY
BENJESTOWN
MEMPHIS
PLUM POINT
OAKVILLE
WHITEHAVEN
Mississippi River
Wolf River
Loosahatchie River
Meeman Shelby Forest State Park
Beef Island
Chicken Island
Robinson Crusoe Island
Hopefield Chute
SHELBY CO.
CRITTENDEN CO.
REDMAN POINT
ST. CLAIR
MOUND CITY
BLANTON
GAMMON
HARVARD
MARION
WEST MEMPHIS
HULBERT
WYANOKE
TENNESSEE
ARKANSAS
SHELBY CO.
DE SOTO CO.
LAKE VIEW
Presidents Island
McKellar Lake
Memphis International Airport
Gen. DeWitt Spain Downtown Airport
Shelby County Airport

Map continues on this page G-2

Scale of Miles
0 1 2 3
©TRAKKER MAPS INC.

Map continues on this page A-5

MEEKER
GERMANTOWN
COLGATE
Donges Bay Rd.
MEQUON
32
43
W
175
41
45
Appleton
WASHINGTON CO.
WAUKESHA CO.
145
Granville
Swan
County Line
OZAUKEE CO.
MILWAUKEE CO.
181
BROWN DEER
RIVER HILLS
BAYSIDE
Rd.
Schlitz Audubon Ctr.

MENOMONEE FALLS
Plainview Rd.
Menomonee
Menominee Co. Park & G.C.
Main St.
100
Dretzka Park & G.C.
Brown Deer
Bradley
100
W
Dean
Rd.
FOX POINT

74
Good Hope Rd.
LANNON
YY
WW
Rd.
91st
145
175
Good Hope
PP
80th
G D
Brown Deer Park
100
32
GLENDALE

SUSSEX
74
J
W. Mill
Silver Spring
VV
Marcy
Pilgrim
Lilly
Rd.
Mill
45
Fond Du Lac
Silver Spring
E
Villard
64th
43rd
S
Hopkins
Teutonia
Bender Rd.
57
Green Bay
Port Washington Rd.
Lake
WHITEFISH BAY

164
K
Town Line
Lannon
Lisbon
K Rd.
KK
BUTLER
Hampton
41
Appleton
Villard
EE
Hopkins
20th
57
SHOREWOOD
190

PEWAUKEE
190
SS
Capitol
Rd.
Capitol
190
100
181
145
Keefe Av.
Edgewood
University of Wisconsin (Milwaukee)
Burleigh St.
Lake Park
190

DUPLAINVILLE
Burleigh
BROOKFIELD
KX
Brookfield City Park
45
Mayfair
92nd
76th
North
Burleigh
60th
Sherman
57
Humboldt
Oakland
McKinley Park
43rd

16
94
Wisconsin River
164
Springdale
M
Gebhardt
North
ELM GROVE
Watertown Plank
Milwaukee Co. Inst.
Milwaukee County Zoo
Vliet
35th
MILWAUKEE
Highland Dr.
City Hall

WAUWATOSA
18
Wisconsin
Blue Mound
Menomonie
Wells
94
Wells St.
Water St.
Marquette Univ.
794

WAUKESHA
18
59
D
Greenfield
East-West
100
Freeway
State Fair Park
Milwaukee County Stadium
41
Greenfield
16th
6th
38
Lake Michigan

NEW BERLIN
Lincoln
Cleveland
Johnsohn Rd.
Racine
D
894
59
Greenfield G.C. Greenfield Park
National
WEST ALLIS
Lincoln
Oklahoma
Jackson Park
Layton
43
SAINT FRANCIS

51
Coffee
Y
FF
KX
Rd.
Calhoun
Moorland
Sunny Slope
T
Zoo
Beloit
N
181
Oklahoma
24
41
NN
Morgan
Holt
43
Morgan
62
32
CUDAHY

XX
Lawnsdale
164
I
Rd.
Moorland
O
45
92nd
84th
Airport
Howard
60th
43rd
894
13th
94
Chase
Whitnell
Sheridan Park

43
Vernon
Glengary
HHH
HI
Small
124th
43
Layton
GREENFIELD
36
General Mitchell International Airport
119
Grant Park

MUSKEGO
College
HH
Corners
North Cape Rd.
100
Grange
HALES CORNERS
GREENDALE
Root River Pkwy.
Whitnall Park
Grobschmidt Park
College
77
Packard

Little Muskego Lake
W. Janesville
OO
St. Martin's Rd.
45
Edgerton
36
Loomis
BB
Rawson
41
119
Howell
SOUTH MILWAUKEE

BIG BEND
Muskego Co. Park
Big Muskego Lake
Durham Dr.
100th St.
U
Drexel
38
100
Chicago

Crowbar
Hillendale
Woods
36
76th
51st
27th
Puetz
V
OAK CREEK
Nicholson
5th

VERNON
43
F
Muskego Lakes G.C.
Ryan
FRANKLIN
100
Rainbow Airport
Oakwood G.C.
Bender Park

24
164
Y
Oakwood
OO
WAUSHEKA CO.
RACINE CO.
County Line
MILWAUKEE CO.
RACINE CO.
J

TICHIGAN
Kee Nong Go Mong Lake
36
UNION CHURCH
Seven Mile
60th
13th
CADDY VISTA
Foley

Wind Lake
KNEELAND
Six Mile
G
V
Six Mile
Nicholson
HUSHER
G

BUENA PARK
Waubeesee Lake
Tichigan Lake
Six Mile
Five and a Half Mile
RAYMOND
94
CALEDONIA
38
TABOR

36
Five Mile
OO
NORTH CAPE
51st
41
THOMPSONVILLE
Pennsylvania
Chicago

Scale of Miles
0 1 2 3

© C.S.C.

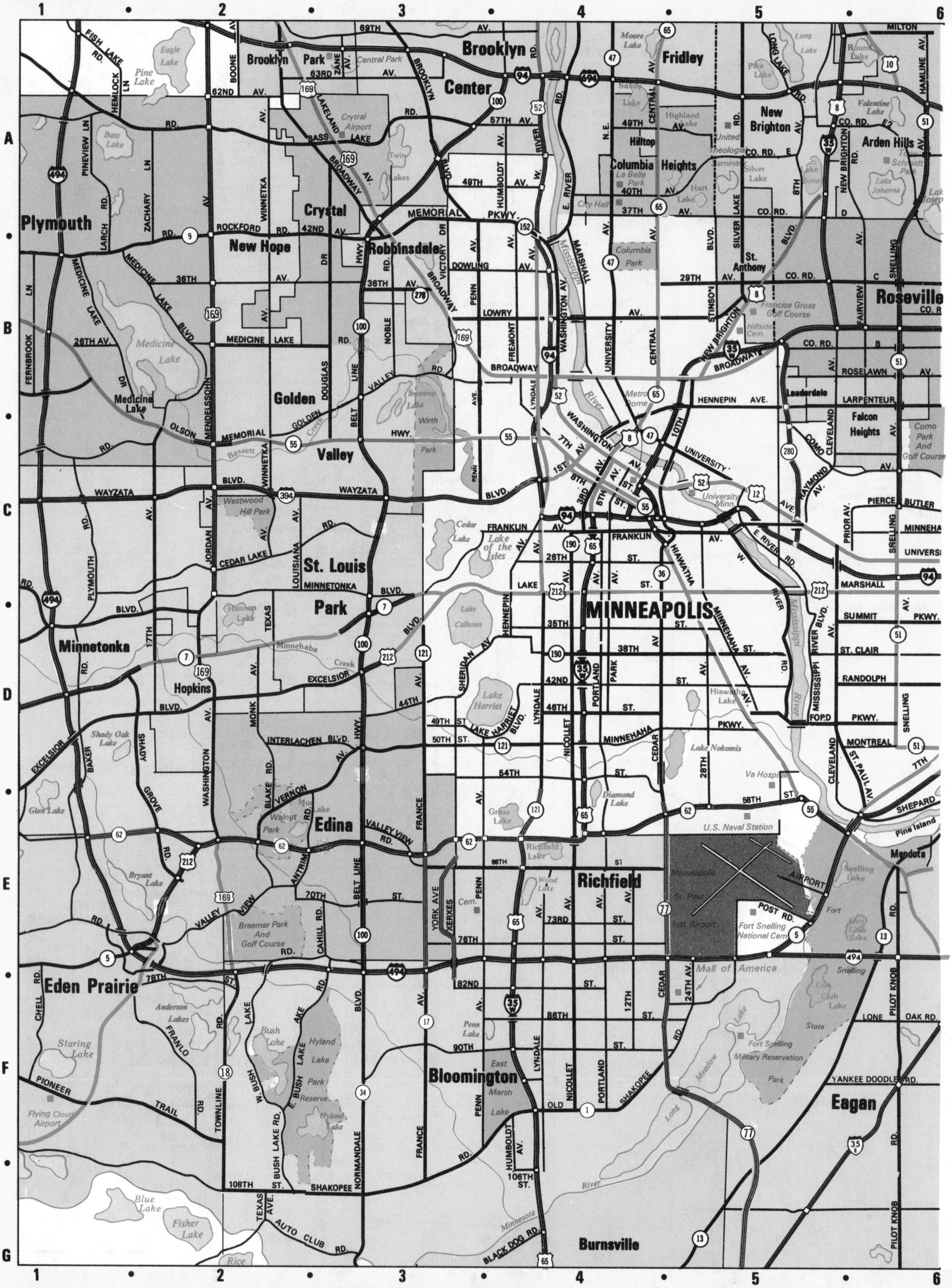

Plymouth

Brooklyn Park

Brooklyn Center

Fridley

New Brighton

Arden Hills

Crystal

New Hope

Robbinsdale

Columbia Heights

Hilltop

St. Anthony

Roseville

Golden Valley

Lauderdale

Falcon Heights

Minnetonka

St. Louis Park

MINNEAPOLIS

Hopkins

Edina

Richfield

Eden Prairie

Bloomington

Eagan

Burnsville

Mendota

Mall of America

U.S. Naval Station

Minneapolis St. Paul Int'l Airport

Fort Snelling National Cem.

Fort Snelling State Park

Fort Snelling Military Reservation

Snail Lake

Shoreview

Vadnais Heights

White Bear Lake

Mahtomedi

Birchwood

Gem Lake

Willernie

White Bear Lake

Pine Springs

DELLWOOD RD.

75TH ST.

KEATS AVE.

MANNING AVE.

Lake Owasso

Lake Vadnais

LITTLE CANADA

Little Canada

Kohlman Lake

Gervais Lake

North St. Paul

Lake De Montreville

Lake Jane

JANE RD.

ELMO AVE.

40TH ST. N.

Maplewood

Silver Lake

Sunfish Lake

30TH ST. N.

Roselawn

Roseland Cem.

Larpenteur

FROST AVE.

Larpenteur

Lake Elmo

Eagle Point Lake

Lake Elmo

10TH ST.

Elmhurst Cem.

ARLINGTON

Como Park Golf Course

Lake Como

Cem.

Phalen Park Golf Course

Lake Phalen

PROSPERITY

Oakdale

HARVESTER AVE.

Eagle Point RD.

MARYLAND AVE.

Maryland

ST. PAUL

Beaver Lake

Minnehaha

Union Cem.

Minnehaha

PIERCE BUTLER RTE.

Calvary Cem.

Oakland Cem.

Ramsey Hosp.

State Off. Bldg.

MINNEHAHA

UNIVERSITY

Concordia Col.

DAYTON AVE.

SUMMIT AVE.

Landfall

HUDSON RD.

BROOKVIEW

Markgrafs Lake

Civic Center

St. Paul Downtown Airport (Holman Field)

Mississippi River

WARNER

BURNS AVE.

UPPER AFTON

LOWER AFTON

Battle Creek Lake

Powers Lake

RADIO DR.

ST. JOHNS DR.

LOWER AFTON RD.

Afton

Lilydale

Highland Park Golf Course

BUTLER AVE.

West St. Paul

South St. Paul

Pigs Eye Lake

LINWOOD AVE.

HIGHWOOD AVE.

CARVER AVE.

STEEPLE VIEW RD.

VALLEY CREEK

Colby Lake

WOODBURY DR.

Woodbury

40TH ST. S.

Mendota

Mendota Heights

Sunfish Lake

Resurrection Cem.

Rogers Lake

THOMPSON AVE.

ANNAPOLIS

CHARLTON

WENTWORTH

SOUTHVIEW BLVD.

Newport

MILITARY RD.

TOWER DR.

DALE RD.

RADIO DR.

KEATS AVE.

COTTAGE GROVE DR.

MANNING AVE.

GLEN RD.

WOODLANE DR.

65TH ST.

70TH

LONE OAK RD.

YANKEE DOODLE RD.

70TH ST.

Inver Grove

So. St. Paul Municipal Airport

66TH ST.

St. Paul Park

70TH ST.

Cottage Grove

80TH ST.

MILITARY RD.

Heights

80TH ST.

COLLEGE TR.

CUNEEN TR.

INVER GROVE TR.

HASTINGS AVE.

HADLEY AVE.

JAMAICA AVE.

100TH ST. S.

DIFFLEY RD.

105TH ST.

N

Scale of Miles
0 1 2

©C.S.C.

A B C D E F G

Benders Ferry Rd.
Cedar Creek
Curd Rd.
Railroad Rd.
Lebanon Rd.
South Mt. Juliet Rd.
Jones Mill Park
Bryant Grove Park
Poole Knobs Park

AVONDALE
SAUNDERSVILLE
HENDERSONVILLE
GREEN HILL
MOUNT JULIET
SEVEN POINTS
LA VERGNE
RUTHERFORD CO.

Old Hickory Lake
Sandersville Rd.
Gallatin Pike
WILSON DAVIDSON
HERMITAGE HILLS
HOPEWELL
LAKEWOOD
CO. CO.
Hope Rd.
New
Central Pike
Union Pike
Earhart Rd.
Granny Wright Park
Vincent Creek Park
Stewarts Creek Park
SMITH SPRINGS
RURAL HILL
FOSTER CORNERS
Couchville Pike
Lavergne-Couchville Pk.
Church Rd.
Smith Springs Rd.
KIMBRO
Hickory Blvd.
Old

SUMNER CO. DAVIDSON CO.
RAYON CITY
OLD HICKORY
Robinson Rd.
Bend
E. N. Peeler Park
Stones River
Stewarts Ferry Pike
DONELSON
Elm Hill Park
Cook Park
Hamilton Creek Park
Anderson Rd. Park
McCrory Ln.
Donelson Pike
ANTIOCH
UNA
BROOKLIN
Franklin Rd.
View
Bell Rd.
Cane Ridge Rd.
Old
WRENCOE

Cinder Rd.
Rio Vista Dr.
31E
Neelans Lane
Briley Parkway
Pennington Bend Rd.
Two Rivers Park
Opryland
Fort Negley
Rosebank Ave.
NASHVILLE
Washington Municipal Airport
Massman Dr.
155
Middle Tennessee Mental Health Institute
PARAGON MILL
PROVIDENCE
Haywood Lane
TUSCULUM
BEACON
OGLESBY
41A
31A
11

GOODLETTSVILLE
65
11
UNION HILL
LICKTON
MADISON
INGLEWOOD
Ellington Pkwy
Greenland Ave.
McGavock Pike
Eastland
S. 10th St.
Lebanon Pike
BERRY HILL
OAK HILL
Harding Pl.
McCall St.
Thompson Lane
Nolensville Pike
65
BRENTWOOD
31
6

Hitt Lane
Little Creek
Due W.
Dickerson Pike
Douglas Ave.
Cleveland St.
2nd Ave. S.
Polk Ave.
Battery Lane
Governors Manbook
Franklin Rd.
Otter Creek Rd.
FOREST HILLS

WHITES CREEK
Whites Creek Pike
Buena Vista Pike
3rd Ave. North
8th Ave. North
Trinity Lane
Ben Allen Rd.
East Trinity Lane
American Baptist Theological
265
440
24
BELLE MEADE
WEST MEADE
Estes Rd.
Harding Rd.
Hillsboro Rd.
WILLIAMSON
DAVIDSON CO.

JOELTON
GERMANTOWN
65
431
112
Clarksville Pike
Hickory
Hydes Ferry Pike
Eaton Creek Rd.
Tennessee State Penitentiary
Centennial
Cockrill Bend Institutional Farm
Bordeaux Hospital
County
51st Ave. North
28th Ave. North
RICHLAND
Charlotte Ave.
West End Ave.
Murphy Rd.
Woodlawn
Harding
Old Hickory Blvd.
VAUGHANS GAP
PASQUO
Hillsboro Rd.
Old Hickory Blvd.
Hicks Rd.
BELLEVUE
106

MOUNT ZION
24
MARROWBONE
12
Charlotte Pike
River Rd.
Old Charlotte Pike
GOWER
Old Hickory Blvd.
Brook Hollow Rd.
Old Harding Rd.
Brown Rd.
40
70
24
CHEATHAM CO. DAVIDSON CO.

N

Scale of Miles
0 1 2 3
© C.S.C.

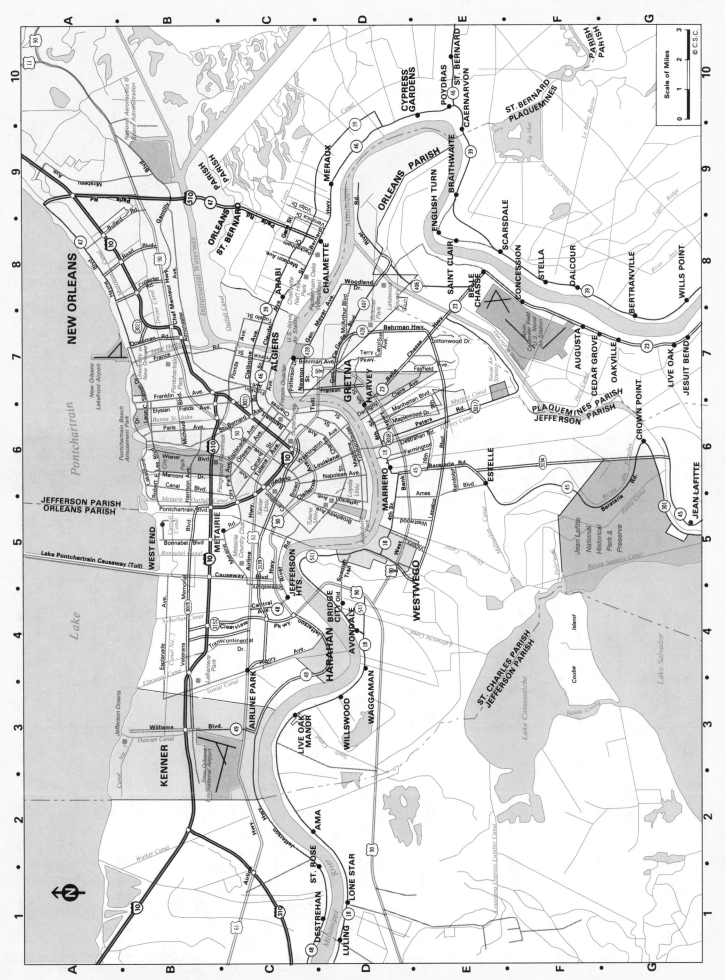

A
B
C
D
E
F
G
H
1
2
3
4
5
6
7
8
9
10
CHAPPAQUA
PLEASANTVILLE
THORNWOOD
HAWTHORNE
MT. PLEASANT
VALHALLA
ELMSFORD
WHITE PLAINS
SCARSDALE
EASTCHESTER
NEW ROCHELLE
LARCHMONT
PELHAM
PELHAM MANOR
MOUNT VERNON
BRONX
WESTCHESTER CO.
BRONX CO.
GREENBURGH
ARDSLEY
IRVINGTON
DOBBS FERRY
HASTINGS-ON HUDSON
YONKERS
BRIARCLIFF MANOR
POCANTICO HILL
OSSINING
ARCHVILLE
N. TARRYTOWN
TARRYTOWN
Hudson
River
Tappan Zee
UPPER NYACK
NYACK
S. NYACK
GRANDVIEW-ON HUDSON
PIERMONT
SPARKILL
PALISADES
NEW YORK
NEW JERSEY
ALPINE
ROCKLEIGH
NORTHVALE
NORWOOD
CLOSTER
DEMAREST
CRESSKILL
TENAFLY
ENGLEWOOD CLIFFS
ENGLEWOOD
FORT LEE
RIVERDALE
VALLEY COTTAGE
CENTRAL NYACK
BLAUVELT
ORANGEBURG
ORANGETOWN
TAPPAN
OLD TAPPAN
HARRINGTON PK.
HAWORTH
DUMONT
BERGENFIELD
TEANECK
LEONIA
PALISADES PK.
BOGOTA
RIDGEFIELD
LITTLE FERRY
HACKENSACK
CLARKSTOWN
BARDONIA
SICKLETOWN
NEW HEMPSTEAD
HILLCREST
SPRING VALLEY
MT. IVY
PEARL RIVER
MONTVALE
RIVER VALE
WESTWOOD
EMERSON
ORADELL
NEW MILFORD
RIVER EDGE
PARK RIDGE
WOODCLIFF LAKE
HILLSDALE
WASHINGTON TWP.
PARAMUS
ROCHELLE PK.
MAYWOOD
SADDLE BROOK
LODI
HASBROUCK HTS.
TETERBORO
MOONACHIE
WOOD RIDGE
WALLINGTON
GARFIELD
PASSAIC
CLIFTON
WESLEY HILLS
MONSEY
VIOLA
LADENTOWN
UPPER SADDLE RIVER
SADDLE RIVER
ROCKLAND CO.
BERGEN CO.
TALLMAN
AIRMONT
HO-HO-KUS
RIDGEWOOD
GLEN ROCK
FAIR LAWN
ELMWOOD PARK
SUFFERN
MAHWAH
ALLENDALE
RAMSEY
WALDWICK
MIDLAND PARK
HAWTHORNE
PATERSON
PROSPECT PK.
HALEDON
NORTH HALEDON
WYCKOFF
FRANKLIN LAKES
WAYNE TWP.
WAYNE
BORO OF TOTOWA
WEST PATERSON
LITTLE FALLS
LITTLE FALLS TWP.
CEDAR GROVE
ESSEX
NORTH CALDWELL
FAIRFIELD
WEST CALDWELL
SLOATSBURG
RAMAPO
HILLBURN
TUXEDO PARK
ORANGE CO.
PASSAIC CO.
RINGWOOD
ERSKINE
HEWITT
BORO OF RINGWOOD
BORO OF WANAQUE
OAKLAND
POMPTON LAKES
BORO OF BLOOMINGDALE
RIVERDALE
PEQUANNOCK
LINCOLN PARK
Harriman State Park
Wanaque Res.
Greenwood Lake Airport
Essex Co. Airport
Taconic State Pkwy.
Tappan Zee Bridge
George Washington Bridge

Scale of Miles
0 1 2 3
10
© C.S.C.

NASSAU CO.

Kings Point
Great Neck Est
Saddle Rock
Bayside
Clearview
Throgs Neck Bridge
Bronx Whitestone Bridge
College Point
Flushing
QUEENS
Queens Village
Springfield Gdns
Jamaica
Rosedale
Inwood
J. F. Kennedy International Airport
Gateway National Recreational Area
Silver Point Park

BRONX
N.Y. CO.
Astoria
Jackson Hts
Long Island City
Maspeth
Forest Hills
Richmond Hill
Ozone Park
Woodhaven
Canarsie
Jamaica Bay
Floyd Bennett Field
U.S. Navy Res.
Fort Tilden
Neponsit
Rockaway Pt.

MANHATTAN
Weehawken
Green Point
BROOKLYN
Flatbush
E. New York
Benson Hurst
Coney Island
New York Aquarium
Marine Parkway Bridge (Toll)
Rockaway Beach

EDGE WATER
Cliffside
Fairview
North Bergen
West New York
Guttenberg
Union City
Hoboken
Jersey City
Bay Ridge
NEW YORK
Verrazano Narrows Bridge
STATEN ISLAND
New Brighton
Castleton Corners
Dongan Hills
New Dorp
New Dorp Beach

Atlantic Ocean

RIDGEFIELD
Fairview
Ridgefield Pk.
North Arlington
Secaucus
Lincoln Tunnel
Holland Tunnel
Liberty State Park
Ellis Is.
Statue of Liberty National Monument
Upper New York Bay
KINGS CO.
RICHMOND CO.
Willow Brook
College of Staten Island
La Tourette Pk.

MOONACHIE
CARLSTADT
EAST RUTHERFORD
RUTHERFORD
LYNDHURST
KEARNY
E. NEWARK
HARRISON
NEWARK
Newark International Airport
ELIZABETH
NEW JERSEY / NEW YORK
PORT RICHMOND
CHELSEA
GREAT KILLS
HUGUENOT
HUGUENOT BEACH

NUTLEY
BELLEVILLE
North Arlington
Irvington
HILLSIDE TWP.
Borough of Roselle
Roselle Park
LINDEN
CARTERET
PORT READING
ROSSVILLE
MIDDLESEX CO.
RICHMOND CO.
PERTH AMBOY

VERONA
GLEN RIDGE
MONTCLAIR
BLOOMFIELD
WEST ORANGE
ORANGE
EAST ORANGE
MAPLEWOOD TWP.
MILBURN
SPRINGFIELD TWP.
ESSEX CO.
UNION CO.
UNION TWP.
BORO OF KENILWORTH
BORO OF GARWOOD
CRANFORD TWP.
WESTFIELD
CLARK TWP.
RAHWAY
SEWAREN
AVENEL
WOODBRIDGE
COLONIA
ISELIN
FORDS

LIVINGSTON TWP.
ROSELAND

Arthur Kill
Raritan River
Hudson River
East River
Harlem River
Newark Bay
Kill Van Kull

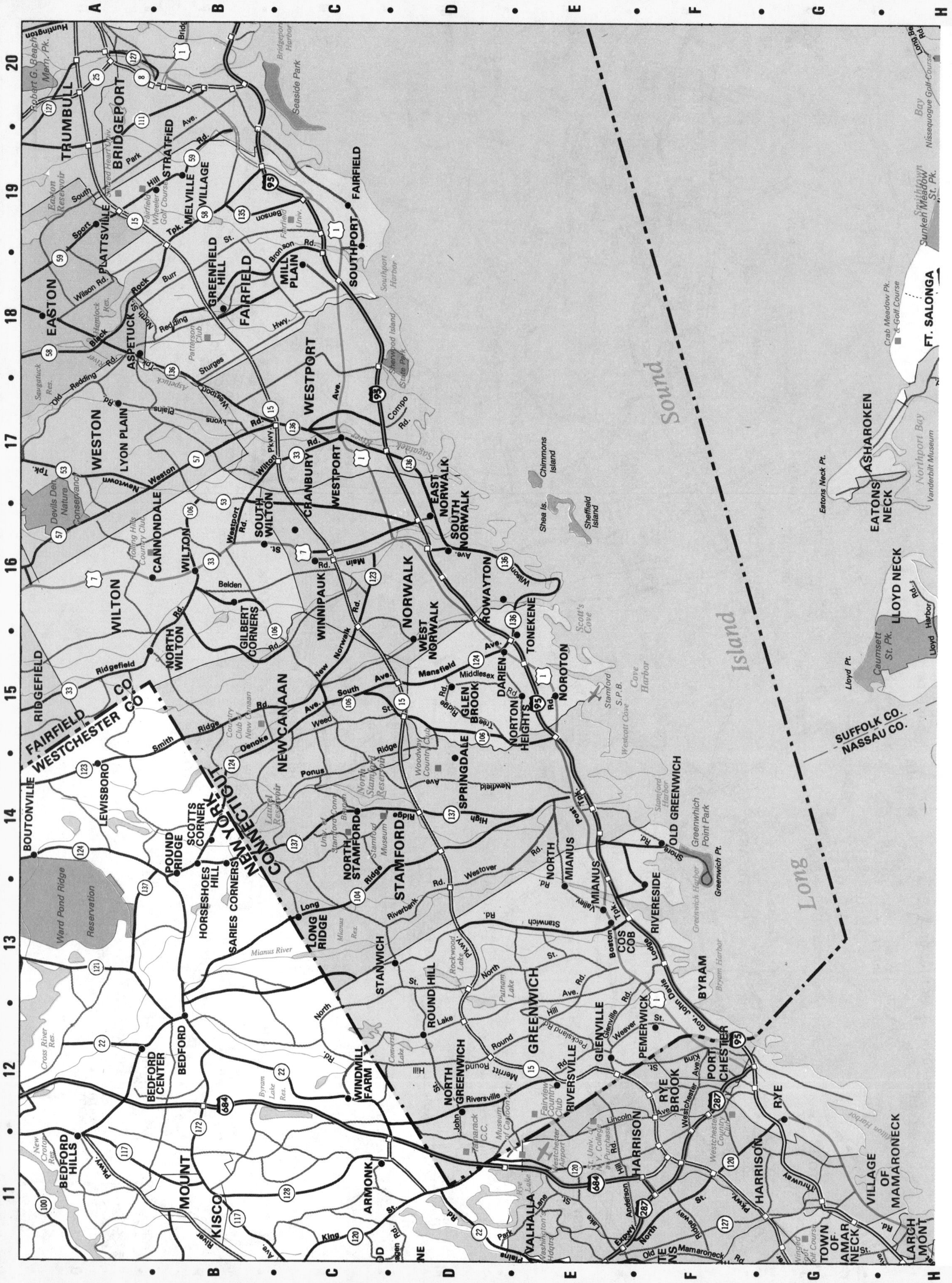
TRUMBULL
BRIDGEPORT
STRATFIED
FAIRFIELD
SOUTHPORT
EASTON
PLATTSVILLE
MELVILLE VILLAGE
GREENFIELD HILL
MILL PLAIN
ASPETUCK
WESTON
LYON PLAIN
WESTPORT
CRANBURY
SOUTH WILTON
CANNONDALE
WILTON
NORTH WILTON
GILBERT CORNERS
WINNIPAUK
EAST NORWALK
SOUTH NORWALK
NORWALK
WEST NORWALK
ROWAYTON
TONEKENE
DARIEN
NOROTON
NORTON HEIGHTS
GLEN BROOK
SPRINGDALE
RIDGEFIELD
FAIRFIELD CO.
WESTCHESTER CO.
NEW CANAAN
BOUTONVILLE
LEWISBORO
POUND RIDGE
SCOTTS CORNER
HORSESHOES HILL
SARIES CORNERS
NEW YORK
CONNECTICUT
NORTH STAMFORD
STAMFORD
OLD GREENWICH
NORTH MIANUS
MIANUS
RIVERESIDE
COS COB
LONG RIDGE
STANWICH
ROUND HILL
GREENWICH
BYRAM
GLENVILLE
PEMERWICK
PORT CHESTER
NORTH GREENWICH
RIVERSVILLE
RYE BROOK
WINDMILL FARM
BEDFORD CENTER
BEDFORD
BEDFORD HILLS
MOUNT KISCO
ARMONK
HARRISON
RYE
VALHALLA
VILLAGE OF MAMARONECK
TOWN OF MAMARONECK
LARCHMONT
Ward Pond Ridge Reservation
Long Island Sound
Chimmons Island
Sheffield Island
Shea Is.
SUFFOLK CO.
NASSAU CO.
FT. SALONGA
ASHAROKEN
EATONS NECK
LLOYD NECK
Caumsett St. Pk.
Seaside Park

POQUOSON

NEWPORT NEWS

HAMPTON

NASA

LANGLEY AIR FORCE BASE

Plum Tree Island Wildlife Refuge

Plumtree Point

Grandview Park

CHESAPEAKE BAY

Scale of Miles
0 1 2 3
© ADC of Alexandria

N

Walker Airfield

Fort Monroe

HAMPTON ROADS

James River Bridge

Newport News Point

Fishing Point

Ragged Island Creek

Batten Bay

CRITTENDEN

JAMES RIVER

NANSEMOND RIVER

Hampton Roads Bridge Tunnel

Fort Wool

WILLOUGHBY

Willoughby Bay

BELLINGER

Norfolk Naval Air Station

OCEAN VIEW

NORFOLK

Little Creek

USN Little Creek Amphibious Base

LYNNHAVEN ROADS

CHESAPEAKE BAY BRIDGE-TUNNEL

Lynnhaven Inlet

Lynnhaven Bay

LITTLE NECK

KINGS GRANT

INT'L TERMINAL

Craney Island Supply Depot

CRANEY

TWIN PINES

HEDGEROW

Elizabeth River

Lafayette Creek

Norfolk International Airport

Little Creek Reservoir

Norview

CHURCHLAND

PORTSMOUTH

Western Branch

Elizabeth River

SAINT MICHAEL

Eastern Branch Elizabeth River

INDIAN RIVER

COLLEGE PARK

VIRGINIA BEACH

Stumpy Lake

SUFFOLK

BOWERS HILL

CRADDOCK

PORTLOCK

Southern Branch Elizabeth River

Portsmouth Chesapeake Airport

GREEN RUN

DEEP CREEK

South Norfolk

CHESAPEAKE

GREAT BRIDGE

Albemarle Canal

FENTRESS

US Naval Airfield Fentress Station

GREAT DISMAL SWAMP

NATIONAL WILDLIFE REFUGE

Deep Creek

Herring Ditch

1 2 3 4 5 6 7

A

B

C

D

E

F

G

H

J

K

ARCADIA

N.E. 178th St.

Arcadia Lake

N.E. 164th St.

N.E. 150th St.

Turner Turnpike

Central State Univ.

Edmond Mem. Hosp.

EDMOND

Okla. Christian College

N.E. 136th St.

136th St.

Kilpatrick Tpke.

(TOLL)

122nd

N.E. 122nd

108th

Mercy Hospital

Quail Creek C.C.

Heritage Hall Sch.

Lone Star Sch.

Eisenhower J.H.S.

Oakdale Sch.

THE VILLAGE

Quail Creek Sch.

Hefner

93rd

JONES

Lake Hefner

Okla. City Art Museum

Britton Rd.

N.E. 78th

Stinchcomb Wildlife Refuge

Wiley Post Airport

Lake Hefner G.C.

Midwest Christian College

National Cowboy Hall of Fame

Expressway Junction Airport

N.E. 63rd

63rd

WARR ACRES

NICHOLS HILLS

Belle Isle Lake

Remington Pk. Race Track

LAKE ALUMA

50th

YUKON

Deaconess Hosp.

Oklahoma City G.C.

50th

Lincoln Park

FOREST PARK

Post

BETHANY

39th

Lincoln Blvd. N.

SPENCER

Anderson

WOODLAWN PARK

Expwy

36th

OKLAHOMA CITY

Twin Hills C.C.

N.E. 23rd

NICOMA PARK

Lake Overholser

Will Rogers Park

Okla. City Univ.

23rd

State Capitol

Bethany Gen. Hosp.

10th

O.S.U. Tech.

Univ. of Okla. Med. Center

King

10th

CHOCTAW

Civic Center

N.E. 4th St.

MIDWEST CITY

Reno

Reno

Midwest City Mem. Hosp.

Pleasant Valley Sch.

Downtown Airport

SMITH VILLAGE

15th

29th

29th

DEL CITY

Rose State College

Western Heights H.S.

South Comm. Hosp.

Grand

44th

Diagonal

Oklahoma City Air Force Station

Airport

MUSTANG

F.A.A. Ctr.

Will Rogers World Airport

59th

Tinker Air Force Base

EXPY

FIREWORKS CITY

Okla. City Comm. College

74th

89th

VALLEY BROOK

89th

OKLAHOMA CO. CLEVELAND CO.

104th

104th

Stanley Draper Lake

119th

N.W. 12th

N.E. 12th

119th

GRADY CO.

CLEVELAND CO. MC CLAIN CO.

134th

MOORE

134th

TUTTLE

Canadian River

173rd

149th

164th

NEWCASTLE

Max Westheimer Field

NORMAN

Lake Thunderbird

HALL PARK

Scale of Miles

0 1 2 3

© C.S.C.

N

1 2 3 4 5 6 7

A
HONEY CREEK
NASHVILLE
WASHINGTON CO.
DOUGLAS CO.
Horseshoe Lake
133
75
183
L-36
G-20
G-30

B
Dutch Hall Rd.
St. St. St. St. St.
Pawnee Rd.
BENNINGTON
Bennington
Bennington
Northern Hills Dr.
84th
North Omaha Airport
McKinley Dr.
Skyranch Airport
132nd
Rainwood
Glen Cunningham Lake and Recreation Area
Dodge Park
CLARA
CRESCENT
Jackson
Rainbow Rd.
WESTON
G-36
L-34
G-36
36
680
29
183
191
36

C
156th
138th
State
126th St.
120th St.
114th St.
Ida
Military St.
Fort
Standing Bear Lake and Recreation Area
Blair
Irvington
Omaha Country Club
SORENSON
PKWY.
Bridge Rd.
Blvd.
DEBOLT
St.
Morman
Redick Ave.
John J. Pershing Dr.
River
STORZ EXPWY
Fort Ave.
Carter
Omaha Airport
Lewis & Clark Monument
Epley Airfield
Rainbow Rd.
8th
Mynster Spring Rd.
Broadway
L-29
6
L-43
191
133
80

D
64
Maple
Tranquility Park
Blondo
144th
132nd
Miracle Hill Golf Course
Dodge
Maple Rd.
108th
98th
Maple St.
N.W. Radial
Hartman Ave.
Benson Park
Ames
Fontenelle Park
Fontenelle
Western Baptist Bible College
Nebraska School for the Deaf
Miller Park
Levi Carter Park
Carter Lake
Locust
Abbott
CARTER LAKE
Lincoln Monument
G St.
25th St.
West
Broadway
Ave.
Iowa Western Community College
McPherson Ave.
6
133
OMAHA
Cumming St.
Dodge St.
64
75
30th

E
West
Center
BOYS TOWN
Pacific
90th
University of Nebraska at Omaha
Happy Hollow Country Club
College of St. Mary
Elmwood Park
Memorial Park
Dodge
Leavenworth
Center Rd.
38
Ed Creighton Blvd.
Martha St.
13th
20th
24th
480
Joslyn Art Museum
Dodge Park
Creighton U.
9th
West
25th Ave.
Nebraska Ave.
23rd
16th Ave.
G St.
COUNCIL BLUFFS
Pierce St.
Pomona Ave.
64
680
38
275
92
192
29
80
375
92
6

F
Q St.
MILLARD
Highland
Applewood Golf Course
Millard Airport
RALSTON
LA VISTA
Main St.
80th
Seymour Smith Park
MAY
DOUGLAS CO
SARPY CO
F St.
Grover St.
Q St.
F St.
75
Missouri Ave.
Rosenblatt Stadium
H. Doorly Zoo
Spring Lake Park
34th Ave.
36th
So. Omaha
31st
55 Ave.
So. 24
Mount Vernon Garden
Mandan Park
68 Ave.
Lake Manawa
Lake Manawa State Park
Fontenelle Forest
Missouri
DUMFRIES
POTTAWATTAMIE CO.
MILLS CO.
L-45
G-86
50
120th
108th
98th
84th
72nd
370
Gifford Rd.
Railroad
48th
275
92

G
166th
156th
144th
132nd
114th
Schram Rd.
CHALCO
Giles
Lincoln
PAPILLION
Old Hwy.
South Omaha Airport
Cornhusker Dr.
Harvell Dr.
Galvan Rd.
Lincoln Rd.
Childs Rd.
BELLEVUE
NEBRASKA
IOWA
Mission Ave.
370
370
85
131
50
80
370

H
Fairview
RICHFIELD
Capehart Rd.
Platteview Rd.
GILMORE
FORT CROOK
Harlan
36th
Gilmore
CAPEHART
Offutt Air Force Base
Hancock
H-12
L-31
L-45
275

J
SPRINGFIELD
SARPY CO.
CASS CO.
Platte River
CULLOM
OREAPOLIS
Missouri River
PACIFIC CITY
GLENWOOD
75
29
34
275

K
CEDAR CREEK MEADOW
PLATTSMOUTH
PACIFIC JUNCTION
50
66

Scale of Miles
0 1 2 3
© C.S.C.

1 2 3 4 5 6 7

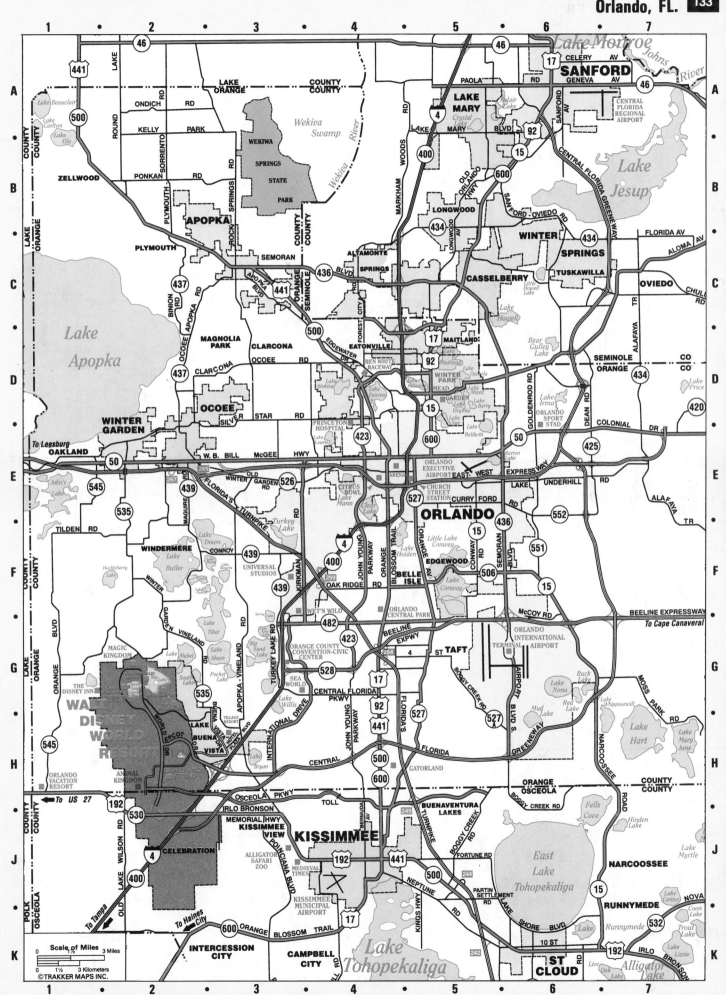

Scale of Miles
0
1
2
3
© ADC of Alexandria
PHILADELPHIA
CAMDEN
PENNSYLVANIA
NEW JERSEY
DELAWARE
RIVER
SCHUYLKILL
Northeast Philadelphia Airport
Philadelphia International Airport
Fairmount Park
Pennypack Park
Neshaminy State Park
Fort Washington State Park
US Naval Reservation
NATIONAL PARK
NORRISTOWN
CONSHOHOCKEN
WEST CONSHOHOCKEN
BRIDGEPORT
KING OF PRUSSIA
JENKINTOWN
CHELTENHAM
GERMANTOWN
MANAYUNK
ROXBOROUGH
CHESTNUT HILL
BRYN MAWR
NARBERTH
ARDMORE
HAVERTOWN
BROOMALL
MEDIA
SWARTHMORE
YEADON
DARBY
LANSDOWNE
COLLINGDALE
ESSINGTON
GLOUCESTER CITY
BROOKLAWN
WESTVILLE
COLLINGSWOOD
HADDONFIELD
HADDON HEIGHTS
AUDUBON PARK
MERCHANTVILLE
PENNSAUKEN
CHERRY HILL
PALMYRA
RIVERTON
BEVERLY
BRISTOL
CROYDON
LEVITTOWN
HULMEVILLE
LANGHORNE MANOR
FEASTERVILLE
TREVOSE
BRYN ATHYN
HUNTINGDON VALLEY
ROCKLEDGE
AMBLER
FORT WASHINGTON
PLYMOUTH MEETING
LAFAYETTE HILL
EDDYSTONE
RIDLEY PARK
PROSPECT PARK
NORWOOD
FOLCROFT
SHARON HILL
CLIFTON HEIGHTS
ALDAN
MORTON
RUTLEDGE
BROOKHAVEN
UPLAND
ROSE VALLEY
WALLINGFORD
NEWTOWN SQUARE
WAYNE
RADNOR
VILLANOVA
ROSEMONT
GLADWYNE
BALA CYNWYD
MERION
WYNNEWOOD
OVERBROOK
WYNNEFIELD
WEST PHILADELPHIA
SOUTH PHILADELPHIA
SOCIETY HILL
KENSINGTON
RICHMOND
FRANKFORD
HOLMESBURG
MAYFAIR
OLNEY
LOGAN
FERN ROCK
OAK LANE
ELKINS PARK
WYNCOTE
GLENSIDE
ABINGTON
WILLOW GROVE
ROSLYN
OREL AND
BENJAMIN FRANKLIN BR (TOLL)
WALT WHITMAN BR (TOLL)
TACONY PALMYRA BR (TOLL)
BETSY ROSS BR (TOLL)
Petty Island
Little Tinicum Island
Pennypack Creek
Wissahickon Creek
Cooper River
Rancocas Creek
Neshaminy Creek

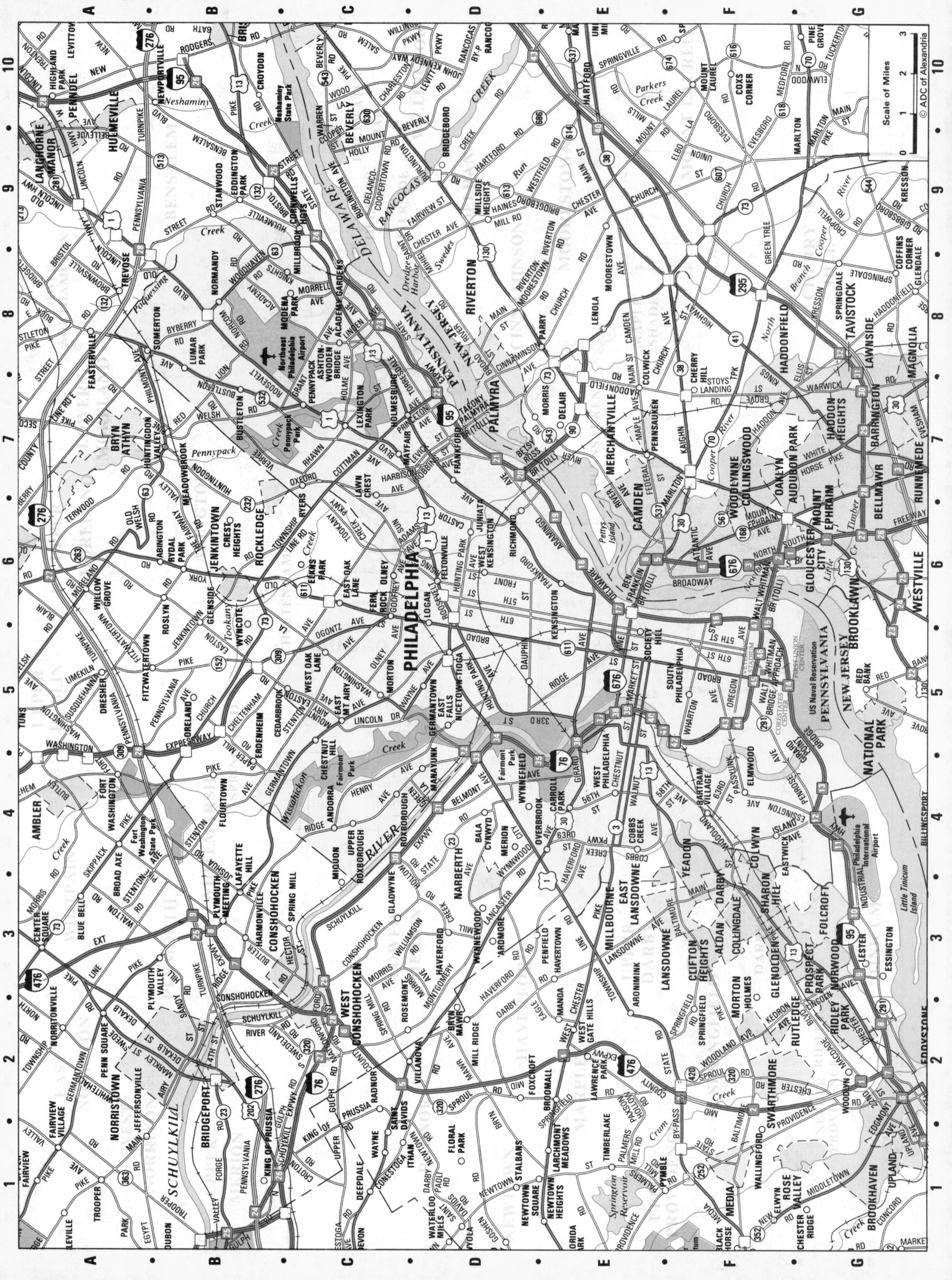

DYNAMITE RD.

JOMAX RD.

HAPPY VALLEY RD.

PINNACLE PEAK RD.

Cave Creek Dam

Arizona Veterans Mem. Cemetery

Currys Corner

PINNACLE PEAK RD.

Peoria

BEARDSLEY RD.

Deer Valley Airport

Adobe Valley

DEER VALLEY RD.

BEARDSLEY RD.

Thunderbird Regional Pk.

UNION HILLS RD.

UNION HILLS RD.

Beardsley

Suprise

Sun City West

Paradise Valley Community College

Paradise City

Paradise Valley Park

BELL RD.

GREENWAY RD.

GREENWAY

Turf Paradise Race Track

Moon Valley C.C.

GREENWAY RD.

Scottsdale Mun. Airport

El Mirage

Sun City

American Inst. for Foriegn Trade

THUNDERBIRD RD.

ASU West

Cactus Pk.

North Mountain Park

THUNDERBIRD

Century C.C.

Youngstown

CACTUS AVE.

Metro Center

CACTUS

SHEA

Scottsdale

PEORIA AVE.

Arizona Canal

Phoenix Mountain Preserve

Squaw Peak Park

DUNLAP

Glendale Com. Col.

Royal Palm Mobile Pk.

Paradise Valley

NORTHERN AVE.

Resthaven Pk. Cem.

Glendale

GLENDALE AVE.

GLENDALE AVE.

PHOENIX

Paradise Valley G.C.

Luke Air Force Base

Glendale Municipal Airport

BETHANY HOME RD.

BETHANY HOME RD.

LINCOLN DR.

MCDONALD DR.

CAMELBACK

Litchfield Park

Holiday Pk.

Grand Canyon Col.

CAMELBACK RD.

Arizona Biltmore

CAMELBACK

Mun. G.C.

INDIAN SCHOOL RD.

V.A. Hospital

Arizona C.C.

INDIAN SCHOOL

Avondale

Eloso Pk.

Encanto Golf Course & Park

Phoenix C.C.

THOMAS RD.

MCDOWELL RD.

Heard Mus.

State Fair Grounds

County Hospital

Military Res.

MCDOWELL

Desert Botanical Gardens

Papago Park

PAPAGO FRWY.

Phoenix Greyhound Pk.

Zoological Park

State Hospital

Goodyear

Avondale

Cashion

Tolleson

VAN BUREN ST.

VAN BUREN

WASHINGTON ST.

State Capitol

Mun. Bldg.

BankOne Ballpark

SKY HARBOR BLVD.

Tempe Park

Mun. Stadium

Goodyear Airfield

BUCKEYE

LOWER BUCKEYE RD.

America West Arena

Sky Harbor Int'l. Airport

Sun Devil Stadium

BROADWAY

UNIVERSITY

APACHE

Ariz. State Univ.

Tempe

BROADWAY RD.

Manzanita Speedway

SOUTHERN AVE.

SOUTHERN AVE.

Casey Abbott Semi-Regional Park

Salt River

BASE LINE RD.

ESTRELLA MOUNTAIN REGIONAL PARK

DOBBINS RD.

Laveen

Phoenix Police Academy

Thunderbird C.C.

GUADULUPE RD.

Guadalupe

ELLIOT RD.

ELLIOT

Ahwatukee

ELLIOT

Gila River

ESTRELLA DR.

Las Ramadas Picnic Area

STEPHEN MATHER RD.

TELEGRAPH PASS

BUENA VISTA RD.

CANYON RD.

WARNER RD.

SAN JUAN RD.

PHOENIX SOUTH MOUNTAIN PARK

Gila Valley Lookout

RAY RD.

KYRENE RD.

GILA

Phoenix South Mountain Park

International Harvester Proving Ground

WILLIAMS RD.

Chandler

PECOS RD.

MARICOPA CO.

PINAL CO.

RIVER

INDIAN

Goodyear Air Force Mil. Field

RESERVATION

© C.S.C.

N

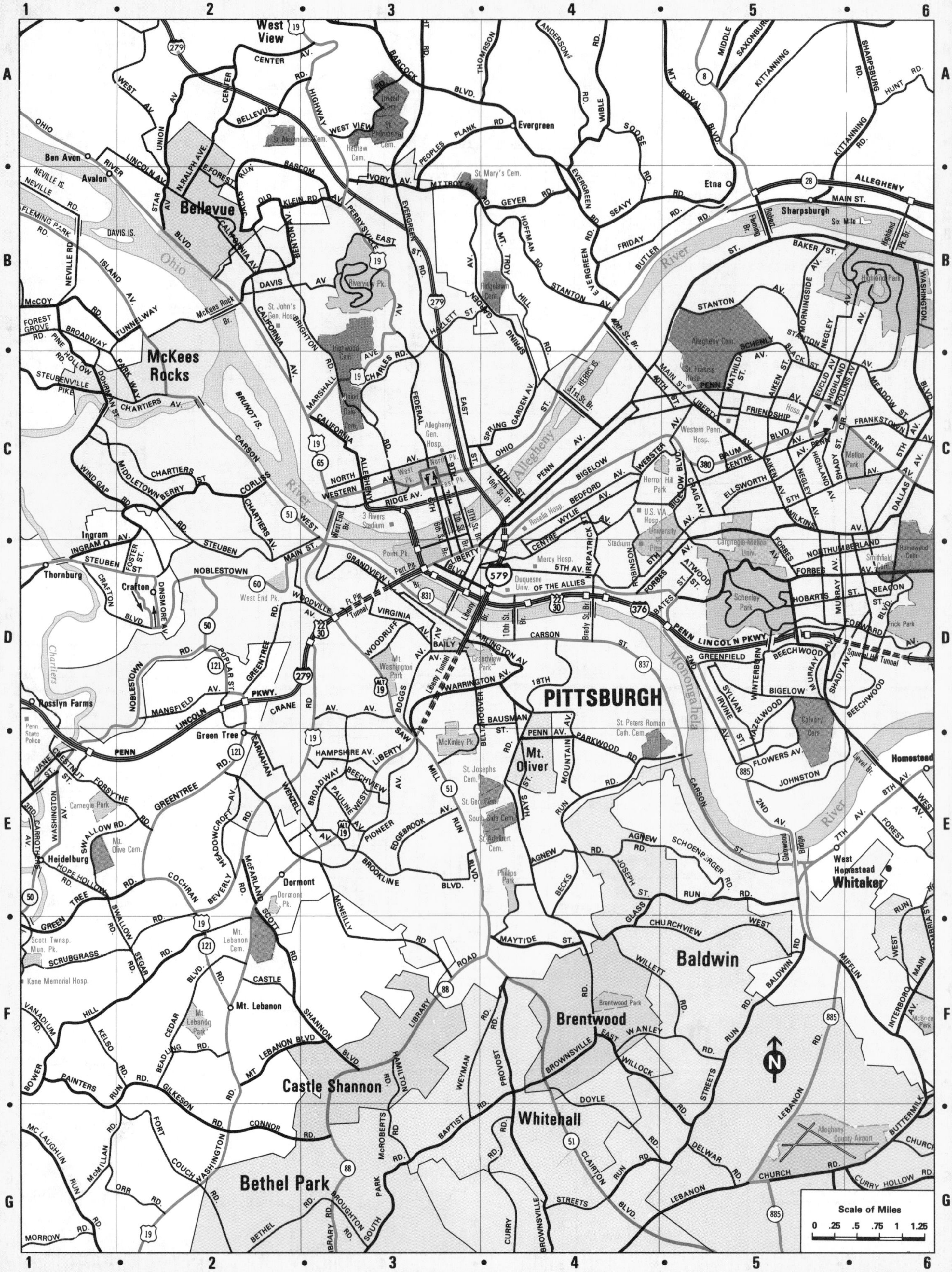

PITTSBURGH

West View
Bellevue
Ben Avon
Avalon
Neville Is.
Davis Is.
McCoy
Forest Grove
McKees Rocks
Ingram
Thornburg
Crafton
Rosslyn Farms
Green Tree
Heidelburg
Dormont
Mt. Lebanon
Castle Shannon
Bethel Park
Whitehall
Brentwood
Baldwin
Mt. Oliver
West Homestead
Whitaker
Homestead
Etna
Sharpsburg
Evergreen

Ohio River
Allegheny River
Monongahela River
Chartiers River

3 Rivers Stadium
Point Pk.
Duquesne Univ.
University of Pitt.
Carnegie-Mellon Univ.
Schenley Park
Frick Park
Highland Park
Riverview Pk.
West End Pk.
McKinley Pk.
Philips Park
Brentwood Park
Allegheny County Airport
Penn State Police

Allegheny Gen. Hosp.
St. John's Gen. Hosp.
St. Francis Hosp.
Western Penn. Hosp.
Mercy Hosp.
3 Rivers Hosp.
Rosalia Hosp.
U.S. V.A. Hosp.
Herron Hill Park
Kane Memorial Hosp.

Allegheny Cem.
St. Mary's Cem.
Hebrew Cem.
St. Philomena Cem.
United Cem.
St. Alexander's Cem.
Highwood Cem.
Union Dale Cem.
Ridgelawn Cem.
Calvary Cem.
Homewood Cem.
Smithfield Cem.
Mt. Lebanon Cem.
Mt. Olive Cem.
St. Joseph's Cem.
St. Geo. Cem.
South Side Cem.
St. Adelbert's Cem.
St. Peters Roman Cath. Cem.

Scale of Miles
0   .25   .5   .75   1   1.25

N

1 2 3 4 5 6

A

SLAVE ISLAND RD.
GILLIMAN
LOOP
Multnomah Channel
MULTNOMAH COUNTY
CLARK COUNTY
MARINE DR.
Hayden Island
VANCOUVER
E. MILL PLAIN BLVD.
500
Pearson Field

SKYLINE BLVD.
NEWBERRY RD.
N.W. SKYLINE BLVD.
GERMANTOWN RD.
COLUMBIA BLVD.
N. FESSENDEN ST.
N. PORTLAND RD.
Columbia Slough
Columbia River
Exposition Center
Delta Park
Portland Tomahawk Yacht Club
Tomahawk Island
Delta Park
Tyee Yacht Club
WASHINGTON
OREGON
Rose City Yacht Club
Columbia River Yacht Club

B

N. LOMBARD ST.
N. COLUMBIA BLVD.
WILLIS BLVD.
N. WILLAMETTE
N. PORTSMITH AVE.
N. PENINSULAR AVE.
N. DENVER BLVD.
Columbia Park
Portland G.C.
N.E. COLUMBIA
Columbia Edgewater G.C.
Riverside G.C.
N.E. MARINE RD.
AVE.
Portland Int'l Airport
Broadmoor G.C.
Portland Air Force Base
Colwood G.C.
BYP 30

Forest Park
Willamette River
30
Univ. of Portland
Swan Island
N. PORTLAND AVE.
GREELEY
N. INTERSTATE AVE.
Peninsula Park
N.E.
Alberta Park
KILLNGSWORTH ST.
N.E. LOMBARD ST.
N.E. SUNDERLAND AVE.
N.E. 42ND AVE.
N.E. CULY RD.
BYP 30

C

YEON AVE.
River
N.W. VAUGHN ST.
Fremont Bridge
Broadway Bridge
UNION
PORTLAND
99E
N.E. FREMONT ST.
N.E. 33RD AVE.
N.E. 39TH AVE.
THE ALAMEDA
N. 57TH
DR 30
Rose City G.C.
84

BRONSON RD.
CORNELL RD.
CORNELL RD.
N.W. CORNELL RD.
MacLeay Park
SKYLINE RD.
N.W. 23RD AVE.
N.W. 19TH AVE.
405
Memorial Coliseum
N.E. BROADWAY
SANDY
N.E. GLISAN ST.
N.E. HALSEY ST.
30
174TH AVE.
WALKER

D

CORNELL AVE.
WALKER RD.
BARNES RD.
S.W. BARNES RD.
26
Zoologocial Gardens and Museum
Portland State Univ.
MARKET
26
405
99E
Laurelhurst Park
E. BURNSIDE
S.E. STARK ST.
S.E. BELMONT ST.
S.E. MORRISON ST.
S.E. HAWTHORNE BLVD.
S.E. DIVISION ST.
Mt. Tabor Park
JENKINS RD.
MURRAY BLVD.
170TH AVE.
CEDAR HILLS BLVD.
8
W. HUMPHREY
S.W. VISTA AVE.
S.W. BROADWAY DR.
S.W. FAIRMONT
Univ. of Oregon Med. Sch.
Ross Is. Bridge
Ross Island
S.E. 26TH AVE.
39TH
POWELL
62ND
71ST
Warner Pacific College

E

FARMINGTON RD.
10
West Slope
8
CENTER RD. S.W. CANYON RD.
HAMILTON
S.W. PATTON RD.
SHATTUCK RD.
DOSCH RD.
SUNSET BLVD.
TERWILLIGER
BALDOCK FWY.
MACADAM AVE.
McLOUGHLIN
Harktack Island
S.E. 28TH AVE.
S.E. 52ND
HOLGATE BLVD.
FOSTER RD.
26
72ND
WALKER RD.
Raleigh Hills
BEAVERTON-HILLSDALE RD.
217
Western AVE.
ALLEN BLVD.
DENNEY RD.
Council Crest
CAMERON RD.
Hillsdale
S.W. VERMONT ST.
Gabriel Park
Multnomah
80TH AVE.
10
S.W.
Pioneer Park
Reed College
WOODSTOCK
S.E. HAROLD BLVD.
S.E. TOLMAN ST.
S.E. FLAVEL DR.
Kendall

170TH
HART RD.
MURRAY BLVD.
WEIR RD.
BEAVERTON
FERRY RD.
HALL BLVD.
SCHOLLS BLVD.
OLESON RD.
GARDEN
HOME
S.W. MULTNOMAH BLVD.
45TH
S.W. BARBUR BLVD.
5
S.W. TAYLORS FERRY RD.
BYBEE BLVD.
S.E. 13TH
TACOMA
Eastmoreland Golf Course
JOHNSON CREEK BLVD.
LINWOOD
32ND AVE.
ALBERTA ST.
BELL
Milwaukie

F

REUSSER RD.
OLD SCHOLLS FERRY RD.
210
Metzger
OAK ST.
WASHINGTON CO.
99
217
Portland Comm. College
MULTNOMAH
Portland Comm. College
KERR
BOONES FERRY RD.
35TH AVE.
STEPHENSON ST.
Tryon Creek State Park
Lewis & Clark College
Waverly C.C.
Riverside Willamette River
Terwilliger
WILLAMETTE
Harrison ST.
KING RD.
RAILROAD
ALDERCHEST
OATFIELD
N. Clackamas Central Park
WEBSTER RD.
HARMONY RD.
Tigard

G

BEEF BEND
BONITA RD.
CARMEN DR.
WAY
KRUSE WAY
Waluga Park
Lake Grove
LAKE OSWEGO
COUNTRY CLUB RD.
Lake Oswego C.C.
Lake Oswego
Oak Grove
OAK GROVE BLVD.
CONCORD RD.
HILL RD.
THIESSEN RD.

KING CITY
BEEF BEND RD.
DURHAM RD.
DURHAM
TUALATIN
99W
CLACKAMAS CO.
5
STAFFORD RD.
ROSE MONT
WEST LINN
43
PORTLAND RD.
Oswego Lake
River
Maryhurst College

Scale of Miles
0 .5 1 1.5

© C.S.C.

Raleigh, NC (top map)

DURHAM, RALEIGH, LEESVILLE, SPRING HILL, PARKWOOD, FAIRFIELD, GENLEE, DURHAM WAKE, MORRISVILLE, THE WOODS OF CHATHAM, GREEN LEVEL, UPCHURCH, PRESTON, CARY, MACGREGOR DOWNS, APEX, GLENRIDGE, FRIENDSHIP, RESEARCH TRIANGLE PARK, RALEIGH-DURHAM INTERNATIONAL AIRPORT, WILLIAM B UMSTEAD STATE PARK, Lake Crabtree, Luther Airstrip, WESTOVER, NEW CHAPEL, MACEDONIA, OAKTON, COUNTY COUNTY, CROSSROADS, STONEBRIDGE, BAYLEAF, WAKE FOREST, WALKERS CROSSROADS, WAKE CROSSROADS, NEUSE, SIX FORKS, BRANDON STATION, RALEIGH, MILLBROOK, BRENTWOOD, NEW HOPE, HEDINGHAM, MILBURNIE, BARCLAY DOWNS, KNIGHTDALE, CARTER FINLEY STADIUM, NC STATE UNIV, TERP, State Capitol, Lake Johnson, Lake Raleigh, CLOVERDALE, GARNER, GREENBRIER ESTATES, EMERALD VILLAGE, BATTLE BRIDGE, AUBURN, Neuse River, Harris Creek, SIX FORKS CROSSROADS

Scale of Miles 0 1 2 3
© ADC of Alexandria

Rochester, NY (bottom map)

GRAND VIEW HEIGHTS, CRESCENT BEACH, RIGNEY BLUFF, Lake Ontario, HILTON, PARMA CENTER, NORTH GREECE, FOREST LAWN, OKLAHOMA BEACH, PARMA CORNERS, WEST GREECE, GREECE, IRONDEQUOIT, WEST WEBSTER, WEBSTER, UNION HILL, SPENCERPORT, SOUTH GREECE, Irondequoit Bay, ROSELAND, OGDEN CENTER, GATE, Durand Eastman Park, Seneca Park, St. Bernard's Seminary, ROCHESTER, Intl. Mus. of Photography, Genesee River, PENFIELD CENTER, WEST WALWORTH, NORTH CHILI, CHILI CENTER, Rochester-Monroe Co. Airport, Susan B. Anthony House, Univ. of Rochester, Univ. of Rochester Med. Cen., BRIGHTON, Highland Park, Ellison Park, PENFIELD, EAST ROCHESTER, EAST PENFIELD, WEST CHILI, CRITTENDEN, Nazareth Coll. of Rochester, PITTSFORD, FAIRPORT, WAYNEPORT, Cobbs Hill Park

Scale of Miles 0 1 2 3
© C.S.C.

N

ROCKVILLE
HYLAS
ELMONT
Hanover County Municipal Airport
POINDEXTERS
ASHCAKE
PEARSONS CORNER
OAK FOREST
RURAL POINT
STUDLEY
Chickahominy
Crump
Pollard Creek
Totopotomoy
Montile
GLEN ALLEN
FRANCIS
INNSBROOK
HUNGARY
WEST CREEK CORPORATE CENTER
SHORT PUMP
LAUREL
CHAMBERLAYNE HEIGHTS
MECHANICSVILLE
POLE GREEN
NEWMANS
HUGHES CORNER
BRANDY CREEK ESTS
SIMPKINS CORNER
Cold Harbor
National Battlefield Park
DUMBARTON
CRESTVIEW
Upham Brook
Beaverdam
BUCKINGHAM
Tuckahoe Creek
JAMES RIVER
Cherokee Lake
RICHMOND STADIUM
RICHMOND UNIV
BON AIR
RICHMOND
ROBIOUS
State Police Airport
OTTERDALE
MIDLOTHIAN
Richmond International Airport
ARROWHEAD
SWAN HILL
FALLING CREEK
Falling Creek Reservoir
BENSLEY
DREWRYS BLUFF
KINGSLAND ACRES
BRANDERMILL
Swift Creek Reservoir
Dorey Park
Four Mile Creek Park
Richmond National Battlefield Park
LEES VILLAGE
FIVE FORKS
Chesterfield Airport
Iron Bridge Pk
POCAHONTAS
Swift Creek Lake
Pocahontas State Park
STATE FOREST
CHESTERFIELD
CENTRALIA
MEADOWVILLE
James River Old Channel
CHESTER
VICTORIA HILLS
WALTHALL
BERMUDA HUNDRED
ENON
Andrews Pond
Federal Corrections Inst
HOPEWELL
PICKADAT CORNER
Scale of Miles
0 1 2 3
© ADC of Alexandria

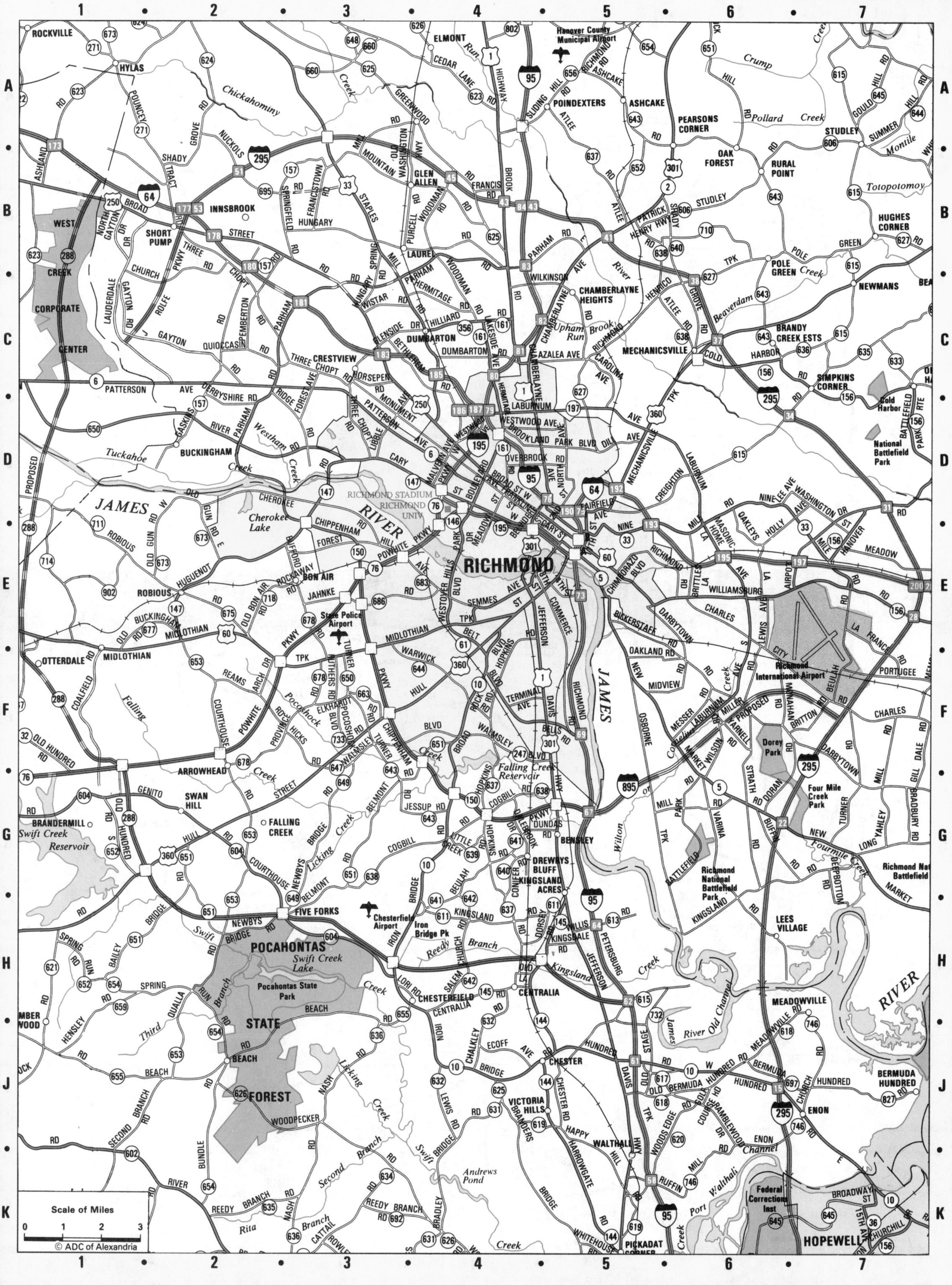

St. Charles
Hazelwood
Florissant
Black Jack
Bridgeton
Berkeley
Ferguson
Dellwood
Bellefontaine Neighbors
Kinloch
Moline Acres
Riverview
Edmundson
Woodson Terr.
St. Ann
Cool Valley
Normandy
Jennings
Breckenridge Hills
St. John
Bel-Ridge
Charlack
Bel-Nor
Northwoods
Maryland Heights
Overland
Vinita Park
Pine Lawn
Velda City
Hanley Hills
Olivette
University City
Pagedale
Wellston
Creve Coeur
Clayton
Ladue
Brentwood
Richmond Heights
Frontenac
Town and Country
Huntleigh
Des Peres
Warson Woods
Rock Hill
Maplewood
Webster Groves
Kirkwood
Glendale
Shrewsbury
Oakland
Marlborough
Crestwood
Grantwood Village
Lakeshire
Sunset Hills
Fenton
Bella Villa
St. George
ST. LOUIS
Arnold
Columbia
Madison
Venice
Granite City
Brooklyn
National City
East St. Louis
Sauget
Alorton
Cahokia
Centreville
East Carondelet
Dupo
Sugar Loaf Heights
North Dupo
Stolle
Chouteau Island
Mosenthein Island
Gabaret Island
Mississippi River
Meramec River
MISSOURI ILLINOIS
MADISON COUNTY ST. CLAIR COUNTY
ST. LOUIS COUNTY ST. CLAIR COUNTY
ST. LOUIS COUNTY MONROE COUNTY
ST. CLAIR COUNTY MONROE COUNTY
ST. LOUIS CO JEFFERSON CO
ST. CHARLES COUNTY ST. LOUIS COUNTY
LAMBERT-ST. LOUIS INTERNATIONAL AIRPORT
Scale of Miles
0 1 2 3 4
© C.S.C.

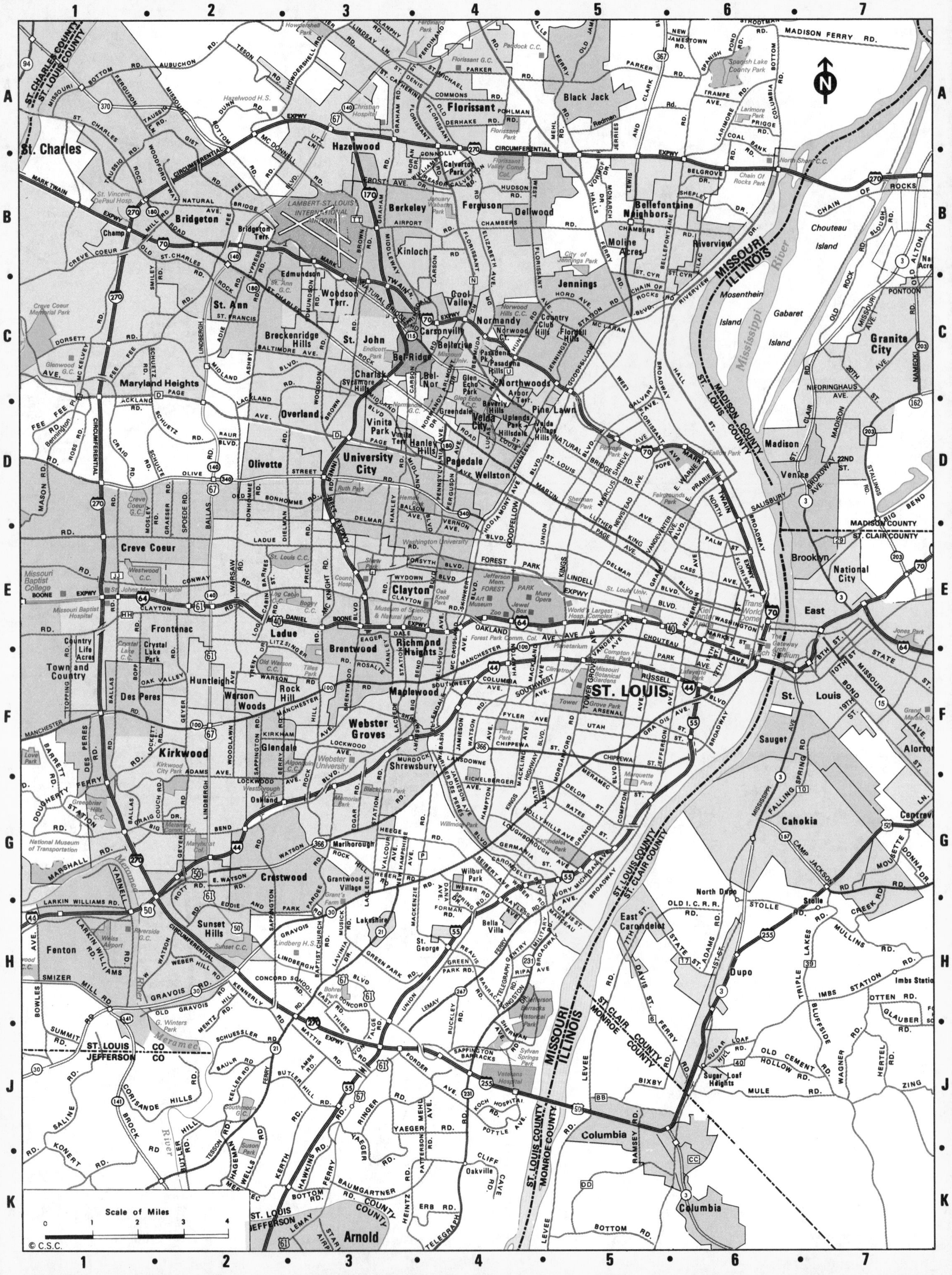

1 2 3 4 5 6 7

Sacramento map (top)

Sacramento Municipal Airport

RIO LINDA
NORTH HIGHLANDS
FOOTHILL FARMS
ORANGEVALE
VALLEY VIEW ACRES
ROBLA
McClellan Air Force Base
FAIR OAK
Northridge C.C.
Madison Ave.
Sunset
Winding Way
Greenback Ln.
Roseville
Auburn
CARMICHAEL
Robertson
Del Paso Country Club
Marconi Ave.
El Camino
Arden
Garfield
Ancil Hoffman Park
El Dorado
NIMBUS
ALDER CREEK
CITRUS
Haggin Oaks G.C.
Carl Johnston Park
Discovery Park
Old Sacramento St. Hist. Park
Sacramento
Exposition Blvd.
California Exposition
SACRAMENTO
Arden Way
C.M. Goethe Park
Coloma
White Rock Rd.
RANCHO CORDOVA
WEST SACRAMENTO
Capitol Ave.
Folsom Blvd.
California St. Univ. at Sacramento
American River
Folsom Blvd.
Old Placerville Rd.
Douglas Rd.
Greens Lake
ARLINGTON OAKS
Linden Rd.
Land Park
PERKINS
ROSEMONT
Mather Air Force Base
Broadway
Tahoe Park
Power
Florin
SOUTH PORT
Sutterville
Fairy Tale Town
Fruitridge
Sacramento Army Depot
Kiefer Blvd.
Bradshaw
Jackson Rd.
Excelsior
Eagles Nest Rd.
RIVERVIEW
Riverside
Sacramento Executive Airport
Stockton
Elder
Perkins Creek
Meadowview
FLORIN
Florin Rd.
Gerber Rd.
Mack Rd.
Elk Grove-Florin Rd.

Scale of Miles
0 1 2 3

N

Salt Lake City map (bottom)

Antelope Island
WOODS CROSS
BOUNTIFUL
NORTH SALT LAKE
DAVIS COUNTY
SALT LAKE COUNTY
Orchard Dr.
DAVIS CO.
SALT LAKE CO.
Wasatch Bountiful Nat'l Forest
Great Salt Lake
2400 N.
Beck St.
Canyon Rd.
Victory Rd.
SALT LAKE CITY
Salt Lake City International Airport
4000 W. St.
Riverside Park
6th. N. St.
State Fair Ground
City Creek
Salt Palace
Utah State Capitol
Elks Cemetery
Fort Douglas Military Res.
SALT LAKE CITY
North Temple
South Temple St.
University of Utah
3rd.
4th. St.
172
Jordan Park
Liberty Park
Mount Olivet Cemetery
Pioneer Trail State Park
Hogle Zoo
Bonneville Golf Course
13th South
California Ave.
700 E.
Foothill
MAGNA
21st South
ALT 50
201
South
2700
9th.
9th.
11th
21st South
Fairmont Park
Sugarhouse Park
Parley's Way
WEST VALLEY CITY
154
3100 South
215
SOUTH SALT LAKE
Forest Dale Golf Course
Salt Lake Country Club Golf Course
EAST MILLCREEK
3500 South
171
33rd South
39th South
VAN
4100 South
1300 South
23rd
45th South
HOLLADAY
181
215
4700

Scale of Miles
0 1 2 3

N

© C.S.C.

1 • 2 • 3 • 4 • 5 • 6 • 7

A

GREY FOREST

Camp Bullis Military Reservation

BRACKEN

HOLLYWOOD PARK

SELMA

B

HELOTES

Univ. of Texas at San Antonio

SHAVANO PARK

HILL COUNTRY VILLAGE

LIVE OAK

CONVERSE

C

LEON VALLEY

S. Texas Medical Center

CASTLE HILLS

San Antonio International Airport

WINDCREST

D

BALCONES HEIGHTS

St. Mary's University

Assumption Seminary

OLMOS PARK

ALAMO HEIGHTS

TERRELL HILLS

KIRBY

E

SAN ANTONIO

Our Lady of the Lake College

San Fernando Cem.

City Hall
The Alamo

Joe Freeman Coliseum

MARTINEZ

GARDENDALE

CHINA GROVE

F

Lackland Training Annex

Lackland AFB

Kelly AFB

East Kelly AFB

Billy Mitchell Dr.

Lions Park

Pecan Valley G.C.

G

MACDONA

Brooks AFB

San Antonio State Hospital

Aerospace Med. Center

Sinson Field

SOUTHTON

Calaveras Lake

H

MANGUS CORNER

VON ORMY

Mitchell Lake

BUENA VISTA

Blue Wing

Braunig Lake

J

SOMERSET

Medina River

CASSIN

Blue Wing Lake

LOSOYA

ELMENDORF

K

BEXAR CO.
ATASCOSA CO.

THELMA

N

Scale of Miles
0   1   2   3

©C.S.C.

1 • 2 • 3 • 4 • 5 • 6 • 7

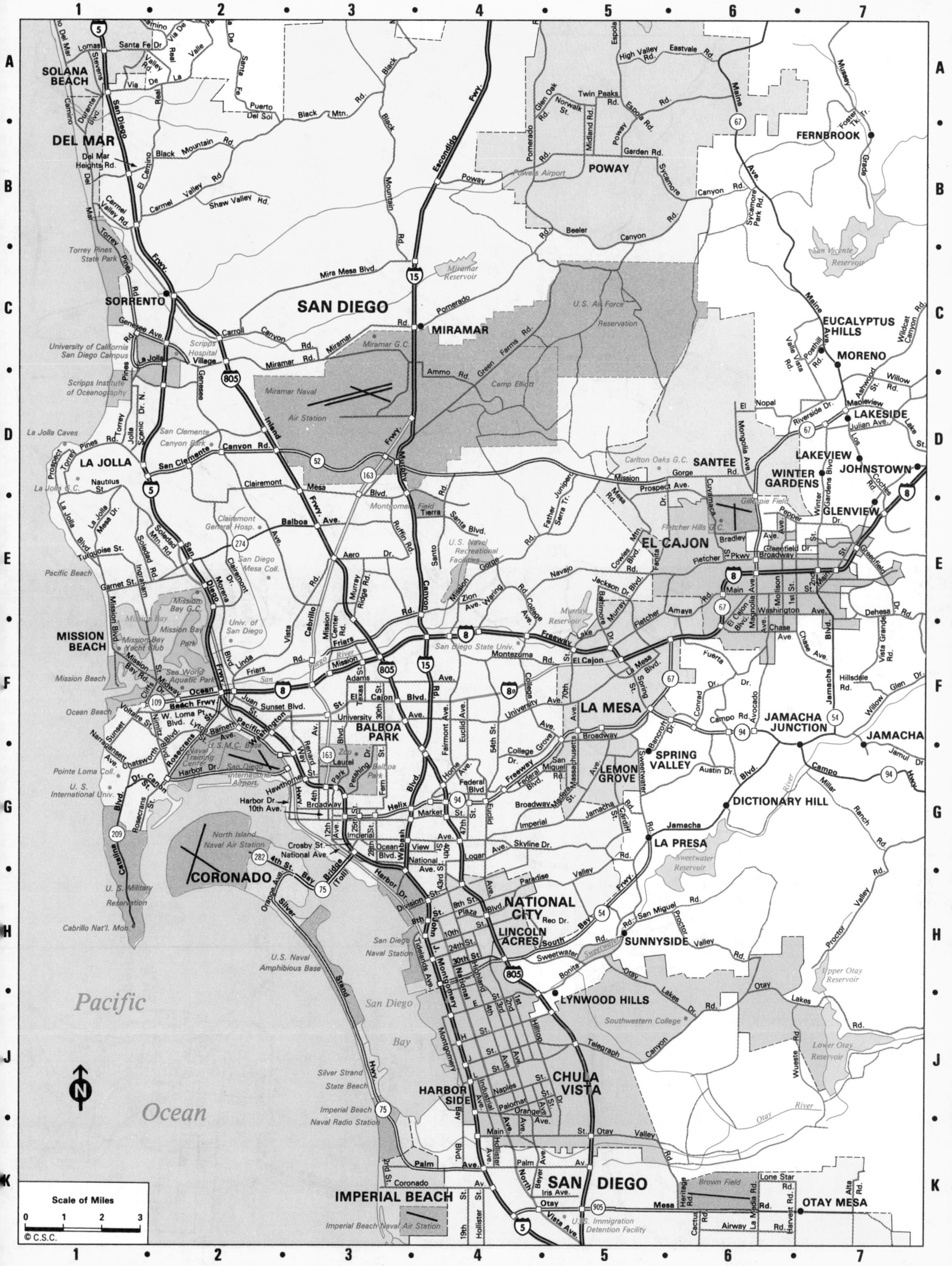
SOLANA BEACH
DEL MAR
SORRENTO
SAN DIEGO
MIRAMAR
POWAY
FERNBROOK
EUCALYPTUS HILLS
MORENO
LAKESIDE
LAKEVIEW
JOHNSTOWN
WINTER GARDENS
GLENVIEW
SANTEE
LA JOLLA
EL CAJON
MISSION BEACH
LA MESA
JAMACHA JUNCTION
JAMACHA
SPRING VALLEY
LEMON GROVE
BALBOA PARK
DICTIONARY HILL
LA PRESA
CORONADO
NATIONAL CITY
LINCOLN ACRES
SUNNYSIDE
LYNWOOD HILLS
CHULA VISTA
HARBOR SIDE
IMPERIAL BEACH
SAN DIEGO
OTAY MESA
Torrey Pines State Park
University of California San Diego Campus
Scripps Institute of Oceanography
La Jolla Caves
Miramar Naval Air Station
U.S. Air Force Reservation
Camp Elliott
Miramar Reservoir
San Vicente Reservoir
Gillespie Field
U.S. Naval Recreational Facilities
San Diego State Univ.
Mission Bay
Sea World Aquatic Park
Ocean Beach
Pointe Loma Coll.
U. S. International Univ.
North Island Naval Air Station
U. S. Military Reservation
Cabrillo Nat'l. Mon.
San Diego Naval Station
U.S. Naval Amphibious Base
San Diego Bay
Silver Strand State Beach
Imperial Beach Naval Radio Station
Imperial Beach Naval Air Station
Sweetwater Reservoir
Upper Otay Reservoir
Lower Otay Reservoir
Southwestern College
Brown Field
U.S. Immigration Detention Facility
Pacific Ocean
Scale of Miles
0 1 2 3
© C.S.C.

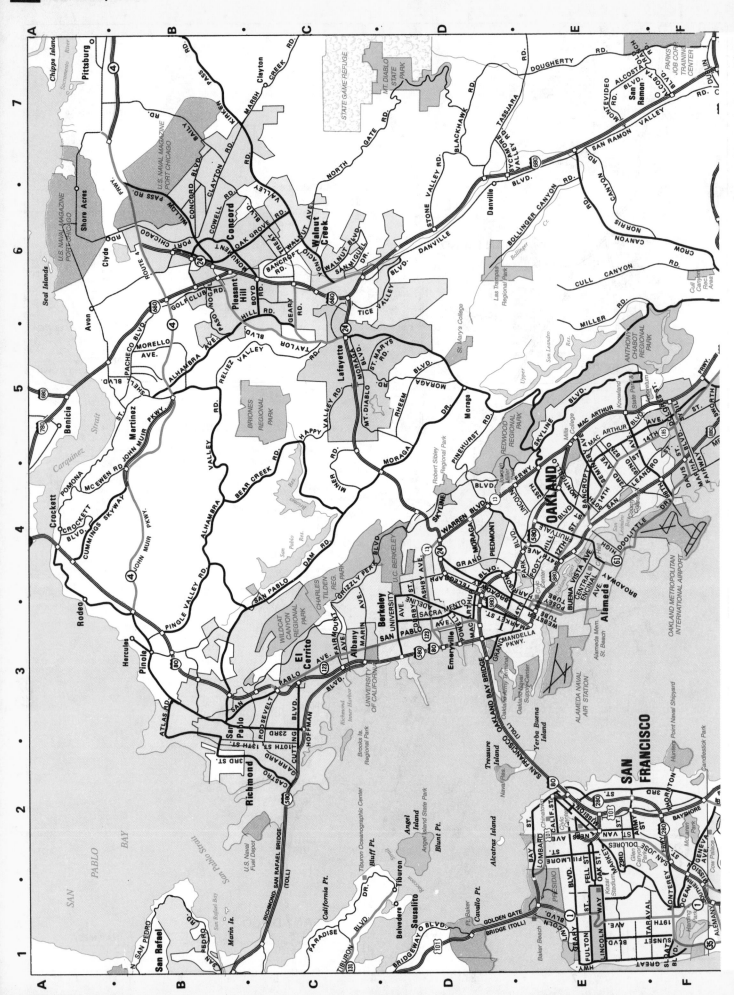

Scale of Miles

© C.S.C.

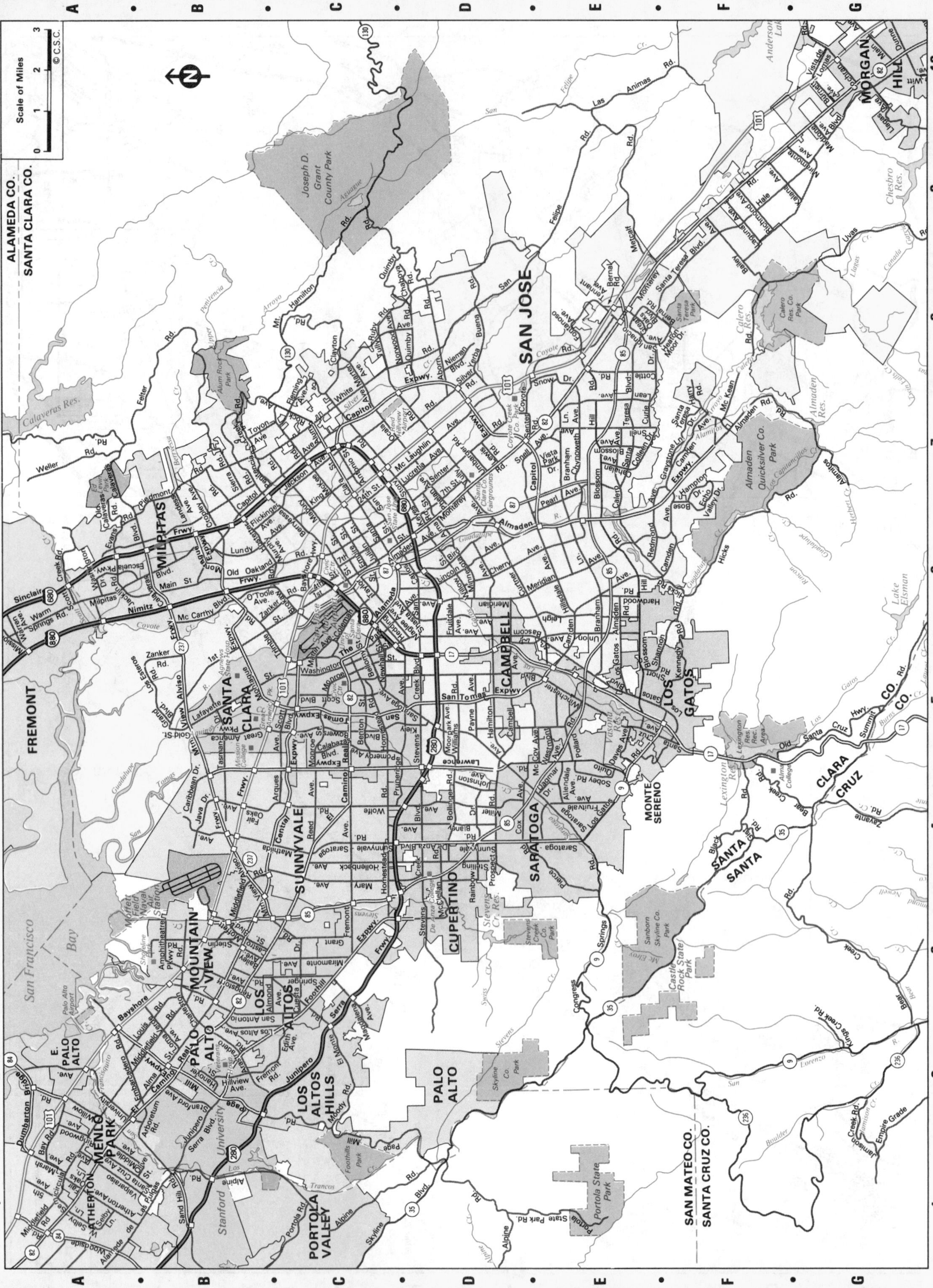

Scale of Miles
© C.S.C.

ALAMEDA CO.
SANTA CLARA CO.

Joseph D. Grant County Park

Calaveras Res.

SAN JOSE

MILPITAS

FREMONT

SANTA CLARA

Moffett Field Naval Station

MOUNTAIN VIEW

SUNNYVALE

CUPERTINO

CAMPBELL

SARATOGA

LOS GATOS

MONTE SERENO

PALO ALTO

E. PALO ALTO

MENLO PARK

ATHERTON

LOS ALTOS

LOS ALTOS HILLS

PORTOLA VALLEY

SANTA CLARA CO.
SANTA CRUZ CO.

SAN MATEO CO.
SANTA CRUZ CO.

MORGAN HILL

Anderson Lake

Chesbro Res.

Calero Res.

Calero Res. Co. Park

Almaden Res.

Almaden Quicksilver Co. Park

Lexington Res. Rec.

Stevens Cr. Res.

Sanborn Co. Park

Castle Rock State Park

Portola State Park

San Francisco Bay

Palo Alto Airport

Almaden Res.

Lake Elsman

West Valley College

Scale of Miles
0 1 2 3
© C.S.C.

Puget Sound

EDMONDS
LYNNWOOD
WOODWAY
MOUNTLAKE TERRACE
BRIER
KINGSTON
Appletree Cove
Jefferson Pt. Rd.
Tulin Rd.
Edmonds Point
Main St.
196th St. S.W.
212th St. S.W.
220th St. S.W.
Richmond Beach N.E.
88th Ave.
9th Ave.
104
99
524
5
405
527
Filbert Rd.
Larch Way
Cedar Way
Maltby Rd.
524
9
522
MALTBY
Paradise Lake Rd.
Echo Lake Rd.
Lost Lake Rd.
Welch Rd.
Fales Rd.
228th St. S.W.
Canyon Park Rd.
228th St.
Swamp Creek
North Rd.
Bothell Way
SNOHOMISH CO.
KING CO.
45th Ave.
175th Ave.
Woodinville Duvall Rd.
BOTHELL
KENMORE
522
WOODINVILLE
Woodinville
Cottage Lake
SHORELINE
LAKE FOREST PARK
N. 175th St.
Simonds Rd.
170th St.
Brier Rd.
Locust Way
Ballinger Way
Lake Ballinger
St. Edward State Park
Juanita-Woodinville Rd. N.E.
100th Ave.
132nd St.
N.E. 124th St.
N.E. 116th St.
Holmes Pt. Dr. N.E.
202
116th Ave.
Novelty Hill Rd.
N. 145th St.
N. 130th St.
N. 105th St.
Carkeek Park
Golden Gardens Park
Shilshole Bay
Seaview Ave.
15th Ave. N.W.
Holman Rd. N.W.
N. 85th St.
Greenwood Ave.
Roosevelt Way
Lake City Way
35th Ave. N.E.
N.E. 65th St.
Magnusson Park
Sand Point Way
Market St.
513
99
Green Lake
Green Lake
N. 45th
KIRKLAND
REDMOND
Market St.
Bridle Trails State Park
908
405
132nd Ave. N.E.
140th Ave. N.E.
148th Ave. N.E.
134th Ave. N.E.
202
228th Ave. N.E.
Redmond Rd.
Union Hill Rd.
196th Ave. N.E.
208th Ave. N.E.
Brier
ROLLINGBAY
Discovery Park
West Point
Murden Cove
Bainbridge Island
Thorndyke Ave.
15th Ave. W.
Gilman Ave. W.
Queen Anne Ave.
10th Ave.
Aurora
Fremont Ave.
Wallingford Ave.
Pacific St.
University of Washington
Lake Union
N.E. 45th St.
Union
Bay
Evergreen Point Floating Bridge (Toll)
HUNTS PT.
MEDINA
CLYDE HILL
520
76th Ave.
84th Ave.
92nd Ave.
104th Ave. N.E.
Bellevue-Redmond Rd.
Northrup Rd.
W. Lake Sammamish
Lake Sammamish
Inglewood Hill Rd.
Eagle Harbor
Seattle-Winslow Ferry
Seattle-Victoria Ferry
U.S. Naval Supply Depot
Key Arena
Seattle Aquarium
Seattle
Safeco Field
Elliott Bay
Madison St.
Yesler Way
23rd Ave.
Boren Ave.
Lake Washington
Lake Washington Floating Bridge
MERCER ISLAND
BEAUX ARTS
BELLEVUE
S.E. 24th St.
Phantom Lake
Pine Lake
SEATTLE
Bremerton-Seattle Ferry
Alki Beach Park
Alki Point
California Ave. S.W.
Fauntleroy Way S.W.
Chilberg
Delridge Way
35th Ave. S.W.
16th Ave. S.W.
Marginal Way
15th Ave. S.
4th Ave. S.
West Seattle Freeway
West Seattle Freeway
99
5
90
Seward Park
East Mercer Way
West Mercer Way
Kalakala Rd.
Newport Way
405
EASTGATE
Lake Sammamish State Park
164th Ave. S.E.
S.E. 60th St.
90
Country Club Rd.
Vashon-Southworth Ferry
Fauntleroy-Vashon Ferry
Lincoln Park
Puget Sound
Seattle Bainbridge Island Ferry
Passenger Ferry Only
SOUTHWORTH
VASHON HEIGHTS
NEWCASTLE
New Castle Rd.
N. 30th St.
Coalfield Way
ISSAQUAH
900
Creek
BURIEN
16th Ave. S.W.
Ambaum Blvd. S.W.
1st Ave. S.
Military Rd.
Des Moines Way
S.W. Barton S.W. Henderson
152nd St.
509
599
99
SKYWAY
TUKWILA
RENTON
900
W. Valley
S.E.
Renton-Issaquah Rd.
148th Ave. S.E.
128th St.
164th Ave. S.E.
Coalfield Issaquah Rd.
Issaquah-Hobart Rd.
Pine Lk. Rd.
Lake Desire
Otter Lake
NORMANDY PARK
SEA TAC
Three Tree Point
Marine View Dr. S.W.
Sylvester Rd.
518
99
Seattle Tacoma Intl. Airport
S. 176th St.
S. 188th St.
Pacific Hwy.
5
181
KENT
169
180th St.
192nd St.
208th St.
River
Cedar Grove Rd.
Lake Youngs
S.W. 168th St.
S.W. 176th St.
S.W. 196th St.
S.W. 204th St.
91st Ave. S.W.
Vashon Island
PORTAGE
Tramp Harbor
DES MOINES
S. 200th St.
S. 212th St.
S. 216th St.
509
515
516
167
S.E. 208th St.
S.E. 224th St.
S.E. 240th St.
116th Ave. S.E.
132nd Ave. S.E.
148th Ave. S.E.
140th Ave. S.E.
Petrovitsky Rd.
Crosson Sweeney Rd.
18
VASHON ISLAND
131st
S.W. 232nd St.
248th St.
220th St. S.W.
Weitzel Wick Rd.
Kent-Des Moines Rd.
MAURY ISLAND
S.E. 240th St.
Kent Kangley Rd.
North Rd.
169
MAPLE VALLEY

ANCLOTE KEY STATE PRESERVE
RABBIT KEY
SPONGEORAMA EXHIBIT CENTER
ST. NICHOLAS GREEK ORTHODOX CATHEDRAL
To West Pasco Hospital
TARPON SPRINGS
CHAMBER OF COMMERCE
PINELLAS COUNTY
KEYSTONE RD
TARPON AV
KLOSTERMAN RD
582
TARPON SPRINGS LAKE FERN RD
LUTZ LAKE FERN RD
MICHIGAN
ANGEL LA
SIERRA BLVD
41
LUTZ
SUNSET LA
GARDEN ISLAND
BOGGY BAYOU
BOY SCOUT RD
CHANLEY RD
VAN DYKE RD
GUNN HWY
MABRY RD
45
Lake Stemper
LIVINGSTON AV
CRYSTAL BEACH
PALM HARBOR NEBRASKA AV
19
Keystone Lake
N MOBLEY
HUTCHINSON RD
WILCOX RD
TOBACCO RD
CITRUS PARK
41 BUS
E FLETCHER AV
HONEYMOON ISLAND
Little Bayou
OZONA
TAMPA RD
595
S MOBLEY RD
Church Lake
RACE TRACK RD
EHRLICH RD
BEARSS AV
41
W FLETCHER AV
FLORIDA AV
UNIVERSITY SOUTH
DUNEDIN CSWY
Sutherland Bayou
CURLEW RD
55
589
GUNN
587
LINEBAUGH AV
DALE MABRY HWY
FLORIDA
BUSCH
Smith Bayou
Hurricane Pass
CALADESI ISLAND STATE PARK
OLDSMAR
TAMPA BAY DOWNS THOROUGHBRED RACING
580
WATERS AV
VETERANS
ANDERSON RD
SLIGH
92
TAMPA GREYHOUND TRACK
CHILDREN'S MUSEUM
LOWRY PARK ZOO
NEBRASKA
CLEARWATER BEACH ISLAND
DUNEDIN
MAIN ST
OLD MEMORIAL HWY
HILLSBOROUGH
SHELDON
W HILLSBOROUGH AV
LAMBRIGHT ST
McKINLEY
CLEARWATER BEACH
CLEARWATER
PATRICIA
SUNSET POINT RD
MAIN ST
10 ST
SAFETY HARBOR
Safety Harbor
Mobbly Bay
Double Branch Bayou
MEMORIAL HWY
EISENHOWER BLVD
TAMPA INTERNATIONAL AIRPORT
HOULIHAN'S STADIUM
TAMPA
574
CAUSEWAY BLVD
CHAMBER OF COMMERCE
DREW ST
HERCULES AV
COACHMAN RD
McMULLEN BOOTH RD
60
COURTNEY CAMPBELL PARKWAY
Old Tampa Bay
COLUMBUS DR
MARTIN LUTHER
MELBOURNE
GULF TO BAY BLVD
DRUID RD
501
BAYSIDE BRIDGE
49TH ST
275
J.F. KENNEDY BLVD
BROADWAY
BELLEAIR BEACH
BELLEAIR
1
BELLEAIR RD
E BAY DR
Largo Inlet
BOATYARD VILLAGE
686
ROOSEVELT
ST. PETERSBURG-CLEARWATER INTERNATIONAL AIRPORT
HOWARD FRANKLAND BRIDGE
SWANN AV
HENDERSON
BAYSHORE BLVD
618
PETER O KNIGHT AIRPORT
BELLEAIR SHORES
BELLEAIR BLUFFS
W BAY DR
LARGO
BELCHER RD
ULMERTON RD
688
49 ST
Tampa Bay
DALE MABRY HWY
MACDILL AV
TAMPA JAI ALAI
INDIAN ROCKS BEACH
697
WALSINGHAM RD
595
693
BRYAN DAIRY RD
HAINES RD
28 ST N
93
92
600
GANDY BRIDGE
BOUNDARY BLVD N
699
OAKHURST RD
102 AV
STARKEY RD
19
275
687
MACDILL AIRFORCE BASE
INDIAN SHORES
THE SUNCOAST SEABIRD SANCTUARY
78 AV
694
PARK BLVD
PINELLAS PARK
9 ST N
83 AV N
Riviera Bay
WEEDON ISLAND
Sunken Island
REDINGTON SHORES
SEMINOLE
113 ST
66 ST
49 ST
54 AV N
62 AV NE
ROSS ISLAND
PINE KEY
NORTH REDINGTON BEACH
BAY PINES BLVD
46 AV N
KENNETH CITY
55
38 AV N
40 AV NE
Placido Bayou
REDINGTON BEACH
GULF BLVD
BAY PINES
TYRONE BLVD
611
22 AV N
4 ST N
Smacks Bayou
MADEIRA BEACH
JOHN'S PASS VILLAGE AND BOARDWALK
John's Pass
9 AV N
5 AV N
SUNKEN GARDENS
Coffee Pot Bayou
TREASURE ISLAND CSWY
SOUTH PASADENA
GULFPORT BLVD
CENTRAL AV
49 ST
5 AV S
SUNCOAST DOME
375
ST. PETERSBURG
ST. PETERSBURG THUNDER DOME CHAMBER OF COMMERCE
Tampa Bay
TREASURE ISLAND
GULFPORT
Boca Ciega Bay
22 AV S
175
ALBERT WHITTED AIRPORT
SALVADOR DALI MUSEUM
Bayboro Harbor
GREAT EXPLORATIONS, HANDS ON MUSEUM
TROPICANA FIELD
22 AV S
26 AV S
Lake Maggiore
Big Bayou
Double Bayou Pass
Hunter Pass
Pelican Cove
ST. PETE BEACH
54 AV S
5 ST S
COQUINA KEY ISLAND
Little Bayou
RUSKIN
PINELLAS BAYWAY
GULF BLVD
62 AV S
PINELLAS POINT DR
PINELLAS COUNTY STATE AQUATIC PRESERVE
INDIAN KEY
Main Channel
Intracoastal Waterway
PINELLAS COUNTY
HILLSBOROUGH COUNTY
Cockroach Channel
Beacon Pass
SUN CITY
North Channel
SHELL KEY
PARDEE KEY
South Channel
TARPON KEY
19
TAMIAMI TRAIL
SAWYER KEY
CABBAGE KEY
Bunces Pass
MADELAINE KEY
93
BUCKEYE RD
75
MULLET KEY
ST. JEAN KEY
BONNE FORTUNE KEY
679
ANDERSON BLVD
275
SUNSHINE SKYWAY BRIDGE
HILLSBOROUGH
MANATEE COUNTY
93A
683
MOCCASIN
FORT DE SOTO COUNTY PARK
WALLOW
EGMONT KEY NATIONAL WILDLIFE REFUGE
Bishop Harbor
Gulf of Mexico

Scale of Miles
0 1 2 3
© C.S.C.

N

Airport

Coronado National Forest

Tucson Florence

Camino De Oesta
Naranja Rd.
Lambert Dr.
Magee La-Chola
Linda Vista Blvd.
Thornydale
Overton Romero Rd.
Hardy Rd.
Cortaro Farms Rd.
Magee Sage St.
Ina Blvd. Rd.
Orange Grove Dr.
Casa Grande Hwy
Shannon Rd.
La-Chola
JAYNES
Rillito
Skyline Dr.
Campbell
Hacienda Del Sol
Pontatoc Rd.
Sunrise Rd.
Kolb Rd.
Snyder
Sunset Rd.
Silverbell Rd.
Del Cerro
Ruthrauff Rd.
Wetmore
River Rd.
Crc.
Swan
Craycroft
River Rd.
Cloud Rd.
El Camino
Camino De Oesta
El Morago Dr.
Goret Rd.
Tucson Rd.
Flowing Wells Rd.
Fairview
Oracle Rd.
1st Ave.
Roger Rd.
Prince Rd.
Water
Sweet
Freeway Airport
Miracle Mile
Ft. Lowell Rd.
Ft. Lowell
Dodge Blvd.
Ft. Lowell Rd.
Wrightstown
Ironwood Hill Dr.
Grant Rd.
Stone Ave.
Grant Rd.
Grant Rd.
Tangue Verde
TUCSON
Miracle Mile
Speedway Blvd.
Campbell Blvd.
Speedway Blvd.
Speedway
Blvd.
W. Speedway Blvd.
W. Anklam Rd.
Greasewood Rd.
Marys Rd.
University of Arizona
Club Dr.
Broadway
Alverson
Wilmot Rd.
Pantano Rd.
Camino Seco St.
W. Congress
Shannon Rd.
22nd St.
Freeway
22nd
Aviation Way
Randolph Park Municipal Golf Course
Swan Rd.
22nd
Golf Links Rd.
San Juan Trail
36th St.
Silver Lake Rd.
36th
Fairfield Strav
Davis-Monthan Air Force Base
Kolb Rd.
Escalante Rd.
John F. Kennedy Blvd.
Lachola Park
Ajo
Downtown Airport
Country Club Blvd.
Verde
Golf Links Rd.
SOUTH TUCSON
Veterans Hospital
Hwy
Tucson Ajo Hwy
86
De Oeste
Irvington Rd.
Tucson-Benson Hwy
Irvington
Dakota
Valley Rd.
Drexel Rd.
S. Park Ave.
Palo Verde Rd.
EMERY PARK
Valencia Blvd.
LITTLETOWN
Cardinal Ave.
Valencia Rd.
Valencia
12th Ave.
Tucson-Nogales Hwy
Tucson International Airport
Los Reales Rd.
Alverson
Wilmot Rd.
Kolb Rd.
Valen
19
Mission Rd.
6th Ave.
Missiondale
Access Rd.
Vail Rd.
10
San Xavier Indian Reservation
Hughes
Tucson
San Xavier Indian Reservation
19

Left panel:

581
75
275
93
93A
BRUCE B DOWNS BLVD
Creek Clay
FLETCHER AV
FOWLER AV
UNIVERSITY OF SOUTH FLORIDA
CANOE ESCAPE ON THE HILLSBOROUGH R.
56 ST
MUSEUM OF SCIENCE AND INDUSTRY MOSI
ADVENTURE ISLAND
BUSCH GARDENS
HARNEY RD
BLVD
301
FLORIDA EXPO PARK
600
KING R BLVD
50 ST
ORIENT RD
75
93A
FRANK ADAMO DR
618
CAUSEWAY BLVD
MADISON ST AV
PROVIDENCE
RIVERVIEW RD
DR
TAMIAMI TRAIL
BIRD ISLAND
GIBSONTON
GIBSONTON DR
SYMMES RD
RHO
The Kitchen
BIG BEND
SIMMONS LOOP
Little Manatee River
APOLLO BEACH
41
93A
301
75
43
COLLEGE AV E
SUN CITY CENTER
67
LITTLE MANATEE RIVER CANOE OUTPOST
LIGHTFOOT RD
62

Scale of Miles

© ADC of Alexandria

Maryland
Virginia
WASHINGTON D.C.

PATUXEN · SCIENCE · NATIONAL AGRICULTURAL RESEARCH CENTER · GREENBELT · BELTSVILLE · BOWIE · ENTERPRISE · LANHAM · GLENARDEN · LARGO · LANDOVER · NEW CARROLLTON · SEAT PLEASANT · CAPITOL HEIGHTS · DISTRICT HEIGHTS · ANDREWS AIR FORCE BASE · CLINTON · MORNINGSIDE · SILVER VALLEY · FOREST HEIGHTS · OXON HILL · TEMPLE HILLS · SUITLAND · MARLOW HEIGHTS · HILLCREST HEIGHTS · ANACOSTIA · CHEVERLY · FAIRMOUNT HGTS · BLADENSBURG · RIVERDALE · EDMONSTON · COLMAR MANOR · COTTAGE CITY · MOUNT RAINIER · BRENTWOOD · NORTH BRENTWOOD · HYATTSVILLE · UNIVERSITY PARK · COLLEGE PARK · BERWYN HGTS · TAKOMA PARK · SILVER SPRING · WHITE OAK · COLESVILLE · WHEATON · KENSINGTON · GARRETT PARK · CHEVY CHASE · BETHESDA · ROCKVILLE · POTOMAC · GREAT FALLS · MC LEAN · LANGLEY · ARLINGTON · ROSSLYN · GEORGETOWN · ALEXANDRIA · CRYSTAL CITY · MOUNT VERNON · FRANCONIA · SPRINGFIELD · ANNANDALE · BAILEYS CROSSROADS · SEVEN CORNERS · FALLS CHURCH · VIENNA · TYSONS CORNER · FAIRFAX · BURKE · RAVENSWORTH · WEST SPRINGFIELD

POTOMAC RIVER · ANACOSTIA RIVER

INDEX
To The United States
Index to Canadian Cities and Towns on Pages 8-9.
Index to Mexican Cities and Towns on Page 11.

ALABAMA
Page 13
Population: 3,893,888
Capital: Montgomery
Land Area: 50,767 sq. mi.

Abanda ... E-6
Abbeville ... H-6
Action ... Pg. 92, J-4
Ada ... G-5
Adamsville ... Pg. 92, C-2
Addison ... B-4
Akron ... E-3
Alabaster ... D-4
Albertville ... B-5
Alden ... Pg. 92, C-2
Aldrich ... C-4
Alexander City ... E-5
Aliceville ... C-3
Allgood ... C-5
Almond ... E-6
Altoona ... C-5
Andalusia ... H-4
Anderson ... A-4
Anniston ... C-5
Arab ... B-5
Arcus ... C-5
Ardilla ... H-6
Ardmore ... A-4
Argo ... D-5
Arkadelphia ... C-4
Arley ... C-4
Ashby ... C-6
Ashford ... H-7
Ashland ... D-6
Ashville ... C-5
Athens ... A-4
Atmore ... J-3
Attalla ... C-5
Auburn ... F-6
Awin ... G-4
Axis ... J-2
Babbie ... H-5
Bailyton ... B-4
Bakerhill ... G-7
Ballplay ... C-6
Bangor ... C-4
Banks ... G-6
Bankston ... D-6
Barfield ... D-6
Barton ... A-3
Bass ... A-6
Batesville ... G-7
Bay Minette ... J-2
Bay View ... Pg. 92, D-2
Bayou LaBatre ... K-2
Bear Creek ... B-4
Beatrice ... G-3
Belgreen ... B-3
Belk ... D-3
Bellamy ... F-2
Belleville ... F-4
Benton ... C-3
Berry ... C-3
Bessemer ... D-4
  Vicinity ... Pg. 92, H-2
Bessie ... Pg. 92, C-1
Big Cove ... B-5
Billingsley ... E-4
Birmingham ... D-4
  Vicinity ... Pg. 92
Blacksher ... H-3
Blount Springs ... C-4
Blountsville ... C-4
Blue Mountain ... D-5
Bluff ... C-3
Boaz ... C-5
Bolinger ... G-2
Bon Secour ... K-3
Borden Springs ... C-6
Boyd ... F-2
Braggs ... G-6
Brantley ... H-5
Bremen ... C-4
Brent ... E-4
Brewton ... J-4
Bridgeport ... A-6
Brighton ... Pg. 92, G-2
Brilliant ... B-3
Brinn ... B-3
Brooklyn ... H-4
Brookside ... Pg. 92, G-6
Brooksville ... C-5
Brookwood ... D-3
Browns ... F-4
Brownsville ... Pg. 92, G-6
Brundidge ... G-6
Bryant ... A-6
Butler ... G-2
Bynum ... D-5
Cahaba Heights ... Pg. 92, G-6
Calera ... E-4
Calvert ... H-2
Camden ... G-3
Campbell ... G-2
Camphill ... E-6
Carbon Hill ... C-3
Cardiff ... Pg. 92, C-2
Carrollton ... D-2

Carrville ... F-6
Castleberry ... H-4
Catalpa ... G-6
Catherine ... F-3
Cedar Bluff ... B-6
Center Point ... Pg. 92, C-6
Centre ... C-6
Centreville ... E-4
Chalkville ... Pg. 92, B-7
Chastang ... J-2
Chatom ... H-2
Chelsea ... D-5
  Vicinity ... Pg. 92, J-7
Cherokee ... A-3
Chickasaw ... J-2
Childersburg ... D-5
Chrysler ... H-3
Citronelle ... H-2
Claiborne ... G-3
Clanton ... E-4
Claud ... F-5
Clayton ... G-6
Cleveland ... C-5
Clinton ... E-2
Clio ... G-6
Clopton ... H-6
Cloverdale ... A-3
Coalburg ... Pg. 92, D-3
Cochrane ... C-2
Coden ... K-2
Coffeeville ... G-2
Collinsville ... B-6
Columbia ... H-7
Columbiana ... D-5
Consul ... F-3
Cooper ... E-5
Cordova ... C-4
Cottonwood ... J-6
Courtland ... B-4
Coxey ... A-4
Creola ... J-2
Crossville ... B-6
Cuba ... F-2
Cullman ... C-4
Cullomburg ... G-2
Dadeville ... E-6
  Vicinity ... Pg. 92, C-7
Damascus ... H-4
Dancy ... E-2
Danville ... B-4
Daphne ... J-3
Dauphin Island ... K-2
Davenport ... G-5
Daviston ... E-6
Davisville ... F-6
Dawes ... J-2
Dayton ... F-3
Deans ... H-4
Deatsville ... F-5
Decatur ... B-4
Deer Park ... H-2
Dees ... K-2
Delta ... D-6
Demopolis ... F-3
Dill ... H-7
Divide Station ... Pg. 92, B-3
Dixie ... J-4
Dixons Mill ... G-2
Dixonville ... J-4
Docena ... Pg. 92, E-2
Dolomite ... Pg. 92, G-2
Dora ... D-4
Dothan ... H-7
Double Springs ... C-3
Dry Forks ... G-3
Dublin ... D-5
Duke ... C-6
Duncanville ... E-3
E. Brewton ... J-4
Eastern Valley ... Pg. 92, J-2
Easton ... E-6
Echola ... E-2
Eclectic ... F-5
Edgewater ... Pg. 92, E-2
Eight Mile ... J-2
Elamville ... H-6
Elba ... H-5
Elberta ... K-3
Elias ... E-5
Eliska ... H-3
Elmore ... F-5
Elrod ... D-3
Elvira ... Pg. 92, K-3
Emelle ... E-2
Enterprise ... H-5
Eoline ... E-4
Epes ... E-2
Equality ... F-5
Ethelsville ... D-2
Eufaula ... G-7
Eunola ... J-6
Eutaw ... E-3
Evergreen ... H-4
Ewell ... H-6
Fairfax ... F-6
Fairfield ... D-4
  Vicinity ... Pg. 92, F-2
Fairhope ... K-2
Falkville ... B-4
Fatama ... G-4
Fayette ... D-3
Fieldstown ... Pg. 92, C-4
Flat Rock ... A-6

Flint City ... B-4
Flomaton ... J-4
Florala ... J-5
Florence ... A-3
Foley ... K-3
Forkland ... F-2
Forkville ... B-3
Fort Mitchell ... F-7
Fort Payne ... B-6
Francisco ... A-5
Frisco City ... H-3
Fruitdale ... H-2
Fulton ... G-3
Fultondale ... D-4
  Vicinity ... Pg. 92, C-4
Gadsden ... C-6
Gainesville ... E-2
Gallant ... C-5
Gallion ... F-3
Gantt ... H-5
Gardendale ... C-4
  Vicinity ... Pg. 92, B-5
Geiger ... E-2
Genery ... Pg. 92, K-3
Geneva ... J-5
Georgiana ... G-4
Geraldine ... B-5
Glencoe ... C-6
Goodwater ... E-5
Gordo ... D-3
Grand Bay ... K-2
Grants Mill ... Pg. 92, F-7
Graysville ... Pg. 92, C-2
Green Bay ... H-5
Green Pond ... D-4
Greens Station ... Pg. 92, C-6
Greensboro ... E-3
Greenville ... G-5
Greenwood ... Pg. 92, K-2
Grove Hill ... G-3
Guin ... C-3
Gulf Shores ... K-3
Guntersville ... B-5
Gurley ... B-5
Hackleburg ... B-3
Haleyville ... B-3
Halsell ... F-2
Halsos Mill ... G-5
Hamilton ... B-2
Hammondville ... B-6
Hanceville ... C-4
Harpersville ... D-5
Harrisburg ... E-3
Hartford ... J-6
Hartselle ... B-4
Hatton ... B-3
Havana ... E-3
Hawk ... D-6
Hayneville ... F-4
Hazel Green ... A-5
Hazen ... F-4
Headland ... H-7
Helena ... D-4
  Vicinity ... Pg. 92, K-4
Henagar ... A-6
Hobson City ... D-6
Hodges ... B-3
Hokes Bluff ... C-6
Hollis ... D-6
Hollywood ... A-6
Holt ... D-3
Holy Trinity ... F-7
Homewood ... D-4
  Vicinity ... Pg. 92, F-4
Hoover ... D-4
  Vicinity ... Pg. 92, F-4
Hueytown ... D-4
  Vicinity ... Pg. 92, G-1
Hulaco ... B-4
Hunter ... F-5
Huntsville ... A-5
Hurtsboro ... F-6
Huxford ... H-3
Hybart ... G-3
Ider ... B-6
Ino ... H-5
Intercourse ... F-2
Irondale ... D-4
  Vicinity ... Pg. 92, E-7
Isney ... G-2
Ishkooda ... Pg. 92, G-6

Jachin ... F-2
Jack ... H-5
Jackson ... H-3
Jacksonville ... C-6
Jasper ... C-4
Jefferson ... F-2
Jefferson Park ... Pg. 92, E-7
Jemison ... E-4
Jenkins Crossroads ... G-6
Jones ... C-4
Jones Chapel ... C-4
Kellerman ... D-4
Kelly's Crossroads ... E-5
Kellyton ... E-5
Kennedy ... D-2
Ketona ... Pg. 92, B-6
Kilgore ... Pg. 92, B-1
Kimberly ... C-4
Kimbrough ... G-3
Kinsey ... H-6
Kinston ... H-5
Knoxville ... E-3
Koenton ... H-2
La Place ... F-6
Lafayette ... E-6
Lanett ... E-6
Langdale ... E-7
Lawrenceville ... H-6
Leeds ... D-5
Leighton ... A-3
Letohatchee ... G-4
Lewisburg ... Pg. 92, D-4
Lexington ... A-4
Lillian ... K-3
Lincoln ... D-5
Lindbergh ... Pg. 92, C-1
Linden ... F-3
Lineville ... D-6
Linn Crossing ... Pg. 92, B-2
Lipscomb ... Pg. 92, H-3
Littleville ... B-3
Livingston ... F-3
Lockhart ... J-5
Lottie ... H-3
Louisville ... G-6
Lowndesboro ... F-5
Loxley ... K-3
Luverne ... G-5
Lyefflon ... H-4
Lynn ... C-3
Magnolia ... F-3
Malvern ... J-6
Maplesville ... E-4
Marbury ... E-5
Marion ... E-3
Marvyn ... F-6
Maytown ... Pg. 92, E-2
McCalla ... Pg. 92, J-1
McDade ... H-2
McIntosh ... H-2
McKenzie ... H-5
Mentone ... A-6
Meridianville ... A-5
Midfield ... Pg. 92, G-3
Midland City ... H-6
Midway ... G-4
Midway ... G-5
Millerville ... E-5
Millport ... D-2
Millry ... G-2
Mineral Springs ... Pg. 92, C-3
Mitchell ... F-6
Mobile ... J-2
Monroeville ... H-4
Monrovia ... $UP
Montevallo ... D-4
Montgomery ... F-5
Montrose ... K-2
Mooresville ... B-5
Morgan ... F-4
Morgan City ... Pg. 92, J-3
Morris ... B-5
Morvin ... G-3
Moulton ... B-4
Moundville ... E-3
Mount Andrew ... G-6
Mount Olive ... E-5
  Vicinity ... Pg. 92, B-4
Mount Vernon ... J-2
Mount Willing ... G-4
Mountain Brook ... D-4
  Vicinity ... Pg. 92, F-5
Mulberry ... H-4
Mulga ... Pg. 92, E-1
Munford ... D-6
Muscle Shoals ... A-3
Muscoda ... Pg. 92, H-2
Nanafalia ... G-2
Natural Bridge ... B-4
New Brockton ... H-5
New Castle ... Pg. 92, B-5
New Hope ... A-5
  Vicinity ... Pg. 92, J-4
New Lexington ... D-3
New Market ... A-5
Newburg ... B-3
Newsite ... E-5
Newton ... H-6
Newtonville ... D-3
Newville ... H-6
Northport ... D-3
Oak Grove ... Pg. 92, B-4
Oakland ... B-4
Oakman ... C-3
Oakwood ... F-5
Odenville ... D-5
Ohatchee ... C-5
Omaha ... G-7
Oneonta ... C-5
Opelika ... F-6
Opp ... H-5
Overton ... Pg. 92, F-6
Owens Crossroads ... B-5
Oxford ... D-5
Oxmoor ... Pg. 92, G-3
Ozark ... H-6
Palmerdale ... Pg. 92, C-4
Parrish ... C-3
Patton Chapel ... Pg. 92, H-4
Pelham ... Pg. 92, K-4
Pell City ... D-5

Pennington ... F-2
Perdido ... J-3
Peterman ... H-3
Peterson ... D-3
Petersville ... A-3
Phenix City ... F-7
Phil Campbell ... B-3
Pickensville ... C-2
Piedmont ... C-6
Pine Apple ... G-4
Pine Grove ... E-3
Pine Hill ... G-3
Pinson ... Pg. 92, B-6
Pisgah ... B-6
Plantersville ... E-4
Pleasant Grove ... D-2
  Vicinity ... Pg. 92, F-1
Prattville ... F-5
Priceville ... B-4
Prichard ... J-2
Pt. Clear ... K-2
Rabun ... J-3
Rainbow City ... C-5
Rainsville ... B-6
Ranburne ... D-6
Range ... H-4
Red Bay ... B-2
Red Level ... H-4
Reece City ... C-6
Reform ... D-3
Repton ... H-3
Republic ... Pg. 92, D-3
Riley ... G-4
River Falls ... H-5
River View ... J-4
Roanoke ... E-6
Robertsdale ... K-3
Robinwood ... Pg. 92, C-5
Rockdale ... H-2
Rockford ... E-5
Rocky Ridge ... Pg. 92, H-5
Roebuck Plaza ... Pg. 92, D-7
Rogersville ... A-3
Rome ... H-5
Romulus ... E-3
Russellville ... B-3
Rutledge ... G-5
Saco ... G-5
Safford ... F-3
Saint Elmo ... K-2
Salitpa ... G-2
Samson ... H-5
Sanford ... H-4
Santuck ... E-5
Saraland ... J-2
Sardis ... F-4
Satsuma ... J-2
Sayre ... Pg. 92, A-2
Scottsboro ... B-5
Seale ... F-6
Section ... B-5
Selma ... E-4
Shannon ... Pg. 92, H-3
Shawmut ... E-7
Sheffield ... A-3
Shelby ... D-5
Shepardville ... G-4
Shorter ... F-6
Silver Hill ... K-3
Simcoe ... B-4
Sipsey ... C-4
Sledge ... Pg. 92, F-5
Slocomb ... J-6
Smut Eye ... G-6
Snead ... C-5
Snowdown ... F-5
Somerville ... B-4
Southside ... C-5
Spring Hill ... H-6
Springville ... C-5
Sprott ... E-3
Spruce Pine ... B-3
Stafford ... D-2
Steele ... C-5
Stevenson ... A-6
Stewartville ... E-5
Stockton ... J-3
Sulligent ... C-2
Sumiton ... C-4
Summerdale ... K-3
Sunflower ... H-2
Suttle ... G-3
Sweet Water ... G-3
Sylacauga ... D-5
Sylvan Springs ... Pg. 92, E-1
Sylvania ... B-6
Talladega ... D-5
Tallassee ... F-6
Tarrant City ... Pg. 92, D-7
Tensaw ... H-3
Terese ... H-2
Theodore ... K-2
Thomaston ... F-3
Thomasville ... G-3
Thorsby ... E-4
Three Notch ... G-6
Tibbie ... H-2
Town Creek ... B-4
Toxey ... G-2
Trinity ... B-4
Troy ... G-5

Trussville ... D-5
Tuscaloosa ... D-3
Tuscumbia ... A-3
Tuskegee ... F-6
Union Grove ... B-5
  Vicinity ... Pg. 92, D-1
Union Springs ... G-6
Uniontown ... F-3
Uriah ... H-3
Valley Head ... B-6
Vance ... E-3
Vernon ... C-2
Vestavia Hills ... D-4
  Vicinity ... Pg. 92, G-5
Victoria ... H-6
Vidette ... G-5
Village Springs ... C-5
Vineland ... G-3
Vinemont ... B-4
Wadley ... E-6
Wagarville ... H-2
Walker Chapel ... Pg. 92, C-4
Walnut Grove ... C-5
Walnut Hill ... E-6
Warrior ... C-4
Weaver ... C-6
Wedowee ... C-6
Wenonah ... Pg. 92, G-3
West Blocton ... D-4
West Point ... B-4
Wetumpka ... F-5
Whatley ... G-3
Whiteoak ... B-2
Whitson ... D-3
Wicksburg ... H-6
Wilburn ... C-4
Wilmer ... J-2
Wilton ... E-4
Windham Springs ... D-3
Winfield ... C-3
Wing ... J-4
Winterboro ... D-5
Woodville ... B-5
Wren ... B-3
Yantley ... F-2
Yarbo ... H-2
York ... F-2
Zip City ... A-3

ALASKA
Page 14
Population: 401,851
Capital: Juneau
Land Area: 570,883 sq. mi.

Akhiok ... F-5
Akolmiut ... D-4
Akulurak ... D-4
  Inset Map ... B-1
Akutan ... F-2
Alakanuk ... C-4
Alaktak ... A-7
Aleknagik ... E-4
Alice Arm ... H-10
Allakaket ... C-6
Ambler ... B-6
Anaktuvuk Pass ... B-7
Anchorage ... D-6
  Inset Map ... B-2
Anderson ... D-7
Angoon ... G-9
Aniak ... D-4
Anvik ... D-5
Arctic Village ... C-8
Atka ... H-8
Atkasuk ... A-6
Attu ... H-5
Baranof ... G-9
Barrow ... A-7
Beaver ... C-7
Beechey Pt ... A-7
Bethel ... D-4
Bettles ... C-7
Big Delta ... D-7
Big Port Walter ... G-9
Black ... D-7
Brevig Mission ... B-4
Buckland ... C-5
Candle ... C-5
Cantwell ... D-6
Cape Romanzof ... D-3
Cape Yakataga ... F-8
Caro ... C-7
Chalkyitsik ... C-8
Chatanika ... D-7
Chenik ... E-5
Chevak ... D-4
Chicken ... D-8
Chignik ... F-4
Chitina ... E-7
Christian ... C-8
Christochina ... D-7
Chugiak ... B-2
Circle ... D-8
Circle Hot Springs ... D-8
Clarks Pt ... E-5
College ... D-7
Copper Center ... E-7

Cordova ... E-7
Craig ... H-9
Crooked Creek ... D-5
Deadhorse ... B-7
Deering ... B-5
Delta Junction ... D-7
Dillingham ... E-4
Donnelly ... D-7
Dot Lake ... D-8
Douglas ... G-9
Dutch Harbor ... F-2
Eagle ... D-8
Eagle River ... E-6
  Inset Map ... B-2
Edna Bay ... H-9
Eek ... E-4
Egavik ... C-5
Elfin Cove ... G-9
Emmonak ... C-4
English Bay ... F-6
Eureka ... D-7
  Inset Map ... D-4
Fairbanks ... D-7
False Pass ... F-3
Farewell ... D-6
Flat ... D-5
Fort Yukon ... C-8
Gakona ... E-7
Galena ... C-6
Gambell ... C-3
Glen Alps ... E-6
Glennallen ... E-7
Golovin ... C-5
Goodnews Bay ... E-4
Gordon ... B-8
Grayling ... D-5
Gulkana ... E-7
Gustavus ... G-9
Haines ... F-9
Hawk Inlet ... G-9
Healy ... D-7
Homer ... E-6
  Inset Map ... C-1
Hoonah ... G-9
Hooper Bay ... D-3
Hope ... E-6
  Inset Map ... B-2
Houston ... A-2
Hughes ... C-6
Huslia ... C-6
Hydaburg ... H-9
Itullilick ... E-5
Juneau ... G-9
  Inset Map
Kachemak ... E-6
Kake ... G-9
Kaktovik ... B-8
Kalla ... A-7
Kaltag ... C-5
Karluk ... F-5
Kasegaluk ... E-5
Kasilof ... E-6
  Inset Map ... B-1
Kaskanak ... F-4
Katalla ... E-7
Kenai ... E-6
Ketchikan ... H-10
  Inset Map ... A-1
Kiana ... B-5
Kinegnak ... E-4
King Cove ... F-3
King Salmon ... E-5
Kipnuk ... E-4
Kivalina ... B-5
Klawock ... H-9
Knik ... B-2
Kobuk ... C-6
Kodiak ... F-6
Kokrines ... C-6
Koliganek ... E-4
Kotlick ... C-4
Kotzebue ... B-5
Koyuk ... C-5
Koyukuk ... C-6
Kuliuk ... C-6
Kwethluk ... D-4
Kwigillingok ... E-4
Larsen Bay ... F-5
Latouche ... E-7
Levelock ... E-5
Lime Village ... D-6
Livengood ... C-7
Long ... D-6
Lower Tonsina ... E-7
Manley Hot Springs ... D-6
Manokotak ... E-4
McCarthy ... E-8
McGrath ... D-5
McKinley Park ... D-7
Medfra ... D-6
Mekoryuk ... D-3
Mentasta Lake ... D-8
Metlakatla ... H-10
Minto ... D-7
Moose Pass ... B-2
Mount Edgecumbe ... G-9
Mountain Village ... D-4
Naknek ... E-5
Napakiak ... D-4
Napaskiak ... D-4
Nenana ... D-7
New Stuyahok ... E-5
Newhalen ... E-5
Nikolai ... D-6
Nikolski ... F-1

Noatak ... B-5
Nogamut ... E-5
Nome ... C-4
Nondalton ... E-5
Noorvik ... B-5
North Pole ... D-7
Northeast Cape ... C-4
Northway ... E-8
Nulato ... C-5
Old Harbor ... F-5
Ooliktok ... A-7
Ouzinkie ... F-6
Palmer ... E-7
  Inset Map ... A-2
Pedro Bay ... E-5
Pelican ... G-9
Perryville ... F-4
Petersburg ... G-9
Pilgrim Springs ... C-4
Pilot Point ... E-5
Platinum ... E-4
Point Hope ... A-5
Point Lay ... A-5
Porcupine ... F-9
Port Alexander ... G-9
Port Lions ... F-5
Portlock ... F-6
Prudhoe Bay ... B-8
Quinhagak ... E-4
Rampart ... C-7
Rampart House ... C-8
Richardson ... D-7
Ruby ... C-6
Russian Mission ... D-4
Sagwon ... B-7
Salchaket ... D-7
Sand Pt ... F-4
Saroonga ... C-3
Selawik ... B-5
Seward ... E-7
  Inset Map ... C-2
Shageluk ... D-5
Shaktoolik ... C-5
Shishmaref ... B-4
Shungnak ... B-6
Sinuk ... C-4
Sitka ... G-9
Skagway ... F-9
Sleetmute ... D-5
Soldotna ... E-6
  Inset Map ... B-1
St. George ... E-2
St. Marys ... D-4
St. Michael ... D-4
St. Paul ... E-2
Stebbins ... C-4
Stevens Village ... C-7
Stony River ... D-5
Stuyahok ... D-5
Susitna ... D-6
Takotna ... D-5
Talkeetna ... D-7
Tanalian Pt ... E-5
Tanana ... C-6
Tatitlek ... E-7
Teller ... C-4
Tetlin ... E-8
Tetlin Junction ... E-8
Togiak ... E-4
Tok ... D-8
Toksook Bay ... D-3
Tonsina ... E-7
Tuluksak ... D-4
Tununak ... D-3
Tyonek ... E-6
  Inset Map ... B-1
Ugashik ... F-4
Umiat ... B-7
Unalakleet ... C-5
Unalaska ... F-2
Valdez ... E-7
Venetie ... C-8
Wainwright ... A-6
Wales ... B-4
Wasilla ... A-2
White Mountain ... C-4
Whittier ... B-2
Willow ... E-6
  Inset Map ... A-1
Wiseman ... C-7
Wrangell ... G-10
Yakutat ... F-8

ARIZONA
Pages 16-17
Population: 2,718,215
Capital: Phoenix
Land Area: 113,508 sq. mi.

Aguila ... J-3
Ajo ... L-4
Ak Chin ... K-5
Alpine ... J-10
Amado ... N-7
Anegam ... L-5

ARIZONA

Angell F-7
Apache Jct. K-6
Arivaca Jct. N-7
Arizona City L-6
Arlington K-4
Artesia M-6
Ash Fork F-5
Ashurst K-9
Avondale K-5
  Vicinity . . . Pg. 135, E-2
Bagdad G-4
Bapchule K-6
Beaverhead J-10
Bellemont F-6
Benson M-8
Bisbee N-9
Black Canyon City . . H-5
Bonita L-9
Bouse J-2
Bowie M-10
Brenda K-2
Buckeye K-5
Bullhead City F-2
Bylas K-9
Cameron E-7
Camp Verde H-6
Carefree J-6
Carmen N-7
Carrizo J-8
Casa Grande K-6
Cashion L-7
Catalina L-7
Cave Creek J-6
Cedar Creek J-9
Cedar Ridge D-7
Cedar Springs F-8
Central L-9
Chambers F-9
Chandler K-6
Chandler Heights . . K-6
Chilchinbito D-9
Childs L-4
Chinle E-10
Chino Valley G-5
Chloride F-2
Christmas K-8
Christopher Creek . . H-7
Chuichu L-6
Circle City J-4
Clarkdale G-5
Clay Spring H-8
Claypool K-7
Clifton K-10
Cochise M-9
Colorado City C-4
Concho H-9
Congress H-4
Continental M-7
Coolidge K-6
Cordes Jct. H-5
Cornville G-6
Cortaro L-7
Cottonwood G-6
Covered Wells M-5
Cow Springs D-8
Cross Canyon E-10
Curtis M-8
Dateland K-3
Desert View E-6
Dewey H-5
Dilkon F-8
Dinnehotso D-9
Dolan Springs F-2
Dome L-2
Dos Cabezas M-10
Douglas N-10
Dragoon M-9
Dudleyville L-7
Duncan H-10
Eager H-10
Eden K-9
Ehrenberg J-2
Elfrida N-9
Eloy L-6
Fairbank N-8
Flagstaff F-7
Florence K-7
Florence Jct. K-7
Fort Apache J-9
Fort Defiance E-10
Fort Grant L-9
Fort McDowell J-6
Fort Thomas K-8
Fountain Hills J-6
Francisco Grande . . K-5
Franklin L-10
Fredonia C-5
Gadsden L-1
Ganado F-9
Gila Bend K-4
Gilbert K-6
Glendale J-5
  Vicinity . . . Pg. 135, C-3
Globe K-8
Golden Shores G-2
Goldroad F-2
Goodyear K-5
  Vicinity . . . Pg. 135, E-1
Grand Canyon E-5
Gray Mountain E-7
Greasewood (Lower) . F-9
Green Valley M-7
Greer J-10
Guadalupe K-5
  Vicinity . . . Pg. 135, F-5
Hackberry F-3
Hannigan Meadow . . K-10
Harcuvar J-3
Hawley Lake J-9
Hayden K-7
Heber H-8
Higley K-6
Hillside H-4
Holbrook G-8

Hope J-3
Hotevilla E-8
Houck F-10
Huachuca City N-8
Humboldt H-5
Indian Wells F-8
Jacob Lake D-5
Jerome G-5
Johnson M-8
Joseph City G-8
Katherine F-2
Kayenta D-8
Keams Canyon E-9
Kearney K-7
Kelvin K-7
Kingman F-2
Kirkland H-4
Kirkland Jct. H-5
Kohls Ranch H-7
La Palma L-6
Lake Havasu City . . G-2
Lake Montezuma . . G-6
Lakeside H-9
Laveen K-5
  Vicinity . . . Pg. 135, F-3
Leupp F-7
Litchfield Park J-5
Littlefield C-3
Littletown . . . . Pg. 149, H-5
Lukeville M-4
Lupton F-10
Mammoth L-8
Many Farms D-10
Marana L-6
Marble Canyon . . . D-6
Maricopa K-5
Mayer H-5
McGuireville G-6
McNeal N-9
Meadview E-2
Mesa J-6
Mexican Water C-9
Miami K-7
Moenkopi E-7
Moqui E-7
Morenci K-10
Morristown J-4
Mountainaire G-6
Mt. View M-7
Munds Park G-6
Naco N-9
Navajo G-10
Nelson F-3
New River J-5
Nicksville N-8
Nogales N-7
North Rim E-6
Nutrioso J-10
Oatman G-2
Ocotillo K-6
Olberg K-6
Old Oraibi E-8
Oracle L-7
Oracle Jct. L-7
Oraibi E-8
Oro Valley L-7
Overgaard H-8
Page C-7
Palm Springs K-6
Palo Verde K-4
Palominas N-8
Pantano M-8
Paradise City Pg. 135, B-5
Paradise Valley . . . J-5
  Vicinity . . . Pg. 135, C-5
Parker H-2
Parks F-6
Patagonia N-7
Paul Spur N-9
Paulden G-5
Payson H-6
Peach Springs F-3
Peeples Valley H-4
Peoria J-5
  Vicinity . . . Pg. 135, B-2
Peridot K-8
Phoenix J-5
  Vicinity . . . . Pg. 135
Picacho L-6
Pima L-9
Pine H-6
Pine Springs F-5
Pinedale H-8
Pinetop H-9
Pirtleville N-9
Polacca E-8
Pomerene M-8
Prescott G-5
Prescott Valley . . . G-5
Punkin Center J-7
Quartzsite J-2
Queen Creek K-6
Quijotoa M-5
Randolph K-6
Red Lake D-7
Red Rock L-7
Rillito L-7
Riverside K-7
Riviera F-2
Rock Point D-10
Rock Springs J-5
Roosevelt J-7
Rough Rock D-9
Round Rock D-10
Rye H-7
Sacaton K-6
Safford L-9
Sahuarita M-7
Saint David M-9
Saint Johns H-10
Saint Michaels F-10
Salome J-3
San Carlos K-8
San Luis (Yuma Cty) . L-1
San Luis (Pima Cty) . L-5

San Manuel L-8
San Simon M-10
Sanders F-10
Sasabe N-6
Scottsdale J-6
  Vicinity . . . Pg. 135, D-6
Seba Dalkai E-8
Second Mesa E-8
Sedona G-6
Seligman F-4
Sells M-5
Sentinel K-3
Shonto D-8
Show Low H-9
Shumway H-9
Sierra Vista N-8
Silver Bell N-6
Snowflake H-9
Solomon L-9
Somerton L-1
Sonoita N-7
South Tuscon M-7
  Vicinity . . . Pg. 149, G-2
Springerville H-10
Stanfield L-6
Star Valley H-7
Stargo K-10
Strawberry H-6
Sun City J-5
  Vicinity . . . Pg. 135, C-2
Sun City West J-5
Sun Lake K-6
Sun Valley G-9
Sunflower J-6
Sunizona M-9
Sunsites M-9
Superior K-7
Surprise J-5
  Vicinity . . . Pg. 135, B-1
Tacna L-2
Taylor H-9
Teec Nos Pas D-10
Tempe K-6
  Vicinity . . . Pg. 135, E-6
Tes Nez Iha C-9
Thatcher L-9
The Gap D-7
Three Points (Robles) M-6
Tolleson . . . . Pg. 135, E-4
Tombstone N-9
Tonalea D-7
Tonopah J-4
Topock G-2
Tortilla Flat J-7
Tracy M-5
Truxton F-3
Tsaile D-10
Tsegi D-8
Tuba City E-7
Tubac N-7
Tucson M-7
  Vicinity . . . . . Pg. 149
Tumacacori N-7
Tusayan E-5
Vail M-8
Valentine F-3
Valle F-5
Vernon H-9
Vicksburg J-2
Wellton L-1
Wenden J-3
Whiteriver J-9
Why M-4
Wickenburg J-4
Wikieup G-3
Wilhoit H-5
Willcox M-9
Williams F-5
Window Rock F-10
Winkelman K-8
Winona F-7
Winslow H-7
Wintersburg K-4
Wittmann J-4
Yampai F-3
Yarnell H-4
Young H-7
Youngtown J-5
  Vicinity . . . Pg. 135, C-2
Yucca G-2
Yuma L-1

Blue Springs D-4
Bluff City F-4
Blytheville B-9
Booneville D-8
Boxley B-4
Bradley F-3
Brashears B-3
Brinkley D-7
Bryant D-5
Bull Shoals A-5
Cabot D-6
Calico Rock B-6
Calion F-4
Camden F-4
Carlisle D-6
Carthage E-5
Cash C-7
Caulksville C-3
Cave City B-7
Cedarville C-2
Centerville C-4
Charleston C-3
Cherry Valley C-8
Clarksville C-3
Clinton C-5
Conway C-5
Corning A-8
Cotton Plant D-7
Cove E-2
Crossett G-6
Crossroads C-3
Crows B-3
Cushman B-6
Dalark E-4
Damascus C-5
Danville D-4
Dardanelle D-4
DeQueen E-2
DeWitt E-7
Decatur A-2
Delight E-3
Deluce E-3
Dermott F-6
Des Arc D-7
Dierks E-2
Dodridge G-3
Dover C-4
Dumas F-7
Earle C-8
El Dorado G-5
Elaine E-8
Emerson G-4
England D-6
Eudora G-7
Eureka Springs A-3
Falcon F-4
Fallsville B-4
Farmington B-2
Fayetteville B-3
Fisher C-7
Flippin A-5
Florence F-6
Fordyce F-5
Foreman F-2
Forrest City D-8
Fouke G-3
Fountain Hill F-6
Ft. Smith C-2
Garland G-3
Gentry A-2
Gillett E-7
Gilmore B-8
Glenwood E-3
Gosnell B-9
Gould F-6
Grady E-6
Grapevine E-5
Gravette A-2
Green Forest A-4
Greenbrier C-5
Greenwood C-2
Greers Ferry C-6
Gurdon E-4
Hackett C-2
Hagarville C-4
Hamburg G-6
Hampton F-5
Hardy A-7
Harrisburg C-8
Harrison A-4
Hartford C-2
Haskell E-5
Hazen D-7
Heber Springs C-6
Helena D-8
Hermitage F-5
Holly Grove D-7
Hope F-3
Horatio E-2
Horseshoe Bend . . . A-6
Hot Springs E-4
Hoxie B-7
Hughes D-8
Humnoke E-6
Humphrey E-6
Huntsville B-3
Huttig G-5
Jacksonville D-6
Jasper B-4
Jonesboro B-8
Judsonia C-6
Junction City G-5
Keiser B-9
Kensett C-6
Kingsland F-5
Lake City B-8
Lake Village G-7
Lavaca C-3
LePanto C-8
Lead Hill A-5
Leslie B-5
Lewisville F-3
Lincoln B-2
Little Rock D-5
Lockesburg E-3

Lonoke D-6
Lowell A-3
Luxora B-9
Madison D-7
Magnolia G-4
Malvern E-5
Mammoth Spring . . A-7
Manila B-9
Mansfield C-2
Marianna D-8
Marion C-9
Marked Tree C-8
Marmaduke B-8
Marshall B-5
Marvell D-8
Maumelle D-5
Maynard A-7
McCrory C-7
McGehee F-7
Melbourne B-6
Mena D-2
Mineral Springs . . . F-3
Monette B-8
Monticello F-6
Montrose G-6
Morrilton C-5
Mountain Home . . . A-5
Mountain View B-6
Mt. Ida D-3
Mt. Pleasant B-6
Murfreesboro E-3
N. Little Rock D-5
Nashville E-3
Needmore D-3
Newport C-7
Nola D-3
Norman E-3
Oark B-3
Ola D-4
Onyx B-9
Osceola B-9
Oxford B-6
Ozark C-3
Pansy F-6
Paragould B-8
Paris C-3
Parkdale G-6
Parkin C-8
Pea Ridge A-3
Pelsor B-4
Perryville D-5
Piggot A-9
Pine Bluff E-6
Pleasant Plains . . . C-7
Pocahontas A-7
Pollard A-9
Ponca B-4
Portland G-8
Poughke B-7
Prairie Grove B-2
Prattsville E-5
Prescott F-4
Princeton F-5
Quitman C-6
Rector A-8
Reed F-7
Rison F-5
Rogers A-3
Rose Bud C-6
Rosston F-4
Rushing B-6
Russellville C-4
Salem A-6
Salesville A-6
Scranton C-3
Searcy C-6
Sherdian E-5
Shirley C-5
Siloam Springs . . . A-2
Smackover F-5
Snow Lake E-7
Springdale A-2
St. Francis A-9
Star City E-6
Stephens F-4
Story D-3
Strawberry B-7
Strong G-5
Stuttgart E-6
Success A-8
Taylor F-3
Texarkana G-2
Timbo B-5
Trumann B-8
Tupelo C-7
Turrell C-9
VanBuren C-2
Vilonia D-5
Waldo G-4
Waldron D-2
Walker A-4
Walnut Ridge B-8
Warren F-5
Washington F-3
Watson F-7
West Fork B-3
West Helena D-8
West Memphis D-9
Western Grove B-4
White Hall E-6
Wickes E-2
Williams Jct. D-5
Willisville F-4
Wilmar F-6
Wilmot G-6
Wilson B-9
Winslow B-3
Witt Springs B-5
Wynne C-8
Y City D-2
Yellville B-5

CALIFORNIA

CALIFORNIA
Pages 18-21
Population: 23,667,902
Capital: Sacramento
Land Area: 156,299 sq. mi.

Acton S-10
Adelanto S-11
Adin C-7
Agoura Hills S-9
Ahwahnee L-8
Alameda . . . Pg. 144, E-3
Alamorio V-15
Albany . . . . Pg. 144, C-3
Alberhill T-12
Alder Creek . Pg. 141, B-7
Alder Springs F-3
Alderpoint E-2
Alhambra . . . Pg. 114, C-5
Alleghany F-6
Almanor E-6
Alpaugh N-9
Alpine V-12
Alta Loma . . Pg. 116, C-11
Altadena . . . Pg. 114, B-6
Altaville J-6
Alton D-1
Alturas C-7
Amboy S-15
Anaheim T-11
  Vicinity . . . Pg. 117, G-7
Anderson D-4
Angels Camp J-7
Angwin H-3
Annapolis H-2
Antioch J-4
Apple Valley S-12
Aptos L-4
Arbuckle G-4
Arcadia . . . Pg. 116, C-7
Arcata C-1
Arlington Oaks
  . . . . Pg. 141, D-2
Arnold J-7
Arroyo Grande Q-6
Artesia . . . Pg. 115, F-3
Artois F-4
Arvin Q-9
Atascadero P-6
Atherton . . . Pg. 146, A-1
Atwater L-6
Auberry L-8
Auburn H-6
Avalon U-10
Avenal N-7
Avon . . . . . Pg. 144, A-6
Azusa . . . . Pg. 116, C-8
Badger M-9
Baker Q-14
Bakersfield Q-9
Balboa Park . Pg. 143, J-4
Baldwin Park Pg. 116, C-7
Banning T-13
Barstow R-12
Bartlett Sprs. G-3
Bass Lake L-8
Baxter G-6
Baywood Park Q-5
Bear Valley K-7
Beaumont T-12
Beckwourth F-7
Bel Air . . . . Pg. 114, C-4
Belden E-6
Bell . . . . . . Pg. 115, E-5
Bell Gardens Pg. 115, E-5
Bella Vista D-4
Bellflower . . Pg. 115, F-6
Bells Station L-4
Belmont . . . Pg. 145, J-3
Belvedere . . Pg. 144, D-1
Ben Lomond L-4
Bend E-4
Benicia . . . Pg. 144, A-6
Benton K-10
Berenda L-7
Berkeley J-4
  Vicinity . . Pg. 144, D-3
Berry Creek F-6
Bertsch Terr. A-1
Beverly Hills S-10
  Vicinity . . Pg. 114, D-3
Bieber C-6
Big Bar D-3
Big Bear Lake S-13
Big Bend C-5
Big Creek L-9
Big Oak Flat K-7
Big Pine L-10
Big Sur N-4
Biggs G-5
Bishop L-10
Blackwells Corner . . P-7
Blairsden F-7
Bloomington Pg. 116, B-10
Blue Lake C-2
Blythe U-16
Bodega Bay H-2
Bodfish P-10
Bolinas J-3
Boonville G-2
Boron R-11
Borrego Springs . . U-13
Boulder Creek L-4
Boulevard V-13
Bowman G-6
Brawley V-15
Brea . . . . . . Pg. 117, E-8
Brentwood J-5
  Vicinity . . Pg. 145, G-1
Bridgeport J-9
Bridgeville D-2
Broderick H-5

Browns Valley G-5
Brownsville G-6
Bryn Mawr . Pg. 116, B-12
Buellton R-6
Buena Park . Pg. 117, F-7
Burbank . . . Pg. 114, B-4
Burlingame . Pg. 145, H-2
Burney D-5
Burnt Ranch C-3
Butte City F-4
Butte Meadows . . . E-5
Buttonwillow Q-8
Cabazon T-13
Cahuilla U-13
Calavo Gardens
  . . . . Pg. 143, F-6
Calexico V-15
Caliente Q-10
California City Q-11
Calipatria V-15
Calistoga H-3
Callahan C-4
Calpella G-2
Calpine F-7
Cambria P-5
Cameron Park H-6
Camino H-7
Camp Nelson N-10
Camp Richardson . . H-8
Campbell . . Pg. 146, E-8
Campo V-13
Camptonville G-6
Canby C-7
Canoga Park . Pg. 114, B-1
Cantil Q-10
Canyon Dam E-6
Capay H-4
Capetown D-1
Capitola L-4
Carlotta D-1
Carlsbad U-11
Carmel Valley P-4
  Vicinity . . Pg. 143, C-6
Carmichael . . Pg. 141, B-5
Carnelian Bay G-7
Carpinteria S-8
Carson . . . . Pg. 115, F-2
Carson Hill - Cartago N-11
Caruthers M-7
Casmalia R-6
Caspar F-1
Castaic S-9
Castella C-4
Castroville M-4
Cayucos P-5
Cedar Grove M-10
Cedarville C-8
Century City Pg. 114, D-3
Ceres K-6
Chalfant L-10
Challenge G-6
Chatsworth . Pg. 114, B-1
Chester E-6
Chico F-5
China Lake P-11
Chino . . . . . Pg. 116, D-10
Cholame P-7
Chowchilla L-7
Chula Vista V-12
  Vicinity . . Pg. 143, J-5
Cima Q-15
Citrus . . . . Pg. 141, B-5
Claremont . . Pg. 116, C-10
Clarksburg H-5
Clay J-6
Clayton . . . Pg. 144, C-7
Clearlake H-3
Clio F-7
Clovis M-8
Clyde . . . . . Pg. 144, A-6
Coachella U-14
Coalinga N-6
Coarsegold L-8
Cobb H-3
Colfax G-6
Coloma H-6
Colton . . . . Pg. 116, B-11
Colusa G-4
Commerce . . Pg. 114, D-5
Compton . . Pg. 115, F-4
Concord J-4
  Vicinity . . Pg. 144, B-6
Copperopolis J-7
Copper Farms Pg. 141, A-5
Corcoran N-8
Corning E-4
Corona . . . Pg. 117, F-11
Coronado V-12
  Vicinity . . Pg. 143, H-2
Costa Mesa . Pg. 117, H-8
Cottonwood D-4
Coulterville K-7
Courtland J-5
Covelo E-3
Covina . . . . Pg. 116, C-8
Crannell C-1
Crescent City B-1
Crescent Mills E-6
Crestmore . . Pg. 116, B-11
Crockett . . . Pg. 144, A-4
Cucamonga Pg. 116, C-11
Cudahy . . . Pg. 115, E-5
Culver City . Pg. 114, D-3
Cummings E-2
Cupertino . . Pg. 146, D-4
Cutler N-9
Cutten C-1
Cuyama R-8
Cypress . . . Pg. 115, G-6
Daggett R-12
Dairyville E-4
Dales E-4
Daly City K-3
  Vicinity . . Pg. 145, G-1
Dana Point U-10
Danville . . . Pg. 144, D-6
Darwin N-11

Davis H-5
Davis Creek B-8
Death Valley Jct. . . N-13
Del Mar V-11
  Vicinity . . Pg. 143, B-1
Delano P-9
Desert Center T-15
Desert Hot Springs . T-13
Desert Shores U-14
Devils Den P-7
Diamond Bar Pg. 116, D-8
Diamond Sprs. H-6
Dictionary Hill
  . . . . Pg. 143, G-6
Dillon Beach J-2
Dinkey Creek L-9
Dixon H-5
Dobbins G-6
Dominguez . Pg. 115, F-5
Dorris B-5
Dos Palos L-6
Dos Rios F-2
Douglas City D-3
Downey . . . Pg. 115, G-6
Doyle F-8
Duarte . . . . Pg. 116, C-7
Ducor P-9
Dulzura V-12
Dunsmuir C-4
Durham F-5
Eagle Rock . Pg. 114, C-5
Eagleville C-8
Earlimart P-9
Earp T-17
East Highlands
  . . . . Pg. 116, A-12
East Los Angeles
  . . . . Pg. 114, D-5
East Palo Alto
  . . . . Pg. 146, A-2
Edison Q-9
El Cajon V-12
El Centro V-15
El Cerrito . . Pg. 144, C-3
El Granada . . Pg. 145, J-1
El Monte . . . Pg. 114, C-6
El Nido L-7
El Portal K-8
El Segundo . Pg. 114, D-3
Elk Creek F-4
Elk Grove J-5
Elmira J-4
Emeryville . . Pg. 144, D-3
Encinitas V-11
Encino . . . . Pg. 114, C-2
Enterprise D-4
Escalon K-6
Escondido U-11
Esparto H-4
Essex R-15
Etiwanda . . Pg. 116, C-12
Etna B-4
Eucalyptus Hills
  . . . . Pg. 143, C-6
Eureka C-1
Exeter N-9
Fair Oak . . . Pg. 141, A-6
Fairfield J-4
Fall River Mills . . . C-6
Fallbrook U-12
Farmersville N-9
Farmington J-6
Fawnskin S-12
Feather Falls F-6
Fellows Q-8
Fenner R-15
Ferndale D-1
Fields Landing D-1
Fillmore S-9
Firebaugh M-6
Fish Camp L-8
Fish Rock G-2
Five Points N-7
Flintridge . . Pg. 114, B-6
Florence . . . Pg. 115, G-6
Florin J-5
  Vicinity . . Pg. 141, E-4
Floriston G-8
Flournoy E-4
Folsom H-6
Fontana . . . Pg. 116, C-12
Foothill Farms Pg. 141, A-5
Forbestown F-6
Ford City Q-8
Forest Glen D-3
Forest Ranch F-5
Foresthill G-6
Forks Of Salmon . . C-3
Fortuna C-1
Foster City . Pg. 145, H-4
Fountain Valley
  . . . . Pg. 117, H-7
Fowler M-8
Frazier Park R-9
Fredericksburg . . . H-8
Fremont K-4
  Vicinity . . Pg. 145, A-5
Frenbrook . . Pg. 143, B-7
French Gulch D-4
Fresno M-8
Ft. Bidwell B-8
Ft. Bragg F-1
Ft. Dick A-1
Ft. Jones B-4
Fullerton T-11
  Vicinity . . Pg. 117, F-7
Furnace Creek Ranch
  . . . . N-13
Galt J-5
Garberville E-2
Garden Grove
  . . . . Pg. 117, G-7
Gardena . . . Pg. 115, F-4
Gasquet A-2

ARIZONA *(continued column)*

ARKANSAS
Page 15
Population: 2,286,435
Capital: Little Rock
Land Area: 52078 sq. mi.

Alpena A-4
Altheimer E-6
Amity E-4
Arkadelphia E-4
Arkansas City F-7
Ash Flat A-7
Ashdown F-2
Athens E-3
Atkins C-4
Augusta C-7
Bald Knob C-6
Banks F-5
Barling C-2
Batesville B-6
Bay B-8
Bearden F-5
Beebe C-6
Benton D-5
Bentonville A-3
Bergman A-4
Berryville A-4
Bismark E-4
Black Rock B-7

CALIFORNIA

COLORADO

Gaviota R-7
Gazelle B-4
Georgetown H-6
Gerber E-4
Geyserville H-3
Giant Forest Village . N-10
Gilroy L-5
Glamis V-16
Glen Avon . . Pg. 116, D-12
Glen Ellen H-3
Glendale S-10
Vicinity . . . . Pg. 114, B-4
Glendora S-11
Vicinity . . . . Pg. 116, C-8
Glenn H-4
Glennville P-10
Glenview . . . . Pg. 143, B-8
Goffs R-16
Goleta S-7
Gonzales M-5
Gorman R-9
Goshen N-8
Graeagle F-7
Granada Hills . Pg. 114, A-1
Grand Terrace
. . . . Pg. 116, B-11
Graniteville G-7
Grass Valley G-6
Green Acres Q-9
Greenfield N-5
Greenview B-4
Greenville F-7
Grenada B-4
Gridley G-4
Grimes G-4
Groveland K-7
Grover City Q-6
Guadalupe Q-6
Gualala G-2
Guerneville H-2
Guinda H-3
Gustine L-6
Hacienda Heights
. . . . Pg. 116, D-7
Half Moon Bay K-3
Hallelujah Jct. F-8
Hamburg B-3
Hamilton City G-4
Hanford N-8
Happy Camp B-3
Harbor Side . . Pg. 143, J-4
Harden Flat K-7
Hawaiian Gardens
. . . . Pg. 115, G-6
Hawthorne . . . Pg. 115, F-3
Hayfork D-3
Hayward H-4
Vicinity . . . . Pg. 145, G-6
Healdsburg H-3
Heber V-15
Helena D-3
Helendale R-12
Hemet T-12
Hercules . . . . Pg. 144, B-3
Herlong E-8
Hermosa Beach
. . . . Pg. 115, F-3
Herndon M-7
Hesperia . . . . Pg. 116, A-12
Highland . . . Pg. 116, A-12
Highland Park
. . . . Pg. 114, C-5
Hillsborough . . Pg. 145, H-2
Hilmar L-6
Hilt A-4
Hinkley R-12
Hobart Mills G-7
Hollister M-5
Hollywood . . . Pg. 114, D-4
Holtville V-15
Homewood G-7
Honcut G-5
Honeydew D-1
Hoopa C-2
Hopland H-2
Hornbrook B-4
Hornitos K-7
Hume M-9
Huntington Beach . . T-10
Vicinity . . . . Pg. 117, H-7
Huntington Park
. . . . Pg. 114, E-5
Huron N-7
Idyllwild T-13
Igo D-4
Imperial V-15
Imperial Beach V-12
Vicinity . . . . Pg. 143, K-3
Independence M-10
Indio T-14
Industry . . . . Pg. 116, D-7
Inglewood . . . Pg. 115, E-3
Ingot D-5
Inverness H-2
Inyokern P-11
Ione J-6
Irvine . . . . . Pg. 117, H-9
Isleton J-5
Ivanpah Q-15
Jackson J-6
Jamacha . . . . Pg. 143, F-7
Jamacha Junction
. . . . Pg. 143, F-7
Jamestown K-7
Jamul V-13
Janesville E-7
Johannesburg Q-11
Johnstonville E-7
Johnstown . . . Pg. 143, D-7
Jolon N-5
Joshua Tree S-13
Julian V-13
Junction City D-3
June Lake K-9
Keddie E-6

Keeler N-11
Keene Q-10
Kelseyville G-3
Kelso R-15
Kenwood H-3
Kerman M-7
Kernville P-10
Kettleman City N-7
King City N-5
Kings Beach G-8
Kingsburg N-8
Kirkwood H-7
Kit Carson H-7
Klamath Glen B-2
Klamath River B-4
Kneeland D-2
Knights Ferry K-6
Knights Landing H-5
Kyburz H-7
La Canada . . . Pg. 114, B-5
La Crescenta Pg. 114, B-4
La Grange K-7
La Habra . . . . Pg. 117, E-7
La Honda L-3
La Jolla . . . . Pg. 143, D-1
La Jolla Mesa
. . . . Pg. 143, D-1
La Mesa . . . . Pg. 143, F-5
La Mirada . . . Pg. 117, F-7
La Palma . . . . Pg. 115, F-6
La Presa . . . . Pg. 143, G-5
La Puente . . . Pg. 116, D-7
La Quinta T-13
Lafayette . . . . Pg. 144, C-5
Laguna Beach U-10
Lake City B-8
Lake Elsinore T-12
Lake Forest T-11
Lakehead D-4
Lakeport G-3
Lakeside . . . . Pg. 143, D-7
Lakewood . . . Pg. 115, F-5
Lamont Q-9
Lancaster R-10
Lawndale . . . Pg. 115, F-3
Laytonville F-2
Lee Vining K-9
Leggett E-2
Lemon Grove Pg. 143, G-5
Lemoore N-7
Lenwood R-12
Leucadia V-11
Likely C-7
Lincoln H-5
Lincoln Acres Pg. 143, H-4
Linda G-5
Linden J-6
Lindsay N-9
Litchfield E-7
Little Lake P-11
Live Oak G-5
Livermore K-4
Livingston L-6
Lockeford J-6
Lockwood N-5
Lodi J-5
Loleta D-1
Loma Linda Pg. 116, B-11
Lomita . . . . . Pg. 115, G-4
Lompoc R-6
Lone Pine N-10
Long Beach T-10
Vicinity . . . . Pg. 115, G-5
Longvale F-2
Lookout C-6
Loomis H-6
Los Alamos R-7
Los Altos . . . . Pg. 145, C-3
Los Altos Hills
. . . . Pg. 146, C-2
Los Angeles . . Pg. 114, D-4
Vicinity . . . . Pg. 114-117
Los Banos L-6
Los Gatos L-4
Vicinity . . . . Pg. 146, F-5
Los Molinos E-4
Los Olivos R-7
Lost Hills P-8
Lower Lake G-3
Loyalton F-7
Lucerne G-3
Lucerne Valley S-12
Ludlow R-14
Lynwood . . . . Pg. 115, G-5
Lynwood Hills Pg. 143, J-5
Macdoel B-5
Mad River D-2
Madeline D-7
Madera M-7
Malaga M-8
Malibu S-9
Mammoth Lakes K-9
Manchester G-2
Manhattan Beach
. . . . Pg. 115, F-3
Manteca K-5
Manton D-5
Maricopa Q-8
Marina M-4
Markleeville H-8
Martinez . . . . Pg. 143, D-1
Maxwell G-4
Maywood . . . . Pg. 114, E-5
McArthur D-6
McCloud C-5
McFarland P-9
McKinleyville C-1
McKittrick P-8
Meadow Valley F-6
Meadow Vista H-6
Mecca U-14
Meeks Bay H-6
Mendocino F-2

Mendota M-7
Menlo Park . . . Pg. 146, A-2
Merced L-7
Mercy Hot Springs . . M-6
Meridian G-5
Meyers H-8
Mi-wuk Village K-7
Middletown H-3
Midpines K-8
Milford E-7
Millbrae . . . . Pg. 145, H-2
Millville D-4
Milpitas K-4
Vicinity . . . . Pg. 146, B-6
Mineral E-5
Mira Loma . . . Pg. 116, E-12
Miramar . . . . Pg. 143, C-4
Miranda E-2
Mission Beach
. . . . Pg. 143, F-1
Mission Hills Pg. 114, B-2
Mission Viejo T-11
Modesto K-6
Mojave R-10
Mokelumne Hill J-7
Mono Hot Springs . . L-9
Mono Lake K-9
Monolith . . . . Pg. 116, C-7
Montague B-4
Montara . . . . Pg. 145, H-1
Montclair . . . Pg. 116, D-10
Monte Rio H-2
Monte Serona
. . . . Pg. 146, E-4
Montebello . . . Pg. 114, D-6
Montecito R-7
Monterey M-4
Monterey Park
. . . . Pg. 114, D-5
Montgomery Creek . . C-5
Montrose . . . . Pg. 114, B-5
Moorpark S-9
Moraga . . . . . Pg. 144, D-5
Moreno . . . . . Pg. 143, C-7
Moreno Valley T-12
Morgan . . . . . Pg. 146, G-10
Morgan Hill L-5
Mormon Bar L-8
Morongo Valley T-13
Morro Bay Q-5
Moss Beach Pg. 145, J-1
Moss Landing M-4
Mountain View
. . . . Pg. 146, B-3
Mt. Bullion K-7
Mt. Laguna V-13
Mt. Shasta C-4
Mugginsville B-4
Murphys J-7
Murrieta U-12
Napa J-4
National City Pg. 143, H-4
Navarro G-2
Needles R-16
Nevada City G-6
New Cuyama R-7
New Idria M-5
Newark . . . . . Pg. 145, J-6
Newberry Springs . . . R-13
Newell B-6
Newport Beach U-10
Vicinity . . . . Pg. 117, J-8
Nice G-3
Niland U-15
Nimbus . . . . . Pg. 141, B-7
Nipomo Q-6
Nipton Q-15
Nord F-5
Norco . . . . . . Pg. 117, E-11
North Edwards R-11
North Fork L-8
North Highlands
. . . . Pg. 141, A-4
North Hollywood
. . . . Pg. 114, C-3
Northridge . . Pg. 114, B-1
Norwalk . . . . Pg. 115, F-6
Novato J-3
Noyo F-2
Nubieber C-6
O'Neals L-8
Oakdale K-6
Oakhurst L-8
Oakland K-4
Vicinity . . . . Pg. 144, C-6
Oasis L-11
Oceano Q-6
Oceanside U-11
Ocotillo V-14
Ocotillo Wells V-14
Ojai S-8
Olancha N-11
Old Station D-6
Olema J-3
Olinda D-4
Ono D-4
Ontario T-11
Vicinity . . . . Pg. 116, D-10
Onyx P-10
Orange . . . . . Pg. 117, G-8
Orange Cove N-9
Orangevale . . Pg. 141, A-6
Orcutt R-6
Ordbend F-5
Orick C-1
Orland F-4
Orleans C-2
Oro Grande R-12
Orosi N-9
Otay . . . . Pg. 143, K-5
Otay Mesa . . . Pg. 143, K-5
Oxnard S-8
Pacific Grove M-4

Pacific Palisades
. . . . Pg. 114, D-1
Pacifica K-3
Vicinity . . . . Pg. 145, G-1
Paicines M-5
Pala U-12
Palermo G-5
Palm Desert T-13
Palm Springs T-13
Palmdale S-10
Palms . . . . . . Pg. 114, D-3
Palo Alto K-4
Vicinity . . . . Pg. 146, B-2
Palo Verde U-16
Palomar Mountain . . U-13
Palos Verdes Estates
. . . . Pg. 115, G-3
Panamint Sprs. N-12
Panoche M-6
Panorama City
. . . . Pg. 114, B-2
Paradise F-5
Paramount . . . Pg. 115, F-5
Parker Dam S-17
Parkfield P-6
Pasadena S-10
Vicinity . . . . Pg. 114, C-5
Paskenta E-4
Paso Robles P-6
Patterson L-5
Patton . . . . . Pg. 116, A-12
Pauma Valley U-12
Pearblossom S-11
Pebble Beach M-4
Pedley . . . . . Pg. 117, E-12
Penn Valley G-6
Perkins . . . . . Pg. 141, D-4
Perris T-12
Petrolia D-1
Phelan S-11
Philo G-2
Pico Rivera . Pg. 114, E-6
Piedmont . . . . Pg. 144, D-4
Piercy E-2
Pine Grove J-6
Pine Valley V-13
Pinecrest J-8
Pinedale M-8
Pinole . . . . . . Pg. 144, B-3
Pioneer Station J-7
Pismo Beach Q-6
Pittsburg . . . . Pg. 144, A-7
Pixley P-9
Placentia . . . Pg. 117, F-8
Placerville H-6
Planada L-7
Pleasant Hill . . Pg. 144, B-6
Plymouth H-6
Point Arena G-2
Pollock Pines H-7
Pomona T-11
Vicinity . . . . Pg. 116, D-9
Pondosa C-5
Poplar P-9
Port Hueneme S-8
Porterville N-9
Portola F-7
Portola Valley Pg. 146, C-1
Portuguese Bend
. . . . Pg. 115, H-3
Potter Valley G-3
Poway V-12
Vicinity . . . . Pg. 143, B-5
Pozo Q-7
Princeton G-4
Project City D-4
Pulga F-6
Pumpkin Center Q-9
Quincy . . . . . Pg. 117, E-11
Raisin M-7
Ramona V-12
Rancho Cordova
. . . . Pg. 141, C-6
Rancho Palos Verdes . T-9
Randsburg Q-11
Ravendale D-7
Red Bluff E-4
Red Mountain Q-11
Redcrest D-1
Redding D-4
Redlands . . . . Pg. 116, B-12
Redondo Beach T-9
Vicinity . . . . Pg. 115, G-3
Redway E-2
Redwood City Pg. 145, J-4
Redwood Valley G-2
Requa B-1
Reseda . . . . . Pg. 114, B-1
Rialto . . . . . Pg. 116, A-10
Richmond . . . . Pg. 144, C-2
Richvale F-5
Ridgecrest Q-11
Rio Dell D-1
Rio Linda H-5
Vicinity . . . . Pg. 141, A-3
Rio Oso H-5
Rio Vista J-5
Ripley U-16
Ripon K-5
River Pines H-6
Riverdale N-7
Riverside T-12
Vicinity . . . . Pg. 117, E-12
Riverview . . . Pg. 141, E-1
Robla . . . . . . Pg. 141, A-3
Rock Haven . . Pg. 143, A-6
Rocklin H-5
Rockport F-2
Rodeo . . . . . Pg. 144, A-3
Rohnert Park J-3
Rolling Hills . Pg. 115, G-3
Rolling Hills Estate
. . . . Pg. 115, G-3
Romoland T-12

Rosamond R-10
Rosemead . . . Pg. 114, D-6
Rosemont . . . . Pg. 141, C-5
Roseville H-5
Rough And Ready . . . G-6
Round Mountain D-5
Rovana L-10
Rowland Heights
. . . . Pg. 116, E-8
Rutherford H-4
Sacramento H-5
Vicinity . . . . Pg. 141
Salinas M-5
Salton City U-14
Salyer C-2
San Andreas J-7
San Ardo N-5
San Bernardino T-12
Vicinity . . . . Pg. 116, A-11
San Carlos . . . Pg. 145, J-3
San Clemente U-11
San Diego V-12
Vicinity . . . . Pg. 143
San Dimas . . . Pg. 116, C-9
San Fernando S-10
Vicinity . . . . Pg. 114, A-2
San Francisco K-3
Vicinity . . . . Pg. 145
San Gabriel . . Pg. 114, C-6
San Jacinto T-12
San Joaquin M-7
San Jose L-5
Vicinity . . . . Pg. 146, D-8
San Juan Bautista . . M-5
San Juan Capistrano U-11
San Leandro Pg. 145, F-5
San Lorenzo Pg. 145, G-5
San Lucas N-5
San Luis Obispo Q-6
San Marcos U-12
San Marino . . Pg. 114, C-6
San Martin L-5
San Mateo . . . Pg. 145, H-3
Vicinity . . . . Pg. 145, H-3
San Miguel P-6
San Pablo . . . Pg. 144, B-3
San Pedro . . . Pg. 115, H-4
San Rafael J-3
Vicinity . . . . Pg. 144, B-1
San Simeon P-5
Sanger M-8
Santa Ana T-11
Vicinity . . . . Pg. 117, H-8
Santa Barbara S-7
Santa Clara L-4
Vicinity . . . . Pg. 146, C-5
Santa Clarita S-9
Santa Cruz L-4
Santa Fe Springs
. . . . Pg. 115, E-6
Santa Margarita Q-6
Santa Maria Q-6
Santa Monica . . Pg. 114, E-2
Santa Nella L-6
Santa Paula S-8
Santa Rosa H-3
Santa Ysabel V-13
Santee V-12
Vicinity . . . . Pg. 143, D-6
Saratoga L-4
Vicinity . . . . Pg. 146, E-4
Saticoy S-9
Sattley F-7
Sausalito J-3
Vicinity . . . . Pg. 144, D-1
Sawyers Bar C-3
Scotia D-1
Scotts Valley L-4
Scottys Castle M-12
Seeley V-14
Selma M-8
Shafter Q-8
Shandon P-6
Shasta D-4
Shaver Lake L-8
Shelter Cove E-1
Sherman Oaks
. . . . Pg. 114, C-2
Shingletown D-5
Short Acres . . Pg. 144, A-6
Shoshone P-14
Sierra City F-7
Sierra Madre Pg. 114, B-6
Sierraville F-7
Signal Hill . . Pg. 115, G-5
Simi Valley S-9
Simmler Q-7
Sisquoc R-7
Sites G-4
Sloat F-7
Smith River A-2
Snelling K-7
Soda Springs G-7
Solana Beach
. . . . Pg. 143, A-1
Soledad N-5
Solvang R-7
Somers D-3
Somes Bar B-3
Sonora K-7
Soquel . . . . . Pg. 143, C-1
Sorrento . . . . Pg. 143, C-1
South El Monte
. . . . Pg. 114, D-6
South Gate . . . Pg. 115, E-5
South Lake Tahoe . . . H-8
South Pasadena
. . . . Pg. 114, C-5
South Port . . . Pg. 141, D-1
South San Francisco
. . . . Pg. 145, G-2
Spring Valley Pg. 143, G-6
Springville N-9

Squaw Valley G-7
St. Helena H-3
Standish E-7
Stanton . . . . . Pg. 117, G-7
Stewarts Point H-2
Stirling City F-5
Stockton K-5
Stonyford F-4
Stovepipe Wells N-12
Stratford N-8
Strathmore N-9
Studio City . . Pg. 114, C-3
Suisun City J-4
Summerland S-8
Summit City D-4
Sun City T-12
Sun Valley . . Pg. 114, B-3
Sunland . . . . Pg. 114, A-3
Sunnyvale K-5
Vicinity . . . . Pg. 146, C-4
Surf R-6
Susanville E-7
Sutter G-5
Sutter Creek J-6
Taft Q-8
Tahoe City G-7
Talmage G-3
Tarzana . . . . Pg. 114, C-1
Taylorsville E-6
Tecopa P-14
Tehachapi Q-10
Temecula U-12
Temple City . . Pg. 114, C-6
Templeton P-6
Terminous J-5
Termo D-7
Terra Bella P-8
Thornton J-5
Thousand Oaks S-9
Thousand Palms T-13
Three Rivers N-9
Tiburon . . . . . Pg. 144, D-1
Tipton N-8
Tomales J-3
Toms Place L-10
Topanga Beach
. . . . Pg. 114, D-1
Topaz H-8
Torrance . . . . Pg. 115, F-3
Tracy K-5
Vicinity . . . . Pg. 117, H-8
Tranquillity M-7
Tres Pinos M-5
Trinity Center C-1
Trona P-12
Truckee G-7
Tujunga . . . . Pg. 114, A-4
Tulelake B-6
Tuolumne K-7
Turlock L-6
Tustin . . . . . Pg. 117, G-9
Tuttletown K-7
Twain F-6
Twain Harte K-7
Twentynine Palms . . . S-14
Ukiah G-2
Union City . . Pg. 145, H-6
Universal City Pg. 114, C-3
Upland . . . . . Pg. 116, C-10
Upper Lake G-3
Vacaville H-4
Vallejo J-4
Valley Springs J-6
Valley View Acres
. . . . Pg. 141, A-2
Van Nuys . . . . Pg. 114, B-2
Venice . . . . . Pg. 114, E-2
Ventura S-8
Victorville S-12
Vidal T-17
Vina E-4
Vinton F-8
Visalia N-8
Vista U-12
Walker J-8
Walnut . . . . . Pg. 116, D-8
Walnut Creek J-4
Vicinity . . . . Pg. 144, C-6
Walnut Grove J-5
Wasco P-8
Washington G-7
Waterford K-6
Waterloo J-6
Watsonville L-4
Watts . . . . . . Pg. 115, E-4
Wawona L-8
Weaverville D-3
Weed C-4
Weitchpec C-2
Wendel E-8
Weott D-1
West Covina Pg. 116, D-8
West Hollywood
. . . . Pg. 114, D-3
West Los Angeles
. . . . Pg. 114, D-2
West Point J-7
West Riverside
. . . . Pg. 116, D-12
West Sacramento
. . . . Pg. 141, C-4
Westley K-6
Westminister Pg. 117, G-7
Westmorland V-14
Westport F-2
Westwood E-6
Wheatland H-5
Whitmore D-5
Whittier . . . . . Pg. 117, E-7
Williams G-4
Willits F-2
Willow Creek C-2
Willow Ranch B-8

Willow Springs R-10
Willows F-4
Wilmington . . . Pg. 115, G-4
Winter Gardens
. . . . Pg. 143, D-6
Winterhaven V-16
Winters H-4
Winton L-6
Wofford Heights P-10
Woodfords H-8
Woodlake N-9
Woodland H-4
Woodville N-9
Woody P-9
Wrightwood S-11
Yermo R-12
Yolo H-5
Yorba Linda . . . Pg. 117, F-9
Yorkville G-2
Yosemite Village K-8
Yreka B-4
Yuba City G-5
Yucaipa T-12
Yucca Valley S-13

COLORADO
Pages 22-23
Population: 2,889,964
Capital: Denver
Land Area: 103,595 sq. mi.

Abarr S-12
Agate D-10
Aguilar J-9
Akron C-11
Alamosa J-7
Allison J-5
Alma E-7
Almont F-6
Amherst B-12
Antero Jct. F-7
Anton D-11
Antonito J-7
Arapahoe F-12
Arboles J-5
Arlington G-11
Aroya F-11
Arriba E-11
Arriola J-3
Arvada D-8
Vicinity . . . . Pg. 103, C-6
Aspen E-6
Atwood B-11
Ault B-9
Aurora D-9
Vicinity . . . . Pg. 103, E-7
Austin F-4
Avon D-6
Avondale G-9
Bailey E-8
Barnesville B-9
Bartlett H-12
Basalt E-6
Baxter G-9
Bayfield J-5
Bedrock G-3
Bellvue B-8
Bennett D-9
Berthoud C-8
Beshoar Jct. J-10
Bethune D-12
Black Hawk D-8
Blanca H-8
Blue Mountain C-3
Blue River D-7
Bond D-7
Boone G-10
Boulder C-8
Bow Mar . . Pg. 103, H-4
Bowie F-5
Boyero E-11
Brandon F-12
Branson J-10
Breckenridge D-7
Breen J-4
Briggsdale B-9
Brighton C-8
Bristol G-12
Broomfield C-8
Brush C-10
Buckingham B-9
Buena Vista F-7
Buford D-5
Burlington D-12
Byers D-9
Cahone H-4
Calhan E-10
Cameo E-4
Campo J-12
Canon City F-8
Capulin J-7
Carbondale E-6
Carlton G-12
Castle Rock D-8
Cedaredge F-4
Center H-7
Chama J-8
Cheney Center G-12
Cheraw G-11
Cherry Hill Village
. . . . Pg. 103, E-6
Cheyenne Wells F-12
Chimney Rock J-5
Chipita Park E-8
Chivington F-12
Chromo J-6
Cimarron G-5
Clarkville B-12
Clifton E-4
Climax E-7
Coaldale G-7

Coalmont C-6
Collbran E-4
Colorado City G-9
Colorado Springs . . . F-9
Columbine Valley
. . . . Pg. 103, J-3
Commerce City D-9
Vicinity . . . . Pg. 103, D-6
Como E-7
Conejos J-7
Conifer D-8
Cope D-11
Cortez J-3
Cotopaxi G-7
Cowdrey B-6
Craig B-5
Crawford F-5
Creede H-6
Crested Butte F-6
Cripple Creek F-8
Crook B-11
Crowley G-10
Cuchara J-9
Dailey B-11
DeBeque E-4
Deckers E-8
Deer Ridge C-7
Deer Trail D-10
Del Norte H-7
Delhi H-10
Delta F-4
Denver D-8
Vicinity . . . . Pg. 103
Dillon D-7
Dinosaur C-3
Divide E-8
Dolores H-4
Dotsero D-5
Dove Creek H-3
Dowd D-6
Doyleville F-6
Drake C-8
Dunton H-4
Dupont . . . . . . Pg. 103, D-6
Durango J-5
Eads F-12
Eagle D-6
Eaton B-9
Echo Lake D-7
Eckley C-12
Edgewater . . . Pg. 103, E-3
Edwards D-6
Egnar H-3
Eldorado Springs . . . D-8
Elizabeth E-9
Elk Springs C-4
Ellicott F-9
Empire D-7
Englewood D-8
Vicinity . . . . Pg. 103, G-5
Estes Park C-7
Evans C-9
Fairplay E-7
Falcon E-9
Farisita H-8
Federal Heights
. . . . Pg. 103, B-4
Fenders . . . . . . Pg. 103, J-1
Firstview F-12
Flagler E-11
Fleming B-11
Florence G-8
Florissant E-8
Ford G-10
Fort Collins B-8
Fort Garland H-8
Fort Lewis J-4
Fort Lupton C-9
Fort Lyon G-11
Fort Morgan C-10
Fountain F-9
Fowler G-10
Franktown E-9
Fraser D-7
Frederick C-8
Frisco D-7
Fruita E-3
Galatea F-11
Garcia J-8
Gardner H-8
Garfield F-7
Garo Park E-7
Gateway F-3
Genoa E-11
Georgetown D-7
Gilcrest C-9
Gilman D-6
Gladstone H-5
Glendale . . . . Pg. 103, F-5
Glenwood Springs . . . D-5
Golden D-8
Vicinity . . . . Pg. 103, E-1
Goodrich C-10
Gould C-7
Granada G-12
Granby C-7
Grand Junction E-3
Grand Lake C-7
Grandview Estates
. . . . Pg. 103, J-7
Granite E-7
Grant E-7
Greeley C-9
Vicinity . . . . Pg. 103, H-5
Greenwood Village . . D-8
Guffey F-7
Gunnison F-6
Gypsum D-6
Hamilton C-5
Hartsel E-7
Hasty G-11
Haswell F-11
Hawley G-10
Haxtun B-12
Hayden C-5

Hermosa J-5
Hesperus J-4
Hiawatha B-3
Hillrose C-10
Hillside G-8
Hoehne J-9
Holly G-12
Holyoke B-12
Homelake H-7
Hooper H-7
Hot Sulphur Springs C-7
Hotchkiss F-5
Howard F-7
Hudson C-9
Hugo E-11
Idaho Sprs. D-8
Idalia D-12
Idledale .... Pg. 103, G-1
Ignacio J-5
Iliff B-11
Indian Hills Pg. 103, H-1
Jansen J-9
Jaroso J-8
Jefferson E-7
Joes D-12
Johnson Village .. F-7
Julesburg A-12
Keenesburg C-9
Kersey C-9
Kim J-11
Kiowa E-9
Kit Carson F-12
Kline J-4
Komman G-12
Kremmling C-7
La Jara J-7
La Junta G-11
La Salle C-9
La Veta H-9
Lafayette C-8
Laird C-12
Lake City G-5
Lake George F-8
Lakewood D-8
  Vicinity ... Pg. 103, F-2
Lamar G-12
Larkspur E-9
Las Animas G-11
Last Chance D-10
Lay C-4
Lazear F-5
Leadville E-7
Lebanon J-4
Lewis J-4
Limon E-10
Lindon D-11
Littleton D-8
  Vicinity ... Pg. 103, H-4
Lochbule C-9
Log Lane Village . C-10
Loma E-3
Longmont C-8
Loveland C-8
Lucerne C-9
Lycan H-12
Lyons E-3
Mack E-3
Maher F-5
Malta E-6
Manassa J-7
Mancos J-4
Manitou Springs .. F-8
Manzanola G-10
Marble E-5
Marvel J-4
Masters C-9
Matheson E-10
Maybell B-4
McClave G-11
McCoy D-6
Meeker C-4
Meeker Park C-8
Merino B-10
Mesa E-4
Mesita J-8
Milliken C-8
Milner B-5
Mineral Hot Springs . G-7
Minturn D-6
Model J-10
Moffat G-7
Molina E-4
Monte Vista H-7
Montrose G-4
Monument E-9
Monument Park J-9
Morrison .... Pg. 103, G-2
Mosca H-7
Mount Princeton Hot Spr.
  .... F-7
Mountain View
  .... Pg. 103, D-3
Nathrop F-7
Naturita J-3
Nederland D-7
New Castle D-5
Northglenn G-4
Norwood G-4
Nucla G-4
Nunn B-9
Oak Creek C-6
Olathe F-4
Olney Springs G-11
Ophir H-4
Orchard C-9
Orchard City F-4
Ordway F-10
Otis C-11
Ouray G-4
Ovid A-12
Oxford J-5
Pagosa Sprs. J-6
Palisade E-4
Palmer Lake E-9
Paoli B-12

Paonia F-5
Parachute E-4
Paradox G-3
Park F-9
Parkdale F-8
Parker D-9
Parlin F-6
Parshall C-7
Peetz A-11
Penrose F-9
Peyton E-9
Phippsburg C-6
Pierce B-9
Pinewood Springs . C-8
Placerville G-4
Platoro J-6
Platteville C-9
Pleasant View H-3
Poncha Springs ... F-7
Poudre Park B-8
Powderhorn G-6
Pritchett H-12
Proctor B-11
Prospect Valley .. C-9
Pryor H-9
Pueblo G-9
Pueblo West G-9
Punkin Center F-10
Ramah E-9
Rand C-7
Rangely C-3
Raymer B-10
Raymond C-8
Red Mountain H-5
Redcliff E-6
Redmesa J-4
Redstone E-5
Redvale G-4
Rico H-4
Ridgway D-4
Rifle D-4
Rio Blanco D-4
Rockport B-9
Rockwood H-5
Rocky G-10
Roggen C-9
Rollinsville D-7
Romeo J-7
Royal Gorge G-8
Rush F-10
Rustic B-7
Rye H-8
Saguache G-7
Salida F-7
San Acacio J-8
San Francisco J-8
San Luis J-8
San Pablo J-8
Sanford J-7
Sapinero G-5
Sargents G-7
Saw Pit G-4
Sedalia E-8
Sedgewick A-11
Segundo J-9
Seibert E-11
Shawnee E-8
Sheridan F-12
  Vicinity ... Pg. 103, G-4
Sheridan Lake F-12
Silt D-5
Silver Cliff G-8
Silverthorne D-7
Silverton H-5
Simla E-10
Skyway E-4
Slick Rock G-3
Snow Mass E-6
Snow Mass Village E-6
Snyder C-10
Somerset F-5
South Fork H-6
Spar City H-6
Springfield H-12
Starkville J-9
State Bridge D-6
Steamboat Springs B-5
Sterling B-11
Stoneham B-10
Stoner H-4
Stonewall J-9
Strasburg D-9
Stratton D-12
Sugar City G-11
Summitville H-6
Sunbeam B-4
Swink G-10
Tabernash D-7
Telluride H-5
Texas Creek G-8
Thatcher H-10
The Forks B-8
Thornton D-8
  Vicinity Pg. 103, B-3
Timpas H-10
Tiny Town Pg. 103, H-1
Tobe J-10
Toonerville H-11
Toponas C-6
Towaoc J-3
Towner F-12
Trinidad J-9
Twin Forks Pg. 103, H-1
Twinlakes E-6
Two Buttes H-12
Tyrone J-10
Utleyville J-11
Vail D-7
Valdez J-9
Vancorum G-3
Victor F-8
Vilas H-12

Villa Grove G-7
Vineland G-9
Virginia Dale B-8
Vona E-11
Wagon Wheel Gap .. H-6
Walden B-6
Walsenburg H-9
Walsh H-12
Watkins D-9
Welby ...... Pg. 103, C-5
Weldona C-10
Westcliffe G-8
Westcreek E-8
Westminster D-8
  Vicinity ... Pg. 103, B-3
Weston J-9
Wetmore G-8
Wheat Ridge D-8
  Vicinity ... Pg. 103, E-3
Whitewater F-4
Wiggins C-10
Wild Horse F-11
Wiley G-12
Windsor B-8
Winter Park D-7
Wolcott D-6
Woodland Park E-8
Woodrow C-10
Woody Creek E-6
Wray C-12
Yampa C-6
Yellow Jacket H-3
Yoder F-9
Yuma C-12

CONNECTICUT
Page 24
Population: 3,107,576
Capital: Hartford
Land Area: 4,872 sq. mi.

Andover F-6
Ansonia H-3
Ashford F-7
Avon F-4
Barkhamsted E-4
Berlin G-4
Bethel H-2
Bethlehem G-3
Bloomfield F-4
Branford J-4
Bridgeport J-2
  Vicinity ... Pg. 128, A-19
Bristol G-4
Brookfield H-2
Brooklyn F-7
Burlington F-4
Byram ...... Pg. 128, F-13
Canaan E-2
Cannondale Pg. 128, B-16
Canterbury F-7
Canton F-4
Chaplin F-7
Cheshire G-4
Chester H-6
Clinton J-5
Colchester G-6
Colebrook E-3
Columbia F-6
Cornwall F-2
Cornwall Bridge .. F-2
Cos Cob ... Pg. 128, E-13
Coventry F-6
Cranbury . Pg. 128, C-17
Cromwell G-5
Danbury H-1
Darien H-1
  Vicinity ... Pg. 128, D-15
Dayville F-8
Deep River H-6
Derby H-3
Durham G-5
E. Hartland F-4
East Granby F-4
East Hampton G-5
East Hartford F-5
East Haven J-4
East Lyme H-3
East Norwalk
  .... Pg. 128, D-16
Eastford F-7
Easton ... Pg. 128, A-18
Ellington E-5
Enfield E-5
Essex H-6
Fairfield J-3
  Vicinity ... Pg. 128, B-18
Falls Vill. E-2
Farmington F-4
Franklin G-7
Georgetown J-2
Glastonbury F-5
Glen Brook Pg. 128, E-12
Glenville .. Pg. 128, E-12
Goshen E-3
Granby E-4
Greenfield Hill
  .... Pg. 128, B-18
Greenwich K-1
  Vicinity ... Pg. 128, E-14
Groton H-7
Guilford H-5
Haddam H-5
Hamden H-4
Hampton F-7
Hartford F-5
Harwinton F-3
Hebron G-6
Kent F-2
Killingworth H-5
Lebanon G-7
Ledyard Ctr. H-7

Litchfield F-3
Long Ridge Pg. 128, C-13
Madison H-5
Manchester F-5
Marlborough G-6
Melrose F-5
Meriden G-4
Mianus .... Pg. 128, E-14
Middlefield G-5
Middletown G-5
Milford J-3
Mill Plain Pg. 128, C-18
Monroe H-2
Morris G-3
N. Canton E-4
Naugatuck G-3
New Britain G-4
New Canaan J-1
New Fairfield G-2
New Hartford F-3
New Haven H-4
New London H-7
New Milford G-2
Newington F-4
Newtown H-2
No. Stonington ... H-8
Norfolk E-3
Noroton ... Pg. 128, E-15
Noroton Heights
  .... Pg. 128, E-15
North Branford ... H-4
North Haven H-4
North Stamford
  .... Pg. 128, C-14
North Wilton Pg. 128, B-15
Norwalk J-2
  Vicinity ... Pg. 128, D-16
Norwich G-7
Old Saybrook J-6
Plainfield G-7
Plymouth F-3
Pomfret F-7
Prospect H-3
Putnam F-8
Redding H-2
Ridgefield H-1
  Vicintiy ... Pg. 128, A-15
Riverside .. Pg. 128, F-14
Rocky Hill G-5
Round Hill Pg. 128, D-12
Rowayton .. Pg. 128, D-16
Salem H-6
Salisbury E-2
Scotland F-7
Seymour H-3
Sharon E-2
Shelton H-3
Simsbury F-4
Somers E-6
South Norwalk
  .... Pg. 128, D-16
South Wilton
  .... Pg. 128, B-16
South Windsor F-5
Southbury G-2
Southington G-4
Southport . Pg. 128, C-18
Springdale Pg. 128, D-14
Stafford E-6
Stamford K-1
  Vicinity ... Pg. 128, D-14
Sterling F-8
Stratford J-3
Suffield E-5
Thomaston G-3
Thompson E-8
Tolland F-6
Torrington F-3
Trumbull H-2
  Vicinity ... Pg. 128, A-19
Union E-7
Vernon F-5
Voluntown G-8
Wallingford H-4
Warren F-2
Washington G-3
Waterbury G-3
Waterford H-7
Watertown G-3
West Hartford F-4
West Haven J-4
West Norwalk
  .... Pg. 128, D-15
Westbrook H-5
Westchester G-6
Weston J-2
  Vicinity ... Pg. 128, A-17
Westport J-2
  Vicinity ... Pg. 128, C-17
Wethersfield F-5
Willington F-6
Wilton J-2
  Vicinity ... Pg. 128, B-16
Windsor F-4
Windsor Locks F-5
Winnipauk Pg. 128, C-16
Wolcott G-4
Woodbridge H-3
Woodbury G-2
Woodstock E-7

DELAWARE
Page 43
Population: 594,338
Capital: Dover
Land Area: 1,932 sq. mi.

Angola F-15
Bethany Beach F-15
Blades E-13
Bowers Beach D-14
Bridgeville E-14
Camden D-13
Cheswold C-13
Clayton C-13
Delaware City B-13
Dewey Beach E-15
Dover C-13
Ellendale D-14
Elsmere A-13
Felton D-13
Fenwick Is. F-15
Frankford F-15
Frederica D-14
Georgetown E-14
Greenwood E-13
Gumboro F-15
Harbeson E-15
Hardscrabble F-14
Harrington D-13
Hartly D-13
Houston D-14
Laurel E-14
Leipsic C-14
Lewes E-15
Middletown B-13
Milford D-14
Millsboro F-15
Millville E-15
Milton E-14
Mission F-14
New Castle A-13
Newark A-13
Newport A-13
Odessa B-13
Porter B-13
Seaford F-13
Selbyville F-15
Slaughter Beach .. E-15
Smyrna C-14
Staytonville E-14
Townsend C-14
Wilmington A-14
Wyoming D-13

DIST. OF COLUMBIA
Page 43
Population: 638,333
Capital: Washington
Land Area: 63 sq. mi.

Washington E-8
Vicinity ...... Pg. 150

FLORIDA
Pages 26-27
Population: 9,746,324
Capital: Tallahassee
Land Area: 58,560 sq. mi.

Alachua C-5
Altamonte Springs
  .... Pg. 133, C-4
Apalachicola Q-6
Apollo Beach H-5
  Vicinity ... Pg. 148, G-5
Apopka F-7
  Vicinity ... Pg. 133, B-3
Arcadia J-6
Archer D-5
Atlantic Beach ... B-7
Aventura .. Pg. 120, D-5
Avon Pk. H-7
Bal Harbor . Pg. 120, E-6
Baldwin B-6
Bartow G-6
Bay Harbor Island
  .... Pg. 120, E-5
Bay Pines .. Pg. 148, G-3
Bellair ... Pg. 111, H-2
Belle Glade K-9
Belle Isle . Pg. 133, F-5
Belleair .. Pg. 148, D-2
Belleair Beach
  .... Pg. 148, E-2
Belleair Bluffs Pg. 148, E-2
Belleair Shores
  .... Pg. 148, E-2
Belleview E-6
Biscayne Gardens
  .... Pg. 120, E-5
Biscayne Park
  .... Pg. 120, E-5
Blountstown P-6
Bloxham B-1
Boca Grande Pg. 108, A-1
Boca Raton L-10
Boca West . Pg. 120, G-2
Bokeelia .. Pg. 108, B-3
Bonifay N-5
Bonita Spr. L-6
Boynton Beach K-10
  Vicinity ... Pg. 120, E-2
Bradenton A-6
Brandon G-5
Branford C-5
Briny Breezes Pg. 120, E-3
Bristol P-6
Brooksville F-5
Buenaventure Lakes
  .... Pg. 133, J-5
Bunnell D-7
Bushnell F-6
Callahan B-6
Callaway P-5
Campbell City Pg. 133, K-4
Cantonment N-2

Cape Coral K-6
  Vicinity ... Pg. 108, C-5
Captiva ... Pg. 108, E-2
Carol City . Pg. 120, E-5
Carrabelle C-6
Casselberry . Pg. 133, K-3
  Vicinity ... Pg. 133, C-5
Cedar Key E-5
Celebration . Pg. 133, J-2
Chattahoochee A-1
Chiefland D-4
Chipley N-5
Citrus Park Pg. 148, B-5
Citrus Spr. E-5
Clarcona .. Pg. 133, D-3
Clearwater . Pg. 148, C-3
Clearwater Beach
  .... Pg. 148, C-2
Clermont F-6
Clewiston K-8
Cloud Lake Pg. 120, D-2
Cocoa Beach F-8
Coconut Creek
  .... Pg. 120, B-5
Cooper City . Pg. 120, C-4
  Vicinity ... Pg. 120, D-4
Coral Gables M-9
  Vicinity ... Pg. 120, C-5
Coral Springs Pg. 120, B-4
Crawfordsville ... C-2
Crescent City D-7
Crestview N-3
Cross City D-4
Crystal Beach
  .... Pg. 148, C-3
Crystal River E-5
Cutler Ridge M-9
Dade City F-5
Dania ..... Pg. 120, D-5
Davie ..... Pg. 120, D-4
Daytona Beach E-8
DeBary E-7
DeFuniak Springs . N-4
DeLeon Springs ... E-7
Deerfield Beach
  .... Pg. 120, A-5
Delray Beach . Pg. 120, A-5
  Vicinity ... Pg. 120, F-2
Deltona E-7
Dover ..... Pg. 120, B-6
  Vicinity ... Pg. 120, B-6
Dunedin H-4
  Vicinity ... Pg. 148, C-3
Dunnellon E-5
East Palatka D-7
Eastpoint Q-6
Eatonville . Pg. 133, D-4
Edgewater E-8
Edgewood .. Pg. 133, F-5
El Portal . Pg. 120, E-5
Ellenton H-5
Englewood J-5
Ensley N-2
Eustis E-6
Everglades City .. M-7
Fellsmere H-9
Fernandina Beach . B-7
Flagler Beach D-7
Florida City M-9
Fort Basinger H-8
Fort Lauderdale .. L-9
  Vicinity ... Pg. 120, C-6
Fort Myers K-6
  Vicinity ... Pg. 108, C-8
Fort Myers Beach . K-6
  Vicinity ... Pg. 108, F-6
Fort Pierce H-9
Fort Walton Beach N-3
Fort White C-5
Freeport N-4
Frost Proof H-7
Gainesville D-5
Gifford H-9
Glen Ridge Pg. 120, D-2
Golden Beach Pg. 120, E-6
Golden Shores
  .... Pg. 120, E-6
Golf ...... Pg. 120, E-2
Golfview .. Pg. 120, D-2
Graceville M-5
Green Cove Spr. .. C-6
Greenacres City
  .... Pg. 120, E-2
Greenville B-3
Gretna B-1
Grove City J-5
Gulf Stream Pg. 120, E-3
Gulfport .. Pg. 148, H-5
Haines City G-7
Hallandale . Pg. 120, D-5
Hastings D-7
Havana B-2
Haverhill Pg. 120, D-2
Hawthorne D-6
Hialeah ... Pg. 120, E-4
Hialeah Gardens
  .... Pg. 120, E-3
High Springs C-5
Highland Beach
  .... Pg. 120, F-3
Hilliard A-6
Hillsborough Beach
  .... Pg. 148, A-6
Hobe Sound J-10
Hollywood . Pg. 120, D-5
  Vicinity ... Pg. 120, D-5
Holmes Beach H-5
Homestead M-9
Homosassa E-5
Hosford P-6
Hudson F-5
Hypoluxo .. Pg. 120, E-2
Indian Creek Pg. 120, E-5
Indian Harbour Beach G-8
Indian Rocks Beach
  .... Pg. 148, E-2
Indian Shores Pg. 148, F-2

Indiantown J-9
Inglis E-5
Intercession City
  .... Pg. 133, K-3
Inverness E-5
Islamorada P-9
Jacksonville B-7
Jacksonville Beach B-7
  Vicinity ... Pg. 111, G-7
Jasper B-5
Jay M-1
Juno Beach Pg. 120, B-3
Jupiter ... Pg. 120, A-2
Jupiter Inlet Colony
  .... Pg. 120, A-3
Kenneth City Pg. 148, F-4
Key Biscayne Pg. 120, G-5
Key Largo N-9
Key West P-6
Keystone Hts. C-6
Kissimmee F-7
  Vicinity ... Pg. 133, J-4
Kissimmee View
  .... Pg. 133, J-3
LaBelle K-7
Lacoochee F-6
Lake Buena Vista . F-7
  Vicinity ... Pg. 133, H-2
Lake City C-5
Lake Clarke Shores
  .... Pg. 120, D-2
Lake Mary Pg. 133, A-5
Lake Park K-9
  Vicinity ... Pg. 120, B-3
Lake Wales G-7
Lake Worth . Pg. 120, D-3
Lakeland G-6
Lantana K-10
  Vicinity ... Pg. 120, D-3
Largo G-4
  Vicinity ... Pg. 148, E-2
Lauderdale Lakes
  .... Pg. 120, B-6
Lauderdale-By-The-Sea
  .... Pg. 120, B-6
Lauderhill . Pg. 120, B-6
Leesburg E-6
Lehigh Acres K-7
Lighthouse Pt. ... L-10
  Vicinity ... Pg. 120, B-6
Live Oak B-4
Longboat Key J-5
Longwood .. Pg. 133, B-5
Lutz ...... Pg. 148, A-7
Lynn Haven P-5
Macclenny B-6
Madison B-3
Magnolia Park
  .... Pg. 120, E-5
Maitland .. Pg. 133, D-5
Manalapan Pg. 120, E-3
Mangonia Park
  .... Pg. 120, C-3
Marathon P-8
Marco Is. L-6
Margate ... Pg. 120, B-5
Marianna N-5
Matlacha Pg. 108, C-3
Mayo D-4
Medley .... Pg. 120, E-4
Melbourne G-9
Merritt Island ... G-8
Miami M-9
  Vicinity ... Pg. 120, F-5
Miami Beach M-10
  Vicinity ... Pg. 120, F-6
Miami Lakes Pg. 120, E-4
Miami Shores Pg. 120, E-5
Miami Springs M-9
  Vicinity ... Pg. 120, F-4
Milton N-2
Mims F-8
Miramar ... Pg. 120, D-3
Monticello B-3
Moore Haven K-8
Mount Dora E-7
Naples L-6
Naples Pk. L-6
Narcoossee . Pg. 133, J-4
Neptune Beach B-7
  Vicinity ... Pg. 111, G-7
New Port Richey .. G-5
New Smyrna Beach . E-8
Niceville N-3
North Bay Village
  .... Pg. 120, E-5
North Fort Myers
  .... Pg. 108, B-7
North Lauderdale . L-9
  Vicinity ... Pg. 120, B-5
North Miami Pg. 120, E-5
North Miami Beach
  .... Pg. 120, E-5
North Palm Beach . K-10
  Vicinity ... Pg. 120, B-3
North Port J-6
North Redington Beach
  .... Pg. 148, F-2
Oakland ... Pg. 133, E-1
Oakland Park L-10
  Vicinity ... Pg. 120, B-5
Ocala E-6
Ocean Ridge Pg. 120, E-3
Ocoee ..... Pg. 133, D-3
Okeechobee J-8
Oldsmar ... Pg. 148, C-5
Opa-Locka L-9
Orange Pk. C-6
Orlando F-7
  Vicinity ...... Pg. 133
Ormand by the Sea D-8
Ormond Beach D-8

Osprey J-5
Oviedo .... Pg. 133, C-7
Ozona ..... Pg. 148, B-3
Pace N-2
Palatka D-6
Palm Bay G-9
Palm Beach Gardens
  .... Pg. 120, B-2
Palm Harbor Pg. 148, B-3
Palm Springs Pg. 120, D-2
Panama City P-5
Parkland .. Pg. 120, A-5
Pembroke G-6
Pembroke Park
  .... Pg. 120, D-5
Pembroke Pines ... G-6
  Vicinity ... Pg. 120, D-3
Pensacola N-2
Perrine M-9
Perry C-3
Pineland .. Pg. 108, B-3
Pinellas Park Pg. 148, F-4
Plant City G-6
Plantation . Pg. 120, C-5
Plymouth .. Pg. 133, C-2
Pompano Beach L-10
  Vicinity ... Pg. 120, B-5
Port Charlotte ... J-6
Port St. Joe Q-5
Port St. Lucie ... H-9
Punta Gorda L-6
Quincy B-1
Reddick D-5
Redington Beach
  .... Pg. 148, G-2
Redington Shores
  .... Pg. 148, F-2
Richmond Hts. M-9
Ridge Manor F-6
Riviera Beach K-10
  Vicinity ... Pg. 120, C-2
Rockledge F-8
Rotonda K-6
Royal Palm Beach
  .... Pg. 120, C-1
Runnymede Pg. 133, K-7
Ruskin H-5
  Vicinity ... Pg. 148, H-7
Safety Harbor Pg. 148, C-4
Sanford E-7
Sanibel K-6
  Vicinity ... Pg. 108, F-4
Sarasota J-5
Satellite Beach .. G-8
Sea Ranch Lakes
  .... Pg. 120, B-6
Sebastian H-9
Sebring H-7
Seminole Pg. 148, F-2
Semoran ... Pg. 133, C-3
Sneads N-6
Sopchoppy C-1
South Bay K-9
South Miami Pg. 120, G-4
South Palm Beach
  .... Pg. 120, D-3
South Pasadena
  .... Pg. 148, G-3
South Venice J-5
Spring Lake H-7
Springfield P-5
St. Augustine C-7
St. Augustine Beach . C-7
St. Cloud G-7
  Vicinity ... Pg. 133, K-6
St. James City
  .... Pg. 108, E-4
St. Pete Beach Pg. 148, H-3
St. Petersburg ... G-4
  Vicinity ... Pg. 148, G-5
Stuart J-10
Sun City Pg. 148, J-7
Sun City Ctr. H-5
  Vicinity ... Pg. 148, H-8
Sunny Isles Pg. 120, E-5
Sunrise ... Pg. 120, B-4
Surfside .. Pg. 120, E-6
Sweetwater . Pg. 120, F-3
Taft ...... Pg. 133, G-5
Tallahassee B-2
Tamarac ... Pg. 120, B-4
Tampa G-5
  Vicinity ... Pg. 148, D-7
Tarpon Springs ... G-4
  Vicinity ... Pg. 148, A-2
Temple Terrace ... G-5
Tennille C-3
Thomas City B-2
Tice K-6
Titusville F-8
Treasure Island
  .... Pg. 148, G-3
Trenton C-4
Truckland Pg. 108, E-6
Tuskawilla Pg. 133, C-6
Umitilla E-6
Valparaiso N-3
Venice J-5
Vero Beach H-9
Virginia Gardens
  .... Pg. 120, F-4
Warrington N-2
Watertown C-5
Wauchula H-6
Wausau N-5
Waverly G-7
West Melbourne ... G-9
West Miami Pg. 120, F-4
West Palm Beach
  .... Pg. 120, C-2
Westwood Lake M-9
Wewahitchka P-5
White City Q-5
Wildwood E-6

FLORIDA

Williston D-5
Wilma P-6
Wilton Manors
. . . . Pg. 120, B-6
Windermere Pg. 133, F-2
Winter Garden . . . Pg. F-7
Vicinity . . . . . Pg. 133, D-2
Winter Park . . . . . . Pg. F-7
Vicinity . . . . . Pg. 133, D-5
Winter Springs . . . Pg. F-7
Vicinity . . . . . Pg. 133, C-6
Woodville B-2
Zellwood . . . . Pg. 133, B-1
Zephyrhills G-5
Zolfo Spr. H-6

GEORGIA
Pages 28-29
Population: 6,478,216
Capital: Atlanta
Land Area: 54,153 sq. mi.

Abbeville K-5
Acworth F-3
Adairsville E-2
Adams Park . . Pg. 90, G-3
Adamsville . . . Pg. 90, F-2
Adel M-5
Adrian J-7
Alamo K-6
Alapaha L-5
Albany L-3
Aldora H-4
Allentown J-5
Alma L-7
Alpharetta E-4
Alston K-7
Alto E-5
Alvaton H-3
Ambrose L-6
Americus K-4
Amsterdam N-3
Andersonville K-3
Apalachee F-5
Apple Valley . Pg. 90, K-4
Appling G-7
Arabi K-4
Aragon F-2
Arlington L-3
Arnoldsville F-6
Ashburn L-4
Ashford Park . Pg. 90, C-5
Ashley Farms Pg. 90, H-3
Athens F-5
Atlanta F-4
Vicinity . . . . Pg. 90
Attapulgus N-3
Augusta G-7
Austell F-3
Avalon E-6
Avondale Estates
. . . . Pg. 90, F-6
Axson M-7
Baconton M-4
Bainbridge N-3
Baldwin E-5
Ball Ground E-4
Barnesville H-4
Barney M-5
Barwick M-5
Baxley L-7
Bellview L-2
Belvedere Gardens
. . . . Pg. 90, F-6
Benevolence K-3
Ben Hill . . . . . Pg. 90, H-2
Berkeley Lake Pg. 90, A-7
Berlin M-5
Berryton E-1
Between F-5
Bishop F-5
Blackshear L-8
Blakely L-2
Blue Creek . Pg. 90, H-6
Blue Ridge D-3
Bluffton L-3
Bonaire J-5
Boston M-5
Boulder Park . Pg. 90, F-2
Bowden G-2
Bowersville E-6
Bowman E-6
Boykin M-3
Bradley Acres Pg. 90, D-1
Bremen F-2
Briarcliff Woods
. . . . Pg. 90, D-6
Bridgeboro L-4
Bristol L-7
Bronwood L-3
Brookhaven . Pg. 90, D-5
Brookstone . Pg. 90, J-7
Brook Hollow Pg. 90, D-4
Brook Glen Pg. 90, H-7
Broxton L-6
Brunswick M-9
Buchanan F-2
Buckhead . . . Pg. 90, D-4
Buena Vista J-3
Buford E-5
Butler J-3
Byron J-5
Cadwell J-6
Cairo N-4
Calhoun E-2
Calvary N-3
Camilla M-3
Candler E-4
Canon E-6
Canoochee H-7
Canton E-3

Cardinal Woods
. . . . Pg. 90, D-7
Carnegie L-2
Carrollton G-2
Cartersville E-2
Cascade Knolls
. . . . Pg. 90, G-1
Cave Spring E-2
Cecil M-5
Cedar Springs M-2
Cedartown F-2
Center D-6
Center Hill . . . Pg. 90, F-3
Centerville M-2
Chamblee . . . Pg. 90, C-5
Chatsworth D-2
Chauncey K-5
Cherokee Pines
. . . . Pg. 90, C-1
Chester J-6
Chickamauga D-2
Cisco D-2
Clarkesville D-5
Clarkston . . . Pg. 90, E-7
Claxton J-8
Clayton D-5
Cleveland D-4
Climax N-3
Clyattville N-5
Clyo J-9
Cobbtown J-8
Cochran J-5
Cogdell M-6
Cohutta D-2
Colemans Lake H-7
College Park . Pg. 90, H-3
Collier Heights Pg. 90, F-3
Colquitt M-3
Columbia Valley
. . . . Pg. 90, G-6
Columbus J-2
Comer E-6
Commerce E-5
Conley . . . . . . Pg. 90, J-5
Conyers F-5
Coolidge M-4
Cordele K-4
Cornelia E-5
Cotton M-4
Covena J-7
Covington G-5
Crandall D-2
Crawford F-5
Crawfordville G-6
Creekwood Hills
. . . . Pg. 90, H-7
Culloden H-4
Cumberland . Pg. 90, C-3
Cumming E-4
Cusseta J-2
Cuthbert L-2
Dacula F-4
Dahlonega D-4
Dallas F-3
Dalton D-2
Damascus M-3
Danielsville E-5
Darien L-9
Dasher N-6
Davis Woods Pg. 90, C-4
Davisboro H-7
Dawson L-3
Dawsonville E-4
Decatur . . . . . Pg. 90, E-6
Demorest D-5
Dexter J-6
Doerun M-4
Donalsonville M-2
Doraville . . . . Pg. 90, C-6
Douglas L-6
Douglasville F-3
Dublin J-6
Duluth . . . . . . Pg. 90, E-7
Dunaire . . . . . Pg. 90, E-7
Dunwoody . . . Pg. 90, B-5
Dupont M-6
East Atlanta . Pg. 90, G-5
East Dublin J-6
East Point G-4
Vicinity . . . . Pg. 90, H-3
Eastglen . . . . Pg. 90, H-7
Eastman K-6
Eatonton G-5
Edgehill H-7
Edgewood . . . Pg. 90, F-5
Edison L-3
Elberton E-6
Elko J-5
Ellaville K-3
Ellenton M-5
Ellenwood . . . Pg. 90, J-6
Ellijay D-3
Emerson F-3
Empire J-6
Enigma L-6
Enon Forest . Pg. 90, H-1
Evans F-8
Faceville N-3
Fair Oaks . . . Pg. 90, B-1
Fairburn . . . . . Pg. 90, K-1
Fairmount E-3
Falconhurst . . Pg. 90, J-2
Fargo N-7
Fayetteville G-3
Feldwood Pines
. . . . Pg. 90, K-2
Fernandina Beach . . N-9
Fernwood . . . Pg. 90, J-2
Finleyson K-5
Fitzgerald L-5
Flairsville D-4
Flemington K-8
Folkston N-8
Forest Park . . Pg. 90, H-4
Vicinity . . . . . Pg. 90, J-4

Forsyth H-4
Fort Gaines L-2
Fort Gillem . . Pg. 90, J-5
Fort Oglethorpe . . . D-2
Fort Valley J-4
Franklin G-2
Franklin Springs E-6
Gainesville E-4
Garden City K-9
Geneva J-3
Georgetown K-2
Gibson G-7
Gillsville E-5
Girard H-9
Glennville K-8
Glenwood K-7
Gordon H-5
Gracewood G-8
Grantville G-3
Grant Park . . Pg. 90, G-4
Gray H-5
Green Oaks . Pg. 90, H-6
Greenbriar . . Pg. 90, H-2
Greensboro F-6
Greenville H-3
Gresham . . . . Pg. 90, E-1
Griffin G-3
Grovania J-5
Grove Park . . Pg. 90, F-3
Grove Town G-7
Haddock H-6
Hagan K-8
Hahira M-5
Hamilton H-2
Hampton G-4
Hapeville . . . Pg. 90, H-4
Haralson H-3
Harlem G-7
Harrison H-6
Hartwell E-6
Hawkinsville K-5
Haynes Manor Pg. 90, E-4
Hazelhurst K-7
Heatherwood . Pg. 90, K-3
Helen D-5
Helena K-6
Hephzibah G-7
Herod L-3
Hiawassee D-5
Hickox M-8
Hilltonia H-9
Hilton M-2
Hinesville K-9
Hoboken M-8
Hogansville G-2
Holly Springs E-3
Hollydale . . . Pg. 90, K-3
Homeland M-8
Homer E-5
Homerville M-7
Horseshoe Bend
. . . . Pg. 90, A-4
Ideal J-4
Idlewood . . . Pg. 90, K-5
Ila E-6
Indian Crossing
. . . . Pg. 90, B-7
Irwinton H-5
Irwinville L-5
Ivey H-6
Jackson G-4
Jacksonville K-6
Jasper E-3
Jefferson E-5
Jeffersonville J-5
Jesup L-8
Jonesboro G-3
Juno D-4
Kingsland N-9
Kingston E-2
Kirkwood . . . Pg. 90, F-5
Kite H-7
Knight Park . . Pg. 90, E-3
Knoxville H-4
La Grange H-2
LaFayette D-2
Lake City . . . Pg. 90, K-5
Lake Park N-6
Lakeland M-6
Lakemont D-5
Lakeshore Estates
. . . . Pg. 90, D-1
Lakewood . . . Pg. 90, H-4
Lavonia E-6
Lawrenceville F-4
Leary L-3
Leesburg L-4
Leland . . . . . Pg. 90, E-1
Lenox M-5
Lenox Park . . Pg. 90, E-4
Leslie K-4
Lexington F-6
Lilburn F-4
Lilly K-4
Lincolndale . . Pg. 90, J-6
Lincolnton F-7
Lindmoor . . . Pg. 90, E-6
Lithonia F-6
Lockheed . . . Pg. 90, B-1
Locust Grove G-4
Loganville F-5
London Park . Pg. 90, F-7
Lovett H-6
Ludowici L-8
Lula E-5
Lumber City K-6
Lumpkin K-3
Luthersville G-3
Lyons J-7
Macon H-5
Manchester H-3
Mangum Manor Pg. 90, G-2
Manor M-7

Margret D-4
Marietta F-3
Vicinity . . . . Pg. 90
Marshallville J-4
Maxeys F-5
Maysville E-5
McCaysville D-3
McIntire H-6
McRae K-6
Meadow Lake Pg. 90, B-5
Meigs M-4
Menlo Park . . Pg. 90, K-6
Merrillville M-4
Metcalf N-4
Metter J-8
Middleton H-7
Midtown . . . . Pg. 90, E-4
Midville H-7
Milan K-6
Milledgeville H-6
Millen H-8
Mineral Bluff D-4
Modoc H-7
Molena H-3
Moncrief N-4
Monroe F-5
Montevista . . Pg. 90, J-5
Montezuma J-4
Monticello G-5
Morgan L-3
Morganton D-4
Morningside . Pg. 90, E-4
Morris K-2
Morrow . . . . . Pg. 90, K-5
Morven M-5
Moultrie M-4
Mountain City D-5
Mountain View Pg. 90, J-4
Mt. Airy D-5
Mt. Vernon K-7
Mt. Zion F-2
Nahunta M-8
Nashville M-6
Naylor N-6
Nelson E-4
Newington J-9
Newnan G-2
Newton M-3
Nicholls L-7
Norcross . . . Pg. 90, B-7
Norman Park M-4
Norristown J-7
North Atlanta Pg. 90, C-5
Northlake . . . Pg. 90, D-6
Northridge . . Pg. 90, A-5
Oak Park J-7
Oakfield L-4
Oakland City . Pg. 90, G-3
Oakman D-3
Oakwood E-5
Ochlocknee M-4
Ocilla L-5
Odum L-8
Offerman L-8
Oglethorpe J-4
Ohoopee J-7
Oliver J-9
Omaha K-2
Omega L-5
Orchard Knob Pg. 90, H-4
Oxford G-4
Palmetto G-3
Panola Woods Pg. 90, H-6
Panthersville . Pg. 90, H-6
Parrott K-3
Patterson L-8
Pavo M-4
Peachtree City G-3
Pearson M-6
Pebblebrook Estates
. . . . Pg. 90, E-2
Pelman M-4
Pembroke K-9
Penhurst . . . Pg. 90, A-3
Percale . . . . . Pg. 90, H-4
Perkerson . . . Pg. 90, H-4
Perry J-5
Philomath F-6
Piedmont Heights
. . . . Pg. 90, E-4
Pine Lake . . . Pg. 90, F-7
Pine Park N-4
Pinehurst K-4
Pineview K-5
Vicinity . . . . . Pg. 90, J-2
Pitts K-5
Pittsburg . . . Pg. 90, C-7
Plains K-3
Ponderosa . . Pg. 90, K-2
Pooler K-9
Portal J-8
Poulan L-5
Preston K-3
Pulaski J-8
Quitman N-5
Radium Springs L-4
Raleigh H-3
Ranger D-2
Ray City M-6
Rayle F-6
Red Oak . . . . Pg. 90, K-1
Regency Park Pg. 90, G-1
Reidsville K-8
Resaca D-2
Revecca K-5
Rex . . . . Pg. 90, K-6
Reynolds J-3
Richland K-3
Richmond Hill K-9
Richmond Oaks
. . . . Pg. 90, G-4
Rincon J-9
Riverdale . . . Pg. 90, K-4
Roberta H-4
Robins J-5

Rochelle K-5
Rockmart F-2
Rocky Ford H-8
Rome E-2
Roopville G-2
Roswell F-3
Round Hill . . Pg. 90, C-4
Saffold M-2
Sale City M-4
Sandersville H-6
Sandy Springs Pg. 90, B-4
Sardis H-9
Sasser L-3
Savannah K-10
Scarborough Crossroads
. . . . Pg. 90, J-7
Scottdale . . . Pg. 90, E-6
Screven L-8
Senoia G-3
Seville K-5
Shady Dale G-5
Shellman L-3
Shiloh H-3
Six Flags . . . . Pg. 90, F-1
Smithville K-4
Smyrna . . . . . Pg. 90, C-2
Social Circle F-5
Somerset . . . Pg. 90, B-3
Soperton J-7
Southwest . . Pg. 90, G-2
Spalding Bridge
. . . . Pg. 90, A-7
Sparks M-5
Sparta G-6
Springfield J-9
Vicinity . . . . . Pg. 90, K-5
St. George N-8
St. Marys N-9
St. Simons Island . . M-9
Stagecoach Hills
. . . . Pg. 90, K-7
Statenville N-6
Statesboro J-8
Stillmore J-7
Stockbridge G-4
Stockton M-6
Stone Mountain F-4
Stonewall . . . Pg. 90, K-1
Strasburg . . . Pg. 90, H-2
Suches D-4
Sugar Hill E-4
Summertown H-7
Summerville D-2
Sumner L-4
Sun Valley . . Pg. 90, J-2
Surrency L-8
Suwanee E-4
Swainsboro J-7
Sycamore L-4
Sylvan Hills . Pg. 90, G-3
Sylvania H-9
Sylvester L-4
Talbotton J-3
Tallulah Falls D-5
Talmo L-7
Tarrytown J-6
Tarver N-6
Tarversville J-5
Tazewell J-3
Tecal . . . . . . Pg. 90, H-2
Tenille H-6
Tennga D-3
Thomaston H-4
Thomasville N-4
Thomson G-7
Thornhedge . Pg. 90, K-3
Thunderbolt K-10
Tifton L-5
Tignall F-7
Toccoa D-5
Toco Hills . . Pg. 90, E-5
Toombsboro H-6
Towns J-7
Toyston J-5
Trenton D-1
Trion D-2
Turin G-2
Tuxedo Park . Pg. 90, D-4
Twin City J-7
Ty Ty L-5
Unadilla K-5
Union City F-3
Vicinity . . . . . Pg. 90, K-1
Union Point F-6
Uvalda K-7
Valdosta N-6
Van Wert F-2
Vanna E-6
Vidalia J-7
Vienna K-5
Villa Rica F-2
Vinings . . . . . Pg. 90, D-3
Wadley H-7
Waleska E-3
Waresboro M-7
Warlick . . . . Pg. 90, H-2
Warner F-6
Warrenton G-6
Warthen H-6
Warwick K-4
Washington F-6
Watkinsville F-5
Watts Road . . Pg. 90, J-2
Waycross M-7
Waynesboro H-8
Wayside H-5
Wesley Chapel
. . . . Pg. 90, G-7
West End . . . Pg. 90, G-4
West Point H-2
Whigham N-3
White E-3
Whitesburg G-3
Wildwood . . . Pg. 90, B-7
Willacoochee L-6

HAWAII
Page 30
Population: 964,691
Capital: Honolulu
Land Area: 6,425 sq. mi.

Aiea G-6
Anahola D-3
Apole Pt C-9
Apua Pt G-10
Barbers Pt F-5
Cape Halawa A-6
Cape Hanamanioa . . C-8
Captain Cook F-9
Eleele F-2
Ewa G-5
Glenwood F-9
Haena D-2
Haena Pt. D-2
Haiku A-8
Hakalau F-10
Halawa A-6
Haleiwa F-5
Hana B-10
Hanalei D-2
Hanamalo Pt G-9
Hanamaulu E-3
Hanapepe F-1
Hauula F-6
Hawaii Kai G-6
Hawi E-9
Hekili Pt. B-7
Hilo F-10
Honaunau F-9
Honohina E-10
Honokaa E-9
Honokahua A-7
Honolulu G-5
Honuapo G-9
Hookena F-8
Ka Lae G-9
Kaalualu G-9
Kaena Pt G-10
Kahakuloa Pt A-8
Kahaluu F-6
Kahana A-7
Kahana Pt A-4
Kahe Pt A-4
Kahuku E-5
Kahuku Pt. E-5
Kahului A-8
Kailua (Hawaii) F-8
Kailua (Oahu) G-6
Kaimu F-10
Kainaliu F-8
Kaka Pt E-7
Kalae A-5
Kalaheo F-2
Kalahu Pt B-10
Kalalau D-2
Kalaoa F-8
Kalapana G-10
Kamalo A-5
Kamiloloa A-5
Kaneohe G-6
Kapaa E-3
Kaumakani F-1
Kauna Pt G-8
Kaunakakai A-5
Kaupo B-9
Kawahae E-8
Keaau F-10
Keahole Pt. F-8
Kealia E-3
Keauhou F-8
Kekaha E-1
Keokea B-8
Keomuku D-7
Kepuhi Pt. F-4
Kihei B-8
Kikipua Pt A-5
Kilauea D-2
Kipahulu B-10
Koele D-6
Koheo Pt F-2
Koko Head G-7
Kolo A-4
Koloa F-2
Kualapa A-4
Kualapuu A-4
Kualoa Pt F-6
Kukaiau E-9
Kukuihaele E-9
Kurtistown F-10
Laau Pt A-4
Lahaina A-7
Laie E-5
Lamaloa Head A-6
Lanai City D-6
Lawai F-2
Lihue E-3
Lilo Pt A-3
Maalaea B-8
Mahukona E-8
Maili G-4
Makaha F-4
Makahuena Pt F-3
Makakilo City G-4

Makanalua Pen A-5
Makapuu Pt. G-7
Makawao A-9
Makena B-8
Mana E-1
Mauna Loa A-4
Mililani Town F-5
Milolii G-8
Mokapu Pt. F-7
Moloaa D-3
Mopua B-7
Mountain View F-10
Muolea Pt. B-10
Naalehu G-9
Nakalele Pt. A-7
Nanakuli G-4
Napoopoo F-8
Nawiliwili E-3
Ninini Pt. E-3
Niulii E-9
Nukele Pt. C-8
Olowalu B-7
Ookala E-9
Opihikao F-10
Pahala G-9
Pahoa F-10
Paia A-8
Papa G-9
Papaaloa E-10
Papaikou F-10
Paukaa F-10
Pauwalu A-6
Pauwela A-8
Pauwela Pt. A-8
Pearl City F-5
Pearl Harbor G-5
Pepeekeo F-9
Pepeekeo Pt. F-10
Pohoiki F-10
Port Allen F-2
Puako E-8
Puhi E-3
Pukaulua Pt. A-10
Pukoo A-5
Puunene A-8
Puuwai B-1
Spreckleisville A-8
Sunset Beach E-5
Ulapue A-5
Ulupalakua B-9
Upola Pt. E-8
Wahiawa F-5
Waiahukini G-9
Waiaka E-9
Waialae F-10
Waialua (Molokai) . . A-6
Waialua (Oahu) F-5
Waianae F-4
Waihee Pt. A-8
Waikiki G-6
Wailea B-8
Wailua (Kauai) E-3
Wailua (Maui) A-9
Wailuku A-8
Waimanalo G-7
Waimea (Hawaii) . . . E-9
Waimea (Kauai) E-1
Waiohinu G-9
Walpahu G-5

IDAHO
Page 31
Population: 943,935
Capital: Boise
Land Area: 82,413 sq. mi.

Ahsahka D-2
American Falls J-5
Arco H-5
Arimo J-6
Ashton G-7
Atlanta H-3
Atomic City H-5
Avery C-3
Bellevue H-4
Bigby H-6
Blackfoot H-6
Bliss J-4
Blue Dome G-5
Boise H-3
Bonners Ferry A-2
Bovill D-2
Bruneau J-3
Burley J-4
Butte City H-5
Caldwell H-2
Cambridge G-2
Cape Horn F-4
Carey H-4
Cascade G-3
Cataldo C-2
Challis G-4
Chubbuck J-6
Coeur D'Alene C-2
Colburn B-2
Cottonwood E-2
Craigmont E-2
Deary D-2
Declo J-5
Downey J-6
Dubois G-6
Eagle H-2
Eastport A-3
Elba J-5
Elk City E-3
Elk River D-2
Emmett H-2
Fernan Lake B-2
Garden City H-2
Gibbonsville E-4
Golden E-3

Gooding J-4
Grand View J-2
Grangeville E-3
Hagerman J-4
Hailey H-4
Hamer G-6
Harpster E-3
Harvard C-2
Headquarters D-3
Hill City H-3
Holbrook K-6
Hollister J-4
Homedale H-2
Hope B-3
Horseshoe Bend . . . G-2
Howe H-5
Idaho City H-3
Idaho Falls H-6
Jerome J-4
Kamiah E-2
Kellogg C-3
Ketchum H-4
King Hill J-3
Kooskia E-3
Kuna H-2
Lamb Creek A-2
Leadore F-5
Lemhi F-5
Lewiston D-2
Lowell D-3
Lowman G-3
Mackay G-5
Malad City K-5
Malta J-5
May G-4
McCall F-3
Meridian H-2
Middleton H-2
Minidoka J-4
Montpelier J-7
Moreland H-6
Moscow D-2
Mountain Home H-3
Moyie Springs A-3
Mud Lake H-6
Mullan C-3
Murphy H-2
Myrtle D-2
Nampa H-2
Naples A-3
New Meadows F-2
New Plymouth G-2
North Fork E-4
Orofino D-2
Osburn C-3
Patterson G-5
Payette G-2
Pierce D-3
Plummer C-2
Pocatello J-6
Pollock F-2
Porthill A-2
Portneuf J-6
Preston J-7
Rexburg H-6
Ririe H-6
Roberts H-6
Rock Creek J-4
Rockland J-5
Salmon F-4
Samaria J-6
Sandpoint B-2
Shoshone J-4
Silver City J-2
Soda Springs J-7
Spencer G-6
Spirit Lake B-2
Springfield B-2
St. Joe C-3
Sunbeam G-4
Troy D-2
Twin Falls J-4
Victor H-7
Wallace C-3
Weiser G-2
White Bird E-2
Woodland D-3
Worley C-2

ILLINOIS
Page 32-33
Population: 11,426,518
Capital: Springfield
Land Area: 55,645 sq. mi.

Abingdon C-5
Addison . . . . . Pg. 98, H-4
Albany D-3
Albion H-11
Aledo B-4
Alexis C-4
Algonquin . . . Pg. 96, E-2
Alhambra D-10
Allendale H-11
Allerton H-7
Alma F-11
Alorton . . . . Pg. 140, G-7
Alpha C-4
Alpine . . . . . Pg. 99, L-5
Alsip . . . . . . Pg. 96, E-5
Altamont F-10
Alto Pass E-14
Alton D-10
Alvin H-7
Amboy E-3
Andover C-4
Anna E-14
Annawan D-4
Antioch G-1
Aptakisic . . . Pg. 96, E-5
Arcola G-8
Argenta F-7

Arlington E-3
Arlington Heights
    Pg. 96, F-4
Arthur G-8
Ashland D-8
Ashley F-12
Ashmore H-8
Ashton E-2
Assumption F-9
Astoria C-7
Athens D-7
Atkinson D-3
Atlanta E-7
Atwood G-8
Auburn D-8
Aubury Hills . Pg. 99, N-6
Augusta B-7
Aurora E-2
  Vicinity .... Pg. 98, J-2
Ava E-13
Avon C-6
Baldmond H-1
Bannockburn . Pg. 97, D-4
Barrington . Pg. 96, E-3
Barrington Hills Pg. 96, F-3
Barry B-8
Bartlett .... Pg. 96, G-3
Bartonville D-6
Batavia .... Pg. 98, H-2
Beardstown C-7
Beckemeyer E-11
Bedford Park . Pg. 99, J-6
Beecher City F-9
Belle Rive F-12
Belleville D-11
Bellflower G-6
Bellmont H-11
Bellwood . Pg. 99, H-5
Belvidere F-1
Bement G-7
Bensenville . Pg. 96, G-4
Benson E-6
Benton F-12
Berkeley . Pg. 99, H-6
Berwyn H-2
  Vicinity .... Pg. 99, H-6
Bethalto D-10
Bethany F-8
Biggsville B-6
Bloomingdale Pg. 96, G-4
Bloomington E-6
Blue Island . Pg. 99, K-7
Blue Mound E-8
Bluffs C-8
Bolingbrook H-2
  Vicinity .... Pg. 98, K-4
Bourbonnais H-4
Bowen B-7
Bradford E-4
Bradley H-4
Braidwood H-4
Bridgeview . Pg. 99, J-6
Brighton C-10
Brimfield D-5
Broadview . Pg. 99, H-5
Brookfield . Pg. 99, J-6
Brookport G-15
Brownstown F-10
Buckley H-4
Buffalo Grove Pg. 96, E-4
Bull Valley F-2
Bunker Hill D-10
Burbank ... Pg. 99, J-6
Burnham ... Pg. 99, L-8
Burr Ridge . Pg. 98, J-5
Burtons Bridge Pg. 96, D-3
Bush F-13
Bushnell C-6
Byron E-2
Cabery G-5
Cahokia C-11
  Vicinity .... Pg. 140, G-7
Cairo F-15
Calumet City . Pg. 99, L-8
Calumet Park . Pg. 99, H-6
Cambridge C-4
Camden B-7
Camp Point B-7
Campbell Hill . E-13
Canton D-6
Capron F-1
Carbondale E-13
Carlinville D-9
Carlyle E-11
Carmi H-12
Carol Stream . Pg. 98, H-3
Carpentersville Pg. 96, F-2
Carriers Mills . F-13
Carrollton C-9
Carterville E-13
Carthage A-6
Cary .... Pg. 96, E-2
Casey H-9
Caton Farm . Pg. 98, L-3
Cave-In-Rock . H-14
Cedarville D-1
Central City F-11
Centralia E-11
Cerro Gordo F-7
Chadwick D-2
Champaign G-7
Chandlerville C-7
Channel Lake . B-3
Chapin C-8
Charleston H-8
Chatham D-8
Chatsworth G-6
Chebanse H-5
Chenoa F-6
Cherry Valley F-1
Chester D-13
Chesterfield D-9
Chicago J-2
  Vicinity .... Pg. 96

Chicago Heights J-3
  Vicinity .... Pg. 99, M-7
Chicago Ridge Pg. 99, K-6
Chillicothe E-5
Chrisman H-8
Cicero .... Pg. 99, H-6
Cisco F-7
Cisne G-11
Clarendon Hills Pg. 98, J-5
Clay City G-11
Clayton B-7
Clifton H-5
Clinton F-7
Cloverdale . Pg. 98, F-2
Coal Village C-4
Cobden E-14
Coffeen E-10
Colchester B-6
Colfax G-6
Collinsville D-11
Columbia C-11
  Vicinity .... Pg. 140, J-5
Compton E-3
Cordova C-3
Cornell F-5
Coulterville E-12
Country Club Hills
    Pg. 99, L-6
Countryside . Pg. 99, J-5
Cowden F-9
Creal Springs . F-13
Crest Hill . Pg. 98, L-3
Crestwood . Pg. 99, L-6
Crete H-4
  Vicinity .... Pg. 99, M-7
Creve Coeur E-6
Crystal Lake G-1
  Vicinity .... Pg. 96, D-2
Cuba C-6
Cullom G-5
Cutler E-12
Dakota E-1
Dallas City B-6
Damiansville E-11
Danville J-7
Darien .... Pg. 98, J-5
De Kalb F-2
De Soto E-13
Decatur F-8
Deer Grove E-3
Deer Park . Pg. 96, E-4
Deerfield . Pg. 97, E-5
Delavan E-6
Des Plaines . Pg. 97, F-5
Diamond Lake E-4
  Vicinity .... Pg. 96, D-4
Dieterich G-10
Divernon E-9
Dix F-11
Dixmoor . Pg. 99, L-7
Dixon E-2
Dolton .. Pg. 99, L-7
Donovan H-5
Downers Grove H-3
  Vicinity .... Pg. 98, J-4
Du Quoin E-12
Dunfermline D-6
Dunlap D-5
Dupo .... Pg. 140, H-6
Dwight G-4
Earlville F-3
East Carondelet
    Pg. 140, H-6
East Chicago Heights
    Pg. 99, K-7
East Dubuque C-1
East Dundee . Pg. 96, F-2
East Hazelcrest
    Pg. 99, K-7
East Peoria E-5
East St. Louis . D-11
  Vicinity .... Pg. 140, G-7
Easton D-7
Eddyville G-14
Edgewood G-10
Edinburg E-8
Effingham G-10
El Paso F-5
Eldorado G-13
Elgin G-2
  Vicinity .... Pg. 96, F-2
Elizabeth C-1
Elizabethtown . G-14
Elk Grove Village
    Pg. 96, G-4
Elkhart E-7
Elkville E-13
Elliot G-6
Ellis Grove D-12
Elmhurst H-2
  Vicinity .... Pg. 98, H-5
Elmwood Park Pg. 99, H-6
Enfield G-12
Eola .... Pg. 98, J-3
Equality G-13
Erie D-3
Eureka E-5
Evanston J-2
  Vicinity .... Pg. 97, G-5
Evansville D-12
Evergreen Park
    Pg. 99, K-7
Fairbury G-5
Fairfield G-11
Fairmont . Pg. 98, L-4
Fairview C-6
Farina F-10
Farmer City F-7
Farmersville E-9
Fayetteville D-11
Fieldon C-10
Fisher G-6

Flanagan F-5
Flat Rock H-10
Flora G-11
Flossmoor . Pg. 99, M-7
Flowerfield . Pg. 98, H-4
Forest Park H-6
Forest View . Pg. 99, J-6
Forrest G-5
Forreston E-2
Fox Lake G-1
  Vicinity .... Pg. 96, C-3
Fox Lake Hills . Pg. 96, C-3
Fox River Grove
    Pg. 96, E-3
Fox River Valley Gardens
    Pg. 96, D-3
Frankfort . Pg. 99, M-5
Franklin D-8
Franklin Park Pg. 99, H-5
Freeburg D-11
Freeport D-1
Fremont Center
    Pg. 96, D-4
Frontenac . Pg. 98, K-3
Fulton D-2
Gages Lake C-4
Galatia G-13
Galena C-1
Galesburg D-4
Galva D-4
Gardner G-4
Geneseo C-3
Geneva G-2
  Vicinity .... Pg. 98, H-2
Genoa F-2
Georgetown H-7
Germantown E-11
Gibson City G-6
Gilberts .. Pg. 96, F-1
Gillespie D-10
Gilman H-5
Gilmer .... Pg. 96, D-4
Girard D-9
Gladstone B-5
Glasford D-6
Glen Ellyn . Pg. 98, H-4
Glencoe .... Pg. 97, E-6
Glendale Heights
    Pg. 98, H-4
Glenview .. Pg. 97, F-6
Glenwood . Pg. 99, M-7
Golconda G-14
Golden B-7
Golf F-6
Good Hope B-6
Goodings Grove
    Pg. 98, L-5
Goreville F-14
Gorham E-13
Grafton C-10
Grand Ridge F-4
Grand Tower . E-13
Granite City D-11
  Vicinity .... Pg. 140, C-7
Grayslake . Pg. 96, C-4
Grayville H-12
Green Oaks . Pg. 96, D-5
Greenfield C-9
Greenup H-9
Greenview D-7
Greenville E-10
Greenwood C-1
Gridley F-5
Griggsville B-8
Gurnee . Pg. 97, C-5
Hainesville . Pg. 96, C-4
Half Day . Pg. 97, E-5
Hamel D-10
Hamilton A-6
Hammond G-8
Hampshire G-2
Hanaford F-13
Hanover C-1
Hanover Park Pg. 96, G-3
Hardin B-9
Harrisburg G-13
Harristown F-8
Harvard F-1
Harvey .. Pg. 99, L-7
Harwood Heights
    Pg. 97, G-6
Hastings . Pg. 98, K-5
Havana D-6
Hawthorn Woods
    Pg. 96, E-4
Hazel Crest . Pg. 99, L-7
Hebron F-1
Hecker D-12
Hegeler J-7
Hennepin E-4
Henning H-6
Henry E-5
Herrin F-13
Herscher H-5
Heyworth F-6
Hickory Hills . Pg. 99, K-6
Highland E-11
Highland Hills Pg. 98, H-4
Highland Park H-1
  Vicinity .... Pg. 97, E-6
Highwood . Pg. 97, E-6
Hillsboro E-9
Hillside H-6
Hinckley G-3
Hinsdale . Pg. 98, J-5
Hodgkins . Pg. 99, J-5
Hoffman Estates
    Pg. 96, F-3
Holiday Hills . Pg. 96, D-3
Homer H-7
Hometown . Pg. 99, K-7
Homewood . Pg. 99, L-7
Hoopeston J-6
Hoopole D-3

Hopedale E-6
Hoyleton E-11
Hudson F-6
Hull A-8
Humboldt G-8
Huntley E-1
Hurst F-13
Hutsonville H-10
Iliopolis E-8
Industry B-6
Ingalls Park . Pg. 98, M-4
Inverness . Pg. 96, F-4
Irvington F-11
Island Lake . Pg. 96, D-3
Itasca .... Pg. 96, G-4
Ivanhoe .... Pg. 96, D-4
Jacksonville C-8
Jerseyville C-9
Johnsburg . Pg. 96, C-2
Joliet H-3
  Vicinity .... Pg. 98, M-4
Jonesboro E-14
Junction City H-13
Justice .... Pg. 99, J-6
Kampsville B-9
Kankakee H-4
Kansas H-8
Karnak F-14
Kaskaskia D-13
Keeneyville . Pg. 96, G-3
Kenilworth . Pg. 97, F-7
Kenney F-7
Kewanee D-4
Kilbourne D-7
Kildeer .... Pg. 96, E-4
Kinderhook B-8
Kingston F-2
Kinmundy F-10
Kirkland F-2
Knollwood . Pg. 97, D-5
Knoxville C-5
La Fayette E-4
La Fox H-1
La Grange . Pg. 99, G-4
La Grange Park
    Pg. 99, J-5
La Harpe A-6
La Moille E-3
La Salle F-4
Lacon E-4
Ladd E-4
Lake Barrington
    Pg. 96, E-3
Lake Bluff . Pg. 97, D-6
Lake Forest H-1
  Vicinity .... Pg. 97, D-6
Lake Villa . Pg. 96, C-4
Lake Zurich . Pg. 96, E-4
Lake in the Hills
    Pg. 96, E-2
Lakemoor . Pg. 96, C-3
Lakewood . Pg. 96, E-1
Lanark D-2
Lansing .. Pg. 99, L-8
Latham E-8
Lawrenceville J-10
Le Roy F-6
Lee Center E-3
Lemont .. Pg. 98, K-4
Lena D-1
Lewistown C-6
Lexington F-6
Liberty A-8
Libertyville H-1
  Vicinity .... Pg. 96, D-5
Lilymoor . Pg. 96, C-3
Lima A-7
Lincoln E-7
Lincoln Estates
    Pg. 99, N-8
Lincolnshire . Pg. 97, E-5
Lincolnwood . Pg. 97, G-6
Lindenhurst . Pg. 96, C-4
Lisle .... Pg. 98, J-4
Litchfield D-9
Little York B-5
Livingston D-10
Lockport .. Pg. 98, L-4
Lombard .. Pg. 98, H-4
Long Grove . Pg. 96, E-4
Long Lake .. Pg. 96, C-3
Loon Lake .. Pg. 96, C-3
Loraine A-7
Louisville G-10
Lovington F-8
Ludlow H-6
Lynwood . Pg. 99, M-8
Lyons .... Pg. 99, J-6
Machesney Park .. E-1
Mackinaw E-6
Macomb B-6
Madison .. Pg. 140, D-6
Magnolia E-4
Mahomet G-7
Manhattan H-4
Manito D-6
Manlius D-3
Manteno H-4
Maquon C-5
Marengo G-1
Marine D-10
Marion F-13
Marissa D-12
Markham .. Pg. 99, L-6
Marley .... Pg. 98, M-5
Maroa F-7
Marseilles G-4
Marshall H-9
Martinsville H-9
Martinton H-5
Marywood .. Pg. 98, J-2

Mascoutah D-11
Mason G-10
Mason City D-7
Matteson . Pg. 99, M-6
Mattoon G-9
Maywood .. Pg. 99, H-6
Mazon G-4
McClure E-14
McCook .. Pg. 99, J-6
McCullom Lake
    Pg. 96, C-2
McHenry G-1
  Vicinity .... Pg. 96, C-2
McHenry Shores
    Pg. 96, B-1
McLean E-6
McLeansboro G-12
McQueens F-1
Medinah .. Pg. 96, G-4
Medora C-9
Melrose Park . Pg. 99, H-5
Melvin G-6
Mendon A-7
Mendota E-3
Meredosia C-8
Merrionette Park
    Pg. 99, K-7
Metamora E-5
Metropolis F-15
Mettawa . Pg. 97, D-5
Midlothian . Pg. 99, L-6
Milan B-4
Milford H-5
Mill Shoals G-12
Millbrook B-4
Milledgeville D-2
Millburn B-4
Milton B-8
Minonk F-5
Minooka . Pg. 98, M-2
Mokena . Pg. 99, M-5
Moline C-3
Momence J-4
Monmouth B-5
Monticello G-7
Montgomery . Pg. 98, K-2
Montrose G-9
Mooseheart . Pg. 98, J-2
Morris G-4
Morrison D-2
Morrisonville E-9
Morristown F-2
Morton E-6
Morton Grove Pg. 97, F-6
Mound City F-15
Mount Carmel H-11
Mount Carroll D-2
Mount Morris E-2
Mount Olive D-10
Mount Prospect
    Pg. 96, F-5
Mount Pulaski E-7
Mount Vernon F-12
Mount Zion F-8
Moweaqua F-8
Mundelein G-1
  Vicinity .... Pg. 96, D-4
Murphysboro E-13
Murrayville C-8
Naperville G-3
Nashville E-12
National City . Pg. 140, D-7
Nauvoo A-6
Neoga G-9
New Athens D-12
New Baden E-11
New Boston B-4
New Burnside . F-14
New Canton B-8
New Haven H-13
New Holland E-7
New Lenox . Pg. 98, M-5
New Windsor C-4
Newark F-3
Newman H-8
Newton G-10
Niles .... Pg. 97, F-6
Nilwood D-9
Noble G-11
Nokomis E-9
Normal F-6
Normantown . Pg. 98, K-2
Norridge . Pg. 97, G-6
Norris D-6
Norris City G-13
North Aurora . Pg. 98, J-2
North Barrington
    Pg. 96, E-3
North Chicago H-1
North Dupo . Pg. 140, H-6
North Riverside
    Pg. 99, H-6
North Wood River
    Pg. 140, A-7
Northbrook E-9
  Vicinity .... Pg. 97, E-6
Northfield .. Pg. 97, E-6
Northlake . Pg. 99, H-5
Oak Brook . Pg. 98, J-5
Oak Forest . Pg. 99, L-6
Oak Lawn . Pg. 99, K-6
Oak Park .. Pg. 99, H-6
Oakbrook Terrace
    Pg. 98, H-4
Oakford D-7
Oakland H-8
Oakwood H-7
Oakwood Hills Pg. 96, D-2
Oblong H-10
Oconee F-9
Odell G-5
Odin F-11
Ogden H-7

Oglesby F-4
Ohio E-3
Okawville D-11
Old Mill Creek Pg. 96, B-4
Olmsted F-15
Olney H-10
Olympia Fields
    Pg. 99, M-7
Omaha G-13
Onarga H-5
Oquawka B-5
Orangeville E-1
Oreana F-7
Oregon E-2
Orion C-4
Orland Hills . Pg. 99, L-6
Orland Park . Pg. 99, L-5
Oswego F-3
Ottawa F-4
Owaneco F-9
Palatine G-2
  Vicinity .... Pg. 96, F-4
Palestine J-10
Palmyra D-9
Palos Heights . Pg. 99, K-6
Palos Hills . Pg. 99, K-6
Palos Park . Pg. 99, K-6
Pana E-9
Paris J-8
Park City . Pg. 97, C-5
Park Forest J-3
  Vicinity .... Pg. 99, M-7
Park Ridge . Pg. 97, G-6
Parkersburg H-11
Patoka F-10
Pawnee E-8
Paxton G-6
Payson A-8
Pearl City D-1
Pekin D-6
Peoria D-5
Peotone H-4
Perry B-8
Pesotum G-7
Petersburg D-7
Phoenix .. Pg. 99, L-7
Pierron E-10
Pinckneyville E-12
Pingree Grove F-1
Piper City G-5
Pittsfield B-8
Plainfield G-3
  Vicinity .... Pg. 98, L-1
Plano G-3
Plato Center . Pg. 96, G-1
Plattville M-1
Pleasant Hill B-9
Plymouth B-6
Pocahontas E-10
Polo E-2
Pontiac G-5
Port Byron C-3
Posen .... Pg. 99, L-7
Prairie Grove . Pg. 96, D-2
Prairie View . Pg. 96, E-5
Prairie du Rocher . F-12
Preston Heights
    Pg. 98, M-4
Prince Crossing
    Pg. 98, E-4
Princeton E-4
Princeville D-5
Prophetstown D-3
Prospect Heights
    Pg. 96, F-5
Pulaski E-15
Quincy A-7
Ramsey F-9
Rankin H-6
Ransom F-4
Rantoul H-6
Rapids City C-3
Raymond E-9
Red Bud D-12
Reynolds C-4
Richton Park . Pg. 99, M-6
Richview E-11
Ridge Farm H-7
Ridgefield . Pg. 96, D-2
Ridgeway G-13
Ridgewood . Pg. 98, M-4
Ringwood . Pg. 96, C-2
River Forest . Pg. 99, H-6
River Grove . Pg. 99, H-6
Riverdale .. Pg. 99, L-7
Riverside .. Pg. 99, J-6
Riverwoods . Pg. 97, E-5
Roanoke E-5
Robbins .. Pg. 99, L-7
Roberts G-6
Robinson H-10
Rochelle E-2
Rochester E-8
Rockbridge C-9
Rockdale . Pg. 98, M-3
Rockford D-1
Rockton E-1
Rolling Meadows
    Pg. 96, F-4
Romeoville H-3
  Vicinity .... Pg. 98, K-4
Rondout . Pg. 97, D-5
Roodhouse C-9
Roscoe E-1
Roselle .. Pg. 96, G-4
Rosemont . Pg. 97, G-5
Roseville B-5
Rosiclare G-14
Rossville H-6
Round Lake . Pg. 96, C-3
Round Lake Beach
    Pg. 96, C-3

Round Lake Heights
Round Lake Park
    Pg. 96, C-4
Royalton E-13
Rushville C-7
Rutland F-5
Sag Bridge . Pg. 98, K-5
St. Anne H-4
San Jose E-6
Sandoval E-11
Sandwich F-3
Sauget .... Pg. 140, F-6
Sauk Village . Pg. 99, M-8
Savanna D-2
Savoy G-7
Schaumburg
  Vicinity .... Pg. 96, G-4
Schiller Park . Pg. 97, G-5
Schram City E-9
Sesser F-12
Shabbona F-2
Shannon D-2
Shawneetown G-13
Sheffield D-4
Shelbyville F-9
Sheldon J-5
Shorewood
  Vicinity .... Pg. 98, M-3
Shumway F-9
Sibley G-6
Sigel G-9
Silvis C-3
Simpson F-14
Sims G-11
Skokie
  Vicinity .... Pg. 97, F-6
Sleepy Hollow . Pg. 96, F-2
Smithton D-11
Solon Mills B-2
Somonauk F-3
South Barrington
    Pg. 96, F-5
South Beloit E-1
South Chicago Hts.
    Pg. 99, M-7
South Elgin . Pg. 96, G-2
South Holland . Pg. 99, L-7
South Lockport Pg. 98, L-4
Sparland E-5
Sparta D-12
Spencer .. Pg. 98, M-5
Spring Grove . Pg. 96, C-2
Spring Valley E-4
Springfield D-8
  Vicinity .... Pg. 98, H-3
St. Augustine C-5
St. Charles G-2
  Vicinity .... Pg. 98, H-2
St. Elmo F-10
St. Francisville . H-11
St. Johns E-12
St. Peter F-10
Stanford E-6
Starks F-2
Staunton D-10
Steeleville D-12
Steger F-9
  Vicinity .... Pg. 99, M-7
Sterling D-2
Stewardson F-9
Stickney .. Pg. 99, J-6
Stillman Valley E-2
Stockton D-1
Stolle .... Pg. 140, H-7
Stone Park . Pg. 99, H-5
Stonefort G-13
Stonington F-8
Strasburg F-9
Streamwood . Pg. 96, G-3
Streator F-4
Stronghurst B-5
Sublette E-3
Sugar Grove G-2
Sugarloaf Hts. Pg. 140, J-6
Sullivan G-8
Summit .... Pg. 99, J-6
Sumner H-11
Sunnyside .. Pg. 96, A-2
Sunrise Ridge . Pg. 96, A-1
Swansea D-11
Sycamore G-2
Table Grove C-6
Tallula D-7
Tamaroa E-12
Tamms E-14
Tampico D-3
Taylor Springs E-9
Taylorville E-8
Teutopolis G-9
Thawville G-5
Third Lake . Pg. 96, C-4
Thompsonville . G-13
Thomson D-2
Thornton .. Pg. 99, L-7
Tilton J-7
Tinley Park . Pg. 99, L-6
Toledo G-9
Tolono G-7
Toluca E-5
Tonica E-4
Toulon D-4
Tower Hill F-8
Tower Lakes . Pg. 96, E-3
Trenton E-11
Troy D-11
Troy Grove E-4
Tuscola G-8
Udina .... Pg. 96, G-2
Ullin E-14
University Park
    Pg. 99, M-6
Urbana H-7
Valley View . Pg. 96, G-2

Valmeyer C-12
Vandalia F-10
Venetian Village
    Pg. 96, C-4
Venice .... Pg. 140, D-7
Vernon F-10
Vernon Hills . Pg. 96, D-5
Versailles B-8
Victoria D-4
Vienna F-14
Villa Grove H-8
Villa Park . Pg. 98, H-5
Viola C-4
Virden D-9
Virginia C-7
Volo .... Pg. 96, C-3
Wadsworth D-5
  Vicinity .... Pg. 96, B-5
Waggoner D-9
Walnut E-3
Waltonville F-12
Wapella F-7
Warren D-1
Warrensburg F-7
Warrenville . Pg. 98, J-3
Warsaw A-6
Wasco G-1
Washburn E-5
Washington E-5
Waterloo C-12
Waterman F-3
Watseka H-5
Watson G-10
Wauconda . Pg. 96, D-3
Waukegan H-1
  Vicinity .... Pg. 96, C-6
Waverly D-8
Wayne .... Pg. 96, G-3
Wayne City G-11
Weldon F-7
Wellington H-6
Wenona F-4
West Chicago Pg. 98, H-3
West City F-12
West Dundee . Pg. 96, F-2
West Frankfort . F-13
West Miltmore Pg. 96, C-4
Westchester . Pg. 98, H-5
Western Springs
    Pg. 98, J-5
Westfield H-9
Westmont . Pg. 98, J-5
Westville J-7
Wheaton G-2
  Vicinity .... Pg. 98, H-3
Wheeler G-10
Wheeling . Pg. 96, F-5
White Hall C-9
Wildwood . Pg. 96, C-5
Willow Hill H-10
Willow Springs Pg. 98, K-5
Willowbrook . Pg. 98, J-5
Wilmette . Pg. 97, F-7
Wilmington H-4
Winchester C-8
Winfield . Pg. 98, H-3
Winnebago E-1
Winnetka H-2
  Vicinity .... Pg. 97, F-6
Winslow D-1
Winthrop Harbor .. D-5
Wolfs .... Pg. 98, K-2
Wonder Lake . Pg. 96, C-2
Wood Dale . Pg. 96, G-4
Wood River . Pg. 140, B-7
Woodhull C-4
Woodridge . Pg. 98, K-4
Woodson C-8
Woodstock G-1
Worth .... Pg. 99, K-6
Wyoming D-5
Xenia G-11
Yates City D-5
York Center . Pg. 98, H-4
Yorkville G-3
Zeigler F-13
Zion H-1

INDIANA
Pages 34-35
Population: 5,490,224
Capital: Indianapolis
Land Area: 35,932 sq. mi.

Akron D-7
Albany F-9
Albion B-8
Alexandria F-8
Allisonville . Pg. 110, B-5
Alton P-6
Alvarado B-10
Ambia F-3
Americus F-4
Anderson G-8
Andersonville . J-9
Andrews D-8
Angola A-10
Antrim .. Pg. 110, F-2
Arcadia G-7
Argos C-6
Atherton J-3
Attica F-3
Auburn B-10
Augusta . Pg. 110, A-4
Austin M-7
Avilla B-9
Bainbridge H-4
Bargersville J-6
Bass Lake C-5
Batesville K-9
Battletown P-6

INDIANA

Place	Grid	Place	Grid
Bedford	L-5	Elwood	F-7
Beech Grove	H-6	Emporia	G-8
Vicinity	Pg. 110, E-5	English	N-6
Beechwood	P-6	Enos	D-3
Belleview	H-6	Evansville	P-2
Belmont	K-6	Fairfield	J-10
Ben Davis	Pg. 110, E-2	Fairmount	F-8
Bennett Switch	E-7	Ferdinand	P-5
Berne	E-10	Fickle	F-5
Beverly Shores	B-4	fishers	Pg. 110, A-5
Bicknell	M-3	Five Points	Pg. 110, B-4
Birdseye	N-5	Flora	E-6
Bloomfield	L-4	Fort Branch	P-2
Blooming Grove	J-9	Fort Wayne	C-9
Bloomingdale	G-3	Fortville	H-7
Bloomington	K-5	Foster	G-6
Bluffton	E-9	Fountain City	G-10
Boonville	P-3	Fowler	E-3
Boston	H-10	Francesville	D-4
Boswell	E-3	Frankfort	F-6
Bourbon	C-6	Franklin	J-7
Bowling Green	K-4	Frankton	G-7
Branchville	P-5	Freedom	K-4
Brazil	J-4	Freetown	L-6
Bremen	B-6	Fremont	A-10
Bristol	A-7	French Lick	M-5
Brook	D-3	Fulton	D-6
Brooklyn	J-6	Galveston	E-6
Brookston	E-5	Garrett	B-9
Brookville	J-10	Gary	B-3
Brownsburg	H-6	Vicinity	Pg. 97, C-7
Brownstown	L-6	Gas City	E-8
Bruceville	M-3	Geneva	E-10
Bryant	E-10	Gentryville	P-4
Bryantsburg	L-8	Glenns Valley	Pg. 110, G-3
Burlington	F-6	Goodland	E-3
Burnettsville	E-5	Goshen	B-7
Burns City	M-5	Gosport	K-5
Butler	B-10	Grandview	Q-4
Cadiz	G-8	Grass Creek	D-6
Cambridge City	H-10	Grayford	M-8
Camby	Pg. 110, F-1	Graysville	K-3
Cannelton	Q-5	Greencastle	H-4
Carbon	J-4	Greendale	K-10
Carbondale	F-3	Greenfield	H-7
Carefree	P-6	Greensboro	H-8
Carlisle	L-3	Greensburg	K-8
Carmel	G-6	Greentown	E-7
Vicinity	Pg. 110, A-4	Greenwood	J-7
Carp	J-5	Griffin	P-2
Castleton	G-7	Griffith	Pg. 97, D-7
Vicinity	Pg. 110, B-5	Grovertown	B-5
Cayuga	H-3	Hagerstown	H-9
Cedar Grove	J-10	Hammond	B-3
Cedar Lake	B-3	Vicinity	Pg. 97, L-8
Centerville	H-10	Hanna	B-5
Chalmers	E-4	Hanover	M-8
Chandler	P-3	Hardinsburg	D-9
Charlestown	N-8	Harlan	C-10
Chester	H-10	Harmony	J-4
Chesterfield	G-8	Harrodsburg	L-5
Chesterton	B-4	Hartford City	F-9
Chrisney	P-4	Hartsville	K-8
Churubusco	C-9	Haysville	N-4
Cicero	G-7	Hazelwood	D-6
Cincinnati	L-5	Hazleton	N-2
Clarks Hill	F-5	Hebron	C-4
Clarksville	N-7	Hedrick	F-3
Vicinity	Pg. 118, A-2	Hemlock	F-7
Clay City	K-4	Henryville	M-8
Clayton	H-5	Heusler	Q-2
Clermont	Pg. 110, C-1	Highland	Pg. 97, C-7
Clinton	H-3	Highwood	Pg. 110, C-3
Cloverdale	J-5	Hillsboro	G-3
Coatesville	H-5	Hindustan	K-5
Collegeville	D-4	Hobart	B-3
Columbia City	C-8	Hobbs	F-7
Columbus	K-7	Holland	P-4
Connersville	H-9	Homecroft	Pg. 110, F-4
Converse	E-7	Hope	K-7
Cory	J-4	Howe	A-9
Corydon	P-7	Hudson	B-9
Covington	G-3	Hudson Lake	A-5
Crawfordsville	G-4	Huntertown	C-9
Crothersville	M-7	Huntingburg	N-4
Crown Point	B-3	Huntington	D-8
Vicinity	Pg. 97, E-7	Huron	M-5
Crows Nest	Pg. 110, C-3	Indianapolis	H-6
Crystal	N-5	Vicinity	Pg. 122
Cumberland	H-7	Jamestown	H-5
Vicinity	Pg. 122	Jasonville	K-3
Cynthiana	P-2	Jasper	N-4
Cypress	Q-2	Jeffersonville	N8
Dale	P-4	Vicinity	Pg. 118, A-2
Dana	H-1	Johnson	N-2
Danville	H-5	Jonesboro	F-8
Darmstadt	P-2	Jonesville	L-7
Dayton	F-4	Kempton	F-6
Decatur	D-10	Kendallville	B-9
Decker	N-3	Kentland	D-3
Deep River	D-8	Kewanna	D-6
Deerfield	F-10	Kingman	G-3
Degonia Springs	P-4	Kingsbury	B-5
Delphi	E-5	Kingsford Hts.	B-5
Demotte	C-4	Knightstown	H-8
Denver	D-7	Knox	C-5
Derby	Q-5	Kokomo	E-6
Dillsboro	K-9	Kouts	C-4
Dogwood	P-7	La Crosse	C-4
Dover	G-5	La Fontaine	E-8
Dublin	H-9	La Paz	B-6
Dugger	L-3	La Porte	B-5
Dunfee	C-9	Vicinity	Pg. 97, C-8
Dunkirk	F-9	Lafayette	F-4
Dunlap	A-7	Lagrange	A-8
E. Mt. Carmel	N-2	Lake Station	B-3
Earl Park	E-3	Vicinity	Pg. 97, C-8
East Gary	Pg. 97, B-7	Lake Village	C-3
Economy	G-9	Lakeville	B-6
Edinburgh	K-7	Lawrence	H-6
Effner	E-3	Vicinity	Pg. 110, C-5
Elberfeld	P-3	Lawrenceburg	L-10
Elizabeth	P-7	Lebanon	G-5
Elizabethtown	K-7	Leota	M-7
Elkhart	A-7	Leroy	B-3
Ellettsville	K-5		

Place	Grid	Place	Grid
Lewistown	D-4	Ossian	D-9
Liberty	H-10	Otis	A-4
Libertyville	J-3	Otwell	N-4
Ligonier	B-8	Owensville	P-2
Linden	G-5	Oxford	E-3
Linton	L-4	Palmyra	N-6
Lizton	H-5	Paoli	M-6
Logansport	E-6	Paris Crossing	L-8
Loogootee	M-4	Parr	D-4
Lowell	C-3	Patriot	L-10
Luther	D-8	Patronville	E-11
Lynn	G-10	Pence	F-3
Lynnville	P-3	Pendleton	G-8
Madison	L-9	Peoria	E-7
Majenica	D-8	Perrysburg	D-7
Malden	B-4	Perrysville	G-3
Manhattan	J-4	Peru	E-7
Marengo	N-6	Petersburg	N-3
Marion	E-8	Pierceton	C-8
Markle	D-9	Pike	G-6
Markleville	G-8	Pine Village	F-3
Mars Hill	Pg. 110, E-2	Plainfield	H-5
Marshall	H-4	Pleasant	L-9
Martinsville	J-5	Pleasant Mills	D-10
Mauckport	P-6	Pleasant View	H-7
Maxwell	H-7	Plymouth	B-6
Maywood	Pg. 110, E-3	Point Isabel	F-7
Mecca	H-3	Portage	B-4
Medaryville	C-5	Porter	B-4
Memphis	N-7	Portland	F-10
Mentone	C-7	Poseyville	P-2
Meridian Hills	Pg. 110, B-3	Prairie City	J-4
Merom	L-3	Prairie Creek	K-3
Merriam	C-8	Prairieton	K-3
Merrillville	B-3	Princeton	N-2
Vicinity	Pg. 97, D-7	Ramsey	N-6
Metamora	K-9	Raub	E-3
Metea	D-6	Ravenswood	Pg. 110, B-4
Michiana Shores	A-5	Rays Crossing	J-8
Michigan City	A-4	Reiffsburg	E-9
Michigantown	F-6	Rensselaer	D-4
Mickeyville	Pg. 110, E-2	Reynolds	E-4
Middlebury	A-8	Richmond	H-10
Middlefork	F-6	Rising Sun	L-10
Middletown	G-8	Riverside	F-3
Milan	K-9	Roachdale	H-5
Millersburg	B-8	Roann	D-7
Milport	M-7	Rochester	C-6
Mishawaka	B-7	Rockfield	E-5
Mitchell	M-6	Rockport	Q-4
Monon	D-4	Rockville	H-3
Monroe	E-9	Rocky Ripple	Pg. 110, C-3
Monroeville	D-10	Rogersville	G-9
Montezuma	H-3	Rome City	B-9
Monticello	E-5	Romney	F-4
Montmorenci	F-4	Rosedale	J-3
Montpelier	E-9	Roseland	A-6
Mooresville	J-6	Roselawn	C-3
Morgantown	K-6	Rosston	G-6
Morocco	D-3	Rossville	F-5
Morristown	H-8	Royal Center	D-5
Morton	H-4	Royalton	H-6
Moscow	J-8	Rushville	J-8
Mt. Ayr	D-3	Russellville	H-4
Mt. Carmel	J-10	Salem	M-6
Mt. Comfort	H-7	Sandusky	J-8
Mt. Etna	D-8	Santa Claus	P-4
Mt. Meridian	J-5	Santa Fe	E-7
Mt. Pleasant (Cass Cty)	D-6	Schererville	B-3
Mt. Pleasant (Perry Cty)	P-5	Vicinity	Pg. 97, D-7
Mt. Vernon	Q-2	Schneider	C-3
Mt. Zion	E-9	Scipio	J-10
Mulberry	F-5	Scott	A-8
Muncie	G-9	Scottsburg	M-7
Munster	B-3	Seelyville	J-3
Vicinity	Pg. 109, M-8	Sellersburg	N-7
N. Liberty	B-6	Sexton	H-8
N. Manchester	D-7	Seymour	L-7
N. Vernon	L-8	Shelburn	K-3
Napoleon	K-9	Shelbyville	J-7
Nappanee	B-7	Sheridan	G-6
Nashville	K-6	Shoals	M-5
New Albany	N-7	Shore Acres	Pg. 110, A-5
Vicinity	Pg. 118, A-4	Sidney	C-7
New Amsterdam	P-6	Silver Lake	C-7
New Augusta	Pg. 110, B-2	Solitude	P-2
New Boston	P-7	South Bend	A-6
New Carlisle	A-6	South Whitley	C-7
New Castle	G-9	Southport	H-6
New Chicago	C-8	Vicinity	Pg. 110, G-4
New Frankfort	J-9	Speedway	H-6
New Goshen	J-3	Vicinity	Pg. 110, D-2
New Harmony	P-2	Spencer	K-5
New Haven	C-10	Spiceland	H-8
New Liberty	M-7	Spring Hills	Pg. 110, C-3
New Market	G-5	St. Croix	P-5
New Pekin	M-7	St. Joe	C-10
New Providence	N-7	St. John	Pg. 99, D-6
New Richmond	G-4	St. Leon	K-10
New Ross	G-5	St. Paul	J-8
New Whiteland	J-6	Stewartsville	P-2
Newberry	L-4	Stilesville	H-5
Newburgh	Q-3	Story	K-6
Newport	H-3	Sullivan	K-3
Newtown	G-4	Sulphur Springs	G-8
Nine Mile	D-9	Summitville	F-8
Nobelsville	G-7	Sunman	K-9
Nora	Pg. 110, B-4	Swayzee	E-7
Norristown	K-7	Syracuse	B-8
North Crows Nest	Pg. 110, B-3	Tell City	Q-5
North Judson	C-5	Templeton	E-4
Oakland City	N-3	Terre Haute	J-3
Oaktown	M-3	Thorntown	G-5
Odell	E-4	Tipton	F-7
Odon	L-4	Topeka	B-8
Ogden Dunes	B-4	Traders Point	Pg. 110, B-1
Ogilville	K-7	Trafalgar	J-6
Oolitic	L-5	Tremont	Pg. 110, G-2
Orleans	M-5	Troy	Q-5
Osceola	A-7	Union City	G-10
Osgood	K-9	Uniondale	D-9
		Unionport	Q-1
		Unionville	K-6
		Upland	F-8

Place	Grid
Urbana	D-7
Valparaiso	B-4
Van Buren	E-8
Veedersburg	G-3
Versailles	L-9
Vevay	M-9
Vincennes	M-3
W. College Corner	J-10
W. Lebanon	F-3
W. Terre Haute	J-3
Wabash	D-7
Waco	M-4
Wakarusa	B-7
Walkerton	B-6
Walton	E-6
Wanatah	B-4
Warren	E-8
Warsaw	C-7
Washington	M-4
Waterford	B-4
Waterloo	B-10
Waynetown	G-4
Webster	H-10
West Lafayette	F-4
West Newton	Pg. 110, G-2
West Point	F-4
Westfield	G-7
Westphalia	M-4
Westport	K-8
Westville	B-4
Wheatfield	C-4
Whitestown	G-6
Whiting	B-3
Vicinity	Pg. 99, K-8
Wilkinson	H-8
Williams	L-5
Williams Creek	Pg. 110, B-4
Williamsport	F-3
Wilmot	B-8
Winamac	C-5
Winchester	G-10
Windfall City	F-7
Wingate	G-4
Winona Lake	C-7
Winslow	N-3
Wolcott	D-4
Woodburn	C-10
Woodstock	Pg. 110, C-3
Worthington	K-4
Wynnedale	Pg. 110, C-3
Yorktown	G-8
Zionsville	G-6
Vicinity	Pg. 110, A-2

IOWA
Page 36
Population: 2,913,808
Capital: Des Moines
Land Area: 55,965 sq. mi.

IOWA

Place	Grid	Place	Grid
Abingdon	F-7	Belle Plaine	D-7
Ackley	C-6	Bellevue	D-9
Adair	E-4	Belmond	C-5
Adel	E-4	Bennett	E-9
Afton	F-4	Bettendorf	E-10
Agency	F-6	Bevington	E-5
Ainsworth	E-8	Blairsburg	C-5
Akron	C-1	Blakesburg	F-7
Albia	F-6	Blencoe	D-2
Alden	C-5	Bloomfield	F-7
Algona	B-4	Bonaparte	F-8
Allendorf	B-2	Boone	D-5
Allerton	G-5	Boyden	B-2
Allison	C-6	Bradford	C-6
Alta	C-3	Brayton	E-3
Alta Vista	B-7	Breda	C-3
Alton	B-1	Bridgewater	F-4
Altoona	E-5	Brighton	F-8
Amana	D-8	Britt	B-5
Ames	D-5	Brooklyn	D-6
Anamosa	D-8	Brooks	F-3
Anderson	F-3	Brunsville	C-1
Andrew	D-10	Bryant	D-10
Anita	E-3	Buffalo Center	A-5
Ankeny	D-5	Burlington	F-8
Vicinity	Pg. 132, C-5	Burr Oak	A-8
Anthon	C-2	Burt	B-4
Aplington	C-6	Bussey	E-6
Arcadia	D-3	Calamus	D-9
Archer	B-2	Calmar	B-8
Aredale	C-6	Camanche	D-9
Arispe	F-4	Cantril	G-7
Arlington	C-8	Carbon	F-3
Armstrong	B-4	Carlisle	E-5
Arnolds Park	A-3	Carpenter	B-6
Arthur	D-3	Carroll	D-3
Asbury	C-9	Carson	E-2
Ashton	B-2	Carter Lake	E-1
Athelstan	G-4	Carter Lake	Pg. 132, D-5
Atkins	D-7	Cascade	D-9
Atlantic	E-3	Casey	E-4
Attica	E-6	Cedar	F-7
Auburn	D-3	Cedar Falls	C-7
Audubon	E-3	Cedar Rapids	D-8
Aurelia	C-2	Center Point	D-8
Avery	F-6	Centerville	F-6
Avoca	E-2	Central City	D-8
Badger	C-4	Chapin	C-5
Baldwin	D-9	Chariton	F-5
Bancroft	B-4	Charles City	B-6
Barnes City	E-6	Charlotte	D-10
Barnum	C-4	Charter Oak	D-2
Battle Creek	D-2	Chatsworth	B-1
Baxter	D-6	Chelsea	D-7
Bayard	D-4	Cherokee	C-2
Beaver	D-5	Churdan	D-4
Bedford	F-4	Cincinnati	G-6
Beech	E-6	Clara	Pg. 132, C-5
		Clare	C-4
		Clarence	D-9
		Clarinda	F-3
		Clarion	C-5
		Clarksville	C-7
		Clear Lake	B-6
		Clearfield	F-4
		Cleghorn	C-2
		Clinton	D-10
		Clutier	D-7
		Coggon	D-8
		Colesburg	C-9
		Colfax	E-6
		Collins	D-6
		Colo	D-5
		Columbia	F-6
		Columbus Jct.	E-8
		Colwell	B-7
		Conesville	E-8
		Conrad	D-6
		Conroy	E-8
		Conway	F-4
		Coon Rapids	D-3
		Cooper	D-4
		Coppock	F-8
		Coralville	E-8
		Corley	E-2
		Corning	F-3
		Correctionville	C-2
		Corwith	B-5
		Corydon	F-6
		Vicinity	Pg. 132, E-6
		Crescent	E-1
		Cresco	B-7
		Creston	F-4
		Curlew	C-4
		Dakota City	C-4
		Dana	D-4
		Danbury	D-2
		Danville	F-8
		Davenport	E-9
		Davis City	G-5
		Dayton	D-4
		De Soto	E-5
		De Witt	D-9
		Decorah	B-8
		Dedham	D-3
		Defiance	D-3
		Delhi	C-8
		Delmar	D-9
		Deloit	D-3
		Delta	E-7
		Denison	D-2
		Denver	C-7
		Des Moines	E-5
		Dexter	E-4
		Dickens	B-3
		Dike	C-6
		Dolliver	A-4
		Donnellson	F-8
		Doon	B-1
		Dorchester	A-8
		Dow City	D-2
		Dows	C-5
		Drakesville	F-7

Place	Grid	Place	Grid
Dubuque	C-9	Imogene	F-3
Dumfries	Pg. 132, G-7	Independence	C-8
Dumont	C-6	Indianola	E-5
Duncombe	C-4	Inwood	B-1
Dunkerton	C-7	Iowa Center	D-6
Dunlap	D-2	Iowa City	E-8
Dyersville	C-9	Iowa Falls	C-6
Dysart	D-7	Ireton	B-1
Eagle Grove	C-5	Irwin	E-3
Earlham	E-4	Jackson Jct.	B-7
Earling	E-3	Jamaica	D-4
Early	C-3	Janesville	C-7
Eddyville	F-7	Jefferson	D-4
Edgewood	B-8	Jerico	B-7
Eldon	F-7	Jesup	C-7
Eldora	C-6	Jewell	C-5
Eldridge	E-10	Joice	B-5
Elgin	B-7	Kalona	E-8
Elk Horn	E-3	Kamrar	C-5
Elkader	C-8	Kanawha	B-4
Elkhart	D-5	Kellogg	D-6
Elliott	F-3	Kendallville	B-8
Ellsworth	D-5	Kent	F-4
Emerson	F-2	Keokuk	G-8
Emmetsburg	B-4	Keosauqua	F-7
Epworth	C-9	Keota	E-8
Essex	F-3	Keswick	E-7
Estherville	B-4	Keystone	D-7
Everly	B-2	Killduff	E-6
Exira	E-3	Kingsley	C-2
Fairbank	C-7	Kirkman	E-3
Fairfield	F-8	Kiron	D-3
Farley	C-8	Klemme	B-5
Farnhamville	C-4	Knoxville	E-6
Farragut	F-2	La Porte City	D-7
Fayette	B-7	Lake City	C-3
Fenton	B-4	Lake Mills	B-5
Floyd	B-6	Lake Park	A-3
Fonda	C-3	Lake View	D-3
Fontanelle	E-3	Lamoni	G-4
Forest City	B-5	Lamont	C-8
Fort Dodge	C-4	Lansing	B-9
Fort Madison	F-9	Larchwood	A-1
Fostoria	B-3	Larrabee	C-2
Frankville	B-8	Laurel	D-6
Fraser	D-5	Laurens	C-3
Fredericksburg	B-7	Le Claire	D-9
Fremont	E-7	Le Mars	C-2
Froelich	B-8	Ledyard	B-4
Frytown	E-8	Lehigh	D-5
Fulton	D-9	Leighton	E-7
Garden City	D-6	Lenox	F-4
Garnavillo	C-9	Leon	F-5
Garner	B-5	Lester	B-1
Garwin	D-6	Lewis	E-3
George	B-2	Liberty Center	F-6
Gibson	E-7	Lime Springs	B-7
Gilman	D-6	Lineville	G-5
Gilmore City	C-4	Lisbon	D-8
Gladbrook	D-6	Little Rock	B-2
Glenwood	F-2	Little Sioux	D-2
Vicinity	Pg. 132, J-7	Livermore	C-4
Glidden	D-4	Logan	E-2
Goldfield	C-5	Lohrville	C-3
Goodell	B-5	Long Grove	E-9
Gowrie	D-4	Long Tree	E-8
Graettinger	B-4	Lorimor	F-4
Grafton	B-6	Lost Nation	D-9
Grand Jct.	D-4	Lovilia	F-6
Grand River	G-5	Lowden	D-9
Grandview	E-9	Lucas	F-5
Grant	F-3	Luther	D-5
Green Mountain	D-6	Luxemburg	C-9
Greene	C-6	Lyman	F-3
Greenfield	E-4	Lytton	C-3
Grimes	D-5	Macedonia	E-2
Grinnell	E-7	Macksburg	E-4
Griswold	F-3	Madrid	D-5
Grundy Center	C-6	Mallard	B-4
Guernsey	E-7	Malcom	E-7
Guthrie Center	E-4	Malvern	F-2
Guttenberg	B-8	Manchester	C-8
Hamburg	G-2	Manilla	E-2
Hamilton	E-5	Manly	B-5
Hamlin	E-3	Manning	D-3
Hampton	C-6	Manson	C-4
Hancock	E-2	Mapleton	D-2
Hanlontown	B-5	Maquoketa	D-10
Harcourt	D-4	Marathon	C-3
Harlan	E-3	Marcus	C-2
Harper's Ferry	B-9	Marengo	E-7
Hartley	B-3	Marne	E-3
Hartwick	D-7	Marshalltown	D-6
Harvey	E-6	Mason City	B-6
Havelock	C-4	Massena	E-4
Hawarden	B-1	Matlock	B-1
Hawkeye	B-7	Maxwell	D-5
Hazleton	C-8	May City	A-3
Hedrick	F-7	Maynard	C-8
Henderson	F-2	McGregor	B-9
Hepburn	F-3	McIntire	B-7
Hesper	B-8	Mechanicsville	D-8
Hiawatha	D-7	Mediapolis	F-8
Hillsboro	F-8	Melbourne	D-6
Hinton	C-1	Melcher	F-6
Holmes	C-5	Melvin	B-2
Holstein	C-2	Meriden	C-2
Honey Creek	Pg. 132, A-5	Merrill	C-1
Hopeville	F-5	Milford	B-3
Hopkinton	C-8	Millerton	G-5
Hospers	B-1	Millville	B-8
Hubbard	C-5	Milo	E-5
Hudson	C-7	Milton	G-7
Hull	B-1	Minburn	E-4
Humboldt	C-4	Minden	E-2
Humeston	F-5	Mingo	E-5
Huxley	D-5	Missouri Valley	E-2
Iconium	F-6	Mitchellville	D-5
Ida Grove	C-2	Mondamin	E-2
		Moneta	B-3
		Monona	B-8

IOWA

Monroe E-6
Montezuma E-7
Monticello D-8
Montrose G-8
Moorhead D-2
Moravia F-6
Morning Sun F-9
Morse E-8
Moulton G-7
Mount Ayr F-4
Mount Etna F-4
Mount Sterling G-8
Mount Union F-8
Moville C-1
Mt. Pleasant F-8
Mt. Vernon D-8
Murray F-4
Muscatine E-9
Nashua B-7
Neola E-2
Nevada D-5
Nevinville F-4
New Albin A-8
New Hampton B-7
New Haven B-7
New London F-9
New Market F-3
New Providence D-6
New Sharon E-7
New Virginia F-5
Newburg D-7
Newkirk B-2
Newton E-6
Nichols E-9
Nora Springs B-6
North English E-8
Northboro G-3
Northwood B-6
Norwalk E-5
Norway D-7
Oakland E-3
Ocheyedan A-2
Odebolt D-3
Oelwein C-8
Ogden D-4
Olin D-9
Onawa D-2
Onslow D-9
Orange City B-2
Orient F-4
Osage B-6
Osceola F-5
Oskaloosa E-7
Otho D-5
Oto D-2
Ottumwa F-7
Oxford E-8
Oyens C-2
Pacific City Pg. 132, J-6
Pacific Junction Pg. 132, K-6
Panama E-3
Panora E-4
Park View E-10
Parkersburg C-7
Parnell E-7
Paullina B-2
Pella E-6
Percival F-2
Perkins B-1
Perry D-5
Persia E-2
Pierson C-2
Pilot Mound D-5
Pisgah D-2
Plain View E-9
Plainfield C-7
Plano F-6
Pleasant Plain F-7
Pleasantville E-5
Pocahontas C-4
Polk City E-5
Pomeroy C-4
Popejoy C-6
Portsmouth E-3
Postville B-8
Prairie City E-6
Preston D-10
Primghar B-2
Prole E-5
Pulaski F-7
Quasqueton C-8
Quimby C-2
Rathbun F-6
Reasnor E-6
Red Oak F-3
Redding G-4
Redfield E-4
Reinbeck D-7
Rembrandt C-3
Remsen C-2
Renwick C-5
Rhodes D-6
Riceville B-6
Richland E-7
Rickardsville C-9
Ridgeway B-8
Ringsted A-3
Rippey D-4
Rochester E-9
Rock Rapids B-2
Rock Valley B-1
Rockford B-6
Rockwell B-6
Rockwell City C-4
Roland C-5
Rolfe C-4
Roselle D-3
Rossie B-3
Rossville B-8
Royal B-3
Russell F-6
Ruthven B-3
Ryan C-8
Sabula C-10
Sac City C-3
Sanborn B-2
Saratoga B-7
Schaller C-3
Schleswig D-2
Schley B-7
Scranton D-4
Searsboro E-7
Selma F-7
Sergeant Bluff C-2
Seymour F-5
Shambaugh G-3
Sharpsburg F-3
Sheffield B-6
Sheldon B-2
Shell Rock B-6
Shellsburg D-8
Shenandoah F-3
Sibley A-2
Sidney F-2
Sigourney E-7
Sioux Center B-1
Sioux City C-1
Sioux Rapids B-3
Sloan D-1
Smithland D-2
Soldier D-2
Solon D-8
Somers C-4
Spencer B-3
Spirit Lake B-3
Springville D-8
St. Ansgar B-6
St. Charles E-5
St. Joseph B-4
St. Marys E-5
Stacyville A-6
Stanton E-2
Stanwood D-8
State Center D-6
Steamboat Rock C-6
Storm Lake C-3
Story City D-5
Stout C-7
Strawberry Point C-8
Stuart E-4
Sully D-6
Sulphur Springs C-3
Sumner C-7
Superior B-3
Sutherland B-2
Swea City B-4
Tabor F-2
Tama D-7
Templeton D-3
Terril B-3
Thompson B-5
Thornton B-5
Thurman F-2
Tiffin E-8
Tipton D-9
Titonka B-5
Toledo D-6
Traer D-7
Trenton F-8
Tripoli C-7
Truesdale C-3
Truro F-5
Turin D-2
Ulmer D-3
Underwood E-2
Union D-6
Urbana D-7
Urbandale E-5
Ute D-2
Vail D-3
Valeria E-6
Van Horne D-7
Van Wert F-5
Varina C-3
Ventura B-5
Victor E-7
Villisca F-3
Vining D-7
Vinton D-7
W. Burlington F-8
Walford D-8
Walker D-8
Wall Lake C-2
Wallingford B-4
Wapello F-9
Washington E-8
Washta C-2
Waterloo C-7
Waukee E-5
Waukon B-8
Waverly C-7
Webster E-7
Webster City C-5
Weldon F-5
Wellman E-8
Welton D-10
Wesley B-5
West Bend B-4
West Des Moines E-5
West Grove F-7
West Liberty E-9
West Point F-8
West Union B-8
Westfield C-1
Weston Pg. 132, J-7
Wheatland D-9
Whiting D-2
Whittemore B-4
Wick B-5
Willey E-3
Williams C-5
Williamsburg E-8
Williamson F-5
Winfield F-8
Winterset E-4
Wiota E-3
Woodbine E-2
Woodburn F-5
Woodward E-4
Woolstock C-5
Wyoming D-9
Yale D-4
Zwingle C-9

KANSAS
Page 37
Population: 2,363,679
Capital: Topeka
Land Area: 81,781 sq. mi.

Abbeyville E-5
Abilene D-7
Admire D-8
Agenda C-6
Agra C-4
Alden E-5
Alexander D-4
Allen D-8
Alma D-8
Almena B-4
Alta Vista D-8
Altamont F-9
Alton C-5
Altoona E-8
Americus E-8
Andale E-6
Andover E-7
Anthony F-6
Arcadia E-9
Argonia F-6
Arkansas City F-7
Arlington E-5
Ashland F-4
Athol C-5
Atlanta F-7
Attica F-5
Atwood B-2
Augusta E-7
Axtell C-7
Baldwin City D-9
Barnard D-6
Barnes C-7
Bartlett F-9
Basehor D-9
Bassett E-8
Baxter Springs F-9
Bazine D-4
Beattie C-7
Belle Plaine F-7
Belleville C-6
Beloit C-6
Belpre E-4
Belvue D-8
Benedict E-8
Bennington D-6
Bentley E-6
Benton E-7
Bern C-8
Beverly D-6
Bird City B-2
Bison D-4
Blue Mound E-9
Blue Rapids C-7
Bluff City F-6
Bogue C-4
Brewster C-2
Bronson E-9
Brookville D-6
Brownell D-4
Bucklin F-4
Buffalo E-8
Buhler E-6
Bunker Hill D-5
Burden F-7
Burdett E-4
Burlingame D-8
Burlington E-8
Burns E-7
Burr Oak C-5
Burrton E-6
Bushong D-8
Bushton D-5
Byers E-5
Caldwell F-6
Cambridge F-7
Caney F-8
Canton E-6
Carbondale D-9
Carlton D-7
Cassoday E-7
Cawker City C-5
Cedar C-5
Cedar Point E-7
Cedar Vale F-8
Centralia C-8
Chanute E-8
Chapman D-7
Chase E-5
Chautauqua F-8
Cheney E-6
Cherokee E-9
Cherryvale F-8
Chetopa F-9
Cimarron E-3
Circleville C-8
Claflin D-5
Clay Center C-7
Clayton C-3
Clearwater F-6
Clifton C-6
Climax F-7
Clyde C-6
Coats F-5
Coffeyville F-9
Colby C-2
Coldwater F-4
Collyer C-3
Colony E-9
Columbus F-9
Concordia C-6
Conway Springs F-6
Coolidge E-1
Copeland F-3
Cottonwood Falls E-7
Council Grove D-8
Countryside Pg. 112, H-2
Courtland C-6
Cuba C-6
Cullison F-5
Culver D-6
Cunningham F-5
De Soto D-9
Dearing F-8
Deerfield E-2
Delphos C-6
Denison C-9
Denton C-9
Derby F-7
Dexter F-7
Dighton D-3
Dodge City E-3
Douglass F-7
Downs C-5
Dresden C-3
Dunlap D-8
Dwight D-7
Earlton E-9
Easton C-9
Edgerton D-9
Edmond C-4
Edna F-9
Effingham C-8
El Dorado F-7
Elbing E-7
Elgin F-8
Elk City F-8
Elk Falls F-8
Elkhart F-1
Ellinwood E-5
Ellis D-4
Ellsworth D-5
Elmdale E-7
Emmett C-8
Emporia E-8
Englewood F-3
Ensign E-3
Enterprise D-7
Erie F-9
Esbon C-5
Eskridge D-8
Eudora D-9
Eureka E-8
Fairview C-8
Florence E-7
Fontana E-9
Ford F-4
Formoso C-6
Fort Scott E-9
Fowler F-3
Frankfort C-7
Fredonia E-8
Freeport F-6
Frontenac F-9
Fulton E-9
Galatia D-4
Galena F-9
Galesburg E-8
Galva E-6
Garden City E-2
Garden Plain F-6
Gardner D-9
Garfield E-4
Garnett E-9
Gaylord C-5
Gem C-2
Geneseo D-5
Girard E-9
Glade C-4
Glasco C-6
Glen Elder C-5
Goessel E-6
Goodland C-1
Gorham D-5
Gove D-3
Grainfield C-3
Grandview Plaza D-7
Great Bend E-5
Greenleaf C-7
Greensburg F-4
Gridley E-8
Grinnell C-2
Halstead E-6
Hamilton E-8
Hamlin C-8
Hanover C-7
Hanston E-4
Hardtner F-5
Harper F-6
Harris E-8
Hartford D-8
Harveyville D-8
Havana F-8
Haven E-6
Havensville C-8
Haviland F-4
Hays D-4
Haysville F-6
Hazelton F-5
Healy D-3
Herington D-7
Herndon B-2
Hesston E-6
Hiawatha C-8
Highland C-8
Hill City C-4
Hillsboro E-6
Hoisington D-5
Holcomb E-2
Hollenberg C-7
Holton C-8
Holyrood D-5
Hope D-7
Horton C-9
Howard F-8
Hoxie C-3
Hoyt C-8
Hudson E-5
Hugoton F-2
Humboldt F-9
Hunter C-5
Huron C-9
Hutchinson E-6
Independence F-8
Ingalls E-3
Inman E-6
Iola E-9
Isabel F-5
Jamestown C-6
Jennings C-3
Jetmore E-3
Jewell C-6
Johnson City E-1
Junction City D-7
Kanapolis D-6
Kansas City D-9
  Vicinity Pg. 112, E-1
Kensington C-5
Kincaid E-9
Kingman F-5
Kinsley E-4
Kiowa F-5
Kirwin C-4
Kismet F-2
La Crosse D-4
La Cygne E-9
La Harpe E-9
Lakin E-2
Lane E-9
Langdon E-5
Larned E-4
Latham F-7
Latimer D-7
Lawrence D-9
Le Roy E-9
Leavenworth C-9
Leawood Pg. 112, K-3
Lebanon C-5
Lebo D-8
Lecompton D-9
Lehigh E-6
Lenexa Pg. 112, J-1
Lenora C-3
Leon F-7
Leona C-9
Leonardville C-7
Leoti D-2
Lewis E-4
Liberal F-2
Lincoln D-6
Lincolnville E-7
Lindsborg D-6
Linn C-7
Linwood D-9
Little River E-6
Logan C-4
Lone Elm E-9
Long Island B-4
Longford D-7
Longton F-8
Lorraine D-5
Lost Springs D-7
Louisburg E-9
Louisville C-8
Lucas D-5
Luka F-5
Luray D-5
Lyndon D-9
Lyons E-6
Macksville E-4
Madison E-8
Maize E-6
Manchester D-7
Manhattan D-8
Mankato C-5
Manter E-1
Maple Hill D-8
Mapleton E-9
Marion E-7
Marquette D-6
Marysville C-7
Matfield Green E-7
Mayetta C-8
Mayfield F-6
McCracken D-4
McCune F-9
McDonald B-2
McFarland D-8
McPherson E-6
Meade F-3
Medicine Lodge F-5
Melvern D-8
Meriden C-9
Merriam Pg. 112, H-2
Milan F-6
Mildred E-9
Milford D-7
Miltonvale D-6
Minneapolis D-6
Minneola E-3
Mission Pg. 112, H-2
Mission Hills Pg. 112, G-3
Moline F-8
Montezuma E-3
Morganville C-7
Morland C-3
Morrill C-8
Morrowville C-7
Moscow F-2
Mound City E-9
Mound Valley F-9
Moundridge E-6
Mount Hope E-6
Mullinville F-5
Mulvane F-7
Munden C-6
Muscotah C-9
Narka C-6
Nashville F-5
Natoma C-4
Neodesha F-8
Neosho Falls E-9
Ness City D-3
Netawaka C-8
New Cambria D-6
New Strawn D-8
Newton E-6
Nickerson E-6
Norcatur C-3
Norton C-3
Nortonville C-9
Norwich F-6
Oak Hill C-7
Oakley C-2
Oberlin C-3
Offerle E-4
Ogden D-7
Oketo C-7
Olmitz D-5
Olpe E-8
Olsburg C-7
Onaga C-7
Osage City D-8
Osawatomie E-9
Osborne C-5
Oskaloosa C-9
Oswego F-9
Otis D-4
Ottawa D-9
Overbrook D-9
Overland Park Pg. 112, J-2
Oxford F-7
Palco C-4
Palmer C-7
Paola E-9
Paradise D-5
Park C-3
Park City E-7
Parker E-9
Parsons F-9
Paxico D-8
Peabody E-7
Perry D-9
Peru F-8
Phillipsburg C-4
Pittsburg F-10
Plains F-3
Plainville C-4
Pleasanton E-9
Plevna E-5
Pomona D-9
Portis C-5
Potwin E-7
Powhattan C-8
Prairie View C-4
Prairie Village Pg. 112, H-3
Pratt F-5
Prescott E-9
Preston F-5
Pretty Prairie E-6
Princeton E-9
Protection F-4
Quenemo D-8
Quinter C-3
Ramona D-7
Randall C-6
Randolph C-7
Ransom D-3
Rantoul E-9
Raymond E-5
Reading D-8
Redfield E-9
Republic C-6
Rexford C-3
Richfield F-1
Richmond E-9
Riley D-7
Robinson C-9
Roeland Park
  Vicinity Pg. 112, G-3
Rolla F-1
Rose Hill F-7
Rossville D-8
Rozel E-4
Rush Center D-4
Russell D-5
Russell Springs D-2
Sabetha C-8
Salina D-6
Satanta F-2
Sawyer F-5
Scandia C-6
Schoenchen D-4
Scott City D-2
Sedan F-8
Sedgwick E-6
Selden C-3
Seneca C-8
Severy E-8
Seward D-5
Sharon F-5
Sharon Springs D-1
Shawnee Pg. 112, H-1
Silver Lake D-8
Simpson C-6
Smith Center C-5
Smolan D-6
Solomon D-7
South Haven F-6
Spearville E-3
Spivey F-5
Spring Hill D-9
St. Francis B-1
St. John E-5
St. Marys D-8
St. Paul F-9
Stafford E-5
Stark F-9
Sterling E-6
Strong City E-8
Sublette F-2
Summerfield C-8
Sun City F-5
Sylvan Grove C-5
Sylvia E-5
Syracuse E-1
Tampa E-7
Tescott D-6
Thayer F-9
Timken D-4
Tipton C-5
Tonganoxie D-9
Topeka D-8
Toronto E-7
Towanda E-7
Tribune D-1
Troy C-9
Turon E-5
Tyro F-8
Udall F-7
Ulysses E-2
Uniontown E-9
Utica D-3
Valley Center E-6
Valley Falls C-9
Vermillion C-7
Victoria D-4
Vining C-7
Virgil E-8
WaKeeney D-4
Wakefield C-7
Waldo D-5
Waldron F-5
Wallace D-2
Walnut F-9
Walton E-7
Wamego D-8
Washington C-7
Waterville C-7
Wathena C-9
Waverly E-9
Webber C-6
Weir Scammon F-9
Wellington F-7
Westmoreland C-8
Westphalia E-9
Wetmore C-8
Wheaton C-8
White City D-7
Whitewater E-7
Whiting C-8
Wichita F-6
Williamsburg D-9
Willowbrook E-6
Wilmore F-5
Wilsey D-7
Wilson D-5
Winchester C-9
Windom E-7
Winfield F-7
Winona C-3
Woodbine D-7
Woodston C-4
Yates Center E-8
Zenda F-5
Zurich C-4

KENTUCKY
Pages 38-39
Population: 3,660,777
Capital: Frankfort
Land Area: 39,669 sq. mi.

Adairville F-6
Albany F-9
Alexandria B-10
Allen D-12
Allensville F-6
Arlington F-3
Ashland C-12
Auburn F-7
Audubon Park Pg. 118, D-3
Augusta B-10
Barbourville F-11
Bardstown D-8
Bardwell F-3
Barlow F-3
Beattyville D-11
Beaver Dam E-6
Bedford B-8
Beech Grove D-6
Bellefonte C-12
Bellevue Pg. 100, E-4
Benham E-12
Benton F-4
Berea D-10
Berry B-10
Bloomfield D-9
Bonnieville E-8
Boone D-10
Boonesboro D-10
Booneville E-11
Bowling Green F-7
Bradfordsville D-9
Brandenburg D-7
Breckinridge C-10
Bremen E-6
Broadfields Pg. 118, C-5
Brodhead E-10
Bromley A-10
Brooksville B-10
Brownsville E-7
Buckhorn E-11
Buffalo E-8
Burgin D-9
Burkesville F-8
Burnside F-10
Burton E-12
Butler B-10
Cadiz F-5
Calhoun D-6
Callaway F-11
Calvert City E-4
Campbellsburg B-8
Campbellsville E-8
Campton D-11
Caneyville E-7
Carlisle C-10
Carrollton B-9
Carrsville E-4
Carter C-11
Caseyville D-4
Catlettsburg C-12
Centertown E-6
Central City E-6
Cerulean F-5
Clairfield F-10
Clay E-5
Clay City D-10
Clearfield C-11
Clinton F-3
Cloverport D-7
Cold Spring Pg. 100, G-5
Columbia E-8
Columbus F-3
Concord B-11
Constance Pg. 100, F-1
Corbin F-10
Corydon D-5
Covington B-9
  Vicinity Pg. 100, F-2
Crab Orchard E-9
Crescent Springs Pg. 100, F-2
Crestview Hills Pg. 100, G-2
Crestwood C-8
Crittenden B-10
Crofton F-5
Cumberland E-12
Cynthiana C-10
Danville D-9
Dawson Springs E-5
Dayton Pg. 100, F-4
Dexter F-4
Dixon D-5
Dover B-11
Drakesboro E-6
Druid Hills Pg. 118, B-5
Dry Ridge B-10
Dunmor E-6
Dycusburg E-4
Earlington E-5
Eddyville E-4
Edmonton F-8
Ekron D-7
Elizabethtown D-8
Elkhorn City E-13
Elkton E-6
Elsmere B-10
Eminence C-9
Erlanger Pg. 100, G-2
Eubank E-10
Evarts F-12
Fairdale C-8
Fairfield D-8
Fairview F-6
Falmouth B-10
Ferguson E-10
Flatwoods C-12
Fleming-Neon E-12
Flemingsburg C-11
Florence B-10
Fordsville D-7
Fountain Run F-8
Frankfort C-9
Franklin F-6
Fredonia E-5
Freeburn D-13
Frenchburg D-11
Frogue F-9
Ft. Mitchell Pg. 100, G-3
Ft. Thomas Pg. 100, F-5
Ft. Wright Pg. 100, F-3
Fulton F-3
Gamaliel F-8
Georgetown C-10
Ghent B-9
Glasgow E-8
Golden Pond F-5
Goshen C-8
Grand Rivers E-4
Gratz C-9
Grayson C-12
Greensburg E-8
Greenup B-12
Greenville E-6
Guthrie F-6
Hanson E-5
Hardin F-4
Hardinsburg D-7
Harlan F-11
Harned D-7
Harrodsburg D-9
Hartford D-6
Hawesville D-6
Hazard E-11
Hazel F-4
Hazel Green E-11
Hellier E-12
Henderson D-5
Hickman F-3
Highland Hts. Pg. 100, G-5
Hindman E-12
Hodgenville D-8
Hopkinsville F-6

KENTUCKY

Horse Cave ... E-8
Hustonville ... E-9
Hyden ... E-11
Independence ... B-10
Inez ... D-12
Irvine ... D-10
Irvington ... D-7
Island ... E-6
Jackson ... D-11
Jamestown ... E-9
Jeffersontown ... C-8
Jenkins ... E-12
Junction City ... D-9
Kenton Vale ... Pg. 100, G-3
Kirkmansville ... E-6
Knob Creek ... D-8
Kuttawa ... E-4
La Fayette ... F-5
La Grange ... C-8
LaCenter ... E-3
Lackey ... E-12
Lakeside Park ... Pg. 100, G-3
Lakeview ... Pg. 100, G-3
Lancaster ... D-10
Lawrenceburg ... C-9
Leatherwood ... E-11
Lebanon ... D-9
Lebanon Jct. ... D-8
Lee City ... D-11
Leitchfield ... D-7
Lewisburg ... C-11
Lewisport ... D-6
Lexington ... D-9
Liberty ... E-9
Livermore ... D-6
Livingston ... E-10
Lockport ... C-9
London ... E-10
Loretto ... D-8
Lothair ... E-11
Louisa ... C-12
Louisville ... C-8
  Vicinity ... Pg. 118
Loyall ... F-11
Lucas ... F-8
Ludlow ... Pg. 100, F-3
Lynch ... F-12
Lynnview ... Pg. 118, E-4
Madisonville ... E-5
Manchester ... E-10
Marion ... E-5
Martin ... D-12
Mason ... B-10
Mayfield ... F-4
Maysville ... B-11
McCreary ... B-10
McHenry ... E-6
McKee ... E-10
McRoberts ... E-12
Middlesboro ... F-10
Middletown ... C-8
Midway ... C-9
Midway ... F-4
Millersburg ... C-10
Milton ... B-8
Mockingbird Valley ... Pg. 118, B-5
Monkeys Eyebrow ... E-3
Monroe ... F-4
Monterey ... C-9
Monticello ... F-9
Morehead ... C-11
Moreland ... D-9
Morgan ... B-10
Morganfield ... D-5
Morgantown ... E-6
Mortons Gap ... E-5
Mount Olivet ... B-10
Mount Sterling ... C-11
Mount Vernon ... E-10
Mount Washington ... C-8
Muldraugh ... D-8
Munfordville ... E-8
Murray ... F-4
Nebo ... E-5
New Castle ... C-9
New Haven ... D-8
Newport ... A-10
  Vicinity ... Pg. 100, F-4
Nicholasville ... D-9
North Middletown ... C-10
Nortonville ... E-5
Oak Grove ... F-5
Oakland ... E-7
Olive Hill ... C-11
Owensboro ... D-6
Owenton ... C-9
Owingsville ... C-10
Paducah ... E-4
Paintsville ... D-12
Paris ... C-10
Park City ... E-8
Park Hills ... Pg. 100, F-3
Parkers Lake ... F-10
Parkway Village ... Pg. 118, D-3
Pembroke ... F-5
Perryville ... D-9
Phelps ... D-13
Pikeville ... E-13
Pine Knot ... F-11
Pineville ... F-11
Pleasureville ... C-9
Prestonsburg ... D-12
Prestonville ... B-8
Princeton ... E-5
Prospect ... C-8
Providence ... E-5
Raceland ... B-12
Radcliff ... D-8
Ravenna ... D-11
Reidland ... E-4
Renfro Valley ... E-10

Richmond ... D-10
Rockcastle ... F-5
Rockport ... D-6
Rolling Fields ... Pg. 118, B-5
Russell ... B-12
Russell Springs ... E-9
Russellville ... F-6
Sadieville ... C-10
Salt Lick ... C-11
Salyersville ... D-12
Sanders ... B-9
Sandy Hook ... C-12
Sardis ... C-11
Science Hill ... E-9
Scottsville ... F-7
Sebree ... D-5
Seco ... E-12
Sedalia ... F-4
Sharpsburg ... C-11
Shelby City ... D-9
Shelbyville ... C-9
Shepherdsville ... C-8
Shively ... Pg. 100, G-3
  Vicinity ... Pg. 118, D-1
Silver Grove ... Pg. 100, G-6
Simpsonville ... C-8
Slaughters ... E-5
Smithland ... E-4
Smiths Grove ... E-7
Somerset ... E-10
Sonora ... D-7
South Shore ... B-12
South Williamson ... D-13
Springfield ... D-9
Stamping Ground ... C-9
Stanford ... D-10
Stanton ... D-11
Stearns ... F-9
Sturgis ... D-5
Taylorsville ... D-9
Tompkinsville ... F-8
Trenton ... F-6
Trimble ... E-9
Tyner ... E-11
Union ... B-9
Uniontown ... D-5
Upton ... E-6
Valley Station ... C-8
Van Lear ... D-12
Vanceburg ... B-11
Vancleve ... D-11
Versailles ... C-9
Villa Hills ... Pg. 100, F-2
Vine Grove ... D-7
Wallins Creek ... F-11
Walton ... B-10
Warfield ... D-13
Warsaw ... B-9
Washington ... B-11
Water Valley ... F-4
Waverly ... D-5
Wayland ... D-12
Webster ... D-7
West Beauchel ... Pg. 118, D-5
West Liberty ... D-11
West Point ... D-8
Wheatley ... B-9
Wheelwright ... E-12
Whitesburg ... E-12
Whitesville ... D-6
Whitley City ... F-10
Wickliffe ... E-3
Wilder ... Pg. 100, F-4
Willard ... C-12
Williamsburg ... F-10
Williamstown ... B-10
Wilmore ... D-9
Winchester ... C-10
Wingo ... F-4
Woodburn ... F-7

LOUISIANA
Page 40
Population: 4,205,9000
Capital: Baton Rouge
Land Area: 44,521 sq. mi.

Abbeville ... F-5
Abington ... B-2
Abita Springs ... E-8
Acme ... D-5
Acy ... E-7
Ada ... B-3
Addis ... E-6
Adeline ... F-6
Afton ... B-6
Aimwell ... C-4
Airline Park ... Pg. 125, C-4
Ajax ... C-3
Albany ... E-7
Alco ... D-3
Alden Bridge ... A-2
Alexandria ... D-4
Alsatia ... A-6
Alto ... B-5
Ama ... Pg. 125, C-2
Amelia ... G-7
Amite ... E-8
Anacoco ... D-3
Angie ... D-9
Angola ... D-6
Ansley ... B-4
Antioch ... A-4
Arabi ... F-9
  Vicinity ... Pg. 125, C-6
Archibald ... B-5
Arcola ... D-8
Archie ... C-5
Armistead ... B-3
Arnaudville ... E-5

Ashland ... B-3
Athens ... A-3
Atlanta ... C-4
Augusta ... Pg. 125, F-7
Avery Island ... F-5
Avondale ... Pg. 125, D-4
Aycock ... A-3
Bains ... D-6
Baker ... E-6
Baldwin ... F-6
Ball ... C-4
Bancroft ... E-2
Barataria ... F-8
Basile ... E-4
Baskin ... B-5
Bastrop ... A-5
Batchelor ... D-6
Baton Rouge ... E-7
Bayou Cane ... G-7
Bayou Chicot ... D-5
Bayou Sorrel ... F-6
Bayou Vista ... G-6
Baywood ... E-7
Beaver ... E-4
Beekman ... A-5
Beggs ... E-5
Bell City ... F-3
Belle Chasse ... F-9
Belle Rose ... F-7
Bellwood ... C-3
Belmont ... C-2
Benson ... C-2
Bentley ... C-4
Benton ... A-2
Bernice ... A-4
Bertrandville ... F-9
  Vicinity ... Pg. 125, G-7
Berwick ... F-6
Bienville ... B-3
Blackburn ... A-3
Blanchard ... A-2
Bogalusa ... D-9
Bohemia ... G-9
Bolinger ... A-2
Bonita ... A-5
Book ... D-5
Boothville ... G-10
Bordelonville ... D-5
Bosco ... B-5
Bossier City ... A-2
Bourg ... G-8
Boyce ... C-4
Braithwaite ... Pg. 125, E-9
Branch ... E-5
Breaux Bridge ... E-5
Bridge City ... Pg. 125, D-4
Broussard ... F-5
Brusly ... E-6
Bryceland ... B-3
Bunkie ... D-5
Buras ... G-9
Burnside ... E-7
Burr Ferry ... D-2
Bush ... E-8
Cade ... F-5
Caernarvon ... Pg. 125, E-9
Calhoun ... B-4
Calvin ... C-4
Cameron ... F-3
Campti ... C-3
Caney ... D-2
Carencro ... E-5
Carlisle ... E-7
Carville ... E-7
Caspiana ... B-2
Castor ... B-3
Cedar Grove ... Pg. 125, F-7
Center Point ... D-5
Centerville ... F-6
Chacahoula ... F-7
Chackbay ... F-7
Chalmette ... F-9
  Vicinity ... Pg. 125, D-8
Chase ... B-5
Chataignier ... E-4
Chatham ... B-4
Chauvin ... G-8
Cheneyville ... D-5
Chestnut ... B-3
Chipola ... D-7
Chopin ... C-3
Choudrant ... B-4
Church Point ... E-5
Clarence ... C-3
Clarks ... B-5
Clay ... C-6
Clayton ... C-6
Clifton ... D-8
Clinton ... D-7
Cloutierville ... C-4
Cocodrie ... G-7
Colfax ... C-4
Collinston ... A-5
Colquitt ... A-3
Columbia ... B-4
Concession ... Pg. 125, F-8
Convent ... E-7
Converse ... C-2
Cotton Valley ... A-3
Cottonport ... D-5
Coushatta ... B-3
Covington ... E-8
Cravens ... D-3
Creole ... F-3
Creston ... B-3
Crowley ... E-4
Crown Point ... Pg. 125, G-6
Crowville ... B-5
Cullen ... A-3
Cut Off ... G-8
Cypress ... C-3
Dalcour ... Pg. 125, F-9

Darlington ... D-7
Darnell ... A-6
Davant ... F-9
De Quincy ... E-3
De Ridder ... D-3
Deer Park ... C-6
Delacroix ... F-9
Delcambre ... F-5
Delhi ... A-6
Derry ... C-3
Des Allemands ... Pg. 125, D-1
Deville ... D-5
Diamond ... G-9
Dixie Inn ... A-2
Dodson ... B-4
Donaldsonville ... F-7
Downsville ... A-4
Dry Creek ... E-3
Dry Prong ... C-4
Dubach ... A-4
Dubuisson ... E-5
Dulac ... G-7
Dupont ... D-5
Duson ... F-5
Duty ... C-5
Easlyville ... D-7
Eastwood ... B-2
Echo ... D-5
Edgerly ... F-2
Effie ... D-5
Elizabeth ... D-4
Elm Grove ... B-2
Elton ... E-4
Empire ... G-9
Englishturn ... Pg. 125, E-8
Enon ... D-8
Enterprise ... C-5
Erath ... F-5
Eros ... B-4
Estelle ... Pg. 125, E-6
Estherwood ... F-4
Esto ... D-2
Ethel ... E-6
Eunice ... E-4
Eva ... C-5
Evangeline ... E-4
Evans ... D-3
Evelyn ... B-2
Evergreen ... D-5
Farmerville ... A-4
Felps ... D-7
Fenton ... E-3
Ferriday ... C-6
Fields ... E-2
Fillmore ... A-2
Fisher ... C-3
Flatwoods ... D-4
Flora ... C-3
Florien ... D-2
Folsom ... E-8
Fondale ... B-5
Fordoche ... E-5
Forest ... A-5
Forest Hill ... D-4
Fort Jesup ... C-3
Fort Necessity ... B-5
Foules ... D-5
Franklin ... F-6
Franklinton ... D-8
French Settlement ... E-7
Frenier ... F-8
Frogmore ... C-5
Frost ... E-7
Galbraith ... C-4
Galion ... A-5
Galliano ... G-8
Gandy ... D-2
Gardner ... D-4
Georgetown ... C-4
Gheens ... F-7
Gibsland ... B-3
Gibson ... G-7
Gilbert ... B-5
Gillis ... E-3
Glade ... D-4
Glenmora ... D-4
Gloster ... B-2
Golden Meadow ... G-8
Goldonna ... B-3
Gonzales ... E-7
Gordon ... A-3
Gorum ... C-3
Goudeau ... D-5
Grambling ... A-4
Grand Bayou ... B-3
Grand Cane ... B-2
Grand Chenier ... F-4
Grand Coteau ... E-5
Grand Isle ... G-9
Grand Lake ... F-4
Grangeville ... E-7
Grayson ... B-5
Greensburg ... D-7
Gretna ... F-8
  Vicinity ... Pg. 125, D-7
Grosse Tete ... E-6
Gueydan ... F-4
Hackberry ... F-3
Haile ... A-5
Hall Summit ... B-3
Hamburg ... D-5
Hammond ... E-8
Hanna ... C-3
Harahan ... F-8
  Vicinity ... Pg. 125, D-4
Harrisonburg ... C-5
Harvey ... Pg. 125, D-6
Hathaway ... E-4
Hayes ... F-4
Haynesville ... A-4
Hebert ... B-5
Henderson ... E-5
Hermitage ... G-8

Hessmer ... D-5
Hickory ... E-9
Hicks ... D-3
Hico ... A-4
Highland ... A-6
Hodge ... B-4
Holloway ... D-5
Holly Beach ... F-2
Holmwood ... F-3
Holton ... F-3
Holum ... A-3
Homer ... A-3
Hornbeck ... D-2
Hosston ... A-2
Hot Wells ... D-4
Houma ... G-7
Humphreys ... G-7
Hutton ... D-3
Ida ... A-2
Independence ... E-8
Indian Mound ... C-3
Indian Village ... E-4
Iota ... F-4
Iowa ... F-3
Ivan ... A-2
Jackson ... D-6
Jamestown ... B-3
Jean Lafitte ... F-8
  Vicinity ... Pg. 125, G-5
Jeanerette ... F-5
Jefferson Hts. ... Pg. 125, C-4
Jena ... C-5
Jennings ... E-4
Jesuit Bend ... Pg. 125, G-7
Jigger ... B-5
Johnsons Bayou ... F-2
Jones ... A-5
Jonesboro ... B-4
Jonesville ... C-5
Kaplan ... F-4
Keatchie ... B-2
Keithville ... B-2
Kenner ... F-8
  Vicinity ... Pg. 125, B-3
Kentwood ... D-7
Kilbourne ... A-6
Killian ... E-7
Kinder ... E-4
Kingston ... B-2
Kisatchie ... D-3
Krotz Springs ... E-5
Kurthwood ... D-3
La Place ... F-8
Labadieville ... F-7
Labarre ... E-6
Lacamp ... C-4
Lacassine ... F-3
Lacombe ... E-8
Lafayette ... F-5
Lafitte ... F-8
Lafourche ... F-7
Lake Arthur ... F-4
Lake Charles ... F-3
Lake End ... C-2
Lake Providence ... A-6
Lakeland ... E-6
Larose ... G-8
Larto ... D-5
Latanier ... D-4
Lawtell ... E-5
Le Blanc ... E-3
LeMoyen ... E-5
Leander ... D-4
Lebeau ... E-5
Lecompte ... D-4
Leesville ... D-3
Leeville ... G-8
Leonville ... E-5
Libuse ... D-4
Lillie ... A-4
Lisbon ... A-3
Lismore ... C-5
Live Oak ... Pg. 125, G-7
Live Oak Manor ... Pg. 125, C-3
Livingston ... E-7
Livonia ... E-6
Lockport ... F-8
Logansport ... C-2
Lone Star ... Pg. 125, D-1
Longstreet ... B-2
Longville ... E-3
Lottie ... E-6
Louisa ... F-6
Lucas ... B-2
Lucky ... B-4
Luling ... Pg. 125, D-1
Luna ... B-5
Lutcher ... F-7
Madisonville ... E-8
Mamou ... E-4
Manchac ... E-8
Mandeville ... E-8
Mangham ... B-5
Manifest ... C-5
Mansfield ... C-2
Many ... C-3
Maringouin ... E-6
Marion ... A-5
Marksville ... D-5
Marrero ... Pg. 125, D-5
Marsalis ... A-3
Martin ... B-3
Mathews ... F-8
Maurepas ... E-7
Maurice ... F-5
Maxie ... F-4
Mayna ... C-5
McDade ... D-6
McNary ... D-4
Melder ... D-4
Melrose ... C-3
Melville ... E-5
Mer Rouge ... A-5

Meraux ... Pg. 125, D-9
Mermentau ... F-4
Merryville ... E-2
Metairie ... F-8
  Vicinity ... Pg. 125, C-5
Midland ... F-4
Midway ... B-4
Mill ... B-4
Minden ... A-3
Mira ... A-2
Mitchel ... C-6
Mittie ... E-4
Mix ... E-6
Monroe ... A-5
Montegut ... G-8
Monterey ... C-6
Montgomery ... C-3
Montpelier ... E-7
Mooringsport ... A-2
Moreauville ... D-5
Morgan City ... G-6
Morganza ... E-6
Morrow ... E-5
Mount Carmel ... C-3
Myrtle Grove ... G-8
Nairn ... G-9
Naomi ... F-7
Napoleonville ... F-7
Natchez ... C-3
Natchitoches ... C-3
Negreet ... C-2
New Era ... D-5
New Iberia ... F-6
New Llano ... D-3
New Orleans ... F-8
  Vicinity ... Pg. 125, A-7
New Roads ... E-6
Newellton ... B-6
Newlight ... B-6
Noble ... C-2
North Hodge ... B-4
Norwood ... D-6
Oak Grove (Cameron Cty) ... F-3
Oak Grove (West Carroll Cty) ... A-6
Oak Ridge ... A-5
Oakdale ... E-4
Oakland ... A-4
Oakville ... Pg. 125, G-7
Oberlin ... E-4
Oil City ... A-2
Olivier ... F-6
Olla ... C-4
Opelousas ... E-5
Oscar ... E-6
Oxford ... C-4
Packton ... C-4
Paincourtville ... F-7
Parks ... F-5
Patterson ... F-6
Pearl River ... E-9
Pecan Island ... G-4
Perryville ... A-5
Phoenix ... F-9
Pickering ... D-3
Pierre Part ... F-6
Pigeon ... F-6
Pilot Town ... G-10
Pine ... D-8
Pine Grove ... E-7
Pine Prairie ... E-4
Pineville ... D-4
Pitkin ... D-3
Plain Dealing ... A-2
Plaquemine ... E-6
Pleasant Hill ... C-2
Pointe a La Hache ... G-9
Pollock ... C-4
Ponchatoula ... E-8
Port Allen ... E-6
Port Barre ... E-5
Port Sulphur ... G-9
Port Vincent ... E-7
Powhatan ... C-3
Poydras ... Pg. 125, E-10
Provencal ... C-3
Quitman ... B-4
Raceland ... F-7
Ragley ... E-3
Ramah ... E-6
Rayne ... F-5
Rayville ... A-5
Readhimer ... B-3
Reddell ... E-4
Reeves ... E-3
Reggio ... F-9
Reserve ... F-8
Richmond ... B-6
Richwood ... B-5
Ridgecrest ... C-6
Ringgold ... B-3
Riverton ... B-5
Robeline ... C-3
Robert ... E-8
Rocky Mountain ... A-2
Rodessa ... A-1
Rosedale ... E-6
Rosefield ... C-5
Rosepine ... D-3
Ruddock ... F-8
Ruston ... B-4
Sailes ... B-3
Saint Bernard ... Pg. 125, E-10
Saint Clair ... Pg. 125, E-8
Saint Francisville ... E-6
Saint Gabriel ... E-7
Saint Joseph ... B-6
Saint Martinville ... F-5
Saint Rose ... Pg. 125, D-1
Saline ... B-3
Sarepta ... A-3
Scarsdale ... Pg. 125, E-8

Scott ... F-5
Shaw ... D-6
Sheridan ... D-9
Shongaloo ... A-3
Shreveport ... A-2
Sibley ... A-3
Sicily Island ... C-5
Sieper ... D-4
Sikes ... B-4
Simmesport ... D-5
Simpson ... D-3
Singer ... E-3
Slagle ... D-3
Slaughter ... E-6
Slidell ... E-9
Slocum ... D-6
Somerset ... B-6
Sondheimer ... A-6
Sorrento ... F-7
Spearsville ... A-4
Spencer ... A-5
Spokane ... C-6
Spring Ridge ... B-2
Springfield ... E-7
Springhill ... A-2
Stanley ... B-2
Starks ... F-2
Start ... B-5
State Line ... D-9
Stella ... Pg. 125, F-8
Sterlington ... A-5
Stonewall ... B-2
Sugartown ... E-3
Sulphur ... F-3
Summerfield ... A-3
Sun ... E-9
Sunset ... E-5
Supreme ... F-7
Talisheek ... E-9
Tallulah ... B-6
Tangipahoa ... D-8
Tannehill ... B-4
Taylortown ... B-2
Terry ... E-6
Tete ... E-6
Thibodaux ... F-7
Tidewater ... G-9
Tioga ... C-4
Toomey ... F-2
Toro ... D-2
Transylvania ... A-6
Triumph ... G-10
Truxno ... A-4
Tullos ... C-5
Turkey Creek ... D-4
Union ... F-7
Union Hill ... D-4
Urania ... C-4
Vacherie ... F-7
Varnado ... D-9
Venice ... G-10
Verda ... C-6
Vidalia ... C-6
Vienna ... A-4
Ville Platte ... E-5
Vinton ... F-2
Violet ... F-9
Vivian ... A-2
Vixen ... B-5
Waggaman ... Pg. 125, D-6
Wakefield ... D-6
Waldheim ... E-8
Walters ... C-5
Warnerton ... D-8
Washington ... E-5
Waterproof ... C-6
Watson ... E-7
Waverly ... B-6
Weeks ... F-5
Welsh ... F-4
West End ... Pg. 125, B-4
Weston ... B-4
Westwego ... F-8
  Vicinity ... Pg. 125, E-4
Weyanoke ... D-6
White Castle ... F-7
Whitehall ... C-5
Williana ... D-4
Wills Point ... Pg. 125, G-8
Willswood ... Pg. 125, E-3
Wilmer ... D-8
Wilson ... D-6
Winnfield ... C-4
Winnsboro ... B-5
Woodworth ... D-4
Worden ... D-6
Wye ... E-3
Youngsville ... F-5
Yscloskey ... F-9
Zenoria ... C-4
Zwolle ... C-2

MAINE

MAINE
Page 41
Population: 1,124,660
Capital: Augusta
Land Area: 30,995 sq. mi.

Acton ... J-2
Addison ... F-6
Albion ... G-3
Alexander ... E-6
Allagash ... B-4
Andover ... G-2
Anson ... F-3
Appleton ... G-4
Ashland ... C-4
Athens ... F-3
Auburn ... H-3
Augusta ... G-3
Avon ... F-2

Bailey Island ... H-3
Balleyville ... E-6
Bangor ... F-5
Bar Harbor ... G-5
Baring ... E-6
Bath ... H-3
Beddington ... F-5
Belfast ... G-4
Belgrade ... G-3
Benton ... F-3
Berwick ... J-2
Bethel ... G-2
Biddeford ... J-3
Bigelow ... F-2
Bingham ... F-3
Blaine ... C-5
Blanchard ... F-3
Blue Hill ... G-4
Boothbay Harbor ... H-4
Bradford ... F-4
Bradley ... F-5
Brewer ... F-4
Bridgewater ... C-5
Bridgton ... H-2
Brighton ... F-3
Bristol ... H-4
Brooks ... G-4
Brownfield ... H-2
Brownville ... E-4
Brownville Jct. ... E-4
Brunswick ... H-3
Buckfield ... G-3
Bucks Harbor ... F-6
Bucksport ... G-5
Burlington ... F-5
Burnham ... F-4
Buxton ... J-2
Byron ... G-2
Calais ... E-6
Cambridge ... F-3
Camden ... G-4
Canton ... G-2
Cape Elizabeth ... J-3
Cape Porpoise ... J-2
Caratunk ... F-3
Caribou ... B-5
Carmel ... F-4
Carrabassett ... F-3
Carroll ... F-5
Cary ... C-5
Casco ... H-2
Castine ... G-4
Cherryfield ... G-6
Chester ... F-5
Chisolm ... G-2
Clayton Lake ... C-3
Clinton ... G-4
Coburn Gore ... E-2
Colby ... E-6
Columbia ... G-6
Conner ... B-5
Cooper ... F-6
Corea ... G-6
Corinna ... F-4
Cornish ... H-1
Costigan ... F-5
Crawford ... F-6
Crouseville ... B-5
Cumberland Center ... H-2
Cutler ... F-6
Daigle ... B-4
Dallas ... F-2
Damariscotta ... H-4
Danforth ... D-5
Deblois ... F-5
Dedham ... F-5
Deer Isle ... G-5
Dennistown ... E-2
Dennysville ... E-6
Dickey ... A-4
Dixfield ... G-2
Dixmont ... G-4
Dover Foxcroft ... E-4
Durham ... H-3
Eagle Lake ... B-4
East Hampden ... F-5
East Machias ... F-6
East Millinocket ... E-4
East Sumner ... G-2
East Wilton ... G-3
Eastbrook ... F-5
Easton ... C-5
Eastport ... F-7
Eaton ... E-6
Eddington ... F-5
Ellsworth ... G-5
Estcourt Sta. ... A-4
Eustis ... E-2
Fairfield ... F-3
Farmingdale ... G-2
Farmington ... G-2
Fort Fairfield ... B-5
Fort Kent ... A-4
Franklin ... F-5
Freeport ... H-3
Frenchville ... A-4
Friendship ... H-4
Frye ... G-2
Fryeburg ... H-2
Gardiner ... G-3
Gilead ... G-1
Glenburn Center ... F-4
Gorham ... H-2
Gouldsboro ... G-6
Grand Isle ... A-5
Grand Lake Stream ... D-5
Gray ... H-3
Greenville ... E-3
Grindstone ... D-4
Grove ... F-6
Guerette ... B-4
Guilford ... F-3
Hallowell ... G-3

MAINE

Hamlin . . . B-5
Hampden . . . F-4
Hancock . . . G-5
Hanover . . . G-2
Harrington . . . F-5
Harrison . . . H-2
Hartford Center . . . G-2
Hartland . . . F-3
Haven . . . G-5
Haynesville . . . D-5
Hersey . . . D-5
Hinckley . . . G-3
Hiram . . . H-2
Hogdon . . . C-5
Houghton . . . F-2
Houlton . . . D-5
Howland . . . E-4
Island Falls . . . D-5
Jackman . . . E-2
Jay . . . G-3
Jefferson . . . H-4
Jemtland . . . B-5
Jonesboro . . . F-6
Jonesport . . . G-6
Keegan . . . B-5
Kenduskeag . . . F-4
Kennebago Lake . . . F-2
Kennebunk . . . J-2
Kennebunkport . . . J-3
Kingfield . . . F-2
Kingman . . . E-5
Kingsbury . . . F-3
Kittery . . . K-2
Kittery Point . . . K-2
Knowles Corner . . . C-4
Kokadjo . . . E-4
Lagrange . . . F-4
Lake Parlin . . . E-2
Lambert Lake . . . E-6
Larone . . . G-3
Lee . . . E-5
Lewiston . . . H-2
Liberty . . . G-4
Lille . . . A-5
Lily Bay . . . E-3
Limerick . . . J-2
Limestone . . . B-5
Limington . . . J-2
Lincoln . . . E-5
Lincolnville . . . G-4
Linneus . . . D-5
Lisbon . . . H-3
Lisbon Falls . . . H-2
Littleton . . . C-5
Livermore Falls . . . G-3
Long Pond . . . E-3
Lovell . . . H-2
Lubec . . . F-7
Ludlow . . . D-5
Lynchville . . . G-2
Machias . . . F-6
Macwahoc . . . D-5
Madawaska . . . A-4
Madison . . . F-3
Madrid . . . F-2
Manchester . . . G-3
Mapleton . . . B-5
Marion . . . F-6
Mars Hill . . . C-5
Masardis . . . C-4
Mattawamkeag . . . D-4
Mayfield . . . F-3
Medford . . . E-4
Medway . . . E-4
Mexico . . . G-2
Milbridge . . . G-5
Milford . . . F-5
Millinocket . . . D-4
Milo . . . E-4
Molunkus . . . E-5
Monarda . . . D-5
Monroe . . . G-4
Monson . . . E-3
Monticello . . . C-5
Moose River . . . E-2
Morrill . . . F-3
Moscow . . . F-3
Naples . . . H-2
New Gloucester . . . H-2
Newcastle . . . H-4
Newfield . . . J-2
Newport . . . F-4
Newry . . . G-2
Nobleboro . . . G-3
Norcross . . . E-4
Norridgewock . . . G-3
North Amity . . . D-6
North Anson . . . F-2
North Berwick . . . J-2
North Enfield . . . E-5
North Lovell . . . H-2
North Lyndon . . . B-5
Northeast Carry . . . D-3
Northeast Harbor . . . G-5
Northfield . . . F-6
Norway . . . H-2
Oakland . . . G-3
Ogunquit . . . J-2
Old Orchard Beach . . . J-2
Old Town . . . F-5
Oquossoc . . . F-2
Orient . . . D-5
Orland . . . G-4
Orono . . . F-5
Orrington . . . G-4
Ouelette . . . B-4
Oxbow . . . C-4
Oxford . . . H-2
Palmyra . . . F-3
Paris . . . G-2
Parkman . . . F-3
Patten . . . D-4
Pittston . . . H-3
Portage . . . B-4

Portland . . . J-3
Presque Isle . . . B-5
Princeton . . . E-6
Quimby . . . B-4
Randolph . . . G-3
Rangeley . . . F-2
Raymond . . . H-2
Readfield . . . G-3
Red Beach . . . E-7
Reed . . . D-5
Richmond . . . H-3
Ripley . . . F-3
Ripogenus Dam . . . D-4
Robbinston . . . E-7
Robinsons . . . C-5
Rockland . . . H-4
Rockport . . . H-4
Rockwood . . . E-3
Rome . . . G-3
Roxbury . . . G-2
Rumford . . . G-2
Sabattus . . . H-3
Saco . . . J-3
Saint Albans . . . F-3
Saint David . . . A-5
Saint Francis . . . B-4
Saint George . . . G-4
Saint John . . . B-4
Salem . . . F-2
Sanford . . . J-2
Sangerville . . . F-4
Saponac . . . E-5
Scarborough . . . J-2
Searsmont . . . G-4
Searsport . . . G-4
Sebago . . . H-2
Sebec Lake . . . E-4
Seboeis . . . E-4
Seboomook . . . D-3
Sedgewick . . . G-4
Selden . . . D-5
Sheridan . . . B-4
Sherman . . . D-4
Sherman Mills . . . D-5
Sherman Sta. . . . D-4
Shin Pond . . . D-4
Shirley Mills . . . E-3
Sidney . . . G-3
Skowhegan . . . F-3
Smyrna Mills . . . C-5
Soldier Pond . . . B-4
Solon . . . F-3
South Arm . . . F-2
South Bancroft . . . D-5
South China . . . G-4
South Hope . . . G-4
South Paris . . . H-2
South Portland . . . J-3
Southwest Harbor . . . G-5
Springfield . . . E-5
Springvale . . . J-2
Squa Pan . . . C-4
Stacyville . . . D-4
Standish . . . J-2
Starboard . . . F-6
Stetson . . . F-4
Steuben . . . G-6
Stockton Springs . . . G-4
Stonington . . . G-5
Stow . . . H-2
Stratton . . . F-2
Strong . . . F-2
Sweden . . . H-2
The Forks . . . E-3
Thomaston . . . H-4
Topsfield . . . E-6
Topsham . . . H-3
Tremont . . . G-5
Turner . . . H-2
Union . . . G-3
Unity . . . G-4
Upton . . . G-2
Van Buren . . . B-5
Vanceboro . . . E-6
Vienna . . . G-3
Vinalhaven . . . G-4
Waite . . . E-6
Waldoboro . . . H-4
Waltham . . . F-5
Warren . . . H-4
Washburn . . . B-5
Washington . . . G-3
Waterboro . . . J-2
Waterford . . . H-2
Waterville . . . G-4
Wells . . . J-2
Wesley . . . F-6
West Enfield . . . E-5
West Forks . . . E-3
West Newfield . . . J-2
West Paris . . . G-2
Westbrook . . . J-3
Weston . . . D-5
Whiting . . . F-6
Williamantic . . . F-4
Wilsons Mills . . . F-1
Wilton . . . G-2
Winn . . . E-5
Winslow . . . G-3
Winter Harbor . . . G-5
Winterport . . . G-4
Winterville . . . B-4
Winthrop . . . G-3
Wiscasset . . . H-3
Woodland . . . B-5
Woolwich . . . H-3
Wytopitlock . . . D-5
Yarmouth . . . H-2
York Beach . . . K-2
York Village . . . K-2

MARYLAND
Pages 42-43
Population: 4,216,975
Capital: Annapolis
Land Area: 9,837 sq. mi.

Aberdeen . . . B-12
Accident . . . B-1
Accokeek . . . F-9
Airy . . . F-12
Altamont . . . B-1
Altoona Beach Pg. 91, H-5
Andersontown . . . E-13
Andrews . . . G-12
Annapolis . . . D-11
Annapolis Juction . . . Pg. 91, J-1
Arbutus . . . Pg. 91, F-3
Arnold . . . D-12
Aspen Hill . . . D-9
Avenue . . . G-12
Baltimore . . . C-10
Vicinity . . . Pg. 91, D-4
Barclay . . . D-13
Barnesville . . . C-7
Bay Ridge . . . E-11
Bayard . . . E-10
Bayview . . . B-12
Belair Edison . Pg. 91, D-5
Bel Air . . . B-11
Belltown . . . Pg. 91, B-1
Benfield . . . Pg. 91, J-4
Berlin . . . G-15
Berwyn Heights . . . Pg. 150, B-8
Bethesda . . . C-8
Vicinity . . . Pg. 150, C-5
Betterton . . . C-12
Bladensburg Pg. 150, C-9
Blenheim . . . Pg. 91, A-5
Bloomsbury . . . Pg. 91, F-2
Bonaparte Estates . . . Pg. 91, A-7
Boonsboro . . . B-7
Bowie . . . D-10
Braddock Hts. . . . C-7
Brandywine . . . F-9
Brentwood . . . Pg. 150, C-9
Bristol . . . E-10
Broadwater Beach . . . Pg. 91, K-6
Brooklyn . . . F-13
Brookview . . . F-13
Broomes Island . . . G-10
Brunswick . . . C-7
Bryans Road . . . F-8
Buckeystown . . . C-7
Bucktown . . . G-12
Burkittsville . . . C-7
Butler . . . B-10
California . . . G-11
Cambridge . . . F-12
Cape St. Claire . . . D-11
Capitol Heights . . . Pg. 150, E-8
Carney . . . Pg. 91, C-6
Cascade . . . A-7
Catonsville . . . C-10
Vicinity . . . Pg. 91, F-2
Caves Park . . . Pg. 91, B-2
Cavetown . . . B-7
Cayots . . . B-13
Ceciliton . . . C-13
Centreville . . . D-12
Chaptico . . . G-9
Charlestown . . . B-12
Charlotte Hall . . . F-9
Chesapeake . . . B-13
Chesapeake Beach . F-10
Chestertown . . . C-12
Cheverly . . . Pg. 150, D-9
Chevy Chase Pg. 150, C-5
Church Creek . . . F-12
Church Hill . . . D-12
Clear Spring . . . B-6
Cliffs City . . . D-12
Clinton . . . E-9
Vicinity . . . Pg. 150, G-8
Cobb Island . . . G-9
Cockeysville . . . B-10
Vicinity . . . Pg. 91, A-4
Colesville . . . Pg. 150, A-6
College Park . . . D-9
Vicinity . . . Pg. 150, B-8
Colmar Manor . . . Pg. 150, D-7
Columbia . . . C-9
Columbia Hills Pg. 91, F-1
Cooksville . . . C-9
Corriganville . . . A-3
Cottage City Pg. 150, D-7
Cove Point . . . G-11
Cresaptown . . . B-3
Crisfield . . . J-13
Crofton . . . D-10
Cronhardt . . . Pg. 91, B-3
Cub Hills . . . Pg. 91, B-6
Cumberland . . . B-3
Damascus . . . C-8
Dares Beach . . . F-11
Deale . . . E-10
Delight . . . Pg. 91, B-4
Delmar . . . G-13
Denton . . . E-13
District Heights . . . Pg. 150, E-9
Doncaster . . . F-8
Dorsey . . . Pg. 91, H-2
Drawbridge . . . H-13
Drummond . Pg.150, C-8
Drum Point . . . G-11
Dublin . . . A-11

Dunbrook . . . Pg. 91, J-6
Dundalk . . . C-10
Vicinity . . . Pg. 91, E-6
Dunkirk . . . F-10
Eagle Harbor . . . F-10
East Point . . . Pg. 91, E-6
Easton . . . E-12
Edgemere . . . C-11
Vicinity . . . Pg. 91, F-7
Edgewood . . . C-11
Edmonston Pg. 150, C-8
Eldersburg . . . C-9
Eldorado . . . F-13
Elkridge . . . Pg. 91, G-2
Elkton . . . B-13
Ellicott City . . . C-9
Vicinity . . . Pg. 91, F-1
Elliott . . . G-12
Elmhurst . . . Pg. 91, H-3
Emmitsburg . . . A-8
Essex . . . Pg. 91, E-7
Fair Hill . . . A-12
Fairmont Heights . . . Pg. 150, D-8
Fallston . . . B-11
Federalsburg . . . F-13
Ferndale . . . Pg. 91, G-4
Fishtown . . . Pg. 91, C-2
Font Hill . . . Pg. 91, G-2
Foremans Corner . . . Pg. 91, G-5
Forest Heights . . . Pg. 150, F-7
Fork . . . Pg. 91, B-4
Fort Howard . Pg. 91, G-7
Fountain Head . . . A-7
Foxridge . . . Pg. 91, G-4
Frederick . . . C-8
Friendship Heights . . . Pg. 150, C-5
Friendsville . . . A-1
Frostburg . . . B-3
Fruitland . . . G-14
Fullerton . . . Pg. 91, C-6
Furnace Branch . . . Pg. 91, G-4
Gaithersburg . . . D-8
Galena . . . C-12
Gambrills . . . Pg. 91, K-3
Garrett Park . Pg. 150, A-5
Germantown . . . Pg. 91, B-7
Vicinity . . . Pg. 91, B-7
Gittings . . . Pg. 91, A-6
Glen Burnie . . . D-10
Vicinity . . . Pg. 91, H-4
Glen Echo . . Pg. 150, C-4
Glen Morris . . Pg. 91, A-1
Glenarden . Pg. 150, D-9
Glenarm . . . Pg. 91, A-6
Glenmar (Baltimore Cty) . . . Pg. 91, D-7
Glenmar (Howard Cty) . . . Pg. 91, F-1
Glyndon . . . Pg. 91, A-4
Golden Beach . . . F-10
Goldsboro . . . D-13
Grantsville . . . A-2
Grasonville . . . E-11
Green Haven . Pg. 91, H-5
Green Hill . . . G-13
Green Valley . . . C-8
Green Valley North . . . Pg. 91, A-7
Greenbelt . . . D-9
Vicinity . . . Pg. 150, B-9
Greengate . . . Pg. 91, H-7
Greensboro . . . D-13
Guilford . . . Pg. 91, H-1
Hagerstown . . . B-7
Halethorpe . . Pg. 91, F-3
Halfway . . . B-6
Hampstead . . . B-9
Hampton . . . Pg. 91, B-5
Hancock . . . A-5
Hanover . . . Pg. 91, H-3
Hanover Woods . . . Pg. 91, H-3
Harkins . . . A-11
Harmans . . . Pg. 91, H-3
Harmony . . . E-13
Harrisonville . Pg. 91, C-1
Harundale . . Pg. 91, H-4
Hebbville . . Pg. 91, D-2
Hebron . . . G-13
Hereford . . . B-10
Hillsboro . . . E-12
Hollifield . . . Pg. 91, F-1
Honga . . . G-11
Hoyes . . . B-1
Hurlock . . . F-13
Hyattsville . . Pg. 150, C-7
Hydes . . . Pg. 91, A-6
Ilchester Landing . . . Pg. 91, F-2
Jacobsville . . Pg. 91, J-6
Jarrettsville . . . B-11
Jenkins . . . Pg. 91, H-2
Jessup . . . Pg. 91, H-2
Joppatowne . . . C-11
Josenhans Corner . . . Pg. 91, D-7
Kennedyville . . . C-12
Kensington . Pg. 150, B-6
Kenwood . . . Pg. 91, D-6
Kingsville . . . Pg. 91, A-7
Kitzmiller . . . C-2
Kraft Corner . Pg. 91, D-1
LaPlata . . . F-9
LaVale . . . B-3
Lake Shore . . Pg. 91, J-6
Landover Hills . . . Pg. 150, C-9
Lansdowne . . Pg. 91, F-3

Largo . . . E-10
Laytonsville . . . C-8
Leonardtown . . . G-10
Lexington Pk. . . . G-11
Liberty Manor Pg. 91, D-1
Linthicum . . Pg. 91, G-3
Lipins Corner Pg. 91, J-5
Lochearn . . . Pg. 91, D-2
Lonaconing . . . B-2
Long Beach . . . G-11
Long Green . . Pg. 91, A-6
Longridge . . . G-14
Longwoods . . . E-12
Luke . . . B-2
Lutherville . . . B-10
Vicinity . . . Pg. 91, B-4
Lynch . . . C-12
Maceys Corner Pg. 91, K-6
Manchester . . . B-9
Manor Woods . Pg. 91, A-4
Marbury . . . F-8
Marion . . . H-13
Marston . . . A-8
Maryland City . Pg. 91, K-1
Mays Chapel . Pg. 91, A-4
Mayo . . . E-11
McHenry . . . B-1
Meadowcliff . . Pg. 91, A-6
Melrose . . . A-9
Middle River . Pg. 91, D-7
Middleborough Pg. 91, E-7
Middletown . . . B-7
Midland . . . B-3
Milford . . . Pg. 91, D-2
Millington . . . C-13
Millstone . . . A-5
Morganza . . . G-10
Morningside Pg. 150, F-8
Mt. Airy . . . C-8
Mt. Pleasant . . . A-9
Mt. Rainier . Pg. 150, C-7
Mtn. Lake Park . . . C-1
Myersville . . . B-7
New Carrollton . . . Pg. 150, C-9
New Market . . . C-8
Newburg . . . G-9
Newport . . . G-9
Newtown . . . C-11
Nordeau . . . Pg. 91, H-1
North Brentwood . . . Pg. 150, C-7
North Chevy Chase . . . Pg. 150, B-5
North East . . . B-12
Oakland (Garrett Cty) . . C-1
Oakland (Carroll Cty) . . B-9
Ocean City . . . G-15
Odenton . . . Pg. 91, K-3
Olde Mill . . . Pg. 91, J-4
Olney . . . D-9
Orchard Beach Pg. 91, H-6
Oriole . . . H-13
Overlea . . . Pg. 91, D-6
Owings Mills . . . C-9
Oxford . . . F-12
Oxon Hill . . . E-9
Vicinity . . . Pg. 150, G-7
Park Hill . . . H-11
Parkton . . . B-10
Parkville . . . C-10
Vicinity . . . Pg. 91, C-5
Pasadena . . Pg. 91, J-5
Pasadena Beach . . . Pg. 91, H-7
Patapsco . . . Pg. 91, A-7
Perry Hall . . . B-11
Vicinity . . . Pg. 91, B-6
Perryvale . . . Pg. 91, B-7
Pfeiffer Corner Pg. 91, L-1
Pikesville . . . C-10
Vicinity . . . Pg. 91, C-2
Pine Ridge . . Pg. 91, G-2
Pinehurst on the Bay . . . Pg. 91, J-7
Piney Grove . . . A-4
Piney Point . . . H-11
Pittsville . . . G-14
Pleasant Hills . . . B-11
Plum Point . . . F-11
Pocomoke City . . . H-13
Point Lookout . . . H-11
Poolesville . . . D-7
Port Deposit . . . B-12
Pot Spring . . Pg. 91, B-4
Potomac Park . . . B-3
Powellville . . . G-14
Pratt . . . A-4
Preston . . . E-12
Price . . . D-12
Prince Frederick . . . F-10
Princess Anne . . . G-13
Providence . . Pg. 91, B-5
Queen Anne . . . D-12
Queenstown . . . D-12
Randallstown . . . C-9
Vicinity . . . Pg. 91, C-1
Redhouse . . . C-1
Reisterstown . . . B-9
Relay . . . Pg. 91, F-3
Ridge . . . H-11
Ridgely . . . E-12
Ridgeway . . Pg. 91, J-3
Rising Sun . . . A-11
Riva . . . E-10
Riverdale . . Pg. 150, C-8
Riverside . . . G-8
Riviera Beach . . Pg. 91, J-6
Vicinity . . . Pg. 91, H-6
Rock Hall . . . D-11
Rockdale . . . Pg. 91, D-2

Rockville . . . D-8
Vicinity . . . Pg. 150, A-4
Rodgers Forge Pg. 91, C-4
Roe . . . D-12
Rolling Ridge . Pg. 91, E-1
Rosedale . . . Pg. 91, D-6
Rosemont . . . C-7
Vicinity . . . Pg. 91, E-3
Rush . . . B-4
Ruthsburg . . . D-12
Ruxton . . . Pg. 91, C-4
Salisbury . . . G-13
Sandy Bottom . . . C-11
Savage . . . Pg. 91, H-1
Seat Pleasant . . . E-9
Vicinity . . . Pg. 150, D-9
Secretary . . . F-12
Seven Oaks . . Pg. 91, J-2
Severn . . . D-10
Vicinity . . . Pg. 91, J-3
Severna Park . . . D-11
Vicinity . . . Pg. 91, K-5
Shady Side . . . E-11
Sharonville . . Pg. 91, J-6
Sharpsburg . . . C-6
Sharptown . . . F-13
Silver Spring . . . D-9
Vicinity . . . Pg. 150, B-6
Snow Hill . . . H-14
Solley . . . Pg. 91, H-5
Somerset . . Pg. 150, C-5
Southgate . . . D-10
Sparrows Point . . . Pg. 91, G-6
Springbrook . Pg. 91, C-1
St. Charles . . . F-9
St. Michaels . . . E-11
Stevenson . . Pg. 91, B-3
Stockton . . . H-14
Stonecrest Hills . . . Pg. 91, F-1
Suburbia . . . Pg. 91, A-1
Sudlersville . . . C-13
Sunrise Beach Pg. 91, K-4
Swanton . . . B-1
Sykesville . . . C-9
Takoma Park Pg. 150, C-7
Taneytown . . . B-8
Taylors Island . . . F-11
Taylorsville . . . B-8
Templeville . . . D-13
Texas . . . Pg. 91, A-4
The Oaks . . . Pg. 91, L-1
The Provinces Pg. 91, J-2
Thurmont . . . B-8
Timonium . . Pg. 91, B-4
Towson . . . C-10
Vicinity . . . Pg. 91, C-4
Turner . . . G-10
Union Bridge . . . B-8
University Park . . . Pg. 150, C-7
Upper Marlboro . . E-10
Valleywood . . Pg. 91, B-4
Venice on the Bay . . . Pg. 91, H-7
Ventnor . . . F-13
Vienna . . . F-13
Waldorf . . . F-9
Walkersville . . . B-8
Warren . . . Pg. 91, A-4
Waterloo . . . Pg. 91, H-1
Waterview . . . G-13
Wenona . . . H-12
Wesley . . . D-13
Westerlee . . Pg. 91, E-2
Westernport . . . B-2
Westminster . . . B-9
Westover . . . H-13
White Marsh . Pg. 91, C-7
White Oak . . Pg. 150, A-7
White Plains . . . F-9
Whiteford . . . A-11
Widgeon . . . G-13
Willards . . . G-15
Windemere . . Pg. 91, A-5
Woodlawn . . Pg. 91, E-2
Woodmoor . . Pg. 91, D-2

MASSACHUSETTS
Pages 24-25
Population: 5,737,037
Capital: Boston
Land Area: 7,824 sq. mi.

Abington . . . D-11
Acton . . . B-9
Acushnet . . . F-11
Adams . . . B-3
Vicinity . . . Pg. 93, J-7
Agawam . . . E-5
Amesbury . . . A-11
Amherst . . . C-5
Andover . . . B-10
Arlington . . Pg. 93, D-3
Ashburnham . . . B-8
Ashfield . . . B-4
Athol . . . B-7
Attleboro . . . E-10
Auburn . . . D-8
Avon . . . D-11
Ayer . . . B-9
Baldwinville . . . B-7
Barnstable . . . F-13
Barre . . . C-7
Becket . . . C-3
Bedford . . . C-9
Vicinity . . . Pg. 93, B-1
Belchertown . . . C-6
Bellingham . . . E-9
Belmont . . . Pg. 93, D-3
Berkley . . . F-11

Bernardston . . . B-5
Beverly . . . B-12
Billerica . . . B-10
Vicinity . . . Pg. 93, A-1
Blackstone . . . E-9
Blanford . . . D-4
Bolton . . . C-9
Boston . . . C-11
Vicinity . . . Pg. 93
Bourne . . . F-13
Boxborough . . . C-9
Boxford . . . B-11
Boylston . . . C-8
Braintree . . . D-11
Vicinity . . Pg. 93, J-6
Brewster . . . F-14
Bridgewater . . . E-11
Brimfield . . . D-7
Brockton . . . D-11
Vicinity . . . Pg. 93, K-1
Brookfield . . . D-7
Brookline . . Pg. 93, F-3
Buckland . . . B-4
Burlington . . Pg. 93, B-2
Buzzards Bay . . . F-12
Cambridge . . Pg. 93, E-4
Canton . . . D-11
Vicinity . . . Pg. 93, K-3
Carlisle . . . B-10
Carver . . . E-12
Centerville . . . G-13
Charlemont . . . B-4
Charlton . . . D-7
Chatham . . . F-15
Chelmsford . . . B-10
Chelsea . . . C-11
Cheshire . . . B-3
Chesterfield . . . C-4
Chicopee . . . D-5
Chilmark . . . H-12
Clarksburg . . . A-3
Cliftondale . . Pg. 93, C-6
Clinton . . . C-9
Cochituate . . . C-9
Cohasset . . . D-12
Colrain . . . A-5
Concord . . . C-10
Conway . . . B-5
Cummington . . . C-4
Dalton . . . C-3
Danvers . . . B-11
Dartmouth . . . G-11
Dedham . . . Pg. 93, H-3
Deerfield . . . B-5
Dennis . . . F-14
Dennis Port . . . G-14
Dighton . . . E-11
Dover . . . Pg. 93, J-1
Dracut . . . B-10
Dudley . . . E-7
Duxbury . . . E-12
East Bridgewater . E-11
East Falmouth . . . G-13
East Longmeadow . E-6
Eastham . . . E-14
Easthampton . . . C-4
Easton . . . E-11
Edgartown . . . H-13
Essex . . . B-12
Everett . . . Pg. 93, D-5
Fairhaven . . . G-11
Fall River . . . F-10
Falmouth . . . G-12
Fitchburg . . . B-8
Framingham . . . D-9
Freetown . . . F-11
Gardner . . . B-7
Gay Head . . . H-12
Georgetown . . . A-11
Gilbertville . . . C-6
Gill . . . B-5
Gloucester . . . B-13
Grafton . . . D-9
Granby . . . D-5
Granville . . . E-4
Great Barrington . . . C-2
Greenfield . . . B-5
Groton . . . B-9
Groveland . . . A-11
Hadley . . . C-5
Halifax . . . E-12
Hamilton . . . B-12
Hampden . . . E-6
Hanover . . . D-12
Hardwick . . . C-6
Harvard . . . B-9
Harwich . . . F-15
Hatfield . . . C-5
Haverhill . . . A-11
Hawley . . . B-4
Heath . . . A-4
Hingham . . . D-11
Vicinity . . . Pg. 93, J-7
Holbrook . . . D-11
Holden . . . C-8
Holland . . . E-7
Holyoke . . . D-5
Hopedale . . . D-9
Hopkinton . . . D-9
Hudson . . . C-9
Hull . . . C-11
Huntington . . . D-4
Hyannis . . . G-14
Ipswich . . . B-11
Kingston . . . E-12
Lee . . . C-3
Leicester . . . D-8
Lenox . . . C-2
Leominster . . . B-8
Leverett . . . C-5
Lexington . . . C-10
Vicinity . . . Pg. 93, C-2
Leyden . . . A-5
Lincoln . . . C-10
Vicinity . . . Pg. 93, D-1

Littleton . . . B-9
Longmeadow . . . D-5
Lowell . . . B-10
Lunenburg . . . B-8
Lynn . . . C-11
Vicinity . . . Pg. 93, B-6
Lynnfield . . . B-11
Vicinity . . . Pg. 93, A-5
Malden . . . Pg. 93, D-4
Manchester . . . B-12
Mansfield . . . E-10
Marblehead . . . B-12
Marion . . . F-12
Marlborough . . . C-9
Marshfield . . . D-12
Mattapoisett . . . G-12
Maynard . . . C-9
Medfield . . . D-10
Medford . . . Pg. 93, D-4
Medway . . . D-10
Melrose . . . Pg. 93, C-5
Mendon . . . D-9
Merrimac . . . A-11
Methuen . . . A-10
Middleborough . . . F-11
Middlefield . . . C-3
Middleton . . . B-11
Milford . . . D-9
Millbury . . . D-8
Millers Falls . . . B-6
Millis . . . D-10
Milton . . . D-11
Vicinity . . . Pg. 93, H-4
Monson . . . D-6
Montague . . . B-5
Monterey . . . D-3
N. Attleborough . . . E-10
Nahant . . . C-11
Vicinity . . . Pg. 93, D-7
Nantucket . . . H-14
Natick . . . D-10
Needham . . Pg. 93, G-2
New Bedford . . . G-11
New Braintree . . . C-7
Newbury . . . A-12
Newton . . . B-7
Vicinity . . . Pg. 93, F-2
Norfolk . . . D-10
North Adams . . . A-3
North Brookfield . . . C-7
North Reading . . . B-11
Northampton . . . C-4
Northborough . . . C-8
Northbridge . . . D-9
Northfield . . . A-6
Norton . . . E-10
Norwood . . . D-10
Vicinity . . . Pg. 93, K-2
Oak Bluffs . . . H-13
Oakham . . . C-7
Orange . . . B-6
Orleans . . . F-15
Osterville . . . G-13
Otis . . . D-3
Oxford . . . D-8
Palmer . . . D-6
Paxton . . . C-8
Peabody . . . B-11
Vicinity . . . Pg. 93, A-7
Pepperell . . . B-9
Petersham . . . B-7
Pinehurst . . Pg. 93, A-2
Pittsfield . . . B-4
Plainfield . . . B-4
Plymouth . . . E-12
Plympton . . . E-12
Princeton . . . C-8
Provincetown . . . E-14
Quincy . . . D-11
Vicinity . . . Pg. 93, J-6
Randolph . . . D-11
Vicinity . . . Pg. 93, K-5
Raynham . . . E-11
Reading . . . B-11
Vicinity . . . Pg. 93, A-4
Rehoboth . . . E-10
Revere . . . C-11
Vicinity . . . Pg. 93, D-5
Richmond . . . C-2
Rochester . . . F-12
Rockland . . . D-11
Rockport . . . B-13
Rowley . . . A-12
Royalston . . . A-7
Rutland . . . C-7
Sagamore . . . F-13
Salem . . . B-12
Vicinity . . . Pg. 93, B-7
Salisbury . . . A-12
Sandisfield . . . D-3
Sandwich . . . F-13
Saugus . . . C-11
Vicinity . . . Pg. 93, C-6
Savoy . . . B-4
Scituate . . . D-12
Seekonk . . . F-10
Sharon . . . D-10
Sheffield . . . D-2
Shelburne . . . B-5
Shirley . . . B-9
Shrewsbury . . . C-9
So. Yarmouth . . . G-14
Somerset . . . F-10
Somerville . . Pg. 93, E-4
South Hadley . . . C-5
Southborough . . . C-9
Southbridge . . . E-7
Spencer . . . D-7
Sterling . . . C-8
Stockbridge . . . C-2
Stoneham . . Pg. 93, B-4
Vicinity . . . Pg. 93, D-1
Stoughton . . . D-11

MASSACHUSETTS

Stow . . . C-9
Sturbridge . . . D-7
Sunderland . . . C-5
Sutton . . . D-8
Swampscott . . . C-12
Vicinity . . . Pg. 93, B-7
Swansea . . . F-10
Taunton . . . E-10
Templeton . . . B-7
Tewksbury . . . B-10
Three Rivers . . . D-6
Tisbury . . . H-12
Topsfield . . . B-11
Townsend . . . B-9
Truro . . . E-15
Tyngsborough . . . A-10
Upton . . . D-9
Uxbridge . . . E-9
Vineyard Haven . . . H-13
Wakefield . . . C-11
Vicinity . . . Pg. 93, B-5
Wales . . . D-6
Walpole . . . D-10
Vicinity . . . Pg. 93, K-1
Waltham . . . Pg. 93, E-2
Ware . . . D-6
Wareham . . . F-12
Warren . . . D-7
Warwick . . . A-6
Washington . . . C-3
Watertown . . . Pg. 93, E-3
Wayland . . . C-10
Webster . . . E-7
Wellesley . . . C-10
Vicinity . . . Pg. 93, G-1
Wellfleet . . . E-14
Wendell . . . B-6
Wenham . . . B-11
West Boylston . . . C-8
West Brookfield . . . D-7
West Dennis . . . G-14
West Newbury . . . A-11
West Springfield . . . D-5
West Stockbridge . . . C-3
West Tisbury . . . H-12
Westborough . . . D-8
Westfield . . . D-5
Westford . . . B-9
Westhampton . . . C-4
Westminster . . . B-7
Weston . . . Pg. 93, E-1
Westport . . . G-11
Westwood . . . D-10
Vicinity . . . Pg. 93, J-2
Weymouth . . . D-11
Vicinity . . . Pg. 93, J-7
Whately . . . C-5
Whitinsville . . . D-8
Whitman . . . E-11
Wilbraham . . . D-6
Williamstown . . . C-3
Wilmington . . . B-10
Vicinity . . . Pg. 93, A-3
Winchendon . . . A-7
Winchester . . . Pg. 93, C-3
Windsor . . . B-3
Winthrop . . . C-11
Vicinity . . . Pg. 93, E-6
Woburn . . . C-10
Vicinity . . . Pg. 93, B-3
Worcester . . . C-7
Worthington . . . C-5
Wrentham . . . D-10
Yarmouth . . . F-14

MICHIGAN
Pages 44-45
Population: 9,262,078
Capital: Lansing
Land Area: 56,954 sq. mi.

Acme . . . F-6
Adamsville . . . L-4
Adrian . . . L-8
Afton . . . E-7
Agnew . . . J-4
Ahmeek . . . A-2
Akron . . . H-8
Alabaster . . . G-8
Alanson . . . E-7
Alaska . . . J-5
Alba . . . F-6
Alberta . . . B-2
Albion . . . L-6
Alcona . . . F-9
Alger . . . G-8
Algonac . . . K-10
Allegan . . . K-5
Allen . . . L-6
Allen Park . . . Pg. 107, J-8
Allendale . . . J-5
Allenville . . . D-7
Allouez . . . A-2
Alma . . . J-7
Almena . . . L-5
Almont . . . K-9
Aloha . . . E-7
Alpena . . . F-9
Alpha . . . D-2
Alston . . . B-2
Alto . . . K-6
Alverno . . . E-7
Amador . . . J-10
Amasa . . . C-2
Amble . . . H-6
Anchorville . . . K-10
Ann Arbor . . . L-8
Vicinity . . . Pg. 106, H-1
Antrim . . . F-6
Applegate . . . J-10
Arbutus Beach . . . F-7

Arcadia . . . G-4
Argentine . . . K-7
Argyle . . . J-9
Arnheim . . . B-2
Arnold . . . D-3
Arthur . . . J-8
Ashley . . . J-7
Ashton . . . H-6
Assinins . . . B-2
Athens . . . L-6
Atlanta . . . F-8
Atlantic Mine . . . B-2
Attica . . . J-9
Atwood . . . E-6
Au Gres . . . H-8
Au Sable . . . G-9
Au Train . . . C-4
Auburn . . . H-8
Austin . . . C-3
Averill . . . H-7
Bad Axe . . . H-9
Bailey . . . J-5
Baldwin . . . H-5
Banat . . . D-3
Bancroft . . . K-8
Banfield . . . K-6
Bangor . . . L-5
Baraga . . . B-2
Bark River . . . D-3
Barker Creek . . . F-6
Barryton . . . H-6
Barton City . . . F-8
Batavia . . . L-6
Bates . . . F-6
Bath . . . K-6
Battle Creek . . . K-6
Bay City . . . H-8
Bay Mills . . . C-7
Bay Park . . . H-7
Bay Port . . . H-8
Bay View . . . E-7
Beacon . . . C-2
Bear Lake . . . G-5
Beaverton . . . H-7
Beechwood . . . C-2
Belding . . . J-6
Belleville . . . Pg. 106, K-4
Bellevue . . . K-6
Bendon . . . F-5
Bennington . . . J-7
Benton Harbor . . . L-4
Benzonia . . . F-5
Bergland . . . A-10
Berkley . . . Pg. 107, D-8
Berrien Sprgs. . . . L-4
Bessemer . . . B-9
Bethel . . . L-6
Beulah . . . F-5
Beverly Hills . Pg. 106, C-7
Big Bay . . . B-3
Big Rapids . . . H-6
Birch Creek . . . E-3
Birch Run . . . J-8
Birmingham . Pg. 107, C-8
Bitley . . . H-5
Black River . . . F-9
Blanchard . . . H-6
Blaney Park . . . D-5
Blissfield . . . L-8
Bloomfield Hills
. . . Pg. 106, B-7
Boyne City . . . E-6
Boyne Falls . . . E-7
Bradley . . . K-5
Brampton . . . D-3
Branch . . . H-5
Bravo . . . K-5
Breckenridge . . . J-7
Brethren . . . G-5
Brevort . . . D-6
Bridgeport . . . J-8
Bridgeton . . . J-5
Bridgman . . . L-4
Brighton . . . K-8
Brimley . . . C-7
Britton . . . L-8
Brockway . . . J-9
Brohman . . . H-5
Bronson . . . L-6
Brooklyn . . . L-7
Brown City . . . J-9
Bruce Crossing . . . C-1
Brunswick . . . H-5
Brutus . . . E-7
Buchanan . . . L-4
Buckley . . . G-5
Burlington . . . L-6
Burnside . . . J-9
Burt . . . J-8
Burton . . . J-8
Byron Center . . . J-5
Cadillac . . . G-6
Cadmus . . . L-7
Caledonia . . . K-6
California . . . L-6
Calumet . . . A-2
Camden . . . M-6
Capac . . . J-9
Carbondale . . . E-3
Carleton . . . L-8
Carney . . . E-3
Caro . . . J-9
Carp Lake . . . E-7
Carsonville . . . J-9
Casco . . . K-5
Casnovia . . . J-5
Cass City . . . H-9
Cassopolis . . . L-4
Cathro . . . F-8
Cedar . . . F-5
Cedar River . . . E-3
Cedar Springs . . . J-6
Cedarville . . . D-8
Center Line Pg. 107, D-11

Centreville . . . L-5
Ceresco . . . L-6
Channing . . . C-2
Charlevoix . . . E-6
Charlotte . . . K-6
Chase . . . H-6
Chatham . . . C-4
Cheboygan . . . E-7
Chelsea . . . L-7
Chesaning . . . J-7
Christmas . . . C-4
Cilo . . . J-8
Clare . . . H-6
Clarendon . . . L-6
Clarion . . . E-7
Clarksville . . . K-6
Clawson . . . Pg. 107, C-9
Clayton . . . L-7
Cliff . . . A-2
Climax . . . L-5
Clinton . . . L-8
Cloverdale . . . K-6
Coldwater . . . L-6
Coleman . . . H-7
Coloma . . . L-4
Colon . . . L-5
Comins . . . F-8
Concord . . . L-7
Constantine . . . L-5
Conway . . . E-7
Coopersville . . . J-5
Copemish . . . G-5
Copper Harbor . . . A-3
Cornell . . . D-3
Corunna . . . J-8
Covert . . . K-4
Covington . . . C-2
Cross Village . . . E-7
Croswell . . . J-10
Croton . . . H-5
Crump . . . H-7
Crystal Falls . . . C-2
Cunard . . . D-3
Curran . . . F-8
Curtis . . . D-6
Custer . . . H-4
Dafter . . . C-7
Daggett . . . E-3
Dansville . . . K-7
Darragh . . . F-6
Davison . . . J-8
Dayton . . . L-4
DeTour Village . . . D-8
Dearborn . . . L-9
Dearborn Heights
. . . Pg. 106, G-7
Decatur . . . L-5
Deer Park . . . C-6
Deerton . . . C-4
Deford . . . J-9
Delano . . . G-8
Delton . . . K-5
Denton . . . L-8
Detroit . . . L-9
Vicinity . . . Pg. 107, F-8
Devereaux . . . L-6
Dewitt . . . K-7
Dexter . . . L-7
Dighton . . . G-6
Disco . . . K-9
Dixboro . . . C-8
Donaldson . . . C-8
Donken . . . B-1
Dorr . . . K-5
Douglas . . . K-4
Dowagiac . . . L-4
Dowling . . . K-5
Drayton Plains . . . K-8
Drummond . . . D-8
Dublin . . . G-5
Dundee . . . L-8
Dunningville . . . K-5
Durand . . . K-8
Eagle Harbor . . . A-3
Eagle River . . . A-2
East Detroit Pg. 107, E-12
East Gilead . . . L-6
East Grand Rapids . . J-5
East Jordan . . . E-6
East Lake . . . G-5
East Leroy . . . L-6
East Tawas . . . G-8
Eastport . . . E-6
Eaton Rapids . . . K-7
Eckerman . . . C-7
Ecorse . . . Pg. 107, J-9
Edenville . . . H-7
Edmore . . . J-6
Edwardsburg . . . L-5
Elba . . . J-9
Elberta . . . F-5
Elk Rapids . . . F-6
Elkton . . . H-9
Elmer . . . J-9
Elmira . . . F-7
Elwell . . . J-7
Emmett . . . K-9
Empire . . . F-5
Engadine . . . D-6
Ensign . . . D-3
Epoufette . . . D-6
Erie . . . H-4
Escanaba . . . D-4
Essexville . . . H-8
Estey . . . H-7
Estral Beach . . . L-9
Evans . . . J-6
Evart . . . H-6
Ewen . . . C-1
Fair Haven . . . K-9
Fairfield . . . L-8
Fairgrove . . . J-9
Fairview . . . F-8
Farmington . Pg. 106, D-5

Farmington Hills
. . . Pg. 106, D-5
Farwell . . . H-6
Fawn River . . . L-6
Fayette . . . D-4
Felch . . . D-3
Felch Mountain . . . D-3
Fennville . . . K-5
Fenton . . . K-8
Ferndale . . . Pg. 107, E-9
Ferry . . . H-5
Ferrysburg . . . J-4
Fibre . . . D-7
Fife Lake . . . G-6
Filer City . . . G-4
Filion . . . H-9
Filmore . . . K-5
Flat Rock . . . L-8
Flint . . . J-8
Flushing . . . J-8
Ford River . . . D-4
Forest Hill . . . J-7
Forest Lake . . . C-4
Forester . . . J-10
Forestville . . . H-10
Foster City . . . D-3
Fouch . . . F-5
Fountain . . . G-5
Fowler . . . J-7
Fowlerville . . . K-8
Frankenmuth . . . J-8
Frankfort . . . F-5
Franklin . . . Pg. 106, H-6
Fraser . . . Pg. 107, C-12
Frederick . . . F-7
Freeland . . . H-7
Freesoil . . . G-5
Fremont . . . J-5
Frontier . . . L-7
Fruitport . . . J-5
Galesburg . . . K-5
Galien . . . L-4
Ganges . . . K-4
Garden . . . D-4
Garden City . Pg. 106, G-6
Garden Corners . . . D-5
Gardendale . . . J-10
Garfield . . . J-7
Garnet . . . D-7
Gaylord . . . F-7
Gera . . . J-8
Germfask . . . C-5
Gibralter . . . L-9
Girard . . . L-6
Gladstone . . . D-4
Gladwin . . . H-7
Glen Arbor . . . F-5
Glen Haven . . . F-5
Glenn . . . K-4
Glennie . . . F-8
Glenwood . . . L-5
Goetzville . . . D-8
Good Hart . . . E-6
Goodrich . . . K-8
Gould City . . . D-5
Gourley . . . D-2
Grand Beach . . . L-4
Grand Haven . . . J-4
Grand Blanc . . . K-8
Grand Ledge . . . K-7
Grand Marais . . . C-5
Grand Rapids . . . J-5
Grange . . . L-6
Granite Bluff . . . D-2
Grant . . . J-5
Grawn . . . F-6
Grayling . . . F-7
Greenbush . . . G-8
Greenland . . . B-1
Greenville . . . J-6
Gregory . . . K-7
Grindstone City . . . H-9
Gros Cap . . . D-7
Grosse Pointe
. . . Pg. 107, F-13
Grosse Pointe Farms
. . . Pg. 107, F-13
Grosse Pointe Park
. . . Pg. 107, G-12
Grosse Pointe Shores . L-9
Vicinity . . . Pg. 107, E-13
Grosse Pointe Woods
. . . Pg. 107, E-13
Gulliver . . . D-5
Gwinn . . . C-3
Hale . . . G-8
Hamburg . . . K-8
Hamilton . . . K-5
Hamlin . . . K-5
Hamlin Lake . . . G-4
Hamtramck Pg. 107, F-10
Hancock . . . B-2
Harbert . . . L-4
Harbor Beach . . . H-10
Harbor Springs . . . E-6
Hardwood . . . D-3
Harper Woods
. . . Pg. 107, E-12
Harris . . . D-3
Harrison . . . H-7
Harrisville . . . F-9
Hart . . . H-4
Hartford . . . L-4
Hartland . . . K-8
Harvey . . . C-3
Hastings . . . K-6
Hawks . . . E-8
Hazel Park . Pg. 107, E-10
Helmer . . . C-5
Hemans . . . J-9
Henderson . . . J-7
Hermansville . . . D-3
Herron . . . F-8
Hesperia . . . H-5

Hessel . . . D-7
Higgans Lake . . . G-7
Highland Park Pg. 107, F-9
Hilliards . . . K-5
Hillman . . . F-8
Hillsdale . . . L-7
Hockaday . . . G-7
Hodunk . . . L-6
Holland . . . K-4
Holly . . . K-8
Holt . . . K-7
Holton . . . H-5
Homer . . . L-6
Honor . . . F-5
Horton . . . L-7
Houghton . . . B-1
Houghton Heights . . G-7
Houghton Lake . . . G-7
Howard City . . . J-5
Howell . . . K-8
Hubbard Lake . . . F-8
Hubbell . . . B-2
Hudson . . . L-7
Hudsonville . . . J-5
Huntington Woods
. . . Pg. 107, D-8
Huron Beach . . . E-8
Huron City . . . H-9
Hyde . . . D-4
Idlewild . . . H-5
Imlay City . . . J-9
Ingalls . . . E-3
Inkster . . . Pg. 106, H-6
Interlochen . . . F-5
Ionia . . . J-6
Iron Mountain . . . D-2
Iron River . . . C-1
Irons . . . G-5
Ironwood . . . B-9
Isabella . . . D-3
Ishpeming . . . C-3
Ithaca . . . J-7
Jackson . . . L-7
Jamestown . . . J-5
Jasper . . . M-8
Jeddo . . . J-10
Johannesburg . . . F-7
Jones . . . L-5
Jonesville . . . L-7
Joppa . . . L-6
Kalamazoo . . . K-5
Kaleva . . . G-5
Kalkaska . . . F-6
Karlin . . . F-5
Kawkawlin . . . H-8
Kearsarge . . . A-2
Kendall . . . K-5
Kent City . . . J-5
Kenton . . . C-1
Kentwood . . . J-5
Kewadin . . . F-6
Keweenaw Bay . . . B-2
Kibbie . . . K-4
Kinde . . . H-9
Kinderhook . . . L-6
Kingsford . . . D-2
Kingston . . . J-9
Kinross . . . C-7
Kiva . . . C-4
L'Anse . . . B-2
La Salle . . . L-8
LaBranche . . . D-3
Lachine . . . F-8
Lacota . . . K-5
Laingsburg . . . K-7
Lake City . . . G-6
Lake George . . . H-6
Lake Leelanau . . . F-5
Lake Linden . . . A-2
Lake Odessa . . . K-6
Lake Orion . . . K-9
Lake Roland . . . B-1
Lakeland . . . K-8
Lakeport . . . J-10
Lakeview . . . J-6
Lambertville . . . M-8
Langston . . . J-6
Lansing . . . K-7
Lapeer . . . J-9
Laporte . . . J-7
Lathrop . . . C-4
Lathrup Village
. . . Pg. 107, D-8
Laurium . . . A-2
Lawton . . . L-5
Le Roy . . . G-6
Leland . . . F-5
Leoni . . . L-7
Leonidas . . . L-5
Leslie . . . K-7
Levering . . . E-7
Lexington . . . J-10
Liberty . . . L-7
Lilley . . . H-5
Lincoln . . . F-9
Lincoln Park Pg. 107, J-8
Linden . . . K-8
Linwood . . . H-8
Litchfield . . . L-7
Little Lake . . . C-4
Livonia . . . K-8
Vicinity . . . Pg. 106, F-6
Long Lake . . . G-8
Long Rapids . . . F-8
Longrie . . . E-3
Loomis . . . H-7
Loretto . . . D-3
Lowell . . . J-6
Lucas . . . G-6
Ludington . . . G-4
Luna Pier . . . M-8
Lupton . . . G-8
Luzerne . . . G-7
Mackinaw City . . . D-7

Madison Heights
. . . Pg. 107, D-9
Mancelona . . . F-6
Mandan . . . A-3
Manistee . . . G-4
Manistique . . . D-5
Manton . . . G-6
Maple Rapids . . . J-7
Marcellus . . . L-5
Marenisco . . . B-10
Marine City . . . K-10
Marion . . . G-6
Marlette . . . J-9
Marne . . . J-5
Marquette . . . C-4
Marshall . . . L-6
Martin . . . K-5
Marysville . . . K-10
Mashek . . . D-3
Mason . . . K-7
Masonville . . . D-4
Mass City . . . B-1
Matchwood . . . B-1
Matherton . . . J-6
Mattawan . . . L-5
Mayville . . . J-9
McBain . . . G-6
McFarland . . . C-3
McMillan . . . C-5
Meade . . . K-9
Mears . . . H-4
Mecosta . . . H-6
Melstrand . . . C-5
Melvin . . . J-9
Memphis . . . K-9
Mendon . . . L-5
Menominee . . . E-3
Meredith . . . G-7
Merriman . . . D-2
Merritt . . . G-6
Merriweather . . . A-10
Mesick . . . G-5
Metz . . . E-8
Michigamme . . . C-3
Michigan Center . . . L-7
Middleville . . . K-6
Midland . . . H-7
Mikado . . . G-8
Milburg . . . L-4
Milford . . . K-8
Vicinity . . . Pg. 107, D-9
Millbrook . . . H-6
Millersburg . . . E-8
Millington . . . J-8
Mineral Hills . . . C-2
Mio . . . F-8
Mohawk . . . A-2
Moline . . . K-5
Monroe . . . L-8
Monroe Center . . . F-6
Montague . . . H-4
Montrose . . . J-8
Moorestown . . . G-6
Moran . . . D-7
Morley . . . H-6
Morneci . . . M-7
Morrice . . . K-7
Moscow . . . L-7
Mottville . . . L-5
Mt. Clemens Pg. 107, B-13
Mt. Forest . . . H-8
Mt. Morris . . . J-8
Mt. Pleasant . . . H-6
Muir . . . J-6
Mullett Lake . . . E-7
Munger . . . H-8
Munising . . . C-5
Muskegon . . . J-4
Muskegon Heights . . J-4
Muttonville . . . K-9
Napoleon . . . L-7
Nashville . . . K-6
Nathan . . . D-3
Naubinway . . . D-6
Negaunee . . . C-3
New Baltimore . . . K-9
New Buffalo . . . L-4
New Era . . . H-4
New Greenleaf . . . H-9
New Haven . . . K-9
Newaygo . . . J-5
Newberry . . . C-6
Newport . . . L-9
Niles . . . L-4
Nirvana . . . H-5
Nisula . . . B-1
North Branch . . . J-9
North Ironwood . . . A-9
North Muskegon . . . J-4
Northland . . . D-3
Northport . . . E-5
Northville . . . Pg. 106, E-4
Norton Shores . . . J-4
Norwalk . . . G-5
Norway . . . D-2
Novi . . . K-8
Vicinity . . . Pg. 106, D-4
Nunica . . . J-5
O'Neil . . . F-6
Oak Grove . . . K-8
Oak Park . . . Pg. 107, E-8
Oakley . . . J-7
Oakwood . . . K-9
Ocqueoc . . . E-8
Ogden Center . . . M-8
Oil City . . . H-7
Okemos . . . K-7
Olivet . . . K-7
Omena . . . F-6
Onaway . . . E-7
Onekama . . . G-4
Onondaga . . . K-7
Ontonagon . . . B-1
Orchard Lake Pg. 106, B-5

Orleans . . . J-6
Ortonville . . . K-8
Oscoda . . . G-9
Oskar . . . A-2
Osseo . . . L-7
Ossineke . . . F-9
Otisville . . . J-8
Otsego . . . K-5
Otsego Lake . . . F-7
Ottawa Lake . . . M-8
Ovid . . . J-7
Owosso . . . J-8
Oxbow . . . H-5
Oxford . . . K-9
Ozark . . . D-7
Painesdale . . . B-2
Palmer . . . C-3
Palmyra . . . L-8
Palo . . . J-6
Paradise . . . C-7
Parchment . . . K-5
Paris . . . H-6
Parisville . . . H-9
Parkdale . . . G-4
Parkville . . . L-5
Paulding . . . C-1
Paw Paw . . . L-5
Peck . . . J-9
Pellston . . . E-7
Pentwater . . . H-4
Perkins . . . D-4
Perrinton . . . J-6
Perronville . . . D-3
Perry . . . K-7
Petersburg . . . L-8
Petoskey . . . E-7
Pewamo . . . J-6
Phoenix . . . A-2
Pickford . . . D-7
Piconning . . . H-8
Pierport . . . G-4
Pierson . . . J-6
Pigeon . . . H-9
Pine River . . . H-8
Pittsford . . . L-7
Plainfield . . . H-6
Plainwell . . . K-5
Pleasant Ridge
. . . Pg. 107, D-9
Plymouth . . . Pg. 106, F-4
Pointe Aux Barques . . H-9
Polaski . . . F-8
Pontiac . . . K-8
Vicinity . . . Pg. 106, A-7
Port Hope . . . H-10
Port Huron . . . K-10
Port Sanilac . . . J-10
Portage . . . K-5
Portland . . . J-6
Posen . . . E-8
Poseyville . . . H-4
Potterville . . . K-6
Powers . . . D-3
Prescott . . . G-8
Princeton . . . C-3
Prudenville . . . G-7
Pullman . . . K-5
Quanicassee . . . H-8
Quimby . . . K-6
Quincy . . . L-7
Quinnesec . . . D-3
Raber . . . C-8
Ralph . . . D-3
Ramsay . . . B-9
Randville . . . D-2
Ransom . . . M-7
Rattle Run . . . K-10
Ray . . . L-6
Reading . . . L-7
Redford . . . Pg. 106, F-7
Reed City . . . H-6
Reese . . . J-8
Remus . . . H-6
Republic . . . C-2
Rexton . . . D-6
Rhodes . . . H-8
Richland . . . K-5
Richmond . . . K-9
Richmondville . . . H-10
Richville . . . J-8
Ridgeway . . . L-8
River Rouge Pg. 107, J-9
Riverdale . . . J-7
Rives Junction . . . K-7
Roberts Landing . . K-10
Rochester . . . K-9
Rock . . . D-4
Rockford . . . J-6
Rockland . . . B-1
Rockwood . . . L-9
Rodney . . . H-6
Rogers City . . . E-8
Rome Center . . . L-7
Romeo . . . K-9
Romulus . . . Pg. 106, J-5
Roosevelt Park . . . J-4
Roscommon . . . G-7
Rose City . . . G-8
Roseburg . . . J-9
Rosebush . . . H-7
Roseville . . . Pg. 107, D-12
Rothbury . . . H-4
Royal Oak . . . Pg. 107, C-9
Rudyard . . . C-7
Rumely . . . C-4
Ruth . . . H-10

Saranac . . . J-6
Saugatuck . . . K-4
Sault Ste. Marie . . . C-8
Sawyer . . . L-4
Schaffer . . . D-3
Schoolcraft . . . L-5
Scottdale . . . L-3
Scottville . . . G-4
Sears . . . H-6
Sebewaing . . . H-9
Seney . . . C-5
Sharon . . . G-6
Shelby . . . H-4
Shelbyville . . . K-5
Shepherd . . . H-7
Sherman . . . G-5
Shingleton . . . C-5
Shore . . . E-6
Sidnaw . . . C-2
Sigma . . . F-6
Silver City . . . A-10
Sister Lakes . . . L-4
Six Lakes . . . J-6
Skandia . . . C-3
Skidway Lake . . . G-8
Smithville . . . G-5
Smyrna . . . J-6
Snover . . . J-9
Somerset . . . L-7
Soo Junction . . . C-6
South Boardman . . F-6
South Branch . . . G-8
South Haven . . . K-4
South Range . . . B-1
Southfield . . . Pg. 106, D-6
Southgate . . . Pg. 107, K-8
Spratt . . . F-8
Spring Lake . . . J-5
Springport . . . K-7
Spruce . . . F-9
St. Clair . . . K-10
Vicinity . . . Pg. 107, D-13
St. Clair Shores . . . L-9
St. Ignace . . . D-7
St. James . . . D-6
St. Johns . . . J-7
St. Louis . . . J-7
Stager . . . D-2
Stalwart . . . D-7
Standish . . . H-8
Stanton . . . J-6
Stanwood . . . H-6
Stephenson . . . E-3
Sterling . . . G-8
Sterling Hts. Pg. 107, B-10
Steuben . . . D-5
Stevensville . . . L-4
Stockbridge . . . K-7
Stronach . . . G-5
Strongs . . . C-7
Sturgis . . . L-5
Stutsmanville . . . E-6
Sundell . . . C-4
Sunfield . . . K-6
Suttons Bay . . . F-6
Swanson . . . E-3
Swartz Creek . . . J-8
Sylvester . . . H-6
Tawas City . . . G-8
Taylor . . . Pg. 106, J-7
Tecumseh . . . L-8
Tekonsha . . . L-6
Theodore . . . D-2
Thompson . . . D-5
Thornville . . . J-9
Three Lakes . . . C-2
Three Oaks . . . L-4
Three Rivers . . . L-5
Tiovola . . . B-1
Tipton . . . L-7
Tower . . . E-7
Traunik . . . C-4
Traverse City . . . F-5
Trenary . . . C-4
Trenton . . . L-9
Triangle Ranch . . . C-2
Trout Creek . . . C-1
Trout Lake . . . D-7
Troy . . . K-9
Vicinity . . . Pg. 107, B-9
Turner . . . G-8
Tustin . . . H-6
Twin Lake . . . J-4
Twin Lakes . . . B-2
Twining . . . G-8
Ubly . . . H-9
Union . . . L-5
Union City . . . L-6
Union Pier . . . L-4
Unionville . . . H-9
Utica . . . K-9
Vicinity . . . Pg. 107, A-11
Vandalia . . . L-5
Vanderbilt . . . F-7
Vassar . . . J-8
Vernon . . . K-7
Verona . . . H-9
Vicksburg . . . L-5
Vienna . . . F-7
Vogel Center . . . G-6
Vriesland . . . K-5
Vulcan . . . D-2
Wacousta . . . K-7
Wadhams . . . K-10
Wakefield . . . B-10
Waldron . . . M-7
Walhalla . . . G-5
Walkerville . . . H-5
Wallace . . . E-3
Walled Lake Pg. 106, C-4
Walton . . . G-6
Warren . . . K-9
Vicinity . . . Pg. 107, D-11
Washington . . . K-9

Waterford .. Pg. 106, A-6
Waterloo ... K-7
Waters ... F-7
Watersmeet ... C-1
Watertown ... J-9
Watervliet ... L-4
Watson (Marquette Cty) ... D-3
Watson (Allegan Cty) ... K-5
Watton ... C-2
Waucedah ... D-3
Wayland ... K-5
Wayne ... Pg. 106, J-5
Webberville ... K-7
Wells ... D-4
Wellston ... G-5
West Branch ... G-7
West Olive ... J-5
Westland ... L-8
Vicinity ... Pg. 106, G-5
Weston ... M-7
Wetmore ... C-4
White ... L-5
White Cloud ... H-5
White Pine ... A-10
White Rock ... H-10
Whitehall ... J-4
Whitney ... D-3
Whittemore ... G-8
Williamston ... K-7
Willis ... L-8
Windsor (Canada) ... Pg. 107, J-11
Winegars ... H-7
Winona ... B-2
Wisner ... H-8
Wixom ... Pg. 106, C-3
Wolf Lake ... G-5
Wolverine ... E-7
Wolverine Lake ... Pg. 106, B-4
Woodbury ... K-6
Woodhaven ... L-9
Woodland ... K-6
Wyandotte .. Pg. 107, K-8
Wyoming ... J-5
Yale ... J-9
Yalmer ... C-4
Ypsilanti ... L-8
Vicinity ... Pg. 106, J-2
Yuma ... G-5
Zeeland ... J-5
Zilwaukee ... J-8

MINNESOTA
Pages 46-47
Population: 4,075,970
Capital: St. Paul
Land Area: 79,548 sq. mi.

Ada ... D-2
Adams ... L-6
Adrian ... L-2
Ah-gwah-ching ... E-4
Aitkin ... F-5
Akeley ... E-4
Albany ... G-4
Albert Lea ... L-5
Alberta ... G-2
Alden ... L-5
Alexandria ... G-3
Alvarado ... C-1
Alvwood ... D-5
Amboy ... K-5
Andover ... H-6
Angle Inlet ... A-3
Angora ... C-7
Annandale ... H-5
Anoka ... H-6
Appleton ... H-2
Arden Hills .. Pg. 122, A-6
Argyle ... C-1
Arlington ... J-4
Ashby ... G-2
Askov ... F-7
Atwater ... H-4
Audubon ... E-2
Aurora ... D-7
Austin ... L-6
Avoca ... K-2
Avon ... G-4
Babbitt ... D-8
Backus ... E-4
Badger ... B-2
Bagley ... D-3
Ball Club ... D-5
Barnesville ... F-1
Barnum ... F-7
Barrett ... G-2
Barry ... G-1
Battle Lake ... F-3
Baudette ... B-4
Baxter ... F-4
Beardsley ... G-1
Beaver Bay ... D-9
Beaver Creek ... L-1
Becker ... H-5
Bejou ... D-2
Belgrade ... H-3
Belle Plaine ... J-5
Bellingham ... H-1
Beltrami ... D-1
Bemidji ... D-4
Bena ... D-5
Benedict ... E-4
Benson ... H-3
Beroun ... G-6
Bertha ... F-3
Big Falls ... C-5
Big Fork ... D-5
Big Lake ... H-5
Bigelow ... L-2
Birchdale ... B-5
Birchwood .. Pg. 123, A-9
Bird Island ... J-4
Biwabik ... D-7
Blackduck ... D-4
Blomkest ... J-3
Blooming Prairie ... K-6
Bloomington Pg. 122, F-3
Blue Earth ... L-5
Bluffton ... F-3
Bock ... G-5
Borup ... D-2
Bovey ... D-5
Bowstring ... D-5
Boy River ... E-5
Boyd ... J-2
Braham ... G-6
Brainerd ... F-4
Branch ... H-6
Brandon ... G-3
Breckenridge ... F-1
Brewster ... L-2
Britt ... D-7
Brook Park ... G-6
Brooklyn Center ... Pg. 122, A-4
Brooklyn Park Pg. 122, A-2
Brooks ... C-2
Brookston ... E-7
Brooten ... H-3
Browerville ... F-4
Browns Valley ... G-1
Brownsdale ... L-6
Brownsville ... L-8
Brownton ... J-4
Bruno ... F-7
Buffalo ... H-5
Buffalo Lake ... J-4
Buhl ... D-6
Burnsville ... J-6
Vicinity ... Pg. 122, G-4
Burtrum ... G-4
Butterfield ... K-4
Buyck ... C-7
Byron ... K-7
Caledonia ... L-8
Callaway ... E-2
Cambridge ... H-6
Campbell ... F-2
Canby ... J-1
Cannon Falls ... J-6
Canyon ... E-7
Carlos ... G-3
Carlton ... F-7
Cass Lake ... D-4
Cedar Mills ... J-4
Centerville ... K-8
Ceylon ... L-4
Chandler ... K-2
Chaska ... J-5
Chatfield ... L-7
Chickamaw Beach ... E-4
Chisholm ... D-6
Clara City ... H-3
Claremont ... K-6
Clarissa ... F-3
Clarkfield ... J-2
Clarks Grove ... L-6
Clear Lake ... H-5
Clearbrook ... D-3
Clearwater ... H-5
Clementson ... B-4
Climax ... D-1
Clinton ... H-1
Clitherall ... F-3
Clontarf ... H-3
Cloquet ... E-7
Cokato ... H-5
Cold Spring ... H-4
Coleraine ... D-6
Cologne ... J-5
Columbia Heights ... Pg. 122, A-4
Comfrey ... K-4
Comstock ... E-1
Cook ... C-7
Coon Rapids ... H-6
Correll ... H-2
Cosmos ... J-4
Cottage Grove ... J-6
Cotton ... E-7
Cottonwood ... J-2
Croftville ... D-10
Cromwell ... E-6
Crookston ... C-2
Crosby ... F-5
Crystal ... Pg. 122, A-3
Currie ... K-2
Cushing ... F-4
Cuyuna ... F-5
Cyrus ... G-2
Dakota ... K-8
Dalton ... F-2
Danube ... J-3
Danvers ... H-2
Darfur ... K-4
Dassel ... H-4
Dawson ... H-2
De Graff ... H-3
Deer River ... D-5
Deerwood ... F-5
Delano ... H-5
Dent ... F-2
Detroit Lakes ... E-2
Dilworth ... E-1
Dodge Center ... K-6
Donaldson ... B-1
Donnelly ... G-2
Doran ... F-2
Dovray ... K-3
Duluth ... E-7
Dumont ... G-2
Dunnell ... L-4
Duquette ... F-7
Eagle Bend ... F-3
Eagle Lake ... K-5
East Bethel ... H-6
East Grand Forks ... C-1
East Gull Lake ... F-4
Easton ... L-5
Echo ... J-3
Eden Prairie Pg. 122, E-1
Eden Valley ... H-4
Edgerton ... K-2
Edina ... Pg. 122, E-3
Effie ... C-5
Elbow Lake ... G-2
Eldred ... D-1
Elgin ... K-7
Elizabeth ... F-2
Elk River ... H-6
Ellendale ... K-6
Ellsworth ... L-2
Elmer ... E-6
Elmore ... L-5
Elrosa ... G-3
Ely ... C-8
Emily ... E-5
Erhard ... F-2
Ericsburg ... B-6
Erskine ... D-2
Evansville ... G-3
Eveleth ... D-7
Eyota ... K-7
Fairfax ... J-4
Fairibault ... K-6
Fairmont ... L-4
Falcon Heights ... Pg. 122, C-6
Farmington ... J-6
Farwell ... G-2
Felton ... E-2
Fergus Falls ... F-2
Fertile ... D-2
Finland ... D-8
Finlayson ... F-6
Fisher ... C-1
Flom ... E-2
Floodwood ... E-6
Florence ... K-2
Foley ... G-5
Forbes ... D-7
Forest Lake ... H-6
Fort Ripley ... F-4
Fosston ... D-3
Fountain ... L-7
Fox Home ... F-2
Franklin ... J-3
Frazee ... E-3
Freeport ... G-4
Fridley ... Pg. 122, A-4
Frost ... L-5
Fulda ... K-3
Funkley ... C-4
Garfield ... G-3
Garrison ... F-5
Garvin ... K-2
Gary ... D-2
Gatzke ... B-3
Gaylord ... J-5
Gem Lake .. Pg. 123, A-8
Geneva ... L-6
Georgetown ... E-1
Gheen ... C-7
Gibbon ... J-4
Gilbert ... D-7
Gilman ... G-5
Glencoe ... J-5
Glenville ... L-6
Glenwood ... G-3
Gluek ... H-3
Glyndon ... E-1
Golden Valley Pg. 122, B-2
Gonvick ... D-3
Good Thunder ... K-5
Goodhue ... K-7
Goodland ... E-6
Goodridge ... C-3
Goodview ... K-8
Graceton ... B-4
Graceville ... G-2
Granby ... G-6
Grand Falls ... C-5
Grand Marais ... D-9
Grand Meadow ... L-7
Grand Portage ... C-10
Grand Rapids ... D-5
Granite Falls ... J-2
Grasston ... G-6
Greenbush ... B-2
Greenfield ... H-5
Grey Eagle ... G-4
Grove City ... H-4
Grygla ... C-3
Gully ... D-3
Guthrie ... D-4
Hackensack ... E-4
Hallock ... B-1
Halma ... B-2
Halstad ... D-1
Ham Lake ... H-6
Hancock ... H-2
Hanley Falls ... J-3
Hanska ... K-4
Harding ... F-5
Hardwick ... L-1
Harmony ... L-7
Harris ... G-6
Hastings ... J-6
Hawley ... E-2
Hayfield ... K-7
Hayward ... L-6
Hazel Run ... J-2
Hector ... J-4
Heidelberg ... J-5
Henderson ... J-5
Hendricks ... J-2
Hendrum ... D-1
Henning ... F-3
Herman ... G-2
Hermantown ... E-7
Heron Lake ... L-3
Hewitt ... F-3
Hibbing ... D-6
Hill City ... E-5
Hills ... L-1
Hilltop ... Pg. 122, A-4
Hinckley ... G-6
Hines ... D-4
Hitterdal ... E-2
Hoffman ... G-2
Hokah ... L-8
Holland ... K-2
Holloway ... H-2
Holt ... C-2
Holyoke ... F-7
Hope ... K-6
Hopkins ... Pg. 122, D-2
Houston ... L-8
Hovland ... C-10
Howard Lake ... H-5
Hoyt Lakes ... D-7
Humboldt ... B-1
Hutchinson ... J-4
Ihlen ... K-1
Independence ... H-5
Indus ... B-5
International Falls ... B-5
Inver Grove Hts. ... Pg. 123, F-8
Iona ... K-2
Ironton ... F-5
Isabella ... D-8
Isanti ... H-6
Isle ... F-5
Ivanhoe ... J-2
Jackson ... L-4
Jacobson ... E-6
Janesville ... K-5
Jasper ... K-1
Jeffers ... K-3
Jenkins ... E-4
Johnson ... G-2
Jordan ... J-5
Karlstad ... B-2
Kasota ... K-5
Kasson ... K-7
Keewatin ... D-6
Kelliher ... C-4
Kellogg ... K-7
Kelsey ... E-7
Kennedy ... B-1
Kensington ... G-2
Kent ... F-1
Kenyon ... K-6
Kerkhoven ... H-3
Kerrick ... F-7
Kettle River ... F-6
Kiester ... L-5
Kimball ... H-5
Kingston ... H-4
Knife River ... E-8
La Crescent ... L-8
La Prairie ... E-6
Lafayette ... J-4
Lake Benton ... K-2
Lake Bronson ... B-1
Lake City ... J-7
Lake Crystal ... K-4
Lake Elmo .. Pg. 123, B-10
Lake George ... D-3
Lake Henry ... H-4
Lake Lillian ... J-4
Lake Park ... E-2
Lake Shore ... F-4
Lake Wilson ... K-2
Lakefield ... L-3
Lakeville ... J-6
Lamberton ... K-3
Lancaster ... A-1
Lanesboro ... L-8
Laporte ... E-4
Larsmont ... E-8
Lastrup ... G-5
Lauderdale . Pg. 122, B-5
Le Center ... K-5
LeRoy ... L-7
LeSueur ... J-5
Lengby ... D-3
Leonard ... D-3
Lester Prairie ... J-5
Lewiston ... K-8
Lilydale .... Pg. 123, D-6
Linden Grove ... C-6
Lindford ... B-5
Lindstrom ... H-6
Lismore ... L-2
Litchfield ... H-4
Little Canada Pg. 123, B-7
Little Falls ... G-4
Little Fork ... B-5
Little Rock ... G-5
Lockhart ... D-2
Loman ... B-5
Long Prairie ... G-4
Longville ... E-5
Lonsdale ... J-5
Lowry ... G-3
Lucan ... J-3
Lutsen ... D-9
Luverne ... L-2
Lyle ... L-6
Lynd ... K-2
Mable ... L-8
Madelia ... K-4
Madison ... H-2
Madison Lake ... K-5
Magnolia ... L-2
Mahnomen ... D-2
Mahtomedi . Pg. 123, A-9
Mahtowa ... F-6
Malmo ... F-6
Manchester ... L-5
Mankato ... K-4
Mantorville ... K-7
Maple Lake ... H-5
Mapleton ... K-5
Mapleview ... L-6
Maplewood . Pg. 123, B-8
Marcell ... D-5
Margie ... C-5
Marietta ... H-1
Markham ... D-7
Marshall ... J-2
McGrath ... F-6
McGregor ... F-6
McIntosh ... D-2
Meadowlands ... E-7
Medford ... K-6
Meire Grove ... G-3
Melrose ... G-4
Menagha ... E-3
Mendota ... Pg. 122, E-6
Mendota Heights ... Pg. 123, E-7
Mentor ... D-2
Middle River ... B-2
Milaca ... G-5
Milan ... H-2
Millvoy ... K-2
Miltona ... G-3
Minneapolis ... J-5
Vicinity ... Pg. 122
Minneota ... J-2
Minnesota Lake ... K-5
Minnetonka . Pg. 122, D-1
Mizpah ... C-5
Montevideo ... H-3
Montgomery ... J-5
Monticello ... H-5
Moorhead ... E-1
Moose Lake ... F-6
Mora ... G-6
Morgan ... J-3
Morris ... G-2
Morton ... J-4
Motley ... F-4
Mountain Iron ... D-7
Mountain Lake ... K-3
Murdock ... H-3
Myrtle ... L-6
Nashua ... G-2
Nashwauk ... D-6
Nassau ... H-1
Nay-Tah-Waush ... D-3
Nevis ... E-4
New Brighton Pg. 122, A-5
New Hope .. Pg. 122, B-2
New London ... H-4
New Prague ... J-5
New Richland ... K-5
New Ulm ... K-4
New York Mills ... F-3
Newfolden ... B-2
Nicollet ... K-4
Nielsville ... D-1
Nimrod ... E-4
Nisswa ... E-4
Norcross ... G-2
North Branch ... H-6
North Mankato ... K-5
North St. Paul Pg. 123, B-9
Northfield ... J-6
Northome ... C-5
Northrop ... L-4
Norwood ... J-5
Noyes ... A-1
Oak Island ... A-4
Oakdale ... Pg. 123, C-9
Odessa ... H-1
Ogema ... E-2
Ogilvie ... G-5
Oklee ... C-2
Olivia ... J-3
Onamia ... G-5
Orleans ... A-1
Ormsby ... K-4
Oronoco ... K-7
Orr ... C-6
Ortonville ... H-2
Osage ... E-3
Osakis ... G-3
Oslo ... C-1
Ottertail ... F-3
Outing ... E-5
Owatonna ... K-6
Palisade ... E-5
Park Rapids ... E-3
Parkers Prairie ... F-3
Paynesville ... H-4
Pelican Rapids ... F-2
Pencer ... B-3
Pennock ... H-3
Perley ... E-1
Pierz ... G-5
Pine City ... G-6
Pine Island ... K-7
Pine River ... E-4
Pine Springs Pg. 123, A-9
Pinewood ... D-4
Pipestone ... K-1
Pitt ... B-4
Plainview ... K-8
Plummer ... C-2
Plymouth ... Pg. 122, A-1
Ponemah ... C-4
Ponsford ... E-3
Porter ... J-2
Preston ... L-7
Princeton ... G-5
Prinsburg ... J-3
Prior Lake ... J-6
Proctor ... E-7
Quamba ... G-6
Randall ... F-4
Randolph ... J-6
Raudette ... B-4
Ray ... B-6
Raymond ... H-3
Red Lake ... C-3
Red Lake Falls ... C-2
Red Wing ... J-7
Redby ... C-4
Redwood Falls ... J-3
Regal ... H-4
Remer ... E-5
Renville ... J-3
Rice ... G-5
Richfield ... Pg. 122, E-4
Richmond ... H-4
Richville ... F-2
Robbinsdale Pg. 122, B-3
Rochester ... K-7
Rock Creek ... G-6
Roosevelt ... B-4
Rose Creek ... L-6
Roseau ... B-3
Roseville ... Pg. 122, B-5
Ross ... B-2
Rothsay ... F-1
Round Lake ... L-3
Round Prairie ... G-4
Royalton ... G-4
Rush City ... G-6
Rushford ... L-8
Russell ... K-2
Ruthton ... K-2
Rutledge ... F-7
Sabin ... E-1
Sacred Heart ... J-3
Saint Anthony Pg. 122, B-5
Saint Charles ... K-7
Saint Clair ... K-5
Saint Cloud ... H-5
Saint Francis ... H-6
Saint Hilaire ... C-2
Saint James ... K-4
Saint Joseph ... G-4
Saint Louis Park ... Pg. 122, D-2
Saint Michael ... H-5
Saint Paul ... H-6
Vicinity ... Pg. 123
Saint Paul Park ... Pg. 123, F-9
Saint Peter ... K-5
Saint Vincent ... A-1
Salol ... B-3
Sanborn ... K-3
Sandstone ... G-7
Sartell ... G-4
Sauk Centre ... G-4
Sauk Rapids ... G-4
Saum ... C-4
Sawyer ... F-6
Scanlon ... F-7
Schroeder ... D-9
Sebeka ... E-3
Sedan ... G-3
Shakopee ... J-5
Shelly ... D-1
Sherburn ... L-4
Shevlin ... D-3
Shoreview .. Pg. 123, A-6
Silver Bay ... D-9
Silver Lake ... J-4
Slayton ... K-2
Sleepy Eye ... K-4
Solway ... D-3
South International ... B-6
South St. Paul ... Pg. 123, E-8
Spicer ... H-4
Spring Grove ... L-8
Spring Lake ... D-5
Spring Valley ... L-7
Springfield ... K-4
Squaw Lake ... D-5
Staples ... F-4
Starbuck ... G-3
Stephen ... B-1
Stewartville ... K-7
Storden ... K-3
Strandquist ... B-2
Strathcona ... B-2
Sturgeon Lake ... F-7
Sunberg ... H-3
Sunfish Lake Pg. 123, E-7
Swan River ... E-6
Swanville ... G-4
Swatara ... E-5
Swift ... B-3
Taconite ... D-6
Taconite Harbor ... D-9
Talmoon ... D-5
Tamarack ... F-6
Taunton ... J-2
Taylors Falls ... H-7
Tenney ... F-1
Tenstrike ... D-4
Terrace ... H-3
Thief River Falls ... C-2
Togo ... C-6
Tommald ... F-5
Toopi ... L-7
Tower ... C-7
Tracy ... K-3
Trail ... C-3
Trimont ... L-4
Trosky ... K-2
Truman ... L-4
Turtle River ... D-4
Twig ... E-7
Twin Lakes ... L-5
Twin Valley ... D-2
Two Harbors ... E-8
Tyler ... K-2
Ulen ... E-2
Underwood ... F-2
Vadnais Hts. Pg. 123, A-7
Verdi ... K-1
Vergas ... E-2
Verndale ... F-4
Vesta ... J-3
Viking ... C-2
Villard ... G-3
Vining ... F-3
Viola ... K-7
Virginia ... D-7
Wabasha ... K-7
Wabasso ... J-3
Waconia ... J-5
Wadena ... F-3
Wahkon ... F-5
Waite Park ... H-4
Walker ... E-4
Walnut Grove ... K-3
Waltham ... L-6
Wanamingo ... K-6
Warba ... E-6
Warraska ... B-3
Warren ... C-1
Warroad ... B-3
Waseca ... K-5
Waskish ... C-4
Watertown ... J-5
Waterville ... K-5
Watkins ... H-4
Watson ... H-2
Waubun ... E-2
Wawina ... E-6
Welcome ... L-4
Wells ... L-5
West Concord ... K-6
West St. Paul Pg. 123, E-7
Westbrook ... K-3
Wheaton ... G-1
Whipholt ... E-4
White Bear Lake ... Pg. 123, A-9
White Earth ... E-2
Wilder ... L-3
Willernie ... Pg. 123, A-9
Williams ... B-4
Willmar ... H-4
Willow River ... F-6
Wilton ... D-3
Windom ... K-3
Winger ... D-2
Winnebago ... L-5
Winona ... K-8
Winthrop ... J-4
Winton ... C-8
Wirt ... D-5
Wolf Lake ... E-3
Wolverton ... F-1
Woodbury ... J-6
Vicinity .. Pg. 123, D-10
Woodland ... G-6
Worthington ... L-3
Wrenshall ... F-7
Wyoming ... H-6
Zemple ... D-5
Zim ... D-7
Zimmerman ... H-6
Zumbro Falls ... K-7
Zumbrota ... K-7

MISSISSIPPI
Page 50
Population: 2,520,638
Capital: Jackson
Land Area: 47,233 sq. mi.

Abbeville ... B-5
Aberdeen ... C-6
Ackerman ... D-5
Alcorn ... G-2
Algoma ... B-5
Alligator ... C-3
Amory ... C-6
Anguilla ... E-3
Arcola ... D-3
Arkabutla ... A-4
Artesia ... D-6
Ashland ... A-5
Askew ... B-3
Avalon ... C-4
Avon ... D-2
Bailey ... F-6
Baird ... D-3
Baldwyn ... B-6
Banner ... B-5
Bassfield ... H-4
Batesville ... B-4
Baxterville ... H-5
Bay Saint Louis ... K-5
Bay Springs ... G-5
Beaumont ... H-6
Beauregard ... G-3
Becker ... C-6
Belden ... B-6
Belen ... B-3
Bellefontaine ... C-5
Belmont ... A-6
Belzoni ... D-3
Benoit ... D-2
Benton ... E-4
Bentonia ... E-3
Beulah ... C-2
Big Creek ... C-4
Bigbee Valley ... D-6
Biloxi ... K-6
Blue Mountain ... A-5
Bogue Chitto ... H-3
Bolton ... F-3
Booneville ... A-6
Boyle ... C-3
Brandon ... F-4
Braxton ... G-4
Brookhaven ... H-3
Brooklyn ... H-5
Brooksville ... D-6
Bruce ... C-5
Buckatunna ... G-6
Bude ... H-3
Burnsville ... A-6
Byhalia ... A-4
Caledonia ... C-6
Calhoun City ... C-5
Call Town ... J-6
Camden ... E-4
Canton ... E-4
Carlisle ... G-3
Carpenter ... G-3
Carriere ... J-5
Carrollton ... D-4
Carson ... H-4
Carthage ... E-4
Cary ... E-3
Cascilla ... C-4
Cedarbluff ... C-5
Centreville ... J-3
Charleston ... C-4
Chatawa ... J-4
Chatham ... E-2
Chunky ... F-6
Church Hill ... G-2
Clara ... G-6
Clarksdale ... B-3
Cleveland ... C-3
Cliftonville ... D-6
Clinton ... F-3
Coahoma ... B-3
Coffeeville ... C-4
Coila ... D-4
Coldwater ... A-4
Collins ... G-5
Collinsville ... E-6
Columbia ... H-4
Columbus ... C-6
Como ... B-4
Conehatta ... F-5
Corinth ... A-6
Courtland ... B-4
Crawford ... D-6
Crenshaw ... B-3
Crosby ... H-2
Cross Roads ... A-6
Crowder ... B-3
Crystal Springs ... G-3
D'Lo ... G-4
Daleville ... E-6
Darling ... B-3
Darlove ... D-3
DeKalb ... E-6
Decatur ... F-5
Dennis ... A-6
Derma ... C-5
Doddsville ... C-3
Dorsey ... B-6
Drew ... C-3
Dublin ... C-3
Duck Hill ... C-4
Dumas ... A-5
Duncan ... C-3
Dundee ... B-3
Durant ... D-4
Eastabuchie ... H-5
Ebenezer ... E-4
Ecru ... B-5
Eden ... E-3
Edinburg ... E-5
Edwards ... F-3
Electric Mills ... E-6
Elizabeth ... D-3
Ellisville ... G-5
Enid ... B-4
Enterprise ... F-6
Ethel ... D-5
Etta ... B-5
Eupora ... D-5
Falcon ... B-3
Falkner ... A-5
Fannin ... F-4
Fayette ... G-2
Fitler ... E-2
Flora ... F-3
Florence ... F-4
Forest ... F-5
Forkville ... F-4
Fort Adams ... H-2
Foxworth ... H-4
French Camp ... D-5
Friar's Point ... B-3
Fruitland Park ... J-5
Fulton ... B-6
Futheyville ... C-4
Gallman ... G-3
Gattman ... C-6
Gautier ... K-6
Georgetown ... G-4
Gillsburg ... J-3
Glen ... A-6
Glen Allan ... E-2
Glendora ... C-3
Gloster ... H-2
Golden ... B-6
Goodman ... E-4
Gore Springs ... C-4
Grace ... E-2
Grand Gulf ... G-2
Greenville ... D-2
Greenwood ... D-4
Grenada ... C-4
Gulfport ... K-6
Gunnison ... C-2
Guntown ... B-6
Hamilton ... C-6
Harperville ... F-5
Harriston ... G-2
Harrisville ... G-4
Hatley ... B-6
Hattiesburg ... H-5

MISSISSIPPI

Hazlehurst G-3
Heidelberg G-6
Helena B-3
Hermanville G-3
Hernando A-4
Hickory F-5
Hickory Flat A-5
Hilhouse C-2
Hillsboro F-5
Hiwannee G-6
Holcomb C-4
Hollandale E-3
Holly Bluff E-3
Holly Springs A-5
Homewood F-5
Horn A-3
Houston C-5
Hurley J-6
Independence A-4
Indianola D-3
Inverness D-3
Isola D-3
Itta Bena A-6
Iuka A-6
Jackson F-3
Jayess H-4
Johnstons Station H-4
Jonestown B-3
Kewanee F-6
Kilmichael D-4
Kiln K-5
Kokomo F-5
Kosciusko E-5
Lafayette Springs B-5
Lake F-5
Lake View Pg. 119, G-2
Lakeshore B-3
Lambert B-3
Lauderdale E-6
Laurel G-5
Lawrence F-4
LeFlore C-4
Leaf H-6
Leakesville H-6
Leland E-3
Lena E-4
Lessley H-2
Lexington D-4
Liberty H-3
Little Rock F-5
Long Beach K-5
Lorman G-2
Louin F-5
Louise E-3
Louisville D-5
Lucedale H-6
Lucien H-3
Ludlow F-4
Lula B-3
Lumberton J-5
Lyman H-5
Lyon B-3
Maben D-5
Macon D-6
Madden E-5
Madison F-4
Magee G-5
Magnolia H-3
Mantachie B-6
Mantee C-5
Marietta B-6
Marion F-6
Marks B-3
Martinsville H-3
Mathiston D-5
McAdams E-4
McCall Creek H-3
McCarley D-5
McComb H-3
McCondy C-5
McCool D-5
McHenry J-5
McLain J-5
McNeill J-5
Meadville H-3
Mendenhall G-4
Meridian F-6
Merigold C-3
Metcalfe C-3
Michigan City A-5
Mineral Wells H-4
Vicinity Pg. 119, G-7
Minter City C-3
Mize G-4
Money C-3
Monticello H-4
Montpelier D-5
Montrose F-5
Mooreville B-6
Moorhead D-3
Morgan City D-3
Morgantown H-4
Morton F-4
Moselle H-5
Moss G-5
Moss Point K-6
Mound Bayou C-3
Mount Olive G-5
Myrtle A-5
Natchez H-2
Necaise J-5
Nesbit A-3
Neshoba E-5
Nettleton B-6
New Albany B-5
New Augusta H-5
New Hebron G-4
New Houlka C-5
New Site A-6
Newton E-5
Nicholson K-5
Nitta Yuma D-3
North Carrollton D-4
Noxapater E-5

Oak Vale H-4
Oakland C-4
Ocean Springs K-6
Ofahoma E-4
Okolona B-6
Olive Branch A-4
Oma G-4
Onward F-2
Osyka J-3
Oxford B-4
Pace C-2
Pachuta F-6
Paden A-6
Panther Burn E-3
Parchman C-3
Paris B-4
Pascagoula K-7
Pass Christian K-5
Paulding F-5
Paulette D-6
Pearl F-4
Pearlington K-5
Pelahatchie F-4
Perkinston J-5
Petal H-5
Pheba C-5
Philadelphia E-5
Philipp C-3
Picayune K-5
Pickens E-4
Pinckneyville J-2
Pinola G-4
Plantersville B-6
Plum Point Pg. 119, G-5
Pocahontas F-3
Pond J-2
Pontotoc B-5
Pope B-4
Poplarville H-5
Port Gibson G-2
Porterville F-6
Potts Camp A-5
Prairie C-6
Prairie Point D-6
Prentiss G-4
Preston E-6
Puckett F-4
Pulaski F-5
Purvis H-5
Quentin H-3
Quitman F-6
Raleigh G-5
Randolph B-5
Raymond F-3
Red Banks A-4
Redwood F-3
Reform D-5
Rena Lara B-2
Richton H-6
Ridgecrest H-2
Ridgeland F-4
Rienzi A-6
Ripley A-5
Robinsonville A-3
Rolling Fork E-3
Rome C-3
Rosedale C-2
Roxie H-2
Ruleville C-3
Runnelstown H-6
Ruth H-4
Sallis E-4
Saltillo B-6
Sandersville G-6
Sandhill F-4
Sandy Hook H-5
Sanford H-5
Sarah B-3
Sardis B-4
Sarepta B-5
Satartia E-3
Saucier J-5
Savage A-3
Schlater C-3
Scobey C-4
Scooba E-6
Scott D-2
Sebastopol F-5
Seminary G-5
Senatobia A-4
Sessums D-6
Seyppel Lake A-3
Shannon B-6
Sharon E-4
Shaw D-2
Shelby C-3
Sherard B-3
Sherman B-6
Shivers G-4
Shubuta G-6
Shuqualak D-6
Sibley H-2
Sidon D-3
Silver City E-3
Silver Creek G-4
Skene C-2
Slate Springs C-5
Slayden A-4
Sledge B-3
Smithdale H-3
Smithville B-6
Sontag G-4
Soso G-5
Southhaven A-3
Star F-4
State Line H-6
Steens D-6
Stewart D-5
Stonewall F-6
Stoneville D-2
Stovall B-3
Stringer G-5

Sturgis D-5
Summit H-3
Sumner C-3
Sumrall H-5
Sunflower D-3
Suqualena F-5
Swan Lake C-3
Swiftown D-3
Sylvarena G-5
Taylor B-4
Taylorsville G-5
Tchula D-4
Terry G-3
Thaxton B-5
Thomastown E-4
Thorn C-5
Thornton D-3
Thyatira A-4
Tie Plant C-4
Tillatoba C-4
Tinsley E-3
Tippo C-3
Tiplersville A-5
Tishomingo A-6
Toccopola B-5
Tomnolen D-5
Toomsuba F-6
Trebloc C-5
Tremont B-6
Tula B-5
Tunica A-3
Tupelo B-5
Tutwiler C-3
Tylertown H-4
Union E-5
Union Church G-3
University B-4
Utica G-3
Vaiden D-4
Valley Park E-3
Van Vleet C-5
Vance C-3
Vancleave J-6
Vardaman C-5
Vaughan E-4
Verona B-5
Vicksburg F-3
Victoria A-4
Vossburg F-6
Wade J-6
Walls A-3
Walnut A-5
Walnut Grove E-5
Walthall C-5
Washington H-2
Water Valley B-4
Waterford A-4
Waveland K-5
Waynesboro G-6
Wayside D-2
Weathersby G-4
Webb C-3
Weir D-5
Wenasoga A-6
Wesson G-3
West Gulfport J-5
West Point D-6
Wheeler A-6
Whitfield F-4
Wiggins J-6
Winona C-4
Winstonville C-3
Woodland C-5
Woodville J-2
Yazoo City E-3

MISSOURI

MISSOURI
Pages 48-49
Population: 4,916,686
Capital: Jefferson City
Land Area: 68,945 sq. mi.

Adair D-5
Adrian H-2
Advance K-9
Agency F-2
Albany D-2
Alexandria D-7
Allendale D-3
Alma G-4
Altamont E-3
Alton L-7
Amoret H-2
Anderson L-2
Annapolis K-8
Anniston K-10
Appleton City H-3
Arab K-9
Arbela D-6
Arbyrd M-9
Arcadia J-8
Archie H-3
Arcola J-3
Arkoe E-2
Arnold Pg. 140, K-3
Vicinity Pg. 140, K-3
Arroll K-6
Arrow Rock G-4
Asbury K-2
Ash Grove K-3
Ashland G-6
Ashley F-7
Athens D-6
Atlanta E-5
Aullville G-3
Aurora K-3
Auxvasse G-6
Ava L-5
Avalon F-4
Avondale Pg. 112, E-4
Bado K-6

Bakersfield L-6
Ballard H-3
Bardley L-7
Baring E-6
Barnard E-1
Battlefield K-4
Bay H-7
Beaufort F-7
Bel Nor Pg. 140, C-4
Bel Ridge Pg. 140, C-3
Bell City K-9
Bella Villa Pg. 140, H-4
Bellair G-5
Belle H-7
Bellefontaine Neighbors Pg. 140, B-5
Bellerive Pg. 140, C-4
Belton G-2
Bem H-7
Bendavis K-5
Bennett Springs J-5
Benton K-10
Berkeley Pg. 140, B-3
Bernie L-9
Bertrand K-10
Bethany D-3
Bethel E-6
Beulah J-6
Beverly Hills Pg. 140, D-4
Bevier E-5
Bible Grove D-6
Bigelow E-1
Bigspring G-7
Birch Tree K-7
Birmingham Pg. 112, E-5
Bismark H-7
Bixby J-7
Black Jack Pg. 140, A-5
Blackburn G-4
Blodgett K-10
Bloomfield K-9
Blue Eye L-4
Blue Springs G-3
Blythedale D-3
Bogard F-4
Bolckow E-2
Bolivar J-4
Bonne Terre J-8
Boonesboro G-4
Boonville G-4
Bosworth F-4
Bourbon H-7
Bowling Green F-7
Boynton D-3
Bradleyville L-4
Branson L-4
Braymer F-3
Brazeau J-10
Breckenridge E-3
Breckenridge Hills Pg. 140, C-3
Brentwood Pg. 140, F-3
Briar L-7
Bridgeton Pg. 140, B-2
Brighton K-4
Brimson D-3
Brinktown H-6
Bronaugh J-2
Brookfield E-4
Broseley L-9
Brownbranch L-5
Browning E-4
Brumley H-5
Bruner K-5
Brunswick F-4
Buckhorn K-6
Bucklin E-5
Buckner G-3
Buffalo J-4
Bunker J-7
Burlington Jct. D-1
Butler H-2
Cabool K-6
Cainsville D-3
Cairo F-5
Calhoun H-3
California F-5
Callao E-5
Calverton Park Pg. 140, B-4
Calwood G-6
Camdenton J-5
Cameron E-3
Campbell L-9
Canton D-7
Cape Girardeau K-10
Caplinger Mills J-3
Cardwell M-9
Carrington E-3
Carrollton F-3
Carsonville Pg. 140, C-4
Carthage K-2
Caruthersville M-10
Cascade K-9
Cassville L-3
Catherine Place J-9
Caulfield L-6
Center F-7
Centerview H-3
Centerville J-8
Centralia F-6
Chadwick L-4
Chaffee K-10
Chain-O-Lakes L-3
Chamois H-6
Champ Pg. 140, B-1
Charlack Pg. 140, C-3
Charleston K-10
Cherryville J-7
Chilhowee H-3
Chillicothe E-4
Chula E-4
Clarence E-5
Clarksdale E-2
Clarksville F-7
Clarkton L-9

Claycomo Pg. 112, D-5
Clayton Pg. 140, E-3
Clearmont D-1
Clever K-4
Clifton City G-4
Climax Springs H-5
Clinton H-3
Clyde D-2
Coal H-3
Coatsville D-5
Coldwater K-8
Cole Camp H-4
Collins J-3
Coloma F-4
Columbia G-6
Concordia G-4
Connelsville D-5
Conway J-5
Cook Station H-7
Cool Valley Pg. 140, C-4
Corder G-4
Corridon K-7
Couch L-7
Country Club Hills Pg. 140, C-5
County Life Acres Pg. 140, E-1
Craig D-1
Crane K-4
Crestwood Pg. 140, G-2
Creve Coeur Pg. 140, E-1
Crocker J-6
Cross Timbers H-4
Crystal Lake Park Pg. 140, E-1
Cuba H-7
Curryville F-7
Cyrene F-7
Dadeville J-3
De Soto H-8
Dearborn F-2
Deerfield J-2
Defiance G-8
Dellwood Pg. 140, B-4
Denver D-3
Des Arc K-8
Des Peres Pg. 140, F-1
Desloge J-8
Dexter K-9
Diamond K-2
Dixon H-6
Doe Run J-8
Dongola K-9
Doniphan L-8
Doolittle J-6
Dorena L-10
Downing D-5
Drexel H-2
Drury K-5
Duenweg K-2
Dunlap F-5
Dunnegan J-4
Durham E-6
Dutchtown K-10
Eagleville D-3
East Prairie L-10
Edgar Springs J-6
Edgerton F-2
Edina E-6
Edinburg E-3
Edmundson Pg. 140, B-3
El Dorado Springs J-3
Eldon H-4
Eldridge J-5
Elkland J-4
Ellington K-7
Ellsinore K-8
Elmira F-3
Elmo D-1
Elsberry F-8
Elwood E-2
Emden E-6
Eminence K-7
Eolia F-7
Essex L-9
Ethel E-5
Eudora J-4
Eunice K-6
Eureka H-8
Everton K-3
Ewing E-6
Excello F-5
Excelsior Springs F-2
Exeter L-3
Fagus L-9
Fair Grove K-4
Fair Play J-4
Fairdealing L-8
Fairfax D-1
Fairmont D-6
Fairview K-6
Farber F-6
Farmersville E-4
Farmington J-8
Faucett F-2
Fayette F-5
Fayetteville G-3
Fenton Pg. 140, H-1
Ferguson Pg. 140, B-4
Festus H-8
Fillmore E-2
Filley F-3
Fisk K-9
Flordell Hills Pg. 140, C-5
Florence H-4
Florida F-6
Florissant Pg. 140, A-4
Foley G-8
Fordland K-4

Forest City E-1
Forest Green F-5
Foristell G-8
Forsyth L-4
Fortescue E-1
Fortuna H-5
Fountain Grove E-4
Frankford F-7
Fredericktown J-9
Freeburg H-6
Fremont K-7
French Village J-9
Frontenac Pg. 140, E-2
Fulton G-6
Gainesville L-5
Galena L-3
Gallatin E-3
Galt E-4
Garden City H-3
Garwood K-8
Gatewood L-7
Gentry D-2
Gerald H-7
Gilliam F-4
Gladden J-7
Gladstone Pg. 112, C-4
Glasgow F-5
Glen Echo Park Pg. 140, C-4
Glenaire Pg. 112, C-5
Glendale Pg. 140, F-2
Glenwood D-5
Glover J-8
Golden City K-3
Goodman L-2
Gower F-2
Graham D-1
Grain Valley G-3
Granby K-3
Grand Pass F-4
Grandin L-8
Granger D-6
Granville F-6
Grassy K-9
Gray Summit H-8
Graysville D-5
Green City D-4
Green Ridge H-4
Greencastle D-5
Greendale Pg. 140, C-4
Greenfield K-3
Greensburg D-6
Greentop D-5
Greenville K-8
Greer L-7
Grovespring K-5
Halfway J-4
Hallsville F-6
Halltown K-3
Hamilton E-3
Hanley Hills Pg. 140, D-4
Hannibal E-7
Hardin F-3
Harris D-4
Harrisburg G-5
Harrisonville G-3
Hartford D-5
Hartville K-5
Hartwell H-3
Harwood J-3
Hatfield D-3
Hawk Point G-7
Hayti M-9
Hayti Heights M-10
Hazelwood Pg. 140, A-3
Helena E-2
Hermann G-7
Hermitage J-4
Higbee F-5
Higginsville G-3
High Point H-5
Hillsboro H-8
Hillsdale Pg. 140, D-4
Hinton G-5
Hitt D-5
Holcomb L-9
Holden G-3
Hollister L-4
Holt F-2
Holts Summit G-6
Hopkins D-2
Hornersville M-9
House Springs H-8
Houston K-6
Houston Lake Pg. 112, D-2
Houstonia G-4
Humansville J-4
Humphreys E-4
Hunter K-8
Huntleigh Pg. 140, F-1
Huntsdale G-5
Huntsville F-5
Hurdland E-6
Hurricane Deck H-5
Iberia H-6
Idlewild K-9
Independence G-3
Vicinity Pg. 112, F-6
Ironton J-8
Jackson J-10
Jacksonville F-5
Jameson E-3
Jamesport E-3
Jamestown G-5
Jane L-2
Jasper K-2
Jefferson City H-5
Jenkins L-3
Jennings Pg. 140, C-4

Jerico Springs J-3
Joplin K-2
Kahoka D-6
Kansas City G-2
Vicinity Pg. 124-125
Kearney F-2
Kendricktown K-3
Kennett M-9
Kewanee L-10
Keytesville F-5
Kidder E-3
Kimberling City L-4
King City E-2
Kingston F-3
Kinloch Pg. 140, B-3
Kirksville E-5
Kirkwood Pg. 140, F-2
Kliever G-5
Knob Noster G-3
Knox City E-6
Knoxville F-3
Koshkonong L-6
La Grange E-7
La Plata E-5
La Tour G-3
LaBelle E-6
LaMonte G-4
Laddonia F-6
Ladue Pg. 140, E-3
Lake Lotawana G-2
Lake Saint Louis G-8
Lake Spring J-7
Lake Waukomis Pg. 112, C-2
Lakenan F-6
Lakeshire Pg. 140, H-4
Lamar J-3
Lancaster D-5
Lanton L-6
Lathrop F-2
Latty J-8
Lawson F-3
Leadwood J-8
Leasburg H-7
Lebanon J-5
Lee's Summit Pg. 112, K-6
Leeper K-8
Leeton H-3
Lemons D-4
Lentner F-6
Leonard E-5
Lewistown E-6
Lexington F-3
Liberal J-2
Liberty F-2
Vicinity Pg. 112, C-6
Licking K-6
Lilbourn L-10
Lincoln H-4
Linn H-6
Linneus E-4
Lockwood K-3
Lone Jack G-3
Long Lane J-5
Longrun L-5
Longwood G-4
Louisiana F-7
Lowry City H-3
Ludlow F-3
Luray D-6
Macks Creek J-5
Macon E-5
Madison F-6
Malden L-9
Manchester Pg. 140, G-1
Manes K-5
Mansfield K-5
Maplewood Pg. 140, F-3
Marble Hill K-9
Marceline E-4
March H-2
Marionville K-4
Marlborough Pg. 140, G-3
Marshall F-4
Marshfield K-5
Marthasville G-7
Martinsburg G-6
Maryland Heights Pg. 140, C-1
Maryville D-2
Matthews L-10
Maysville E-2
McBaine G-5
McFall E-3
Melbourne E-3
Memphis D-6
Mercer D-4
Mexico F-6
Miami F-4
Miami Station F-4
Middle Grove F-5
Midway G-5
Milan E-4
Milford J-3
Mill Grove E-3
Millard E-5
Miller K-3
Millersburg G-6
Milo J-3
Mineola G-7
Miner K-10
Mirabile E-3
Moberly F-5
Mokane G-6
Moline Acres Pg. 140, B-5
Monett L-3
Monroe City F-6
Montevallo J-3
Monticello E-6
Montgomery City G-7
Montreal J-5
Montrose H-3
Moody L-6

Morley K-10
Morrisville J-4
Mound City E-1
Moundville J-2
Mount Moriah D-3
Mount Vernon K-3
Mount Zion H-5
Mountain Grove K-5
Mountain View K-7
Myrtle L-7
Mystic E-4
Nashville L-3
Naylor L-8
Nebo K-5
Neelyville L-8
Neosho L-2
Nevada J-2
New Bloomfield G-6
New Boston E-4
New Florence G-7
New Franklin F-5
New Hartford F-7
New Haven G-7
New Hope F-8
New London F-7
New Madrid L-10
New Market F-2
New Melle G-7
New Point E-1
Newburg J-6
Niangua K-5
Nixa K-4
Noel L-2
Norborne F-4
Normandy Pg. 140, C-4
Northmoor Pg. 112, D-3
Northview K-4
Northwoods Pg. 140, C-4
Norwood Court Pg. 140, D-4
Noser Mill H-7
Novelty E-5
Novinger E-5
O'Fallon G-8
Ocie L-5
Odessa G-3
Oermann H-8
Olivette Pg. 140, D-3
Olympian Village H-8
Oran K-10
Orchard Farm G-8
Oregon E-1
Orrick F-3
Osage Beach H-5
Osceola H-3
Osgood E-4
Oskaloosa J-2
Otto H-8
Overland Pg. 140, D-3
Owensville H-6
Ozark K-4
Pacific H-8
Pagedale Pg. 140, D-4
Palmyra E-7
Paris F-6
Parkville Pg. 112, D-2
Parma L-9
Pasadena Hills Pg. 140, C-4
Pasadena Park Pg. 140, C-4
Passaic H-2
Patton J-9
Pattonsburg E-2
Peace Valley L-6
Peach Orchard L-9
Peculiar G-2
Pennsboro K-3
Perry E-2
Perryville J-9
Pevely H-8
Phelps K-3
Philadelphia E-6
Phillipsburg J-5
Piedmont K-8
Pierce City K-3
Pilot Grove G-4
Pilot Knob J-8
Pine Lawn Pg. 140, D-5
Pineville L-2
Plad J-4
Plato K-6
Platte Woods Pg. 112, C-2
Plattsburg F-2
Pleasant Green G-5
Pleasant Valley Pg. 112, C-5
Plevna E-6
Pocahontas J-9
Polk J-4
Pollock D-4
Polo F-3
Pomona L-6
Poplar Bluff L-8
Portageville L-10
Potosi J-8
Prairie Hill F-5
Prairie Home G-5
Preston J-4
Princeton D-4
Protem L-5
Purdin E-4
Purdy L-3
Puxico K-9

MISSOURI

NEBRASKA

Queen City D-5
Quincy H-4
Qulin L-9
Racine K-2
Randolph . . . Pg. 112, E-5
Ravanna D-4
Ravenwood D-2
Raymondville K-6
Raymore G-2
Raytown . . . . . Pg. 112, H-5
Rea E-2
Redford K-8
Reeds Spring L-4
Regal F-3
Reger F-5
Renick F-5
Rensselaer F-7
Republic K-4
Reynolds K-8
Rhineland G-7
Rich Hill H-2
Richland J-5
Richmond F-3
Richmond Heights
. . . . Pg. 140, E-3
Ridgedale L-4
Ridgeway D-3
Risco L-9
Riverside . . . . Pg. 112, F-2
Riverton L-7
Riverview . . . . Pg. 140, B-6
Rock Hill . . . . Pg. 140, F-2
Rock Port D-1
Rockville H-3
Rocky Comfort L-3
Rogersville K-4
Rolla J-6
Romance L-5
Rombauer K-8
Rosati H-7
Rosebud G-7
Rosendale E-2
Rothville K-7
Round Spring K-7
Rover L-7
Rushville F-1
Saint Ann . . . . Pg. 140, C-2
Saint Charles G-8
Vicinity . . . . . Pg. 140, A-1
Saint Clair H-8
Saint Clement F-7
Saint George Pg. 140, F-2
Saint James H-6
Saint John . . . . Pg. 140, C-3
Saint Joseph E-2
Saint Louis G-8
Vicinity . . . . Pg. 140
Saint Marys J-9
Saint Patrick E-7
Saint Robert J-6
Sainte Genevieve H-8
Salem J-7
Saline D-3
Salisbury F-5
Sandy Hook G-5
Santa Fe F-6
Sarcoxie K-3
Savannah E-2
Scott City K-10
Sedalia G-4
Sedgewickville J-9
Seligman L-3
Senath L-9
Seneca L-2
Seymour K-5
Shannondale F-6
Shelbina E-6
Shelbyville E-6
Sheldon J-3
Sheridan D-2
Shirley J-7
Shrewsbury . Pg. 140, F-3
Sikeston K-10
Silva J-9
Silver Lake J-9
Simmons K-6
Skidmore D-1
Slater F-4
Sleeper J-5
Sligo J-7
Smithton G-4
Smithville F-2
South Fork L-6
South Gifford E-5
South Lineville D-4
Southwest City L-2
Sparta K-4
Spickard E-4
Spokane L-4
Springfield K-4
Squires K-5
Stanberry E-2
State Line M-9
Steele M-9
Steelville J-7
Stockton J-3
Stoutsville F-6
Stover H-4
Strafford K-4
Strasburg G-3
Sturgeon F-5
Sugar Creek Pg. 112, H-5
Sullivan H-7
Summersville K-7
Sumner F-4
Sunset Hills . Pg. 140, H-2
Sweet Springs G-4
Sycamore L-6
Sycamore Hills
. . . . Pg. 140, C-3
Tarkio D-1
Tebbetts G-6
Thayer L-7
Theodosia L-5

Thomas Hill F-5
Thomasville L-6
Thompson F-6
Thornfield L-5
Tiffin J-3
Tina F-4
Tindall E-4
Tipton G-5
Town & Country
. . . . Pg. 140, F-1
Townley L-9
Trenton E-4
Troy G-8
Truesdale G-7
Truxton G-7
Tunas J-4
Turney F-2
Tuscumbia H-5
Tyrone K-6
Union H-7
Union Star E-2
Unionville D-4
Unity Village Pg. 112, J-6
University City
. . . . Pg. 140, D-3
Uplands Park Pg. 140, D-4
Urich H-3
Utica E-3
Van Buren K-8
Vandalia F-7
Vanzant K-6
Velda City . . . Pg. 140, D-4
Velda Village Hills
. . . . Pg. 140, D-4
Versailles H-5
Viburnum J-7
Vichy H-6
Vienna H-6
Vinita Park . . Pg. 140, D-3
Vinita Terrace Pg. 140, D-3
Vulcan K-8
Wainwright G-6
Walnut Grove K-4
Wardsville H-6
Warren E-6
Warrensburg G-3
Warrenton G-7
Warsaw H-4
Warson Woods
. . . . Pg. 140, F-2
Washington G-7
Wasola L-5
Waverly F-4
Wayland D-6
Waynesville J-6
Weatherby Lake
. . . . Pg. 112, C-2
Weaubleau J-4
Webb City K-2
Weber Hill H-8
Webster Groves
. . . . Pg. 140, F-3
Wellston . . . . Pg. 140, D-4
Wellsville G-7
Wentworth K-3
West Plains L-6
Westboro D-1
Weston F-1
Westphalia H-6
White Oak L-9
Wilbur Park Pg. 140, G-4
Wilcox D-2
Willard K-4
Williamsburg G-6
Williamsville K-8
Willow Springs K-6
Wilson City K-10
Windsor H-4
Winfield G-8
Winigan E-4
Winona K-7
Winston E-3
Winthrop F-1
Woodlawn F-6
Woods Heights F-3
Woodson Terrace
. . . . Pg. 140, C-3
Wooldridge G-5
Worth D-2
Wyaconda D-6
Yarrow E-6
Yount J-9
Yukon K-6
Zalma K-9

MONTANA
Page 51
Population: 786,690
Capital: Helena
Land Area: 145,398 sq.mi.

Absarokee E-6
Acton E-6
Alberton D-2
Alder E-4
Alzada D-10
Anaconda E-3
Angela D-8
Antelope B-10
Arlee D-2
Ashland E-8
Augusta C-4
Avon D-3
Babb B-3
Bainville B-10
Baker D-10
Basin D-4
Bearcreek F-6
Belfry F-6
Belgrade E-5
Belt C-5

Biddle E-9
Big Fork C-2
Big Sandy C-5
Big Sky E-4
Big Timber E-6
Bighorn E-7
Billings E-6
Birney E-8
Black Eagle C-5
Blackfoot B-3
Bloomfield C-9
Bonner D-2
Boulder E-4
Box Elder F-4
Bozeman E-5
Brady C-4
Bridger F-6
Broadus E-9
Broadview E-6
Brockton C-9
Brockway C-9
Browning B-3
Busby E-8
Butte E-3
Bynum C-4
Cameron F-4
Canyon Creek D-4
Capitol D-10
Carter C-5
Cartersville D-8
Cascade C-4
Checkerboard D-5
Chester F-4
Chico Hot Springs F-5
Chinook B-6
Choteau C-4
Christina C-6
Churchill E-4
Circle C-9
Cleveland C-6
Clinton D-2
Clyde Park E-5
Coffee Creek C-5
Cohagen D-8
Colstrip E-8
Columbia Falls B-2
Columbus E-6
Conner E-2
Conrad C-4
Cooke City F-6
Corvallis D-2
Craig D-4
Crane C-10
Crow Agency E-7
Culbertson B-9
Custer E-7
Cut Bank B-4
Darby E-2
DeBorgia C-1
Dean F-6
Decker F-8
Deer Lodge D-3
Dell F-3
Denton C-5
Dillon F-3
Divide E-3
Dixon C-2
Dodson B-7
Drummond D-3
Dupuyer C-4
Dutton C-4
East Glacier Park B-3
East Helena D-4
Edgar E-6
Ekalaka D-10
Elliston D-3
Elmo C-2
Emigrant E-5
Ennis E-4
Ethridge B-4
Eureka B-2
Fairfield C-4
Fairview C-10
Fallon D-9
Flatwillow D-7
Flaxville B-9
Florence D-2
Ford C-9
Forestgrove D-6
Forsyth E-8
Fort Belknap Agency . . C-6
Fort Benton C-5
Fort Peck C-8
Fort Shaw C-4
Fortine B-2
Frenchtown D-2
Froid C-9
Fromberg F-6
Galen D-3
Gallatin Gateway E-4
Gardiner F-5
Garneill D-6
Garrison D-3
Garryowen E-8
Geraldine C-5
Geyser C-5
Glasgow C-8
Glen E-4
Glendive D-10
Grant F-3
Grantsdale D-2
Grassrange D-6
Great Falls C-4
Hall D-3
Hamilton D-2
Hammond D-10
Happy's Inn C-2
Hardin E-7
Harlem B-6
Harlowton D-6
Harrison E-4
Hathaway D-9
Havre B-6
Helena D-4

Helmville D-3
Heron C-1
Hilger D-6
Hingham B-4
Hinsdale C-8
Hobson D-5
Homestead B-9
Hot Springs C-2
Hungry Horse B-2
Huntley E-7
Huson D-2
Hysham D-8
Ingomar D-8
Jackson E-3
Jefferson City D-4
Joliet F-6
Joplin B-4
Jordan C-8
Judith Gap D-6
Kalispell B-2
Kiowa B-3
Klein D-7
Kremlin B-5
Lakeside C-2
Lambert C-9
Lame Deer E-8
Laurel E-6
Laurin E-4
Lavina E-6
Lewistown D-6
Libby B-1
Lima F-3
Lincoln D-3
Lindsay C-9
Livingston E-5
Lloyd B-6
Lodge Grass E-7
Lohman B-6
Lolo D-2
Lolo Hot Springs D-2
Loma C-5
Loring B-7
Lothair B-4
Malta B-7
Manhattan E-4
Marion C-2
Martin City B-2
McLeod E-5
Medicine Lake B-9
Melrose E-3
Melstone D-7
Melville E-6
Miles City D-9
Missoula D-2
Moccasin D-5
Monarch D-5
Montague C-5
Montana City D-4
Moore D-6
Musselshell D-7
Nashua C-8
Neihart D-5
Niarada C-2
Norris E-4
Noxon C-1
Nye E-6
Olney B-2
Opheim B-8
Oswego C-9
Ovando D-3
Pablo C-2
Paradise C-2
Pendroy C-4
Philipsburg D-3
Plains C-1
Plentywood B-9
Plevna D-10
Polebridge B-2
Polson C-2
Pompeys Pillar E-7
Poplar C-9
Port of Del Bonita B-3
Port of Morgan B-7
Port of Opheim B-8
Port of Raymond B-9
Potomac D-3
Powderville E-9
Power C-4
Pray E-5
Rapelie E-6
Raymond B-9
Raynesford C-5
Red Lodge F-6
Redstone B-9
Reedpoint E-6
Rexford B-1
Richey C-9
Richland B-8
Ringling E-5
Roberts F-6
Rock Springs D-8
Rollins C-2
Ronan C-2
Rosebud E-8
Roundup D-6
Roy D-7
Rudyard B-4
Ryegate E-6
Saco B-8
Saint Ignatius D-2
Saint Mary B-3
Saint Regis C-1
Saltese D-1
Santa Rita B-4
Savage C-10
Scobey B-9
Seeley Lake D-3
Shawmut D-6
Shelby B-4
Sheridan E-4
Sidney C-10
Silesia E-6
Silver Star E-4
Simms C-4

Somers C-2
Springdale E-5
Stanford D-5
Stevensville D-2
Stryker B-2
Suffolk C-6
Sumatra D-7
Sun River C-4
Sunburst B-4
Superior C-2
Swan Lake C-2
Sweetgrass B-4
Tarkio D-2
Teigen D-7
Terry D-9
Thompson Falls C-2
Three Forks E-4
Toston E-4
Townsend D-4
Trego B-2
Trout Creek C-1
Troy B-1
Turner B-7
Twin Bridges E-4
Twodot D-5
Valier C-4
Vaughn C-5
Victor D-2
Vida C-9
Virginia City E-4
Volborg E-9
Walkerville E-3
Warmsprings D-3
Waterloo E-4
West Glacier B-3
West Yellowstone F-4
Westby B-10
White Hall E-4
White Sulphur Springs . D-5
Whitefish B-2
Whitetail B-9
Wibaux D-10
Willow Creek E-4
Wilsall E-5
Winifred C-6
Winnett D-7
Winston D-4
Wisdom E-3
Wise River E-3
Wolf Creek D-4
Wolf Point C-9
Worden E-7
Wyola F-8
Yaak B-1
Zurich B-6

NEBRASKA
Pages 52-53
Population: 1,569,825
Capital: Lincoln
Land Area: 76,664 sq. mi.

Abie F-11
Adams H-12
Ainsworth D-7
Albion E-10
Alda G-9
Alexandria H-11
Allen D-11
Alliance E-3
Alma H-8
Almeria E-8
Amelia D-8
Ames F-12
Amherst G-8
Angora E-3
Anoka C-8
Anselmo E-7
Ansley F-8
Antioch D-3
Arapahoe H-7
Arcadia F-8
Archer F-9
Arlington F-12
Arnold F-7
Arthur E-5
Ashby D-4
Ashland G-12
Ashton F-9
Atkinson D-8
Atlanta H-8
Auburn H-12
Aurora G-10
Axtell H-8
Ayr H-9
Bancroft E-11
Barneston J-12
Bartlett E-9
Bartley H-7
Bassett D-8
Battle Creek E-10
Bayard E-3
Bazile Mills D-10
Beatrice H-11
Beaver City H-7
Beaver Crossing G-11
Beemer E-11
Belden D-11
Belgrade F-9
Bellevue G-12
Vicinity . . . . . Pg. 132, G-5
Belvidere H-10
Benedict G-10
Benkelman H-5
Bennet H-12
Bertrand H-8
Berwyn F-8
Big Springs F-4
Bingham D-4
Bladen H-9
Blair F-12

Bloomfield D-10
Blue Hill H-9
Blue Springs H-11
Boelus G-9
Boone F-10
Boys Town F-12
Vicinity . . . . . Pg. 132, E-1
Bradshaw G-10
Brady F-6
Brandon G-4
Brewster E-7
Bridgeport E-3
Bristow C-9
Broadwater E-3
Brock H-12
Broken Bow F-7
Brownlee D-6
Brule F-4
Bruning H-10
Bruno F-11
Brunswick D-10
Burchard H-12
Burr H-12
Burton C-8
Burwell E-8
Bushnell F-2
Butte C-9
Cairo G-9
Callaway F-7
Cambridge H-6
Campbell H-9
Capehart . . . Pg. 132, H-4
Carleton H-10
Carroll D-11
Carter lake . . Pg. 132, D-4
Cedar Bluffs F-11
Cedar Creek Pg. 132, K-1
Cedar Rapids F-9
Center D-10
Central City G-9
Ceresco G-12
Chadron C-3
Chalco . . . . . Pg. 132, F-1
Chambers D-9
Champion G-5
Chapman G-9
Chappell F-4
Chester J-10
Clarks F-10
Clarkson E-11
Clatonia H-11
Clay Center H-10
Clearwater D-10
Clinton C-4
Cody C-6
Coleridge D-11
Columbus F-11
Comstock F-8
Concord D-11
Cook H-12
Cornlea F-10
Cortland H-11
Cotesfield F-9
Cowles H-9
Cozad G-7
Crab Orchard H-12
Craig E-12
Crawford C-3
Creighton D-10
Creston E-11
Crete H-11
Crofton C-10
Crookston C-6
Culbertson H-6
Cullom . . . . Pg. 132, K-2
Curtis G-6
Dakota City D-12
Dalton E-3
Danbury H-6
Dannebrog G-9
Davenport H-10
David City F-11
Dawson J-13
Daykin H-11
Debolt . . . . Pg. 132, C-3
Decatur E-12
Denton G-11
Deshler H-10
Dewitt H-11
Dickens G-6
Diller H-11
Dix F-2
Dodge E-11
Doniphan G-9
Dorchester G-11
Douglas H-12
DuBois J-12
Dunbar G-12
Duncan F-10
Dunning E-7
Dwight G-11
Eddyville G-7
Edgar H-10
Edison H-7
Elba F-9
Elgin E-9
Eli C-5
Elk Creek H-12
Elkhorn F-12
Ellsworth D-4
Elm Creek G-8
Elmwood G-12
Elsie G-5
Elsmere D-7
Elwood H-7
Elyria E-8
Emerson D-12
Emmet D-9
Enders H-5
Endicott J-11
Ericson E-9
Eustis G-7
Exeter G-10
Fairbury H-11

Fairfield H-10
Fairmont H-10
Falls City J-13
Farnam G-7
Farwell F-9
Filley H-11
Firth H-11
Fordyce D-11
Fort Crook . . Pg. 132, H-4
Foster D-10
Franklin H-8
Fremont F-12
Friend G-10
Fullerton F-10
Funk H-8
Gandy F-6
Garrison F-11
Geneva H-10
Genoa F-10
Gering E-2
Gilmore . . . . Pg. 132, H-4
Giltner G-9
Glenvil H-9
Goehner G-11
Gordon C-5
Gothenburg G-7
Grafton G-10
Grainton G-5
Grand Island G-9
Grant G-5
Greeley F-9
Greenwood G-12
Gresham G-11
Gretna F-12
Guide Rock J-9
Gurley F-3
Hadar E-11
Haigler H-4
Hallam H-11
Halsey E-7
Hamlet H-5
Hampton G-10
Harrisburg E-2
Harrison C-2
Hartington D-11
Harvard H-9
Hastings H-9
Hay Springs C-4
Hayes Center H-5
Hazard F-8
Hebron H-10
Hemingford D-3
Henderson G-10
Herman F-12
Hershey F-6
Hildreth H-8
Holdrege H-7
Holstein H-9
Hooper F-11
Hoskins E-11
Howells E-11
Humboldt J-12
Humphrey E-10
Huntley H-8
Hyannis D-5
Imperial G-5
Inavale J-9
Indianola H-6
Inman D-9
Ithaca F-11
Johnson H-12
Johnstown D-7
Juniata H-9
Kearney G-8
Kenesaw G-9
Kennard F-12
Keystone F-5
Kilgore C-6
Kimball F-2
La Vista . . . . Pg. 132, F-2
Lakeside D-4
Laurel D-11
Lawrence H-9
Lebanon H-5
Leigh E-11
Lemoyne F-5
Lewellen F-4
Lewiston H-12
Lexington G-7
Liberty J-12
Lincoln G-11
Linwood F-11
Lisco E-4
Litchfield F-8
Lodgepole F-4
Long Pine D-7
Loomis H-7
Louisville G-12
Loup City F-8
Lyman E-2
Lynch C-9
Lyons E-12
Madison E-11
Madrid G-5
Magnet D-10
Malmo F-11
Marquette G-10
Martell H-11
Martinsburg D-11
Mason City F-8
Max H-5
Maxwell F-6
May . . . . . . Pg. 132, G-6
Maywood G-6
McCook H-6
McCool Jct. G-10
McGrew E-2
Mead F-12
Meadow . . . Pg. 132, K-2
Melbeta E-2
Memphis G-12
Merna F-7
Merriman C-5
Milford G-11

Millard . . . . . Pg. 132, F-1
Miller G-8
Milligan H-10
Mills C-8
Minden H-8
Minitare E-2
Mitchell D-2
Monowi C-9
Moorefield G-6
Morrill D-2
Mullen D-6
Murray G-12
Naper C-8
Naponee H-8
Nashville . . . Pg. 132, B-3
Nebraska City H-12
Neligh E-10
Nelson H-10
Nenzel C-6
Newman Grove E-10
Newport D-8
Nickerson F-12
Niobrara C-10
Norden C-7
Norfolk E-11
North Bend F-11
North Loup F-9
North Platte F-6
O'Neill D-9
Oak H-10
Oakdale E-10
Oakland E-12
Obert D-11
Oconto F-7
Octavia F-11
Odell J-11
Odessa G-8
Ogallala F-5
Ohiowa H-10
Omaha F-12
Vicinity . . . . Pg. 132
Ong H-10
Oreopolis . . . Pg. 132, J-5
Orleans H-8
Osceola F-10
Oshkosh E-4
Osmond D-11
Overton G-8
Oxford H-7
Page D-9
Palisade H-5
Palmer F-9
Palmyra G-12
Panama H-12
Papillion G-12
Vicinity . . . . . Pg. 132, G-3
Parks H-4
Pawnee City J-12
Paxton F-5
Pender E-11
Petersburg E-10
Phillips G-10
Pickrell H-11
Pierce D-10
Pilger E-11
Plainview D-10
Platte Center F-10
Plattsmouth G-12
Vicinity . . . . . Pg. 132, K-5
Pleasanton G-8
Plymouth H-11
Polk G-10
Poole G-8
Potter F-3
Prague F-11
Primrose F-9
Prosser G-9
Purdum D-7
Raeville E-10
Ragan H-8
Ralston . . . . Pg. 132, F-2
Randolph D-11
Ravenna G-9
Raymond G-11
Red Cloud H-9
Republican City H-8
Reynolds J-11
Richfield . . . Pg. 132, H-2
Richland F-11
Rising City F-11
Riverdale G-8
Riverton H-9
Roca G-11
Rockville F-8
Rogers F-11
Rosalie E-12
Rose D-8
Roseland H-9
Rushville C-4
Ruskin H-9
Saint Edward F-10
Saint Helena C-11
Saint Libory G-9
Saint Mary H-12
Saint Paul F-9
Santee C-10
Sargent E-8
Saronville H-10
Schuyler F-11
Scotia F-9
Scottsbluff D-2
Scribner F-11
Seneca D-6
Seward G-11
Shelby F-10
Shelton G-8
Shickley H-10
Sholes D-11
Shubert H-12
Sidney F-3
Silver Creek F-10
Smithfield G-7
Snyder E-11

NEBRASKA

NEW JERSEY

South Bend ... G-12
South Souix City ... D-12
Spalding ... E-9
Sparks ... C-7
Spencer ... C-9
Springfield ... G-12
  Vicinity ... Pg. 132, J-1
Springview ... C-8
Stamford ... H-7
Stanton ... E-11
Staplehurst ... G-11
Stapleton ... F-6
Steele City ... J-11
Steinauer ... H-12
Stockville ... G-6
Strang ... H-10
Stratton ... H-5
Stromsburg ... F-10
Stuart ... D-8
Summerfield ... J-12
Sumner ... G-8
Superior ... J-10
Surprise ... G-10
Sutherland ... F-6
Sutton ... H-10
Syracuse ... H-12
Table Rock ... H-12
Tarnov ... F-10
Taylor ... E-8
Tecumseh ... H-12
Tekamah ... E-12
Terrytown ... D-2
Thayer ... G-10
Thedford ... E-6
Thurston ... E-12
Tilden ... E-10
Tobias ... H-11
Trenton ... H-6
Trumbull ... G-9
Tryon ... E-6
Uehling ... E-12
Ulysses ... G-11
Unadilla ... H-12
Upland ... H-8
Valentine ... C-7
Valley ... F-12
Valparaiso ... G-11
Venango ... G-4
Verdel ... C-10
Verdigre ... D-10
Verdon ... J-13
Waco ... G-10
Wahoo ... F-12
Wakefield ... D-11
Wallace ... G-5
Walthill ... D-12
Wauneta ... H-5
Wausa ... D-10
Waverly ... G-11
Wayne ... D-11
Weeping Water ... G-12
Weissert ... F-8
Wellfleet ... G-6
West Point ... E-11
Western ... H-11
Westerville ... F-8
Whitman ... D-5
Whitney ... C-3
Wilber ... H-11
Wilcox ... H-8
Willow Island ... G-6
Wilsonville ... H-7
Winnebago ... D-12
Winnetoon ... D-9
Winside ... E-11
Winslow ... F-12
Wisner ... E-11
Wolbach ... G-10
Wood Lake ... C-7
Wood River ... G-8
Wymore ... J-12
Wynot ... C-10
York ... G-10

NEVADA
Page 54
Population: 800,493
Capital: Carson City
Land Area: 109,893 sq. mi.

Adaven ... F-5
Alamo ... G-5
Arden ... Pg. 113, G-1
Ash Springs ... G-5
Austin ... D-4
Babbitt ... E-2
Baker ... E-6
Battle Mountain ... C-4
Beatty ... H-4
Beowawe ... C-4
Blue Diamond ... J-5
Boulder City ... J-6
Bracken ... Pg. 113, G-8
Bunkerville ... H-6
Cactus Springs ... H-5
Cal Nev Ari ... J-6
Caliente ... G-6
Carlin ... C-5
Carp ... G-6
Carson City ... E-1
Carver's ... E-3
Caselton ... F-6
Cherry Creek ... D-6
Coaldale ... F-3
Cold Spring ... D-3
Contact ... A-6
Crescent Valley ... C-4
Currant ... E-5
Currie ... C-6
Deeth ... B-5
Duckwater ... E-5

Dyer ... F-3
Eagle Picher Mine ... C-2
East Ely ... E-6
East Las Vegas ... Pg. 113, E-6
Elko ... C-5
Ely ... E-6
Empire ... C-1
Eureka ... D-5
Fallon ... D-2
Fernley ... E-3
Gabbs ... E-3
Gerlach ... C-2
Glendale ... H-6
Golconda ... B-3
Gold Point ... G-3
Goldfield ... G-3
Goodsprings ... J-5
Halleck ... B-5
Hawthorne ... E-2
Henderson ... J-6
  Vicinity ... Pg. 113, G-8
Hiko ... G-5
Imlay ... C-3
Indian Springs ... H-5
Ione ... E-3
Jack Creek ... B-5
Jackpot ... A-6
Jarbidge ... A-5
Jean ... J-5
Jiggs ... C-5
Kimberly ... E-5
Lage's ... D-6
Lamoille ... C-5
Las Vegas ... J-6
  Vicinity ... Pg. 113
Las Vegas Beach ... Pg. 113, E-9
Laughlin ... K-6
Lee ... C-5
Lida ... G-3
Lovelock ... C-2
Lund ... E-6
Luning ... F-3
Major's Place ... E-6
McDermitt ... A-3
McGill ... D-6
Mercury ... H-5
Mesquite ... H-6
Midas ... B-4
Middle Gate ... E-3
Mill City ... C-3
Mina ... F-3
Moapa ... H-6
Montello ... B-6
Mountain City ... A-5
Nelson ... J-6
Nixon ... D-2
North Las Vegas ... J-6
  Vicinity ... Pg. 113, B-3
Nyala ... F-5
Oasis ... B-6
Oreana ... C-3
Orovada ... B-3
Overton ... H-6
Owyhee ... A-5
Panaca ... G-6
Paradise Valley ... B-3
Pioche ... F-6
Preston ... E-6
Rachel ... G-5
Reno ... D-1
Round Mt. ... E-4
Ruby Valley ... C-5
Ruth ... E-6
Sandy ... J-5
Schurz ... E-2
Scotty's Jct. ... G-4
Searchlight ... K-6
Shantytown ... C-5
Silver City ... D-2
Silver Peak ... F-3
Silver Springs ... D-2
Sloan ... J-5
Sparks ... D-2
Sulphur ... B-2
Sutcliffe ... D-1
Thousand Springs ... B-6
Tonopah ... F-3
Tuscarora ... B-4
Unionville ... C-3
Ursine ... F-6
Valmy ... C-4
Virginia City ... D-2
Wadsworth ... D-2
Warm Springs ... F-4
Weed Heights ... E-2
Wellington ... E-2
Wells ... B-6
Winnemucca ... B-3
Yerington ... E-2

NEW HAMPSHIRE
Page 55
Population: 920,610
Capital: Concord
Land Area: 8,993 sq. mi.

Albany ... E-6
Allenstown ... H-6
Alstead ... H-3
Alton ... G-6
Alton Bay ... G-6
Amherst ... J-5
Andover ... G-5
Antrim ... J-4
Ashland ... F-5
Ashuelot ... K-3
Atkinson ... J-6
Auburn ... J-6

Barnstead ... H-6
Bartlett ... E-6
Bath ... E-4
Bayside ... J-7
Bedford ... J-5
Belmont ... G-5
Bennington ... J-4
Berlin ... D-6
Bethlehem ... D-5
Boscawen ... H-5
Bow Center ... H-5
Bradford ... H-4
Brentwood ... J-6
Bretton Woods ... E-5
Bridgewater ... G-5
Bristol ... G-5
Brookfield ... G-6
Brookline ... K-5
Canaan ... G-4
Canaan Center ... F-4
Candia ... J-6
Carroll ... D-5
Cascade ... D-6
Center Conway ... E-6
Center Ossipee ... F-6
Charlestown ... H-3
Cheever ... G-5
Chester ... J-6
Chesterfield ... J-3
Chichester ... H-5
Chocorua ... F-6
Cilleyville ... G-4
Claremont ... G-4
Coburn ... G-6
Cold River ... H-3
Colebrook ... B-5
Columbia ... B-5
Concord ... H-5
Contoocook ... H-5
Conway ... E-6
Coos Junction ... D-5
Cornish City ... G-3
Cornish Flat ... G-3
Crystal ... C-6
Danbury ... G-4
Davisville ... H-5
Derry ... J-6
Derry Village ... J-6
Dixville ... B-6
Dorchester ... F-4
Dover ... H-7
Drewsville ... H-3
Dublin ... J-4
Dummer ... C-6
Durham ... H-7
East Alton ... G-6
East Barrington ... H-6
East Grafton ... G-4
East Hebron ... F-5
East Kingston ... J-6
East Lempster ... H-3
East Madison ... F-6
Easton ... E-5
Eaton Center ... F-6
Effingham Falls ... F-6
Elkins ... G-4
Epping ... J-6
Epsom ... H-6
Epsom Four Corners ... H-6
Errol ... C-6
Exeter ... J-7
Fabyan ... D-5
Farmington ... G-7
Fish Market ... G-4
Francestown ... J-4
Franconia ... D-5
Franklin ... G-5
Freedom ... F-6
Fremont ... J-6
Gerrish ... H-5
Gilford ... G-6
Gilmans Corner ... F-4
Gilmanton ... G-6
Gilsum ... H-4
Glen ... E-6
Glen House ... D-6
Glendale ... G-6
Goffs Falls ... J-5
Goffstown ... J-5
Gorham ... D-6
Goshen ... H-4
Gossville ... H-6
Grafton ... G-4
Grantham ... G-4
Greenfield ... J-4
Greenville ... K-4
Groton ... F-4
Groveton ... C-5
Guild ... G-4
Guildhall ... C-5
Hampton ... J-7
Hampton Beach ... J-7
Hancock ... J-4
Hanover ... F-4
Hanover Center ... F-4
Harts Location ... E-6
Haverhill ... E-4
Hebron ... F-4
Henniker ... H-4
Hillsborough ... H-4
Hinsdale ... J-3
Hooksett ... H-6
Hopkinton ... H-5
Hoyts Corner ... H-4
Hudson ... J-6
Jackson ... D-6
Jaffrey ... J-4
James City ... H-6
Jefferson ... D-5
Jefferson Highlands ... D-5
Keene ... J-3
Kensington ... J-6
Kidderville ... B-5
Kingston ... J-6

Laconia ... G-5
Lancaster ... D-5
Laskey Corner ... H-6
Leavitts Hill ... H-6
Lebanon ... G-4
Lincoln ... E-5
Lisbon ... E-4
Little Boars Head ... J-7
Littleton ... D-5
Loudon ... H-5
Lower Shaker Village ... G-4
Lower Village ... H-4
Lyme ... F-4
Lyme Center ... F-4
Madbury ... H-7
Madison ... F-6
Manchester ... J-5
Marlborough ... J-4
Marlow ... H-4
Martin ... H-5
Mason ... K-5
Meadows ... D-5
Meredith ... F-5
Meriden ... G-3
Merrimack ... J-5
Milan ... C-6
Milford ... J-5
Milton ... G-6
Mirror Lake ... F-6
Monroe ... D-4
Mont Vernon ... J-5
Moultonborough ... F-6
Moultonville ... F-6
Mount Sunapee ... H-4
Munsonville ... H-4
Nashua ... K-5
New Durham ... G-6
New Hampton ... G-5
New Ipswich ... K-4
New London ... G-4
New Rye ... H-6
Newbury ... H-4
Newfields ... J-7
Newington ... H-7
Newmarket ... J-7
Newport ... G-4
Newton ... J-7
North Chatham ... D-6
North Conway ... E-6
North Grantham ... G-4
North Groton ... F-5
North Haverhill ... E-4
North Rochester ... H-6
North Sandwich ... F-6
North Stratford ... C-5
North Sutton ... H-4
North Wakefield ... G-6
North Woodstock ... E-5
Northfield ... H-5
Northumberland ... C-5
Northwood ... H-6
Orford ... F-4
Orfordville ... F-4
Ossipee ... F-6
Otterville ... G-6
Pages Corner ... H-5
Parker ... J-5
Pearls Corner ... K-6
Pelham ... K-6
Pembroke ... H-6
Penacook ... H-5
Peterborough ... J-4
Pinardville ... J-5
Pittsburg ... B-6
Pittsfield ... H-6
Plainfield ... G-3
Plaistow ... J-6
Plymouth ... F-5
Portsmouth ... H-7
Potter Place ... G-4
Province Lake ... F-7
Randolph ... D-6
Raymond ... J-6
Redstone ... E-6
Richmond ... K-3
Rindge ... K-4
Riverton ... B-6
Rochester ... H-6
Rollinsford ... H-7
Rumney ... F-5
Rye ... J-7
Rye Beach ... J-7
Salem ... K-6
Salisbury ... H-5
Sanbornton ... G-5
Sanbornville ... G-7
Sandwich ... F-6
Seabrook Beach ... J-7
Sharon ... J-4
Shelburne ... D-6
Somersworth ... H-7
South Acworth ... H-4
South Cornish ... G-3
South Danbury ... G-4
South Stoddard ... J-4
South Weare ... J-5
Spofford ... J-3
Springfield ... G-4
Squantum ... J-4
Stark ... C-6
Stewartstown ... B-6
Stoddard ... H-4
Stratford ... C-5
Stratham ... J-7
Sunapee ... H-4
Surry ... J-3
Sutton ... H-4
Swiftwater ... E-4
Tamworth ... F-6
Temple ... J-4
Thornton ... F-5
Tilton ... H-5
Trapshire ... H-3
Troy ... J-4

Tuftonboro ... F-6
Twin Mountain ... D-5
Union ... G-7
Wakefield ... G-7
Wallis Sands ... J-7
Walpole ... H-3
Warner ... H-5
Warren ... F-4
Washington ... H-4
Weare ... J-5
Wendell ... H-4
Wentworth ... F-4
Wentworths Location ... B-6
West Campton ... F-5
West Lebanon ... F-4
West Milan ... C-6
West Ossipee ... F-6
West Rindge ... K-4
West Rumney ... F-5
West Stewartstown ... B-5
West Swanzey ... J-4
Westmoreland ... J-3
Westville ... J-6
Willey House ... E-5
Wilton ... J-5
Winchester ... J-3
Windsor ... H-4
Winnisquam ... G-5
Wolfeboro ... G-6
Wonalancet ... F-6
Woodman ... F-7
Woodsville ... E-4

NEW JERSEY
Pages 56-57
Population: 7,364,823
Capital: Trenton
Land Area: 7,468 sq. mi.

Absecon ... M-6
Adelphia ... H-7
Allamuchy ... C-4
Allendale ... Pg. 126, D-4
Allentown ... H-6
Alloway ... M-2
Alpha ... E-3
Alpine ... B-6
  Vicinity ... Pg. 126, F-7
Andover ... C-5
Asbury Park ... G-8
Atlantic City ... N-7
Atlantic Highlands ... F-8
Atsion ... K-5
Audubon ... K-4
Audubon Park ... Pg. 134, F-7
Avalon ... P-5
Avenel ... Pg. 127, P-1
Baptistown ... F-4
Barnegat ... K-8
Barnegat Light ... K-8
Barrington ... Pg. 134, G-7
Bay Head ... H-8
Bay Point ... N-3
Bayonne ... E-7
  Vicinity ... Pg. 127, M-4
Beach Haven ... M-7
Beachwood ... J-7
Bedminster ... E-5
Beesley's Pt. ... N-5
Belleplain ... N-4
Belleville ... D-7
  Vicinity ... Pg. 127, J-3
Bellmawr ... K-3
  Vicinity ... Pg. 134, G-6
Belmar ... H-8
Belvidere ... D-3
Bergenfield ... C-8
  Vicinity ... Pg. 126, F-6
Berlin ... K-4
Bernardsville ... D-6
Beverly ... H-4
  Vicinity ... Pg. 134, C-9
Blairstown ... C-4
Blawenburg ... F-5
Bloomfield ... D-7
  Vicinity ... Pg. 127, J-3
Bloomingdale ... C-7
  Vicinity ... Pg. 126, D-1
Bloomsbury ... E-3
Bogota ... Pg. 126, H-6
Boonton ... C-7
Bordentown ... H-5
Bound Brook ... F-6
Bradley Beach ... H-8
Branchville ... B-5
Bridgeboro ... Pg. 134, D-9
Bridgeport ... K-2
Bridgeton ... M-2
Brielle ... H-8
Brigantine ... N-6
Broadway ... D-3
Brooklawn ... Pg. 134, G-4
Browns Mills ... J-6
Budd Lake ... C-5
Buena ... M-4
Burlington ... H-4
Buttzville ... D-3
Caldwell ... Pg. 127, H-1
Califon ... E-4
Camden ... J-3
  Vicinity ... Pg. 134, G-6
Cape May ... Q-4
Cape May Court House ... Q-4

Cedar Bridge ... K-7
Cedar Grove ... J-8
  Vicinity ... Pg. 126, G-2
Cedarville ... N-3
Centerton ... M-3
Chatham ... D-6
Chatsworth ... K-6
Cherry Hill ... J-3
  Vicinity ... Pg. 134, F-7
Chesilhurst ... K-4
Chester ... D-5
Cinnaminson ... J-4
Clark ... Pg. 127, N-1
Clarksburg ... H-6
Clarksville ... G-5
Clayton ... L-3
Clermont ... P-5
Cliffside Park ... Pg. 127, J-6
Clifton ... D-8
  Vicinity ... Pg. 126, H-3
Clinton ... E-4
Closter ... Pg. 126, E-7
Coffins Corner ... Pg. 134, G-9
Colesville ... A-5
Collingswood ... J-3
  Vicinity ... Pg. 134, F-7
Colonia ... Pg. 127, P-1
Colts Neck ... G-7
Columbus ... H-5
Colwick ... Pg. 134, E-8
Corbin City ... N-5
Coxs Corner ... Pg. 134, F-10
Cranbury ... G-6
Cranford ... Pg. 127, M-1
Cresskill ... Pg. 126, E-7
Croton ... F-4
Crestwood Village ... J-7
Cumberland ... N-4
Deacons ... J-5
Deerfield ... M-3
Delaware ... D-2
Demarest ... Pg. 126, F-7
Denville ... C-6
Dividing Creek ... N-3
Dover ... C-6
Dumont ... Pg. 126, F-6
Dunellen ... E-6
East Newark ... Pg. 127, K-4
East Orange ... D-7
  Vicinity ... Pg. 127, J-3
East Rutherford ... Pg. 127, H-4
East Vineland ... M-4
Eatontown ... G-8
Edgewater Park ... J-4
Edinburg ... G-5
Edison ... F-6
Egg Harbor ... M-6
Elizabeth ... E-7
  Vicinity ... Pg. 127, M-3
Elmer ... L-3
Elmwood Park ... Pg. 126, G-4
Elwood ... M-5
Emerson ... Pg. 126, E-6
Englewood ... C-9
  Vicinity ... Pg. 126, F-6
Englewood Cliffs ... A-6
Englishtown ... G-7
Erskine ... Pg. 126, B-2
Estell Manor ... N-5
Everittstown ... E-3
Ewingville ... G-5
Fair Haven ... G-8
Fair Lawn ... C-8
  Vicinity ... Pg. 126, G-5
Fairfield ... Pg. 126, G-1
Fairmount ... D-5
Fairton ... N-3
Farmingdale ... H-7
Flemington ... F-4
Florham Park ... D-7
  Vicinity ... Pg. 127, J-1
Folsom ... L-4
Fords ... Pg. 127, P-1
Forked River ... K-8
Fort Dix ... J-6
Fort Lee ... D-9
  Vicinity ... Pg. 126, H-6
Four Mile ... F-6
Franklin ... B-6
Franklin Lakes ... Pg. 126, D-4
Franklinville ... L-3
Fredon ... C-5
Freehold ... G-7
Freewood Acres ... H-7
Frenchtown ... F-4
Garfield ... C-8
  Vicinity ... Pg. 126, G-4
Garwood ... Pg. 127, M-1
Gibbsboro ... K-4
Gilford Park ... J-8
Glassboro ... L-3
Glen Gardner ... E-4
Glen Ridge ... Pg. 127, H-3
Glen Rock ... Pg. 126, F-4
Glendale ... Pg. 134, G-8
Gloucester City ... K-3
  Vicinity ... Pg. 134, G-5
Gouldtown ... M-3
Great Meadows ... D-4
Green Bank ... K-6
Guttenberg ... Pg. 127, J-5
Hackensack ... Pg. 127, C-8
  Vicinity ... Pg. 126, G-6
Hackettstown ... D-4
Haddon Heights ... Pg. 134, G-7

Haddonfield ... K-4
  Vicinity ... Pg. 134, F-8
Hainesburg ... C-4
Haledon ... C-7
  Vicinity ... Pg. 126, F-3
Hamburg ... B-6
Hamilton Sq. ... G-6
Hammonton ... L-5
Hampton ... E-4
Hanover ... D-6
Harmony ... D-3
Harrington Park ... Pg. 126, E-6
Harrison ... Pg. 127, K-1
Harrisonville ... L-1
Harvey Cedars ... L-8
Hasbrouck Hts. ... Pg. 126, G-5
Haworth ... Pg. 126, E-6
Hawthorne ... C-8
  Vicinity ... Pg. 126, F-3
Helmetta ... G-7
Hewitt ... A-6
  Vicinity ... Pg. 126, B-1
High Bridge ... E-4
Highland Park ... F-7
Highlands ... F-9
Hightstown ... G-6
Hillsdale ... B-6
  Vicinity ... Pg. 126, D-5
Ho-Ho-Kus ... Pg. 126, E-4
Hoboken ... D-7
  Vicinity ... Pg. 127, K-5
Holmdel ... G-7
Hopatcong ... C-5
Hope ... C-4
Hopewell ... F-5
Hurdtown ... C-6
Irvington ... D-7
  Vicinity ... Pg. 127, L-2
Iselin ... Pg. 127, P-1
Island Heights ... J-8
Jamesburg ... G-6
Jersey City ... D-8
  Vicinity ... Pg. 127, H-3
Johnsonburg ... C-4
Keansburg ... F-8
Kearny ... D-8
  Vicinity ... Pg. 127, K-4
Kenilworth ... E-7
  Vicinity ... Pg. 127, M-1
Kenvil ... C-6
Keyport ... G-8
Kinnelon ... C-6
Lafayette ... B-5
Lakehurst ... J-7
Lakeside ... B-7
Lakewood ... H-7
Lambertville ... G-4
Larisons Cor. ... F-4
Laurence Harbor ... F-7
Lavallette ... J-8
Lawnside ... Pg. 134, G-8
Lawrence ... G-5
Lebanon ... E-4
Lenola ... Pg. 134, D-8
Liberty Cor. ... E-5
Lincoln Park ... C-7
  Vicinity ... Pg. 126, F-1
Linden ... E-7
  Vicinity ... Pg. 127, N-2
Lindenwold ... K-4
Linwood ... N-6
Little Egg Harbor ... M-7
Little Falls ... Pg. 126, G-2
Little Ferry ... Pg. 126, H-5
Livingston ... Pg. 127, J-1
Lodi ... Pg. 126, G-4
Long Branch ... G-9
Long Valley ... D-5
Longport ... N-6
Lumberton ... J-5
Lyndhurst ... Pg. 127, J-4
Madison ... D-6
Magnolia ... F-4
Mahwah ... A-6
Manahawkin ... L-7
Manalapan ... G-6
Manasquan ... H-8
Mantoloking ... J-8
Manville ... F-5
Maple Shade ... J-3
Maplewood ... Pg. 127, K-2
Marcella ... C-6
Margate City ... N-6
Marlboro ... G-7
Marlton ... Pg. 134, E-9
Marshallville ... N-5
Matawan ... F-7
Maurice River ... N-4
Mays Landing ... M-5
Maywood ... Pg. 126, G-5
McAfee ... B-6
Medford ... K-5
Medford Lakes ... K-5
Mendham ... D-6
Merchantville ... Pg. 134, E-7
Metuchen ... F-6
Mickleton ... K-3
Middletown ... Pg. 134, G-7
Midland Park ... Pg. 126, E-4
Milburn ... Pg. 127, K-1
Milford ... E-3
Millside Heights ... Pg. 134, D-9
Millstone ... F-6
Milltown ... F-6
Millville ... N-3
Monmouth Jct. ... G-6
Monroe ... Pg. 126, G-6
Montague ... A-5
Montclaire ... Pg. 127, H-3
Montvale ... Pg. 126, D-5

Montville ... C-7
Moorestown ... J-4
  Vicinity ... Pg. 134, E-8
Morris ... Pg. 134, E-7
Morris Plains ... D-6
Morristown ... D-6
Morrisville ... E-3
Mt. Arlington ... C-6
Mt. Ephraim ... Pg. 134, G-6
Mt. Holly ... J-5
Mt. Laurel ... Pg. 134, F-10
Mullica Hill ... L-3
National Park ... K-3
  Vicinity ... Pg. 134, G-6
Neptune ... H-8
Neshanic ... F-5
Netcong ... C-5
New Brunswick ... F-6
New Egypt ... J-6
New Gretna ... E-6
New Milford ... Pg. 126, F-6
New Providence ... E-6
New Rochelle ... Pg. 126, G-8
Newark ... D-8
  Vicinity ... Pg. 127, K-3
Newfield ... M-4
Newfoundland ... B-6
Newton ... B-5
North Arlington ... Pg. 127, J-4
North Bergen ... Pg. 127, J-6
North Caldwell ... Pg. 126, G-2
North Cape May ... Q-4
North Dennis ... P-4
North Haledon ... C-7
  Vicinity ... Pg. 126, F-3
North Wildwood ... Q-5
Northfield ... N-6
Northvale ... Pg. 126, D-7
Norwood ... C-9
  Vicinity ... Pg. 127, E-7
Nutley ... D-8
  Vicinity ... Pg. 127, H-3
Oakland ... Pg. 126, D-3
Oaklyn ... Pg. 134, F-7
Ocean City ... N-6
Ocean Gate ... J-8
Oceanport ... G-8
Ogdensburg ... B-5
Old Bridge ... F-7
Old Tappan ... Pg. 126, D-6
Oldwick ... E-4
Oradell ... Pg. 126, F-6
Orange ... D-7
  Vicinity ... Pg. 127, K-2
Oxford ... D-4
Palisades Park ... Pg. 126, H-6
Palmyra ... Pg. 134, D-7
Paramus ... C-8
  Vicinity ... Pg. 126, F-5
Park Ridge ... Pg. 126, D-5
Parry ... Pg. 134, D-8
Parsippany-Troy Hill ... D-6
Passaic ... D-8
  Vicinity ... Pg. 126, H-4
Paterson ... C-7
  Vicinity ... Pg. 126, F-3
Paulsboro ... K-2
Peapack ... E-5
Pemberton ... J-5
Pennington ... G-5
Penns Grove ... L-2
Pennsauken ... Pg. 134, E-7
Pennsville ... L-1
Penny Pot ... M-5
Pequannock ... Pg. 126, F-1
Perth Amboy ... Pg. 127, Q-2
Phillipsburg ... E-3
Pine Beach ... H-1
Pine Grove ... Pg. 134, G-10
Pine Hill ... K-4
Pitman ... L-3
Pittstown ... F-4
Plainfield ... E-6
Plainsboro ... G-6
Pleasantville ... N-6
Pole Tavern ... L-3
Pomona ... N-6
Pompton Lakes ... C-7
  Vicinity ... Pg. 126, D-1
Pompton Plains ... B-6
  Vicinity ... Pg. 126, E-1
Port Elizabeth ... N-4
Port Norris ... P-3
Port Reading ... Pg. 127, P-2
Port Republic ... M-6
Princeton ... G-5
Princeton Jct. ... G-5
Prospect Park ... C-8
Pt. Pleasant ... H-8
Pt. Pleasant Beach ... H-8
Quinton ... M-2
Rahway ... E-7
  Vicinity ... Pg. 127, N-2
Ramsey ... Pg. 126, C-4
Raritan ... E-5
Readington ... E-5
Red Bank ... G-8
  Vicinity ... Pg. 134, G-8
Red Lion ... K-5
Ridgefield ... Pg. 127, H-6
Ridgefield Park ... Pg. 126, G-6
Ridgewood ... C-8
  Vicinity ... Pg. 126, B-2
Ringwood ... B-7
Rio Grande ... Q-5

NEW JERSEY

River Edge . Pg. 126, F-5
River Vale B-6
  Vicinity . . . . . Pg. 126, E-6
Riverdale C-7
Riverside J-4
Riverton J-4
  Vicinity . . . . . Pg. 134, D-8
Robertsville G-7
Rochelle Park Pg. 126, F-5
Rockaway C-7
Rockleigh . Pg. 126, E-7
Rocky Hill F-5
Roosevelt H-6
Roseland . . Pg. 127, H-1
Roselle E-7
  Vicinity . . . . . Pg. 127, M-2
Roselle Park E-7
  Vicinity . . . . . Pg. 127, M-2
Ross Corners B-5
Rumson G-8
Runnemede K-3
  Vicinity . . . . . Pg. 134, G-7
Rutherford . Pg. 127, H-4
Saddle Brook Pg. 126, G-5
Saddle River B-6
  Vicinity . . . . . Pg. 126, D-4
Salem M-1
Sayreville F-7
Sea Isle City P-5
Seabrook M-3
Seaside Heights . . . J-8
Seaside Park J-8
Seaville P-5
Secaucus . . Pg. 127, J-5
Sewaren . . . Pg. 127, P-2
Sharptown L-2
Shiloh M-2
Ship Bottom L-8
Shrewsbury G-8
Silverton J-8
Smithburg H-7
Smithville M-6
Somerdale K-3
Somers Pt. N-6
Somerville F-5
South Amboy F-7
South Brunswick . . F-6
South Dennis P-5
South Hackensack
. . . . Pg. 126, G-5
South Orange
. . . . Pg. 127, K-2
South Plainfield . . . E-6
South River F-6
South Toms River . . J-7
Sparta C-5
Speedwell D-4
Spotswood F-6
Spring Lakes Heights H-8
Spring Mills E-3
Springdale B-5
  Vicinity . . . . . Pg. 134, G-8
Springfield . Pg. 127, L-1
Stanhope C-5
Stockholm B-6
Stockton F-4
Stone Harbor Q-5
Stratford K-4
Summit D-7
Surf City L-8
Sussex B-6
Swedesboro K-2
Tabernacle L-6
Tavistock . . Pg. 134, G-8
Teaneck . . . Pg. 126, G-6
Tenafly C-9
  Vicinity . . . . . Pg. 126, F-7
Teterboro . . Pg. 126, H-5
Tinton Falls J-7
Toms River J-7
Totowa C-7
  Vicinity . . . . . Pg. 126, G-3
Trenton G-5
Tuckerton L-7
Tuttles Cor. F-8
Union Beach F-7
  Vicinity . . . . . Pg. 127, L-2
Union City D-8
  Vicinity . . . . . Pg. 127, K-5
Upper Saddle River
. . . . Pg. 126, C-4
Ventnor City N-6
Vernon B-6
Verona . . . . Pg. 127, H-2
Villas Q-5
Vineland M-4
Waldwick C-7
  Vicinity . . . . . Pg. 126, D-4
Wallington . Pg. 126, H-4
Wanaque B-7
  Vicinity . . . . . Pg. 126, D-1
Waretown K-8
Warren E-6
Warren Grove K-7
Washington D-4
Washington Crossing G-4
Watchung C-8
Wayne C-8
  Vicinity . . . . . Pg. 126, F-2
Weehawken . Pg. 127, K-5
Welchville L-2
Wells Mills K-7
Wenonah K-3
West Caldwell
. . . . Pg. 126, H-1
West Cape May . . . Q-4
West Long Branch . . H-8
West Milford B-6
West New York
. . . . Pg. 127, J-6
West Orange C-7
  Vicinity . . . . . Pg. 127, J-2
West Patterson . . . C-7
West Portal E-4

Westfield E-7
Westville K-3
  Vicinity . . . . . Pg. 134, G-8
Westwood C-8
  Vicinity . . . . . Pg. 126, E-6
Weymouth M-6
Wharton C-6
White Horse H-5
Whitehouse E-5
Whitesboro Q-4
Whitesville H-7
Wildwood Q-5
Wildwood Crest . . . Q-5
Williamstown L-4
Winslow L-4
Wood Ridge Pg. 126, H-5
Woodbine P-4
Woodbridge C-6
Woodbury K-3
Woodbury Heights . . K-3
Woodcliff Lake
. . . . Pg. 126, D-5
Woodlynne . Pg. 134, F-6
Woods Tavern F-5
Woodstown L-2
Woodsville G-4
Wrightstown J-6
Yardville H-5

NEW MEXICO
Page 62
Population: 1,302,894
Capital: Santa Fe
Land Area: 121,335 sq. mi.

Abbott C-5
Abeytas E-3
Abiquiu C-3
Abo E-4
Alameda D-3
Alamo E-2
Alamogordo G-4
Albuquerque D-3
Alcalde C-4
Algodones D-3
Alma G-1
Alto G-4
Amalia B-4
Ambrosia Lake D-2
Amistad C-7
Anapra J-3
Ancho F-4
Angus G-4
Animas J-1
Antelope Wells J-1
Apache Creek F-1
Aqua Fria D-4
Arabela E-6
Aragon F-1
Arch E-7
Archuleta B-2
Armijo D-3
Arrey H-2
Arroyo Hondo B-4
Arroyo Seco B-4
Artesia G-6
Atoka H-6
Aztec B-2
Bayard H-2
Beklabito B-1
Belen E-3
Bellview D-7
Bent G-4
Berino J-3
Bernal D-5
Bernalillo D-3
Bernardo E-3
Bingham F-4
Black Lake C-5
Black River Village . H-6
Black Rock D-2
Blanco B-2
Blanco Trading Post . C-2
Bloomfield B-2
Bluewater D-2
Bosque Farms E-3
Brazos B-3
Broadview E-7
Buckhorn G-1
Bueyeros C-6
Caballo G-3
Canjilon B-3
Canon C-3
Canon Plaza B-4
Capitan F-4
Caprock F-7
Capulin B-6
Carlsbad H-6
Carlsbad Caverns . . H-6
Carrizozo F-4
Causey F-7
Cebolla B-3
Cebolleta D-2
Cebolletita D-2
Cedar Crest D-4
Cedar Hill B-2
Cedarvale E-4
Central H-2
Cerro B-4
Chacon C-5
Chama B-3
Chamberino J-3
Chamizal J-3
Chaparral J-4
Chililí D-4
Chimayo C-4
Cimarron B-5
Clapham C-6
Claunch F-4
Clayton B-7

Cleveland C-4
Cliff G-1
Clines Corners D-4
Cloudcroft G-4
Clovis E-7
Cochiti Lake C-3
Columbus J-2
Conchas D-6
Coolidge D-1
Corona E-4
Costilla B-4
Cotton City J-1
Counselors C-2
Coyote C-3
Coyote Canyon . . . C-1
Crossroads F-7
Crownpoint D-1
Cruzville F-1
Crystal C-1
Cuba C-3
Cuchillo G-3
Cuervo D-6
Cundiyo C-4
Datil F-2
Deming H-2
Derry H-3
Des Moines B-6
Dexter G-6
Dilia D-5
Domingo D-3
Dona Ana H-3
Dora F-7
Dulce B-3
Dunken G-5
Duran E-5
Dwyer H-2
Eagle Nest B-5
Edgewood D-4
El Morro D-2
El Paso Gap J-5
El Porvenir D-1
El Rito C-4
El Vado B-3
Elephant Butte G-3
Elida E-6
Elk G-5
Elk Silver E-6
Elkins E-6
Embudo C-4
Encino E-5
Endee D-7
Engle G-3
Ensenada B-3
Escobosa D-3
Escondida F-3
Espanola C-4
Estancia E-4
Eunice H-7
Fairacres H-3
Farley B-6
Farmington B-1
Fence Lake E-1
Flora Vista B-1
Floyd E-7
Folsom B-6
Forrest E-5
Fort Stanton G-4
Fort Sumner E-6
Fort Wingate D-1
Frijoles C-4
Gage H-2
Galisteo D-4
Gallina C-3
Gallinas C-4
Gallup D-1
Gamerco D-1
Garfield H-3
Gila H-1
Gladstone B-6
Glenrio D-7
Glenwood G-1
Golden D-4
Grady D-7
Gran Quivira E-4
Grants D-2
Greenfield G-6
Grenville B-6
Guadalupita C-5
Hachita J-2
Hagerman G-6
Hanover H-2
Hatch H-3
Hayden C-7
Hernandez C-4
High Rolls G-4
Hilburn City G-7
Hill H-3
Hillsboro H-2
Hobbs G-7
Holman C-5
Hondo G-5
Hope G-6
House E-6
Humble City H-7
Hurley H-2
Jal H-7
Jarales E-3
Jemez Springs C-3
Jicarilla F-4
Kenna E-6
Kingston H-2
Kirtland B-1
Knowles G-7
La Cienega D-4
La Cueva C-5
La Jara C-3
La Joya E-3
La Luz G-4
La Madera C-4
La Mesa J-3
La Mesilla J-3
La Plata B-1
La Puente B-3
La Union J-3

Laborcita F-3
Laguna E-3
Lake Arthur G-6
Lake Valley C-2
Lamy C-4
Las Cruces H-3
Las Nutrias E-3
Las Palomas H-3
Las Vegas C-5
Ledoux C-5
Lemitar F-3
Lincoln G-4
Lindrith C-3
Lingo F-7
Loco Hills G-6
Logan D-7
Lordsburg H-1
Los Alamos C-4
Los Cerrillos D-4
Los Chavez E-3
Los Lunas E-3
Los Ojos B-3
Los Padillas D-3
Loving H-6
Lovington G-7
Luis Lopez F-3
Lumberton B-3
Luna F-1
Madrid D-4
Magdalena F-3
Malaga H-6
Maljamar G-6
Manuelito D-1
Manzano E-4
Maxwell B-5
Mayhill G-5
McAlister E-6
McCartys D-2
McDonald G-7
Melrose E-5
Mentmore D-1
Mesa E-6
Mescalero G-4
Mesita D-3
Mesquite H-3
Mexican Springs . . C-1
Miami B-5
Miera D-4
Milan D-2
Mills C-6
Milnesand E-7
Mimbres H-2
Mineral Hill D-4
Mogollon G-1
Monero B-3
Montezuma C-5
Monticello G-2
Montoya D-6
Monument H-7
Mora C-5
Moriarty D-4
Mosquero C-6
Mountainair E-4
Mt. Dora B-6
Mule Creek G-1
Nadine H-7
Nageezi C-2
Nara Visa C-7
Naschitti C-1
Navajo C-1
Navajo C-1
Newcomb C-1
Newkirk D-6
Ocate C-5
Oil Center H-7
Ojo Caliente C-4
Ojo Feliz C-5
Old Horse Springs . F-2
Omega F-3
Organ H-3
Orogrande H-4
Oscuro F-4
Paguate D-2
Paraje D-2
Pastura E-5
Pecos D-4
Pena Blanca D-3
Penasco C-4
Pep F-7
Peralta E-3
Pescado D-1
Picacho G-5
Pie Town F-2
Pine Lodge E-6
Pinon G-5
Pinos Altos H-1
Placita G-2
Placitas D-3
Pleasant Hill E-7
Pleasanton G-1
Pojoaque C-4
Portales E-7
Prewitt D-1
Pueblo D-1
Pueblo Bonito C-2
Puerto De Luna . . . E-5
Punta E-4
Quay D-6
Quemado E-1
Questa B-4
Radium Springs . . . H-3
Ragland D-6
Rainsville C-5
Ramah D-1
Ramon E-5
Ranchos De Taos . . B-4
Ranchvale E-7
Raton B-5
Rayado B-5
Red Hill F-1
Red River B-4
Red Rock H-1
Regina C-3
Reserve F-1

Rincon H-3
Rinconada C-4
Rio Rancho D-3
Riverside G-6
Rociada C-4
Rodeo J-1
Rogers F-7
Romeroville D-5
Roswell F-6
Rowe D-4
Roy D-4
Ruidoso G-4
Ruidoso Downs . . . G-4
Rutheron B-3
Sabinal E-3
Sacramento H-4
Saint Vrain E-7
Salem H-3
Salt Lake E-1
San Acacia E-3
San Antonio F-3
San Antonito D-4
San Fidel D-2
San Ignacio D-4
San Jon D-7
San Juan H-2
San Lorenzo H-2
San Mateo D-2
San Miguel D-4
San Patricio G-4
San Rafael D-2
Santa Cruz C-4
Santa Fe C-4
Santa Rita H-2
Santa Rosa D-5
Sapello C-5
Sedan C-6
Sena D-5
Seneca B-7
Separ H-1
Seven Rivers H-6
Shadybrook C-4
Sheep Springs C-1
Shiprock B-1
Silver City H-1
Socorro F-3
Solano C-6
Springer B-5
Standing Rock D-1
Stanley D-4
Sunset C-4
Sunshine J-2
Sunspot H-4
Taiban E-6
Tajique D-4
Talpa B-4
Taos B-4
Tatum G-7
Terrero C-4
Tesuque C-4
Thoreau D-1
Three Rivers G-4
Tierra Amarilla B-3
Tierra Monte C-4
Tijeras D-4
Tinnie G-5
Tohatchi C-1
Tolar E-6
Tome E-3
Torreon D-3
Torreon E-3
Tres Piedras B-4
Tres Ritos C-4
Truchas C-4
Trujillo D-5
Truth or Consequences
. . . . G-3
Tucumcari D-6
Tularosa G-4
Turley B-2
Turn E-3
Tyrone H-1
Ute Park B-5
Vado J-3
Valencia E-3
Vallecitos C-3
Valmora C-5
Variadero D-5
Vaughn E-5
Veguita E-3
Velarde C-4
Villanueva D-5
Virden H-1
Wagon Mound C-5
Watrous C-5
Weed G-5
Wheatland D-7
White Horse D-2
White Oaks F-4
White Rock C-4
White Sands Missile
Range G-4
Whites City H-6
Whitewater D-1
Willard E-4
Williamsburg G-3
Winston G-2
Yeso E-5
Youngsville C-3

NEW YORK
Pages 58-61
Population: 17,558,072
Capital: Albany
Land Area: 47,377 sq. mi.

Adams F-12
Addison N-8
Afton M-13
Airmont . . Pg. 126, B-4
Akron J-5

Albany K-18
Albion H-6
Alden K-5
Alexander K-5
Alexandria Bay . D-12
Alfred M-7
Allegany N-5
Almond M-7
Altamont K-18
Altmar G-12
Amagansett C-9
Amenia O-19
Ames K-16
Amherst . . Pg. 94, C-5
Amityville . . Pg. 129, N-16
Amsterdam J-18
Andes M-16
Andover N-7
Angelica M-6
Angola L-3
Angola-on-the-Lake . L-3
  Vicinity . . Pg. 94, K-1
Antwerp D-13
Apalachin N-12
Arcade L-5
Archville . . Pg. 126, B-8
Ardsley . . . Pg. 126, D-9
Argyle H-20
Arkport M-7
Arlington O-19
Armonk . . . Pg. 128, C-11
Armor . . . . Pg. 94, H-5
Asharoken . . Pg. 128, G-17
Astoria . . . Pg. 127, M-6
Athens M-19
Athol Springs Pg. 94, H-4
Atlantic Beach E-4
Attica K-5
Atwell G-15
Auburn K-10
Aurora K-10
Avoca M-8
Avon K-7
Babylon E-4
  Vicinity . . Pg. 129, P-13
Bainbridge M-13
Baldwin E-4
  Vicinity . . Pg. 129, P-13
Baldwinsville J-11
Ballston Spa J-18
Balmville A-3
Bardonia . . Pg. 126, B-6
Barker J-6
Barneveld H-14
Barnum Island
. . . . Pg. 129, Q-13
Batavia J-6
Bath M-8
Bay Park . . Pg. 129, P-12
Bay Ridge . Pg. 127, M-6
Bay Shore E-4
  Vicinity . . Pg. 129, M-19
Bay View . . Pg. 94, H-4
Bayberry J-11
Bayside . . . Pg. 127, K-10
Bayville D-5
  Vicinity . . Pg. 129, H-14
Beach Ridge . Pg. 94, A-4
Beacon A-3
Bedford . . . Pg. 128, B-13
Bedford Hills Pg. 128, A-11
Bellevue . . Pg. 94, E-6
Bellmore . . Pg. 129, N-14
Belmont N-6
Bemus Pt. N-2
Benson Hurst Pg. 127, N-5
Bergen J-6
Berkholtz . . Pg. 94, A-3
Bethpage D-5
  Vicinity . . Pg. 129, L-15
Big Flats N-9
Big Tree . . Pg. 94, G-5
Binghamton N-12
Black River E-13
Blasdell E-4
  Vicinity . . Pg. 94, G-4
Blauvelt . . . Pg. 126, C-7
Bloomingburgh . . . A-2
Bloomingdale C-18
Bloomington N-18
Blossom . . Pg. 94, F-7
Bolivar N-6
Boonville H-14
Bovsen Bay J-11
Bowmansville Pg. 94, D-7
Brasher Falls B-16
Brentwood D-6
  Vicinity . . Pg. 129, L-19
Brewerton J-11
Brewster B-4
Briarcliff Manor . . C-4
Bridgehampton . . C-9
Bridgewater K-14
Brighton . . Pg. 138, K-4
Brightwaters Pg. 138, M-19
Broadalbin J-18
Brockport J-6
Brocton M-2
Bronx . . . . Pg. 126, D-9
  Vicinity . . Pg. 129, K-14
Brooklyn . . Pg. 127, L-7
  Vicinity . . Pg. 129, K-14
Brownsville E-12
Brushton B-16
Buchanan B-3
Buffalo J-4
  Vicinity . . . . . . Pg. 94
Burdett M-10
Burke B-17

Camden H-13
Camillus J-11
Canajoharie K-16
Canandaigua K-8
Canarsie . . Pg. 127, M-8
Canaseraga M-7
Canastota J-13
Candor M-11
Canisteo M-7
Canton C-14
Cape Vincent E-11
Carnegie . . Pg. 94, H-4
Carthage E-13
Cassadaga M-2
Castile L-6
Castleton Corners
. . . . Pg. 127, N-4
Castleton-on-Hudson L-18
Castorland F-13
Cato J-10
Catskill M-19
Cattaraugus M-4
Cayuga K-10
Cayuga Heights . . L-11
Cazenovia K-13
Cedarhurst . Pg. 129, P-11
Celoron N-2
Center Moriches . . D-7
Center Port . Pg. 129, H-17
Centereach D-6
Central Islip . Pg. 129, K-20
Central Nyack
. . . . Pg. 126, C-7
Central Square . . . H-12
Central Valley B-3
Champlain A-19
Chappaqua . . Pg. 126, A-9
Chateaugay A-17
Chatham M-19
Chaumont E-12
Cheektowaga Pg. 94, E-6
Chelsea . . . Pg. 127, N-3
Cherry Creek M-3
Cherry Valley K-16
Chester B-3
Chili Center . Pg. 138, K-2
Chippawa (Canada)
. . . . Pg. 94, B-1
Chittenango J-13
Churchville J-7
Clarence Center . . J-4
Clarkstown . Pg. 126, B-6
Claverack M-19
Clayton D-12
Clayville J-14
Cleveland H-13
Clifton Heights Pg. 94, H-3
Clifton Knolls K-18
Clifton Springs . . . K-8
Clinton J-14
Clintondale O-18
Clyde J-10
Cobleskill K-17
Cohocton L-8
Cohoes K-19
Cold Brook H-15
Cold Springs J-11
Coldspring Harbor
. . . . Pg. 129, J-16
College Point Pg. 127, J-9
Colonie K-18
Commack . . Pg. 129, J-18
Coney Island Pg. 127, P-6
Constableville G-14
Constantia H-12
Cooperstown K-15
Copenhagen F-13
Copiague . . Pg. 129, N-17
Coram D-6
Corfu K-5
Corinth H-18
Corning N-9
Cornwall-on-Hudson . A-3
Cortland L-11
County Knolls J-18
Cove Neck . Pg. 129, J-15
Coxsackie M-19
Crescent Beach
. . . . Pg. 94, D-3
Crescent Park (Canada)
. . . . Pg. 138, F-3
Crittenden . . Pg. 138, K-3
Croton-on-Hudson . B-3
Crystal Beach (Canada)
. . . . Pg. 94, F-1
Cuba N-5
Cutchogue C-8
Dannemora B-18
Dansville L-7
DeRuyter K-13
Deer Park D-6
  Vicinity . . Pg. 129, L-18
Deferiet E-13
Delanson K-17
Delevan M-4
Delhi M-15
Delmar L-18
Depew . . . . Pg. 94, E-6
  Vicinity . . Pg. 94, E-6
Deposit N-14
Derby . . . . Pg. 94, G-2
Dexter E-12
Dobbs Ferry C-3
  Vicinity . . Pg. 126, D-8
Dolgeville J-16
Dongan Hills Pg. 127, N-4
Dover Plains O-19
Dresden L-9
Dryden L-11
Duells Corners Pg. 94, H-6
Dundee L-9

Dunkirk M-2
Earlville K-13
East Amherst Pg. 94, B-6
East Aurora K-4
East Bloomfield . . . K-8
East Glenville J-18
East Hamburg Pg. 94, H-6
East Hampton C-9
East Hills . . Pg. 129, K-13
East Marion C-9
East Meadow
. . . . Pg. 129, M-14
East New York
. . . . Pg. 127, M-8
East Northport D-5
East Penfield Pg. 138, J-7
East Quogue D-8
East Randolph . . . N-3
East Rochester . . . J-7
  Vicinity . . Pg. 138, J-6
East Rockaway
. . . . Pg. 129, P-12
East Seneca . Pg. 94, F-6
East View . . Pg. 126, C-9
Eastchester . Pg. 126, E-9
Eatons Neck C-7
Eatons Neck
. . . . Pg. 128, H-17
Ebenezer . . Pg. 94, F-6
Echota . . . . Pg. 94, A-2
Eden L-4
Eden Valley . Pg. 94, K-4
Edgemere . . Pg. 129, Q-11
Edgewater . Pg. 94, B-3
Edwards D-14
Eggertsville . Pg. 94, C-5
Elba J-6
Elbridge J-11
Ellenville N-17
Ellicott . . . . Pg. 94, H-6
Ellicott Heights Pg. 94, H-7
Ellicottville M-4
Ellisburg F-12
Elma K-4
  Vicinity . . Pg. 94, F-7
Elma Center . Pg. 94, F-7
Elmira N-10
Elmira Hts. N-10
Elmont . . . Pg. 129, N-12
Elmsford . . Pg. 126, C-9
Elsers Corners Pg. 94, A-7
Elwood . . . Pg. 129, J-17
Endicott N-12
Endwell N-12
Erie Beach (Canada)
. . . . Pg. 94, E-3
Esperance K-17
Evans . . . . Pg. 94, K-2
Evans Mills E-12
Fabius K-12
Fair Haven H-10
Fairport J-8
  Vicinity . . Pg. 138, K-6
Falconer N-3
Farmingdale Pg. 129, M-16
Farnham L-3
Fayetteville J-12
Fernwood H-5
Ferry Village Pg. 94, C-3
Fillmore M-6
Firthcliffe A-3
Fishkill A-3
Flatbush . . Pg. 127, M-7
Fleischmanns N-17
Floral Park . Pg. 129, M-11
Florida B-2
Flower Hill . Pg. 129, K-12
Flushing . . Pg. 127, K-9
Fonda J-17
Forest Hills . Pg. 127, L-9
Forest Lawn Pg. 138, F-5
Forestville M-3
Fort Ann G-19
Fort Edward H-19
Fort Erie (Canada)
. . . . Pg. 94, E-3
Fort Erie North (Canada)
. . . . Pg. 94, D-3
Fort Johnson J-17
Fort Plain K-16
Fort Salonga
. . . . Pg. 128, H-18
Frankfort J-15
Franklin M-15
Franklinville M-5
Freeport E-4
  Vicinity . . Pg. 129, P-14
Frewsburg N-3
Friendship N-6
Fulton H-11
Fultonville J-17
Gainesville L-6
Galway J-18
Gang Mills N-9
Garden City Pg. 129, M-12
Gardenville . Pg. 94, F-6
Gate . . . . . Pg. 138, J-2
Geneseo K-7
Geneva K-9
Getzville . . Pg. 94, B-6
Gilbertsville L-14
Glasco N-18
Glen Cove D-4
  Vicinity . . Pg. 129, H-13
Glen Head . Pg. 129, K-13
Glen Park E-12
Glenham A-3
Glens Falls H-19
Gloversville J-17
Goldens Bridge . . B-4
Goshen B-2
Gouverneur D-14
Gowanda M-3

NEW YORK

NEW YORK

Grand View Heights . . . . Pg. 138, F-3
Grandview-on-Hudson . . . . Pg. 126, C-8
Grandyle Village . . . . Pg. 94, A-3
Granville G-20
Great Kills . . . Pg. 127, P-4
Great Neck D-4
Vicinity . . . Pg. 129, K-11
Greece J-7
Vicinity . . . Pg. 138, G-2
Green Island K-19
Green Lawn . Pg. 129, J-17
Green Point . Pg. 127, K-7
Greenburgh . Pg. 126, D-9
Greene M-13
Greenport C-9
Greenwich J-20
Greenwood Lake B-2
Griffins Mills . Pg. 94, J-2
Groton L-11
Hadley H-19
Hagaman J-18
Halesite . . . Pg. 129, H-16
Hamburg L-4
Vicinity . . . Pg. 94, J-4
Hamilton K-14
Hammond C-13
Hammondsport M-8
Hampton Bays D-8
Hancock O-15
Hannibal H-10
Harriman B-2
Harris Hill . Pg. 94, C-7
Harrison C-4
Vicinity . . . Pg. 128, F-11
Harrisville E-14
Hastings-On-Hudson . . . . Pg. 126, E-8
Hauppage . Pg. 129, K-19
Haverstraw B-3
Haviland O-19
Hawthorne . Pg. 126, B-10
Hempstead K-4
Vicinity . . . Pg. 129, N-13
Herkimer J-15
Hermon C-14
Herrings E-13
Heuvelton C-14
Hewlett Bay Park . . . . Pg. 129, P-12
Hewlett Harbor . . . . Pg. 129, P-12
Hicksville D-5
Vicinity . . . Pg. 129, L-15
Highland O-18
Highland Falls B-3
Highland Mills B-3
Highland-on-the-Lake . . . . Pg. 94, J-2
Hillburn C-2
Hillcrest . . . Pg. 126, A-6
Hillside Lake P-19
Hilton D-7
Vicinity . . . Pg. 138, F-1
Hobart M-16
Hoffman . . . Pg. 94, A-5
Holbrook D-6
Holcomb K-8
Holland L-5
Holland Patent H-14
Holley J-6
Homer L-11
Honeoye Falls K-7
Hoosick Falls J-20
Hornell M-7
Horseheads N-10
Houghton M-6
Hudson M-19
Hudson Falls H-19
Hugenot Park Pg. 127, Q-3
Huguenot . . Pg. 127, Q-2
Hunter M-17
Huntington D-5
Vicinity . . . Pg. 129, J-16
Huntington Sta. D-5
Hurley O-18
Hyde Park O-18
Ilion J-15
Interlaken M-10
Inwood . . . Pg. 129, P-11
Irondequoit . Pg. 138, F-1
Irvington . . Pg. 126, D-8
Island Park Pg. 129, Q-12
Islip D-6
Ithaca M-11
Jamaica . . . Pg. 129, N-11
Jamesport C-8
Jamestown N-3
Jefferson Hts M-18
Jefferson Valley B-4
Jeffersonville O-15
Jericho D-5
Vicinity . . . Pg. 129, L-14
Jerusalem Corners . . . . Pg. 94, K-1
Jewittville . . . Pg. 94, J-6
Johnson City N-12
Johnstown J-17
Jones Island . . . . Pg. 129, Q-14
Jordan J-11
Keeseville C-19
Kenmore K-3
Vicinity . . . Pg. 94, C-4
Kensington . Pg. 129, L-12
Kerhonkson O-18
Keuka Park L-9
Kinderhook M-19
Kings Park . Pg. 129, J-16
Kings Point Pg. 129, K-11
Kingston N-18
Kiryas Joel B-2

La Salle . . . . . Pg. 94, A-3
Lackawanna K-4
Vicinity . . . Pg. 94, G-4
Lacona G-12
Ladentown . Pg. 126, A-5
Lake Carmel C-3
Lake Erie Beach L-3
Lake George G-19
Lake Luzerne H-18
Lake Placid D-18
Lake Ronkonkoma . . . D-6
Lakeview . . . Pg. 94, J-3
Lakewood N-2
Lancaster K-4
Vicinity . . . Pg. 94, E-7
Lansing L-11
Larchmont . Pg. 126, F-9
Latham K-18
Lattington . Pg. 129, H-13
Laurel Hollow . . . . Pg. 129, J-15
Laurens . . . Pg. 129, Q-11
Lawrence . Pg. 129, Q-11
LeRoy K-6
Leicester K-6
Levittown E-5
Vicinity . . . Pg. 129, M-15
Lewiston J-3
Liberty O-16
Lido Beach Pg. 129, Q-13
Lima K-7
Lime Lake M-5
Limestone N-4
Lincoln Park N-18
Lindenhurst E-5
Vicinity . . . Pg. 129, N-17
Lisle M-12
Little Falls J-16
Little Valley M-4
Liverpool J-11
Livingston Manor . . . O-16
Livonia K-7
Lloyd Harbor D-5
Vicinity . . . Pg. 129, H-15
Lloyd Neck Pg. 128, H-16
Lockport J-4
Locksley Park Pg. 94, H-3
Locust Grove . . . . Pg. 129, K-15
Locust Valley Pg. 129, J-13
Lodi L-10
Long Beach E-4
Vicinity . . . Pg. 129, Q-12
Long Island City . . . . Pg. 127, K-7
Lorenz Pk M-19
Lowville F-14
Lynbrook . . Pg. 129, P-12
Lyndonville H-5
Lyons J-9
Lyons Falls G-14
Macedon J-8
Machias M-5
Madison K-14
Mahopac B-4
Malone B-17
Malverne . Pg. 129, N-12
Mamaroneck C-4
Vicinity . . . Pg. 126, E-10
Manchester J-8
Manhasset Pg. 129, K-12
Manhattan . Pg. 127, J-7
Manlius J-12
Mannsville F-12
Manorhaven Pg. 129, K-11
Marathon M-12
Marcellus J-11
Margaretville N-16
Marlboro P-18
Martinsville . Pg. 94, B-5
Massapequa E-5
Vicinity . . . Pg. 129, N-15
Massapequa Park . . . . Pg. 129, N-16
Massena B-15
Mastic D-7
Mastic Beach D-7
Matinecock Pg. 129, J-14
Mattituck C-8
Mattydale J-11
Maybrook A-2
Mayfield M-2
Mayville M-2
McGraw L-12
Meadow Island . . . . Pg. 129, Q-14
Mechanicville K-19
Medford D-6
Medina J-5
Melville . . Pg. 129, L-16
Menands K-19
Meridian J-11
Merrick . . . Pg. 129, P-14
Merriewold Lake B-2
Mexico H-11
Middle Hope P-18
Middleburgh L-17
Middleport J-5
Middletown A-2
Middleville J-15
Milford L-15
Mill Neck . Pg. 129, H-14
Millbrook O-19
Millersport . Pg. 94, A-7
Millerton N-19
Millport M-10
Milton O-18
Mineola . Pg. 129, M-13
Minetto H-11
Mineville D-18
Minoa J-12
Mohawk J-15
Monroe B-2
Monsey C-3
Vicinity . . . Pg. 126, B-5

Montauk C-10
Montgomery A-2
Monticello P-16
Montour Falls M-10
Mooers A-19
Moravia L-11
Morris L-15
Morristown C-13
Morrisville K-13
Mount Ivy . . . Pg. 126, A-6
Mount Kisco B-4
Mount Morris L-7
Mount Pleasant . . . . Pg. 126, C-9
Mount Vernon D-4
Vicinity . . . Pg. 126, F-9
Mt. Vernon . . . Pg. 94, H-3
Munnsville J-13
Muttontown Pg. 129, K-14
Nanuet C-3
Napanoch O-17
Naples L-8
Nashville . . . Pg. 94, A-4
Nassau L-19
Nelliston J-16
New Berlin L-14
New Brighton . . . . Pg. 127, M-5
New Cassel Pg. 129, M-14
New Dorp . . Pg. 127, P-4
New Dorp Beach . . . . Pg. 127, P-4
New Hartford J-14
New Hempstead . . . . Pg. 126, A-5
New Hyde Park . . . . Pg. 129, M-12
New Paltz O-18
New Rochelle D-4
Vicinity . . . Pg. 126, F-10
New Suffolk C-8
New York City E-3
Vicinity . . . Pg. 126-129
New York Mills J-14
Newark J-9
Newark Valley M-12
Newburgh A-3,P-18
Newfane H-4
Newport H-15
Niagara Falls J-3
Niagara Falls (Canada) . . . . Pg. 94, A-1
Nichols N-11
Norfolk B-15
North Bailey . Pg. 94, C-4
North Boston . Pg. 94, K-6
North Chili . . Pg. 138, J-1
North Collins L-3
North Evans Pg. 94, J-5
North Greece Pg. 138, G-2
North Haven C-9
North Hills Pg. 129, L-12
North Hornell M-7
North New Hyde Park . . . . Pg. 129, M-12
North Sea C-9
North Syracuse J-12
North Tarrytown . . . . Pg. 126, B-8
North Tonawanda K-4
Vicinity . . . Pg. 94, B-4
Northville H-17
Norwich (Chenango Cty) L-13
Norwich (Nassau Cty) . . . . Pg. 129, J-14
Norwood B-15
Noyack C-9
Nunda L-6
Nyack C-3
Vicinity . . . Pg. 126, B-7
Oak Beach Pg. 129, P-19
Oakfield J-5
Ocean Beach E-6
Oceanside . Pg. 129, P-13
Odessa M-10
Ogden Center . . . . Pg. 138, H-1
Ogdensburg B-13
Olcott H-4
Old Bethpage . . . . Pg. 129, L-16
Old Brookville . . . . Pg. 129, K-13
Old Forge G-14
Old Westbury . . . . Pg. 129, K-13
Olean N-5
Oneida J-13
Oneida Castle J-13
Oneonta M-15
Orange Lake P-18
Orangeburg Pg. 126, D-7
Orangetown . Pg. 126, C-6
Orchard Park L-4
Vicinity . . . Pg. 94, H-6
Orient C-9
Oriskany J-14
Oriskany Falls J-14
Ossining C-4
Oswego H-10
Otego M-14
Otisville A-1
Ovid L-10
Owego N-11
Oxford M-13
Oyster Bay Pg. 129, J-14
Oyster Bay Cove . . . . Pg. 129, J-15
Ozone Park . Pg. 127, L-9
Painted Post N-9
Palatine Bridge K-16
Vicinity . . . Pg. 126, B-5

Palisades . . . Pg. 126, D-8
Palmyra J-9
Panama N-2
Parish H-12
Parma Center Pg. 138, F-1
Parma Corners . . . . Pg. 138, G-1
Patchin . . . Pg. 94, K-6
Patchoque D-6
Pawling A-4
Peach Haven . Pg. 94, A-3
Pearl River C-3
Vicinity . . . Pg. 126, C-6
Peconic C-8
Peekskill B-3
Pelham . . . Pg. 126, F-9
Pelham Manor . . . . Pg. 126, G-9
Pendleton . . Pg. 94, A-6
Penfield . . Pg. 138, J-6
Penfield Center . . . . Pg. 138, H-7
Penn Yan L-9
Perry L-6
Perrysburg M-3
Peru C-19
Phelps K-9
Philadelphia E-13
Philmont M-19
Phoenix H-11
Piermont . . Pg. 126, C-8
Pike L-6
Pine Bush P-17
Pine Hill N-17
Pine Plains N-19
Pinehurst . . Pg. 94, J-3
Pittsford J-8
Vicinity . . . Pg. 138, K-5
Plainview D-5
Vicinity . . . Pg. 129, L-16
Plandome Manor . . . . Pg. 129, K-11
Plattsburgh B-19
Pleasantville C-4
Pocantico Hill Pg. 126, B-9
Poestenkill K-20
Point Abino (Canada) . . . . Pg. 94, E-1
Poland H-15
Pomona B-3
Port Byron J-10
Port Chester Pg. 128, F-12
Port Dickinson N-13
Port Ewen N-18
Port Henry E-19
Port Jefferson C-6
Port Jervis B-1
Port Leyden G-14
Port Richmond . . . . Pg. 127, M-3
Port Washington . . . . Pg. 129, K-12
Port Washington North . . . . Pg. 129, K-12
Portville N-5
Potsdam B-15
Poughkeepsie O-19
Pound Ridge B-4
Prospect H-14
Pulaski G-12
Quaker . . Pg. 127, K-9
Quogue D-8
Ramapo . . . Pg. 126, A-3
Randolph N-3
Ransomville H-4
Rapids . . . Pg. 94, A-7
Ravena L-18
Red Creek H-10
Red Hook N-19
Red Oaks Mill O-19
Remsen H-15
Rensselaer L-19
Rensselaer Falls C-14
Rhinebeck N-19
Richburg N-6
Richfield Springs K-15
Richmond Hill Pg. 127, L-9
Richmondville L-17
Richville C-14
Ridge D-7
Ridgeway (Canada) . . . . Pg. 94, E-1
Rigney Bluff . Pg. 138, F-2
Riverdale . . Pg. 126, H-7
Riverhead D-8
Riverside N-9
Rochester J-7
Vicinity . . . Pg. 138
Rockville Center . . . . Pg. 129, N-13
Rocky Pt. C-7
Roessleville K-18
Rome J-13
Roosevelt . Pg. 129, N-14
Rosendale O-18
Roslyn . . . Pg. 129, K-12
Roslyn Harbor . . . . Pg. 129, K-13
Roslyn Hts. Pg. 129, L-13
Rossville . . Pg. 127, P-2
Round Lake J-19
Rouses Point A-19
Ruby N-18
Rushville K-9
Rye C-4
Vicinity . . . Pg. 128, G-12
Rye Brook C-4
Vicinity . . . Pg. 128, F-12
Sackets Harbor F-12
Sag Harbor C-9
Saint Johnsville J-16

Saint Lawrence Park D-12
Salamanca N-4
Salem H-20
Saltaire . . . Pg. 129, P-20
San Remo . . Pg. 129, J-19
Sand Ridge J-11
Sands Point Pg. 129, J-11
Sandy Beach . Pg. 94, B-2
Sandy Creek G-12
Saranac Lake D-18
Saratoga Springs J-18
Saugerties N-18
Savona M-9
Sawyer . . . Pg. 94, A-4
Sayville D-6
Scarsdale C-4
Vicinity . . . Pg. 126, E-10
Schaghticoke K-18
Schenectady K-18
Schenevus L-15
Schoharie L-17
Schuylerville J-19
Scotch Town A-2
Scotia K-18
Scottsville J-7
Scranton . . . Pg. 94, H-4
Sea Cliff . . . Pg. 129, J-12
Seaford . . . Pg. 129, P-15
Searington Pg. 129, L-12
Selden D-6
Seneca Falls K-10
Sharon Springs K-16
Shelter Island C-9
Sherburne L-14
Sherman N-1
Sherrill J-13
Shirley D-7
Shortsville K-8
Sidney M-14
Silver Creek L-3
Silver Springs L-6
Sinclairville M-2
Skaneateles K-11
Sloan . . . . Pg. 94, E-5
Sloatsburg C-2
Vicinity . . . Pg. 126, A-3
Smithtown D-6
Smyrna L-13
Snyder . . . . Pg. 94, D-5
Snyder (Canada) . . . . Pg. 94, D-1
Sodus J-10
Sodus Point H-9
Solvay J-11
Sound Beach C-6
South Corning N-9
South Fallsburg O-16
South Farmingdale . . . . Pg. 129, M-16
South Glens Falls . . H-19
South Greece . . . . Pg. 138, H-2
South Nyack Pg. 126, C-8
Southampton D-9
Southold C-8
Southport N-10
Sparkill . . . Pg. 126, D-7
Speculator G-17
Spencer N-11
Spencerport J-7
Vicinity . . . Pg. 138, H-1
Spring Valley C-3
Vicinity . . . Pg. 126, B-6
Springbrook . Pg. 94, G-7
Springfield Gdns. . . . . Pg. 127, M-10
Springs D-10
Springville L-4
St. Johnsburg Pg. 94, A-3
Stamford M-16
Stannards N-6
Star Lake D-15
Staten Island Pg. 127, N-5
Stevensville (Canada) . . . . Pg. 94, D-1
Stillwater J-19
Stony Brook C-6
Vicinity . . . Pg. 128, H-20
Stony Pt. B-3
Stottville M-19
Success . . . Pg. 129, L-12
Suffern C-3
Vicinity . . . Pg. 126, B-4
Swormville . . Pg. 94, B-7
Sylvan Beach J-13
Syosset . . . Pg. 129, K-15
Syracuse J-12
Tall Man . . Pg. 126, B-4
Tannersville M-18
Tarrytown C-4
Vicinity . . . Pg. 126, C-8
Theresa D-13
Thornwood Pg. 126, B-10
Thunder Bay (Canada) . . . . Pg. 94, F-2
Ticonderoga F-19
Tillson O-18
Tivoli N-18
Tonawanda K-4
Vicinity . . . Pg. 94, C-3
Town Line K-5
Tribes Hill J-17
Troy K-19
Trumansburg L-10
Tuckahoe D-8
Tully K-12
Tupper Lake F-17
Turin F-14
Tuxedo Park B-2
Unadilla M-14
Union Hill . Pg. 138, G-7*
Union Springs K-10
Uniondale Pg. 129, M-13
Unionville B-15

University Gardens . . . . Pg. 129, L-11
Upper Brookville . . . . Pg. 129, J-14
Upper Nyack Pg. 126, B-7
Utica J-15
Valatie L-19
Valhalla . . Pg. 128, E-11
Valley Cottage . . . . Pg. 126, B-7
Valley Falls J-20
Valley Stream E-4
Vicinity . . . Pg. 129, N-11
Van Etten N-11
Vernon J-14
Verona J-12
Victor K-8
Victory J-10
Village of the Branch . . . . Pg. 129, J-20
Viola . . . . Pg. 126, A-5
Voorheesville L-18
Waddington B-14
Wading River C-7
Walden A-2
Wallkill A-2
Walton N-15
Walton Park B-2
Wampsville J-13
Wanakah . . Pg. 94, H-3
Wantagh . . Pg. 129, N-15
Wappinger Falls A-3
Warrensburg G-19
Warsaw K-6
Warwick B-2
Washingtonville A-2
Water Valley . Pg. 94, J-4
Waterford K-19
Waterloo K-9
Watertown E-12
Watervale K-14
Watervliet K-19
Watkins Glen M-10
Waverly N-11
Wayland L-7
Wayneport . Pg. 138, K-7
Webster J-8
Vicinity . . . Pg. 138, G-7
Webster Corners . . . . Pg. 94, H-6
Weedsport J-10
Wellsburg N-10
Wellsville N-6
Wendelville . . Pg. 94, A-5
Wesley Hills Pg. 126, A-5
West Carthage F-13
West Chili . . Pg. 138, K-1
West End L-15
West Falls . . Pg. 94, K-6
West Greece Pg. 138, G-2
West Plattsburgh . . . B-19
West Point B-3
West Sand Lake L-19
West Seneca . Pg. 94, F-5
West Walworth . . . . Pg. 138, J-7
West Webster . . . . Pg. 138, G-5
West Winfield K-14
Westampton D-8
Westbury . . Pg. 129, M-13
Westfield M-2
Westhampton D-8
Westmere K-17
Westons Mills N-5
Westport D-19
White Plains C-4
Vicinity . . . Pg. 126, D-10
Whitehall G-20
Whitesboro J-14
Whitney Point M-12
Willard L-10
Williamsville K-4
Vicinity . . . Pg. 94, D-5
Williston Park . . . . Pg. 129, L-13
Willow Brook Pg. 127, N-4
Wilson H-4
Vicinity . . . Pg. 94, G-5
Windom J-6
Windsor N-13
Winthrop B-16
Witherbee E-19
Wolcott H-10
Woodbury . Pg. 129, K-15
Woodhull N-8
Woodlawn . . Pg. 94, G-4
Woodmere . Pg. 129, P-11
Woodridge O-17
Woodstock N-18
Wurlitzer Park Pg. 94, A-4
Wyandanch Pg. 129, L-17
Wyoming K-6
Yonkers D-3
Vicinity . . . Pg. 126, E-8
Yorkshire L-5
Yorktown Hts. B-4
Yorkville J-14
Youngstown H-3
Zena N-18

NORTH CAROLINA
Pages 64-65
Population: 5,881,766
Capital: Raleigh
Land Area: 48,843 sq. mi.

NORTH CAROLINA

Abbotsburg E-10
Aberdeen D-8
Acre C-12
Ahoskie A-12
Albemarle D-7

Alexis . . . . Pg. 95, A-1
Allen D-7
Allenton E-9
Andrews D-2
Apex . . . . Pg. 138, D-2
Arapahoe D-12
Archdale C-7
Arcola B-10
Arlington B-6
Asheboro C-8
Ashland B-12
Asheville C-4
Askin D-12
Auburn . . . Pg. 138, E-6
Aurora C-12
Avent Ferry Pg. 138, D-4
Avery Creek D-4
Avon C-14
Ayden C-11
Badin D-7
Bagley C-10
Bald Creek C-4
Baldwin B-5
Bandana B-4
Banner Elk B-5
Barclay Downs . . . . Pg. 138, C-6
Barco A-13
Bat Cave C-4
Battleboro B-11
Bayleaf . . . Pg. 138, A-5
Bear Creek C-9
Beaufort D-13
Belgrade D-11
Belhaven C-12
Belmont C-5
Vicinity . . . Pg. 95, E-2
Benson C-9
Bertha A-13
Bessemer City D-6
Bethel B-11
Bethel Hill A-9
Bethlehem C-6
Beulaville D-11
Biscoe D-8
Black Mtn. C-4
Bladenboro E-9
Blowing Rock B-5
Bolton E-10
Boone B-5
Bottom A-6
Bowdens D-10
Brandon Station . . . . Pg. 138, A-4
Brasstown . . Pg. 138, C-5
Brentwood . . Pg. 138, C-5
Brevard D-4
Bridgeton D-12
Bridgewater C-5
Brookford C-5
Brooks Cross Roads . B-6
Brooksdale B-9
Browns Summit B-8
Brunswick F-10
Bryson City D-2
Bulade B-4
Bullock A-9
Bunn B-10
Burgaw E-10
Burlington B-8
Burnsville B-4
Buxton C-14
Calypso D-10
Camden A-13
Cameron D-9
Candler C-4
Candor D-8
Canto C-3
Canton C-3
Carolina Beach F-11
Carr B-8
Carrboro B-9
Cary C-9
Vicinity . . . Pg. 138, D-3
Casville B-8
Cedar Creek D-10
Celo C-4
Centerville B-10
Chadbourn F-10
Chapel Hill C-9
Charlotte D-7
Vicinity . . . Pg. 95
Cherokee D-2
Cherryville D-5
China Grove C-7
Chinquapin D-11
Chocowinity C-12
Churchland C-7
Cid C-7
Clemmons B-7
Clinton D-10
Cloverdale . Pg. 138, E-5
Coinjock A-13
Colerain B-12
College B-8
Columbia B-13
Columbus D-4
Comfort D-11
Concord D-7
Conover C-6
Conway A-12
Corapeake A-12
Cornelius D-6
Council E-10
Cove Creek C-3
Cramerton . Pg. 95, D-1
Creedmoor B-9
Creswell B-13
Culberson D-1
Currie E-10
Dalton B-7
Darden B-12
Davidson C-6
Deep Gap B-5
Del Mar Beach E-12

Delway E-10
Derita . . . . Pg. 95, C-7
Diane . . . . Pg. 138, A-2
Dillsboro D-3
Dixie . . . . Pg. 95, D-3
Dobson B-7
Dortches B-10
Dudley D-10
Dunn D-9
Durham B-9
Vicinity . . . Pg. 138, A-1
East Lake B-13
East Laport D-3
Eastwood D-8
Eden A-8
Edenhouse B-12
Edenton B-12
Edneyville D-4
Edward C-12
Ela D-3
Eldorado C-7
Elizabeth City A-13
Elizabethtown[?] . . . E-10
Elk Park B-4
Elkin B-6
Emerald Village . . . . Pg. 138, E-6
Emery D-8
Enfield B-11
Englehard C-13
Erwin D-9
Essex B-10
Ether C-8
Evergreen E-9
Fair Bluff E-9
Fairfield . . Pg. 138, B-1
Fairmont E-9
Faison D-10
Falls . . . . Pg. 138, A-6
Farmville C-11
Fayetteville D-9
Flat Rock D-4
Fletcher D-4
Folkston E-11
Fontana Village D-2
Forest City D-5
Fountain C-11
Franklin D-2
Freeman E-6
Fremont C-10
Friendship Pg. 138, E-1
Frisco C-14
Fuquay-Varina C-9
Garner . . . Pg. 138, E-5
Garysburg A-11
Gastonia D-6
Vicinity . . . Pg. 95, D-1
Gates A-12
Genlee . . . Pg. 138, B-1
Gilkey D-5
Glade Valley B-6
Glenridge Pg. 138, E-3
Glenview B-10
Glenwood C-5
Gneiss D-3
Godwin D-9
Gold Rock B-11
Goldsboro C-10
Goldston C-8
Gordonton B-9
Graingers C-11
Grandy A-13
Granite Falls C-5
Granite Quarry C-7
Grantham D-10
Green Level Pg. 138, D-1
Greenbrier Estates . . . . Pg. 138, E-5
Greensboro B-8
Greenville C-11
Grifton C-11
Grissettown F-10
Guilford B-8
Halifax A-11
Hamlet D-8
Hampstead E-11
Harbinger B-14
Harmony B-6
Harrells E-10
Harrisburg D-7
Hatteras C-14
Hazelwood D-3
Heartsease B-11
Hedingham . Pg. 138, C-6
Henderson B-10
Hendersonville D-4
Henrietta D-5
Hertford B-12
Hester B-9
Hickory C-6
Hickory Grove Pg. 95, C-8
High Hampton D-3
High Point C-7
Hightowers B-8
Hill Crest B-9
Hillsborough B-9
Hiwassee D-2
Hoffman D-8
Holly Ridge E-11
Hollyville (Cash Corner) D-12
Hope Mills D-9
House D-9
Hubert D-11
Hudson C-5
Huntersville D-6
Vicinity . . . Pg. 95, A-6
Ingleside B-10
Jackson A-11
Jacksonville D-11
Jamesville B-12
Jarvisburg A-13
Jason C-11
Johns E-9

Jonas Ridge C-5
Jonesville B-6
Julian B-8
Justice B-10
Kannapolis D-7
Keener D-10
Kelley E-10
Kenansville D-11
Kenly C-10
Kernersville B-7
Kilkenny B-13
King B-7
Kings Mountain D-5
Kinston D-11
Kittrell B-10
Knightdale .. Pg. 138, D-7
Kuhns D-12
Kure Beach F-11
La Grange D-11
Lake Landing C-13
Lakeview D-9
Landis C-7
Lauada D-3
Laurinburg E-9
Lawrence B-11
Leasburg A-9
Leechville C-12
Leesville ... Pg. 138, A-4
Lemon Springs C-8
Lenoir C-5
Level Cross B-8
Lewis A-9
Lexington C-7
Liberia B-10
Liberty B-8
Lilesville D-8
Lillington C-9
Lincolnton D-5
Linwood C-7
Lizzie C-11
Logan D-5
Long Beach F-10
Longview C-5
Louisburg B-10
Lowell .... Pg. 95, D-1
Lowesville .... Pg. 95, A-3
Lucama C-11
Lucia .... Pg. 95, B-3
Luck C-3
Lumber Bridge D-9
Lumberton E-9
Lynn Crossroads
.... Pg. 138, A-3
Macedonia . Pg. 138, D-4
Macgregor Downs
.... Pg. 138, D-2
Maco E-10
Madison B-7
Magnolia D-10
Maiden C-6
Mamie B-13
Manns Harbor B-13
Manteo B-14
Maple Hill E-11
Marble D-2
Marion C-5
Mars Hill C-4
Marshall C-3
Marshville D-7
Marston D-8
Matthews D-7
Vicinity .... Pg. 95, G-8
Maxton E-9
Mayodan B-8
Maysville D-12
Mesic C-12
Micro C-10
Middleburg A-10
Midway B-12
Midway Park E-11
Milburnie .. Pg. 138, C-6
Mint Hill D-6
Vicinity .... Pg. 95, F-9
Mocksville C-7
Moncure C-9
Monroe D-7
Monticello B-8
Mooresville C-6
Morehead City D-12
Morgans Corner A-13
Morganton C-5
Morrisville .. Pg. 138, C-2
Mount Airy A-7
Mount Gilead D-7
Mount Holly D-6
Vicinity .... Pg. 95, D-3
Mount Mourne C-6
Mount Olive D-11
Mountain Home D-4
Mulberry B-6
Murfreesboro A-11
Nags Head B-14
Nakina F-10
Nantahala D-2
Nashville B-10
Nelson .... Pg. 138, B-2
Neuse .... Pg. 138, B-6
New Bern D-12
New Holland C-13
New Hope .. Pg. 138, C-6
New Salem D-7
Newell .... Pg. 95, D-7
Newport D-12
Newton C-6
Newton Grove C-10
Norlina A-10
Norman D-8
North Wilkesboro B-6
Northside B-9
Oak Grove B-9
Oakboro D-7
Oakton .. Pg. 138, E-4
Ocracoke D-14
Old Dock F-10

Old Ford C-12
Old Fort C-4
Olivia D-9
Osceola B-8
Oswalt C-6
Oteen C-4
Otto D-3
Oxford B-9
Pantego C-12
Parkwood ... Pg. 138, A-1
Patterson B-5
Peachtree D-2
Pembroke E-9
Penderlea E-10
Picks B-9
Pilot Mountain B-7
Pine Ridge A-6
Pinebluff D-8
Pineola B-5
Pinetops B-11
Pineville D-6
Pinnacle B-7
Pireway F-10
Pittsboro C-9
Pleasant Hill A-11
Plymouth B-12
Point Harbor B-13
Polkton D-7
Pollocksville D-11
Portsmouth D-13
Postell D-1
Powells Point B-14
Preston .... Pg. 138, C-2
Raeford D-9
Rainbow Springs D-2
Raleigh B-9
Vicinity ... Pg. 138, B-5
Randleman C-8
Ranger D-1
Ransomville C-12
Rapids A-11
Red Hill B-4
Red Springs E-9
Reidsville B-8
Rheasville A-11
Rich Square B-11
Roanoke Rapids A-11
Robbinsville D-2
Robersonville B-11
Rockingham D-8
Rocky Mount B-11
Rodanthe B-14
Roduco A-12
Roper B-12
Rose Hill D-10
Roseboro D-10
Roseneath B-11
Rougemont B-9
Rowan E-10
Rowland E-9
Roxboro A-9
Ruth D-5
Rutherfordton D-4
Saint Pauls E-9
Salemburg D-10
Salisbury C-7
Salvo B-14
Sanford C-9
Schley B-9
Scotland Neck B-11
Scott's Hill E-11
Scranton C-13
Seabreeze F-11
Seagrove C-8
Selma C-10
Shallotte F-10
Sharpsburg B-11
Shelby D-5
Shopton .... Pg. 95, F-3
Siler City C-8
Sioux B-4
Six Forks B-10
Six Forks Crossroads
.... Pg. 138, B-4
Skyland C-4
Smith F-10
Smithfield C-10
Snow Hill C-11
Southern Pines D-8
Southport F-10
Sparta A-6
Spencer C-7
Spivey's Corner D-10
Spout Springs D-9
Spring Hill D-9
Vicinity ... Pg. 138, A-1
Spring Lake D-9
Spruce Pine C-5
Stanhope B-10
Stanley .... Pg. 95, B-1
Stanleyville B-7
State Road B-6
Statesville C-6
Steeds C-8
Stocksville C-4
Stokes C-11
Stonebridge Pg. 138, A-5
Stony Point C-6
Stovall A-10
Stratford A-6
Sunbury A-12
Supply F-10
Surf City E-11
Surl B-9
Swann C-8
Swannanoa C-4
Swansboro E-12
Swiss C-4
Sylva D-3
Tabor City F-10
Tapoco D-2
Tar Heel E-9
Tarboro B-11
Taylorsville C-6

Teachey D-10
Terp .... Pg. 138, D-4
The Woods of Chatham
.... Pg. 138, C-1
Thomasville C-7
Tillery B-11
Tin City E-10
Tobaccoville B-7
Toluca C-5
Topsail Beach E-11
Topton D-2
Tramway C-9
Trent Woods D-12
Trenton D-11
Trust C-3
Tryon D-4
Turnersburg C-6
Tuxedo D-4
Twin Oaks A-6
Ulah C-8
Unaka D-2
Upchurch .. Pg. 138, C-2
Uwharrie C-8
Valdese C-5
Vanceboro C-11
Vander D-9
Violet D-9
Wadesboro E-7
Wadeville D-8
Wagram D-9
Wake Crossroads
.... Pg. 138, B-7
Wake Forest B-10
Vicinity .. Pg. 138, A-7
Walkers Crossroads
.... Pg. 138, A-7
Wallace E-11
Walnut C-4
Walnut Creek C-11
Wanchese B-14
Wards Corner E-10
Warsaw D-10
Waves B-14
Waynesville D-3
Weldon A-11
Wendell C-10
Wesser D-2
West Concord
.... Pg. 95, A-10
West Onslow Beach E-12
Westminster D-5
Westover .. Pg. 138, C-4
Whalebone B-14
White Lake E-10
White Oak E-10
Whiteville F-10
Wilbar B-6
Wilkesboro B-6
Willard E-10
Williamsburg B-8
Williamston B-12
Wilmar C-12
Wilmington F-10
Wilmington Beach ... F-11
Wilson C-11
Windsor B-12
Wingate D-7
Winnabow F-10
Winston-Salem B-7
Winterville C-11
Winton A-12
Wise A-10
Wise Fork D-11
Woodland B-11
Woodley B-13
Wrightsville Beach . F-11
Yadkinville B-7
Yancyville A-8
Yeatesville C-12
Youngsville B-10
Zebulon B-10

NORTH DAKOTA
Page 63
Population: 652,717
Capital: Bismarck
Land Area: 69,300 sq. mi.

Abercrombie F-9
Adams B-8
Alamo B-2
Alexander C-2
Alice E-9
Almont D-4
Alsen B-7
Ambrose A-2
Amenia E-9
Amidon E-2
Anamoose D-6
Aneta D-8
Antler B-5
Ardoch C-9
Arena D-6
Argusville E-10
Arnegard C-2
Arthur E-9
Ashley F-6
Ayr E-9
Balfour C-5
Balta C-6
Bantry B-5
Barney F-9
Barton B-6
Bathgate B-9
Battleview B-3
Beach D-1
Belcourt B-6
Belfield D-2
Benedict C-5
Berlin F-6
Berthold B-4

Berwick C-6
Beulah D-4
Binford D-8
Bisbee B-7
Bismarck D-5
Bottineau B-6
Bowbells B-3
Bowden D-6
Bowman E-2
Braddock E-6
Breien D-7
Bremen D-7
Brinsmade C-7
Brocket C-8
Bucyrus F-2
Buffalo E-9
Burlington B-4
Butte C-5
Buxton D-9
Calio B-7
Calvin B-7
Cando C-7
Carbury B-5
Carpio B-4
Carrington D-7
Carson E-4
Casselton E-9
Cathay D-7
Cavalier B-9
Cayuga F-9
Center D-5
Charlson C-3
Churchs Ferry C-7
Cleveland E-7
Clifford E-9
Colehabor D-5
Colfax F-9
Columbus A-3
Conway C-9
Cooperstown D-8
Courtenay D-8
Crary C-8
Crosby A-2
Crystal B-9
Davenport E-9
Dawson E-6
Dazey D-8
Deering B-5
Des Lacs B-4
Devils Lake C-7
Dickey E-7
Dickinson D-3
Dodge D-3
Donnybrook B-4
Douglas C-5
Drake D-6
Drayton B-9
Driscoll E-5
Dunn Center D-3
Dunseith B-6
Dwight F-10
Edgeley F-7
Edinburg C-9
Edmore C-8
Elgin E-4
Ellendale F-7
Elliott E-8
Emerado C-9
Enderlin E-9
Epping B-2
Esmond D-7
Fairdale B-8
Fairfield D-2
Fargo E-10
Fairmont F-10
Fessenden D-6
Fingal E-8
Finley D-8
Flasher E-4
Flaxton A-3
Fordville C-8
Forest River C-9
Forman F-8
Fort Ransom E-8
Fort Yates F-5
Fortuna A-2
Freda E-5
Fredonia F-7
Fullerton F-8
Gackle E-7
Galesburg E-9
Gardena B-5
Garrison C-4
Gascoyne F-2
Gilby C-9
Gladstone D-3
Glen Ullin E-4
Glenfield D-7
Golden Valley D-3
Golva D-1
Goodrich D-6
Grafton C-9
Grand Forks C-9
Grandin E-9
Grano B-4
Grassy Butte C-2
Great Bend F-10
Grenora B-1
Gwinner F-8
Hague F-6
Haley F-2
Halliday D-4
Hamberg C-7
Hampden B-8
Hankinson F-9
Hanks B-2
Hannaford D-8
Hannah B-8
Harlow C-7
Harvey D-6
Harwood E-10
Hatton D-9
Havana F-8

Haynes F-3
Hazelton E-5
Hazen D-4
Hebron D-4
Heimdal C-6
Hensel B-9
Hettinger F-2
Hillsboro D-9
Hoopie B-9
Hope D-9
Hunter D-9
Hurdsfield D-6
Inkster C-9
Jamestown E-8
Jud E-7
Karlsruhe C-5
Kathryn E-8
Kenmare B-4
Kensal D-7
Killdeer D-3
Kindred E-9
Kramer B-5
Kulm F-7
La Moure F-8
Lakota C-8
Landa B-5
Langdon B-8
Larimore C-8
Larson A-3
Lawton C-8
Leal D-8
Leeds C-7
Lehr F-7
Leith E-4
Leonard E-9
Lidgerwood F-9
Lignite A-3
Lincoln E-5
Linton F-6
Lisbon F-9
Litchville E-8
Loma B-8
Ludden F-8
Maddock C-7
Makoti C-4
Mandan E-5
Mandaree C-3
Manning D-3
Mantador F-9
Manvel C-9
Marion E-8
Marmarth E-1
Marshall D-3
Martin C-6
Max C-4
Maxbass B-5
Mayville D-9
Maza B-7
McClusky D-5
McHenry D-7
McVille D-8
Medina E-7
Medora D-2
Mercer D-5
Merricourt F-7
Michigan C-8
Milnor F-9
Milton B-8
Minnewaukan C-7
Minot C-4
Minto C-9
Mohall B-4
Monango F-8
Montpelier E-7
Mooreton F-9
Mott E-3
Mountain B-9
Munich B-7
Mylo B-6
Napoleon E-6
Neche B-9
Nekoma B-8
New England E-2
New Leipzig E-3
New Rockford D-7
New Salem E-4
New Town C-3
Newburg B-5
Nome E-8
Noonan A-3
Northwood D-9
Oakes F-8
Oberon C-7
Oriska E-8
Osnabrock B-8
Page E-9
Palermo B-3
Park River C-9
Parshall C-4
Pekin D-8
Pembina B-9
Perth B-7
Petersburg C-8
Pettibone D-6
Pick City D-4
Pillsbury D-8
Pingree D-7
Pisek C-9
Plaza C-4
Portal A-3
Portland D-9
Powers Lake B-3
Prairie Rose E-9
Ray B-2
Rawson C-2
Reeder F-2
Regan D-6
Regent E-3
Rhame E-1
Richardton D-3
Riverdale D-4
Robinson D-6
Rock Lake B-7

Rogers E-8
Rolette B-6
Rolla B-6
Ross B-3
Rugby C-6
Ruso C-5
Rutland F-9
Ryder C-4
Saint Thomas B-9
Sanborn E-8
Sarles B-7
Sawyer C-5
Scranton E-2
Selfridge F-4
Sentinel Butte D-1
Sharon D-8
Shields F-4
Sheldon E-9
Sherwood A-4
Sheyenne C-7
Sibley D-8
Solen E-5
Souris B-5
South Heart D-2
Spring Brook B-2
Stanley B-3
Stanton D-4
Starkweather B-7
Steele E-6
Strasburg F-6
Streeter E-7
Surrey C-5
Sydney E-7
Sykeston D-7
Tappen E-6
Thompson D-9
Tioga B-2
Tolley B-4
Tolna C-8
Tower City E-8
Towner B-5
Turtle Lake D-5
Tuttle D-6
Underwood D-5
Upham B-5
Valley City E-8
Velva C-5
Venturia F-6
Verendrye C-5
Verona F-8
Voltaire C-5
Wahpeton F-10
Walcott E-9
Wales B-8
Walhalla B-8
Walseth B-5
Warwick C-7
Washburn D-5
Watford City C-2
West Fargo E-9
Westfeild F-5
Westhope B-5
Wheelock B-2
White Earth B-3
Wildrose B-2
Williston B-2
Willow City B-6
Wilton D-5
Wimbledon D-7
Wing D-6
Wishek F-6
Wolford B-6
Woodworth D-7
Wyndmere F-9
York C-6
Ypsilanti E-7
Zap D-4

OHIO
Pages 66-67
Population: 10,797,630
Capital: Columbus
Land Area: 41,004 sq. mi.

Abbeyville ... Pg. 101, J-1
Aberdeen N-3
Ada G-3
Addyston M-1
Adena J-9
Akron G-8
Albany M-7
Alexandria J-5
Alger H-3
Alliance G-9
Amanda L-5
Amberley ... Pg. 100, C-5
Amelia M-2
Amesville L-7
Amherst F-6
Amsterdam H-9
Andover E-10
Anna J-2
Ansonia J-1
Antwerp F-1
Apple Creek H-7
Arcadia F-4
Arcanum K-1
Archbold E-2
Arlington G-3
Ashland G-6
Ashley H-5
Ashtabula D-9
Ashville K-5
Athalia O-6
Athens M-7
Attica G-5
Aurora F-8
Avon Lake E-7
Bainbridge M-4
Baltic H-8
Baltimore K-6

Barberton G-8
Barnesville K-9
Barnsburg .. Pg. 100, B-2
Batavia M-2
Bath .... Pg. 101, K-4
Bath Center . Pg. 101, K-4
Bay View E-5
Beach City H-8
Beallsville K-9
Beavercreek K-2
Beaverdam G-3
Bedford ... Pg. 101, E-6
Bedford Heights
.... Pg. 101, E-6
Beechwood . Pg. 101, C-6
Beliot G-9
Bellaire K-10
Bellbrook L-2
Belle Center H-3
Bellefontaine H-3
Bellevue F-5
Bellville H-6
Belmont J-9
Belpre M-8
Belvis .... Pg. 100, A-2
Bennetts Corner
.... Pg. 101, H-2
Berea F-7
Vicinity ... Pg. 101, F-1
Bergholz H-9
Berlin Heights F-6
Bethel N-2
Bethesda J-9
Bettsville F-4
Beverly L-8
Bexley J-5
Blanchester M-3
Bloomdale F-4
Bloomingburg L-4
Bloomville G-5
Blue Ash ... Pg. 101, B-6
Bluffton G-3
Bolivar H-8
Boston Heights
.... Pg. 101, H-6
Botkins H-2
Botzum ... Pg. 101, K-5
Bowersville L-3
Bowling Green F-3
Bradford J-2
Bradner
.... Pg. 100, C-4
Brathenal .. Pg. 101, B-5
Brecksville . Pg. 101, F-6
Bremen K-6
Brewster H-8
Bridgetown . Pg. 100, D-1
Brilliant J-10
Broadview Heights
.... Pg. 101, E-6
Brook Park . Pg. 101, E-2
Brooklyn ... Pg. 101, D-3
Brooklyn Heights
.... Pg. 101, D-4
Brunswick F-7
Vicinity ... Pg. 101, J-2
Bryan E-1
Buchtel L-7
Bucyrus G-5
Burton E-9
Butler H-5
Byesville K-8
Cadiz J-9
Cairo G-2
Caldwell K-8
Caledonia H-5
Cambridge J-8
Camden L-1
Campbell F-10
Canal Fulton G-8
Canal Winchester . K-5
Vicinity ... Pg. 102, J-7
Canfield F-9
Canton H-8
Cardington H-5
Carey G-4
Carroll K-6
Carrollton H-9
Castalia F-5
Cedarville K-3
Celina H-1
Center Village Pg. 102, B-7
Centerburg J-5
Centerville L-2
Chardon E-9
Chauncey L-7
Chesapeake O-6
Chesterhill L-7
Cheviot M-1
Vicinity ... Pg. 100, D-2
Chillicothe L-5
Christiansburg J-3
Cincinnati M-2
Vicinity ... Pg. 100, H-2
Circleville K-5
Clarington K-9
Clarksville L-3
Cleveland E-7
Vicinity ... Pg. 101, D-5
Cleveland Heights ... E-8
Vicinity ... Pg. 101, D-5
Cleves L-1
Clyde F-5
Coal Grove O-6
Coalton M-6
Coldwater H-1
Columbiana G-10
Columbus J-4
Vicinity ... Pg. 102, E-6
Columbus Grove ... G-2
Commercial Point
.... Pg. 102, K-3
Conneaut D-10
Continental F-2

Convoy G-1
Coolville M-7
Corning L-7
Cortland F-10
Coshocton J-7
Covington J-2
Craig Beach G-9
Crestline G-5
Cridersville H-2
Crooksville K-7
Crown City O-6
Cuyahoga Falls G-8
Vicinity ... Pg. 101, K-7
Cuyahoga Heights
.... Pg. 101, D-5
Cygnet F-3
Dalton G-8
Danville H-6
Darbydale
Vicinity ... Pg. 102, J-1
Dayton K-2
De Graff J-3
Delaware J-4
Delphos G-2
Delta E-3
Dennison H-9
Derby .... Pg. 102, K-1
Deshler F-3
Dover H-8
Dresden J-7
Dublin J-4
Vicinity ... Pg. 102, C-2
Dunkirk G-3
Dunlap .... Pg. 100, A-1
Duvall .... Pg. 102, K-5
East Canton G-9
East Cleveland E-8
Vicinity ... Pg. 101, B-5
East Liverpool H-10
East Palestine G-10
East Sparta H-8
Eastlake E-8
Eaton K-1
Edgerton E-1
Edgewater Park
.... Pg. 102, G-6
Edison H-5
Edon E-1
Eldorado K-1
Elmore E-4
Elmwood Place
.... Pg. 100, C-4
Elyria F-7
Emery .... Pg. 101, D-6
Englewood K-2
Enon K-3
Euclid E-8
Vicinity ... Pg. 101, B-5
Evendale ... Pg. 100, B-5
Everett .... Pg. 101, J-5
Fairfax L-1
Fairfield L-1
Fairlawn H-8
Fairport Harbor D-9
Fairview Park Pg. 101, D-1
Fayette E-2
Felicity N-2
Findlay G-3
Flint .... Pg. 102, C-4
Flushing J-9
Forest G-4
Forest Park M-1
Vicinity ... Pg. 100, A-3
Fostoria F-4
Frankfort L-4
Franklin L-2
Frazeysburg J-7
Fredericksburg H-7
Fredericktown H-6
Freeport J-8
Fremont F-5
Ft. Jennings G-2
Ft. Loramie J-2
Ft. Recovery H-1
Ft. Shawnee H-2
Gahanna J-5
Vicinity ... Pg. 102, E-6
Galena .... Pg. 102, A-6
Galion H-5
Gallipolis N-7
Galloway ... Pg. 102, G-2
Gambier J-6
Garfield Heights E-8
Vicinity ... Pg. 101, D-5
Garrettsville F-9
Geneva D-9
Geneva-on-the-Lake . D-9
Genoa E-4
Georgetown N-3
Georgeville . Pg. 102, H-1
Germantown L-1
Gettysburg J-2
Ghent .... Pg. 101, K-4
Gibsonburg F-8
Girard F-10
Glandorf G-2
Glendale ... Pg. 100, A-4
Glenwillow . Pg. 101, G-7
Glouster L-7
Gnadenhutten J-8
Golf Manor . Pg. 100, C-5
Gould Park . Pg. 102, D-6
Grafton F-7
Grand Rapids F-3
Grandview Heights
.... Pg. 102, F-4
Granger ... Pg. 101, K-3
Granville J-6
Gratis L-1
Green Springs F-5
Greenfield L-4
Greenhills . Pg. 100, A-3
Greenville J-1
Greenwich G-6

Grove City K-4
  Vicinity . . . . . Pg. 102, H-3
Groveport K-5
  Vicinity . . . . . Pg. 102, J-6
Hamden M-6
Hamersville N-3
Hamilton L-1
Hamler F-3
Hanover J-6
Hanoverton H-10
Harlem . . . . . Pg. 102, B-6
Harrisburg . . . . Pg. 102, K-1
Harrison M-1
Harrod H-3
Hartville G-9
Hayden . . . . Pg. 102, D-1
Hayesville G-7
Heath K-6
Hebron K-6
Hicksville F-1
Higginsport N-3
Highland Heights
  . . . . Pg. 101, B-7
Hilliard J-4
  Vicinity . . . . . Pg. 102, H-3
Hillsboro M-3
Hinckley . . . . . Pg. 101, H-2
Hiram F-9
Holgate F-2
Holland E-3
Hopedale J-9
Hubbard F-10
Huber Heights K-2
Huber Ridge . Pg. 102, C-6
Hudson . . . . . Pg. 101, H-7
Huron E-6
Hyatts . . . . . Pg. 102, A-3
Independence
  . . . . Pg. 101, F-4
Ironton O-6
Jackson M-5
Jackson Center H-3
Jacksonville L-7
Jamestown L-3
Jefferson E-9
Jeffersonville L-4
Jerome . . . . . Pg. 102, B-1
Jeromesville G-7
Jewett J-9
Johnstown J-6
Junction City K-6
Kalida G-2
Kellys Island E-6
Kent F-8
Kenton H-3
Kettering K-2
Kileville . . . . Pg. 102, C-1
Killbuck H-7
Kingston L-5
Kirkersville K-6
Kirtland Hills E-9
Lagrange F-7
Lakemore G-8
Lakeview H-3
Lakewood E-7
  Vicinity . . . . . Pg. 101, C-1
Lancaster K-6
Laurelville L-5
Lebanon L-2
Leesburg L-4
Leetonia G-10
Leipsic G-3
Lewis Center Pg. 102, A-4
Lewisburg K-1
Lexington H-6
Liberty Center E-2
Lima G-2
Lincoln Heights
  . . . . Pg. 100, B-4
Lindsey F-5
Linworth . . . . Pg. 102, C-3
Lisbon H-9
Lithopolis . . . . Pg. 102, K-7
Lockbourn . . . . Pg. 102, K-4
Lockland . . . . . Pg. 100, B-4
Lodi G-7
Logan L-6
London K-4
Lorain E-6
Lordstown F-9
Loudonville H-6
Louisville G-9
Loveland M-2
Lowell L-8
Lowellville G-10
Luckey F-4
Lynchburg M-3
Lyndhurst . . . Pg. 101, B-7
Lyons E-2
Macedonia F-8
  Vicinity . . . . . Pg. 101, G-6
Madei . . . . . Pg. 100, C-6
Madeira M-2
Madison E-9
Magnolia H-8
Malta K-7
Malvern H-9
Manchester N-3
Mansfield H-6
Maple Heights
  . . . . Pg. 101, E-5
Marble Cliff . Pg. 102, F-3
Marblehead E-5
Marietta L-8
Marimet . . . . Pg. 100, D-4
Marion H-4
Martins Ferry J-10
Martinsville L-3
Marysville J-4
Mason L-2
Massillon G-8
Maumee E-3
Mayfield Heights
  . . . . Pg. 101, B-7

McArthur M-6
McClure F-3
McConnelsville L-7
McGuffey H-3
Mechanicsburg J-4
Medina F-7
  Vicinity . . . . . Pg. 101, K-1
Mentor E-8
Mentor-on-the-Lake . . E-8
Metamora E-3
Miamisburg L-2
Middle Point G-2
Middleburg Hts
  . . . . Pg. 101, F-3
Middleport M-7
Middletown L-1
Midvale H-8
Midway K-4
Milan F-6
Milford M-2
Milford Center J-4
Millersburg H-7
Millersport K-6
Millville L-1
Mineral City . . . . . . H—8
Minerva G-9
Minerva Park J-5
  Vicinity . . . . . Pg. 102, D-4
Mingo Junction J-10
Minster H-2
Monroe L-2
Monroeville F-5
Montpelier E-1
Moraine K-2
Moreland Hills
  . . . . Pg. 101, D-7
Morrow L-2
Mt. Air . . . . Pg. 102, B-3
Mt. Blanchard G-4
Mt. Gilead H-5
Mt. Healthy . Pg. 100, B-3
Mt. Orab M-3
Mt. Sterling K-4
Mt. Vernon H-6
Mt. Victory H-4
Mudsock . . . . Pg. 102, E-1
Murray City L-7
Napoleon F-2
Navarre G-8
Nelsonville L-6
Nevada G-5
New Albany . . Pg. 102, C-7
New Boston N-5
New Bremen H-2
New Carlisle K-3
New Concord K-7
New Holland L-4
New Knoxville H-2
New Lebanon K-1
New Lexington L-7
New London G-6
New Madison K-1
New Matamoras L-9
New Miami L-1
New Middletown G-10
New Paris K-1
New Philadelphia H-8
New Richmond N-2
New Rome . . . Pg. 102, F-2
New Straitsville L-7
New Vienna L-3
New Washington G-5
New Waterford G-10
Newark J-6
Newburgh Heights
  . . . . Pg. 101, D-4
Newcomerstown J-7
Newton M-2
Newton Falls F-9
Niles F-10
North Baltimore F-3
North Bend M-1
North Canton G-8
North College Hill
  . . . . Pg. 100, C-3
North Fairfield F-6
North Kingsville D-10
North Lewisburg J-4
North Olmsted F-7
North Randall
  . . . . Pg. 101, D-6
North Ridgeville F-7
North Royalton
  . . . . Pg. 101, F-3
Northfield . . . Pg. 101, G-6
Northwood F-4
Norton G-8
Norwalk F-6
Norwood . . . . Pg. 100, D-4
Oak Harbor E-4
Oak Hill N-6
Oakwood
  (Paulding Cty) F-2
Oakwood
  (Montgomery Cty) . . K-2
  Vicinity . . . . . Pg. 101, F-6
Oberlin F-6
Obetz K-5
  Vicinity . . . . . Pg. 102, H-5
Ohio City G-1
Ontario H-6
Orange . . . . . Pg. 101, D-7
Orangeville F-10
Oregon E-4
Orient . . . . . Pg. 102, K-2
Orrville G-7
Orwell E-9
Ottawa G-3
Ottawa Hills E-4
Ottoville G-2
Otway N-4
Owensville M-2
Oxford L-1
Painesville E-9

Pandora G-3
Parma F-8
  Vicinity . . . Pg. 101, E-3
Parma Heights
  . . . . Pg. 101, E-2
Pataskala K-6
Paulding F-1
Payne G-1
Pemberville F-4
Peninsula . . . . Pg. 101, J-5
Pepper Pike . Pg. 101, C-7
Perry E-9
Perrysburg E-4
Perrysville H-6
Philo K-7
Pickerington K-5
Piketon M-5
Pioneer E-2
Piqua J-2
Plain City J-4
Pleasant Corners
  . . . . Pg. 102, J-2
Pleasant Hill J-2
Pleasantville K-6
Plymouth G-6
Poland G-10
Pomeroy M-7
Port Clinton E-5
Port Washington J-8
Portsmouth N-5
Powell . . . . . . Pg. 102, B-3
Powhatan Point K-9
Proctorville O-6
Prospect H-4
Put-in-Bay E-5
Quaker City K-8
Quincy J-3
Racine M-7
Rathbone . . . . Pg. 102, A-2
Ravenna F-9
Reading M-2
  Vicinity . . . . Pg. 100, B-5
Reese . . . . . . Pg. 102, H-5
Remsen Corners
  . . . . Pg. 101, K-3
Republic F-5
Reynoldsburg K-5
  Vicinity . . . . Pg. 102, F-7
Richfield . . . . . Pg. 101, H-5
Richmond J-8
Richmond Heights
  . . . . Pg. 101, A-6
Rio Grande N-6
Ripley N-3
Rising Sun F-4
Rittman G-7
Riverlea . . . . . Pg. 102, D-4
Roaming Shores E-10
Rock Creek E-9
Rockford H-1
Rocky River . . Pg. 101, C-1
Rome N-4
Roseville K-7
Rossford E-4
Rushsylvania H-3
Russells Point H-3
Rutland M-7
Sabina L-3
Sagamore Hills
  . . . . Pg. 101, G-5
Saint Bernard Pg. 100, D-4
Saint Clairsville J-9
Saint Henry H-1
Saint Marys H-2
Saint Paris J-3
Salem G-9
Salineville H-9
San Margherita
  . . . . Pg. 102, F-2
Sandusky E-6
Sarahsville K-8
Sardinia N-3
Scio H-9
Seaman N-4
Sebring G-9
Senecaville K-8
Seven Hills . . . Pg. 101, E-4
Seven Mile L-1
Seville G-7
Shadeville . . . Pg. 102, J-4
Shadyside K-9
Shaker Heights F-8
  Vicinity . . . Pg. 101, C-6
Sharonville . . . Pg. 100, A-5
Shawnee L-7
Shawnee Hills
  . . . . Pg. 102, B-1
Sheffield Lake E-6
Shelby G-6
Sherwood F-1
Shiloh G-6
Shreve H-7
Sidney J-2
Silverton . . . Pg. 100, C-5
Sinking Spring N-4
Smithfield J-10
Solon . . . . Pg. 101, E-7
Somerset K-6
South Bloomfield K-5
South Charleston K-3
South Euclid Pg. 101, B-6
South Lebanon L-2
South Point O-6
South Russell F-9
South Webster N-5
South Zanesville K-7
Spencer F-7
Spencerville H-2
Spring Valley L-3
Springboro L-2
Springdale . . . Pg. 100, A-4
Springfield K-3
Stockport L-7
Stoutsville L-5

Stow F-8
  Vicinity . . . Pg. 101, K-7
Strasburg H-8
Streetsboro F-9
Strongsville F-7
  Vicinity . . . Pg. 101, G-1
Struthers G-10
Stryker E-2
Stuebenville H-10
Sugar Grove L-6
Sugarcreek H-8
Sunbury J-5
Swanton E-3
Sycamore G-4
Sylvania E-3
Syracruse M-7
Tallmadge G-8
Terrace Park M-2
Thornville K-6
Tiffin G-5
Tiltonsville J-10
Tipp City K-2
Toledo E-4
Toronto H-10
Trenton L-1
Trimble L-7
Trotwood K-2
Troy J-2
Tuscarawas H-8
Twinsburg . . . Pg. 101, G-6
Uhrichsville J-8
Union K-2
Union City J-1
University Heights
  . . . . Pg. 101, C-6
Upper Arlington K-4
  Vicinity . . . Pg. 102, E-3
Upper Sandusky G-4
Urbana J-3
Urbancrest K-4
  Vicinity . . . . Pg. 102, H-3
Utica J-6
Valley View . . Pg. 101, E-5
Valleyview . . . Pg. 102, F-2
Van Wert G-1
Vandalia K-2
Vermilion F-6
Versailles J-2
Vinton M-6
Wadsworth G-7
Wakeman F-6
Walbridge F-4
Walton Hills Pg. 101, F-6
Wapokoneta H-2
Warren F-10
Warrensville Heights
  . . . . Pg. 101, D-6
Warsaw J-7
Washington C.H. L-4
Washingtonville H-9
Waterloo . . . . Pg. 102, J-7
Waterville E-3
Wauseon E-2
Waverly M-5
Wayne F-4
Waynesburg G-9
Waynesfield H-3
Waynesville L-3
Wellington F-6
Wellston M-6
Wellsville H-10
West Alexandria K-1
West Carrollton K-2
West Farmington F-9
West Jefferson K-4
West Lafayette J-8
West Liberty J-3
West Mansfield H-4
West Milton K-2
West Richfield
  . . . . Pg. 101, H-4
West Salem G-7
West Union N-4
West Unity E-2
Westerville J-5
  Vicinity . . . . Pg. 102, C-5
Westfield Center G-7
Weston F-3
Whitehall K-5
  Vicinity . . . Pg. 102, F-6
Whitehouse E-3
Wickliffe . . . . Pg. 101, A-7
Wilkesville M-6
Willard G-5
Williamsburg M-2
Williamsport L-4
Willoughby E-8
Willoughby Hills E-8
Willowby Hills Pg. 101, A-7
Willowick E-8
Willshire H-1
Wilmington L-3
Winchester N-3
Windham F-9
Wintersville H-10
Woodlawn . . Pg. 100, B-4
Woodmere . . Pg. 101, D-7
Woodsfield K-9
Woodville F-4
Wooster G-7
Worthington J-5
  Vicinity . . . Pg. 102, D-4
Wyoming . . Pg. 100, B-4
Xenia L-3
Yellow Springs K-3
Yorkville J-10
Youngstown F-9
Zanesville K-7

OKLAHOMA
Pages 68-69
Population: 3,025,487
Capital: Oklahoma City
Land Area: 68,655 sq. mi.

Achille J-11
Acme G-8
Ada G-10
Adair C-13
Addington G-9
Afton C-13
Agawam G-9
Agra E-10
Ahloso G-11
Albany H-11
Albert F-8
Albion G-13
Alcorn C-9
Alderson G-12
Aledo E-7
Alex F-8
Alfalfa F-8
Aline C-8
Allen G-11
Alpers D-8
Altus G-6
Alva C-7
Amber F-8
Ames D-8
Amorita B-8
Anadarko F-8
Angora G-9
Antioch G-9
Apache F-7
Apperson C-10
Apple H-12
Aqua Park E-13
Arapaho E-7
Arcadia E-9
  Vicinity . . . Pg. 131, A-7
Ardmore H-10
Arnett D-6
Arpelar F-12
Asher F-10
Ashland G-11
Atoka H-11
Atwood F-11
Avant C-11
Avard C-7
Avery E-10
Aydelotte E-10
Babbs F-7
Bache F-12
Bado D-7
Bald Hill E-12
Balko C-5
Barnesdall C-11
Barr D-8
Bartlesville C-11
Battiest G-13
Baum H-11
Bearden F-11
Beggs E-11
Bellvue E-9
Belva C-7
Bengal G-13
Bennington H-11
Bernice C-13
Bessie E-7
Bethany . . . . Pg. 131, D-2
Bethel H-13
Bethel Acres F-10
Big Cabin C-13
Big Cedar G-13
Bigheart C-11
Billings C-9
Binger F-8
Bison D-9
Bixby D-12
Blackburn D-11
Blackwell C-10
Blair G-6
Blanchard F-9
Blocker F-12
Blue H-11
Boise City C-2
Boley E-11
Bomar J-10
Boswell H-11
Bowlegs F-10
Box E-13
Boyd C-4
Boynton E-12
Brace C-7
Braggs E-12
Braman C-9
Bray G-8
Briartown F-13
Bridgeport E-8
Brinkman F-6
Bristow E-11
Broken Arrow D-11
Broken Bow H-13
Bromide H-11
Brooksville F-10
Brown H-11
Brushy E-13
Bryan's Corner B-4
Bryant F-11
Buffalo C-6
Bugtussle F-12
Bunch E-13
Burbank C-10
Burlington B-7
Burmah F-8
Burns Flat F-7
Butler E-7
Byars G-10
Byng G-11
Byron C-8
Cabiniss F-11

Cache G-8
Caddo H-11
Calvin F-11
Camargo D-7
Canadian F-12
Canadian Club City . . F-9
Caney H-11
Canton D-8
Capron C-8
Carleton D-8
Carmen C-8
Carnegie F-8
Carney E-10
Carrier C-8
Carter F-7
Cartwright J-10
Cashion E-9
Castle E-11
Caston F-13
Catesby C-6
Catoosa D-12
Cedar Springs D-8
Cement F-8
Centrahoma G-11
Centralia C-12
Ceres D-10
Cestos D-7
Chandler E-10
Chattanooga G-7
Checotah E-12
Chelsea C-12
Cherokee C-8
Chester D-7
Cheyenne E-6
Chickasha F-8
Childers C-12
Chilocco B-10
Chisney F-10
Chloeta C-13
Chockie G-11
Choctaw . . . . Pg. 131, E-7
Choska E-12
Chouteau D-12
Cimmaron City E-9
Claremore D-12
Clayton G-12
Clemscott H-10
Cleo Springs D-8
Cleveland D-11
Clinton E-7
Cloud Chief F-7
Coalgate G-11
Cogar F-8
Colbert J-11
Cole F-9
Coleman H-11
Collinsville D-12
Colony F-8
Comanche H-9
Commerce B-13
Connerville G-11
Cookietown H-8
Cookson E-13
Cooperton G-7
Cora C-7
Cordell F-7
Corinne H-13
Corn E-7
Cornish H-9
Corum H-8
Council Hill E-12
Courtney J-9
Covington D-9
Cowden F-8
Coweta D-12
Cowlington F-13
Coyle D-10
Crawford E-6
Crekola E-12
Crescent D-9
Creta G-6
Criner F-9
Cromwell F-11
Crowder F-12
Curtis C-7
Cushing D-10
Custer City E-7
Cyril G-8
Dacoma C-8
Daisy G-12
Dale F-10
Darwin H-12
Davenport E-10
Davidson H-7
Davis G-10
Deer Creek C-9
Del City . . . . Pg. 131, F-5
Delaware C-12
Dempsey E-7
Denman F-13
Depew E-11
Devol H-7
Dewey C-12
Dibble F-9
Dickson H-10
Dill City F-7
Dillworth B-10
Dougherty G-10
Douglas D-9
Dover D-9
Doxey F-6
Drake H-12
Driftwood C-8
Drummond D-8
Drumright E-11
Duke G-6
Dunbar F-12
Duncan G-8
Durant H-11
Durham E-6
Durwood H-10
Dustin F-11
Eagle City D-8
Eakly F-8

Earlsboro F-10
Eason F-10
Eddy C-9
Edith C-7
Edmond . . . . Pg. 131, A-5
El Reno E-8
Eldon D-13
Eldorado G-6
Elgin G-8
Elk City E-6
Elmer G-6
Elmore City G-9
Elmwood C-5
Emet H-10
Empire City G-8
Enid D-9
Enterprise F-12
Erick F-6
Eubanks G-12
Eufaula F-12
Eva C-3
Hulah B-11
Evening Star E-8
Fair Oaks D-12
Fairfax C-10
Fairland C-13
Fairmont D-9
Fairview D-8
Fallis E-10
Fallon F-12
Fanshawe F-13
Fargo D-6
Farris H-12
Faxon G-8
Fay E-7
Featherston F-12
Felt C-2
Fewell G-13
Fillmore H-11
Finley H-12
Fireworks City
  . . . . Pg. 131, G-2
Fittstown G-10
Fitzhugh G-10
Fleetwood H-9
Fletcher G-8
Floris D-7
Folsom H-11
Foraker C-10
Forest Park . . Pg. 131, D-5
Forgan B-5
Fort Arbuckle G-9
Fort Cobb F-8
Fort Gibson E-13
Fort Supply C-6
Fort Towson H-13
Forty One F-7
Foss E-7
Four Corners C-3
Fowler E-10
Foyil C-12
Fox H-9
Francis G-10
Frederick G-7
Freedom C-7
Gage D-6
Gans F-13
Gansel D-9
Garber D-9
Garvin H-13
Gate B-5
Gay H-12
Geary E-8
Gene Autry H-10
Gerty G-11
Gibbon B-8
Gideon D-13
Gideon B-13
Glencoe D-10
Glenpool D-11
Glover H-13
Goldsby F-9
Goltry C-8
Goodland H-12
Goodwell C-3
Goodwin D-6
Gore E-13
Gotebo F-7
Gould G-6
Gowen G-12
Gracemont F-8
Grady H-9
Grainola B-11
Grandfield H-7
Granite F-6
Grant H-11
Gray C-4
Grayson E-12
Greenfield E-8
Griggs C-3
Grove C-13
Guthrie E-9
Guymon C-3
Haileyville G-12
Hall Park . . . . Pg. 131, F-7
Hammon E-6
Hanna F-12
Harden City G-10
Hardesty C-4
Hardy B-10
Harmon D-6
Harrah E-10
Hartshorne G-12
Haskell E-12
Hastings H-8
Haworth J-13
Haywood G-11
Headrick G-7
Healdton H-9
Heavener G-13
Hectorville E-12
Helena C-8
Hendrix J-11
Hennepin G-9
Hennessey D-9
Henryetta E-11
Hickory G-10

Higgins G-12
Hillsdale C-8
Hinton E-8
Hitchcock D-8
Hobart F-7
Hodgen G-13
Holdenville F-11
Hollis G-6
Hollister H-7
Hollow C-12
Homestead D-8
Hominy D-11
Honobia G-13
Hooker B-4
Hoot Owl D-13
Hopeton C-7
Hough B-3
Howe F-13
Hucmac D-7
Hugo H-12
Hulbert D-13
Hulen G-8
Humphreys G-7
Hunter C-9
Huskey H-12
Hydro E-8
Idabel H-13
Indiahoma G-7
Indianola F-12
Ingersoll C-8
Inola D-12
Isabella D-8
Jay C-13
Jefferson C-9
Jenks D-11
Jennings D-11
Jesse G-11
Jet C-8
Jones . . . . Pg. 131, C-7
Joy G-10
Kansas D-13
Karma J-11
Karns E-8
Kellyville E-11
Kendrick E-10
Kent H-12
Kenton B-2
Keota F-13
Keyes C-3
Kiamichi G-12
Kildare C-10
Kingfisher E-9
Kingston H-10
Kinta F-13
Kiowa G-11
Knowles C-5
Konawa F-10
Kosoma H-12
Kremlin C-9
Kusa E-12
Lacey D-8
Lahoma D-8
Lake Aluma . Pg. 131, C-5
Lake Valley F-7
Lamar F-11
Lambert C-8
Lamont C-9
Lane H-11
Langston E-10
Latta G-10
Laverne C-6
Lawrie G-8
Leach D-13
Lebanon H-10
Leedey E-6
Lehigh G-11
Lela D-10
Lenapah C-12
Leon H-9
Leonard E-11
Lequire F-13
Letitia G-8
Lewisville F-12
Lexington F-10
Lima F-10
Lincoln G-6
Lindsay G-9
Little Axe F-10
Little City H-10
Loco H-9
Locust Grove D-12
Lone Grove H-9
Lone Wolf F-7
Longdale D-8
Lookeba F-8
Lookout B-7
Lovedale C-6
Loveland H-7
Lovell D-9
Loyal D-8
Lucien D-9
Lugert F-7
Lula G-11
Luther E-10
Lyman C-10
Lyons E-13
Macomb F-10
Madill H-10
Manchester B-9
Mangum F-6
Manitou G-7
Mannsville H-10
Maramac D-10
Marietta J-9
Marland C-10
Marlow G-8
Marshall D-9
Martha G-6
Mason E-11
Maud F-10
Mayfield F-6
Maysville G-9

OKLAHOMA

Mazie D-12
McAlester F-12
McBride H-11
McCurtain F-13
McLoud E-10
McQueen G-6
McWillie C-8
Mead H-10
Medford C-9
Meeker E-10
Meers G-8
Meno D-8
Meridian E-10
Messer H-12
Miami C-13
Middleberg F-9
Midwest City Pg. 131, E-6
Milburn H-11
Milfay E-11
Mill Creek G-10
Millerton H-13
Milo H-9
Milton F-13
Minco F-9
Mocane B-5
Moore Pg. 131, H-5
Mooreland C-7
Morris E-12
Morrison D-10
Mounds E-11
Mountain View F-7
Moyers H-12
Mulhall D-9
Muskogee E-12
Mustang F-9
Mutual D-7
Narcissa C-13
Nardin C-9
Nash C-8
Nashoba G-13
Navina E-10
Nebo H-10
New Alluwe C-12
New Eucha D-13
New Prue D-11
New Ringold H-13
New Tulsa D-12
New Woodville H-10
Newcastle F-9
  Vicinity Pg. 131, J-2
Newkirk C-10
Nichols Hills Pg. 131, C-4
Nicoma Park Pg. 131, D-7
Nida H-11
Ninnekah F-9
Noble F-9
Norge F-8
Norman F-9
  Vicinity Pg. 131, K-5
North Miami B-13
Nowata C-12
Numa C-9
Oakland H-10
Oaks D-13
Oakwood D-7
Ochelata C-12
Octavia G-13
Oilton D-11
Okeene D-8
Okemah F-11
Okesa C-11
Okfuskee E-11
Oklahoma City E-9
  Vicinity Pg. 131
Okmulgee E-11
Oleta H-12
Olney G-11
Olustee G-6
Omega E-8
Onapa F-12
Oneta D-12
Oologah C-12
Optima C-4
Ord H-12
Orienta D-8
Orion D-7
Orlando D-9
Osage D-11
Ottawa C-13
Overbrook H-10
Owasso D-12
Owen B-11
Ozark E-11
Paden E-11
Panama F-13
Panola F-12
Paoli G-10
Patton C-13
Pauls Valley G-10
Pawhuska C-11
Pawnee D-10
Payne G-9
Pearson F-10
Pearsonia C-11
Peggs D-13
Peoria B-13
Perkins D-10
Perry D-10
Pershing C-11
Petersburg H-9
Pharoah F-11
Phillips G-11
Picher B-13
Pierce F-12
Pink F-10
Pittsburg G-12
Plainview H-11
Platter H-11
Poccasset F-8
Pocola C-10
Pond Creek C-9
Pontotoc G-11
Pooleville G-9
Porter E-12

Porum F-13
Poteau F-13
Prague E-10
Preston E-11
Proctor D-13
Pryor D-12
Pumpkin Center G-8
Purcell F-9
Purdy G-9
Putnam E-7
Pyramid Corners C-12
Quapaw B-13
Quay D-10
Quinlan C-7
Quinton F-12
Ralston C-10
Ramona C-11
Randlett H-8
Rankin E-6
Ratliff City G-9
Rattan H-12
Ravia H-10
Reagan H-10
Red Bird E-12
Red Oak F-13
Red Rock D-10
Redden G-12
Reed F-6
Remus F-10
Renfrow B-9
Retrop F-7
Reydon E-6
Rhea E-7
Richards Spur G-8
Ringling H-9
Ringold H-12
Ringwood D-8
Roberta H-11
Rocky C-8
Roff G-10
Roll E-6
Roosevelt G-7
Rose D-13
Rosedale G-10
Rosston C-6
Rubottom H-9
Rush Springs G-9
Ryan H-9
Saddle Mountain G-7
Saint Louis F-10
Salem F-12
Salina D-13
Sallisaw E-13
Salt Fork C-9
Sand Springs D-11
Sapulpa D-11
Sasakwa F-10
Sayre F-6
Scraper D-13
Scullin G-10
Seiling D-7
Selman C-6
Seminole E-11
Sentinel F-7
Shamrock E-11
Sharon D-6
Shattuck D-6
Shawnee F-10
Shidler C-11
Skedee D-10
Skiatook D-11
Slapout C-6
Slaughterville F-10
Slick E-11
Smithville G-13
Smith Village Pg. 131, E-6
Snow G-12
Snyder G-7
Soper H-12
South Coffeyville C-12
Southard D-8
Sparks E-10
Spear H-12
Spencer Pg. 131, D-6
Sperry D-11
Spiro F-13
Springer H-10
Stanley G-12
Steadman G-11
Stecker F-8
Sterling G-8
Stidham F-12
Stigler F-13
Stillwater D-10
Stilwell E-13
Stonewall G-11
Stratford G-10
Stringtown G-11
Strong City E-6
Stroud E-11
Stuart G-11
Sturgis B-3
Sugden H-9
Sulphur G-11
Summerfield G-13
Summit E-11
Sumner D-10
Sumpter C-10
Surrey Hills B-3
Sweetwater E-6
Sylvian F-11
Tabler F-9
Taft E-12
Tahlequah E-13
Talala C-12
Talihina G-13
Tallant C-11
Taloga D-7
Tangier C-7
Tatums G-9
Taylor H-8
Tecumseh F-10
Tegarden C-7
Temple H-8

Terlton D-11
Terral H-9
Texola F-6
The Village Pg. 131, C-3
Thomas E-7
Three Sands C-10
Tiawah D-12
Tipton G-7
Tonkawa C-10
Trail D-7
Tribbey F-10
Trousdale F-10
Troy H-10
Tryon E-10
Tullahassee E-12
Tulsa D-11
Tupelo G-11
Turpin C-4
Tushka H-11
Tuskahoma G-13
Tuttle F-9
Tyrone B-4
Unger H-12
Union City F-8
Utica H-11
Valley Brook Pg. 131, F-5
Valliant H-13
Vanoss G-10
Velma G-9
Vera C-12
Verdigris D-12
Vernon F-11
Vian E-13
Vici D-7
Vinita C-12
Vinson F-6
Wade H-11
Wadena H-12
Wagoner D-12
Wakita C-9
Wanette F-10
Wapanucka H-11
Warner E-12
Warr Acres Pg. 131, C-2
Warren G-7
Warwick E-10
Waters G-9
Watonga E-8
Watova G-13
Watson G-13
Waukomis D-8
Waurika H-9
Wayne F-10
Waynoka C-7
Weatherford E-7
Webb City C-10
Webbers Falls E-12
Welch C-13
Weleetka F-11
Wellston E-10
Welty E-11
Westport D-11
Wetumka F-11
Wewoka F-11
Wheeless C-2
White Bead G-9
White Oak C-12
Whitefield G-13
Whitesboro G-13
Wilburton F-12
Willis J-10
Willow F-6
Wilson H-9
Wolco E-11
Woodford H-10
Woodlawn Park Pg. 131, D-2
Woodward D-7
Wyandotte C-13
Wynnewood G-10
Wynona D-12
Yale D-10
Yeager H-11
Yewed C-8
Yost D-10
Yuba J-11
Yukon F-9
Zeb E-13
Zena C-13

OREGON
Pages 70-71
Population: 2,633,105
Capital: Salem
Land Area: 98,184 sq. mi.

Adair Village D-3
Adams C-9
Adel J-7
Adrian G-11
Agness H-1
Albany D-3
Algoma J-4
Alicel C-10
Allegany F-2
Alpine E-3
Alsea E-3
Amity D-3
Andrews J-9
Antelope D-6
Applegate J-2
Arlington C-7
Arock H-10
Ashland J-3
Ashwood D-6
Astoria A-3
Athena C-9
Aurora C-4
Austin D-9
Azalea H-3
Baker E-10

Bandon G-1
Banks B-3
Barlow C-4
Bay City B-2
Beatty J-5
Beaver C-2
Beaverton Pg. 137, E-2
Belknap Springs E-4
Bend F-5
Biggs C-6
Birkenfeld B-3
Blalock C-7
Blodgett D-2
Blue River E-4
Bly J-5
Boardman B-8
Bonanza J-5
Bonneville C-6
Boring C-5
Breitenbush Springs D-5
Bridge G-2
Bridgeport E-10
Brightwood C-5
Broadbent G-2
Brogan E-10
Brookings J-1
Brooks D-4
Brothers F-6
Brownsville E-4
Burns H-8
Burns Jct. J-9
Butte Falls H-4
Buxton B-3
Camas Valley G-2
Camp Sherman E-5
Canby C-4
Cannon Beach B-2
Canyon City E-9
Canyonville H-2
Carlton C-3
Cascade Locks C-5
Cascadia E-4
Cave Junction J-2
Cecil C-7
Central Point J-3
Charleston G-1
Chemult G-5
Cheshire E-3
Chiloquin H-5
Christmas Valley G-6
Clackamas Pg. 137, G-6
Clatskanie A-3
Cloverdale C-2
Coburg E-3
Colton C-4
Columbia City B-3
Condon D-7
Coos Bay F-1
Coquille G-2
Corvallis D-2
Cottage Grove F-3
Council Crest Pg. 137, E-4
Cove D-10
Crabtree D-4
Crane G-9
Crawfordsville E-4
Crescent G-5
Crescent Lake G-4
Creswell F-3
Culp Creek F-3
Culver E-5
Curtin F-3
Cushman E-2
Dairy J-5
Dallas D-3
Days Creek H-3
Dayton C-3
Dayville E-8
Dee C-5
Deer Island B-3
Denmark H-1
Depoe Bay D-2
Detroit D-4
Dexter F-3
Diamond H-9
Diamond Lake G-4
Dillard H-3
Disston F-4
Donald C-4
Dorena F-4
Drain F-3
Drew H-3
Drewsey F-9
Dufur C-6
Dunes City F-1
Durkee E-10

Eagle Creek C-4
Eagle Point J-3
Eastside F-1
Echo C-8
Eddyville D-3
Elgin C-10
Elk City D-2
Elkton F-2
Elmira E-3
Enterprise C-11
Estacada C-5
Eugene F-3
Falls City D-3
Falls Creek F-4
Fields J-8
Flora B-11
Florence E-2
Forest Grove C-3
Fort Klamath H-4
Fort Rock G-6
Fossil D-7
Fox E-8
Frenchglen H-8
Friend C-6
Gales Creek B-3
Gardiner F-2
Garibaldi B-2
Gaston C-3
Gates D-4
Gaylord H-2
Gearhart A-2
Gervais C-4
Gibbon C-9
Gilchrist G-5
Gladstone Pg. 137, G-6
Glenada E-2
Glendale H-2
Gleneden Beach D-2
Glenwood B-3
Glide G-3
Goble B-4
Gold Beach H-1
Gold Hill H-3
Goshen F-3
Government Camp C-5
Grand Ronde C-3
Grangeville B-12
Granite D-9
Grants Pass H-2
Grass Valley C-6
Gravelford G-2
Greenhorn E-9
Gresham C-4
Haines D-10
Halfway D-11
Halsey E-3
Hamilton D-8
Hammond A-2
Hampton G-6
Harbor J-1
Hardman D-7
Harlan E-2
Harper F-10
Harrisburg E-3
Hebo C-2
Heceta Beach E-2
Helix B-9
Heppner C-8
Hereford E-10
Hermiston B-8
Hillsboro C-3
Hillsdale Pg. 137, E-4
Hines G-8
Holley E-4
Homestead D-11
Hood River B-5
Horton Blachly E-3
Hoskins D-3
Hubbard C-4
Huntington E-10
Idanha D-5
Ideyld Park G-3
Imbler C-10
Imnaha C-11
Independence D-3
Ione C-8
Ironside E-10
Island City C-10
Jacksonville J-3
Jamieson F-10
Jasper E-3
Jefferson D-4
Jewell B-3
John Day E-9
Jordan Valley H-10
Joseph D-11
Junction City E-3
Juntura G-9
Kamela C-9
Keizer D-3
Keno J-4
Kent D-6
Kerby J-2
Kernville D-2
Kimberly D-7
King City Pg. 137, G-2
Kings Valley D-3
Kinzua D-7
Klamath Agency H-4
Klamath Falls J-4

La Grande D-9
La Pine G-5
Lacomb D-4
Lafayette C-3
Lake Grove Pg. 137, G-3
Lakecreek J-3
Lakeside F-1
Lakeview J-7
Langlois G-1
Lawen G-9
Leaburg E-4
Lebanon D-4
Lexington C-7
Lincoln Beach D-2
Lincoln City D-2
Lonerock C-7
Long Creek E-8
Lorane F-3
Lostine C-11
Lowell F-4
Lyons D-4
Mabel E-4
Madras D-5
Malin K-5
Manning B-4
Manzanita B-2
Mapleton E-2
Marcola E-4
Marion D-4
Maupin C-6
Mayville D-7
McCredie Springs F-4
McKenzie Bridge E-5
McMinnville C-3
McNary B-8
Meacham C-9
Medford J-3
Medical Springs D-10
Merlin H-2
Merrill K-5
Metolius E-6
Metzger Pg. 137, F-2
Midland J-5
Mikkalo C-7
Mill City D-4
Millersburg D-3
Millican F-6
Milo H-3
Milton Freewater B-10
Milwaukie Pg. 137, F-5
Minam C-10
Mission E-9
Mist B-3
Mitchell E-7
Mohawk E-4
Mohler B-2
Molalla C-4
Monmouth D-3
Monroe E-3
Monument D-8
Moro C-6
Mosier C-6
Mount Hood C-5
Mount Vernon E-8
Mt. Angel C-4
Mulino C-4
Multnomah Pg. 137, E-3
Murphy J-2
Myrtle Creek G-3
Myrtle Point G-1
Nehalem B-3
Neskowin C-2
Netarts C-2
New Bridge E-11
New Princeton G-9
Newberg C-3
Newport D-2
North Bend F-2
North Plains B-4
North Powder D-10
Norway G-1
Noti E-3
Nyssa F-11
O'Brien J-2
Oak Grove Pg. 137, G-5
Oakland G-3
Oakridge F-4
Oceanside C-2
Odell C-5
Olene J-5
Ontario F-11
Ophir H-1
Oregon City C-4
Otis C-2
Otter Rock D-2
Owyhee F-11
Pacific City C-2
Paisley H-6
Parkdale C-5
Paulina F-7
Pendleton C-8
Philomath D-3
Phoenix J-3
Pilot Rock C-9
Pinehurst J-4
Pistol River J-1
Pleasant Hill F-4
Pleasant Valley E-10
Plush J-7
Port Orford H-1
Portland C-4
  Vicinity Pg. 137
Post E-6
Powell Butte E-6
Powers G-1
Prairie City E-9
Prescott B-4
Prineville E-6
Prospect H-4
Rainier B-4
Raleigh Hills Pg. 137, E-3
Redmond D-5
Reedsport F-2
Remote G-2
Rhododendron C-5
Richland E-11
Riddle H-3
Riley H-7
Ritter D-8
Riverton G-1
Rockaway B-2
Rogue River H-3
Rome H-10
Roseburg G-3
Rufus C-7
Saginaw F-3
Saint Helens B-4
Saint Paul C-4
Salem D-3
Sandy C-4
Scappoose B-3
Scio D-4
Scottsburg F-2
Seal Rock D-2
Seaside A-2
Selma J-2
Seneca E-9
Shady Cove H-3
Shaniko D-6
Sheaville H-11
Shedd E-4
Sheridan C-3
Sherwood C-3
Siletz D-2
Siltcoos F-2
Silver Lake G-6
Silverton D-4
Sisters E-5
Sitkum G-2
Sixes G-1
Skipanon A-2
Sodaville E-4
South Beach D-2
Sprague River J-5
Spray D-7

Springfield E-3
Stanfield B-8
Stayton D-4
Sublimity D-4
Summer Lake H-6
Summerville C-10
Sumner E-9
Sumpter E-9
Sunriver F-5
Sutherlin G-3
Sweethome E-4
Swisshome E-2
Talent J-3
Tangent D-4
Telocaset D-10
Tenmile G-2
Terrebonne E-5
The Dalles C-6
Tidewater E-2
Tiernan E-2
Tigard Pg. 137, F-2
Tillamook C-3
Tiller H-3
Timber B-3
Toledo D-2
Trail H-3
Troutdale C-5
Troy B-10
Tualatin C-4
Turner D-3
Tygh Valley C-6
Ukiah D-8
Umapine B-9
Umatilla B-8
Umpqua G-3
Union D-10
Union Creek H-3
Unity E-10
Vale F-10
Valley Falls J-6
Valsetz D-3
Veneta E-3
Vernonia B-3
Vida E-4
Waldport E-2
Walker F-3
Wallowa C-10
Walterville E-4
Walton E-2
Wamic C-6
Warm Springs D-5
Warren B-4
Warrenton A-2
Wasco C-7
Waterloo E-4
Wedderburn H-1
Wemme C-5
West Fir F-4
West Linn C-4
West Slope Pg. 137, D-2
West Stayton D-3
Westfall F-10
Weston B-9
Westport A-3
Wheeler B-2
White City J-3
Whitney E-9
Wilbur G-3
Wilderville J-2
Willamina C-3
Williams J-3
Willow Creek F-10
Wilsonville C-4
Winchester G-3
Winchester Bay F-1
Winston H-3
Wolfcreek H-2
Wonder J-2
Woodburn C-4
Yachats E-2
Yamhill C-3
Yoncalla G-3
Zigzag C-5

PENNSYLVANIA

PENNSYLVANIA
Pages 72-73
Population: 11,863,895
Capital: Harrisburg
Land Area: 44,888 sq. mi.

Abington Pg. 134, B-6
Academy Gardens Pg. 134, C-8
Adamstown H-11
Addison K-4
Akron H-11
Alba D-9
Albion C-1
Alburtis G-12
Aldan Pg. 134, F-3
Aliquippa H-2
Allentown G-12
Altoona G-6
Ambler H-13
Ambridge H-2
Andorra Pg. 134, C-4
Archbald D-12
Arendtsville J-8
Armagh G-4
Aronimink Pg. 134, D-3
Ashley E-11
Ashville H-6
Athens C-10
Austin D-7
Avalon Pg. 136, B-1
Avis E-8
Avonmore G-3
Baden H-2
Bala-Cynwyd Pg. 134, D-4

Baldwin Pg. 136, F-5
Bally H-12
Bangor F-13
Barnesboro G-5
Bartram Village Pg. 134, F-4
Bath G-13
Beaver G-1
Beaver Falls F-1
Beavertown F-9
Bedford J-6
Beech Creek E-8
Belle Vernon J-2
Bellefonte F-7
Bellevue
  Vicinity Pg. 136, B-2
Bellwood H-6
Ben Avon Pg. 136, A-1
Bendersville J-8
Benson H-5
Benton E-10
Berlin J-4
Berrysburg F-9
Berwick F-11
Bessemer F-1
Bethel Park H-2
  Vicinity Pg. 136, G-2
Bethlehem G-13
Big Beaver F-1
Big Run F-5
Birdsboro H-12
Black Horse Pg. 134, F-1
Blain H-7
Blairsville G-3
Blakely D-12
Blooming Valley C-2
Bloomsburg F-10
Blossburg C-9
Blue Bell Pg. 134, A-3
Bolivar H-4
Boswell H-4
Bowmanston F-12
Boyertown H-12
Brackenridge G-3
Bradford C-5
Brentwood Pg. 136, F-4
Briar Creek F-11
Bridgeport Pg. 134, B-2
Bridgeville H-2
Bristol J-14
Broad Axe Pg. 134, A-4
Broad Top City H-6
Brockway E-5
Brookhaven Pg. 134, F-3
Brookville D-4
  Vicinity Pg. 134, G-1
Brookville E-4
Broomall Pg. 134, D-2
Brownsville H-5
Brownsville J-2
Bruin E-3
Bryn Athyn Pg. 134, A-7
Bryn Mawr Pg. 134, D-2
Burgettstown H-1
Burlington C-10
Burnham G-8
Burnside F-5
Bustleton Pg. 134, B-7
Butler F-2
Calico Corner Pg. 134, B-9
California J-2
Callensburg E-3
Callery H-2
Cambridge Springs C-2
Canonsburg H-2
Canton D-9
Carbondale D-12
Carlisle H-9
Carmichaels J-2
Carnegie H-2
Carroll Park Pg. 134, D-4
Carroll Valley K-8
Carrolltown G-5
Cassandra H-5
Castle Shannon
  Pg. 136, F-3
Catasauqua G-12
Catawissa F-10
Cedarbrook Pg. 134, B-5
Center Square
  Pg. 134, A-3
Centerville
  (Washington Cty) J-2
Centerville
  (Crawford Cty) C-3
Central City J-5
Centre Hall F-7
Chalfont H-13
Chambersburg H-7
Charleroi H-2
Cherry Tree G-5
Chester J-13
  Vicinity Pg. 134, F-4
Chester Heights J-12
Chester Hill F-6
Chestnut Hill Pg. 134, C-4
Chicora F-3
Clairton H-2
Clarendon C-4
Clarion E-4
Clarks Summit D-12
Clearfield F-6
Cleona H-10
Clifton Heights
  Pg. 134, F-3
Clintonville E-3
Clymer G-5
Coalport G-5
Coatesville H-12
Cobbs Creek Pg. 134, D-4
Cochranton D-2
Cokeburg H-2
Collegeville H-13
Colling Dale Pg. 134, F-3
Columbia J-10
Colwyn Pg. 134, F-4

PENNSYLVANIA

Conneautville C-1
Connellsville J-3
Connoquenessing . . F-2
Conshohocken J-13
  Vicinity . . . Pg. 134, B-3
Conway G-2
Conyngham F-11
Coopersburg G-13
Cooperstown D-3
Coraopolis G-2
Cornwall H-10
Corry C-3
Corsica E-4
Coudersport C-7
Crafton . . . . Pg. 136, D-2
Cranesville C-2
Creekside G-4
Cresson G-5
Cressona G-11
Croydon . . . Pg. 134, B-10
Curwensville F-6
Dallastown J-10
Dalton D-12
Danville F-10
Darby J-13
  Vicinity . . Pg. 134, F-4
Dauphin H-9
Dayton F-4
Deepdale . . . Pg. 134, C-1
Delaware Water Gap F-13
Delta K-11
Denver H-11
Derry H-4
Dickson City D-12
Dillsburg J-9
Donegal J-4
Donora H-2
Dormont H-2
  Vicinity . . . Pg. 136, E-2
Dover J-9
Downingtown J-12
Doylestown H-13
Dresher . . . Pg. 134, A-5
Driftwood E-6
DuBois E-5
Duboistown E-9
Dudley H-6
Dunbar J-3
Duncannon H-9
Duncansville H-6
Dunmore D-12
Dushore D-10
Eagles Mere D-10
Eagleville . . Pg. 134, A-4
East Berlin J-9
East Brady F-3
East Butler F-3
East Falls . . . Pg. 134, D-5
East Greenville . . . H-12
East Lansdowne
  . . . . . . Pg. 134, D-3
East Mt. Airy Pg. 134, C-5
East Oak Lane
  . . . . . . Pg. 134, C-6
East Stroudsburg . . F-13
East Washington . . . H-2
Easton G-13
Eastwick . . . Pg. 134, F-4
Eau Claire E-3
Ebensburg G-5
Economy G-2
Eddington Park
  . . . . . . Pg. 134, B-9
Eddystone . . Pg. 134, G-4
Edinboro C-2
Edwardsville E-11
Eldred C-6
Elizabethtown H-10
Elizabethville G-10
Elkland C-7
Ellport F-2
Ellwood City F-2
Elmwood . . . Pg. 134, F-4
Elwyn . . . Pg. 134, F-1
Emlenton E-3
Emmaus G-12
Emporium D-6
Ephrata H-11
Erie . . . . . . Pg. 136, B-5
Etna . . . . . . Pg. 136, B-5
Evans City F-2
Everett J-6
Everson J-3
Factoryville D-12
Fairchance J-3
Fairfield K-8
Fairview B-2
Fairview Village
  . . . . . . Pg. 134, A-1
Falls Creek E-5
Farrell E-1
Fawn Grove K-10
Fentonville . . Pg. 134, D-6
Fern Rock . . Pg. 134, C-9
Fitzwatertown Pg. 134, A-5
Fleetwood G-12
Flemington E-8
Flourtown . . Pg. 134, B-4
Folcroft . . . Pg. 134, G-3
Ford City F-3
Ford Cliff F-3
Forest City D-12
Forksville D-10
Fort Washington
  . . . . . . Pg. 134, A-4
Forty Fort E-12
Fountain Hill G-13
Foxcroft . . . Pg. 134, D-2
Frackville G-11
Frankford . . Pg. 134, D-7
Franklin D-3
Franklin Park G-2
Freeburg G-9
Freeland F-12

Freemansburg G-13
Freeport G-3
Galeton C-8
Gallitzin G-5
Garrett J-4
Geistown H-5
Germantown Pg. 134, D-5
Gettysburg K-9
Girard B-2
Gladwyne . . Pg. 134, C-3
Glen Campbell F-5
Glen Hope F-6
Glen Rock K-10
Glenolden . . Pg. 134, F-3
Glenside . . . Pg. 134, B-6
Gordon G-11
Grampian F-5
Gratz G-10
Great Bend C-12
Greencastle K-7
Greensboro J-2
Greensburg H-3
Greentree . . Pg. 136, E-2
Greenville D-1
Grove City E-2
Halifax G-9
Hallstead C-12
Hamburg G-11
Hanover K-9
Harmonville . Pg. 134, B-3
Harmony F-2
Harrisburg H-9
Harrisville E-2
Harveys Lake D-11
Hastings G-5
Hatboro H-13
Havertown . . Pg. 134, D-3
Hawley D-13
Hawthorn F-4
Hazleton F-11
Heidelberg . . Pg. 136, E-1
Herndon G-9
Hershey H-10
Holidaysburg H-6
Holmesburg . Pg. 134, C-7
Homer City G-4
Homestead . . Pg. 136, E-6
Honesdale D-13
Honey Brook J-12
Hooversville H-5
Hop Bottom C-12
Hopewell H-7
Houston H-2
Houtzdale F-6
Hughesville E-10
Hulmeville . . Pg. 134, A-9
Hummelstown H-10
Huntingdon G-7
Huntingdon Valley
  . . . . . . Pg. 134, B-7
Hydetown C-3
Hyndman K-5
Indian Lake J-5
Indiana G-4
Industry G-1
Ingram . . . . Pg. 136, D-1
Irvona F-5
Ithan . . . . . Pg. 134, C-1
Jackson Center . . . E-2
Jacobus J-10
Jamestown D-1
Jeanette H-3
Jeddo E-1
Jefferson H-2
Jeffersonville Pg. 134, A-2
Jenkintown . . Pg. 134, B-6
Jennerstown H-4
Jermyn D-12
Jersey Shore E-9
Jim Thorpe F-12
Johnsonburg D-5
Johnstown H-5
Jonestown H-10
Juniata . . . Pg. 134, D-6
Kane D-6
Karns City F-3
Kennett Square . . . J-12
Kensington . . Pg. 134, E-6
King of Prussia
  . . . . . . Pg. 134, B-1
Kingston E-11
Kistler H-7
Kittanning F-3
Knox E-3
Knoxville C-7
Kulpmont F-10
Kutztown G-12
Lake City B-2
Lancaster J-11
Landisburg H-8
Lanesboro C-12
Langhorne H-14
Langhorne Manor
  . . . . . . Pg. 134, A-9
Lansdale H-13
Lansdowne . . Pg. 134, J-13
  Vicinity . . . Pg. 134, E-3
Lansford F-12
Laporte D-10
Larchmont Meadows
  . . . . . . Pg. 134, E-1
Latrobe H-4
Laureldale G-12
Lawn Crest . . Pg. 134, C-7
Lawrence Park B-2
Le Raysville C-11
Lebanon H-10
Leesport G-11
Lehighton F-12
Lemoyne H-9
Levittown H-14
Lewisburg F-9
Lewistown G-8

Lexington Park
  . . . . . . Pg. 134, C-7
Liberty D-9
Ligonier H-4
Lilly H-5
Lincoln H-11
Linesville C-1
Lititz J-11
Little Meadows C-11
Littlestown K-9
Liverpool G-9
Lock Haven E-8
Logan . . . . Pg. 134, D-6
Loganton E-8
Loretto G-5
Lower Burrell G-3
Lumar Park . . Pg. 134, B-8
Lumber City F-5
Lykens G-10
Macungie G-12
Mahanoy City F-11
Manayunk . . Pg. 134, D-4
Manchester J-10
Manheim J-11
Manns Choice J-5
Mansfield C-9
Marble Hall . Pg. 134, B-4
Marcus Hook K-13
  Vicinity . . . Pg. 134, F-3
Marianna J-2
Marietta J-10
Marion Center F-4
Marklesburg H-6
Mars G-2
Martinsburg H-6
Marysville H-9
Masontown J-2
Matamoras D-14
Mayfair . . . Pg. 134, C-7
McKean B-2
McKeesport H-2
McSherrytown K-9
McVeytown G-7
Mckee's Rocks
  . . . . . . Pg. 136, D-2
Meadville D-2
Mechanicsburg H-9
Media . . . . . Pg. 134, F-1
Mercer E-2
Mercersburg K-7
Meshoppen D-11
Meyersdale K-4
Middleburg G-9
Middletown H-10
  Vicinity . . Pg. 147, A-10
Midland G-1
Mifflinburg F-9
Mifflintown G-8
Milesburg F-7
Milford E-14
Mill Creek H-7
Mill Hall E-8
Mill Village C-2
Millbourne . . Pg. 134, D-3
Millerbrook . . Pg. 134, C-8
Millersburg G-9
Millerstown G-9
Millersville J-10
Millheim F-8
Millridge . . . Pg. 134, D-2
Milton F-9
Minersville G-11
Mohnton H-11
Monaca G-2
Monessen H-2
Monroe C-10
Monroeville G-3
Mont Alto J-8
Montoursville E-9
Montrose C-12
Moosic D-12
Morrisville H-14
Morton . . . Pg. 134, C-5
Moscow E-12
Mountville J-10
Mt. Carmel F-10
Mt. Holly Springs . . J-9
Mt. Jewett C-5
Mt. Joy J-10
Mt. Pleasant H-3
Mt. Pocono E-13
Mt. Union H-7
Mt. Wolf J-10
Murrysville G-3
Myerstown H-11
Nanticoke E-11
Nanty-Glo G-5
Narberth J-13
  Vicinity . . . Pg. 134, D-3
Nazareth G-13
Nescopeck F-11
New Albany D-10
New Alexandra H-3
New Beaver F-1
New Berlin F-9
New Bethlehem F-4
New Brighton F-2
New Buffalo G-9
New Castle F-1
New Centerville . . . J-4
New Cumberland . . . H-9
New Eagle H-2
New Florence H-4
New Freedom K-10
New Holland J-11
New Kensington . . . G-3
New Lebanon D-2
New Milford C-12
New Oxford K-9
New Paris J-5
New Philadelphia . . G-11
New Salem J-2
New Stanton H-3
New Wilmington . . . E-1

Newburg F-5
Newburg J-8
Newport G-9
Newry H-6
Newtown Heights
  . . . . . . Pg. 134, E-1
Newtown Square
  . . . . . . Pg. 134, D-1
Newville H-8
Nicetown-Tioga
  . . . . . . Pg. 134, D-5
Nicholson D-12
Normandy . . Pg. 134, B-8
Norristown J-13
  Vicinity . . . Pg. 134, A-2
Norritonville Pg. 134, A-2
North Apollo G-3
North Belle Vernon . H-3
North East B-2
North Hills . . Pg. 134, B-5
North Wales H-13
North York J-10
Northampton G-12
Northumberland . . . F-10
Norwood . . . Pg. 134, G-3
Nuangola E-11
Oakland C-12
Oakmont G-3, D-4
Ohiopyle J-3
Oil City D-3
Old Forge D-12
Olyphant D-12
Orangeville E-10
Orbisonia H-7
Orrstown J-8
Orwigsburg G-11
Osceola Mills F-6
Oswayo C-7
Overbrook . . Pg. 134, D-4
Oxford K-11
Palmerton G-12
Palmyra H-10
Parker E-3
Parkesburg J-11
Parkside . . . Pg. 134, G-3
Patton G-5
Paxton G-9
Pen Argyl F-13
Penfield . . . Pg. 134, D-3
Penn Square . Pg. 134, A-2
Pennsburg H-13
Perkasie H-13
Petersburg G-7
Petrolia F-3
Philadelphia . . . Pg. 134
Philipsburg F-6
Phoenixville H-12
Picture Rocks E-10
Pillow G-9
Pine Grove G-10
Pittsburgh G-2
  Vicinity . . . . Pg. 136
Pittston E-12
Platea B-2
Pleasantville
  (Venango Cty) . . . D-3
Pleasantville
  (Bedford Cty) H-5
Plum G-3
Plumville F-4
Plymouth Valley
  . . . . . . Pg. 134, B-3
Point Marion K-2
Polk D-2
Port Allegany C-6
Port Carbon G-11
Port Matilda F-7
Port Royal G-8
Portage H-5
Portersville F-2
Portland F-13
Pottstown H-12
Pottsville G-11
Prospect Park
  . . . . . . Pg. 134, G-3
Punxsutawney F-4
Pymble . . . Pg. 134, F-1
Quakertown G-13
Quarryville J-11
Radnor . . . . Pg. 134, C-2
Rainsburg J-5
Ramey F-6
Reading H-12
Red Hill H-13
Red Lion J-10
Renovo E-7
Reynoldsville E-5
Rices Landing J-2
Richland H-11
Richlandtown H-13
Richmond . . Pg. 134, D-6
Ridgway D-5
Ridley Park . Pg. 134, G-3
Rimersburg E-3
Ringtown F-11
Riverside F-10
Roaring Spring H-6
Robesonia H-11
Rockledge . . Pg. 134, B-6
Rockwood J-4
Rome C-11
Rose Valley . Pg. 134, F-1
Rosemont . . Pg. 134, C-2
Roseto F-13
Roslyn . . . . Pg. 134, B-6
Rosslyn Farms
  . . . . . . Pg. 136, D-1
Rouseville D-3
Roxborough . Pg. 134, C-4
Royersford H-12
Rural Valley F-4
Rutledge . . . Pg. 134, G-2
Saegertown C-2

Saint Clair G-11
Saint Marys D-5
Saint Petersburg . . . E-3
Salisbury K-4
Salladasburg E-9
Saltillo H-7
Saltsburg G-3
Sandy Lake D-2
Sankertown G-5
Saxonburg F-3
Saxton H-6
Sayre C-10
Scalp Level H-5
Schuylkill Haven . . . G-11
Scottdale H-3
Scranton D-12
Selinsgrove F-9
Sellersville H-13
Seward H-4
Shade Gap H-7
Shamokin F-10
Shamokin Dam F-9
Sharon E-1
Sharon Hill . Pg. 134, F-3
Sharpsburg . . Pg. 136, B-5
Shenandoah F-11
Shickshinny E-11
Shillington H-11
Shinglehouse C-6
Shippensburg J-8
Shippenville E-3
Shirleysburg H-7
Shoemakersville . . . G-11
Shrewsbury K-10
Sligo E-3
Slippery Rock E-2
Smethport C-6
Smithfield K-3
Snow Shoe F-7
Society Hill . Pg. 134, D-5
Somerset J-4
Somerton . . . Pg. 134, B-8
Souderton H-13
South Bethlehem . . . G-13
South Coatesville . . J-12
South Connellsville . J-3
South Fork H-5
South Philadelphia
  . . . . . . Pg. 134, F-5
South Renovo E-7
South Waverly B-10
South Williamsport . E-9
Spangler G-5
Spartansburg C-3
Spring City H-12
Spring Grove J-9
Spring Mill . . Pg. 134, C-3
Springboro C-1
Springfield . . Pg. 134, F-2
Stanwood . . . Pg. 134, B-9
State College F-7
Stillwater E-12
Stoneboro D-2
Stoystown J-4
Strasburg J-11
Strattanville E-4
Strausstown G-11
Stroudsburg F-13
Sugar Grove B-4
Sugarcreek D-3
Summerhill H-5
Summerville E-4
Summit Hill F-12
Sunbury F-9
Suscon . . . . Pg. 134, E-4
Susquehanna C-12
Swarthmore . . Pg. 134, F-2
Sykesville E-5
Sylvania B-9
Tamaqua G-12
Tatamy G-13
Taylor D-12
Telford H-13
Temple H-12
Terre Hill H-11
Thompsontown G-9
Thornburg . . Pg. 136, D-1
Three Springs H-7
Tidioute C-4
Timberlake . Pg. 134, E-1
Tioga C-9
Tionesta D-3
Titusville D-3
Topton G-12
Towanda C-10
Tower City G-10
Townville C-3
Trainer J-13
Trappe H-12
Tremont G-10
Trooper . . . Pg. 134, A-1
Troutville F-5
Troy C-10
Tullytown H-14
Tunkhannock D-11
Tyrone G-6
Union City C-3
Union Dale C-11
Uniontown J-3
Upland . . . . Pg. 134, G-1
Upper Fairview
  . . . . . . Pg. 134, A-1
Upper Roxborough
  . . . . . . Pg. 134, C-4
Ursina K-4
Vandergrift G-3
Venango C-2
Villanova . . Pg. 134, C-2
Walnutport G-12
Wampum F-1
Warren C-4
Washington H-2
Waterford C-2
Waterloo Mills Pg. 134, D-1

Watsontown E-9
Wattsburg B-3
Waymart D-13
Wayne . . . . Pg. 134, C-1
Waynesboro K-8
Waynesburg J-2
Weatherly F-12
Wellersburg K-5
Wellsboro C-8
Wellsville J-9
Wesleyville B-2
West Brownsville . . . J-2
West Chester J-12
West Conshohocken
  . . . . . . Pg. 134, C-2
West Easton G-13
West Gate Hills
  . . . . . . Pg. 134, D-2
West Grove K-12
West Hazleton F-11
West Homestead
  . . . . . . Pg. 136, E-5
West Kensington
  . . . . . . Pg. 134, D-6
West Kittanning F-3
West Liberty F-2
West Middlesex E-1
West Mifflin G-3
  Vicinity . . . Pg. 136, G-5
West Newton H-3
West Oak Lane
  . . . . . . Pg. 134, C-5
West Philadelphia
  . . . . . . Pg. 134, D-4
West Pittston E-12
West Reading H-11
West View . . Pg. 136, A-2
West York J-10
Westfield C-8
Westmont H-5
Westover G-5
Wheatland E-1
White Haven E-12
White Marsh . Pg. 134, A-6
White Oak H-3
Whitehall J-13
  Vicinity . . . Pg. 136, G-4
Wilkes-Barre E-12
Wilkinsburg G-3
Williamsburg G-6
Williamsport E-9
Williamstown G-10
Willow Grove Pg. 134, A-6
Wilson G-13
Wind Gap F-13
Windber H-5
Winterstown K-10
Womelsdorf H-11
Woodbury H-6
Worthington F-3
Wrightsville J-10
Wyalusing D-11
Wyola . . . . Pg. 134, D-1
Wyomissing H-11
Yardley H-14
Yeadon J-13
  Vicinity . . . Pg. 134, F-4
York J-10
York Springs J-9
Youngsville C-4
Youngwood H-3
Zelienople F-2

RHODE ISLAND
Page 25
Population: 947,154
Capital: Providence
Land Area: 1055 sq. mi.

Ashton E-8
Auburn F-9
Barrington F-10
Berkeley E-9
Bristol F-10
Carolina H-9
Charlestown H-9
Chepachet E-8
Clayville F-8
Cranston F-9
East Greenwich G-9
East Providence . . . F-10
Esmond F-9
Exeter G-9
Fiskeville F-9
Foster Center F-8
Glocester E-8
Harmony E-9
Harrisville E-9
Homestead E-9
Hope F-9
Hope Valley G-9
Jamestown G-10
Lippitt F-9
Little Compton G-11
Mapleville E-9
Middletown G-10
Millville E-8
Narragansett Pier . . H-9
Nasonville E-9
Newport G-10
Nooseneck G-9
North Foster F-8
North Scituate F-9
North Tiverton G-10

Pascoag E-8
Pawtucket F-10
Portsmouth G-10
Providence F-10
Usquepaug G-9
Vernon F-8
Wakefield H-9
Warren F-10
Warwick G-10
Washington F-9
West Greenwich . . . G-8
Westerly H-8
Wickford G-9
Wood River Jct. . . . H-8
Woodville H-8
Woonsocket E-9

SOUTH CAROLINA
Pages 64-65
Population: 3,121,820
Capital: Columbia
Land Area: 30,203 sq. mi.

Abbeville F-4
Adams Run J-7
Aiken G-5
Allendale H-6
Almeda J-6
Anderson F-4
Andrews G-9
Antreville F-4
Appleton H-6
Awendaw H-8
Aynor G-9
Ballentine F-6
Bamberg H-6
Barnwell H-6
Batesburg G-5
Bayboro G-9
Belton E-4
Bennettsville E-8
Bethany D-6
Bethune F-7
Bishopville F-7
Blacksburg D-5
Blackville H-6
Blenheim E-8
Bonneau H-8
Bowman H-7
Boykin F-7
Bradley F-4
Branchville H-7
Brownsville E-8
Buffalo E-5
Bullock Creek E-6
Cades G-8
Cainhoy H-8
Calhoun Falls F-4
Camden F-7
Canadys H-7
Carlisle E-6
Cassatt F-7
Cayce G-6
Centenary F-9
Central E-3
Chappells F-5
Charleston J-8
Chelsea K-7
Cheraw E-8
Chesnee D-5
Chester E-6
Chesterfield E-8
Clarkshill G-5
Clemson E-3
Cleveland D-4
Clinton F-5
Clio E-8
Clover D-6
Columbia F-6
Conway G-9
Cool Spring F-9
Cresent Beach G-10
Cross H-7
Cross Hill F-5
Cross Keys E-5
Dalzell F-7
Darlington F-7
De Kalb F-7
Debidue Beach H-9
Denmark H-6
Dillon F-8
Dovesville E-8
Due West F-4
Edgefield G-5
Edgemoor E-6
Edisto Beach J-8
Edisto Island J-7
Effingham F-8
Ehrhardt H-6
Elgin F-7
Enoree E-5
Estill J-6
Eureka G-5
Evergreen F-7
Fair Bluff F-9
Fairfax J-6
Filbert D-6
Florence F-8
Floydale F-8
Folly Beach J-8
Forest Beach K-7
Foreston G-7
Fork F-8
Fork Shoals E-4
Fort Mill E-5
Fountain Inn E-4
Furman J-6
Gaffney D-5
Galivants Ferry F-9
Garden City G-9

Gardens Corner . . . J-7
Garnett J-6
Georgetown G-9
Givhans H-7
Goose Creek H-8
Gourdin G-8
Gownesville D-4
Grays J-6
Great Falls E-6
Greeleyville G-8
Green Pond J-7
Green Sea F-9
Greenville E-4
Greenwood F-5
Greer E-4
Hampton J-6
Hanahan H-8
Hannah G-8
Hardeeville K-6
Hartsville F-7
Hemingway G-8
Hickory Grove F-9
Hickory Grove D-5
Hilda H-6
Hilton Head Island . . K-7
Holly Hill H-7
Honea Path E-4
Indiantown G-8
Inman D-4
Islandton H-7
Isle of Palms J-8
Iva F-4
Jackson H-5
Jacksonboro J-7
James Island J-8
Jamestown H-8
Jefferson E-7
Jenkinsville F-6
Joanna F-5
Johnston G-5
Jonesville E-5
Kershaw E-7
Kingsburg F-7
Kingstree G-8
Kitchings Mill G-6
Kline H-6
Lake City G-8
Lamar F-7
Lancaster E-6
Landrum D-4
Lane G-8
Latta F-8
Laurens E-4
Leeds E-5
Lena J-6
Lesslie E-6
Lewis E-6
Lexington G-6
Liberty E-4
Litchfield Beach . . . G-9
Little River F-10
Lockhart E-5
Lodge H-6
Loris F-9
Manning G-7
Manville F-7
Marietta D-4
Marion F-9
Martin H-5
Mauldin E-4
Mayesville F-7
McBee E-7
McColl E-8
McConnells E-6
McCormick G-4
Moncks Corner H-8
Mount Pleasant J-8
Mountville F-5
Mt. Carmel F-4
Mullins F-8
Myrtle Beach G-10
New Ellenton H-5
New Prospect D-5
Newberry F-5
Nichols F-9
Nine Times E-3
Nixonville F-9
North G-6
North Augusta G-5
North Charleston . . . J-8
Oatland G-9
Oats F-8
Olanta F-8
Olar H-6
Orangeburg G-6
Outland G-3
Owdoms G-5
Pacolet E-5
Pageland E-7
Pamplico F-8
Parksville G-5
Patrick E-7
Pauline E-5
Pawleys Island G-9
Pelion G-6
Pendleton E-3
Pickens E-3
Pineland J-6
Pineville H-8
Pinewood G-7
Plum Branch G-4
Pontiac F-6
Prosperity F-5
Pumpkintown E-4
Rantowles J-8
Rhems G-9
Richburg E-6
Ridgeland J-6
Ridgeway F-6
Rock Hill E-6
Rockton F-6
Rockville J-8
Rocky Bottom E-3

SOUTH CAROLINA

Ruby E-7
Salters G-8
Saluda F-5
Sampit H-9
Sandy Run G-6
Santee G-7
Sardinia G-8
Sardis F-8
Scranton F-8
Seneca E-3
Sharon E-6
Simpson F-6
Simpsonville E-4
Smallwood F-6
Smoaks H-7
Society Hill E-8
Spartanburg E-5
Springfield G-6
St. George H-7
St. Matthews G-7
St. Stephen G-8
Starr F-4
Stateburg F-7
Steedman G-6
Stoney Hill F-5
Stuckey G-9
Sullivans Island . . . J-8
Summerton G-7
Summerville H-7
Sumter G-7
Surfside Beach G-9
Switzerland K-6
Sycamore H-6
Tamassee E-3
Tatum E-8
Taylor E-4
Tillman J-6
Timmonsville F-8
Tradesville E-7
Travelers Rest E-4
Trenton G-5
Ulmer H-6
Union E-5
Varnville J-6
Wagener G-6
Walhalla E-3
Walterboro J-7
Ward G-5
Ware Shoals F-4
Wateree G-7
Wells H-7
Westminster E-3
Westville E-7
Whitehall J-8
Whitmire E-5
Willington F-4
Williston H-5
Winnsboro F-6
Woodruff E-5
Yauhannah G-9
Yemassee J-7
Yonges Island J-8
York D-6

SOUTH DAKOTA
Page 74
Population: 690,768
Capital: Pierre
Land Area: 75,952 sq. mi.

Aberdeen C-8
Agar C-6
Akaska C-10
Albee F-10
Alcester E-8
Alexandria D-8
Alpena D-10
Altamont C-9
Andover C-9
Arlington D-10
Armour F-8
Artas B-6
Artesian E-8
Ashton C-8
Astoria D-10
Aurora D-10
Badger D-9
Bancroft D-9
Batesland F-4
Belle Fourche C-2
Belvidere E-5
Beresford F-10
Bison B-3
Blunt D-6
Bonesteel F-7
Bowdle C-7
Bradley C-9
Brandon E-10
Brandt D-10
Brentford C-8
Bristol C-9
Britton B-9
Broadland D-8
Brookings D-10
Bruce D-10
Bryant D-9
Buffalo B-2
Buffalo Gap E-2
Burke F-7
Bushnell D-10
Butler C-9
Camp Crook B-2
Canova E-9
Canton E-10
Carthage D-9
Castle Rock C-2
Cavour D-8
Centerville E-9
Central City D-2
Chamberlain E-7
Chelsea C-8

Claire City B-9
Clark C-9
Clear Lake D-10
Colman E-10
Colton E-9
Columbia B-8
Conde C-8
Corona C-10
Corsica E-8
Cottonwood E-4
Cresbard C-7
Crooks E-10
Custer E-2
Dallas F-6
Dante F-8
De Smet D-9
Deadwood D-2
Dell Rapids E-10
Delmont F-8
Dimock E-8
Doland C-8
Dolton E-9
Draper E-5
Dupree C-4
Eagle Butte C-5
Eden B-9
Edgemont E-2
Elk Point G-10
Elm Springs D-3
Emery E-9
Enning D-3
Erwin D-9
Estelline D-9
Ethan E-8
Eureka B-7
Fairburn E-2
Fairfax F-7
Fairpoint C-3
Fairview F-10
Faith C-4
Farmer E-9
Farmingdale D-3
Faulkton C-7
Flandreau E-10
Florence C-9
Fort Pierre D-6
Fort Thompson D-7
Frankfort C-8
Frederick B-8
Freeman F-9
Fruitdale C-2
Fulton E-8
Gann Valley E-7
Garden City C-9
Garretson E-10
Gary D-10
Gayville F-9
Geddes F-8
Gettysburg C-6
Glad Valley B-4
Glenham B-6
Goodwin C-10
Greenwood F-8
Gregory F-7
Grenville C-9
Groton C-8
Hammer B-9
Harrisburg F-10
Harrold D-6
Hayti D-9
Hecla B-8
Hermosa E-2
Herreid B-7
Herrick F-7
Highmore D-7
Hill City D-2
Hillsview B-7
Hitchcock D-8
Hosmer B-7
Hot Springs E-2
Houghton B-8
Hoven C-6
Howard E-9
Howes D-4
Huron D-8
Interior E-4
Ipswich C-7
Irene F-9
Iroquois D-9
Isabel B-5
Java B-6
Jefferson G-10
Kadoka E-4
Kennebec E-6
Keystone D-2
Kimball E-7
Kranzburg C-10
Kyle E-4
La Bolt C-10
La Plant C-6
Lake Andes F-8
Lake City B-9
Lake Preston D-9
Lane E-8
Langford B-9
Lead D-2
Lebanon C-6
Lee's Corner E-7
Lemmon B-4
Lennox F-10
Leola B-7
Letcher E-8
Lily C-9
Little Eagle B-5
Lodgepole B-3
Long Lake B-7
Long Valley F-4
Lowry C-6
Loyalton B-7
Ludlow B-3
Lyman E-6
Madison E-9
Marion F-9
Martin F-4

Marty F-8
Marvin C-10
Maurine C-3
McIntosh B-5
McLaughlin B-5
Meadow B-4
Mellette C-8
Menno F-9
Midland D-5
Milbank C-10
Miller D-7
Mission F-5
Mitchell E-8
Mobridge B-6
Monroe E-9
Montrose E-9
Morristown B-4
Mound City B-6
Mount Vernon E-8
Mud Butte C-3
Murdo E-5
Naples D-9
New Effington B-10
Newell C-2
Nisland C-2
North Sioux City . . . G-10
Northville C-8
Nunda E-9
Oacoma E-6
Oelrichs E-2
Oglala F-3
Okreek E-5
Oldham D-9
Olivet F-8
Onaka C-7
Onida D-6
Opal C-3
Orient C-7
Ortley C-9
Parker E-9
Parkston F-8
Parmelee E-5
Philip D-4
Pierpont C-9
Pierre D-6
Pine Ridge F-3
Plainview D-10
Plankinton E-8
Platte F-7
Pollock B-6
Prairie City B-3
Presho E-6
Pringle E-2
Provo E-1
Pukwana E-7
Quinn D-4
Ramona E-9
Rapid City D-3
Ravinia F-8
Raymond C-9
Red Owl C-3
Red Shirt E-3
Redfield C-8
Redig B-2
Ree Heights D-7
Reliance E-7
Revillo C-10
Ridgeview C-5
Rockerville D-2
Rockham C-8
Roscoe C-7
Rosebud F-5
Roslyn C-9
Roswell C-8
Saint Charles F-7
Saint Francis F-5
Saint Lawrence D-7
Salem E-9
Scenic E-3
Scotland F-8
Selby B-6
Seneca C-6
Shadehill B-4
Sharp Corner B-4
Sherman E-10
Sioux Falls E-10
Sisseton B-10
Sorum B-3
South Shore C-10
Spearfish D-2
Springfield F-8
Stephan D-7
Stickney E-7
Stockholm C-10
Stoneville C-3
Stratford C-8
Sturgis D-2
Summit C-10
Tabor F-8
Tea F-10
Timber Lake C-5
Tolstoy C-7
Toronto D-10
Trail City B-5
Trent E-10
Tripp F-8
Tulare D-8
Turton C-8
Tyndall F-9
Union Center D-3
Veblen B-9
Verdon C-8
Vermillion F-9
Viborg F-9
Vienna D-9
Vilas E-9
Vivian E-6
Wagner F-8
Wakonda F-9
Wall D-4
Wallace C-9
Ward E-10
Wasta D-3
Watertown D-9

Waubay C-9
Webster C-9
Wessington D-7
Wessington Springs . E-8
Westport B-8
Wetonka B-8
Wewala H-6
White D-10
White Butte B-4
White Lake E-8
White River E-5
Whitewood D-2
Willow Lake D-9
Wilmot C-10
Winner F-6
Wood E-5
Woonsocket E-8
Worthing F-10
Yale D-9
Yankton F-9
Zeona C-3

TENNESSEE
Pages 38-39
Population: 4,591,120
Capital: Nashville
Land Area: 41,155 sq. mi.

Adams F-6
Adamsville J-4
Aetna H-5
Alamo H-3
Alcoa H-11
Alexandria G-8
Algood G-8
Allardt G-8
Allens H-5
Allisona H-7
Allred G-9
Alpine G-9
Altamont J-8
Alto J-7
Antioch . . Pg. 124, F-7
Arlington J-2
Vicinity . . Pg. 119, A-10
Arrington H-7
Arthur F-11
Ashland City G-6
Ashport H-2
Athens H-10
Atoka J-2
Atwood G-3
Avondale . . Pg. 124, A-9
Bailey . . . . Pg. 119, F-9
Banner Hill G-13
Bartlett J-2
Vicinity . . Pg. 119, C-6
Beacon . . . Pg. 124, G-6
Bean Station G-12
Beardstown H-5
Beersheba Springs . . H-8
Belfast H-7
Bell Buckle H-7
Belle Meade G-6
Vicinity . . Pg. 124, E-4
Bellevue . . Pg. 124, F-2
Bells H-3
Belvidere J-7
Benjestown . Pg. 119, B-3
Benton J-10
Berry Hill . . Pg. 124, E-6
Bethel J-6
Bethel Springs J-4
Big Sandy G-4
Big Springs J-9
Birchwood J-9
Blaine G-11
Bluff City F-13
Bogota H-3
Bolivar J-3
Bolton . . . Pg. 119, A-9
Bon Air H-8
Braden H-2
Bradford G-3
Brentwood G-6
Vicinity . . Pg. 124, G-5
Briceville G-9
Brighton H-2
Bristol F-13
Brooklin . Pg. 124, G-6
Brownsville H-3
Bruceton G-4
Brunswick . Pg. 119, B-8
Bulls Gap G-12
Bumpus Mills F-5
Burlison H-2
Burns G-6
Byrdstown F-9
Calhoun J-9
Camden G-5
Camelot J-9
Capleville J-2
Vicinity . . Pg. 119, G-6
Carlisle J-3
Carthage G-8
Caryville G-10
Cash Point J-6
Cedar Hill F-6
Celina F-8
Center Point J-6
Centertown H-8
Centerville H-6
Central G-5
Charleston J-9
Charlotte G-5
Chattanooga J-9
Church Hill F-12
Clarksburg H-4
Clarksville F-5
Cleveland J-9
Clifton J-5

Clinton G-10
Coalmont J-8
Collegedale J-9
Collierville J-2
Vicinity . . Pg. 119, F-10
Collinwood J-5
Columbia H-6
Cookeville G-8
Copperhill J-10
Cordova . . Pg. 119, D-8
Cornersville J-6
Cosby H-11
Covington H-2
Crab Orchard H-9
Cross Plains F-6
Crossville H-9
Culleoka H-6
Cumberland City . . . G-5
Cumberland Furnace . G-5
Cumberland Gap . . . F-11
Dancyville H-3
Dandridge G-11
Dayton H-9
Decatur H-9
Decaturville H-5
Decherd J-8
Dibrell H-8
Dickson G-5
Dixon Springs G-8
Donelson G-6
Vicinity . . Pg. 124, D-7
Dover F-5
Dowelltown G-8
Doyle H-8
Dresden G-3
Ducktown J-10
Dunlap J-9
Dyer G-3
Dyersburg G-3
Eads . . . . . Pg. 119, C-10
Eagan F-10
East Ridge J-9
Eastview J-4
Egypt . . . . Pg. 119, B-6
Elizabethton G-13
Elkton J-6
Ellandale . Pg. 119, B-7
Elmore Park . Pg. 119, C-7
Elora J-7
Elza G-10
Englewood J-10
Erin G-5
Erwin G-13
Estill Springs J-7
Ethridge J-6
Etowah J-10
Evensville H-9
Fairview G-6
Farmington H-6
Fayetteville J-6
Finley G-2
Fisherville . Pg. 119, D-10
Flat Woods H-5
Flatcreek J-7
Forbus F-9
Forest Hill . Pg. 119, F-8
Forest Hills . Pg. 124, F-4
Foster Corners J-3
. . . . Pg. 124, F-8
Franklin H-6
Friendship G-3
Fruitvale H-3
Gadsden H-3
Gainesboro G-8
Gallatin G-7
Gates H-3
Gatlinburg H-11
Germanton . Pg. 124, B-4
Germantown J-2
Vicinity . . Pg. 119, E-8
Gibson H-3
Gildfield . . Pg. 119, A-8
Gilt Edge H-2
Gleason G-4
Goodlettsville G-7
Vicinity . . Pg. 124, A-6
Goodspring J-6
Gordonsville G-8
Gower . . . Pg. 124, E-3
Grand Junction J-3
Grandview H-9
Gray G-13
Graysville H-9
Green Hill . Pg. 124, C-9
Greenback H-10
Greenbrier G-6
Greeneville G-12
Greenfield G-4
Grimsley G-9
Habersham F-10
Haletown J-8
Halls H-3
Halls Crossroads . . . G-11
Hampshire H-5
Hampton G-13
Hanging Limb G-9
Harriman H-9
Harrogate F-11
Hartsville G-7
Henderson H-4
Hendersonville G-7
Vicinity . . Pg. 124, A-8
Henning H-2
Henry K-8
Hermitage Hills . . . .
. . . . Pg. 124, D-8
Hickory Valley J-3
Highland J-7
Hohenwald H-5
Hopewell . Pg. 124, C-8
Hornsby J-3
Humboldt H-3
Hunter G-13

Huntingdon G-4
Huntland J-7
Huntsville G-10
India G-4
Inglewood G-7
Vicinity . . Pg. 124, C-6
Iron City J-5
Isham F-10
Ivydell G-10
Jacksboro G-10
Jackson H-3
Jamestown G-9
Jasper J-8
Jefferson City G-11
Jellico F-10
Joelton G-6
Vicinity . . Pg. 124, A-4
Johnson City G-13
Jonesboro G-12
Keeling H-2
Kelso J-7
Kenton G-3
Kimbro . . . Pg. 124, G-8
Kingsport F-13
Kingston H-10
Kirkland H-7
Knoxville H-10
Kodak H-11
Kyles Ford F-12
La Vergne G-7
Vicinity . . Pg. 124, G-9
LaFollette G-10
Laager J-8
Lafayette F-8
Lake City G-10
Lake Mont H-10
Lakesite J-9
Lancing G-9
Lascassas H-7
Latham G-4
Lawrenceburg J-5
Leach G-4
Lebanon G-7
Vicinity . . Pg. 119, B-6
Leipers Fork H-6
Lenoir City H-10
Lenow . . . Pg. 119, C-9
Lewisburg H-6
Lexington H-4
Liberty G-8
Lickton . . . Pg. 124, A-5
Linden H-5
Little Creek . Pg. 124, B-5
Livingston G-8
Lobelville H-5
Locke J-2
Loretto J-5
Loudon H-10
Lucy . . . . Pg. 119, A-4
Luttrell G-11
Lutts J-5
Lyles H-6
Lynchburg J-7
Lynnville J-6
Madisonville H-10
Malesus H-3
Manchester H-7
Marrowbone Pg. 124, C-5
Martin G-4
Maryville H-10
Mason H-2
Maury City H-3
Mayland G-8
Maynardville G-11
McBurg J-6
McEwen G-5
McKenzie G-4
McMinnville H-8
Medina H-3
Medon H-3
Memphis J-1
Vicinity . . . . Pg. 119
Mercer H-3
Michie J-4
Middleton J-3
Midtown H-10
Milan G-3
Milledgeville J-4
Milligan College . . . G-13
Millington J-2
Vicinity . . Pg. 119, B-6
Minor Hill J-6
Miston G-2
Monteagle J-8
Monterey G-9
Morgantown H-9
Morris Chapel J-4
Morrison H-7
Morristown G-11
Moscow J-2
Mosheim G-12
Moss F-8
Mound City . Pg. 119, C-2
Mount Carmel F-12
Mount Crest H-9
Mount Juliet G-7
Vicinity . . Pg. 124, C-10
Mount Olive H-11
Mount Pleasant H-6
Mount Vernon H-8
Mount Zion . Pg. 124, A-2
Mountain City F-14
Munford H-2
Murfreesboro H-7
Nashville G-6
Vicinity . . . . Pg. 124
New Hope K-8
New Johnsonville . . . G-5
New Market G-11
New River G-10
New Tazwell G-11
Newbern G-3
Newport G-12
Niota H-10
Nixon J-4
Nobles G-4

Norris G-10
Nunnelly H-5
Oak Hill . . Pg. 124, F-6
Oak Ridge G-10
Oakdale G-9
Oakland J-2
Vicinity . . Pg. 119, F-5
Oakville . . Pg. 119, F-5
Oakwood F-5
Obion G-3
Ocoee J-9
Oglesby . . Pg. 124, G-6
Old Hickory . Pg. 124, B-8
Olivehill J-4
Oliver Springs G-10
Oneida F-10
Palmer J-8
Palmyra F-5
Parago Mill . Pg. 124, F-7
Paris G-4
Parrottsville G-12
Parsons H-4
Pasquo . . . Pg. 124, F-3
Peakland H-9
Pegram G-6
Pelham J-8
Petersburg J-7
Philadelphia H-10
Pigeon Forge H-11
Pikeville H-9
Pinewood H-6
Pinson H-4
Pisgah . . . Pg. 119, D-10
Pleasant Hill G-8
Pleasant View G-6
Portland F-7
Providence J-7
Vicinity . . Pg. 124, G-7
Pulaski J-6
Puncheon Camp . . . G-11
Puryear F-4
Quebeck H-8
Raleigh J-2
Vicinity . . Pg. 119, B-6
Ramer J-4
Ramsey . . Pg. 119, A-4
Raus H-7
Rayon City . Pg. 124, B-7
Red Bank J-9
Red Boiling Springs . F-8
Riceville J-10
Richland . . Pg. 124, D-3
Rickman G-8
Ridgely G-3
Ridgetop G-6
Ripley H-2
Rives G-3
Roan Mountain G-13
Robbins G-10
Rockwood H-9
Rocky Fork G-12
Rogersville G-12
Rossville J-2
Rural Hill . Pg. 124, C-9
Russellville G-12
Rutherford G-3
Rutledge G-11
Saint Bethlehem . . . F-5
Saint Joseph J-5
Sale Creek J-9
Saltillo H-4
Sardis H-4
Saundersville Pg. 124, A-9
Savannah J-4
Scotts Hill H-4
Selmer J-4
Seven Points Pg. 124, E-9
Sevierville H-11
Sewanee J-8
Shacklett G-5
Shady Valley F-13
Sharon G-3
Shelby Farms Pg. 119, D-7
Shelbyville H-7
Shooks Gap H-11
Shop Springs G-7
Signal Mtn. J-8
Silver Point G-8
Skiem J-6
Smartt H-8
Smith Springs Pg. 124, F-8
Smithville H-8
Smyrna G-7
Sneedville F-11
Soddy-Daisy J-9
Somerville J-2
South Carthage G-8
South Dyersburg . . . G-3
South Fulton G-4
South Pittsburg J-8
Sparta H-8
Spencer H-8
Spring City H-9
Spring Creek H-4
Spring Hill H-6
Spring Lake Pg. 119, B-7
Springfield F-6
Stanton H-3
Sullivan Gdn. F-12
Summertown J-6
Sunbright G-10
Surgoinsville F-12
Sweetwater H-10
Sycamore . . Pg. 124, A-1
Taft J-6
Tarpley F-8
Tazewell F-11
Tellico Plains J-10
Tennessee Ridge . . . G-5
Timberlake F-5
Tiptonville F-3
Toone J-3
Tracy City J-8
Trenton G-3

Trezevant G-4
Triune H-7
Troy G-3
Tullahoma J-7
Tusculum G-13
Vicinity . . Pg. 124, F-6
Una . . . . . Pg. 124, F-7
Unicoi G-13
Union City G-3
Union Grove J-9
Union Hill . Pg. 124, A-5
Vaughlans Gap . . . .
. . . . Pg. 124, F-4
Victoria J-8
Viola H-8
Violet J-10
Vonore H-10
Waco J-6
Walden J-9
Walkertown J-4
Walling H-8
Wartburg G-10
Wartrace H-7
Watertown G-8
Waverly G-5
Waynesboro J-5
Webber City J-5
West Meade Pg. 124, E-4
West Shiloh J-4
Westmoreland F-7
White Bluff G-6
White House F-7
White Pine G-12
Whitesburg G-12
Whiteville J-3
Whitwell J-8
Wilder G-9
Williston J-3
Winchester J-7
Winfield F-10
Woodbury H-8
Woodland Mills F-3
Woodstock . . Pg. 119, B-5
Wrencoe . . Pg. 124, G-7
Wyanoke . . Pg. 119, E-1
Wynnburg G-3

TEXAS
Pages 75-79
Population: 14,229,191
Capital: Austin
Land Area: 262,017 sq. mi.

Abernathy E-7
Abilene G-10
Acala J-2
Ackerly G-7
Acme D-10
Adamsville J-12
Addicks L-15
Vicinity . . Pg. 109, D-1
Addison . . Pg. 105, A-8
Adrian C-7
Agua Dulce P-12
Aiken E-8
Alamo Heights . . . .
. . . . Pg. 142, D-5
Alanreed C-9
Alba F-15
Albany G-10
Aldine L-15
Aledo F-12
Alexander H-12
Alfred P-12
Algoa M-16
Alice P-12
Alief . . . . . Pg. 109, E-2
Allamoore J-3
Allen F-14
Alleyton L-14
Allison B-10
Allred D-7
Almeda . . Pg. 109, G-4
Alpine J-4
Altair M-14
Alto H-16
Alvarado F-13
Alvin M-16
Alvord E-12
Amarillo C-7
Ambrose E-13
Ames L-16
Amherst E-7
Anahuac L-16
Anderson K-15
Andice K-12
Andrews G-6
Angleton M-16
Anna E-14
Annona E-16
Anson F-10
Antelope E-12
Anthony H-2
Anton E-7
Apple Springs J-16
Aquilla H-13
Aransas Pass P-13
Archer City E-11
Argyle F-13
Arlington G-13
Vicinity . . Pg. 104, E-5
Arp G-16
Artesia Wells P-10
Arthur City E-15
Asherton N-10
Ashtola C-8
Aspermont F-9
Athens G-15
Atlanta F-17
Aubrey E-13
Austin L-13

TEXAS

Austonio J-15
Austwell N-14
Avery F-16
Avinger F-17
Avoca G-10
Azle G-13
Bacliff M-16
Bagwell E-16
Baird G-10
Bakersfield K-7
Balch Springs G-14
Vicinity Pg. 105, E-11
Balcones Heights Pg. 142, D-3
Ballinger H-10
Balmorhea J-5
Bammel Pg. 109, A-4
Bandera L-11
Bangs H-11
Barclay J-13
Bardwell H-14
Barksdale L-10
Barnhart J-8
Barrett L-16
Vicinity Pg. 109, C-10
Barry H-14
Barstow J-5
Bartlett K-13
Bassett F-16
Bastrop L-13
Batesville N-10
Batson L-16
Bay City M-15
Baytown L-17
Vicinity Pg. 109, E-10
Beasley M-15
Beaumont L-17
Vicinity Pg. 109, C-17
Beckville G-17
Bedias K-15
Bee Cave L-12
Beeville N-12
Belfalls J-13
Bellaire Pg. 109, E-3
Bellevue E-12
Bellmead H-13
Bells E-14
Bellville L-14
Belmont M-13
Belton J-13
Ben G-15
Ben Arnold J-14
Ben Bolt P-12
Benavides Q-11
Benbrook G-13
Benchley K-14
Benjamin F-10
Bertram K-12
Bettie G-16
Big Lake J-7
Big Sandy G-16
Big Spring H-8
Big Wells N-10
Bigfoot M-11
Birthright F-15
Bishop Q-12
Bivins F-17
Black D-7
Blackwell H-9
Blanco L-11
Blanket H-11
Bleakwood K-18
Bledsoe E-6
Blessing N-15
Blewett M-9
Blooming Grove H-14
Bloomington N-13
Blossom E-15
Blue Mound Pg. 104, C-3
Blue Ridge F-14
Bluegrove E-12
Bluff Dale G-12
Bluffton K-11
Boca Chica S-13
Boerne L-11
Bogata F-15
Boling M-14
Bomarton F-10
Bon Wier K-18
Bonham E-14
Booker A-9
Boonsville F-12
Borger B-8
Boston F-17
Bovina D-6
Bowie E-12
Boxelder F-16
Boyd F-13
Boys Ranch Tacosa B-7
Brackettville M-9
Bradshaw H-10
Brady J-10
Brandon H-14
Brashear F-15
Brazoria M-15
Breckenridge G-11
Bremond J-14
Brenham L-14
Brice D-9
Bridge City L-18
Bridgeport F-12
Briggs K-12
Briscoe B-9
Bronco F-6
Bronson J-17
Bronte H-9
Brookeland J-17
Brooksmith H-11
Brookshire L-15
Brookside Village Pg. 109, G-6
Brownfield F-7
Brownsboro G-15

Brownsville S-13
Brownwood H-11
Brundage N-10
Bruni Q-11
Bryan K-14
Bryson F-12
Buchanan Dam K-12
Buckholts K-13
Buda L-12
Buena Vista Pg. 142, H-5
Buffalo J-15
Buffalo Gap G-10
Bula E-6
Bulcher E-13
Bullard H-16
Buna K-17
Bunavista B-8
Bunker Hill Pg. 109, E-3
Burkburnett E-11
Burke J-16
Burkett H-10
Burkeville J-18
Burleson G-13
Vicinity Pg. 104, G-3
Burlington J-14
Burnet K-12
Burton L-14
Bushland C-7
Bustamanete R-11
Butler K-13
Byers E-12
Bynum H-14
Cactus A-7
Caddo G-11
Caddo Mills F-15
Caldwell K-14
Calf Creek J-10
Call K-18
Calliham N-12
Calvert K-14
Camden K-16
Cameron K-14
Camilla L-16
Camp Verde L-11
Camp Wood L-10
Campbell F-15
Campbellton N-12
Canadian B-9
Canton G-15
Canutillo H-1
Canyon C-7
Caps G-11
Carbon G-11
Carlos K-15
Carlsbad H-9
Carlton H-12
Carmine L-14
Carmona K-16
Carrizo Springs N-10
Carrollton G-13
Vicinity Pg. 105, A-8
Carta Valley L-9
Carthage H-17
Cash F-14
Cassin Pg. 142, H-4
Castle Hills M-11
Vicinity Pg. 142, C-4
Castroville M-11
Catarina N-10
Cayuga H-15
Cedar Creek L-13
Cedar Hill Pg. 105, F-7
Cedar Park K-12
Celeste F-14
Celina F-14
Center H-17
Centerville H-15
Champions Pg. 109, A-3
Chandler G-15
Channelview L-16
Vicinity Pg. 109, D-8
Channing B-7
Chapman Ranch P-13
Chappell Hill L-14
Charco N-13
Charlotte N-11
Cherokee K-11
Cherry Spring K-11
Chester J-16
Chico F-12
Childress D-10
Chillicothe D-10
Chilton J-13
China L-17
China Grove Pg. 142, F-7
Chireno J-17
Chisos Basin M-5
Chriesman K-14
Christine N-11
Christoval J-9
Circle Back E-6
Cisco G-11
Cistern L-13
Clairemont H-9
Clairette H-12
Clarendon C-8
Clarksville E-16
Claude C-8
Clayton H-17
Cleburne F-13
Cleveland L-16
Clifton H-13
Clint H-1
Cloverleaf Pg. 109, D-8
Clute M-16
Clyde G-11
Coady Pg. 109, D-10
Coahoma G-8
Cockrell Hill Pg. 105, D-8
Coffey City H-15
Coldspring K-16
Coleman H-10

College Station K-14
Colleyville Pg. 104, B-5
Collinsville F-13
Colmesneil K-17
Colorado City G-9
Columbus L-14
Comanche H-11
Combes R-12
Comfort L-11
Commerce F-15
Como F-15
Comstock L-8
Concan M-10
Concepcion Q-12
Concord H-16
Conroe K-15
Converse L-11
Conway C-8
Cooks Point K-14
Cookville F-16
Coolidge J-13
Cooper F-15
Coppell Pg. 105, A-7
Copperas Cove J-12
Cornudas H-3
Corpus Christi P-13
Corrigan L-16
Corsicana H-14
Coryell City J-13
Cotton Center E-7
Cottonwood K-15
Cottonwood H-11
Cotulla N-10
Country Campus K-16
Coy City N-12
Coyanosa J-5
Crabbs Prairie K-15
Crandall G-14
Crane J-6
Cranfills Gap J-13
Crawford J-13
Cresson G-13
Crews H-10
Crockett J-15
Crosby L-15
Vicinity Pg. 109, B-9
Crosbyton E-8
Cross K-15
Cross Cut H-11
Cross Plains H-11
Cross Roads H-15
Crow G-16
Crowell E-10
Crowley G-13
Vicinity Pg. 104, F-3
Crystal City N-10
Cuero M-13
Cumby F-14
Cut & Shoot K-15
Cypress L-15
Cypress Mill K-12
D'Hanis M-10
Dabney M-9
Dacosta N-14
Daingerfield F-16
Daisetta K-16
Dalhart B-7
Dallas G-14
Vicinity Pg. 105
Dalworthington Gardens Pg. 104, E-5
Damon M-15
Danbury M-15
Danevang M-15
Darrouzett A-9
Dawn C-7
Dawson H-14
De Berry G-17
De Kalb F-16
De Leon H-11
De Wees N-11
DeSoto Pg. 105, F-8
Deanville K-14
Decatur F-13
Deer Park L-16
Vicinity Pg. 109, F-6
Del Rio M-8
Del Valle L-13
Dell City H-3
Denison E-14
Denton F-13
Denver City F-6
Deport F-15
Derby N-11
Desdemona H-12
Devers L-17
Devine M-11
Dew H-15
Deweyville K-18
Diana G-16
Dickens E-9
Dickinson L-15
Dilley N-11
Dime Box K-14
Dimmitt D-7
Dinero P-12
Divot P-12
Dobbin K-15
Dodd City E-15
Dodson C-9
Donie J-14
Doole J-10
Doss K-11
Doucette K-17
Dougherty E-8
Douglass H-16
Douglassville F-17
Dozier C-9
Draw F-8
Dripping Springs L-12

Driscoll P-12
Dryden L-7
Dublin H-12
Dumas B-7
Dumont E-9
Duncanville Pg. 105, F-7
Dundee E-11
Dunlay M-11
Dunn G-9
Dyersdale Pg. 109, B-7
Eagle Lake M-14
Eagle Pass N-9
Early H-11
Earth D-7
East Columbia M-15
Easterly J-14
Eastland G-11
Easton G-16
Edcouch R-12
Eddy J-13
Eden J-10
Edgecliff Pg. 104, E-3
Edinburg R-12
Edmonson D-7
Edna M-14
Edom G-15
Edroy P-13
Egypt M-14
El Campo M-14
El Lago Pg. 109, G-10
El Paso H-2
El Sauz R-10
Elbert E-11
Eldorado K-9
Electra E-11
Elgin L-13
Elkhart H-15
Ellinger L-14
Elmendorf M-12
Vicinity Pg. 142, J-7
Elmo G-14
Elsa R-12
Elysian Fields G-17
Emory F-14
Encinal P-10
Encino Q-12
Energy H-12
Enloe F-15
Ennis G-14
Enochs E-6
Escobas Q-11
Estelline D-9
Etoile J-17
Etter B-7
Euless Pg. 104, C-6
Eureka H-14
Eustace G-15
Evadale K-17
Evant J-12
Evergreen K-16
Everman Pg. 104, F-3
Fabens H-2
Fairbanks Pg. 108, C-2
Fairfield H-15
Fairlie F-15
Fairview F-14
Fairview G-8
Fairy H-12
Falcon R-11
Falfurias Q-12
Falls City N-12
Fannett L-17
Fannin N-13
Farmers Branch Pg. 105, B-8
Farmersville F-14
Farrar J-14
Farwell D-6
Fayetteville L-14
Fedor K-13
Fentress L-13
Ferris G-14
Vicinity Pg. 105, G-10
Fieldton E-7
Fink E-14
Finney E-9
Flatonia M-13
Flomot D-8
Florence K-12
Floresville M-12
Flower Mound Pg. 104, A-6
Floydada E-8
Fluvanna F-8
Follett A-10
Forest J-16
Forest Hill Pg. 104, E-4
Forestburg F-13
Forney G-14
Fort Clark Springs M-9
Fort Davis K-5
Fort Gates J-12
Fort Griffin G-10
Fort Hancock J-2
Fort McKavett K-10
Fort Stockton J-6
Fort Worth G-13
Vicinity Pg. 104
Fostoria K-16
Four Corners Pg. 109, D-10
Fowlerton N-11
Frame Switch K-13
Francitas N-14
Frankel City G-6
Franklin J-14
Frankston H-15
Fransworth A-9
Fred K-17
Fredericksburg L-11
Fredonia K-11
Freeport N-16
Freer P-11
Friday J-16

Frio Town M-10
Friona D-6
Frisco F-13
Fritch B-8
Frost H-14
Fruitland F-12
Fruitvale G-15
Fullbright F-16
Fulton P-13
Funston G-10
Gail G-8
Gainesville F-13
Galena Park Pg. 109, E-7
Galveston M-16
Ganado M-14
Garden City H-8
Garden Valley G-15
Gardendale H-7
Vicinity Pg. 142, E-7
Garland G-14
Vicinity Pg. 105, B-10
Garrison H-16
Garwood M-14
Gary H-17
Gatesville J-12
Gause K-14
Geneva J-17
George West N-12
Georgetown K-13
Geronimo L-12
Giddings L-13
Gilchrist M-17
Gillett M-12
Gilliland E-10
Gilmer G-16
Girard F-9
Girvin J-7
Gladewater G-16
Glazier B-9
Glen Cove H-10
Glen Flora M-15
Glen Rose H-13
Glenn E-9
Glenn Heights Pg. 105, G-8
Glenrio C-6
Glenwood G-16
Glidden L-14
Gober G-13
Godley G-13
Goldsboro H-10
Goldthwaite J-11
Goliad N-13
Gonzales M-13
Goodland E-6
Goodlett D-10
Goodnight C-8
Goodrich K-16
Gordon G-12
Gordonville E-13
Goree F-10
Gorman H-11
Gouldbusk J-10
Graford F-12
Graham F-11
Granbury G-12
Grand Prairie G-13
Vicinity Pg. 105, D-6
Grand Saline G-15
Grandfalls J-6
Granger K-13
Grapeland J-15
Grapevine Pg. 104, B-6
Grassland E-8
Grayback E-11
Greenville F-15
Grey Forest Pg. 142, A-1
Grit K-10
Groesbeck J-14
Groom C-8
Groves L-17
Groveton J-16
Gruver A-8
Gun Barrel City G-15
Gustine H-12
Guthrie E-9
Guy M-15
Hagansport F-15
Hale Center D-7
Halletsville M-14
Hallsville G-16
Haltom City Pg. 104, C-3
Hamilton H-12
Hamlin G-9
Hamshire L-17
Happy C-7
Hardin L-17
Hargill R-12
Harker Heights J-13
Harleton G-16
Harlingen S-13
Harper L-11
Harrold E-11
Hart D-6
Hartley B-7
Harwood L-13
Haskell F-10
Haslet Pg. 104, A-3
Hatchel H-10
Hawkins G-16
Hawley G-10
Hearne K-14
Hebbronville Q-11
Hebron Pg. 105, A-8
Hedley C-9
Hedwig Pg. 109, D-3
Helotes Pg. 142, B-1
Hemleigh G-9
Hemphill J-18
Hempstead L-14
Henderson G-16
Henrietta E-12
Hereford C-6

Hext K-10
Hico H-12
Hidalgo S-12
Higgins B-10
Highbank J-14
Highland Park Pg. 105, C-9
Highlands Pg. 105, E-16
Vicinity Pg. 109, D-9
Hill Country Village Pg. 142, A-5
Hillister K-17
Hillsboro H-13
Hillshire Village Pg. 109, D-3
Hilltop Lakes J-14
Hindes N-11
Hitchcock M-16
Hobson M-13
Hochheim M-13
Hockley K-15
Holland K-13
Holliday E-11
Hollywood Park Pg. 142, A-5
Hondo M-11
Honey Grove E-15
Horizon City H-1
Houmont Park Pg. 109, C-7
Houston L-15
Vicinity Pg. 109
Howe F-14
Howellville Pg. 109, E-1
Hubbard H-14
Huckabay G-12
Hudson J-16
Hughes Springs F-16
Hull L-16
Humble L-16
Vicinity Pg. 109, A-7
Hunt L-10
Hunters Creek Pg. 109, D-3
Huntington J-17
Vicinity Pg. 105, F-9
Huntsville K-15
Hurlwood E-7
Hurst Pg. 104, C-5
Hutchins Pg. 105, E-14
Hutto K-13
Hye L-11
Idalou E-7
Imperial J-6
Inadal G-9
Independence L-14
Indian Gap J-12
Industry L-14
Ingleside P-13
Ingram L-11
Inez N-14
Iola L-15
Iowa Park E-11
Ira G-8
Iraan K-7
Iredell H-12
Ireland J-12
Irving G-13
Vicinity Pg. 105, C-7
Italy H-13
Itasca H-13
Jacinto City Pg. 109, D-7
Jacksboro F-12
Jacksonville H-15
Jamestown J-18
Jarrell K-13
Jasper J-17
Jayton F-9
Jean F-12
Jefferson F-17
Jermyn F-12
Jersey Village Pg. 109, C-2
Jewett J-14
Joaquin H-17
Johnson City L-11
Johntown E-15
Jolly E-12
Jollyville K-12
Jones Creek M-15
Jonesboro J-12
Jonestown K-12
Jourdanton N-11
Joshua G-13
Joy F-13
Junction K-10
Juno L-8
Justiceburg F-8
Justin F-13
Kalgary F-8
Kamay E-11
Kanawha E-16
Karnes City N-12
Katemcy K-10
Katy L-15
Kaufman G-14
Keene G-13
Keller Pg. 104, B-4
Kellerville C-9
Kemp G-14
Kempner J-12
Kendalia L-11
Kendleton M-15
Kenedy N-12
Kennard J-16
Kennedale Pg. 104, E-4
Kenney L-14
Kent J-4
Kenwood Pg. 109, B-6
Kerens H-14
Kermit H-5
Kerrville L-11
Kilgore G-16
Killeen J-13
Kings Mill C-8

Kingsland K-11
Kingston F-14
Kingsville S-12
Kirby Pg. 142, D-6
Kirbyville K-17
Kirkland D-9
Kirvin H-14
Knickerbocker J-9
Knott G-7
Knox City F-10
Kopperl H-13
Kosse J-14
Kountze K-17
Kress D-7
Vicinity Pg. 104, F-5
Krum F-13
Kyle L-12
La Gloria R-11
La Grange L-13
La Grulla R-11
La Joya R-11
La Marque M-16
La Paloma S-13
La Porte Pg. 109, F-10
La Pryor N-10
La Reforma R-12
La Vernia M-12
La Villa R-12
La Ward N-14
Ladonia F-15
Lago Vista K-12
Laguna Park H-13
Lake Hills M-11
Lake Jackson M-15
Lake Worth Pg. 104, C-2
Lakeport G-16
Lakeside Pg. 104, C-1
Lakeside Village H-13
Lakeview D-9
Lamesa G-7
Lamkin H-12
Lampasas J-12
Lancaster G-14
Vicinity Pg. 105, F-9
Lane City M-15
Langtry L-7
Laredo Q-10
Lariat D-6
Lark C-8
Lasara R-12
Latexo J-15
Lavon F-14
Lawn H-10
League City L-15
Leakey L-10
Leander K-12
Leesburg F-16
Leesville M-13
Leggett K-16
Lehman E-6
Leigh G-17
Lela C-9
Lelia Lake C-9
Leming M-12
Lenorah G-7
Leon Springs L-11
Leon Valley L-11
Vicinity Pg. 142, C-2
Leona J-15
Leonard F-14
Levelland E-7
Lewisville F-13
Vicinity Pg. 105, A-6
Lexington K-13
Liberty L-16
Liberty Hill K-12
Libscomb A-9
Lincoln L-13
Lincoln City Pg. 108, C-5
Linden F-16
Lindsay F-13
Lingleville H-12
Linus Pg. 109, D-10
Lipan G-12
Littlefield E-7
Live Oak Pg. 142, B-7
Liverpool M-16
Livingston K-16
Llano K-11
Lobo J-3
Lockhart L-13
Lockney E-8
Lodi F-17
Loma Alta L-8
Lometa J-11
London K-10
Lone Star F-16
Long Branch H-16
Long Mott N-14
Longview G-16
Longworth G-9
Lopeno R-11
Loraine G-9
Lorena J-13
Lorenzo E-8
Los Angeles N-11
Los Fresnos S-12
Losoya Pg. 142, J-5
Lott J-13
Louise M-14
Lovelady J-15
Loving G-11
Loyal Valley K-11
Lubbock E-7
Luckenbach L-11
Lueders F-10
Lufkin J-16
Luling L-13
Lumberton K-17

Lutie C-9
Lydia F-16
Lyford R-13
Lynchburg Pg. 109, E-8
Lyons K-14
Lytle M-11
Mabank G-15
Macdona Pg. 142, G-1
Madisonville J-15
Magnolia L-15
Malakoff H-15
Malta F-16
Mangus Corner Pg. 142, H-2
Mankins E-11
Mansfield G-13
Vicinity Pg. 104, F-5
Maple E-6
Marathon K-5
Marble Falls K-12
Marfa K-4
Marietta F-17
Marion M-12
Markham M-15
Marlin J-14
Marquez J-15
Marshall G-17
Mart J-14
Martindale L-13
Martinez M-12
Vicinity Pg. 142, E-7
Martinsville H-17
Maryneal G-9
Mason K-11
Masterson B-7
Matador E-8
Matagorda N-15
Mathis P-12
Maud F-17
Mauriceville L-17
Maxwell L-12
May H-11
Maydelle H-16
Maypearl G-13
McAdoo E-8
McAllen S-12
McCamey J-7
McCaulley G-9
McDade L-13
McFaddin N-13
McGregor J-13
McKinney F-14
McLean C-9
McLeod F-17
McMahan L-13
McNair Pg. 109, D-10
McNary J-2
McQueeney L-12
Meadow F-7
Medicine Mound D-10
Medina L-11
Megargel F-11
Melissa F-14
Melrose H-17
Melvin J-10
Memphis D-9
Menard K-10
Mendoza L-13
Mentone H-5
Mercedes S-12
Meridian H-13
Merkel G-9
Mertzon J-8
Mesquite G-14
Vicinity Pg. 105, C-11
Mexia J-14
Miami B-9
Mico M-11
Midland H-7
Midlothian G-14
Midway K-15
Milam J-17
Milano K-14
Miles H-9
Milford G-13
Millersview J-10
Millett N-11
Millican K-14
Mineola G-15
Mineral N-12
Mineral Wells G-12
Mingus G-12
Mirando City Q-11
Mission S-12
Missouri City Pg. 109, G-3
Mobeetie B-9
Moline J-12
Monahans H-6
Monkstown E-15
Monroe E-16
Mont Belvieu L-16
Montague E-12
Montalba H-15
Monte Alto R-12
Montgomery K-15
Monthalia M-13
Moody J-13
Moore N-11
Mooring K-14
Moran G-11
Morgan H-13
Morgan Mill G-12
Morgans Point Pg. 109, F-10
Morse B-8
Morton E-6
Morton Valley G-11
Moscow J-16
Moss Hill L-16
Moulton M-13
Mount Calm J-14
Mount Enterprise H-16
Mount Houston Pg. 109, C-6

TEXAS

TEXAS

Mount Pleasant F-16
Mount Sylvan G-15
Mount Vernon F-16
Mountain Home L-10
Muenster E-13
Muldoon L-14
Muleshoe D-6
Mullin J-11
Mumford K-14
Munday F-10
Murchison G-15
Murphy .... Pg. 105, A-11
Myrtle Springs G-15
N. Richland Hills .... Pg. 104, C-4
Nacogdoches H-16
Nada M-14
Naples F-16
Nash F-17
Natalia M-11
Navasota K-14
Nazareth D-7
Neches H-16
Nederland K-17
Needmore E-6
Needville M-15
Nelsonville L-14
New Baden J-14
New Boston F-17
New Braunfels L-12
New Caney L-16
New Deal E-7
New Gulf M-15
New Home F-7
New London G-16
New Summerfield H-16
New Ulm L-14
New Waverly K-15
Newark .... Pg. 104, A-1
Newcastle F-11
Newlin D-9
Newman H-2
Newsome F-16
Newton K-18
Nixon L-12
Nocona E-12
Nolan G-9
Nolanville J-13
Nome K-16
Noodle G-10
Nordheim N-13
Normandy N-9
Normangee J-15
Normanna N-13
North Houston .... Pg. 109, B-3
North Zulch K-14
Northcrest H-13
Northfield D-9
Norton H-9
Notrees H-6
Novice G-11
Nuevo Laredo P-10
Nursery N-13
O'Brien F-10
O'Donnell F-7
Oak Hill J-12
Oakalla J-12
Oakland M-14
Oakwood H-15
Odem P-13
Odessa H-7
Oglesby H-13
Oilton Q-11
Oklaunion E-11
Old Boston F-17
Old Center H-17
Old Glory F-9
Old Ocean M-15
Olden G-12
Oldenburg L-14
Olivia N-14
Olmito S-13
Olmos Park .... Pg. 142, D-4
Olney F-11
Olton E-7
Omaha F-16
Opin H-10
Orange L-18
Orange Grove P-12
Ore City F-16
Orla H-5
Osceola J-13
Ottine M-13
Ovalo G-10
Overton G-16
Ovilla .... Pg. 105, G-8
Ozona K-8
Paducah E-9
Paige L-13
Painview D-7
Palacios N-14
Palestine H-15
Palmer G-14
Palo Pinto G-12
Pampa B-8
Pandora M-13
Panhandle C-8
Panna Maria M-12
Panola G-17
Paradise F-13
Paris E-15
Parnell D-9
Pasadena L-16
Vicinity .... Pg. 109, F-8
Patricia G-7
Patroon H-17
Pattonville F-16
Pawnee N-12
Paxton H-17
Pearland .... Pg. 109, G-6
Pearsall N-11
Pecos J-5
Peggy N-12

Penwell H-6
Perrin F-12
Perry J-13
Perryton A-9
Petersburg E-8
Petrolia E-12
Pettus N-12
Petty E-15
Pflugerville K-13
Phalba G-15
Pharr S-12
Phillips B-7
Pilot Point F-13
Pine Mills G-16
Pinehurst K-17
Pineland H-17
Piney Pt. .... Pg. 109, E-3
Pioneer H-11
Pipecreek L-11
Pittsburg F-16
Placedo N-14
Plains F-6
Plano F-14
Vicinity .... Pg. 105, A-10
Plantersville K-15
Plata L-4
Pleasanton N-12
Point Comfort N-14
Pollok J-16
Ponder F-13
Ponta H-16
Pontotoc K-11
Poolville F-12
Port Aransas P-13
Port Arthur L-17
Port Bolivar L-17
Port Isabel S-13
Port Lavaca N-14
Port Mansfield R-13
Port Neches L-17
Port O'Connor N-14
Porter L-16
Portland P-13
Posey F-8
Post F-8
Poteet N-11
Poth M-12
Pottsboro E-14
Pottsville H-12
Powderly E-15
Powell H-14
Poynor H-15
Prairie Dell K-13
Prairie Hill H-14
Prairie Lea L-13
Prairie View K-15
Premont Q-12
Presidio L-4
Priddy H-11
Princeton F-14
Pritchett G-16
Proctor H-12
Prosper F-14
Purmela J-12
Putnam G-11
Pyote H-5
Quail C-9
Quanah D-10
Queen City F-17
Quemado N-9
Quinlan G-14
Quitaque D-8
Quitman G-15
Rachal R-12
Ralls E-8
Ramirez Q-12
Randado Q-11
Randlett Charlie E-12
Randolph F-14
Ranger G-11
Rankin J-7
Ratcliff J-16
Ravenna E-14
Rayland D-9
Raymondville R-12
Raywood L-17
Reagan J-14
Realitos Q-11
Red Bluff .... Pg. 109, G-11
Red Oak G-13
Vicinity .... Pg. 105, G-8
Red Springs E-10
Redford M-4
Reese Vill. E-7
Refugio P-13
Reklaw H-16
Reno G-15
Retta .... Pg. 104, G-4
Rhome F-13
Ricardo Q-12
Rice H-14
Richardson F-14
Vicinity .... Pg. 105, A-9
Richland H-14
Richland Hills Pg. 104, C-4
Richland Springs J-11
Richmond L-15
Richwood M-16
Ridge J-14
Riesel H-13
Ringgold E-12
Rio Grande City R-11
Rio Vista G-13
Riomedina M-11
Rios Q-12
Rising Star H-11
River Oaks .... Pg. 104, D-2
Riverside K-15
Riviera Q-12
Roans Prairie K-15
Robbins H-17
Robert Lee H-9
Robinson H-13
Robstown P-13
Roby G-9

Rochelle J-11
Rochester F-10
Rock Island M-14
Rockdale K-14
Rockland J-17
Rockport P-13
Rocksprings L-9
Rockwood J-10
Roganville K-17
Rogers K-13
Roma R-10
Romayor K-16
Roosevelt K-9
Ropesville F-7
Rosanky L-13
Roscoe G-9
Rosebud J-14
Rosenberg M-15
Rosevine J-17
Rosser G-14
Rotan G-9
Round Mountain K-12
Round Rock K-13
Round Top L-14
Rowena H-9
Roxton E-15
Royalty J-6
Rule F-10
Runge M-12
Rusk H-16
Rye K-16
Sabinal M-10
Sacul H-16
Sadler E-14
Sagerton F-10
Saginaw G-13
Vicinity .... Pg. 104, C-2
Saint Hedwig M-12
Saint Jo E-13
Salado J-13
Salt Falt H-3
Samnorwood C-9
San Antonio M-12
Vicinity .... Pg. 142
San Augustine H-17
San Benito S-13
San Diego P-12
San Elizario H-1
San Felipe L-14
San Gabriel K-13
San Isidro R-11
San Juan R-12
San Marcos L-12
San Patricio P-12
San Perlita R-13
San Saba J-11
San Ygnacio Q-10
Sanderson L-6
Sandia P-12
Sanford B-8
Sanger F-13
Sansom Park .... Pg. 104, C-2
Santa Anna H-11
Santa Elena R-12
Santa Fe L-15
Santa Maria S-12
Santa Rosa S-12
Saragosa J-5
Saratoga K-17
Sarita Q-12
Satsuma .... Pg. 109, B-1
Savoy E-14
Schertz M-12
Schulenburg L-14
Scotland E-11
Scottsville G-17
Scranton G-11
Seabrook L-16
Vicinity .... Pg. 109, G-9
Seadrift N-14
Seagraves F-6
Sealy L-14
Sebastian R-13
Sebastopol K-16
Segovia K-10
Seguin M-12
Seminole G-6
Seven Points G-15
Seymour E-11
Shafter L-4
Shallowater E-7
Shamrock C-9
Shannon F-12
Shavano Park Pg. 142, A-4
Sheffield J-7
Shelbyville H-17
Sheldon L-16
Vicinity .... Pg. 109, C-9
Sheridan M-14
Sherman E-14
Sherwood J-8
Shiner M-13
Shiro K-15
Shoreacres Pg. 109, G-10
Sidney H-11
Sierra Blanca J-3
Silsbee K-17
Silver H-9
Silverton D-8
Simms F-16
Singleton K-15
Sinton P-13
Sisterdale L-11
Sivells Bend E-13
Skellytown B-8
Skidmore N-12
Slaton F-8
Slidell E-13
Slocum H-16
Smiley M-13
Smyer E-7
Snook K-14
Snyder G-8
Socorro H-1

Somerset M-11
Vicinity .... Pg. 142, J-1
Somerville K-14
Sonora K-9
Sour Lake L-17
South Bend F-11
South Houston .... Pg. 109, F-7
South Padre Island S-13
South Plains D-8
Southlake .... Pg. 104, B-5
Southland E-7
Southon .... Pg. 142, H-6
Spade E-7
Spanish Fort E-12
Speaks M-14
Spearman B-8
Spicewood K-12
Splendora L-16
Spofford M-9
Spring L-15
Spring Branch L-11
Spring Valley .... Pg. 109, D-3
Springlake D-7
Springtown F-13
Spur F-9
Spurger K-17
Stafford M-15
Vicinity .... Pg. 109, G-2
Stamford F-10
Stanton H-7
Star J-12
Stephenville H-12
Sterling City H-8
Stinnett B-8
Stockdale M-12
Stoneburg E-12
Stoneham K-15
Stonewall L-11
Stowell L-17
Stratford A-7
Strawn G-11
Streetman H-14
Study Butte M-5
Sudan E-7
Sugar Land L-15
Vicinity .... Pg. 109, G-1
Sullivan City S-11
Sulphur Sprs. F-15
Summerfield D-6
Sumner E-15
Sundown F-6
Sunray B-8
Sunset F-13
Sutherland Springs M-12
Sweeny M-15
Sweetwater G-9
Swenson F-9
Taft P-13
Tahoka F-7
Talco F-16
Talpa H-10
Tankersley J-9
Tarpley M-11
Tarzan G-7
Tatum G-17
Taylor K-13
Taylor Lake Village .... Pg. 109, G-9
Teague H-14
Telegraph K-9
Telephone E-15
Telferner N-14
Tell D-9
Temple J-13
Tenaha H-17
Tenneseee Colony H-15
Tennyson F-9
Terlingua M-5
Terrell G-14
Terrell Hills .... Pg. 142, D-5
Texarkana F-17
Texas City M-16
Texhoma A-6
Texico D-6
Texline A-6
Thackerville E-14
Thalia D-10
The Grove J-13
The Woodlands L-15
Thelma .... Pg. 142, K-5
Thomaston N-12
Thorndale K-13
Thornton J-14
Thorp Spring G-12
Thrall K-13
Three Rivers N-12
Throckmorton F-10
Tilden N-11
Timpson H-17
Tioga F-13
Tira F-15
Tivoli N-14
Toco E-15
Tolar G-12
Tomball K-15
Tool G-15
Topsey J-12
Tornillo H-1
Toyah J-5
Trent G-9
Trenton F-14
Trickham H-11
Trinidad H-15
Trinity J-15
Troup G-16
Troy J-13
Tucker H-16
Tuleta N-12
Tulia D-7
Turnertown H-16
Tuscola H-10
Twin Sisters L-12
Twitty C-9

Tye G-10
Tyler G-16
Tynan P-12
Umbarger C-7
Unity E-15
Universal City M-12
University Park .... Pg. 105, C-9
Utopia M-10
Uvalde M-10
Valentine K-4
Valera H-10
Valley Mills H-13
Valley Spring K-11
Valley View F-13
Van G-15
Van Alstyne F-14
Van Horn J-3
Van Vleck M-15
Vancourt J-9
Vanderbilt N-14
Vanderpool L-10
Vashti E-12
Vealmoor G-8
Vega C-7
Venus G-13
Vernon E-10
Victoria N-13
Vidor L-17
Village Mills K-17
Vincent G-8
Voca J-11
Von Ormy .... Pg. 142, H-2
Voss H-10
Votaw K-17
Waco H-13
Wadsworth N-15
Waelder L-13
Waka A-9
Wake Village E-17
Wall J-9
Waller L-14
Wallis L-14
Walnut Sprs. H-13
Warda L-13
Warren K-17
Washington K-15
Waskom G-17
Water Valley H-9
Watson K-12
Watsonville .... Pg. 104, F-5
Waxahachie G-14
Wayside D-8
Weatherford G-12
Weaver F-15
Webster M-16
Weches H-16
Weesatche N-13
Weimar L-14
Weinert F-10
Welch F-7
Wellington D-9
Wellman F-7
Wells J-16
Weslaco S-12
West H-13
West Columbia M-15
West Orange K-17
West Point L-13
Westbrook G-8
Westfield L-15
Vicinity .... Pg. 109, A-4
Westhoff M-13
Westlake .... Pg. 104, A-4
Westover F-11
Westworth Village .... Pg. 104, D-2
Wharton M-15
Wheeler C-9
Wheeler G-15
Wheelock K-14
White Deer C-8
Whiteface E-6
Whiteflat E-9
Whitehouse G-15
Whitesboro E-13
Whitewright F-14
Whitharral E-7
Whitney H-13
Whittsett N-12
Wichita Falls E-11
Wickett H-5
Wiergate J-18
Wildorado C-7
Wildwood K-17
Wilkinson F-16
Willow City K-11
Wills Point G-15
Wilmer .... Pg. 105, F-10
Wilson F-8
Wimberly L-12
Winchell J-11
Windcrest .... Pg. 142, C-7
Windom F-15
Windthorst E-12
Winfield F-16
Wingate H-9
Wink H-5
Winnie L-17
Winnsboro F-16
Winona G-16
Winters H-10
Wolfe City F-15
Wolfforth F-7
Woodlake J-16
Woodlawn G-17
Woodsboro P-13
Woodson F-11
Woodville K-17
Woodward N-13
Wortham H-14
Yoakum M-13
Yorktown M-13

Zavalla J-17
Zephyr H-11
Zorn L-12

UTAH
Pages 80-81
Population: 1,461,037
Capital: Salt Lake City
Land Area: 82,073 sq. mi.

UTAH

Abraham H-4
Adamsville K-4
Alpine F-5
Alta F-6
Altamont F-8
Alton L-4
American Fork F-5
Aneth M-9
Angle K-5
Annabella J-5
Antimony K-5
Arcadia F-8
Aurora J-5
Austin J-5
Axtell H-5
Bacchus .... Pg. 141, K-2
Bear River City D-5
Beaver K-4
Benjamin F-5
Beryl K-2
Bicknell K-5
Birdseye G-6
Black Rock J-4
Blanding L-9
Blue Cr. C-4
Bluebell F-8
Bluff L-9
Bluffdale F-5
Bonanza G-9
Boneta F-7
Boulder K-6
Bountiful F-5
Vicinity .... Pg. 141, F-6
Brian Head L-4
Bridgeland F-8
Brigham City D-5
Bryce Canyon L-4
Burmester E-4
Burrville J-5
Cannonville L-4
Carbonville G-7
Castle Dale H-7
Castle Rock E-6
Cave C-5
Cedar City L-3
Cedar Creek C-3
Cedar Fort F-5
Cedar Springs D-4
Cedarview F-8
Center Creek F-6
Centerfield H-5
Centerville E-5
Central J-5
Central L-2
Charleston F-6
Chester H-5
Circleville K-4
Cisco J-9
Clarkston C-5
Clawson H-6
Clear Creek C-3
Clearcreek G-6
Clearfield E-5
Cleveland H-7
Clinton D-5
Clover F-4
Coalville G-6
Colton G-7
Corinne D-5
Cornish C-5
Cove Fort K-4
Crescent Jct. J-8
Croydon F-6
Delle E-4
Delta H-4
Deseret H-4
Desert Mound L-3
Dividend G-5
Draper F-5
Duchesne F-7
Dugway F-4
East Carbon City H-8
East Mill Creek .... Pg. 141, J-7
Eastland L-9
Echo F-6
Elberta G-5
Elmo H-7
Elsinore J-5
Emery J-6
Enoch L-3
Enterprise L-2
Ephraim H-6
Escalante L-5
Etna D-2
Eureka G-5
Fairfield F-5
Fairview H-6
Farmington E-5
Faust F-4
Fayette H-5
Ferron H-7
Fillmore J-4
Fish Springs G-3
Flowell H-4
Fort Duchesne F-8
Fountain Green G-5
Francis F-6
Freedom G-5
Fremont J-6
Fremont Jct. J-6

Fruit Heights E-5
Fruitland F-7
Fry Canyon K-8
Gandy G-2
Garden City C-6
Garrison G-2
Geneva F-5
Genola G-5
Glendale L-4
Glenwood J-5
Goshen G-5
Grantsville E-4
Green Lake E-9
Green River H-8
Greenville K-4
Greenwich J-5
Greenwood J-5
Grouse Creek C-2
Gunlock L-2
Gunnison H-5
Gusher F-8
Hamilton Fort L-3
Hanksville K-7
Hanna F-7
Harrisville D-5
Hatch L-4
Hatton J-4
Heber City F-6
Helper G-7
Henefer E-6
Henrieville L-5
Hiawatha H-7
Hinckley H-4
Holden H-5
Holladay F-5
Vicinity .... Pg. 141, K-7
Honeyville D-5
Hot Springs D-5
Howell D-4
Hoytsville E-6
Huntington H-7
Huntsville D-6
Hurricane M-3
Hyde Park C-5
Hyrum D-5
Indianola G-6
Ioka F-8
Iron Springs L-3
Ivins M-2
Jensen F-9
Jericho G-5
Joseph J-4
Junction K-4
Kamas F-6
Kanab M-4
Kanarraville L-3
Kanosh J-4
Kaysville E-5
Kelton D-4
Kenilworth G-7
Kimball Jct. E-6
Kingston K-4
Knolls E-3
Koosharem J-5
La Sal K-9
La Sal Jct. K-9
La Verkin L-3
Lake Pt. Jct. E-4
Lake Shore F-5
Lake View F-5
Laketown C-6
Lapoint F-8
Leamington H-5
Leeds L-3
Leeton F-8
Lehi F-5
Leota F-9
Levan H-5
Lewiston C-5
Loa J-6
Logan D-5
Long Valley Jct. L-4
Low E-4
Lucin C-2
Lund K-3
Lyman J-6
Lynndyl H-5
Maeser F-9
Magna E-5
Vicinity .... Pg. 141, J-2
Manderfield J-4
Manila E-9
Manti H-6
Mantua D-5
Mapleton F-6
Marion E-6
Marysvale J-4
Mayfield H-6
Meadow J-4
Meadowville C-6
Mendon D-5
Mexican Hat M-8
Midvale E-5
Midway F-6
Milburn G-6
Milford J-3
Mills H-5
Minersville K-3
Moab J-9
Modena K-2
Molen H-7
Mona G-5
Monarch F-8
Monroe J-5
Montezuma Creek M-9
Monticello L-9
Moore H-7
Morgan E-5
Moroni G-5
Mountain Home F-7
Mt. Carmel L-4
Mt. Carmel Jct. L-4
Mt. Emmons F-7
Mt. Pleasant G-6

Murray E-5
Myton F-8
N. Logan C-6
N. Salt Lake F-5
Vicinity .... Pg. 141, J-6
Naples F-9
Neola F-8
Nephi G-5
New Harmony L-3
Newcastle L-2
Newton C-5
Oak City H-5
Oakley E-6
Oasis H-4
Ogden D-5
Orangeville H-6
Orderville L-4
Orem F-6
Ouray F-9
Panguitch K-4
Paradise D-5
Paragonah K-4
Park City E-6
Park Valley C-3
Parowan K-4
Payson G-5
Peoa E-6
Perry Willard D-5
Pigeon Hollow Jct. H-6
Pine Valley L-2
Pintura L-3
Plain City D-5
Pleasant Grove F-6
Pleasant View D-5
Plymouth C-5
Portage C-5
Porterville E-6
Price G-7
Providence D-5
Provo F-6
Randolph D-6
Redmond H-5
Richfield J-5
Richmond C-5
Riverdale D-5
Riverton F-5
Rockville M-3
Roosevelt F-8
Rosette C-3
Rowley Jct. E-4
Roy E-5
Ruby's Inn L-4
Saint George M-3
Saint John Sta. F-4
Salem G-5
Salina H-5
Salt Lake City F-4
Vicinity .... Pg. 141
Sandy F-5
Santa Clara M-2
Santaquin G-5
Scipio H-5
Scofield G-6
Sevier J-4
Shivwits M-2
Sigurd J-5
Silver City J-5
Smithfield C-5
Smyths J-3
Snowville C-4
Soldier Summit G-7
South Jordan F-5
South Ogden D-5
South Salt Lake E-5
Vicinity .... Pg. 141, J-5
Spanish Fork G-6
Spring City H-6
Spring Lake G-5
Springdale M-3
Springville F-6
Sterling H-6
Stockton F-4
Summit K-3
Summit Pt. K-9
Sunnyside G-8
Sunset E-5
Sutherland H-4
Syracuse E-5
Tabiona F-7
Talmage F-7
Teasdale K-6
Terrace D-6
Thistle G-6
Thompson H-9
Tooele F-4
Toquerville L-3
Torrey K-6
Tremonton D-5
Tropic L-5
Trout Cr. G-2
Tucker G-6
Upalco F-8
Uvada L-2
Venice J-5
Vernal F-9
Vernon F-4
Veyo L-2
Virgin M-3
W. Valley City F-5
Wahsatch D-6
Wales H-5
Wanship E-6
Washington M-3
Washington Terrace D-5
Wellington G-7
Wellsville D-5
Wendover E-2
West Jordan F-5
West Point E-5
West Valley City F-5
Vicinity .... Pg. 141, J-4
Whiterocks F-8
Widtsoe Jct. K-5
Woodruff D-6

Woods Cross E-5
Vicinity .... Pg. 141, F-5
Woodside H-8
Zane K-2

VERMONT
Page 55
Population: 511,456
Capital: Montpelier
Land Area: 9,273 sq. mi.

Addison E-1
Albany C-3
Alburg B-1
Arlington J-1
Ascutney G-3
Averill B-5
Bakersfield B-2
Barnard F-3
Barnet D-4
Barre E-3
Barton C-4
Bellows Falls H-3
Bennington J-1
Bethel F-3
Bloomfield C-5
Bomoseen G-1
Bondville H-2
Bradford E-4
Brandon F-2
Brattleboro J-3
Bridgewater Cors. G-3
Bridport E-1
Bristol E-1
Broadford Cen. E-3
Brunswick Sprs. C-5
Burlington D-1
Cambridge J-1
Cambridgeport H-3
Canaan B-5
Castleton G-1
Charlotte D-1
Chelsea E-3
Chester H-3
Chester Depot H-3
Chimney Cor. C-2
Concord D-4
Cornwall E-1
Danby G-2
Dorset H-1
E. Barnet D-4
E. Berkshire B-2
E. Braintree E-3
E. Brookfield E-3
E. Burke C-4
E. Calais D-3
E. Dorset H-2
E. Fairfield C-2
E. Granville E-3
E. Hardwick D-3
E. Haven C-4
Eden C-3
Eden Mills C-3
Enosburg Falls B-2
Essex Jct. D-2
Fair Haven G-1
Fairfax C-2
Ferrisburg E-1
Franklin B-2
Gassetts H-3
Gaysville F-3
Glover C-4
Grafton H-3
Grand Isle C-1
Granville E-2
Groton E-4
Guilford J-3
Hancock F-2
Hardwick D-3
Heartwellville J-2
Hinesburg D-2
Holland B-4
Hubbardton F-1
Hyde Park C-3
Irasburg B-3
Irasville E-2
Island Pond C-4
Jacksonville J-2
Jamaica H-2
Jay B-3
Jeffersonville C-2
Johnson C-3
Lake Elmore C-3
Leicester F-2
Londonderry H-2
Lowell B-3
Ludlow G-2
Lunenberg D-5
Lyndon C-4
Lyndonville C-4
Maidstone C-5
Manchester H-2
Manchester Cen. H-2
Marlboro J-2
Marshfield D-3
Middlebury E-1
Middletown Sprs. G-1
Mill Village E-3
Montgomery Cen. B-3
Montpelier D-3
Morgan Cen. B-4
Morrisville C-3
New Haven E-1
New Haven Jct. E-1
Newbury E-4
Newfane J-2
Newport D-4
North Concord D-4
North Dorset H-2
North Hero C-1
North Hyde Park C-3

North Rupert H-1
Northfield E-2
Norton B-5
Norwich F-3
Orleans B-4
Orwell F-1
Passumpsic D-4
Pawlet H-1
Pittsfield F-2
Pittsford F-2
Pittsford Mills F-2
Plainfield D-3
Plymouth C-2
Plymouth Union G-2
Pompanoosuc E-3
Post Mills E-4
Poultney G-1
Pownal J-1
Pownal Cen. J-1
Putney J-3
Quechee G-3
Randolph F-2
Richford B-2
Richmond D-2
Ripton F-2
Robinson F-2
Rochester F-2
Roxbury E-2
Royalton F-2
Rutland G-2
Saint Albans B-2
Saint George D-2
Saint Johnsbury D-4
Searsburg J-2
Shafsbury J-1
Shafsbury Cen. J-1
Shelburne D-1
Sherburne Cen. G-2
Shoreham F-1
Simonsville H-3
South Burlington D-1
South Dorset G-2
South Hinesburg D-2
South Royalton F-3
South Ryegate E-4
South Shafsbury J-1
South Starksboro E-2
South Walden D-3
South Wallingford G-2
Springfield H-3
Starksboro E-2
Stockbridge F-2
Sudbury F-1
Sunderland J-2
Swanton B-1
Ticonderoga F-1
Townshend J-2
Troy B-3
Tunbridge F-3
Tyson G-2
Underhill Flats D-2
Union Village F-3
Vergennes E-1
Vershire E-3
Waits River E-3
Waitsfield E-2
Wallingford G-2
Waltham E-1
Wardsboro J-2
Warren E-2
Washington E-3
Waterbury D-2
Waterbury Ctr. D-3
Websterville E-3
Wells G-1
West Addison E-1
West Braintree E-2
West Bridgewater G-2
West Burke C-4
West Danville D-3
West Dover J-2
West Fairlee E-3
West Groton E-3
West Hartford F-3
West Rutland G-2
West Topsham E-3
West Wardsboro J-2
Westfield B-3
White River Jct. F-3
Whiting F-1
Wilmington J-2
Windsor G-3
Wolcott C-3
Woodbury D-3
Woodford J-1
Woodstock G-3
Worcester D-3

VIRGINIA
Pages 82-83
Population: 5,346,818
Capital: Richmond
Land Area: 39,703 sq. mi.

Abingdon K-3
Achilles H-12
Alexandria E-12
Vicinity .. Pg. 150, F-6
Altavista J-8
Amber Wood Pg. 139, J-1
Amelia H-10
Amherst J-8
Annandale .. Pg. 150, F-5
Appalachia J-2
Appomattox H-9
Arlington D-12
Vicinity ... Pg. 150, E-4
Ashburn ..... Pg. 139, A-5
Ashland G-10
Bailey's Crossroads
..... Pg. 150, E-4

Ballston ... Pg. 150, E-6
Bassett J-7
Bastian J-4
Bavon H-13
Beach ... Pg. 139, J-4
Bedford H-8
Belle Haven G-13
Bensley ... Pg. 139, G-5
Bermuda Hundred
..... Pg. 139, G-5
Berryville D-10
Big Island H-8
Big Stone Gap J-2
Blacksburg H-6
Blackstone J-11
Bluefield J-4
Bon Air H-11
Vicinity ... Pg. 139, E-3
Boones Mill H-7
Bowling Green F-11
Boydton K-9
Brandermill . Pg. 139, G-4
Brandy Creek Estates
..... Pg. 139, C-6
Bridgewater F-8
Bristol K-3
Broadway F-8
Brodnax J-10
Brookneal J-8
Buchanan H-7
Buckingham G-9
Vicinity ... Pg. 139, D-2
Buena Vista H-8
Burgess G-12
Burke ... Pg. 150, G-2
Burkeville H-10
Cape Charles H-13
Carmel Church G-10
Castlewood J-3
Cedarbluff J-4
Central Garage G-11
Centralia ... Pg. 139, H-4
Chamberlayne Heights
..... Pg. 139, C-5
Charlottesville F-9
Charlottsville F-9
Chase City J-9
Chatham J-8
Cheriton H-13
Chesapeake J-13
Vicinity ... Pg. 130, K-4
Chester H-11
Chesterfield . Pg. 139, H-4
Chilhowie K-4
Chincoteague F-14
Christiansburg J-6
Churchville F-8
Clarksville K-9
Claudville K-6
Clifton Forge G-7
Clinchco H-3
Clintwood J-3
Coeburn J-3
Colonial Beach F-11
Colonial Hts. H-11
Courtland J-11
Covington G-6
Craigsville G-7
Crestview . Pg. 139, C-3
Crewe H-10
Crittenton .. Pg. 130, E-1
Crozet G-9
Culpeper E-10
Cumberland H-9
Dale City E-11
Damascus K-4
Dante J-3
Danville K-7
Dayton F-8
Deltaville G-13
Dillwyn H-9
Drakes Branch J-9
Drewrys Bluff Pg. 139, G-4
Dublin J-5
Dugspur K-6
Dumbarton . Pg. 139, C-4
Eagle Rock G-7
Eastville H-13
Edinburg E-10
Elkton E-9
Elmont ... Pg. 139, A-4
Emporia K-11
Enon ... Pg. 139, J-7
Ewing K-1
Exmore H-13
Fairfax E-12
Vicinity ... Pg. 150, E-1
Falling Creek Pg. 139, G-2
Falls Church . Pg. 150, E-5
Falmouth F-11
Farmville H-9
Fieldale K-7
Five Forks . Pg. 139, H-3
Floyd J-6
Franconia .. Pg. 150, G-4
Franklin K-11
Fredericksburg F-10
Fries K-5
Front Royal D-9
Galax K-5
Gate City K-2
Glade Spring J-4
Gladys H-8
Glasgow G-8
Glen Allen .. Pg. 139, B-4
Gloucester H-12
Gloucester Pt. H-12
Gordonsville F-9
Goshen G-8
Grottoes F-8
Groveton .. Pg. 150, G-5
Grundy H-3

Gum Springs G-10
Gwynn H-13
Halifax J-8
Hampden-Sydney H-9
Hampton J-13
Vicinity ... Pg. 130, A-2
Hanover G-11
Harrisonburg E-8
Herndon D-10
Hillsville J-6
Hollins H-7
Honaker J-3
Hopewell H-11
Vicinity ... Pg. 139, K-7
Hughes Corner
..... Pg. 139, B-7
Hurt J-8
Hylas ... Pg. 139, A-1
Independence K-4
Innsbrook .. Pg. 139, B-2
Iron Gate G-7
Irvington G-12
Jarratt J-11
Jonesville K-1
Keene Mill Heights
..... Pg. 150, G-2
Kenbridge J-10
Keysville J-9
Kilmarnock G-12
King & Queen C.H. .. G-12
Kingsland Acres
..... Pg. 139, G-5
Kiptopeke H-13
La Crosse K-10
Lancaster G-12
Langley . Pg. 150, C-4
Laurel ... Pg. 139, B-3
Lawrenceville J-10
Lebanon J-3
Leesburg D-10
Lees Village . Pg. 139, H-6
Lexington G-7
Lottsburg G-12
Lovingston G-8
Luray E-9
Lynchburg H-8
Madison F-9
Madison Hts. H-8
Manassas E-10
Mappsville G-14
Marion J-4
Marshall E-10
Martinsville K-7
Mathews H-13
McKenney J-10
McLean ... Pg. 150, D-3
Meadowville . Pg. 139, H-7
Mechanicsville G-11
Vicinity ... Pg. 139, C-6
Middleburg D-10
Middletown D-9
Midlothian .. Pg. 139, F-1
Monterey F-8
Montross F-12
Mt. Jackson E-9
Narrows J-5
Nassawadox H-13
New Castle H-7
New Market E-9
Newmans .. Pg. 139, C-7
Newport News J-12
Vicinity ... Pg. 130, A-1
Norfolk J-13
Vicinity ..... Pg. 130
Norton J-2
Oak Forest . Pg. 139, B-6
Oak Grove F-12
Onancock G-13
Onley G-14
Orange F-9
Otterdale . Pg. 139, F-1
Palmyra G-9
Pamplin City H-8
Parksley G-13
Patrick Springs K-7
Pearisburg H-6
Pearsons Corner
..... Pg. 139, A-6
Pembroke H-6
Pennington Gap J-2
Petersburg H-10
Pickadat Corner
..... Pg. 139, K-5
Pimmit Hills . Pg. 150, D-3
Poindexters . Pg. 139, A-5
Pole Green . Pg. 139, B-6
Poquoson J-12
Vicinity ... Pg. 130, A-3
Port Royal F-11
Portsmouth J-12
Vicinity ... Pg. 130, F-3
Pound J-2
Powhatan H-10
Prospect Hill Pg. 150, C-2
Pulaski J-5
Purcellville D-10
Quantico E-11
Radford J-6
Raven J-4
Ravensworth Pg. 150, F-2
Red Ash J-3
Remington E-10
Richlands J-4
Richmond H-10
Ripplemead H-6
Roanoke H-7
Robious .. Pg. 139, E-2
Rockville G-10
Rocky Mount J-7
Ruckersville F-9
Rural Point . Pg. 139, B-6
Rural Retreat J-5
Rustburg H-8

Salem H-7
Saltville J-4
Sandston H-11
Saxis G-13
Seaford H-12
Shady Oak . Pg. 150, B-1
Shenandoah E-9
Shipman G-8
Short Pump . Pg. 139, B-2
Simpkins Corner
..... Pg. 139, C-7
Smithfield J-12
South Boston K-8
Sperryville E-9
Spring Grove H-11
Springfield . Pg. 150, G-3
St. Paul J-3
Stafford F-11
Stanley E-9
Stanleytown J-7
Staunton F-8
Stephens City D-9
Strasburg E-9
Stuart K-6
Stuarts Draft G-8
Studley ... Pg. 139, A-7
Suffolk J-12
Vicinity ... Pg. 130, H-1
Sugar Grove J-4
Surry H-12
Sussex J-11
Swan Hill ... Pg. 139, G-2
Sydnorsville J-7
Tangier G-13
Tappahannock G-11
Tazewell J-4
Timberville E-8
Triangle E-11
Tysons Corner
..... Pg. 150, D-2
Urbanna G-12
Vanderpool F-7
Vansant H-3
Verona F-8
Victoria J-9
Victoria Hills Pg. 139, J-5
Vienna D-11
Vicinity ... Pg. 150, E-2
Vinton H-7
Virginia Beach J-13
Vicinity ... Pg. 130, H-7
Volens J-8
Wakefield J-12
Walthall ... Pg. 139, K-5
Warm Springs F-7
Warrenton E-10
Warsaw F-12
Waverly J-11
Waynesboro F-8
Weber City K-3
West Point H-12
Williamsburg H-11
Winchester D-9
Windsor J-12
Wise J-2
Woodbridge E-11
Woodlawn K-5
Woodstock E-9
Wylliesburg J-9
Wytheville J-5
Zion G-9

WASHINGTON
Pages 84-85
Population: 4,132,156
Capital: Olympia
Land Area: 66,511 sq. mi.

Aberdeen F-3
Acme B-6
Addy B-13
Airway Heights D-14
Albion F-14
Alderwood Maner
..... Pg. 147, A-4
Algona E-5
Almira D-11
Altoona H-3
Anacortes B-5
Anatone H-14
Appleyard E-9
Arlington C-5
Asotin G-14
Auburn F-5
Battle Ground J-5
Bellevue D-6
Vicinity ... Pg. 147, E-4
Bellingham A-5
Benton City H-10
Bickleton H-9
Bingen J-7
Black Diamond E-6
Blaine A-5
Bonney Lake F-6
Bossburg B-13
Bothell D-6
Vicinity ... Pg. 147, B-5
Boundary A-13
Bremerton D-5
Brewster C-10
Bridgeport C-10
Brier ..... Pg. 147, A-4
Vicinity ... Pg. 147, A-4
Bryn Mawr . Pg. 147, H-5
Buckley F-6
Bucoda F-4
Burien ..... Pg. 147, H-3
Burlington B-5
Camas J-5
Carbonado F-6
Carnation D-6

Cashmere E-9
Castle Rock H-4
Cathlamet H-3
Centralia G-5
Chehalis G-4
Chelan D-9
Cheney E-14
Chewelah C-13
Clarkston G-14
Clayton C-13
Cle Elum E-8
Vicinity ... Pg. 147, A-6
College Place H-12
Colton G-14
Colville B-13
Conconully B-10
Concrete B-7
Connell F-12
Copalis Beach E-2
Cosmopolis F-3
Coulee City D-11
Coulee Dam C-11
Coupeville C-5
Crescent Bar E-9
Creston D-12
Cusick C-14
Darrington C-7
Davenport D-13
Dayton H-13
Deer Park C-14
Deming A-6
Des Moines E-6
Vicinity ... Pg. 147, K-3
Disautel C-11
Discovery Bay C-5
Dodge H-13
Duluth J-5
Dusty F-13
Duvall D-6
East Wenatchee E-9
Eastgate . Pg. 147, F-6
Eatonville F-6
Edmonds D-5
Vicinity ... Pg. 147, A-2
Edwall E-13
Elbe F-6
Eldon E-4
Electric City D-11
Ellensburg F-9
Elma F-4
Elmer City C-11
Endicott F-13
Entiat D-9
Enumclaw E-6
Ephrata E-10
Eureka H-12
Everett C-6
Everson A-6
Fairfield E-14
Fairholm C-3
Farmington F-15
Ferndale A-5
Fircrest E-5
Forks C-2
Friday Harbor B-5
Garfield F-14
George F-10
Gifford C-13
Gig Harbor E-5
Glenoma G-5
Gold Bar D-7
Goldendale J-8
Grand Coulee D-11
Grandview H-9
Granger G-9
Granite Falls C-6
Greenwater F-7
Hamilton B-6
Harrah G-9
Harrington E-12
Hartline D-11
Hatton G-11
Hoodsport E-4
Hoquiam E-3
Humptulips E-3
Husum J-7
Hyak E-7
Ilwaco H-2
Index D-7
Ione B-14
Issaquah E-6
Joyce C-3
Juanita .. Pg. 147, C-4
Kahlotus G-12
Kalama H-5
Keller C-12
Kelso H-4
Kenmoore . Pg. 147, B-4
Kennewick H-11
Kent E-6
Vicinity ... Pg. 147, J-4
Kettle Falls B-13
Kingston .. Pg. 147, A-1
Kirkland D-6
Vicinity ... Pg. 147, D-5
Kittitas F-9
Klaus E-13
Klickitat J-7
Krupp E-11
La Center J-5
La Conner B-5
La Crosse F-13
La Push C-2
Lacey F-5
Lake Stevens C-6
Lamont F-13
Langley C-5
Latah F-13
Leavenworth D-9
Lebam G-3
Lind F-12

Littlerock F-4
Long Beach G-3
Longview H-4
Lyman B-6
Lynden A-5
Lynnwood D-6
Vicinity ... Pg. 147, A-3
Mabton H-9
Malone F-4
Maltby .. Pg. 147, A-6
Mansfield D-10
Manson D-9
Maplewood . Pg. 147, H-5
Marcus B-13
Marysville C-6
Mattawa G-10
McCleary F-4
Medical Lake E-13
Megler H-3
Menlo G-3
Mercer Island D-5
Vicinity ... Pg. 147, F-5
Mesa G-11
Metaline A-14
Metaline Falls A-14
Methow C-9
Millwood D-14
Monroe D-6
Montesano F-3
Morton G-6
Moses Lake F-11
Mossyrock G-5
Mount Baker A-7
Mount Vernon B-5
Mountlake Terrace D-5
Moxee City G-9
Mukilteo D-6
Naches F-8
Napavine G-4
Naselle H-3
Neah Bay B-2
Neilton E-3
Newcastle . Pg. 147, G-5
Newport C-14
Normandy Park E-5
North Bend E-7
North Bonneville J-6
North Cove F-2
Northport A-13
Oak Harbor C-5
Oakesdale F-14
Oakville F-4
Ocean Park G-3
Ocean Shores E-2
Odessa E-12
Okanogan C-10
Olympia F-5
Omak B-10
Orchards J-5
Orient A-13
Oroville A-10
Orting F-6
Othello F-11
Ozette C-2
Pacific E-6
Pacific Beach E-2
Packwood G-7
Palouse F-14
Pasco H-11
Pateros C-10
Pe Ell G-4
Pomeroy G-14
Port Angeles C-4
Port Gamble D-5
Port Orchard E-5
Port Townsend C-5
Poulsbo D-5
Prescott H-12
Prosser H-10
Pullman G-14
Puyallup F-5
Queets D-2
Quincy E-10
Rainier F-5
Randle G-6
Raymond G-3
Reardan D-13
Redmond D-6
Vicinity ... Pg. 147, H-4
Republic B-12
Richland H-11
Richland Highlands
..... Pg. 147, B-3
Richmond Beach
..... Pg. 147, B-3
Ridgefield J-5
Rimrock G-7
Ritzville F-12
Riverside B-10
Rochester F-4
Rock Island E-9
Rockford E-14
Rockport D-7
Rollingbay . Pg. 147, D-1
Roosevelt J-9
Rosalia E-14
Rosburg G-3
Roslyn E-8
Roy F-5
Royal City F-10
Ryderwood G-4
Salmon La Sac E-8
Sappho C-2
Seattle D-5
Vicinity ..... Pg. 147
Sedro Woolley B-6
Selah G-9
Sequim C-4
Shelton E-4
Silver Creek G-5
Skykomish D-7

Snohomish D-6
Snoqualmie E-7
Soap Lake E-10
South Bend G-3
South Cle Elum F-8
South Prairie F-6
Spangle E-14
Spokane D-14
Sprague E-13
Springdale C-13
St. John F-14
Stanwood C-6
Starbuck G-13
Steilacoom E-5
Stella H-4
Steptoe F-14
Stevenson J-6
Sultan D-6
Sumas A-6
Sumner E-6
Sunnyside H-10
Tacoma E-5
Taholah E-2
Tekoa E-14
Telma D-8
Tenino F-5
Tieton G-8
Toledo G-5
Tonasket B-10
Toppenish H-9
Trout Lake H-7
Tukwila E-5
Tumwater F-4
Twisp C-9
Union E-4
Union Gap G-9
Uniontown G-14
Vader H-4
Vancouver J-4
Vicinity ... Pg. 137, A-5
Vantage F-9
Vashon Heights
..... Pg. 147, G-2
Vashon Island
..... Pg. 147, K-1
Waitsburg H-13
Walla Walla H-12
Wallula H-11
Wapato G-9
Warden F-11
Washougal J-5
Washtucna G-12
Waterville D-9
Wauconda B-11
Waverly E-14
Wenatchee E-9
Wenatchee Heights E-9
West Richland H-11
Westport F-2
White Salmon J-7
White Swan H-8
Wickersham B-6
Wilbur D-12
Wilkeson F-6
Wilson Creek E-11
Winlock G-4
Winslow D-5
Winthrop B-9
Wishram Heights J-8
Withrow D-10
Woodinville . Pg. 147, A-5
Woodland J-5
Yacolt J-5
Yakima G-9
Yelm F-5
Zillah G-9

WEST VIRGINIA
Pages 82-83
Population: 1,949,644
Capital: Charleston
Land Area: 24,119 sq. mi.

Alderson G-6
Arnoldsburg E-5
Ashton E-4
Athens H-5
Augusta D-8
Baker D-9
Baileysville G-4
Barbourville F-3
Barrackville C-7
Beckley G-5
Belington D-7
Belmont D-5
Bethlehem B-6
Beverly E-7
Big Chimney F-4
Big Otter F-5
Birch River E-6
Blacksville C-7
Bluefield H-5
Bradley G-5
Bramwell H-4
Bridgeport D-7
Buckhannon D-6
Buffalo E-4
Burnsville E-6
Cairo D-5
Camden-on-Gauley F-6
Cameron C-6
Cedar Grove F-5
Center Pt. D-6
Chapmanville G-3
Charles Town D-10
Charleston F-4
Chesapeake F-4
Chester A-6
Clarksburg D-6
Clay E-5
Clendenin E-5

WEST VIRGINIA   WYOMING

Coxs Mills ... D-6
Craigsville ... F-6
Danville ... D-8
Davis ... F-7
Delbarton ... G-3
Dunbar ... E-4
Dunmore ... F-7
Durbin ... E-7
East Bank ... E-4
Eleanor ... E-4
Elk Garden ... C-8
Elkins ... D-7
Ellenboro ... D-5
Fairmont ... C-7
Fairview ... C-6
Farmington ... C-6
Fayetteville ... F-5
Flatwoods ... E-6
Follansbee ... A-6
Forest Hill ... H-5
Franklin ... E-8
Friendly ... D-4
Ft. Ashby ... C-8
Ft. Gay ... F-3
Gandeeville ... E-4
Gap Mills ... H-6
Gary ... H-4
Gassaway ... E-6
Gauley Bridge ... F-5
Gerrardstown ... C-9
Gilbert ... G-4
Gilmer ... E-6
Glen Dale ... B-6
Glenville ... D-5
Grantsville ... D-5
Hambleton ... D-7
Hamlin ... F-4
Harman ... E-8
Harrisville ... D-5
Hedgesville ... C-9
Henderson ... E-3
Hillsboro ... F-6
Hinton ... G-5
Hundred ... C-6
Huntington ... F-3
Hurricane ... F-3
Huttonsville ... E-7
Iaeger ... H-4
Ingleside ... H-5
Inwood ... C-10
Jane Lew ... D-6
Jolo ... H-4
Junction ... C-8
Junior ... D-7
Kenna ... E-4
Kenova ... F-3
Kermit ... G-3
Keyser ... C-9
Keystone ... H-4
Kimball ... H-4
Kingwood ... C-7
Leon ... E-4
Lester ... G-5
Lewisburg ... G-5
Liberty ... E-4
Linn ... D-6
Logan ... G-3
Lost City ... D-8
Lost Cr. ... D-7
Lumberport ... D-6
Mabscott ... G-5
Madison ... G-4
Man ... G-4
Mannington ... C-7
Marlinton ... F-6
Marmet ... F-4
Martinsburg ... C-9
Mason ... D-4
Masontown ... C-7
Matewan ... G-3
Matoaka ... H-5
Meadow Bridge ... G-5
Middlebourne ... C-5
Midkiff ... F-3
Mill Creek ... E-7
Milton ... F-3
Monongah ... C-6
Montgomery ... G-5
Montrose ... D-8
Moorefield ... D-9
Morgantown ... C-7
Mossy ... G-4
Moundsville ... B-6
Mt. Hope ... G-5
Mt. Storm ... D-8
Muddlety ... F-5
Mullens ... H-5
Naoma ... G-4
Neola ... G-7
Nettie ... F-5
New Cumberland ... A-6
New Haven ... D-4
New Martinsville ... C-6
Newton ... E-5
Nitro ... F-4
Nutter Fort ... D-6
Oak Flat ... E-8
Oak Hill ... G-5
Oceana ... G-4
Omar ... G-3
Paden City ... C-5
Parkersburg ... D-5
Parsons ... D-7
Paw Paw ... C-9
Pennsboro ... D-5
Petersburg ... D-8
Peterstown ... H-6
Philippi ... D-7
Piedmont ... C-8
Pine Grove ... C-6
Pineville ... H-4

Poca ... E-4
Pocatalico ... E-4
Prichard ... F-3
Princeton ... H-5
Pt. Pleasant ... E-3
Racine ... F-4
Rainelle ... G-5
Rand ... F-4
Ranson ... D-10
Ravenswood ... D-4
Reedy ... E-5
Renick ... G-6
Rhodell ... H-5
Richwood ... F-6
Ridgeley ... C-9
Ripley ... E-4
Roanoke ... E-6
Rock Cave ... E-6
Romney ... D-9
Ronceverte ... G-6
Rowlesburg ... D-7
Rupert ... G-6
Salem ... D-6
Scherr ... D-8
Seneca Rocks ... E-8
Shepherdstown ... C-10
Shinnston ... C-6
Slatyfork ... F-6
Smithers ... F-5
Smithfield ... C-6
Sophia ... G-5
South Charleston ... F-4
Spencer ... E-5
St. Albans ... F-4
St. Mary's ... C-5
Star City ... C-7
Stonewood ... D-7
Summersville ... F-6
Sylvester ... G-4
Terra Alta ... C-8
Thomas ... D-7
Thornwood ... E-7
Triadelphia ... B-6
Tunnelton ... D-7
Union ... H-6
Valley Head ... E-7
Van ... G-4
Vienna ... D-4
War ... H-4
Wardensville ... D-8
Wayne ... F-3
Webster Spr. ... E-6
Weirton ... A-6
Welch ... H-4
Wellsburg ... A-6
West Hamlin ... F-3
West Logan ... G-4
West Union ... D-5
Weston ... D-6
Westover ... C-7
Wheeling ... B-6
White Sulphur Spr. ... G-6
Whitesville ... G-4
Williamson ... G-3
Williamstown ... D-4
Yawkey ... F-4

WISCONSIN
Pages 86-87
Population: 4,705,767
Capital: Madison
Land Area: 54,426 sq. mi.

Abbotsford ... F-5
Adams ... H-5
Adell ... J-8
Algoma ... G-8
Alma ... G-2
Alma Center ... G-4
Almena ... F-2
Altoona ... G-3
Amery ... F-2
Aniwa ... F-6
Antigo ... F-6
Appleton ... G-7
Arcadia ... H-3
Argyle ... K-5
Arlington ... J-6
Ashland ... D-4
Ashwaubenon ... G-7
Athens ... F-5
Auburndale ... G-5
Augusta ... G-4
Avoca ... K-5
Baldwin ... F-2
Balsam Lake ... E-2
Bangor ... H-4
Baraboo ... J-5
Barneveld ... K-5
Barron ... F-3
Bay City ... F-2
Bayfield ... C-4
Bayside ... J-8
  Vicinity ... Pg. 121, A-6
Beaver Dam ... J-7
Belgium ... J-8
Belleville ... K-6
Belmont ... K-5
Beloit ... L-6
Benton ... L-5
Berlin ... H-6
Big Bend ... Pg. 121, H-1
Birchwood ... E-3
Birnamwood ... F-6
Black Creek ... G-7
Black Earth ... K-5
Black River Falls ... G-4

Blair ... H-3
Blanchardville ... K-5
Bloomer ... F-3
Bloomington ... K-4
Bonduel ... G-7
Boscobel ... K-4
Boyceville ... F-2
Boyd ... F-4
Brandon ... J-7
Brillion ... H-8
Brodhead ... L-6
Brokaw ... F-6
Brookfield ... Pg. 121, D-3
Brown Deer ... Pg. 121, A-5
Browntown ... L-6
Bruce ... F-3
Buena Park ... Pg. 121, K-1
Buffalo ... H-2
Burlington ... K-8
Butler ... Pg. 121, C-3
Butternut ... D-5
Cable ... D-3
Caddy Vista ... Pg. 121, J-6
Cadott ... F-3
Caledonia ... Pg. 121, K-6
Cambra ... J-6
Cambridge ... K-7
Cameron ... F-3
Camp Douglas ... H-5
Campbellsport ... J-8
Cascade ... J-8
Casco ... G-8
Cashton ... J-4
Cassville ... K-4
Catawba ... E-4
Cazenovia ... J-5
Cecil ... G-7
Centuria ... E-1
Chetek ... F-3
Chilton ... H-8
Chippewa Falls ... F-3
Clayton ... F-2
Clear Lake ... F-2
Cleveland ... H-8
Clinton ... L-7
Clintonville ... G-7
Cochrane ... H-3
Colby ... G-5
Coleman ... F-8
Colfax ... F-3
Colgate ... Pg. 121, A-1
Coloma ... H-6
Columbus ... J-7
Coon Valley ... J-4
Cornell ... F-4
Couderay ... E-3
Crandon ... E-7
Crivitz ... F-8
Cross Plains ... K-6
Cuba City ... L-4
Cudahy ... K-8
  Vicinity ... Pg. 121, F-6
Cumberland ... E-2
Dane ... J-6
Darien ... L-7
Darlington ... K-5
De Pere ... G-8
De Soto ... J-4
DeForest ... K-6
Deerfield ... K-6
Delavan ... K-7
Denmark ... G-8
Dickeyville ... L-4
Dodgeville ... K-5
Dorchester ... F-5
Dousman ... K-7
Dresser ... F-1
Duplainville ... Pg. 121, D-2
Durand ... G-2

Eagle ... K-7
Eagle River ... E-6
East Troy ... K-7
Eastman ... K-4
Eau Claire ... G-3
Eden ... J-7
Edgar ... F-5
Edgerton ... K-6
Egg Harbor ... F-9
Elano ... G-7
Eleva ... G-3
Elk Mound ... G-3
Elkhart Lake ... H-8
Elkhorn ... K-7
Ellsworth ... G-2
Elm Grove ... Pg. 121, D-3
Elmwood ... G-2
Elroy ... J-5
Embarrass ... G-7
Ephraim ... F-9
Ettrick ... H-3
Evansville ... K-6
Exeland ... E-3
Fairchild ... G-4
Fall Creek ... G-3
Fall River ... J-6
Fennimore ... K-4
Ferryville ... J-4
Fifield ... E-5
Florence ... E-7
Fond Du Lac ... H-7
Fontana ... L-7
Footville ... L-6
Forestville ... G-8
Fort Atkinson ... K-7
Fountain City ... H-3
Fox Lake ... J-7
Fox Point ... Pg. 121, B-6
Francis Creek ... G-8
Franklin ... K-8
  Vicinity ... Pg. 121, H-4

Frederick ... E-2
Fremont ... H-7
Friendship ... H-6
Galesville ... H-3
Gays Mills ... J-4
Genoa ... J-3
Genoa City ... L-8
Germantown ... J-8
  Vicinity ... Pg. 121, A-3
Gillett ... F-7
Gilman ... F-4
Glen Flora ... E-4
Glendale ... Pg. 121, B-6
Glenwood City ... F-2
Grafton ... J-8
Granton ... G-5
Grantsburg ... E-1
Gratiot ... L-5
Green Bay ... G-8
Green Lake ... H-6
Greendale ... K-8
  Vicinity ... Pg. 121, G-4
Greenfield ... Pg. 121, F-5
Greenwood ... G-5
Gresham ... G-7
Hales Corners
  Vicinity ... Pg. 121, G-4
Hammond ... F-2
Hancock ... H-6
Hartford ... J-7
Hartland ... K-8
Haugen ... E-4
Hawkins ... E-4
Hawthorne ... D-3
Hayward ... E-3
Hazel Green ... L-4
Heafford Jct. ... E-6
Highland ... K-5
Hilbert ... H-8
Hillsboro ... J-4
Holmen ... H-3
Horicon ... J-7
Hortonville ... H-7
Howard ... G-8
Howards Grove ... H-8
Hudson ... F-1
Hurley ... D-5
Husher ... Pg. 121, J-6
Independence ... G-3
Ingram ... F-4
Iola ... G-6
Iron River ... C-3
Jackson ... J-8
Janesville ... K-7
Jefferson ... K-7
Johnson Creek ... K-7
Junction City ... G-5
Juneau ... J-7
Kaukauna ... H-8
Kendall ... J-5
Kennan ... E-4
Kenosha ... L-8
  Vicinity ... Pg. 121, C-1
Keshena ... F-7
Kewaskum ... J-8
Kewaunee ... G-8
Kiel ... H-8
Kimberly ... H-7
Kingston ... J-6
Kneeland ... Pg. 121, J-5
La Crosse ... H-3
La Farge ... J-4
Lac Du Flambeau ... D-5
Ladysmith ... E-3
Lake Delton ... J-5
Lake Geneva ... L-7
Lake Nebagamon ... C-2
Lancaster ... K-4
Lannon ... Pg. 121, B-2
Lena ... F-8
Linden ... K-5
Little Chute ... G-7
Livingston ... K-5
Lodi ... J-6
Loganville ... J-5
Lomira ... J-7
Lone Rock ... J-5
Loyal ... G-5
Lublin ... F-4
Luck ... E-2
Luxemburg ... G-8

Madison ... K-6
Manawa ... G-7
Manitowish ... D-5
Manitowoc ... H-9
Marathon City ... F-5
Marinette ... F-9
Marion ... G-7
Markesan ... J-6
Marshall ... K-6
Marshfield ... G-5
Mason ... D-4
Mauston ... H-5
Mayville ... J-7
Mazomanie ... K-5
Medford ... F-4
Meeker ... Pg. 121, A-2
Mellen ... D-4
Melrose ... H-4
Melvina ... H-4
Menasha ... H-7
Menomonee Falls ... J-7
  Vicinity ... Pg. 121, A-2
Menomonie ... G-2
Mequon ... Pg. 121, A-5
Merrill ... F-5
Merrillan ... G-4
Middleton ... K-6
Milltown ... E-2
Milton ... K-7
Milwaukee ... K-8
  Vicinity ... Pg. 121

Mineral Point ... K-5
Minong ... D-3
Mishicot ... H-8
Mondovi ... G-3
Monico ... E-6
Monroe ... L-5
Montello ... H-6
Montfort ... K-5
Monticello ... K-6
Montreal ... D-4
Mosinee ... G-6
Mount Horeb ... K-6
Mount Sterling ... J-4
Mukwonago ... K-7
Muscoda ... K-5
Muskego ... K-8
  Vicinity ... Pg. 121, G-2
Necedah ... H-5
Neenah ... H-7
Neillsville ... G-4
Nekoosa ... H-5
Nelson ... G-2
Nelsonville ... G-6
Neshkoro ... H-6
New Berlin ... K-7
  Vicinity ... Pg. 121, E-2
New Glarus ... K-5
New Holstein ... H-8
New Lisbon ... J-5
New London ... G-7
New Richmond ... F-2
Niagara ... E-8
North Cape ... Pg. 121, K-4
North Fond du Lac ... H-7
North Hudson ... F-1
Norwalk ... H-4
Oak Creek ... K-8
  Vicinity ... Pg. 121, G-6
Oconomowoc ... K-7
Oconto ... F-8
Oconto Falls ... F-8
Omro ... H-7
Onalaska ... H-3
Ontario ... J-4
Oostburg ... J-8
Orfordville ... K-6
Osceola ... F-1
Oshkosh ... H-7
Osseo ... G-3
Owen ... F-4
Oxford ... H-6
Paddock Lake ... L-8
Palmyra ... K-7
Pardeeville ... J-6
Park Falls ... E-4
Park Ridge ... G-6
Patch Grove ... K-4
Pembine ... E-8
Pepin ... G-2
Peshtigo ... F-8
Pewaukee ... Pg. 121, C-1
Phelps ... D-7
Phillips ... E-5
Pigeon Falls ... G-3
Pittsville ... G-5
Plain ... J-5
Plainfield ... H-6
Platteville ... K-4
Plover ... G-6
Plum City ... G-2
Plymouth ... H-8
Poplar ... C-2
Port Edwards ... H-5
Port Washington ... J-8
Portage ... J-6
Potosi ... K-4
Pound ... F-8
Prairie du Chien ... K-4
Prairie du Sac ... J-5
Prentice ... E-5
Prescott ... G-1
Princeton ... H-6
Pulaski ... G-7
Racine ... K-8
  Vicinity ... Pg. 121, G-6
Radisson ... E-3
Randolph ... J-7
Raymond ... Pg. 121, K-4
Redgranite ... H-6
Reedsburg ... J-5
Reedsville ... H-8
Rhinelander ... E-6
Rib Lake ... E-5
Rice Lake ... E-3
Richland Center ... J-5
Ridgeland ... F-2
Ridgeway ... K-5
Ripon ... H-7
River Falls ... F-1
River Hills ... Pg. 121, A-5
Riverside ... D-2
Roberts ... F-2
Rosendale ... H-7
Rosholt ... G-6
Rothschild ... G-6
Saint Croix Falls ... F-2
Saint Francis ...
  Vicinity ... Pg. 121, F-7
Sauk City ... J-5
Saukville ... J-8
Schofield ... G-6
Seymour ... G-7
Sharon ... L-7
Shawano ... G-7
Sheboygan ... H-8
Sheboygan Falls ... H-8
Sheldon ... F-4
Shell Lake ... E-2
Shiocton ... G-7

Shorewood ... Pg. 121, C-7
Shullsburg ... L-5
Siren ... E-2
Sister Bay ... F-9
Soldiers Grove ... J-4
Solon Springs ... D-3
Somerset ... F-1
South Milwaukee ... K-8
  Vicinity ... Pg. 121, G-7
Sparta ... H-4
Spencer ... G-4
Spooner ... E-3
Spring Green ... J-5
Spring Valley ... G-2
Stanley ... F-4
Stevens Point ... G-5
Stockbridge ... H-7
Stockholm ... G-2
Stoddard ... J-4
Stoughton ... K-6
Stratford ... G-5
Strum ... G-3
Sturgeon Bay ... F-8
Sturtevant ... K-8
Sun Prairie ... K-7
Superior ... C-2
Suring ... F-7
Sussex ... Pg. 121, B-1
Tabor ... Pg. 121, J-7
Taylors Falls ... E-1
Tennyson ... K-4
Theresa ... J-7
Thompsonville ...
  Vicinity ... Pg. 121, K-5
Thorp ... F-4
Tichigan ... Pg. 121, J-7
Tigerton ... G-7
Tomah ... H-4
Tomahawk ... E-6
Tony ... E-4
Trego ... E-3
Trempealeau ... H-3
Turtle Lake ... F-2
Two Rivers ... H-9
Union Center ... J-5
Union Church ... Pg. 121, J-4
Union Grove ... K-8
Unity ... G-5
Valders ... H-8
Vernon ... Pg. 121, G-1
Verona ... K-6
Vesper ... G-5
Village of Superior ... C-2
Viroqua ... J-4
Walworth ... L-7
Washburn ... C-3
Waterford ... K-7
Waterloo ... K-6
Watertown ... J-7
Waukesha ... K-7
  Vicinity ... Pg. 121, E-1
Waunakee ... K-6
Waupaca ... G-7
Waupun ... J-7
Wausau ... F-6
Wausaukee ... F-8
Wautoma ... H-6
Wauwatosa ... K-8
  Vicinity ... Pg. 121, E-5
Webster ... E-2
West Allis ... Pg. 121, E-4
West Bend ... J-8
West Milwaukee ...
  Pg. 121, E-5
Westby ... J-4
Westfield ... H-6
Weyauwega ... G-6
White Lake ... F-7
Whitefish Bay ... K-8
  Vicinity ... Pg. 121, C-6
Whitehall ... G-3
Whitelaw ... H-8
Whitewater ... K-7
Whiting ... G-6
Wild Rose ... H-6
Wind Pt. ... K-8
Winneconne ... H-7
Winter ... E-4
Wisconsin Dells ... J-6
Wisconsin Rapids ... G-5
Withee ... F-4
Wittenberg ... F-6
Wonewoc ... J-5
Woodruff ... E-6
Wrightstown ... H-7
Wyeville ... H-5
Wyocena ... J-6
Yuba ... J-5

WYOMING
Pages 88-89
Population: 469,559
Capital: Cheyenne
Land Area: 96,989 sq. mi.

Acme ... B-8
Afton ... F-3
Aladdin ... B-12
Albany ... J-9
Albin ... H-12
Alcova ... E-8
Alpine Jct. ... E-3
Alva ... B-11
Arapahoe ... F-6
Arlington ... H-9
Arminto ... E-8
Arvada ... B-9
Atlantic City ... G-6

Auburn ... F-3
Baggs ... J-7
Bairoil ... G-7
Banner ... B-8
Bar Nunn ... F-9
Barnum ... D-8
Basin ... C-7
Beckton ... B-8
Bedford ... F-3
Beulah ... B-12
Big Horn ... B-8
Big Piney ... G-4
Big Sandy ... F-5
Big Trails ... D-8
Bill ... E-10
Bitter Creek ... H-6
Bondurant ... E-4
Border ... G-3
Bosler ... H-10
Boulder ... F-5
Boxelder ... F-10
Buffalo ... C-8
Burgess Jct. ... B-7
Burlington ... C-7
Burns ... J-12
Burntfork ... J-4
Burris ... E-5
Byron ... B-6
Calpet ... G-4
Canyon Jct. ... B-4
Carpenter ... J-12
Carter ... J-4
Casper ... F-9
Centennial ... J-9
Cheyenne ... J-11
Chugwater ... H-11
Clareton ... D-11
Clark ... B-5
Clearmont ... B-9
Cody ... B-6
Cokeville ... G-3
Colony ... B-12
Cora ... E-4
Cowley ... B-6
Creston Jct. ... H-7
Crowheart ... E-5
Daniel ... F-4
Dayton ... B-8
Deaver ... B-6
Devil's Tower Jct. ... B-11
Diamondville ... G-3
Dixon ... J-7
Douglas ... F-10
Dubois ... E-5
East Thermopolis ... D-7
Eden ... G-5
Edgerton ... E-9
Egbert ... J-12
Elk Basin ... B-6
Elk Mountain ... H-9
Elkol ... H-4
Elmo ... H-9
Emblem ... C-6
Encampment ... J-9
Ethete ... E-5
Etna ... E-3
Evanston ... J-3
Evansville ... F-9
Fairview ... F-3
Farson ... G-5
Federal ... J-11
Fort Bridger ... J-4
Fort Laramie ... G-11
Fort Washakie ... F-5
Four Corners ... C-12
Frannie ... B-6
Freedom ... F-3
Frontier ... H-4
Garland ... B-6
Gillette ... C-10
Glendo ... F-11
Glenrock ... F-10
Granger ... H-4
Grass Creek ... D-6
Green River ... H-5
Greybull ... C-7
Grover ... F-3
Guernsey ... G-11
Hamilton Dome ... D-6
Hampshire ... D-11
Hanna ... H-9
Hartville ... G-11
Hawk Springs ... H-12
Hiland ... E-8
Hillsdale ... J-12
Hobock Jct. ... E-3
Horse Creek ... H-11
Hudson ... F-6
Hulett ... B-11
Hyattville ... C-8
Iron Mountain ... H-11
Jackson ... E-3
Jay Em ... G-12
Jeffrey City ... G-7
Jenny Lake ... D-3
Kaycee ... D-9
Keeline ... F-11
Kelly ... E-4
Kemmerer ... H-3
Kinnear ... E-6
Kirby ... D-7
La Barge ... G-4
La Grange ... H-12
Lake Jct. ... B-4
Lamont ... G-8
Lance Creek ... E-11
Lander ... F-6
Laramie ... J-10
Leiter ... B-9

Lightning Flat ... B-11
Linch ... D-9
Lingle ... G-12
Little America ... J-4
Lonetree ... J-4
Lost Cabin ... E-8
Lost Springs ... F-11
Lovell ... B-6
Lucerne ... D-7
Lusk ... F-11
Lyman ... J-4
Lysite ... E-7
Madison Jct. ... B-3
Mammoth Springs Jct. ... B-3
Manderson ... C-7
Manville ... F-11
Marbleton ... F-4
Mayoworth ... D-8
McFadden ... H-10
McKinnon ... K-4
Medicine Bow ... H-9
Meeteetse ... C-6
Merna ... F-4
Midwest ... E-9
Millburne ... J-4
Mills ... F-9
Moneta ... E-7
Moorcroft ... C-11
Moose ... D-3
Moran Jct. ... D-4
Morrisey ... D-11
Morton ... E-6
Mountain Home ... J-10
Mountain View ... J-4
Mule Cr. Jct. ... E-12
Natrona ... F-8
New Haven ... B-11
Newcastle ... D-12
Node ... F-12
Norris Jct. ... B-3
Old Faithful ... C-3
Opal ... H-4
Orin ... F-11
Orpha ... F-10
Osage ... D-11
Oshoto ... B-11
Otto ... C-7
Parkman ... B-8
Pavillion ... E-6
Piedmont ... J-4
Pine Bluffs ... J-12
Pine Tree Jct. ... D-10
Pinedale ... F-5
Pitchfork ... D-5
Point of Rocks ... H-6
Powder River ... F-8
Powell ... B-6
Quealy ... J-5
Ralston ... B-6
Ranchester ... B-8
Rawlins ... H-8
Recluse ... B-10
Red Desert ... H-7
Redbird ... E-12
Reliance ... H-5
Reno Jct. ... D-10
Riverside ... J-9
Riverton ... F-7
Robertson ... J-4
Rochelle ... D-11
Rock River ... H-10
Rock Springs ... H-5
Rocky Point ... B-11
Rozet ... C-10
Sage ... H-3
Saint Stephens ... F-6
Saratoga ... J-9
Savageton ... D-10
Savery ... J-8
Shawnee ... F-11
Shell ... C-7
Sheridan ... B-8
Shirley Basin ... G-9
Shoshoni ... E-7
Sinclair ... H-8
Slater ... H-11
Smoot ... F-3
South Pass City ... G-6
Spotted Horse ... B-10
Story ... C-8
Sundance ... C-12
Sunrise ... G-11
Superior ... H-6
Sussex ... D-9
Table Rock ... H-7
Ten Sleep ... D-8
Teton Village ... D-3
Thayne ... F-3
Thermopolis ... D-6
Tie Siding ... J-10
Torrington ... G-12
Tower Jct. ... B-4
Turnerville ... F-3
Ucross ... C-9
Upton ... C-11
Urie ... J-4
Valley ... C-5
Van Tassell ... F-12
Veteran ... G-12
Walcott ... H-9
Waltman ... E-8
Wamsutter ... H-7
Weston ... B-10
Wheatland ... G-11
Wilson ... E-3
Woods Landing ... J-10
Worland ... D-7
Wright ... D-10
Yoder ... H-12